The Bloomsbury Companion to Ethics

Other volumes in the series of Bloomsbury Companions:

Aesthetics, edited by Anna Christina Ribeiro
Analytic Philosophy, edited by Barry Dainton and Howard Robinson
Continental Philosophy, edited by John Ó Maoilearca and Beth Lord
Epistemology, edited by Andrew Cullison
Existentialism, edited by Jack Reynolds, Felicity Joseph and Ashley Woodward
Hegel, edited by Allegra de Laurentiis and Jeffrey Edwards
Hume, edited by Alan Bailey and Dan O'Brien
Hobbes, edited by S.A. Lloyd
Kant, edited by Gary Banham, Dennis Schulting and Nigel Hems
Leibniz, edited by Brendan Look
Locke, edited by S.-J. Savonious-Wroth, Paul Schuurman and Jonathan Walmsley
Metaphysics, edited by Robert W. Barnard and Neil A. Manson
Philosophical Logic, edited by Leon Horston and Richard Pettigrew
Philosophy of Language, edited by Manuel Garcia-Carpintero and Max Kolbel
Philosophy of Mind, edited by James Garvey
Philosophy of Science, edited by Steven French and Juha Saatsi
Plato, edited by Gerald A. Press
Political Philosophy, edited by Andrew Fiala and Matt Matravers
Pragmatism, edited by Sami Pihlström
Socrates, edited by John Bussanich and Nicholas D. Smith
Spinoza, edited by Wiep van Bunge, Henri Krop, Piet Steenbakkers and Jeroen van de Ven

Bloomsbury Academic
An imprint of Bloomsbury Publishing Plc

50 Bedford Square	1385 Broadway
London	New York
WC1B 3DP	NY 10018
UK	USA

www.bloomsbury.com

Bloomsbury is a registered trade mark of Bloomsbury Publishing Plc

First published in 2011 by Continuum

British Library Cataloguing-in-Publication Data
A catalogue record for this book is available from the British Library.

ISBN:	HB:	978-1-4411-2175-2
	PB:	978-1-4725-6779-6
	ePDF:	978-1-4725-6780-2
	ePub:	978-1-4725-6781-9

Library of Congress Cataloging-in-Publication Data
A catalog record for this book is available from the Library of Congress.

Typeset by Newgen Knowledge Works (P) Ltd., Chennai, India
Printed and bound in Great Britain

The Bloomsbury Companion to Ethics

Edited by
Christian B. Miller

Bloomsbury Companions

BLOOMSBURY
LONDON • NEW DELHI • NEW YORK • SYDNEY

Contents

Notes on Contributors

Daniel R. Boisvert is Lecturer of Philosophy at the University of North Carolina Charlotte. His main areas of research are ethics and philosophy of language, especially their intersections and their relations to broader issues in philosophy of mind and logic. His authored or coauthored articles have appeared in outlets such as *Pacific Philosophical Quarterly*, *The Philosophical Quarterly*, and *The Oxford Handbook of Philosophy of Language*.

John Brunero is Associate Professor of Philosophy at the University of Missouri–St. Louis, where he teaches moral, political, and legal philosophy. His research is primarily focused on questions concerning normative reasons and the requirements of practical rationality. His work has appeared in such journals as *Philosophical Quarterly*, *Philosophical Studies*, *Pacific Philosophical Quarterly*, *Journal of Ethics and Social Philosophy*, and *Ethics*.

Matthew Chrisman is Lecturer in Philosophy at the University of Edinburgh. His main areas of research are ethical theory, the philosophy of language, and epistemology. He is also interested in semantics of modals, action theory, political philosophy, deontic logic, the ethics of climate change, and Kant. His work has appeared in such journals as *The Journal of Philosophy*, *Philosophy and Phenomenological Research*, *Oxford Studies in Metaethics*, *Philosophers' Imprint*, and *Philosophical Studies*.

Terence Cuneo is Associate Professor of Philosophy at the University of Vermont. His primary areas of research include metaethics and the history of modern philosophy. His books include *The Normative Web: An Argument for Moral Realism* (Oxford, 2007), *Foundations of Ethics* (edited with R. Shafer-Landau, Blackwell, 2007) and *The Cambridge Companion to Thomas Reid* (edited with R. van Woudenberg, Cambridge, 2004).

Michael DePaul is Professor of Philosophy at the University of Notre Dame, and his main areas of research are ethics and epistemology. He is the author of *Balance and Refinement: Beyond Coherence Methods of Moral Inquiry* (Routledge) and editor (with William Ramsey) of *Rethinking Intuition* (Rowman and Littlefield), *Resurrecting Old-Fashioned Foundationalism* (Rowman and Littlefield), and (with Linda Zagzebski) *Intellectual Virtue* (Oxford).

Kyla Ebels-Duggan is Associate Professor of Philosophy at Northwestern University. She works on moral and political philosophy and their history, especially the work of Immanuel Kant. She has published articles in *Philosophers' Imprint*, *Ethics*, and *The Philosophical Quarterly* and in 2009–2010 held the Laurance S. Rockefeller Visiting Fellowship at the Princeton University Center for Human Values.

William J. FitzPatrick is Associate Professor of Philosophy at the University of Rochester. His research focuses on topics in metaethics, normative ethical theory, and applied ethics, and he has published articles in *Ethics*, *Mind*, *Analysis*, *Philosophical Studies*, *Oxford Studies in Metaethics*, and other journals. Among his current projects are the development of a robust, nonnaturalist ethical realism; a defense of the doctrine of double effect; and an exploration of questions at the intersection of ethical theory and the sciences.

Joshua Gert is Professor of Philosophy at the College of William and Mary. His primary research interests are metaethics, practical rationality and reasons for action, and philosophy of color, all with an emphasis on the relevance of philosophy of language. His publications include *Brute Rationality: Normativity and Human Action* (Cambridge 2004), "Normative Strength and the Balance of Reasons," *Philosophical Review* 2007 and "What Colors Could not Be: An Argument for Color Primitivism," *The Journal of Philosophy* 2008.

Hallvard Lillehammer teaches moral and political philosophy at Cambridge University where he is a University Senior Lecturer, the Sidgwick Lecturer, and Senior Research Fellow at Churchill College. He is the author of *Companions in Guilt: Arguments for Ethical Objectivity* (2007), and coeditor of *Ramsey's Legacy* (2005) and *Real Metaphysics* (2003).

Sean McKeever is Associate Professor of Philosophy at Davidson College. His research interests are in contemporary moral theory and metaethics. He is the author (with Michael Ridge) of *Principled Ethics: Generalism as a Regulative Ideal* (Oxford, 2006).

Alfred R. Mele is the William H. and Lucyle T. Werkmeister Professor of Philosophy at Florida State University and director of the Big Questions in Free Will Project (2010–13). He is the author of *Irrationality* (1987), *Springs of Action* (1992), *Autonomous Agents* (1995), *Self-Deception Unmasked* (2001), *Motivation and Agency* (2003), *Free Will and Luck* (2006), and *Effective Intentions: The Power of Conscious Will* (2009). He also is the editor or coeditor of *The Philosophy of Action* (1997), *Mental Causation* (1993), *The Oxford Handbook of Rationality* (2004), *Rationality and the Good* (2007), and *Free Will and Consciousness: How Might They Work?* (2010).

Christian B. Miller is Professor of Philosophy at Wake Forest University. His main areas of research are meta-ethics, moral psychology, moral character, action theory, and philosophy of religion. His work has appeared in such journals as *Noûs, Philosophy and Phenomenological Research, Philosophical Studies, Philosophical Psychology, The Journal of Ethics, Journal of Ethics and Social Philosophy,* and *Oxford Studies in Philosophy of Religion,* and he is the author of *Moral Character: An Empirical Theory* (Oxford, 2013) and *Character and Moral Psychology* (Oxford, 2014). He is also the director of The Character Project, which is funded by a 4.6 million dollar grant for the study of character from the John Templeton Foundation.

Thomas Nadelhoffer is Assistant Professor of Philosophy at College of Charleston. His main areas of research include moral psychology, the philosophy of action, free will, and neurolaw, and his articles have appeared in journals such as *Analysis, Midwest Studies in Philosophy, Mind & Language, Neuroethics,* and *Philosophy and Phenomenological Research.* He also edited *Moral Psychology: Historical and Contemporary Readings* with Eddy Nahmias and Shaun Nichols (Blackwell), and he is presently editing "The Future of Punishment" (Oxford).

Douglas W. Portmore is an Associate Professor of Philosophy in the School of Historical, Philosophical, and Religious Studies at Arizona State University. His research focuses mainly on morality, rationality, and the interconnections between the two, but he also writes on wellbeing, posthumous harm, and the nonidentity problem. He is the author of *Commonsense Consequentialism: Wherein Morality Meets Rationality*, Oxford University Press, 2011. In addition, he has published several articles in various journals, including *Noûs, Mind, Ethics, Utilitas, Philosophical Studies,* and *Oxford Studies in Normative Ethics.*

J. B. Schneewind is Professor Emeritus of Philosophy at Johns Hopkins University and a Visiting Scholar in Philosophy at NYU. Author of two books and numerous articles on the history of moral philosophy, he has recently published a collection of his essays entitled *Essays on the History of Moral Philosophy* (Oxford).

Russ Shafer-Landau is Professor of Philosophy at the University of Wisconsin-Madison. He works primarily in metaethics, and is the author of *Moral Realism: A Defence* (Oxford), *Whatever Happened to Good and Evil?* (Oxford) and *The Fundamentals of Ethics* (Oxford). He is the editor of *Oxford Studies in Metaethics.*

Walter Sinnott-Armstrong is Chauncey Stillman Professor of Practical Ethics in the Philosophy Department and the Kenan Institute for Ethics at Duke University. He has served as vice-chair of the Board of Officers of the American Philosophical Association and co-director of the MacArthur Project on Law and Neuroscience. He publishes widely in normative moral theory, metaethics, applied ethics, moral psychology and neuroscience, philosophy of law, epistemology, informal logic, and philosophy of religion. His most recent books include *Moral Skepticisms, Morality Without God?*, and, as editor, *Moral Psychology* (3 Volumes) and *Conscious Will and Responsibility* (with Lynn Nadel).

Anita Superson is Professor of Philosophy at the University of Kentucky. She specializes in ethics, particularly metaethics and moral psychology, and in feminism. She is the author of *The Moral Skeptic* (Oxford University Press, 2009), and the coeditor (with Ann Cudd) of *Theorizing Backlash: Philosophical Reflections on the Backlash against Feminism* (Rowman and Littlefield, 2002). She authored an entry on "Feminist Moral Psychology" in the *Stanford Encyclopedia of Philosophy*.

Christine Swanton teaches in the Philosophy Department at the University of Auckland in New Zealand. She is currently working on the virtue ethics of Hume and Nietzsche. Her book on virtue ethics, *Virtue Ethics: A Pluralistic View*, was published with Oxford University Press in 2003.

Pekka Väyrynen is Senior Lecturer in Philosophy at University of Leeds. He works primarily in metaethics and maintains strong interests in metaphysics, epistemology, and philosophy of language. His work has appeared in many journals and volumes including *Ethics, Philosophy and Phenomenological Research, Oxford Studies in Metaethics*, and *Philosophical Quarterly*. His current work on a monograph on the distinction between thick and thin ethical concepts and its significance (tentatively entitled *The Lewd, the Rude, and the Nasty: A Study of Thick Concepts*) is supported by grants from UK Arts and Humanities Research Council and the European Community.

William J. Wainwright is Distinguished Professor of Philosophy Emeritus at the University of Wisconsin-Milwaukee. Major recent publications include *Reason and the Heart* (1995), *Philosophy of Religion*, 2nd ed. (1998), *Religion and Morality* (2005), and the edited volume *The Oxford Handbook of Philosophy of Religion* (2005).

Eric Wiland is Associate Professor of Philosophy at the University of Missouri-St. Louis. He is the author of *Reasons* (Continuum, 2012), and a wide variety of papers on ethics and practical reason. He also organizes SLACRR, the St. Louis Conference on Reasons and Rationality.

Preface: How to Use this Book, the Intended Audience, and Acknowledgments

Christian B. Miller

How to Use this Book

The heart of this *Companion* is the 13 newly commissioned chapters on central topics in metaethics and normative theory. Readers interested in a comprehensive and rich treatment of a given topic are advised to turn directly to that particular chapter. Note as well that there are three chapters on "New Directions in Ethics," which are devoted to moral particularism, experimental ethics, and biology, evolution, and ethics, respectively.

This *Companion* has a number of features which set it apart from other "Handbooks" and "Guides" to ethics:

- An "Overview of Contemporary Metaethics and Normative Ethical Theory," which goes into extensive detail about how to formulate and organize the various positions in the two fields.
- A "Chronology of Ethics" by J. B. Schneewind, one of the leading contemporary historians of philosophy, which provides a very thorough timeline of philosophical milestones in the West, as well as important cultural, political, scientific, literary, and religious developments more broadly.
- A section on "Methodological Issues," which offers a comprehensive and highly informed treatment of the main approach to doing ethical theorizing, reflective equilibrium, written by one of the leading experts on the topic.
- Newly commissioned entries for "Important Technical Terms in Ethics," with extended characterizations for those looking for a quick and accessible guide to some of the most important terminology.
- An extensive overview of "Internet Resources for Research in Ethics," which provides website addresses for ethics centers and institutes, research fellowships in ethics, ethics societies, research projects on ethical

topics, websites with ethics content, ethics-related blogs, regular ethics-related conferences, print journals related to ethics, electronic journals related to ethics, and classic works in ethics available online.
- A resource entitled "Selected Works in Contemporary Metaethics and Normative Theory," with lists of familiar and influential contemporary books and articles pertaining to constructivism, error theory, moral methodology, moral epistemology, moral psychology, moral realism, noncognitivism, practical reason, consequentialism, ethical concepts, feminist ethics, care ethics, Kantian ethics, contractarianism, contractualism, moral pluralism, moral particularism, natural law theory, the structure of ethical theories, theological voluntarism, and virtue ethics.

I hope that these resources will prove to be of great assistance to the further study of ethics.

The Intended Audience

Authors for this volume were instructed to write their chapters in such a way that they would be accessible to nonspecialists in metaethics and ethical theory, and I am thrilled that they have done so without exception. At the same time the entries are also rich in philosophical content, and not only survey the relevant positions but break new philosophical ground as well. Hence I see this volume as being very helpful to at least the following audiences:

- Graduate students and faculty who work in other areas but who want to get up to speed on contemporary work in ethics.
- Advanced undergraduates and early graduate students who want to develop a good comprehensive understanding of contemporary ethics.
- Philosophers who work in metaethics and/or ethical theory and who are interested in the new insights offered by a given author on a particular topic.
- Philosophers who work in applied ethics and who are interested in the approaches, arguments, and objections offered by the authors on the different topics in theoretical ethics.
- Others outside of academic philosophy would wish to develop a good understanding of contemporary ethics for their own personal or professional enrichment.

Please note that those who have not studied ethics before beyond, say, an introductory undergraduate course are advised to start with the "Overview of Contemporary Metaethics and Normative Ethical Theory."

This *Companion* does not cover either applied ethics or the history of ethics in detail, since to do so properly would have required a volume which is two to three times as long.

Acknowledgments

I am very grateful to Sarah Campbell at Continuum for approaching me to edit this volume and to Tom Crick for his assistance. Many thanks to Thom Brooks as well for his support, and to Thom and Dwight Furrow for being positive and encouraging referees of the proposal for this volume. In addition, I want to thank each of the philosophers who contributed to the *Companion*. Everyone worked extremely hard on his or her contribution, and I could not be more pleased with the outcome. Not only that, but we also met the publisher's deadline, a rarity for a project of this size!

For extremely detailed and careful comments on the overview of contemporary metaethics and normative ethical theory, I want to thank Jason Baldwin and Terence Cuneo. Jason also did a great job putting together the Index, for which I am very grateful. Thanks as well to Joshua Seachris for suggestions for the chapter on internet resources. Part of the work on this volume was done during a research leave jointly funded by Wake Forest University and the Thomas Jack Lynch Fund of the Department of Philosophy. I want to thank both my university and department for all of their support. Finally my parents, Charles and Joyous Miller, and my wife, Jessie Lee Miller, were wonderful sources of encouragement and love during the editing of this volume.

Overview of Contemporary Metaethics and Normative Ethical Theory

Christian B. Miller

The study of morality continues to flourish in contemporary philosophy. As the chapters of this *Companion* illustrate, new and exciting work is being done on a wide range of topics from the objectivity of morality to the relationship between morality and religious, biological, and feminist concerns. Along with this vast amount of work has come a proliferation of technical terminology and competing positions. The goal of this chapter is to provide an overview of the terrain in contemporary ethics. More precisely, we shall survey each of the following in the three sections of this chapter:

(i) Leading concepts and distinctions in the ethics literature.
(ii) Central positions in contemporary metaethics, with a focus on what it takes for a position to count as a form of moral realism.
(iii) Central positions in contemporary normative ethical theory, with a focus on the difference between monist versus pluralist theories.

Each of the sections is largely self-contained, and they can be read in any order. My hope is that this chapter as a whole will help the reader with a solid background in other areas of philosophy become better equipped to enter into more advanced work in philosophical ethics.

Two comments should be made before we begin. First, my primary goal in this chapter is taxonomic, and so I do not try to advance any of the substantive debates mentioned below. Nevertheless, there will be plenty of controversy to be had, since there is nothing approaching a widely accepted taxonomy in either metaethics or normative ethical theory. So my way of dividing up the conceptual landscape will differ from that of other contemporary ethicists, and indeed from other writers in this volume. Despite this, I hope that my approach comes across as well motivated and useful for readers trying to make sense of the terrain.

Some Central Concepts and Distinctions

The normative and the descriptive

Let us start at a general level with the distinction between the normative and the descriptive. Here are some descriptive statements:

"2+2=4"
"A water molecule is composed of two hydrogen atoms and one oxygen atom."
"George Washington was the first president of the United States of America."
"Benjamin Franklin was the first president of the United States of America."

These statements, as descriptive, only aim to capture the way the world actually is. Not all of them succeed in doing so (such as the fourth), but the key concern is whether the world is as each statement says it is.

Normative statements, on the other hand, are concerned with *evaluating* the way the world is:

"There should be more charity organizations."
"He is a cowardly person."
"The criminal deserves the death penalty."
"If only he had acted for better reasons."[1]

Sometimes the descriptive and the normative come together. The statement that a person is cowardly may at once seem to describe the person's actual character and also serve to evaluate him as a person. But we know that the descriptive and normative domains are distinct. For as a matter of fact, the world as it is falls short in all kinds of ways from the way that it should be. No examples are needed for such an obvious point.

Let us focus on the normative domain. It is tempting to proceed directly to morality, but the normative encompasses far more than just the moral. We can distinguish at least the following distinct normative domains besides the moral:

Prudential (what is in our long-term self-interest)
"Smoking is bad for you." "Exercise will make you healthier in the long run."
Aesthetic
"That painting is beautiful." "The room is tastefully designed."

Epistemic

"One should not hold a belief based upon insufficient evidence." "Understanding is a good thing to cultivate."

Legal

"This law is unjust." "He should be sent to jail for breaking the law."

Religious

"Communion should be served every Sunday." "It is better for adults to be baptized rather than children."

Competitive (i.e., athletic)

"Traveling with the basketball is wrong." "Mickey Mantle was the greatest baseball player ever."

Customary

"In our culture, forks should be placed to the left of the plate." "He was rude for not bowing."

Political/Economic

"This political party is doing a good job running the country." "A flat tax system is better than a progressive system."

One of the reasons we know that these domains are distinct is that any one of them can require or forbid a certain action or practice without another domain similarly requiring or forbidding it, or even in some cases being applicable at all in the first place. An athlete, for instance, may be required to aim a ball at a certain hole, hoop, or receiver, without this being required or even immediately relevant from a moral, legal, aesthetic, religious, political, or economic perspective. Furthermore, we can devise cases in which, on the surface at least, each of these domains can prescribe a course of action which conflicts with some facet of the moral domain, such as a moral principle. Hence in addition to the moral domain and each of the other normative domains listed above, we also have the concept of the normative *all-things-considered*. Judgments of whether something is good or right all-things-considered often involve a (largely implicit and subconscious) weighing of the various specific kinds of normative considerations involved.

How then do we delimit the strictly moral domain? Unfortunately philosophers have had little success in doing so. Here are some general characterizations:

Moral beliefs are "beliefs [the person] has about how to live her life when she takes into account in a sympathetic way the impact of her life and decisions on others."[2]

Ethics inquires "into what we ought to desire, feel, be, or do."[3]

Morality is concerned with "what are good and bad ends to pursue in life and what is right and wrong to do in the conduct of life."[4]

Morality "compris[es] standards of right and wise conduct whose authority in practical thought is determined by reason rather than custom."[5]

And here are some of the features that the moral has been thought to possess:[6]

(i) Prescriptivity
(ii) Universalizability
(iii) Publicity
(iv) Practicality
(v) Impartiality
(vi) Compassion
(vii) Categoricity
(viii) Overriddingness

The first four of these features are plausibly necessary for a normative concept to be a moral one, although doubts may surround each of them depending on how they are spelled out. But note that they are neither individually nor jointly sufficient for uniquely identifying the moral. Epistemic concepts, for instance, have all the same properties. Epistemic concepts also may involve a requirement of impartiality, but in the moral case, such a feature has been heavily contested in recent years.[7] Compassion does not seem uniquely moral, and in any event would be only one component of morality if it were, not a distinctive feature of morality as such. To say that morality is categorical, or roughly a system of categorical obligations which bind us regardless of whether we desire to follow them or not, is also controversial, and if they exist at all such obligations would also seem to obtain in the epistemic realm as well. The last candidate on the list is admittedly distinctive. But it is also highly contestable among ethicists, as it is not clear that, all-things-considered, morality should always trump prudential or religious considerations, for instance, in certain conflict cases. And in any event, while all these properties might be helpful in clarifying how moral concepts *function*, they do not tell us very much about the *unique subject matter* of the moral domain. Like most philosophers, then, we shall simply adopt the attitude that we know a moral statement when we see it.

A schema for the normative

Here is a general schema we can use to help organize the various elements of normative concern:

(1) Object of evaluation O has normative status S in virtue of bearing dependence relation R to one or more considerations C.

This schema may look daunting, but here are some examples:

(2) The practice of slavery is morally wrong in virtue of causing pain and suffering.
(3) Jones's belief that p is unjustified in virtue of being based on insufficient evidence.
(4) A statue has the property of being beautiful in virtue of certain subvening physical properties of the clay.

Let us take each of these four components of (1) in turn.

Objects of Evaluation. The main object of moral evaluation in recent normative ethics has been *actions*, such as Jones's lying to his friend or Smith's donating money to charity. This evaluation can occur at the level of act-types (lying to a friend, donating to a charity, etc.) or particular act-tokens, such as the particular actions of Jones and Smith.

But the scope of moral appraisal extends much wider than this. We also evaluate the *motives* of agents. If Smith donates to charity, but does so only for selfish reasons like being written up in the newspaper, then while his action might be morally obligatory, we typically will say that it deserves little if any moral praise. And we evaluate the *character* of a person. Is she honest, compassionate, and generous, or dishonest, cruel, and stingy?

There are other objects of evaluation both inside and outside the moral domain. Beliefs and reasoning processes are evaluated epistemically, works of art and music are evaluated aesthetically (and in other ways too), rituals are evaluated religiously and culturally, sporting maneuvers are evaluated athletically, and so forth. A comprehensive list of all objects of evaluation would likely be coextensive with a comprehensive list of all that we experience.

Normative Statuses. There is a vast array of normative statuses which we use in evaluating actions, motives, characters, and the like, including the concepts of good, bad, virtuous, vicious, right, wrong, obligatory, forbidden, honest, kind, slothful, inconsiderate, terrible, perfect, wise, tasteful, and so forth. Fortunately we can organize many of them using three general categories:

The axiological: Concepts of good, bad, better, evil, and the like are axiological concepts. They are typically used to evaluate the consequences of our actions ("that donation made several people much better off") and states of affairs in the world ("that was a bad production of Hamlet"). But they can also be used to evaluate people in various respects. Mother Teresa, for instance, was a morally excellent person, while Tiger Woods is a very good golfer.

When it comes to axiological concepts, it is customary to distinguish between the intrinsic and the instrumental. An intrinsic good is something good in itself (good for its own sake), and leading candidates include pleasure, happiness, love, and virtue. An instrumental good is something that is good as a means to something else. Some philosophers hold that the something else need not itself be intrinsically good, and can even be something intrinsically bad. For instance, a scalpel can be instrumentally good for inflicting brutal torture on someone, or it can be good as a means to saving a person's life during surgery. Others require that an instrumental good be a good means (eventually) to something that is intrinsically good.[8] They might say that a scalpel is a good *instrument* for various purposes (whether good, bad, or neutral), but claim that it is not instrumentally *good*.[9] Regardless of the outcome of this debate, one of the standard examples of an instrumental good is the practice of medicine. In itself it may be intrinsically neutral, but it is an instrumental good for a number of purposes.

Thus we can divide the axiological itself into the following categories:

The intrinsically good (potential candidate: virtue)
The intrinsically bad (potential candidate: vice)
The intrinsically value neutral (potential candidate: a grain of sand)
The instrumentally good (potential candidate: medicine)
The instrumentally bad (potential candidate: a broken watch)
The instrumentally value neutral (potential candidate: a grain of sand outside of our light cone).

Note that these categories are not exclusive. Virtue, for instance, might be both intrinsically good and instrumentally good for achieving happiness.

The deontological. The second category of normative statuses has to do primarily with actions (whether mental or bodily), and includes concepts such as right, wrong, obligatory, permissible, forbidden, prohibited, prescribed, required, dutiful, and allowable. Here the main division of the deontological is the following:

Obligatory (required, prescribed, a duty, ought to do)
Optional (permissible but not required, allowable but not required)
Forbidden (prohibited, wrong, impermissible, contrary to duty, ought not do).

"Optional" is used here rather than "permissible," since obligatory actions are also permissible. The concept of a "right" action is omitted from the list, since we use the term ambiguously—sometimes we label actions "right" only when they are obligatory, and sometimes we label them "right" provided they are not forbidden (i.e., either obligatory or optional).

The concepts of the obligatory, optional, and forbidden form a tight conceptual relationship. An obligatory action is one whose omission would be forbidden. A forbidden action is one whose omission is obligatory. And an optional action is one whose commission and omission are both neither obligatory nor forbidden.

One other important deontological concept is the supererogatory, or that set of actions which are highly praiseworthy in certain respects but not obligatory (colloquially, they go "above and beyond the call of duty"). For instance, according to our ordinary or commonsense morality, we are not required to give away all of our disposable income to famine relief, but we are allowed to do so (other things being equal), and if we do, we are acting in a supererogatory fashion and deserve a great deal of praise for going so far above what morality expects of us. Given such actions, at least according to most ethical frameworks, we can further divide the optional as follows:

Optional (permissible but not required, allowable but not required)
  Supererogatory (praiseworthy)
  Merely optional actions (not praiseworthy).

An example of the merely optional would be choosing one kind of cereal off of the shelf as opposed to another, other things being equal.

Note that the deontological concepts do not have an exclusive connection to morality—they are prevalent in the epistemic and prudential domains as well, for instance. And this may also apply to the supererogatory—presumably we can go above and beyond our epistemic duties.

The characterological. A third category of normative statuses has to do with the character concepts, such as virtuous, vicious, brave, lazy, bold, shy, fearless, understanding, wise, and so forth. What we are evaluating in this area are first and foremost the character traits had by a person, where such traits are dispositions to think, feel, and/or act in certain ways when in trait-relevant circumstances. We call someone kind, for instance, when she has a character trait which disposes her towards regularly thinking, feeling, and acting in certain helpful and beneficent ways when in circumstances that warrant such behavior.

But the characterological concepts are not limited to just evaluating traits. We say that a person acted honestly, for instance, and this may be because the action in question is what we would have expected an honest person to have done in the circumstances. Similarly, we talk about a just outcome of a change in social policy, or a just society, government, or law.[10]

The characterological concepts can also be divided up into their own categories using the familiar notion of a virtue:

Virtues (potential candidates: honesty, compassion)
Vices (potential candidates: sloth, pride)
Character traits which are neither (potential candidates: shyness, extroversion)

While controversial, the virtues can perhaps be further divided into the intrinsically versus the instrumentally good virtues (and same with the vices). On some views, for instance, courage is only instrumentally good, since it may seem as if it can be used for all kinds of bad moral ends.[11]

Finally, we can note that, as with the other normative statues, the charactero-logical concepts are not uniquely moral. Much work is currently being done in epistemology on the epistemic virtues, to take just one illustration.[12]

The three categories above may not be exhaustive of all normative status concepts, depending on how broadly we want to construe them. The concept of rights, for instance, may deserve its own category, or it could be classified under the deontological, and similarly with the concepts of desert, retribution, and rehabilitation. So the above taxonomy is offered only as an initial attempt to helpfully organize the dozens of normative status concepts we have.

Justifying Considerations. When we say that a state of affairs is good or an action forbidden, we do not mean that they have these normative statuses for no reason whatsoever. Rather, states of affairs are good and actions forbidden in virtue of one or more considerations that *makes it the case that* they are this way. Perhaps slavery is wrong, for instance, in virtue of the pain and suffering it causes slaves, or in virtue of how it undermines their dignity, or in virtue of how it violates their rights, or in virtue of some alterative factor or combination of factors. But it is not the case that slavery is wrong for no reason at all—its wrongness, we might say, has an underlying nature, some underlying feature or set of features that makes it the case that it is wrong. And the same applies to the other normative concepts. Determining what precisely the considerations in question are, serves as the primary goal of ethical theorists.[13]

Hence it is a platitude of the normative that it is grounded in further underlying considerations, or to use a common way of speaking, that it supervenes on more fundamental considerations. What immediately grounds a normative property might itself be normative. So in our example above, the wrongness of slavery might be grounded in the dignity of all human beings. But as a normative property, dignity itself will have to be grounded in still further considerations, such as having certain mental capacities or being created in the image of God. Hence, while not uncontroversial, one view is that necessarily, all normative properties are ultimately grounded in nonnormative, merely descriptive properties.[14]

Dependence Relations. What then is this relation of "grounding" that connects the normative with the (ultimately) nonnormative? One question we need to first ask is whether our schema in (1) is concerned with semantic or metaphysical relations. If the former, then the grounding relation could be a relation of semantic meaning. To take our example of slavery, one instance of (1) might be:

(1*) "The practice of slavery is wrong" is equivalent in meaning to "The practice of slavery violates the dignity of slaves."

G. E. Moore famously considered such an approach for something's being "good," but ultimately concluded that no informative and plausible analysis could be given.[15]

But presumably our most basic interest in (1) is as a metaphysical claim about the relationship between normative facts and properties on the one hand, and what metaphysically grounds them on the other. So it is the fact, let us say, that slavery violates the dignity of slaves that *makes it the case that* slavery is wrong. All of these expressions—"in virtue of," "makes it the case that," "grounding," "because"—highlight the claim that a normative fact or property is based in some way on something more fundamental to it, such that were it not for the more fundamental fact obtaining or property being instantiated, the normative fact or property in this instance would not have either (other things being equal). But can anything more be said about this grounding relationship? Here are two of the leading contenders:[16]

Nonreductive Supervenience or Constitution: A normative property is instantiated as a matter of metaphysical necessity in virtue of having certain underlying properties, but is not identical to those underlying properties. For instance, the fact that the action brought about pain instantiated the property of badness, and there is no possible world where, other things being equal, the same action bringing about pain would not instantiate wrongness. But this is compatible with there being other ways in which badness might be instantiated.

Identity: A normative property is instantiated in virtue of being metaphysically identical to one or more nonnormative properties. For instance, on a type-identity view, the property of badness could just be the property of being painful, and so nothing besides being painful could be bad. Or on a token-identity view, this action's property of being wrong could be identical to the action's causing pain in the world.

Versions of these views can even be combined together, i.e., a *token*-identity view combined with a nonreductive constitution account of the relation between *types* of normative and nonnormative properties.

The study of ethics

Having now clarified various aspects of our normative appraisals of the world, let us focus specifically on uniquely *moral* appraisals. I take "ethics" and "moral philosophy" to be synonymous and to mean the study of morality, although I have nothing to offer by way of a definition of morality.[17] Ethicists have typically approached the study of morality in three different ways:[18]

Normative Ethical Theory. The normative ethical theorist (hereafter just "ethical theorist" for short) attempts to develop an understanding of what the relationship is between moral properties and their underlying nonmoral properties. For instance, as we saw above, there are many candidates for what makes it the case that slavery is wrong, and the ethical theorist attempts to sort through them and arrive at the most promising account of the feature(s) which grounds its wrongness. In doing so, such a philosopher does not eschew first-order moral evaluations, but rather carries out her work in part by directly employing moral concepts and forming moral judgments. We can put the main goals of an ethical theory more carefully as follows:

(i) To provide a *theoretical account* of the underlying feature or set of features that ground various axiological, deontological, and characterological moral judgments, concepts, and properties. So for any given moral property, the ethical theorist attempts to determine if there is one single underlying feature that always determines its instantiation (say, maximizing pleasure), whether there is some finite set of features that individually or in combination always determines its instantiation, or whether there is no such finite set of features which always determines its instantiation.

(ii) To provide a *practical decision procedure*, whereby we can resolve controversial moral disputes in society and also find practical guidance for moral questions in our ordinary lives.

Naturally these two goals are typically related. Suppose there is one and only one feature which makes an action morally obligatory, such as maximizing overall net pleasure. Then that feature can be used to formulate a *moral principle*, which articulates the relationship between a moral feature and one or more nonmoral features. So in our example we would have:

(a) An action is morally obligatory if and only if the action, of all the actions which the agent could perform at the time, is such that it maximizes overall net pleasure.

But then we might determine on empirical grounds that the following is true:

(b) Action A is the action which, of all the actions that the agent could perform at the time, is the one that would maximize overall net pleasure.

Hence we can infer that:

(c) Action A is morally obligatory.

Thus meeting the theoretical goal of an ethical theory can help to advance the practical one.[19] Similarly, it is often taken to be a flaw in the theoretical account provided by an ethical theory if it does not turn out to be helpful in resolving practical disputes. At the same time, we have to acknowledge the possibility that the moral domain might be too complex or resistant to neat formulations of principles for us to be able to actually achieve much success in advancing either the theoretical or the practical goal outlined above. As Darwall notes, an ethical theory "attempts to articulate the grounds of value and obligation in a way that is maximally systematic and maximally sensitive to genuine complexity."[20]

Of course, there may be other important goals for an ethical theory. Perhaps it will strengthen our confidence in our moral convictions, especially in the face of temptation. Perhaps it will help us criticize and improve aspects of ourselves, our friends and families, and our society. And perhaps there is simply the goal of attaining satisfaction at discovering how one part of the world works.[21] But the theoretical and practical goals above are certainly widely regarded as central.[22]

Applied Ethics. As its name suggests, applied ethics examines the moral status of specific human actions and practices, with a focus on those which have become prominent in societal debates, such as abortion, the death penalty, cloning, stem cell research, animal consumption, access to scarce medical resources, and so forth.

One natural way to conceive the relationship between normative ethical theory and applied ethics is to look to the former in order to resolve disputes about the latter. And in principle this would be a wise approach. Unfortunately, just as sustained controversy permeates discussions of practical moral questions, so too is there tremendous disagreement among advocates of different theories. So as a matter of fact, applied ethicists sometimes make conditional claims, such as *if* a particular ethical theory is correct, then abortion has such-and-such a moral status. At other times, applied ethics discussions are carried out without explicit appeal to any ethical theory at all, and instead rely on our moral intuitions or general moral principles about which there is wide agreement.

The relationship between ethical theory and applied ethics need not be one-directional. For it can become a constraint on an adequate ethical theory that it be able to adjudicate particular ethical disputes. And in some cases, we might have very specific and deeply held convictions about, say, the immorality of slavery or cloning. These convictions can then become data for constructing a plausible ethical theory, and serve as basic commitments that any such theory must respect.[23]

Metaethics. Roughly half of the chapters in this *Companion* are devoted to metaethics, or the nonmoral study of the metaphysics, epistemology, and semantics of the moral. Unlike normative ethical theory, metaethical approaches are carried out at the second-order level by examining the practice of morality from a disengaged perspective and typically refraining from making moral claims.[24] In other words, metaethics raises and attempts to answer questions *about* morality. To use an analogy, a scientist arrives at first-order scientific conclusions, whereas a philosopher of science examines the practice of science as such, and does not make any scientific discoveries. So too is the metaethicist not concerned, in the first instance, with arriving at new ethical claims, but rather with the answers to various questions about morality such as the following:

Do moral facts and properties exist?
If so, are they objective?
If they are not objective, who or what created them?
How do we learn the content of morality, if there is such content to learn in the first place?
What is the meaning of moral terms, and how do they refer, if they do in the first place?
Are moral statements capable of being true or false?
If so, are any of them true?

The central goal of the leading metaethical positions is to answer questions such as these.

While metaethics clearly seems to be a separate branch of ethics from normative ethical theory, the two are also closely related. If we discover where morality came from and how objective it is, that information can obviously have significant implications for our attempt to better understand the underlying nature of moral properties. Similarly, some metaethical positions might imply that no theoretically informative and practically relevant ethical theories are available in the first place. And what the source of morality turns out to be—such as God, evolution, or our cultural opinions—could make a significant difference for our motivation to comply with our best ethical theory.[25]

This *Companion* is only concerned with metaethics and normative ethical theory, not applied ethics. In the remaining sections of this chapter, I provide a taxonomy of the leading positions in each of these two areas.

A Taxonomy of Metaethical Positions

It has become increasingly difficult to find clear differences between the various positions on offer in the contemporary metaethics literature. In what follows I briefly outline my own approach to sorting out the landscape of views, while remaining neutral on the truth or falsity of the positions themselves.[26]

General realism

The key divide separating metaethical positions is between advocates of moral realism and advocates of various forms of moral antirealism. But first we should note that realism disputes arise with respect to just about every domain of experience—the existence of God, unobservable scientific objects, beautiful paintings, scientific laws, ordinary medium sized objects, and so forth. The *realists* about a given domain have typically argued for the existence and objectivity of the entities in question or, at a semantic level, for the objective truth of the relevant claims. Examples of such realist positions include theism about God, Platonism about properties, and necessitarianism about scientific laws.

Antirealists, on the other hand, usually adopt one of two outlooks in a given domain. Some antirealists will simply deny the existence of the thing(s) in question. Atheists about God are a straightforward example. Others accept the existence of the thing in question or the truth of the relevant statements, but make their existence or truth dependent in certain ways upon the mental activities of human beings. Forms of relativism about aesthetic beauty or about standards of etiquette would count as antirealist positions in this sense.

It is worth noting that neither realism nor either form of antirealism is likely going to turn out to be true in every domain. Realism is extremely plausible about my own existence, for example, whereas the first form of antirealism is plausible with regard to unicorns and the second form with regard to etiquette.

Given the prevalence of realism disputes, we can try to articulate conditions for what might be called *general realism*, i.e., conditions for what it is to be a realist about any domain of experience. While an ambitious project, if successful it would provide a perfectly general and well-motivated framework within which to organize the positions in contemporary metaethics.

It turns out that there have been roughly six different approaches for thinking about general realism:[27]

(i) *Metaphysical Thesis:* Realism about X is true iff and because X exists and[28] X has an existence and nature which are not dependent in certain ways upon human beings.[29]

(ii) *Semantic Thesis:* Realism about X is true iff and because certain claims which putatively refer to X are true (given a certain theory of truth) and/or meaningful (given a certain theory of meaning).[30]

(iii) *Epistemic Thesis:* Realism about X is true iff and because certain epistemic relations can obtain between human beings and X.[31]

(iv) *Explanatory Thesis:* Realism about X is true iff and because X is inelimitable from our best explanation(s) of certain phenomena in that domain.[32]

(v) *Mixed Thesis*: Realism about X is true iff and because more than one of the above kinds of conditions obtains.[33]

(vi) *Quietist Thesis*: The most sophisticated forms of what is often called "antirealism" about some domain can satisfy all the reasonable requirements for being a "realist" about that domain. Thus at the end of the day there is nothing of substance which separates realists from antirealists. The debate, if there even was a genuine one in the first place, has been dissolved.[34]

Which of these approaches should we adopt? For reasons I have outlined elsewhere,[35] my view is that we should favor a metaphysical approach to formulating general realism. Let me only allude to those reasons here using the case of realism disputes about God. Theists and atheists take themselves to be having a substantive debate about God, where both sides have a reasonably clear idea of where the key differences lie. And that debate is at bottom a metaphysical debate about whether in fact there is a divine being who exists, created the universe, and so forth. The primary interest of both parties has to do with the objective existence of such a putative being.

Admittedly, theists and atheists alike are also concerned with the truth-value of statements such as "God created the universe." But intuitively such an interest is parasitic on the more fundamental question of whether God in fact created the universe. Similarly, explanatory considerations will often have a large role to play in adjudicating many realism disputes, including the theistic one. As such, then, they might serve as a test for the truth of realism in a particular domain of experience, and thereby supply us with reasons for or against adopting a realist stance towards the entities in that domain. But what is harder to see is how explanatory considerations are *constitutive* of what it is to be a realist in the first place, and in particular a realist about God. And much the same could be said about epistemic considerations. The obtaining of certain epistemic relations might be helpful in evidentially adjudicating particular realist disputes, such as whether God exists, but it is hard to see such relations as essential to being a realist in the first place. Indeed, it is conceivable that God exists but his existence and activity are all epistemically inaccessible to human beings. Realism about God would then be the correct position in this case, even if we would not have any way of knowing that it is.

This last point raises a more general worry about all nonmetaphysical approaches to general realism. Suppose that such an inaccessible God does exist. Then our statements about God may fail to refer to God and so come out false or neither true nor false if we do not bear the appropriate semantic (and in particular, causal) relations to this entity. And there will not be a wide variety of candidate truth-bearers available; sentence tokens, beliefs, statements, or assertions, which might be employed in a semantic formulation of realism, will not in fact be in the offing. Similarly, we will not bear any epistemic relations to such a being, and God on this conception would not figure into any of our explanatory accounts.[36] Yet it seems clear that a formulation of general realism had better make it be the case that realism turns about to be true about this inaccessible God.

Much more could be said in favor of a metaphysical approach to formulating general realism. But what would such an approach actually look like? A simple starting point is to say that:

(R1) Realism about X is true iff and because:
(i) X exists.

But while offering a plausible necessary condition, (R1) is nowhere near sufficient. Relativists, subjectivists, and constructivists about various normative domains such as the epistemic and aesthetic, as well as about mathematical properties, could all accept (R1), but they are paradigm antirealists in their respective domains.

What is missing is an objectivity condition, which I prefer to formulate in terms of mind-independence.[37] What makes a subjectivist or relativist approach to the property of beauty count as a form of antirealism, for instance, is that it makes the existence and nature of beauty counterfactually dependent upon the mental attitudes that we human beings adopt towards it, such that if those attitudes changed, so too could beauty itself. Beauty, in other words, would be in the eye of the beholder, and so subject to changes in the beholder's actual or improved attitudes. Thus (R1) should be supplemented as follows:

(R2) Realism about X is true iff and because:
(i) X exists.
(ii) The existence and nature of X do not exhibit counterfactual dependence on the intentional attitudes had by human beings in the actual world which pertain to X.[38]

where "counterfactual dependence" is understood in the usual way to mean that for two things, A and B, A's existence counterfactually depends on B's existence iff if B did not exist, then A would not exist.[39] Thus realism about a theistic God would be true on this account so long as a theistic God exists, and his existence and nature are not dependent upon our views which pertain to him. And realism about a particular mental state of mine can be true so long as that mental state exists, and does so in an invariant fashion in light of what other second-order attitudes I (or anyone else) adopt towards it, including thinking that it does not exist at all.

But there is a remaining technical problem concerning the way in which we assess nonactual worlds, and it is important to address this problem here before we turn to the metaethics literature. Suppose we hold a relativist position about beauty, and agree in the actual world that the Mona Lisa is a beautiful painting.

Given (R2), it is natural to think that a relativist position in aesthetics would be a form of antirealism, since although the painting would instantiate the property of beauty, it would only do so in a way that is dependent upon our opinions about beauty in the actual world. For realists, on the other hand, whether the Mona Lisa instantiates the property of beauty is an objective matter that does not change based upon our opinions.

Now consider another possible world just like ours except that everyone in that world is of the opinion that the Mona Lisa is ugly. Then, one would think, the relativist would have to say that the Mona Lisa would be ugly in that world, and so the aesthetic relativist thereby clearly counts as an antirealist given (R2). But not so fast. For one way we assess worlds is to use our *actual* opinions in order to determine what is going on in counterfactual worlds, i.e., in order to determine whether the Mona Lisa is beautiful in a world in which everyone thinks it is ugly. And if the relativist adopts this approach of rigidifying her actual attitudes, then she can *agree* with the aesthetic realist that the instantiation of the property of beauty by the Mona Lisa does not change even in worlds in which people adopt radically different attitudes towards its beauty.

So we need one more move to correctly delineate the difference between the realist and the antirealist. For the realist, what matters concerning objects in nearby possible worlds is their existence and nature as divorced from *any* intentional attitudes whatsoever, whether actual or counterfactual. Given this, a realist thinks that a thing's existence and nature remain invariant in nearby worlds in which we have undergone variations in our intentional attitudes towards it. This leads to a better, although unfortunately more cumbersome, way of stating the conditions for general realism:

(R+) Realism about X is true iff and because:
- (i) X exists.
- (ii) In the nearby worlds in which human beings have different intentional attitudes from those in the actual world which pertain to X, it is the case that:
  - (a) The existence and nature of X remain unchanged from how they are in the actual world.
  - (b) The existence and persistence conditions of X do not result to any extent from any intentional attitudes that pertain to X in the actual world.

With condition (a) by itself, the antirealist could agree that the existence and nature of X do not change in the relevant counterfactual worlds, provided that such an assessment of X in those worlds stems from the attitudes that the antirealist has in the *actual* world. Thus, we need to combine (a) with condition (b), so that realism will be true of X provided only that X is unchanged in these particular counterfactual worlds, and yet, at the same time, X in those worlds does not have existence and persistence conditions that result from our actual intentional attitudes. Provided such conditions are met, then we can say that X exists *mind-independently*.

This is obviously a highly theoretical proposal. An example would help.

Applying the account of general realism to a moral example

We can take an example of a moral property, such as the property of being forbidden, and apply (R+) as follows:

(M+) Moral realism is true about actions of a certain type T (such as torturing an innocent child purely for amusement) having the property of being morally forbidden iff and because:

- (i) Actions of type T have the property of being morally forbidden.
- (ii) In the nearby worlds in which human beings have different intentional attitudes from those in the actual world which pertain to the moral status of actions of type T, it is the case that:
  - (a) These actions having the property of being morally forbidden remains unchanged from the actual world.
  - (b) The existence and persistence conditions for those actions having the property of being morally forbidden do not result to any extent from any intentional attitudes which pertain to actions of type T in the actual world.

Less formally, the idea is that for realism to be true of the moral status of such acts of torture, that status must not vary with what anyone thinks about it. Hence in nearby worlds in which everyone thinks that torturing children in this way is morally obligatory, or that in general morality does not exist at all, these acts of torture still have the property of being morally forbidden, *and* not because of the fact that we in the actual world have the opinion that they are forbidden.

Sorting out the metaethical positions

With such a proposal in hand, we can apply it to some of the leading positions in the metaethics literature. The first two positions—cognitivism and noncognitivism—are views in moral psychology about what is involved in making moral judgments. The next three positions —error theory, response-dependence, and moral realism—are primarily metaphysical views about the existence and nature of moral properties.[40]

Cognitivism. As with all of the views which follow, there is no official characterization of cognitivism. Common themes include the following:[41]

Moral judgments are or are expressions of cognitive mental states such as beliefs.
Moral statements are truth-apt or truth-evaluable.
Moral statements are factual.
Moral statements purport to represent the world as being a certain way.

Hence on cognitivist views, when I say that "Murder is wrong" in an ordinary conversational context, I am typically giving expression to my belief about what is the case with respect to acts of murder. Note, though, that nothing about cognitivism is committed to the actual *existence* of moral facts, properties, or states of affairs (hereafter "moral properties" for the sake of simplicity). So cognitivism does not entail moral realism. Indeed, as we will mention in a moment, an error theory can combine cognitivism with the outright denial of moral facts altogether. For it might turn out, for all that cognitivism by itself is claiming, that moral judgments are expressions of beliefs and represent the world as being in a certain way, but that they are also all systematically false—in the same way that according to atheists, much traditional theological discourse, while cognitive in nature, is simply false.

Noncognitivism.[42] Traditional versions of noncognitivism of the kind developed early in the twentieth century by A. J. Ayer and certain other logical positivists,[43] simply deny one or more of the cognitivist claims above:

Moral judgments are or are expressions of noncognitive mental states such as desires.
Moral statements are not truth-apt or truth-evaluable.
Moral statements are nonfactual.
Moral statements do not purport to represent the world as being a certain way.

So, to take a simple example, my statement "Murder is wrong" could turn out to be an expression of one or more desire-like states which are opposed to murder. As such, then, I am not ascribing a moral property to murder or purporting to represent what is the case factually-speaking with respect to such acts.

While strictly speaking noncognitivism is only making psychological and semantic claims about moral judgments, it is almost inevitably paired with a metaphysical rejection of moral properties, and so does not comport well with moral realism as we have formulated the view above.[44]

Error Theory. According to Mackie, moral concepts and judgments purport to refer to objective (and specifically nonnatural) moral facts, and so Mackie is a cognitivist about moral judgments. But to this he adds the additional claim that no such objective facts actually exist, either because there are no moral facts of any kind, or because the ones which exist are not suitably objective. Hence our moral judgments turn out to be systematically false, and at least this version of the moral error theory clearly counts as an antirealist view using (R+).[45]

But this is not the only form the error theory might take. Suppose it turns out that we are really relativists in our moral thinking, but that on metaphysical grounds objective moral facts do actually exist. Then we would be systematically in error on this picture as well. And other permutations of our moral thought on the one hand, and the metaphysical existence (or not) of moral facts on the other hand, are possible.[46]

Broadly Response-Dependent Views: Subjectivism, Relativism, Constructivism, and Ideal Observer Views. These views tend to accept a cognitivist account of moral judgments. But they are not error theories—they also all accept that moral judgments can come out true in many instances and that moral facts of some kind do exist. Typically what we get on their accounts is a biconditional linking some purported moral rightness or goodness fact with what a paradigm individual or community does or would endorse.[47]

Subjectivism, in at least many leading versions, ties moral properties to our desires, and a crude example of the view would be that:

(i) A consequence of my action is morally good iff I approve of the consequence.

Cultural moral relativists tie moral properties to cultural and social practices, and could accept something like this:

(ii) An action A is morally obligatory for Jones to perform iff Jones's society requires A.

In a broad sense of "constructivism," all response-dependent views are forms of constructivism. But typically *constructivist* approaches have tried to secure some distance from actual human desires and practices. For example, according to John Rawls:

(iii) P is a principle of justice iff P is what free and rational persons concerned to further their own interests would accept in an initial position of equality as defining the fundamental terms of their association.[48]

Similarly, according to Michael Smith's version of the dispositional theory of value:

(iv) We morally ought to x in C iff we would all of us converge, and necessarily so, upon a desire that we x in C if we had a maximally coherent and rational set of pro- and con-attitudes.[49]

And David Lewis claims that:

(v) X is a value iff we would be disposed to value x under conditions of the fullest imaginative acquaintance with X.[50]

The dividing line between constructivist views and *ideal observer views*, as with all of these positions, is not clear either, and perhaps the latter is best understood as an instance of the former. In any event, here is what one leading advocate of an ideal observer view has proposed:

(vi) "Murder is wrong" means "Any ideal observer [omniscient with respect to non-ethical facts, omnipercipient, disinterested, dispassionate, and consistent] would react to murder in such and such a way in such and such conditions."[51]

Numerous other examples of such response-dependent accounts could also be mentioned, but what all these views seem to have in common is a commitment to something like the following version of the basic equation:

(B) X is [moral status] if and only if X tends to elicit [response] from [respondents] in [circumstances].

where the class of [respondents] and [circumstances] is taken to be ideally suited to the kind of moral phenomenon at issue.[52]

There are at least three considerations that figure prominently in evaluating the compatibility of moral realism with response-dependent views. The first is that the relevant biconditional can be proposed either at the level of moral concepts or at the level of moral facts. If the former is the case, however, then response-dependent views are neutral with respect to the truth of moral realism unless, and until, they are supplemented with an ontological thesis about the existence and nature of the moral entities in the extension of the concept.

Secondly, merely positing a biconditional between some moral phenomenon and our responses underdetermines the direction of explanation and thereby falls prey to a familiar Euthyphro dilemma—such biconditionals can be given either a left-to-right "detectivist" reading or a right-to-left "projectivist" reading.[53] And a detectivist reading, according to which the relevant respondents come to have the responses they do *because* the thing in question is morally good or right, is naturally well-suited to a realist outlook. However, it is the projectivist reading that is intended by advocates of most response-dependent views. Thus, for example, it is *because* agents behind a veil of ignorance would endorse a certain principle of justice that such a principle is binding on them.

Finally, the biconditional can be offered either as a *reduction* of some part of the moral, and thereby precludes use of the moral term on the right-hand side on pain of circularity, or as a nonreductive elucidation of some part of the moral, thereby freely appealing to the same term in filling out either the class of respondents or the kind of circumstances. As an example of the latter, consider the following nonreductive account:

(vii) X is good if and only if X tends to elicit the judgment that X is good from good people in circumstances of full imaginative acquaintance with X.

But such an analysis would be compatible with moral realism if the right-hand side appeals to an independently characterizable concept or property of goodness.

In general, then, it turns out that a number of different forms of a broadly response-dependent view are compatible with moral realism. But these are also typically *not* the forms of the view that self-described advocates of response-dependent positions have in mind. Rather, they usually offer a response-dependent biconditional that is ontological, projectivist, and reductive. Since such views purport to tie moral facts to the intentional attitudes of human beings, albeit often vastly improved human beings, they imply claims that are incompatible with condition (ii) of (R+), and thereby count as forms of antirealism.

Realism. What do the options look like for those metaethicists who, using our taxonomy, fall on the moral realist side? First of all, moral realists are inevitably cognitivists about moral judgments—they think that those judgments express beliefs which purport to represent how things are morally. Furthermore, on metaphysical grounds, realists not only accept the existence of moral facts (along with those who advocate response-dependent views), but they also claim that such facts are objective. While there is no one widely accepted approach among moral realists to spell out what objectivity amounts to, my proposal in (M+) is an attempt to get at the heart of the matter.[54]

The main divide separating moral realists is a divide between naturalists versus nonnaturalists. These terms have proven to be difficult to pin down, but for our purposes we can characterize moral naturalism roughly as the view that moral properties are investigable empirically by the sciences. Note that on this approach, moral properties do not have to be identical to descriptive properties. In other words, nonreductive constitution views about the relationship between the moral and the descriptive can still count as forms of naturalism, so long as the supervening moral properties themselves are amenable to scientific inquiry. Nonnaturalists, then, also accept such a nonreductive metaphysical picture, but deny the claim about scientific investigation.[55]

Two leading naturalist positions in metaethics are Cornell realism and moral functionalism. Both agree that objective moral properties exist, and furthermore that these properties are either identical to, or at least constituted by, certain descriptive properties. Their disagreement has to do with the role that conceptual analysis should play, with functionalists affirming and Cornell realists denying that moral predicates and sentences can be analyzed in the form of necessary and sufficient conditions which employ only descriptive and not moral terms.[56]

Nonnaturalist approaches to moral realism divide into secular and religious kinds, and both have seen an increase in attention in recent years. Theological voluntarists have tended to focus their attention on God's psychology or commands as the metaphysical ground for deontological properties, whereas a recent strategy involves grounding axiological properties in resemblance relations to God's own goodness.[57] Secular versions of nonnaturalist moral realism, on the other hand, claim that moral properties exist objectively without any creative source (whether human or divine), while at the same time nonreductively supervening on descriptive properties.[58]

Hopefully the framework developed in (R+) can prove to be a useful tool for organizing these and other important metaethical positions.[59]

A Taxonomy of Normative Ethical Theories

Recall that a normative ethical theory attempts to understand the underlying features in virtue of which something (an action, person, motive, etc.) has the moral status that it does. Unfortunately, as there was with the metaethical positions, there is an equally wide ranging and often confusing array of normative theories. To begin to try to helpfully arrange them, let us return to our schema for organizing the various elements of normative concern:

(1) Object of evaluation O has normative status S in virtue of bearing dependence relation R to one or more considerations C.

And let us simplify the schema for our purposes in this section by focusing just on the deontological status of actions:

(2) An action has the status of being morally obligatory in virtue of one or more considerations C.

We can then divide some of the leading approaches in ethics based upon whether they appeal to *one* fundamental ethically relevant feature, or to *more than one* such feature in their account of moral obligation:

One Feature (Monism):

Traditional Act-Utilitarianism
Ethical Egoism
Kantian Views
Rule-Utilitarianism
Theological Voluntarism
Hybrid Monism

Multiple Features (Pluralism):

Rossian Pluralism
Hybrid Pluralism
Pluralistic Utilitarianism

We will go over each of these views below. But first I want to introduce another distinction.[60] Let us begin with our commonsense folk morality. One feature of that morality is a commitment to:

(i) *Agent-Centered Constraints or Restrictions*: Prohibitions against certain actions even if performing those actions would maximize the overall good or prevent a worse overall outcome.[61]

Suppose that by covertly killing one unsuspecting patient, a doctor can save the lives of three other patients who immediately need organ transplants. Or suppose that in a particular society, the practice of slavery would bring about more overall good than would a focus on equality for all. In either example, ordinary morality would presumably condemn such a practice, other things being equal. Hence ordinary morality accepts the existence of constraints on the permissibility of maximizing the overall good. It may be a matter of debate whether such constraints are to be understood as absolute, and so admit of no exceptions, or have thresholds after which the constraint no longer applies. But either way, it is undeniable that ordinary morality is committed to constraints of some kind.

Ordinary morality also includes:

(ii) *Agent-Centered Options*: Two actions can both be morally optional and not required, even though one of them would bring about more overall good than the other.[62]

In many cases, donating $10 to a famine relief organization would bring about more good than spending the money on a movie ticket, but ordinary morality gives us the option of doing either. With constraints and options in mind,[63] we can take our initial distinction between monist and pluralist positions and further categorize the same ethical theories listed above as follows:

One grounding feature, typically rejects both constraints and options.

Traditional Act-Utilitarianism
Ethical Egoism

One grounding feature, typically accepts both constraints and options.

Kantian Views
Rule-Utilitarianism
Theological Voluntarism

One grounding feature, typically accepts either constraints or options.

Hybrid Monism

Multiple grounding features, typically accepts both constraints and options.

Rossian Pluralism

Multiple grounding features, typically accepts either constraints or options.

Hybrid Pluralism

Multiple grounding features, typically rejects both constraints and options.

Pluralistic Utilitarianism

There are plenty of other ethical theories than the nine approaches listed above. Here my aim is not to provide a comprehensive list, but rather to outline the broad conceptual space which is available for any ethical theory to occupy, and then use the nine specific positions as illustrations of actual views which already fit into that space. Furthermore, some of the positions listed above (or perhaps the labels that I have used for them) are less than familiar, and hence the taxonomy can seem daunting rather than illuminating at this point. The best thing to do is to turn to each of these positions.[64]

Traditional act-utilitarianism

For act-utilitarianism (AU), the only morally relevant underlying feature of an action is the utility it will produce. Other considerations—whether it harms another person, whether it makes one a better person for performing it, whether it conforms to God's will, and so forth—are ethically insignificant except insofar as they bear on the utility that is brought about. Hence we get the following rough framework for filling in our schema (2):

(i) An action A is morally obligatory for agent S to perform iff, and because, of all the actions available for S to perform in the circumstances, A ranks highest in the aggregate utility it would produce.
(ii) An action A is morally optional for agent S to perform iff, and because, of all the actions available for S to perform in the circumstances, A and at least one other action A* rank highest in the aggregate utility they would produce.
(iii) An action A is morally forbidden for agent S to perform iff, and because, of all the actions available for S to perform, A ranks lower in the aggregate utility it would produce than some other action A* that S could also perform in the circumstances.

The "because" clause is added to make it clear that it is the utility of outcomes which is what makes it the case that actions have their ethical status according to AU.

What is utility? Here act-utilitarians diverge, but traditional advocates of the view were hedonists about utility, and so equated it with pleasure. Or, more precisely, utility is a matter of the presence or promotion of pleasure and the absence or prevention of pain, if the act-utilitarian also maintains that preventing pain is an intrinsically good thing too.[65] Note that in some cases, all the available options might involve bringing about a greater balance of pain over pleasure, and so causing the least amount of net pain may be the best option available to an agent. For such cases, the *aggregate* utility might be negative, but the morally obligatory thing to do is still to perform that action which ranks highest in aggregate utility.

A few familiar points should be made about the above framework: first, it is not stated in terms of the *amount* of utility that an action would produce. Advocates of AU can rank utility using a number of criteria, and the quantity of utility need only be one of them. Thus Bentham was a hedonist about utility who used criteria such as intensity, duration, and fecundity in his ranking.[66] Famously, Mill criticized Bentham for not taking into account the quality of pleasures, and argued that the value of higher-quality pleasures can outweigh the value of greater amounts of lower-quality pleasures.[67]

Secondly, the moral status of an action on AU is typically not a matter of what bearing the action has just on the utility of the agent performing it. Rather, it is a function of the utility ranking as impartially construed, and so may require actions which, if performed, would have tremendous utility costs for the agent who carries them out. Hence the perspectives of all beings for whom utility considerations apply and who would be affected in some way by the action are taken into account in grounding its status. If utility is understood in terms of pleasure and pain, for instance, then the perspectives of certain non-human animals would matter to action assessment as well.

Thirdly, it is important to stress that the above are act-utilitarian *moral criteria* for what actually makes an action obligatory, optional, and wrong. They are not necessarily *moral decision procedures*.[68] In other words, it does not follow from AU that we should always employ such criteria in our deliberative reasoning. Whether we *should* or not is itself a matter, presumably, of what would maximize utility. And so, as has been frequently noted, it may be that the principles of ordinary morality serve as a better decision procedure to follow in many cases, even from an act-utilitarian perspective.

Fourthly, and related to the last idea, note that (i) through (iii) above are stated in terms of what *actual utility* an action would produce, as opposed to its *expected utility*, where the latter is (roughly) the sum of taking each distinct set of possible outcomes of an action and multiplying the estimated probability of that set of outcomes by its utility. Hence the above is a version of objective act-utilitarianism. But one could hold a version of *subjective* act-utilitarianism where (i) through (iii) are formulated in terms of expected utility rather than actual utility.

With these clarifications in mind, it should be clear why traditional AU rejects both constraints and options. To use our organ harvesting and slavery examples, if such practices came out as the highest ranked ones, then they would be morally obligatory on (i), thereby violating ordinary morality's constraint on such forms of harming. And given (ii), the only time an action will be optional is if it is tied for first place in the utility ranking with another action. In cases like spending $10 on the movies or on famine relief, such a tie is highly unlikely. And in general, there is no room on (ii) for performing an action which brings about less than the maximal amount of aggregate utility in the circumstances.

AU is a species of *consequentialism*. However, as Douglas Portmore notes in his chapter, there is almost nothing which unites the various species of consequentialism beyond their grounding the normative status of actions in terms of the rankings of the outcomes of those actions. Hence, I have avoided using consequentialism as part of the taxonomy in this section in favor of more concrete instances of the view.

Traditional Ethical Egoism

Ethical egoism bears a noticeable resemblance in structure to act-utilitarianism. Here is one common way of formulating the view:

(i) An action A is morally obligatory for agent S to perform iff, and because, of all the actions available for S to perform in the circumstances, A ranks highest in promoting S's self-interest.

The accounts of the morally optional and morally forbidden would parallel what we saw with AU above. Note that the main change from AU is that what grounds the deontological status of actions is solely what is in the agent's self-interest, and what benefits other human beings, is in accordance with God's will, etc., is relevant only to the extent to which it has a bearing on that self-interest. As with "utility," there is no one understanding of "self-interest" among ethical egoists, although here too the traditional view is to understand it in terms of pleasure and pain.

Ethical egoism is to be contrasted with *psychological egoism*, which holds (roughly) that the ultimate goal of each action performed by every person is to promote his or her own self-interest. As such, psychological egoism is a descriptive claim about how we actually are, rather than a normative view. Furthermore, it is logically independent of ethical egoism—one could hold either view without holding the other. And it is a view which has been cast into doubt by much recent work in social psychology.[69]

We should also note that (i) is not the only way one could formulate an ethical egoist position. One could accept a *threshold* on the promotion of self-interest, such that any action above the threshold is optional even though some would benefit the agent more than others. One could also develop a version of *rule-egoism* where actions are directly assessed by rules which themselves are assessed in terms of the self-interest their acceptance would promote.[70] And one could hold a form of *subjective ethical egoism* where actions are assessed in terms of their bearing on the agent's expected self-interest. But none of these views has found much support.

Traditional ethical egoism also rejects both constraints and options. An agent can be required to perform an action, even if so doing would necessitate killing several innocent people, provided it was ultimately in the agent's self-interest. Anything less than maximizing the agent's self-interest will not be an option, as it is according to commonsense morality.

Kantian Views

One natural place to look for a view which appeals to a single grounding feature for moral obligation while also accepting agent-centered constraints and options is any ethical theory inspired by Kant. Consider, for instance, Kant's second formulation of the categorical imperative: "Act in such a way that you treat humanity, whether in your own person or in any other person, always at the same time as an end, never merely as a means."[71] Now, as with everything from Kant, interpreting such a passage is a matter of much textual dispute which we will eschew here. Some approaches use the idea of shared purposes to unpack what it is to treat another as an end, others the idea of human dignity, and still others the idea of respect for persons.[72] Here, for instance, is one way of fleshing out the view:

(i) An action A is morally obligatory for agent S to perform iff, and because, A treats S and other persons as beings with intrinsic dignity, and not merely as beings with price.

For our purposes, we need only note that a moral theory derived from the second formulation will typically ground moral obligation in a single feature, in this case dignity (which itself is grounded in something further such as an agent's rational capacities). Furthermore, it clearly involves a constraint on maximizing the good, since doing so will be forbidden if it thereby treats a being with dignity merely as a means.

The question of options is a bit trickier. In one place in the *Groundwork* Kant writes: "This harmonizing with humanity as an end in itself would, however, be merely negative and not positive, unless everyone else endeavours, as far as he can, to further the ends of others. For the ends of any person who is an end in himself must, if this idea is to have its full effect in me, be also, as far as possible, my ends."[73] Nevertheless, despite the demandingness of such remarks, a common interpretation of Kant's work as a whole is that the positive duty to promote others' ends is a limited duty, i.e., an imperfect duty. This would make sense in light of Kant's aim to provide a systematic understanding of our commonsense morality.[74] And a similar view is found in the writings of many self-described Kantians who draw on the second formulation.[75]

Here we have focused on Kant's second formulation, but his other formulations of the categorical imperative can also be understood as single-feature views which involve both constraints and options.

Rule-utilitarianism

According to AU, the deontological status of actions is grounded directly in their utility promotion. But for rule-utilitarianism (RU), there is an intermediate step between obligation and utility, namely the assessment of the action by those rules whose acceptance would best promote utility. More formally, one way of stating RU is the following:

(i) An action A is morally obligatory for agent S to perform iff, and because, of all the actions available for S to perform in the circumstances, A is required by a set of moral rules which has an acceptance utility that ranks higher than the acceptance utility associated with any alternative set of moral rules applying to the circumstances.

Parallel criteria could be used for optional and forbidden actions. Acceptance utility is to be understood here roughly as the utility that would be produced in a given society if most of the people in the society were to accept a given set of moral rules.[76] So while actions are directly assessed in terms of their conformity to rules, the fundamental ethically relevant feature for RU is still utility.

Variations are possible. We might formulate (i) in terms of expected rather than actual acceptance utility. And there are various ways of ranking acceptance utility besides aggregating it, such as giving some weight to the distribution of acceptance utility in a society. Brad Hooker adopts both of these variations in his formulation of what he calls rule-consequentialism: "An act is wrong if it is forbidden by the code of rules whose internalization by the overwhelming majority of everyone everywhere in each new generation has maximum expected value in terms of well-being (with some priority for the worst off)."[77]

Other variants of RU result from accepting or rejecting constraints and options. By itself, (i) does not mandate that the moral rules with the highest ranking acceptance utility be ones which have either of these features—indeed, the rule in question could even be the act-utilitarian principle to maximize overall utility. But as a matter of fact, advocates of RU typically motivate their view by claiming that the moral rules it prescribes will likely be simpler, less demanding rules to follow which are closer to those of ordinary morality than are the act-utilitarian principles. In particular, they will be rules which forbid certain actions in some cases even though their performance would maximize the good, and they will be rules which allow people to have enough freedom to choose between multiple options even though some options are more utility promoting than others.[78] Hence, like pure deontologists, advocates of RU typically accept constraints and options, although they ground them in a different way than we saw above.

Theological voluntarism

A rather different monist view from the Kantian and rule-utilitarian approaches is one that grounds moral obligations in facts about God. A range of different voluntarist accounts has emerged in the literature, such as the following:

(i) *Divine Command Theory*: Deontological properties are metaphysically grounded in God's relevant commands.[79]

(ii) *Divine Intention Theory*: Deontological properties are metaphysically grounded in God's relevant intentions.[80]
(iii) *Divine Desire Theory*: Deontological properties are metaphysically grounded in God's relevant desires.[81]
(iv) *Divine Motivation Theory*: Deontological properties are metaphysically grounded in God's relevant emotions.[82]

To expand on just one of them, I have developed a version of divine desire theory according to which:

(iii*) An action A is morally obligatory for agent S to perform iff, and because, after considering all the reasons relevant to S's freely A-ing in the circumstances, God desires that S freely A.[83]

As such, voluntarist views are neutral in their commitment to constraints and options. But as a matter of fact, most voluntarist views take both on board. Constraints are natural to accept, say in the form of the Ten Commandments or a prohibition against blaspheming God. In the case of options, some voluntarists in particular religious traditions claim that, so long as no constraints are violated, we are required to always satisfy certain demanding principles such as loving our neighbors as ourselves.[84] But this approach is controversial in the relevant literature.[85]

Hybrid monism

Constraints and options do not have to be packaged together. One could, for instance, accept *constraints without options*, which would amount to the following:

(i) One is *forbidden* from bringing about the best outcome if doing so would violate one or more constraints.
(ii) But one is *required* to bring about the best outcome if no constraint would be violated.

As a simple example, we can take our formulation of act-utilitarianism's criterion for obligatory actions, and add a single constraint designed to protect the dignity of persons:

(iii) An action A is morally obligatory for agent S to perform iff, and because, of all the actions available for S to perform in the circumstances, A ranks highest in the utility it would produce, so long as A does not violate the dignity of any persons involved in the circumstances.

Such a constraint could render the practices in both the organ harvesting example and the slavery example morally forbidden. Obviously, alternative constraints, additional constraints, and constraints on other positions besides act-utilitarianism are all possible versions of hybrid monism.

Similarly, the opposite strategy of *options without constraints* is also available, which would amount to the following:

(iv) One is not always *obligated* to bring about the best outcome.
(v) But one is always *permitted* to bring about the best outcome.

Samuel Scheffler has developed just such a view, which postulates what he calls an "agent-centred prerogative" that in his words, "would then allow the agent to promote the non-optimal outcome of his choosing, provided only that the degree of its inferiority to each of the superior outcomes he could instead promote in no case exceeded, by more than the specified proportion, the degree of sacrifice necessary for him to promote the superior outcome."[86] Such a view would seek to mitigate the frequently alleged overdemandingness of act-utilitarianism.

Rossian pluralism

At this stage we turn from views which ground deontological moral properties in one fundamental morally relevant feature, to views which ground such properties in multiple features.

Perhaps the most famous such view in the twentieth century was developed by W. D. Ross in his 1930 book *The Right and the Good*. We will consider Ross's view in a moment, but for now let us instead begin with a broadly *Rossian* pluralist view. To take a familiar example, for a Rossian the fact that an action would violate a promise grounds a prima facie duty not to perform it. But suppose that, subsequent to making a promise to meet a friend for lunch in an hour, you find that you are the only person who can drive a desperately ill family member to the hospital. This need of your family member also grounds a prima facie duty to take him to the hospital. Unfortunately, in such a case these two prima facie duties conflict.

According to the Rossian, there is no single, more fundamental morally relevant feature which grounds all prima facie duties and can be used to resolve conflicts between them. Rather there is simply a plurality of bedrock features with no absolute priority ranking between them, such that for any two morally relevant features, in some cases feature F1 outweighs feature F2, whereas in others F2 outweighs F1. In our example above, clearly helping the relative outweighs keeping the promise, but we can easily imagine cases where the opposite is true. Note, though, that the prima facie duty to keep the promise is only outweighed, not eliminated, as is evidenced by our disapproval of you if you never made an attempt afterwards to contact your friend and let him or her know why you were absent at lunch.

Our duties proper, or duties all-things-considered, are a function of the stringency of the relevant prima facie duties which apply in the circumstances:

(i) An action A is morally obligatory (all-things-considered) for agent S to perform iff, and because, of all the prima facie duties which apply to A in the circumstances, the prima facie duty (or duties) to A outweighs any other prima facie duty (or duties) which conflicts with doing A.

The morally optional would then involve either cases of ties between the most stringent prima facie duties, or cases where no prima facie duties obtain.[87]

By postulating multiple morally relevant features, only one of which is typically taken to involve promoting the good of others, and by claiming that there is no fixed ranking between these features, the Rossian pluralist can secure constraints on promoting the good, albeit not absolute ones.[88] Options, however, might be a different matter. If there is a standing prima facie duty to promote the good or to prevent the bad from happening, then given the current state of the world, there will almost never be cases in which no prima facie duty obtains and so no room to be allowed to do what is less than maximally good, barring conflicts with outweighing prima facie duties. Thus to accept both options and constraints, it would appear at an initial glance that the Rossian pluralist has to deny that there are such standing prima facie duties to promote the good and prevent the bad. Or perhaps instead these duties can be understood as limited, imperfect duties for which we only have a prima facie obligation to satisfy them on occasion.

Hybrid pluralism

In the previous section, we were careful to describe a *Rossian* pluralist position. But what we outlined—a position which allows for both constraints and options—does not appear to be Ross's own view. Considerations such as promise keeping can in some cases serve as constraints on maximizing the good. But Ross also seems to hold that in cases where no outweighing prima facie duty applies, we are under the standing prima duty to maximize the good.[89] In other words, according to *Ross's hybrid pluralism*:

(i) An action A is morally obligatory (all-things-considered) for agent S to perform iff, and because, S has a prima facie duty D to perform A in virtue of A ranking highest in the goodness it would produce among the actions available to S in the circumstances, unless (other things being equal) either:

(a) There is another prima facie duty which outweighs D and which mandates that S *not perform* A.

(b) There is another prima facie duty which outweighs D and which mandates that S *perform* A, in which case A is morally obligatory for S to perform primarily because of *this* prima facie duty, and also because of D.[90]

To take an example, suppose I am contemplating whether to send five dollars to charity. If that would produce the most good compared to whatever else I can do with the money, then it is morally obligatory on this account (other things being equal). But if I have promised to give the money to my best friend, then that conflicting duty might outweigh the prima facie duty to maximize the good. Finally, though, suppose I had instead promised my parents that I would use the money for charity. Then if my prima facie duty to keep my promise outweighs my duty to maximize the good in this case, it can be what primarily contributes to my all-things-considered moral obligation to donate, even though the other prima facie duty does as well.

This view seems to leave little room for options. And hence, like traditional act-utilitarianism, it can be accused of being overdemanding. Nevertheless, it is a good illustration of a hybrid pluralist position which accepts constraints without options.

Another version of hybrid pluralism has been offered by David Brink.[91] On *Brink's hybrid pluralistic utilitarianism*, there are three distinct good-making features—reflective pursuit of one's projects, the realization of those projects, or the existence of certain personal and social relationships.[92] Combine such an account of the good with utilitarianism, and we have a view which rejects both constrains and options (to be developed in more detail below). But Brink also adds a Kantian constraint that persons be respected.[93] So his official view becomes roughly the following:

(ii) An action A is morally obligatory for agent S to perform iff, and because, A would result in the promotion of one or more of the goods above to a greater degree than would any alternative action that the agent could perform instead, so long as the projects and relationships in question respect persons.

Hence Brink's view is also a hybrid pluralist position which accepts constraints without options.[94]

Pluralistic utilitarianism

Suppose one accepted Brink's view, but rejected the Kantian constraint to respect persons. Then one would have a straightforward instance of pluralistic utilitarianism:

(i) An action A is morally obligatory for agent S to perform iff, and because, A would result in the promotion of one or more of the goods above to a greater degree than would any alternative action that the agent could perform instead.

G. E. Moore's ideal utilitarianism is an actual version of such a view, in that it appeals to a variety of features which make something good, including knowledge and aesthetic experience.[95]

Such views are pluralist because of the multiple considerations which ground the goodness of states of affairs and so, indirectly, the obligatory status of actions. And they also involve rejecting both agent-centered options and constraints, as did act-utilitarianism way back at the beginning of our taxonomy.

Two other ethical theories

Among the omissions to the taxonomy above, two are worth noting by way of conclusion. First, according to *moral particularism*, at least roughly and in many versions, the moral relevance and valance of at least some considerations is not invariant with context, but rather varies according to features of the particular situation. Hence, to use Jonathan Dancy's well-known example, telling a lie has a negative valence in many contexts. But in certain games where lying is required in order to win, it does not have such a valence.[96] Similarly, some considerations such as telling a lie might be relevant to an action's wrongness in certain situations, but irrelevant to its wrongness in others. Relevance, then, is a matter of whether a consideration bears on something's moral status at all in the first place, whereas valance is a matter of whether, if a consideration is relevant, it counts as a positive or a negative feature, for instance. On a standard particularist approach, then, both the relevance and valence of an action's being an instance of telling a lie to its rightness or wrongness are dependent upon the relations it bears to other properties of the context. This is one way of briefly stating the idea of what particularists call holism about reasons.[97]

On the opposing, atomistic view about reasons, a morally relevant consideration maintains both its relevance and its valence regardless of context. Hence for the act-utilitarian who takes utility to be pleasure, the fact that an action would cause pleasure will always be relevant to its obligatory status, and will always have a positive valance. Similarly for the Rossian pluralist, the fact that an action breaks a promise will always be relevant to its prima facie wrongness, and will always have a negative valance.

In a given situation, there may be morally relevant considerations favoring an action, and others opposing the action, thereby making the deontological status of the action dependent on the balance of such considerations, where each consideration for the particularist is holistically dependent on that particular context. Hence one way of stating their account of moral obligation is as follows:

(i) An action A, in a particular context C, is morally obligatory for agent S to perform iff, and because, the morally relevant features in C favor performing A overall.[98]

The reason we have omitted moral particularism from the above taxonomy is that it is typically stated in such a way as to be compatible in principle with several conceptual options we distinguished for an ethical theory. At least as sketched here, particularism is compatible with there being only one fundamental morally relevant feature whose relevance and valence vary contextually, although typically the view is developed by appealing to multiple morally relevant features. It is also compatible with the morally relevant features allowing or excluding agent-centered options in many contexts.

What does seem ruled out by particularism is the existence of certain kinds of constraints. For absolute constraints on the promotion of the good seem to imply the fixed relevance and valance of a consideration such as torturing a child, and particularism denies that any morally relevant consideration has such fixed relevance and valance. The same is true as well of putative constraints with invariant threshold values, say a constraint against killing an innocent person unless five or more innocent people can be thereby saved. Nevertheless, there may still be room on a particularist view for what we might call contextual constraints, such that in certain contexts the morally relevant features in that context favor not performing an action even though it would bring about the most good of any action available to the agent. While these constraints do not hold fixed in all contexts, it is still the case that within any given context they can be just as strict as they are for Kantian or other nonparticularist positions.

Another theory also not mentioned in our taxonomy is *virtue ethics*. Virtue ethicists typically take as their central moral notion the concept of a virtue, or a stable trait of character that is related in certain ways to right action, good motives, and correct judgments. The virtues can then in turn ground the deontological status of an action, such that on one common formulation used by many virtue ethicists:

(i) An action A is morally obligatory for agent S to perform iff, and because, A is the action that a virtuous person, acting in character, would perform in the circumstances.[99]

Stated this way, virtue ethics clearly seems to ground deontological properties in a single morally relevant feature, namely the behavior of a virtuous person. And hence it seems to belong with monist views in our taxonomy.

But this appearance is misleading, and hence explains why virtue ethics was omitted earlier. For the monism/pluralism divide was developed in terms of *fundamental* morally relevant features, and we have only said what, according to virtue ethics, is *directly* morally relevant. So we next need to examine what is relevant to grounding the virtuousness of a person. Here we find answers all over the conceptual terrain. On the monist side, virtuousness might be grounded in the strength of the person's disposition to maximize pleasure, or to promote his or her self-interest, or to obey God's commands, or to treat others as ends and never merely as means. And so forth. But pluralist options are also available. Virtue might be grounded in the strength of the person's disposition to maximize Brink's three goods, or to be properly responsive to Rossian considerations, or even, taking our cue from the particularist, to be properly responsive to considerations whose relevance and valance are contextually dependent. The options are numerous.[100] Nor is there any clear indication from the leading formulations of virtue-ethical accounts of moral obligation whether or not there have to be agent-centered options. Different advocates of the view can go either way. Hence virtue ethics proves to be the most difficult view, of the ones we have considered, to adapt to our taxonomy.[101]

Of course, there are plenty of other important normative ethical theories out there—natural law theory, care ethics, and scalar consequentialism are just a few. As I stated at the beginning of this section, my goal was not to summarize the entire lay of the land in contemporary normative ethics, but just to offer one map to make sense of the terrain. Hopefully helpful clarification has been provided not only here but throughout this chapter.[102]

Bibliography

Adams, R. (1999), *Finite and Infinite Goods: A Framework for Ethics*. New York: Oxford University Press.

Audi, R. (2004), *The Good in the Right: A Theory of Intuition and Intrinsic Value*. Princeton: Princeton University Press.

—. (2009), "Moral Virtue and Reasons for Action." *Philosophical Issues* 19, 1–20.

Ayer, A. J. (1936/1946), *Language, Truth and Logic*. Second Edition. London: V. Gollancz ltd.

Batson, C. (1991), *The Altruism Question: Toward a Social-Psychological Answer*. Hillsdale: Erlbaum.

Bentham, J. (1948), *An Introduction to the Principles of Morals and Legislation*. New York: Hafner.

Brink, D. (1989), *Moral Realism and the Foundations of Ethics*. Cambridge: Cambridge University Press.

Copp, D. (2006), "Introduction: Metaethics and Normative Ethics," in D. Copp (ed.), *The Oxford Handbook of Ethical Theory*. Oxford: Oxford University Press, 3–35.

Dancy, J. (1993), *Moral Reasons*. Oxford: Oxford University Press.

—. (2004), *Ethics without Principles*. Oxford: Oxford University Press.

Darwall, S. (1998), *Philosophical Ethics*. Boulder: Westview Press.

Deigh, J. (2010), *An Introduction to Ethics*. Cambridge: Cambridge University Press.

Devitt, M. (1991), *Realism and Truth*. Second Edition. Princeton: Princeton University Press.

Dreier, J. (1993), "Structures of Normative Theories." *The Monist* 76, 22–40.

Enoch, D. (2011), *Taking Morality Seriously: A Defense of Robust Realism*. Oxford: Oxford University Press.

Fantl, J. (2006), "Is Metaethics Morally Neutral?" *Pacific Philosophical Quarterly* 87, 24–44.

Firth, R. (1952), "Ethical Absolutism and the Ideal Observer." *Philosophy and Phenomenological Research* 12, 317–45.

FitzPatrick, W. (2008), "Robust Ethical Realism, Non-Naturalism and Normativity," in R. Shafer-Landau (ed.), *Oxford Studies in Metaethics*, Volume 3. Oxford: Oxford University Press, 159–206.

Griffin, J. (1996), *Value Judgement: Improving our Ethical Beliefs*. Oxford: Clarendon Press.

Hill, T. (2006), "Kantian Normative Ethics," in D. Copp (ed.), *The Oxford Handbook of Ethical Theory*. Oxford: Oxford University Press, 480–514.

Hinman, L. (2008), *Ethics: A Pluralistic Approach to Moral Theory*. Belmont: Wadsworth.

Hooker, B. (2000), *Ideal Code, Real World: A Rule-Consequentialist Theory of Morality*. Oxford: Clarendon Press.

Hooker, B. and M. Little (eds.) (2000), *Moral Particularism*. Oxford: Clarendon Press.

Horwich, P. (1998), *Truth*. Second Edition. Oxford: Clarendon Press.

Hospers, J. (1961), "Rule-Utilitarianism," in Louis P. Pojman (ed.), *Human Conduct: An Introduction to the Problem of Ethics*. Reprinted in *Moral Philosophy: A Reader*. Indianapolis: Hackett Publishing Company, 2003.

Hursthouse, R. (1999), *On Virtue Ethics*. Oxford: Oxford University Press.

Joyce, R. (2001), *The Myth of Morality*. Cambridge: Cambridge University Press.

Jackson, Frank. (1998), *From Metaphysics to Ethics: A Defense of Conceptual Analysis*. Oxford: Clarendon Press.

Kagan, S. (1992), "The Structure of Normative Ethics," *Philosophical Perspectives* 6, 223–42.

—. (1998), *Normative Ethics*. Boulder: Westview Press.

Kant, I. (2002), *Groundwork of the Metaphysics of Morals*. Thomas Hill (ed.). Oxford: Oxford University Press.

Lance, M. and M. Little. (2006), "Particularism and Antitheory," in D. Copp (ed.), *The Oxford Handbook of Ethical Theory*. Oxford: Oxford University Press, 567–94.

Lewis, D. (1989), "Dispositional Theories of Value." *The Proceedings of the Aristotelian Society* 63. Reprinted in *Papers in Ethics and Social Philosophy*. Cambridge: Cambridge University Press, 2000, 68–94.

Mackie, J. L. (1977), *Ethics: Inventing Right and Wrong*. New York: Penguin.

McNaughton, D. and P. Rawling. (2000), "Unprincipled Ethics," in Hooker and Little 2000, 256–75.

—. (2006), "Deontology," in D. Copp (ed.), *The Oxford Handbook of Ethical Theory*. Oxford: Oxford University Press, 424–58.

Mill, J. S. (1998), *Utilitarianism*. Roger Crisp (ed.). Oxford: Oxford University Press.

Miller, C. (2007), "The Conditions of Realism." *The Journal of Philosophical Research* 32, 95–132.

—. (2009a), "The Conditions of Moral Realism." *The Journal of Philosophical Research* 34, 123–55.

—. (2009b), "Divine Will Theory: Desires or Intentions?" *Oxford Studies in Philosophy of Religion*. Oxford: Oxford University Press, 185–207.

—. (2009c), "Divine Desire Theory and Obligation," in Y. Nagasawa and E. Wielenberg (eds.), *New Waves in Philosophy of Religion*. Palgrave Macmillan, 105–24.

Moore, G. E. (1903), *Principia Ethica*. Cambridge: Cambridge University Press.

Murphy, Mark. (1998), "Divine Command, Divine Will and Moral Obligation." *Faith and Philosophy* 15, 3-27.

Oakley, J. (1996), "Varieties of Virtue Ethics." *Ratio* 9, 128–52.

Pigden, C. (1991), "Naturalism," in P. Singer (ed.), *A Companion to Ethics*. Oxford: Blackwell Publishers, 421–31.

Pojman, L. and J. Fieser. (2009), *Ethics: Discovering Right and Wrong*. Belmont: Wadsworth.

Putnam, H. (1981), *Reason, Truth and History*. Cambridge: Cambridge University Press.

Quinn, P. (2000), "Divine Command Theory," in H. LaFollette (ed.), *The Blackwell Guide to Ethical Theory*. Malden: Blackwell, 53–73.

Rachels, S. (2010), *The Elements of Moral Philosophy*. New York: McGraw Hill.

Rawls, J. (1971), *A Theory of Justice*. Cambridge: Harvard University Press.

Rosen, G. (1994), "Objectivity and Modern Idealism: What is the Question?" in M. Michael and J. O'Leary-Hawthorne (eds.), *Philosophy in Mind*. Dordrecht: Kluwer Academic Publishers, 277–319.

Ross, W. D. (1930), *The Right and the Good*. Oxford: Oxford University Press.

Sayre-McCord, G. (1988), "Introduction: The Many Moral Realisms," in G. Sayre-McCord (ed.), *Essays on Moral Realism*. Ithaca: Cornell University Press, 1–23.

—. (1991), "Being a Realist about Relativism (in Ethics)," *Philosophical Studies* 61, 155–176.

Scheffler, S. (1993), *The Rejection of Consequentialism*, Revised Edition. Oxford: Oxford University Press.

Shafer-Landau, R. (2003), *Moral Realism: A Defence*. Oxford: Clarendon Press.

Smith, M. (1989), "Dispositional Theories of Value," *Proceedings of the Aristotelian Society*, Supplementary Volume, 89–111.

—. (1995), "Internal Reasons," *Philosophy and Phenomenological Research* 55, 109–31.

Sturgeon, N. (1986), "What Difference Does It Make Whether Moral Realism is True?" *The Southern Journal of Philosophy* 24, 115–41.
—. (2006), "Ethical Naturalism," in D. Copp (ed.), *The Oxford Handbook of Ethical Theory*. Oxford: Oxford University Press, 91–121.
Timmons, M. (2002), *Moral Theory: An Introduction*. Lanham: Rowman and Littlefield Publishers.
Williams, B. (1985), *Ethics and the Limits of Philosophy*. Cambridge: Harvard University Press.
Wright, C. (1992), *Truth and Objectivity*. Cambridge: Harvard University Press.
Zagzebski, L. (1996), *Virtues of the Mind*. Cambridge: Cambridge University Press.
—. (2004), *Divine Motivation Theory*. Cambridge: Cambridge University Press.

Chronology of Ethics

J. B. Schneewind

The Chronology given here is unabashedly Eurocentric. It starts with Greek philosophy and goes up to the present time, but it does not include philosophers still living when the table was constructed. The one-line comments in the third column give, obviously enough, only the barest indication of the thought of the philosopher they describe. The Chronology as a whole is undoubtedly incomplete, often, I am sure, in ways of which I am not even aware.

How were the philosophers picked for inclusion? Well, I looked through histories of moral philosophy and of philosophy in general. If one of them listed someone as doing moral philosophy the name was considered for inclusion. If I thought the contribution to moral philosophy was too slight the name was left off. I have also included the names of the major historians of moral philosophy.

In addition to various histories and encyclopedias of philosophy, I have used some chronologies and handbooks, including *Annals of English Literature*, Oxford: Oxford University Press, 1961; *The Oxford Companion to Classical Literature*, ed. Sir Paul Harvey, Oxford: Oxford University Press, 1946; and Bernard Grun's remarkable *Timetables of History*, New York, 1991.

I also consulted a number of experts on the history of philosophy. I accepted most of their recommendations about inclusions and exclusions, and their proposals for the one-line descriptions. In many respects this chronology is thus a collaborative effort. For their suggestions I am much indebted to Bonnie Kent, Eileen O'Neill, Karl Ameriks, John Cooper, Jill Kraye, Richard Bett, Eckart Förster, and J.-P. Clero. They are of course not responsible for what I did with their advice, nor for errors, omissions, and such disfiguring as my own prejudices have given to the history of moral philosophy.

Dates	Name	Identifying comments	Religious, cultural, social, and political events
?8th Century BCE	Homer	Portrayals of human character as essence of morality	Homeric poems *Iliad* and *Odyssey* basis of Greek education
? 8th Century BCE	Hesiod		Poetic portrayal of Greek gods, daily life; later than *Iliad*
c. 579–475 BCE	Pythagoras	Pseudo-Aristotle says he was the first to discuss the virtues	Wrote nothing. Though a historical person, was shrouded in myth already by Plato's time
525–456 BCE			Aeschylus, Greek tragedian
c. 500–419 BCE			Pericles
496–406 BCE			Sophocles, Greek tragedian
c. 490–c. 420 BCE	Protagoras	The first Sophist	490 Athenians won battle of Marathon
c. 483–376 BCE	Gorgias	Sophist	
c. 480–425 BCE	Herodotus		First historian of Greece 480 Battle of Thermopylae
480–406 BCE			Euripides, tragedian
469–399 BCE	Socrates	Traditionally taken as founder of moral philosophy	
460–370	Democritus	Atomist, materialist; man's happiness depends on himself	
c. 460 BCE–?			Hippocrates: introduced ethical concerns into medicine
c. 460–c. 400 BCE	Thucydides		Historian of Peloponnesian War (431–404 BCE)
c. 455–c. 360 BCE	Antisthenes	Precursor of Cynicism, associate of Socrates	
459–387 BCE	Aristophanes		Wrote comedies, including one on Socrates
c. 444–c. 357 BCE	Xenophon	Wrote on Socrates and Socratic views	
435–356 BCE	Aristippus of Cyrene	Founder of Cyrenaic school	
c. 425–347 BCE	Plato	First written systematic explorations of moral and political philosophy	
c. 400–c. 325 BCE	Diogenes of Sinope	First Cynic	
400–330 BCE			Praxiteles, sculptor

Dates	*Name*	*Identifying comments*	*Religious, cultural, social, and political events*
384–322 BCE	Aristotle	Major theorist of virtue and the virtues, and of political life	Founded Peripatetic school 335 BCE
365–285 BCE	Crates	Cynic, teacher of Stoic Zeno	
c. 365–c. 275 BCE	Pyrrho	Precursor of one version of skepticism	
c. 350–c. 275 BCE	Polemon	Teacher of Zeno, ethics of life according to nature	
341–271 BCE	Epicurus	Founder of Epicureanism	
336 BCE			Alexander the Great (d. 323 BCE) becomes King of Macedonia
c. 334–264 BCE	Zeno	Founder of Stoicism	
330–239 BCE	Cleanthes	Stoic leader	
323 BCE			Euclid's *Elements*
c. 316–c. 242 BCE	Arcesilaus of Pitane	Socratic and skeptic, founder of Middle Academy	
280–204 BCE	Chrysippus	Stoic, systematized doctrine	
c. 250 BCE	Ariston of Chios	Pupil of Zeno, developed cynical element of stoicism	
c. 240–150 BCE	Diogenes of Babylon	Stoic leader after Chrysippus; brought Stoicism to Rome	
218–217 BCE			Hannibal invades Italy, defeats Romans
214–129 BCE	Carneades	Academic: skeptical attacks on Stoicism, Epicureanism	
2nd Century BCE	Antipater of Tarsus	Head of Stoa at Athens	
146 BCE			Greece, Macedonia, become provinces of Rome
c. 130 BCE	Antiochus of Ascalon	Stoicism as proper heir of Platonism	
135 BCE	Posidonius	Stoic, revised older psychology	
110–c. 75 BCE	Philodemos of Gadara	Studied in Athens, taught Epicureanism in Italy	
106–43 BCE	Cicero	Roman orator and philosopher, major transmitter of Greek philosophy	
100–44 BCE			Julius Ceasar; 58–51 BCE, conquest of Gaul
c. 99–c.55 BCE	Lucretius	Epicurean system in poetic form	
70–19 BCE			Virgil, Latin poet: *Aeneid, Georgics*

Dates	Name	Identifying comments	Religious, cultural, social, and political events
65–8 BCE			Horace, Latin poet: *Satires, Epistles, Odes*
43 BCE–18			Ovid, Latin poet: *Metamorphoses*
30 BCE–50 CE	Philo	Synthesis of Jewish and Greek thought	
4 BCE–65 CE	Seneca	Stoic moralist and theorist	
1st C BCE–1st C CE	Arius Didymus	Stoic, source for other philosophers	
30 (33?)			Crucifixion of Jesus
46–120	Plutarch	Platonizing popular moral essays, criticism of Stoics, Epicureans	
51–57			St. Paul on missions
c. 55–135	Epictetus	Stoic teacher	
c. 65–95			Gospels according to Mark, Luke, Matthew, and John
2nd century			Ptolemy, astronomer
121–180	Marcus Aurelius	Stoic	Roman emperor 161–80
c. 150–c. 215	Clement of Alexandria	Early Christian moral theologian	
160–210	Sextus Empiricus	Main source for Pyrrhonian skepticism	
185–254	Origen	Theologian, defended free will, Platonist	
200–250	Diogenes Laertius	Chronicler of older philosophical views, sole source for many	
205–270	Plotinus	Founder of neo-Platonism; evil as privation	
215–77			Mani, founder of Manichaeism
234–305	Porphyry	Student and biographer of Plotinus; theory of virtue	
305–11			Diocletian and Galerius persecuting Christians
312–13			Constantine accepted Christianity, legalized it in Roman Empire
325			Council of Nicea set Nicene Creed
354–430	Augustine	First major system of Christian moral and political thought	Bishop of Hippo, 396–430
381			Revised Nicene Creed
395			Partition of Roman Empire into East and West

Dates	Name	Identifying comments	Religious, cultural, social, and political events
c. 400			Jerome translated Bible into Latin
410			Decline of Roman empire, marked by sack of Rome by Goths under Alaric, 410
Fl. 400–411	Pelagius	Theologian who asserted strong free will	411–31, controversies over Pelagianism
451			Council of Chalcedon issued declaration on person of Christ
c. 480–524	Boethius	Philosophical reflections on evil, fortune, endurance	
490–560	Simplicius	Late neo-platonic commentator on Aristotle	
529–534			Justinian's codifications of Roman law
570–632	Mohammed		Founder of Islam
800			Charlemagne crowned Holy Roman Emperor by Pope Leo III
950–1037	Avicenna	Muslim Aristotle commentator of neo-Platonic bent	
968			Founding of University of Cordoba
1033–1109	Anselm, O.S.B, Archbishop of Canterbury	Taught that justice can be willed for its own sake, not for sake of happiness.	
1054			Eastern Orthodox and Western Catholic churches separated
1079–1144	Abelard	Theological reflections on importance of intention	
c. 1088			Beginnings of University of Bologna
1095			First Crusade called
1100			Chanson de Roland
c. 1100–1160	Peter Lombard	His *Sentences* became standard theology text until 16th century	
1115–76	John of Salisbury	Christian neoplatonist, argued for importance of true philosophy In politics	
c. 1126–1198	Averroes	Muslim Aristotle commentator, attacked for denying free will, immortality	
1138–1204	Maimonides	Leading mediaeval Jewish philosopher, "negative theology"	

Dates	*Name*	*Identifying comments*	*Religious, cultural, social, and political events*
c. 1160			University of Paris founded
1167–68			Oxford University founded
c. 1168–1253	Robert Grosseteste	First complete Latin translation of *Nicomachean Ethics*	
c. 1200–1280	Albertus Magnus	Pioneering Aristotle commentator, teacher of Aquinas	
1215			Magna Carta signed
1217–1274	Bonaventure, O.F.M.	Opposed what he saw as paganizing trends at University of Paris	
1217–93	Henry of Ghent	Criticized Aquinas, defended voluntarism in ethics	
c. 1224–1274	Thomas Aquinas O.P.	Worked to synthesize Aristotelian and Christian thought	
1225			Roman de la Rose by Guillaume de Loris
c. 1240–82	Siger of Brabant	Associated with Latin Averroism	
1240–1302			Cimabue
c. 1243–4–1316	Giles of Rome	Believed to deny free will	1285, Propositio Magistralis taken from Giles, endorsed by Paris theology faculty, denies evil in will without ignorance in intellect
c. 1250–c. 1306/09	Godfrey of Fontaines	Defended intellectualism in ethics, psychology	
1269–1327			Meister Eckhart, German mystic, poet
1265–1321			Dante, his *Divine Comedy*; placed Siger along with Aquinas in Heaven
1270			Thomas Beckett, archbishop of Canterbury, assassinated on king's orders
1277			Most sweeping anti-Aristotelian condemnation of the Middle Ages, by Bishop of Paris
1266–1308	Duns Scotus O.F.M.	Distinguished between logical and empirical claims about ethics	
1287–1347	William of Ockham	Accepted Scotus's distinction but turned to empirical research	

Dates	Name	Identifying comments	Religious, cultural, social, and political events
c. 1290–1349	Thomas Bradwardine	Attacked new "Pelagians"; Archbishop of Canterbury	
c. 1300–1358	Gregory of Rimini O.E.S.A.	More extensive and historically based reading of Augustine	
c. 1300–c. 1360	Buridan	Commented on Aristotle's ethics	
1304–74	Petrarch	Stoic and Christian; encyclopedia of moral philosophy	Poet, humanist
1309–78			Political controversies related to relocation of papacy from Rome to Avignon
1313–75			Boccaccio
1331–1460	Salutati	Italian humanist; Chancellor of Florence	
1338			University of Pisa founded
1343–1400			Chaucer
c. 1348–1350			Bubonic plague killed 30–60 percent of European population
1360–c. 1452	Pletho	Byzantine Platonist; treatise on virtues	
1364–1430	Christine de Pizan	Virtue theory; argued women can exercise political authority	
1369–1444	Bruni	Italian humanist; translator of Plato and Aristotle	
1380–1459	Poggio Bracciolini	Italian humanist, moral dialogues	
1380			Wycliffe's English Bible
1398–1481	Filelfo	Italian humanist; treatise on moral philosophy	
1406–69			Fra Filippp Lippi
1406–57	Valla	On pleasure; ancient ethics inferior to Christian	
1429–1478	Accaiuoli	Florentine Aristotle commentator, Christian ethics	
1431			Joan of Arc burned at stake
1433–99	Ficino	Major translator of Plato; Platonic ethics	
1445–1510			Botticelli
1453			Constantinople falls to Turks; refugees bring Greek texts West, stimulate rebirth of scholarship
1460–1536	Lefevre d'Etaples	Aristotle, Christian ethics, agree	

Dates	Name	Identifying comments	Religious, cultural, social, and political events
1460–1523	Leone Ebreo	Jewish Platonist; dialogue on love	
1462–1525	Pompanazzi	Italian Aristotelian influenced by Stoic ethics	
1463–1494	Pico della Mirandola	Defended philosophical concord, human dignity	
1466–1536	Erasmus	On free will against Luther	Humanist scholar, editor
c. 1467–1550	Mair (Major)	Scottish Aristotelian, lectured in Paris	
1469–99	Laura de Cereta	Letters on virtues	
1469–1527	Machiavelli	Realistic political and moral philosophy	
c. 1469–1538	Nifo	Italian Aristotelian with eclectic leanings	
1472–1543	Clichtove	French textbook writer; treatise on nobility	
1474–1504			Isabella I, Queen of Aragon
1474–1522			Ariosto
1475–1564			Michelangelo
1478–1535	More, Sir Thomas	Humanist, wrote the original Utopia	
1479–1529			Castiglione, on manners (*The Courtier*, 1528)
1483–1520			Raphael
1483–1546	Luther O.E.S.A	Influenced by late mediaeval Augustinianism, started Protestant reformation	1517, Luther posted 95 Theses
1486–1535	Agrippa	German philosopher, wrote on magic, vanity of human learning	
1490–1576			Titian
1491–1547			Henry VIII of England
1491–1556			Ignatius Loyola
1492			Columbus sails from Spain to the Bahamas, Cuba, Haiti
1493–1540	Vives	Spanish humanist	
1494–1553			Rabelais
1495–1569	Soto	Spanish Dominican, school of Salamanca	
1497–1560	Melanchthon	Lutheran expositions of morality	
1499–1599			Amerigo Vespucci sails to South America and back to Spain
1499–1562	Vermigli	Calvinist commentator on Aristotle's ethics	
1505–72			John Knox
1509–64	Calvin	Protestant theologian, reviver of Augustinian moral outlook	

Dates	Name	Identifying comments	Religious, cultural, social, and political events
1523–1607	Piccolomini, Francesco	Italian eclectic Aristotelian	
1525			Tyndale's English *New Testament*
1526–1560	Fox-Morcillo	Spanish philosopher; textbook on ethics	
1526–95	Muret	French humanist, lectures on Aristotle's ethics	
1530–96	Bodin	Theory of sovereignty, defends toleration	
1530–1595	Daneau	Calvinist, based ethics on Bible	
1533–92	Montaigne	Critic of all previous moral philosophies, sometime skeptic	
1533–1603			Queen Elizabeth I of England
1535–1600	Molina	Started major controversy on free will	
1540–1600	Case	Expounded Aristotle's ethics at Oxford	
1541–1603	Charron	Montaignian skeptic	
1545–63			Council of Trent
1547–1616			Cervantes
1548–1600	Bruno	Pantheist	Burnt as heretic
1548–1617	Suarez	Modern Catholic natural law theorist	
1550–1623	Sanches	Spanish skeptic	
1552–99			Edmund Spenser
1554–1600	Hooker	Restatement of Thomistic natural law	Theologian of Church of England
1556–1621	Du Vair	Reviver of Stoicism	
1561–1626	Bacon	Moralist, voluntarist theory	
1564–93			Marlowe
1564–1642			Galileo
1564–1616			Shakespeare
1565–1645	Marie de Gournay	On virtues and moral psychology; edited Montaigne	
1567–1643`			Monteverdi
1568–1639	Campanella	Utopian writer	
1571–1653	Lucrezia Marinella	Neoplatonic views on virtues, moral development	
1572–1637			Ben Jonson
1572–1608	Keckerman	German theologian, writer of textbooks	
1573–1640	Eustachius a Sancto Paolo	Wrote Catholic theological text, probably read by Descartes	
1576–1631	Ames	Puritan casuist	

Dates	Name	Identifying comments	Religious, cultural, social, and political events
1578			Stephanus edition of Plato, source of future page references
1580–1645	Quevedo	Spanish neo-stoic	
1583–1648	Lord Herbert of Cherbury	First central appeal to intuition in ethics	
1583–1645	Grotius	Founder of modern natural law theory	
1585–1638	Jansen	Revived Augustinianism in Catholic church	Jansenism an important theological, ethical, movement
1649			King Charles I beheaded; the Commonwealth began; 1653–8, Cromwell ruled
1588–1679	Hobbes	Apparently strongly egoistic ethics, defense of powerful ruler	
1590–1635	Burgersdijk	Standard Aristotelian textbook on ethics	
1591–1655	Gassendi	Revived Epicure's ethics. edited his texts	
1594–1656	Hall, Joseph	Neo-stoic	
1596–1650	Descartes	Letters on ethics, moral psychology	
1598–1678	Madeleine de Souvre, marguise de Sablè	Moral maxims	
1600–81			Calderon
1606–84			Corneille
1606–69			Rembrandt
1607–1701	Madeleine de Scudéry	Re-conceptualized virtues; moral psychology	
1609–83	Whichcote	Morality independent of God's will	
1611–1677	Harrington	Utopian republican theory of virtue	
1611			King James Bible
1614–1702	Margaret Fell (Fox)	Quaker, argued for spiritual equality of women and men	
1614–87	More, Henry	Axiomatic ethic, intuition of first principles	
1655–1728	Thomasius, C.	Original if fluctuating views on natural law	
1617–88	Cudworth	Cambridge Platonist, critic of voluntarism, determinism	
1616–80	Elisabeth of Bohemia	Correspondence with Descartes on morality	

Dates	Name	Identifying comments	Religious, cultural, social, and political events
1618–52	Smith, John	Cambridge Platonist	
1618–48			Thirty Years War, ended with Peace of Westphalia 1648
1619–51	Culverwell	Natural law theorist	
1622–73			Moliere, dramatist
1623–1662	Pascal	Religious critic of Jesuit casuistry, theorist of probability	
1624–1669	Geulincx	Cartesian ethics	
1624–95	Nicole	Argued that rational self-interest leads to moral behavior	
1626			Peter Minuit purchases island of Manhattan from native Americans
1626–89	Kristina of Sweden	Moral maxims	
1627–91			Robert Boyle
1628–88			John Bunyan
1631–1718	Cumberland	Anti-Hobbes, moved toward utilitarianism	
1632–1704	Locke	Empiricism and voluntarism as basis of morality	
1632–1694	Pufendorf	Major theorist of modern natural law; voluntarist	
1632–77	Spinoza	Morality in wholly determined world	
1632–75			Vermeer
1635			Founding of French Academy
1636			Founding of Harvard College
1638–1715	Malebranche	Occasionalist ethic; separated morality and self-interest	
1639–99			Jean Racine, dramatist
1640–93	Marguerite de Sabliére	Wrote moral maxims	
1642–60			English Civil War
1642–1727			Isaac Newton
1647–1706	Bayle	Defended toleration, asserted atheists can be moral	
1646–1716	Leibniz	Rationalist, anti-voluntarist, consequentialist	
1651–1715	Fenelon	Pure disinterested love of God possible	
1658–1708	Masham, Damaris	Wrote on virtuous life and on love of God	
1659–1724	Wollaston	Morality as truthfulness in action	
1659–1731			Defoe

Dates	Name	Identifying comments	Religious, cultural, social, and political events
1659–1695			Purcell
1660			Restoration of British monarchy
1665			La Rochefoucauld's *Maxims*
1667			Milton's *Paradise Lost*
1666–1731	Astell, Mary	Malebranchian philosopher and feminist	
c. 1666–c. 1723	Drake, Judith	Against subjection of women to men	
1670–1733	Mandeville	Self-interest the source of morals	
1671–1713	Shaftesbury, 3rd Earl	Platonizing moral sense theory	
1672–1729	Carmichael	Scottish educator, Pufendorfian textbook	
1674–1744	Barbeyrac	Translated Grotius, Pufendorf, defended Pufendorf; history of natural law theory	
1675–1729	Clarke, Samuel	Presented self-evident axioms to ground morals	
1676–1729	Collins	Wrote on free will, morals	
1679–1749	Trotter (Cockburn)	On grounds of morality	
1679–1754	Wolff	Leibnizian systematizer opposed by Kant	
1683–1764			Rameau
1685–1753	Berkeley	Essay on rules and ends	
1685–1750			Johann Sebastian Bach
1685–1759			G. F. Händel
1686–1748	Balguy	Objectivist critic of sentimentalist theory	
			1688 William of Orange landed in England; ruled with Queen Mary
1688–1744	Pope, Alexander	Verse "Essay on Man" 1733	
1692–1752	Butler	Critic of egoism, defender of conscience	
1694–1748	Burlamaqui	Natural law theorist	
1694–1746	Hutcheson	Moral sense and proto-utilitarian theory	
1694–1778			Voltaire
1699–1745	Gay	Theological utilitarian	
1700			British Academy of Science founded
1703–58	Edwards	Puritan Calvinist, theory of will and choice	
1703–1791			John Wesley

Dates	Name	Identifying comments	Religious, cultural, social, and political events
1705–57	Hartley	Associationism explains morality	
1706–46	Emilie du Châtelet	On happiness; trans. Mandeville	
1709–84			Samuel Johnson; *Dictionary* 1755
1709–51	LaMettrie	Materialist, hedonist, outraged everyone	
1710–96	Reid	Anti-Humean creator of Scottish commonsense philosophy	
1711–76	Hume	Associationist theory of morality as sentiment, antireligious ethics	
1712–1778	Rousseau	Human nature good, society corrupts, self-legislation for morality	
1713–84	Diderot	Essays on morals, free will; edited *Encyclopaedie*	
1714–62	Baumgarten	Wrote Wolffian ethics texts used by Kant	
1715–75	Crusius	Acute anti-Wolffian voluntarist read by Kant	
1715–71	Helvetius	Proto-utilitarian, argued for equality of intelligence	
1717–83	d'Alembert	Mathematician, radical philosophical program, *Encyclopaedie*	
1720–1805	D'Arconville, Marie	Wrote on friendship, moral psychology	
1723–89	d'Holbach	Atheist, materialist, determinist, moral system	
1723–91	Price	Innovative intuitionist, pluralist on principles	
1723–90	Smith, Adam	Sympathy and moral sentiments	
1724–1804	Kant	Categorical imperative as new formula for moral knowledge	
1729–96			Catherine the Great
1729–81			Lessing, advocate of tolerance, dramatist, literary critic
1729–1786	Mendelssohn	Wolffian moral philosopher	
1731–93	Macaulay, Catherine	On morals, education	
1733–1804	Priestley	Determinism and materialism compatible with religion	Scientist, Unitarian religious leader
1737–94			Edward Gibbon

Dates	*Name*	*Identifying comments*	*Religious, cultural, social, and political events*
1738–94	Beccaria	Utilitarian reformer of criminal law	
1742–98	Garve	"Popular" philosopher; important annotated translation of Cicero	
1743–94	Condorcet	Radical utopian thinker, theorist of probability	
1743–1805	Paley	Theological utilitarian, emphasizes rules	
1744–1803	Herder	Philosophy of history centering on Volk	
1746			Collapse of Stuart uprising against the English government
1748–1832	Bentham	Widely considered the founder of utilitarianism	
1748–93	De Gouges, Olympe	Rights of women; against slavery	
1749–1832			Goethe, poet, dramatist, critic, scientist
1751–72			Diderot and d'Alambert publish *Encyclopaedie*, radical coverage of all major philosophical issues
1754			Founding of King's College NY, eventually Columbia University
1753–1828	Stewart	Scottish commonsense philosopher	
1756–1836	Godwin	Radical utilitarian, utopian political thinker	
1756–91			Mozart
1757–1823	Reinhold	Letters disseminating Kantianism	
1759–1805	Schiller	Against Kant on dignity and worth	Dramatist, poet
1759–97	Wollstonecraft	Rights of women	
1760–1825	St. Simon	Socialism, asserts justice of first benefiting the worst off	
1761–1826	Staüdlin	First modern history of moral philosophy	
1762–1814	Fichte	Major German idealist	
1764–1822	Sophie de Grouchy de Condorcet	Translated and annotated Adam Smith's *Moral Sentiments*	
1766–1817	De Staël	On passions, on German thought	
1766–1834			Malthus

Dates	Name	Identifying comments	Religious, cultural, social, and political events
1767–1835	Humboldt, Wilhelm von	Ideal person as harmonious work of art; sets limits to state	
1768–1834	Schleier-macher	Moral theologian, determinist	
1769–1821			Napoleon Bonaparte
1770–1827			Beethoven
1770–1850			Wordsworth
1771			First edition of Encyclopedia Britannica
1772–1834			Coleridge, poet, helped bring German philosophy to Britain
1773–1836	Mill, James	Utilitarian ethics and associationism	
1775–1854	Schelling	On human freedom and the nature of evil	
1775			Watts' steam engine
1776			USA Declaration of Independence asserts inalienable rights of all; start of American Revolution (to 1783)
1776–1841	Herbart	Ethics as part of aesthetics in realist system	
1777–1811			Kleist
1778–1820	Brown, Thomas	Morality based on feeling	
1779–1831	Hegel	Self-realization as including previous moral outlooks	
1781–1832	Krause	Sought human union based on friendship; free will	
1783			Montgolfiers' balloon flight
1785–1848	Wheeler, Anna	Utilitarian, on rights on women	
1785–1873			Manzoni
1788–1860	Schopen-hauer	Blind will as source of all, including morality	
1788–1824			Byron
1789			George Washington, first US President
1789			French Revolution; Declaration of Rights of Man and Citizen
1790–1859	Austin	Utilitarian jurisprudentialist	
1791			USA Bill of Rights
1792–1867	Cousin	Eclectic, creator of 19th century French philosophy curriculum	

Dates	Name	Identifying comments	Religious, cultural, social, and political events
1792–1822			Shelley
1793			King Louis XVI of France beheaded; "Reign of Terror"
1794–1866	Whewell	Philosophy of science, intuitional system of ethics, anti-utilitarian	
1794–1871	Grote, George	Utilitarian, important Plato scholar	
1795–1881			Carlyle
1795–1821			Keats
1797–1828			Schubert
1798–1857	Comte	Founder of systematic positivism	
1800–78	Beecher, Catherine	Secularized Calvinist ethic	
1802–85			Victor Hugo
1802–76	Martineau, Harriet	Translated Comte; essays on ethics	
1803–82	Emerson	Essays on self-reliance	
1805–1900	Martineau, James	Intuitionist ethical system stressing motives	
1805–72			Mazzini
1806–1873	Mill, John Stuart	Leading utilitarian theorist, public intellectual	
1807–82			Garibaldi
1807–1858	Mill, Harriet Taylor	Defended equality of women	
1809–1882	Darwin	Evolutionist view of humans, morality	*Origin of Species* (1859) had profound impact on moral philosophy
1809–52			Gogol
1809–75	Jenny Poinsard d'Hericourt	Moral philosophy, rights activist	
1810–61			Cavour
1810–49			Chopin
1811–77	Bain	Utilitarian philosopher and psychologist	
1812–70			Dickens
1812–70			Herzen
1813–1855	Kierkegaard	Originated themes of religious existentialism	
1813–66	Grote, John	Intuitionist critic of Utilitarianism	
1813–1901			Verdi
1813–83			Wagner
1815			Final defeat of Napoleon
1815–98			Bismarck

Dates	Name	Identifying comments	Religious, cultural, social, and political events
1815–1903	Renouvier	Revisionary Kantian, free will as phenomenal	
1817–1881	Lotze	Religious pluralistic monadism with values arising from feeling	
1818–1883	Marx	Founder of modern communism; materialist ethic	
1818–83			Turgenev
1819–80			George Eliot
1819–1900			Ruskin
1819–1901			Victoria, Queen of England 1837–1901
1820–95	Engels	Co-worker with Marx	
1820–1903	Spencer	Evolutionary ethics; widely read	
1821–30			Greek war of independence from Turkey
1821–81			Dostoevsky
1821–80			Flaubert
1823–1918	Coignet, Clarice	Book on morality independent of religion	
1825–1895	Huxley, T. H.	Popularized evolutionary ethics	
1828–1910			Tolstoy
1829			Catholic emancipation in England
1830–1902	Royer, Clemence	Annotated Darwin; wrote on ethics	
1831			Bekker edition of Aristotle, source of future page references
1832			First political reform bill in England
1832–1904	Stephen, Leslie	Evolutionary science of ethics, also a history of utilitarianism	
1832–1920	Wundt	Experimental psychologist, published system of ethics	
1832–98			Lewis Carroll
1832–83			Manet
1833–97			Brahms
1833–1911			Dilthey
1833			Abolition of slavery in British Empire
1834–96	Favre, Julie	Books on several moral philosophers	
1836–1882	Green	Idealist ethics, political philosophy	

Dates	Name	Identifying comments	Religious, cultural, social, and political events
1838–1900	Sidgwick	Reconciliation of intuitionist and utilitarian ethics	Leader in higher education for women
1838–1917	Brentano	Intuitional ethical system	
1838–1903	Lecky	Historian of morals and moral philosophy	
1839–1906			Cezanne
1841–1919			Renoir
1842–1918	Cohen	Neo-kantian, sought apriori science of virtue	
1842–1910	James, William	Pragmatist consequentialism	
1842–98			Mallarme
1843–1920			Galdos, Spanish novelist
1844–1900	Nietzsche	Iconoclastic anti-Christian moralist and theorist	
1846–1924	Bradley	Hegelian critic of British thought; self-realization ethics	
1846–1918	Ziegler	History of Christian Ethics	
1846			Irish potato famine
1847			American Medical Assoc. Code of Ethics
1848			Revolutions in many European countries
1848–1922	Jones, Constance	Wrote on Sidgwick, primer on ethics	
1848–1923			Pareto
1848			Seneca Falls (USA) Declaration of Rights of Women
1849–1914	Jodl	Wrote important history of moral philosophy	
1849–1912			Strindberg
1853–1920	Meinong	Value theory; feeling sole basis of values	
1854–1924	Natorp	Neo-kantian, ethics as logic of "ought"	
1854–91			Rimbaud
1855–1916	Royce	Hegelian ethics of loyalty	
1856–1939	Freud	Society as repressive necessity	Psychoanalysis achieved widespread cultural influence
1856–1933	Robertson, J. M.	Historian of moral philosophy	
1856–1959	.		Shaw, G. B
1857–1924			Joseph Conrad
1859–1941			Wilhelm II of Germany
1858–1936	Hall, T. C.	History of ethics within Christianity	
1858			East India Company yielded rule of India to British government

Dates	Name	Identifying comments	Religious, cultural, social, and political events
1859–1938	Alexander	Evolutionary ethics	
1859–1941	Bergson	Vital spirit guides evolution to man as highest being	
1859–1952	Dewey	Major pragmatist moral philosopher	
1859–1932	Ehrenfels	Value theory; desire as key to value	
1859–1935			Housman, A. E.
1860–1935	Gilman, Charlotte Perkins	For utilitarian social ethic valuing "feminine" moral qualities	
1861–65			United States Civil War; 1863, Emancipation Proclamation
1862–1937			Wharton
1862–1939	Westermarck	Anthropologist, philosopher; relativity	
1863–1930	Calkins	Philosopher and psychologist, book on ethics	Pioneer in struggle for women's education
1863–1916	Munsterberg	Psychologist, value theorist	
1863–1936	Rickert	Value theory	
1864–1949			Richard Strauss
1864–1920			Weber
1865–1936			Kipling
1867–1934			Marie Curie
1867–1959			Frank Lloyd Wright
1868–1953			O'Neill, Eugene
1869–1954			Matisse
1870			First Vatican Council's Declaration of Papal Infallibility
1870–71			Franco-Prussian War
1870–1924			Lenin
1871–1947	Prichard	Intuitionist, pluralist on principles	
1871–1945			Dreiser
1871–1922			Proust
1872–1970	Russell	Essays on moral theory and morality	
1873–1958	Moore	Denounces "naturalistic fallacy"; ideal utilitarianism	
1873–1947			Cather
1873–1943			Rachmaninoff
1874–1928	Scheler	Phenomenology of ethics, sympathy	
1874–1937			Marconi
1874–1951			Schönberg
1875–1955			Thomas Mann
1875–1926			Rilke

Dates	Name	Identifying comments	Religious, cultural, social, and political events
1876–1957			Brancusi
1877–1971	Ross	Aristotle scholar, intuitionist moral view	
1878–1965	Buber	Jewish theologian, theorist of "I-thou"	
1878–1953			Josef Stalin
1879–1955			Albert Einstein
1880–1942			Robert Musil
1881–1945			Bartok
1881–1973			Picasso
1882–1950	Hartmann, N	Value theory, free will	
1882–1973	Maritain	Neo-thomist realist ethics	
1882–1936	Schlick	Main logical positivist treatise on ethics	
1882–1941			James Joyce; *Ulysses*, 1922
1882–1941			Virginia Woolf
1883–1969			Gropius
1883–1924			Kafka
1883–1946			Keynes, J. M.
1883–1956	Ortega y Gasset	Critic of modern mass society	
1885–1933			Alban Berg
1888–1965			T. S. Eliot; *The Waste Land,* 1922
1883–1964	Lewis C.I.	Value theory and theory of norms	
1887–1971	Broad	Analytic ethics, historical studies of moral philosophy	
1889–1951	Wittgenstein	The ethical cannot be expressed	
1891–1953			Prokofiev
1892–1975			Franco rules Spain from 1936 until his death
1897–1962			Faulkner
1898–1956			Brecht
1898			Curies discover radium, polonium
1901–81	Lacan	Seminar on ethics of psychoanalysis	
1901–62	Murphy	Wide-ranging critique of ethical theories	
1902			Vol.1 of the Akademie Edition of Kant's works
1903–87	Findlay	Eclectic and acute writings on ethics	
1903–57			Von Neumann
1903–50			George Orwell
1906–1980	Sartre	Existentialism and its ethics	Playwright and novelist
1906–96	Levinas	Reworking of Jewish ethics	

Dates	*Name*	*Identifying comments*	*Religious, cultural, social, and political events*
1906–1975			Shostakovich
1907–73			Auden
1908–1986	De Beauvoir	Feminist; existential ethics	Novelist, critic
1908–94	Frankena	Analytic discussions of major topics in ethics	
1908–79	Stevenson	Carefully elaborated emotivist ethics	
1909–97	Berlin	Pluralist about principles and values	
1909–43	Weil, Simone	Restates religious views in new ways	
1910–97	Brandt	Complex utilitarian views, major textbook	
1910–1989	Ayer	Brought positivist ethics to England	
1913–76			B. Britten
1913–60	Camus	Existentialist theorist, novelist	
1913–2005	Ricoeur	Complex views on ethics, morality, action, will	
1914–18			World War I
1916–2003	Von Wright	Logic of norms and good	
1917–87	Firth	Ideal observer theory of cognitive meaning for moral language	
1917–81	Mackie	Error theory in ethics	
1917			Russian Revolution
1919–2001	Anscombe	Critic of modern moral philosophy, theorist of action	
1919–2002	Hare	Logic of imperatives, defense of utilitarianism	
1919–99	Murdoch	Essays on the good and other moral issues, treatise on ethics	
1920			19th amendment to US Constitution grants women right to vote
1921–2002	Rawls	Major 20th century American moral and political thinker	
1922–2009	Toulmin	Wittgensteinian approach to moral reasoning	
1922			Mussolini comes to power in Italy
1926–2004	Feinberg	Philosophy of law, responsibility	
1926–84	Foucault	Historical critiques of social institutions enforcing norms; morality and sexuality	
1929–2003	Williams	Differences between science and morality	

Dates	Name	Identifying comments	Religious, cultural, social, and political events
1929			Vienna Circle begins meeting
1929			U.S. stock market collapse touches off world depression
1933			Hitler made chancellor of Germany
1933–39			Massive flight of writers, artists, intellectuals, Jews, from Germany
1935			"Show trials" begin in Moscow
1936–39			Spanish Revolution
1938–2002	Nozick	Against Rawls on justice, critic of hedonism	
1939–45			2nd World War; 1941, US enters war
1948			UN Declaration of Universal Human Rights
1954			US Supreme Court declares school racial segregation unconstitutional
1965			Second Vatican Council passes Declaration on Religious Freedom, addressed to all people
1973			US Supreme Court declares abortion legal
1982			UN formulates principles of medical ethics

Methodological Issues: Reflective Equilibrium

Michael DePaul

Introduction

Insofar as philosophers have a consensus about the correct method for moral inquiry, the consensus method is reflective equilibrium (henceforth RE). John Rawls (1971, 46ff) is responsible for the name and a systematic description, but it is not hard to make a case that RE has been employed throughout the history of philosophy. Indeed, when he introduced the term "reflective equilibrium" Rawls himself pointed out that this was, in essence, the method employed by Aristotle and Henry Sidgwick, as well as many figures in between.[1]

And it is not hard to discern the early stages of RE being followed in most any philosophy classroom today where ethics is the topic. The professor writes some plausible sounding moral theory on the board, such as John Stuart Mill's Greatest Happiness Principle, and the cleverer students pretty much immediately describe particular examples where what seems to be right or wrong does not match what application of the principle entails. Or students are presented with a number of trolley type scenarios and set about trying to find a distinction between the cases where they think an intervention that would result in fewer deaths is morally acceptable and cases where the intervention is unacceptable. But significantly, not any distinction will do. The problem is to find a distinction that seems to be morally significant on its own. These very familiar kinds of discussions are easily subsumed under RE.

The proviso preceding my claim that RE is the consensus method for philosophical ethics should indicate that the method is not uncontroversial. Indeed, the method was subjected to "lively" criticism as soon as Rawls articulated it and claimed to employ it in developing his theory of justice. And the criticisms continue to the present, supposedly bolstered by findings from psychology and even neuroscience. Virtually all the criticisms focus on the same element of RE: what *seems to be true* about morality—e.g., what seems right or wrong, either in a particular case or in general—plays a significant role in the method. This has struck many critics as a thinly disguised form of intuitionism (boos and hisses expected here). More moderate critics complain that it is not legitimate to rely on such intuitions unless they can first be shown to be reliable, and indeed they have not been shown to be reliable. The more aggressive critics charge that moral intuitions are in fact unreliable, and have been shown to be such.

I'm getting ahead of myself. Before delving into the objections to RE—some old and some new—I need to present a clear description of the method. I'll state my sympathies right now: I'm a proponent of RE, not a critic. So I'll be doing my best to describe RE in the best possible light. After the description I'll consider the objections that are usually seen as most worrisome. I said I'm a proponent of RE, but I hope I am not a blind devotee. I'll close by turning my attention to the two objections that I consider most troublesome, but that usually are not mentioned.

Reflective Equilibrium

Narrow reflective equilibrium

How are we to begin a philosophical inquiry into morality? We might try to follow Descartes' lead and set aside every moral belief about which there is any possibility of doubt so that we can build our theory upon an absolutely firm foundation. The problem is, we probably have no beliefs in nontrivial moral propositions[2] that are entirely indubitable. So if we followed a Cartesian method, we could expect our efforts to construct a moral theory to fare about as well as Descartes' efforts to reconstruct our knowledge of the "external world."

What's the alternative? According to RE, we should begin where we are—and where else could we begin?—with all the beliefs about morality we happen to have. If you think about it a moment, that's actually where the Cartesian approach would have you begin as well. But the Cartesian asks whether these beliefs can clear the hurdle of indubitability and casts them aside if they cannot. RE begins by asking whether these beliefs, which it terms *initial moral judgments* (IMJs), can clear a much less formidable obstacle: Were they formed in a way that avoids the obvious sources of error that plague our efforts to discover the truth in any area of inquiry? So, if you hold some moral belief now, but don't have a settled opinion about it or have no real confidence in the belief, then set it aside. If you stand to gain or lose something significant depending upon what you believe, then set it aside. If you formed the belief in a heightened emotional state, say when you were enraged or terrified, then set it aside. And so on. The IMJs that survive this initial screening are know as *considered moral judgments* (CMJs).[3]

Before moving on it is worth pausing to emphasize that a typical person's IMJs will include beliefs about a wide range of things: right, wrong, obligation, permission, blame, rights, responsibility, guilt, virtue, vice, character, dignity, etc. And the typical person's IMJs will include beliefs about particular cases, both real and hypothetical, and also beliefs in more general moral propositions. A typical person might believe, e.g., that Bernie Madoff ought not to have run a Ponzi scheme and that the FDNY members who rushed into the World Trade Center on 9/11 were courageous, which are particular moral judgments. Other particular IMJs a typical person might have concern hypothetical or fictional situations. A person might believe, e.g., that Huckleberry Finn had no obligation to turn Jim over to the runaway slave hunters and that a person who steers a runaway trolley onto a track with one workman rather than a track with five workmen does no wrong. A typical person will believe such mid-level moral rules as that one should keep one's promises and that lying is wrong. And it would not be unusual for a typical person to believe a high level principle, such as that one ought never treat another person as a means or that one ought always treat others as one would want to be treated oneself. Finally, many typical persons will believe some version of a principle of supervenience, which is a very high level moral principle, since they will at least tacitly accept that two actions or persons could not differ morally unless there were some nonmoral difference between them. There is no reason to think that any of these types of moral beliefs would face special problems making it through the loose filtering of IMJs that yields CMJs, so we should expect that all these types of moral beliefs will be found among the typical person's CMJs.

What comes next according to RE? Especially after filtering out IMJs about which one has no settled opinion or is insufficiently confident, one's CMJs will likely include gaps—significant moral issues about which one has no CMJs. And even though one would probably have some general principles among one's CMJs, it is extremely unlikely that one of these would provide a fully adequate fundamental moral principle. There is also a good chance that at least some of one's particular judgments do not conform to the general principles one does accept. Finally, if one accepts the usual sort of supervenience principle, which entails that there can be no moral differences without a relevant nonmoral difference, there is a very good chance that the set of one's particular CMJs and this principle is inconsistent. (Note that many moral arguments exploit just this inconsistency, attacking one particular judgment by citing different moral judgments about other cases where it is difficult to find a nonmoral difference that could explain and justify a moral difference.) Hence, it is highly improbable that one's CMJs would constitute a comprehensive moral theory and quite probable that they will not even be internally consistent.

The next step, then, is to try to mold one's CMJs into a consistent, comprehensive system and develop a moral theory that accounts for them all. This will involve formulating a moral principle, or set of principles, that accounts for all of one's more particular CMJs. In the process of attempting to find such a principle, it is significant that according to RE one is not supposed to treat one's more particular CMJs as unrevisable data points that one's theory must accommodate at all costs. After all, as we noted above, one's CMJs will likely include some moral principles. One might expect to use these, or some of them, as one's initial efforts at a moral theory, or at the very least to draw the inspiration for one's initial attempts at a fundamental moral principle from these principles that are CMJs themselves.

Why then would it make sense to always favor particular CMJs over principles, always revising principles to accord with particular judgments? If the principle and particular judgment that conflict are both CMJs, it would seem that they should have the same status. What, then, should one revise to eliminate the conflict? The answer, which is one of the defining features of RE, is that one should revise what seems less plausible or less likely to be true to one upon due consideration and retain the judgment, be it particular or principle, that seems more likely to be true upon due consideration.

At the risk of providing excruciating detail, let's slow down a moment and consider how this process might go for an individual inquirer, S.[4] S begins the process with a set of CMJs, which, as we have seen, are beliefs in moral propositions.[5] We can represent the CMJs S begins with like this: $CMJ_1 = \{cmj_1, cmj_2, cmj_3, \ldots, cmj_n\}$.[6] Faced with the task of constructing a moral theory to account for the elements of CMJ_1, let's suppose S takes her first shot by using a belief in a general principle that is an element of CMJ_1 as her moral theory. Conveniently for us, this is cmj_1. So cmj_1 becomes the first element of S's first moral theory, MT_1, which is just the set of principles constituting S's moral theory. So we can represent the stage S is at with an ordered pair, CMJs first, MT second: $<CMJ_2, MT_1>$ or $<\{cmj_2, cmj_3, cmj_4 \ldots, cmj_n\}, \{mt_1\}>$. Note that it is CMJ_2 rather than CMJ_1, because S has already made a small alteration, taking cmj_1 for her initial moral theory, now relabeled mt_1.

Now suppose that S sets about trying to test MT_1, at first by considering whether applying mt_1 to the various cases about which she has particular judgments in CMJ_1 to see whether the result she gets by applying mt_1 agrees with the CMJs. Unfortunately, she discovers that cmj_2 is inconsistent with the result of applying mt_1 to the same case. Upon reflection, S considers cmj_2 to be more likely to be correct than mt_1, and she sees how she might amend mt_1 so that it's application yields cmj_2. So S adopts the amended version of mt_1, which we'll label mt_2. So S will have moved from $<CMJ_2, MT_1>$ to $<CMJ_2, MT_2> = <\{cmj_2, cmj_3, cmj_4 \ldots, cmj_n\}, \{mt_2\}>$.

Let's make this discussion a little more concrete. Suppose cmj_1 is the belief that it is wrong to use people as means to one's own ends. S takes this as her initial moral theory. But she then recalls that her cousin Suzie donated bone marrow so that Suzie's sister Samantha could have very aggressive chemotherapy that saved Samantha's life. S always believed it was perfectly OK that Samantha accepted the bone marrow from Suzie (let this belief be cmj_2), but S now realizes that Samantha did, in a literal sense, use Suzie as a means to surviving cancer. So strictly applying mt_1 to this case yields a result inconsistent with cmj_2. But Suzie agreed to the whole thing; indeed, she was eager to donate the bone marrow for her sister. So S sees that she can easily revise her moral principle: it is wrong to use a person as a means to one's own ends unless that person consents. Let this be mt_2, and the initial steps of S's moral inquiry match the abstract description above.

Let's follow S for another step or two. Suppose someone presents S with a trolley case, something S has never considered. A trolley driver's brakes fail. He is barreling down the tracks. Ahead are 5 workmen who will be killed if he continues on his present course. At the last minute the driver sees he can take a side track. If he does so, he will ram another workman. But it's one versus five, so he takes the side track. Thinking about this case, S forms a new judgment: The driver did the right thing. We can suppose this judgment passes through the filters used to define CMJs, so it takes its place along side S's other CMJs. Let this be cmj_{n+1}, and S will have taken another step, now holding $<\{cmj_2, cmj_3, cmj_4 \ldots, cmj_n, cmj_{n+1}\}, \{mt_2\}> = <CMJ_3, MT_2>$.

S's next step should be clear. Applying mt_2 to the trolley example, she realizes that the one workman the driver killed was used as a means to save the other five workmen. And being no hero, that one workman would not have consented. So mt_2 conflicts with cmj_{n+1}. Upon consideration, S feels more sure of cmj_{n+1} than mt_2, so mt_2 has got to go. This time around, S sees no easy way of revising mt_2, so she generalizes from her judgment about the trolley case, ending up with a consequentialist principle: One ought to act so as to produce the best consequences. Let's call that mt_3. We can represent S's state as $<CMJ_3, MT_3> = <\{cmj_2, cmj_3, cmj_4 \ldots, cmj_n, cmj_{n+1}\}, \{mt_3\}>$. Notice that we have just seen how counterexamples figure into seeking RE.

Suppose that the person who presented S with the normal trolley example now asks her to think about a trolley case with a twist: There are no side tracks. There is nothing the driver can do to avoid hitting the five workmen. But there are two bystanders on a footbridge over the tracks looking on with horror. One's quick witted, the other enormously fat. The quick witted fellow realizes that if he tips the fat man onto the tracks, the fat man will derail the trolley, saving the five workmen. So the quick witted observer winds up, gives the fat man a mighty shove and over he goes, saving the five workmen. Considering this example, S judges that the quick witted observer did something morally wrong (cmj_{n+2}). So she has added yet another CMJ, now accepting $CMJ_4 = \{cmj_2, cmj_3, cmj_4 \ldots, cmj_n, cmj_{n+1}, cmj_{n+2}\}$. S quickly realizes that cmj_{n+2} conflicts with mt_3; the new case is just like the original trolley case in the sense that someone must choose between one life or five. So applying mt_3 to the new case yields the conclusion that the quick witted observer did the right thing after all. S realizes that she has got to revise something, but this time she is not so sure of her particular judgment, cmj_{n+2}. As she thinks about the two trolley cases and mt_3, she comes to feel more confident that the only thing that really matters here is the number of lives at stake, which is to say that she comes to feel more confident of mt_3 than she is of cmj_{n+2}. So this time S sticks with her principle and rejects cmj_{n+2}, and instead comes to believe cmj_{n+3}, namely, what the quick witted observer did was right. We can represent S's state at this stage like this: $<CMJ_5, MT_3> = <\{cmj_2, cmj_3, cmj_4 \ldots, cmj_n, cmj_{n+1}, cmj_{n+3}\}, \{mt_3\}>$.

We can leave S to pursue her inquiry without our looking on. In the course of the inquiry she will have occasion to make numerous revisions to CMJ_5 and MT_3. As a result she will pass through a whole series of MTs and sets of CMJs. Ideally, this process would come to an end when she has a comprehensive and consistent set of CMJs and a MT that accounts for them. At this point, S would have attained a *narrow reflective equilibrium* (NRE). Let's represent this state as $<CMJ_{NRE}, MT_{NRE}>$.

The fact that the state is labeled *narrow* RE is a give away that this is not the end of the inquiry. But before looking at what more is involved in RE, I want to pause for a moment to raise an important question. What is it exactly that determines what will be revised in cases of conflict? Commentators on RE have not paid enough attention to this question, so there is neither clarity nor consensus about how to answer it. I do not have the space to defend an answer here, or even to carefully examine the alternatives. Fortunately a version of everything I want to say in this chapter will apply to each of the answers—or so I believe. I want to at least mention some of the alternatives, however. There are, I think, three broad ways of answering the question. First, one might appeal to S's degree of belief or degree of confidence in the belief or the belief's credence, where these are understood as different ways of referring to the same feature of beliefs: how sure S feels or how firmly S holds the belief.[7] Second, one might appeal to some sort of meta belief or judgment about the beliefs in question regarding to how plausible, credible or likely to be true S considers the various contending beliefs to be.[8]

A final view is found in more recent discussions of the role of intuition in philosophy. This alternative has it that "seemings" or "appearances" determine revisions.[9] Such seemings are taken to be a mental state distinct from belief, as is indicated by the fact that it is possible for a proposition to seem true to one even after one has been convinced that it is false and no longer believes it. In the perceptual realm, this typically happens with illusions. For example, even after one has measured the arrows in the Müller-Lyer illusion, it still (visually) appears that one of the arrows is longer. A similar thing can happen with purely intellectual seeming, the kind of seeming that would be at work in reflective equilibrium. Even after one understands Russell's paradox, for example, when one considers the proposition that for any property, there is a set of things having that property, this proposition *seems* true.

I shall henceforth refer to the feature that determines belief revisions in RE in terms of seeming. I should confess that this choice does reveal where my sympathies lie, but these are just sympathies, not a settled conviction. Officially I'm using the one terminology throughout this chapter in order to simplify and standardize the presentation. So in what follows a statement such as "p seems more likely to be true than q to S" should be understood as neutral between "S believes p to a higher degree than q," "S judges p to be more plausible than q," and "the degree to which p seems true to S is greater than the degree to which q seems true."[10]

Before picking up my description of RE where I left off, I want to call attention to two significant points about seeming. First, in the case of CMJs what ultimately determines revisions are the degrees to which the conflicting CMJs seem true to S *on their own*, apart from any inferential support the judgments might receive from any MT.[11] The reason for this restriction is fairly clear. If MT is to win one's allegiance, at least in part, because it accounts for one's CMJs, it had better not be the case that the CMJs seem true only because one inferred them by applying that MT itself. Moreover, in the final analysis, what determines revisions, and hence the shape of the position one holds in RE, will have to be what seems true on its own. Inference can serve to "transfer" the appearance of truth, so to speak, from one or more beliefs to one or more other beliefs, but it does not seem to have the power to manufacture the appearance of truth ex nihilo. One might doubt this claim on the ground that a person can consider a system of interconnected propositions and become convinced of the truth of the whole system. But it is more accurate to view this as a way in which a whole system of propositions can come to seem true to a person *on their own*.

Secondly, while it is easy to find authors referencing "*our* considered moral judgments" or "*our* reflective equilibrium," these phrases can be misleading. Because of the way revisions are determined, RE must be a first-person inquiry. Propositions do not seem true to a group of people except in the derivative sense that they seem true to each member of the group. Any disagreement within a group and there will be nothing to determine how conflicts are to be resolved, and hence, nothing to determine the group's state of RE. Moral inquiry can be a joint endeavor according to RE only insofar as we agree or insofar as one person is willing to assist another in her individual attempt to bring her beliefs into equilibrium by doing such things as pointing out potential conflicts in her beliefs, presenting examples that might elicit interesting intuitions or proposing theories that might account for her CMJs. Alternatively, one might approach some other person as a subject, taking that person's beliefs and seemings as data and attempting to work out what that person's state of RE would be.

Wide reflective equilibrium

What's involved in the second stage of reflective equilibrium is not as clear as what was involved in the first. It therefore might be useful to begin by considering what Rawls had to say about it:

> There are, however, several interpretations of reflective equilibrium. For the notion varies depending upon whether one is to be presented only with those descriptions which more or less match one's existing judgments except for minor discrepancies, or whether one is to be presented with all possible descriptions to which one might plausibly conform one's judgments together with all relevant philosophical arguments for them. In the first case we would be describing a person's sense of justice more or less as it is although allowing for the smoothing out of certain irregularities; in the second case a person's sense of justice may or may not undergo a radical shift. Clearly it is the second kind of reflective equilibrium that one is concerned with in moral philosophy. (Rawls 1971, 49).

It is not immediately obvious how consideration of alternative moral conceptions along with the philosophical arguments for and against them might cause a person who has attained NRE to revise her moral beliefs. Suppose S has been thorough and considered the application of MT_{NRE} to all the important types of cases—and being thorough in this way would seem to be required to attain a NRE. Then MT_{NRE} will have to correspond with the CMJs S forms about these cases, since they will be elements of CMJ_{NRE}. So there simply would not be anything left within S's system of moral beliefs that could serve as a fulcrum to lever S off of MT_{NRE} and towards some alternative MT.

In his important work on RE, Norman Daniels (1979) interprets the transition from NRE to wide reflective equilibrium (WRE) as a matter of mobilizing relevant *background theories* (BTs) which are beliefs, judgments, or theories that are elements of neither CMJ_{NRE} nor MT_{NRE}. (The term "theory" is obviously used loosely here. BTs will just be a grab bag that might include anything else S believes.) It is perfectly reasonable, from one perspective, for Daniels to look outside $\langle CMJ_{NRE}, MT_{NRE}\rangle$ in this way for the fulcrum that might force changes to MT_{NRE}. He's clearly thinking that if the consideration of alternative moral conceptions disrupts S's NRE, it must be because of the *arguments* for these conceptions or against MT_{NRE}. And for such an argument to gain purchase with S, forcing an alteration in MT_{NRE}, S must believe the premises. People are not typically or rationally moved to alter their views by arguments with premises they do not accept. These premises would have to be found among S's BTs; there simply is no place else they could be. So Daniels' idea is that while NRE involves coherence between two sets of beliefs, represented by the ordered pair $<CMJ_{NRE}, MT_{NRE}>$, WRE involves coherence among three sets of beliefs, $<CMJ_{WRE}, MT_{WRE}, BT_{WRE}>$.

Let's consider a more specific example of how the transition from NRE to WRE might go according to Daniels. Having attained a state of NRE, S is to consider alternatives to the moral conception constituted by $<CMJ_{NRE}, MT_{NRE}>$. Suppose, that MT_{NRE} is some version of utilitarianism. Then, among other alternative moral conceptions, S will need to consider Rawls' account of justice as fairness. As is well known, Rawls argues for his conception of justice by appeal to what he calls the original position: the correct principles of justice are those rational agents would select, acting in their own self-interest, behind a veil of ignorance that screens them off from knowledge that might bias their decision.

There is no reason to suppose that S would have thought of any of this while working towards NRE. But it is not outlandish to suppose that S might have viewed persons as free and equal; let this be bt_1.[12] Because S accepts bt_1, when S's attention is focused on the original position by considering Rawls' argument, S is willing to accept a high level moral principle stating that the principles of justice that should govern a society would be those such agents would accept in the original position. Supposing that MT_{NRE} for S is $\{mt_1, \ldots, mt_{nre}\}$, we will label this new high level principle mt_{nre+1}. So the result of this initial step beyond NRE for S would be $<\{cmj_1, \ldots, cmj_{nre}\}, \{mt_1, \ldots, mt_{nre}, mt_{nre+1}\}, \{bt_1, \ldots, bt_n\}>$ or $<CMJ_{NRE}, MT_{NRE+1}, BT_1>$. This need not be a huge change for S, since $<CMJ_{NRE}, MT_{NRE+1}, BT_1>$ could very well be a coherent system of beliefs. S might, for example, have never thought much about rational decisions and so might vaguely accept that when deciding under uncertainty, one should assign equal probabilities to the outcomes and maximize expected utility. In this case, S's utilitarian moral theory would be the theory agents would accept in the original position.

But when presented with Rawls' arguments, S will need to consider the arguments in favor of instead employing a maximin rule in conditions of uncertainty. We can suppose that when S engages in reflection about rational decisions, S's considered judgments about which decisions are best militate in favor of adopting the maximin rule. If S's old rule about rational decisions under uncertainty was bt_2, and we label the maximin rule bt_{n+1}, S's foray into the theory of rational decisions will have brought S to this system of beliefs: $<\{cmj_1, \ldots, cmj_{nre}\}, \{mt_1, \ldots, mt_{nre}, mt_{nre+1}\}, \{bt_1, bt_3, bt_4, bt_5, \ldots, bt_n, bt_{n+1}\}> = <CMJ_{NRE}, MT_{NRE+1}, BT_2>$. (In fact, the changes to BT_1 would likely be more extensive than this, since S would no doubt have been forced to form new considered judgments about rational decisions and perhaps also to reject old considered judgments about rational decisions. In short, S would have had to bring his judgments and principles regarding rational decisions under uncertainty into RE, and all this would fall under the broad heading of background theories from our present perspective.) Now, supposing the overall thrust of Rawl's argument is cogent, S is in trouble. $<CMJ_{NRE}, MT_{NRE+1}, BT_{2}>$ will be incoherent. This is because applying the maximin rule, bt_{n+1}, in the original position will not yield a utilitarian theory of justice, which would be part of $\{mt_1, \ldots, mt_{nre}\}$, but will instead yield justice as fairness. And mt_{nre+1} states that the correct principles of justice are those that would be chosen in the original position.

It might be tempting simply to assume that S will be forced to alter MT_{NRE+1} by rejecting her utilitarian principle and adopting justice as fairness in its place. But this would be to suppose that BTs always take precedence over MTs and CMJs. That is not the approach taken by RE. As in the development of a NRE, *revisions are determined by what seems true to one upon reflection*. If the maximin rule and the other relevant beliefs seem likely enough to be true to S, then RE would direct S to reject her utilitarian moral principle. But the utilitarian moral principle and the CMJs with which it coheres might seem more likely to be true to S than the maximin rule and the judgments about rationality that support it. In this case, RE would direct her to revise her background theories instead of her moral principles. Let us suppose that S takes the more expected course, rejecting her utilitarian principle, mt_1, and adopting justice as fairness, mt_{NRE+2}. S's system of beliefs would then be $<\{cmj_1, \ldots, cmj_{nre}\}, \{mt_2, \ldots, mt_{nre}, mt_{nre+1}, mt_{nre+2}\}, \{bt_1, bt_3, bt_4, bt_5, \ldots, bt_n, bt_{n+1}\}>$.

S's work would have only begun. There may be other inconsistencies in her system of beliefs to resolve. And even if there are not, there are other alternative moral conceptions she must consider along with the arguments for and presumably against those conceptions as well as her own going conception. If S persists in her reflective inquiry, she will move through a series of revisions to her CMJs, MTs and BTs and eventually attain a system of beliefs that is coherent and that she would not be induced to revise by consideration of any alternative moral conceptions. This would be her state of WRE: $<CMJ_{WRE}, MT_{WRE}, BT_{WRE}>$.

Radical wide reflective equilibrium

In the previous subsection I described how the transition from NRE to WRE is conceived from Daniels' perspective. I certainly would not want to deny that it is possible for a person's state of NRE to be disrupted in the way Daniels supposes. He definitely captures a part of what is involved in WRE. But I do not think this is the only way for the transition to WRE to go. There is a sense in which Daniels' conception is very conservative, in spite of the effort he made in his article to emphasize that WRE so conceived has considerable resources to force revisions. Notice what serve as the new inputs to the inquiry. These will primarily be existing background beliefs. As I described the process above, I also allowed that S might adopt some new background beliefs along the way, parallel to the way in which I allowed that S might adopt new CMJs in response to the consideration of new examples along the way to NRE. And since non-moral background theories are being put into play, it would also make sense to allow new empirical beliefs, the sorts of beliefs that might provide evidence for some relevant background theory. But on what I'll call the conservative conception of WRE, the new inputs are limited to beliefs of these few kinds.

More significantly, all alterations of beliefs and theories made along the way to WRE, conservatively understood, will be dictated by the degrees to which the relevant beliefs seemed true to S initially. Beliefs and the degrees to which they seem true are only altered when such alteration is required to make an incoherent set of beliefs coherent, and specific revisions are dictated by the prior degrees to which the beliefs seemed true. Thus, if some other person knew all of S's CMJs and BTs along with the degrees to which these beliefs seemed true to S, this person could work out what $\langle CMJ_{WRE}, MT_{WRE}, BT_{WRE}\rangle$ would be for S. S makes her contribution at the beginning, so to speak, and from then on the inquiry could be carried out quite mechanically.

There is another way of thinking about what might happen when S considers alternative moral conceptions, and it coheres nicely with both Rawls' talk of radical shifts and the coherentism that RE so obviously embodies. When S considers an alternative moral conception, the entire package as a coherent whole, or at least parts of it, might come to seem true to S—and the alternative might seem true apart from how things previously seemed to S. Why think S is forever wedded to what initially seemed true to her, so that what seems true, and the degree to which it seems true, can change only when change is required to preserve something that initially seemed even more likely to be true? Why think that philosophy can persuade only by latching onto things one already believes and arguing from these beliefs to further conclusions? Isn't it possible that philosophy can also work by articulating an entirely new perspective that is capable of winning one's allegiance quite on its own, even though there are not sufficient premises among one's existing beliefs to force acceptance of the new perspective?

If philosophy has this potential, as I think it clearly does, then one reason one would be well advised to reflect upon alternatives to the moral conception one accepts in NRE is that one might be led to make a radical, discontinuous break with one's previous mode of thinking and adopt an alternative moral conception that, when one considers it, seems preferable to one's old conception. If some such conception is out there, one's NRE would be unstable. In this case, while one's system of beliefs in NRE might reflect what one *thinks* about morality, at least at a certain point in time, it would not accurately reflect one's broader moral sensibility.

Aldo Leopold's *Sand County Almanac* provides one example of an "argument" that might be interpreted as working in the manner I'm trying to articulate. In "The Upshot," after presenting a series of essays on various aspects of the environment, Leopold proposes a moral principle: "A thing is right when it tends to preserve the integrity, stability and beauty of the biotic community. It is wrong when it tends otherwise" (1949, 224–5). Leopold's work, and specifically this proposal, has had a huge influence on the development of environmental ethics. So even though Leopold was not a philosopher by academic specialization, there is a strong case for thinking that his work culminating in this principle constitutes an alternative philosophical conception that one should consider in order to move towards WRE. But it is not at all clear how anyone who accepted a more conventional MT in NRE might be moved to accept anything like Leopold's land ethic via an argument from a BT. In order to take the land ethic seriously, one needs to assign moral value to collective entities (ecosystems) most of whose elements are insensate. What would a person with a conventional NRE already believe that might induce such a valuation?

Compare the relatively much easier task of bringing someone who accepts a morality that does not extend to nonhuman animals to alter his or her views. Such a person will almost certainly accept that pain and suffering are bad and that actions that cause unnecessary pain and suffering are wrong. And such a person would most likely already have background views regarding the nature of animals that one could use to get him or her to agree that many animals are capable of experiencing pain and suffering. So it is easy to *argue* such a person into extending moral concern to such animals. Not so in the case of the land ethic. Rather, Leopold's task—which he apparently had some success in carrying off for at least some readers—was to bring people to view the environment in a new way that enabled them to value it intrinsically. Many "converts" did not have resources in their prior moral conceptions that prompted such a change, or so it seems to me, and hence, any movement in the direction of a land ethic produced by consideration of Leopold's work would constitute a radical change of the sort that could not be captured by a more conservative understanding of WRE.

Friedrich Nietzsche's critique of conventional "Christian" morality might provide a more familiar example. One could not say that Nietzsche does not offer an argument. It is clear that much of his critique is based on the claim that conventional morality is unhealthy in the sense that it frustrates the development of "higher" human beings (Übermenschen). The problem with this argument, as I see it, is that there is little reason to think that persons who accept a more conventional moral view in NRE would value the flourishing of "higher" humans sufficiently, or have a sufficiently negative view of a conventional mode of life, for Nietzsche's critique to gain any purchase with them. The hard work for him, therefore, was to provide a perspective—on a conventional modern way of life, for example, as well as the higher form of life he envisioned—from which it is natural to assign values in Nietzsche's way. I do not think it is plausible to think that Nietzsche seeks to induce this shift in values by arguing for it from premises that can be found among the CMJs or BTs of an adherent to conventional morality. That's one reason his writing style is so unusual for what's classified as philosophy. So, if consideration of Nietzsche's philosophy has any power to disrupt a person's conventional NRE, which it manifestly does have, it must at least in part operate in the way envisioned by radical rather than conservative RE. Or so it seems to me.

I know it is supposing a lot, but I am going to suppose that I've said enough to make the idea of a radical, discontinuous belief revision clear and also to make the claim that philosophy can provoke such revisions of belief plausible. The radical conception of WRE simply recognizes the possibility of such revisions and takes this as one reason for requiring that an inquirer consider alternatives to her moral conception in NRE. I would like to emphasize, however, that a radical revision need not be sweeping, requiring a complete overturning of one's previous moral conception. The key idea here is that the revision is *discontinuous* in the sense that it is not required by one's previous beliefs and how likely they seemed to be true, and indeed might well run counter to these beliefs and seemings. Such a revision might lead only to a modest alteration of one's previous viewpoint. But of course it might also lead to a kind of moral conversion.[13]

If it is granted that philosophy can lead to radical revisions of one's moral conception, it is a very small step to the recognition that other things can lead to such revisions. Indeed, I expect that philosophy is relatively impotent in this regard when compared with literature, film, music, and art. (Perhaps that's why the two examples I managed to come up with above are very "literary" as far as philosophy goes.) And of course actual life experiences might be most potent of all. What could this have to do with the appropriate method for *philosophical* inquiry into morality, and WRE in particular?

I will simply state my view. Everyone should recognize that the novels and poems one reads, the plays and films one watches, the music one listens to, the art one views and of course the various significant real-life experiences one has enjoyed, all have the potential to influence what seems valuable and disvaluable, right and wrong, virtuous and vicious, etc. But one cannot count on the influence being salutary. Advocates of various censorship regimes going back at least to Socrates in *The Republic* have been mistaken about many things, but they are not mistaken in holding that literature, music, and art have the power to corrupt one's judgment. So it would not make good sense to take exposure to everything as the ideal, and have WRE require such exposure. Instead, as part of the process of seeking radical WRE, S must reflect upon whether she has been exposed to enough of the right sorts of things to adequately refine her capacity for moral judgment. She must seek to determine what sorts of experiences might be beneficial and then seek out those experiences. Part of attaining a radical WRE, therefore, is getting oneself into a state where one's experiences match one's reflective views about what sorts of experiences are necessary or beneficial for moral discernment.[14]

A wider reflective equilibrium

Allow me to quote at length from Rawls' important presidential address to the Eastern Division of the American Philosophical Association, "The Independence of Moral Theory":

> I distinguish between moral philosophy and moral theory; moral philosophy includes the latter as one of its main parts. Moral theory is the study of substantive moral conceptions, that is, the study of how the basic notions of the right, the good, and moral worth may be arranged to form different moral structures. Moral theory tries to identify the chief similarities and differences between these structures and to characterize the way in which they are related to our moral sensibilities and natural attitudes . . .
>
> Now my thought is this: much of moral theory is independent from the other parts of philosophy. The theory of meaning and epistemology, metaphysics and the philosophy of mind, can often contribute very little. In fact, preoccupation with the problems that define these subjects may get in the way and block the path to advance. To be sure, no part of philosophy is isolated from the rest; and so the same is true of that part of moral philosophy I call moral theory. But the study of substantive moral conceptions and their relation to our moral sensibility has its own distinctive problems and subject matter that requires to be investigated for its own sake. At the same time, answers to such questions as the analysis of moral concepts, the existence of objective moral truths, and the nature of persons and personal identity depend upon an understanding of these structures. Thus the problems of moral philosophy that tie in with the theory of meaning and epistemology, metaphysics, and the philosophy of mind must call upon moral theory (1974–5, 5–6).

Rawls' view on the distinction between moral theory and moral philosophy combined with the fact that he was concerned with moral theory when he proposed RE explains why *wide* RE is not really all that wide. As we've seen, the transition from NRE to WRE is mediated by consideration of alternative moral conceptions and the arguments for these conceptions. As Daniels emphasized, one significant thing this does is bring S's BTs into play. But strictly construed, it does not bring all of S's BTs into play; it only brings in those that figure in the arguments for alternative moral conceptions. BTs that might be central to those elements of moral philosophy that fall outside moral theory will not, therefore, be brought into play.

Epistemological background theories and the empirical theories used to apply them provide a significant example for my purposes in this chapter. Efforts to use results from psychology or neuroscience or evolutionary theory to question the reliability of some or all of our CMJs are now extremely prominent. And of course such efforts were preceded and are now accompanied by lower tech efforts to argue for moral skepticism on the basis of more easily observed factors, such as the apparently high level of disagreement regarding morality. As Rawls conceived of WRE, these background theories would not be part of the equilibrium. Because they provide premises for a broad skepticism regarding morality, they would not serve as premises of arguments for, or against, any particular MT. (As we will see in a later section, things are somewhat more complicated than this because some use these BTs to target only some CMJs, and thereby to support particular MTs.) A similar fate befalls BTs from philosophy of language and metaphysics along with the necessary empirical theories that have been used to argue for or against moral relativism, moral realism, noncognitivism, motivational internalism, and so on—in short, the bulk of what is traditionally classified as metaethics: they are not involved in Rawlsian WRE. (Or more precisely, they are not involved except and to the extent that they are employed to argue for or against a particular MT.)

Rawls had his reasons for limiting his conception of RE in this way. Some were contingent. He wrote at the end of a period of time when philosophical inquiry into morality was dominated by the philosophy of language and work on substantive normative theory and substantive normative issues was scarce. Hence, he was keen to set all the metaethical disputes aside, at least for a while, and readjust the balance in the direction of normative ethics. And Rawls obviously succeeded; he clearly played a huge role in achieving the readjustment. He also had a theoretical reason for taking this approach, as the passage quoted above makes clear. Simply put, without an adequate understanding of the morality, or moralities, that people actually accept, speculation about the meaning or nature or justification of morality is not likely to get very far. Finally, there's the fact that Rawls conceived of his project as psychological in an important sense, again as the passage above makes clear. He thought of the MT (or MTs) that would emerge in WRE as characterizing the human moral sensibility (or sensibilities). Regardless of whether there are powerful metaphysical or epistemological arguments against such a MT, if it accounts for S's CMJs, as it must to be in RE, there's reason to think the MT nevertheless succeeds in capturing the moral sensibility that produced the CMJs.

It is easy to see what a wider reflective equilibrium (WrRE) would involve. Simply remove all restrictions on the BTs that must be brought into consideration: S must reflect on the connections between CMJ_{NRE}, MT_{NRE}, and *all* of her

BTs and make the revisions necessary to mold all of this into a coherent system. And it seems that there is some pressure to move towards such a WrRE even within Rawls' narrower conception. For one thing, as noted above, there have been efforts to use the kinds of BTs that Rawls apparently wants to exclude, e.g., BTs from metaphysics and epistemology, to argue for or against particular MTs.[15] So S would have to reflect about these matters even to attain the narrower Rawlsian WRE, and once S has engaged in such reflection it is hard to imagine her not noticing that there are arguments for broader forms of moral skepticism in the near neighborhood. What is S to make of these arguments? They clearly have the potential to undermine S's CMJs, thereby altering her WRE. So it is difficult to see how one approaching a state of Rawlsian WRE would avoid being drawn right on past towards a state of WrRE.

Moreover, Rawls himself saw moral theory as feeding into moral philosophy. And his remarks above make it pretty clear he thought that when we undertake this broader philosophical inquiry, the interaction between moral theory and the kinds of BTs left out of his conception of WRE would not be one way—one would not simply adjust MT_{WRE} and CMJ_{WRE} to bring them into accord with the relevant BTs not included in BT_{WRE}. Instead, consideration of MT_{WRE} might well influence these BTs. This obviously suggests the kind of mutual adjustment characteristic of RE in general, and hence it suggests that Rawls would think that moral philosophy should be pursued by a method of WrRE.

One might expect that anyone who accepts Rawlsian WRE as the method for inquiry into moral theory would also be sympathetic to using WrRE for an inquiry into moral philosophy. But such an expectation may not be fulfilled. WrRE would take more of S's BTs into account; indeed, it would take all of them into account. But it does not privilege any of these BTs. As in all versions of RE, conflicts would be resolved in virtue of how likely the various contending beliefs seem to be true to S. Thus, WrRE allows that S might be led to do such things as revise her epistemological or metaphysical views because they somehow conflict with a CMJ or MT that seems more likely to be true to S, all things considered. (Gasp!). In fact, WrRE allows, at least in principle, for S to revise empirical BTs in the face of conflicting CMJs or MTs if these moral beliefs seem sufficiently likely to be true. (Louder gasp!). Some philosophers—perhaps many—may think it is perfectly OK to make mutual adjustments to judgments and theories in order to attain a coherent system, with no type of judgment or theoretical principle being favored, *provided* these judgments and theories all have some kind of moral content. But how many of these philosophers will be equally egalitarian when other kinds of judgments and theories are thrown into the mix, in particular judgments and theories that are in no sense moral?

More specifically, think of those philosophers who accept Rawlsian WRE because they view its goal as essentially psychological in the way Rawls did.

These will be philosophers who take it that MT_{WRE} provides principles that characterize S's moral sensibility and who are willing to allow the elements in CMJ_{WRE} to play the methodological role WRE assigns them only because they are used to construct a theory characterizing a psychological construct rather than some independent reality. Such philosophers would almost certainly balk at the consequences of the method of WrRE just cited. For they most likely will not take the same view of epistemological BTs as they take of MTs, i.e., they will not think epistemological theories merely provide a psychological theory of some sensibility we have. And they almost certainly will not interpret metaphysical or empirical BTs psychologically.[16] It would be nothing short of bizarre to revise one's views about extra psychological matters so that they cohere with statements that do no more than characterize some sensibility one has. For example, if it were somehow possible for one's views about the nature of persons or what provides adequate evidence for what to conflict with an account of what combinations of sounds we judge to be cheerful as opposed to sad, the proposal that we resolve the conflict in favor of the account of happy sounds seems laughable.

At this point I am only trying to describe the method of RE, so it would not be appropriate to evaluate the position that accepts WRE but rejects WrRE that I just tried to articulate. My reason for presenting it in this context was simply to make it clear that WrRE is significantly different from Rawlsian WRE even though the differences may initially seem minor. Since this is not the place for evaluation, it also would not be appropriate to try to decide between WRE and WrRE at this point. So I'll leave them both on the table for now.

As I have described a number of different versions of RE in the preceding subsections, it might be worth recounting them before proceeding. First, there is narrow reflective equilibrium, NRE. This is a state where one has molded one's CMJs and a MT into a comprehensive, coherent system. Second, there is wide reflective equilibrium, WRE. One moves from NRE to WRE by considering alternatives to the moral conception one holds in NRE along with pertinent philosophical arguments. A state of WRE can be understood as an ordered triple consisting of CMJs, MT, and BTs, where the latter contain the premises for the philosophical arguments regarding one's own and alternative MTs. I also described a conservative and a radical way of understanding the transition from NRE to WRE. On the conservative understanding, more comes into play in WRE than in NRE, specifically BTs are included, but all belief revisions are dictated by how likely to be true the relevant beliefs seemed prior to the start of the inquiry. The radical understanding allows for discontinuous revisions of belief that are not dictated by the inquirer's prior seemings. Having called attention to the radical understanding, I went on to note that other things than philosophical theories have the potential to provoke discontinuous revisions of belief and briefly described how WRE might be extended to take account of such influences. I referred to this extension of WRE as radical WRE, but it will play no role in the discussion below. Finally, I went back to Rawls' presentation of RE to explain how WRE is actually not all that wide since it limits the BTs that come into play. I described a wider reflective equilibrium, WrRE, that takes all BT's into account.

Idealizations

I want to close my description of RE by emphasizing something that should already be obvious. All the versions of RE that I have described are idealizations. They are idealized in various ways. In the first place, no actual inquirer would proceed by first screening IMJs to attain CMJs, then working out a NRE, then moving to WRE, and so on. Our thinking just is nowhere near that regimented. We naturally bring all kinds of considerations, IMJs, CMJs, MTs, and BTs, into play helter skelter as they occur to us.

Even more significantly, no actual human being could pursue any of the methods of RE I've described through to their conclusions. This is already dead obvious in the case of WRE: It just is not humanly possible to consider *all* the alternatives to MT_{NRE}. Rawls recognized this already when he presented WRE in *A Theory of Justice*, and suggested we settle for an approximation of WRE by considering the major alternative moral theories developed in the history of philosophy. It seems obvious that this problem would be even worse for radical WRE and WrRE, even though it is not entirely clear what it might be for something to be even more humanly impossible that what's already humanly impossible. Finally, it is not even humanly possible to pursue NRE to its conclusion. For one thing, to really carry it off, one would need to reflect upon and form CMJs about far too many kinds of hypothetical cases.

Objections and Replies

Preliminaries

Before considering some of the many objections to RE along with possible replies, I'd like to make some assumptions in order to set some parameters for the discussion to follow. First, having paid careful attention to Rawls' psychological interpretation, according to which the point of RE is to provide a set of principles characterizing one's moral sensibility, I am going to set this idea aside. I'll ultimately be most concerned to defend WrRE, and the psychological interpretation just does not sit well with this method for the reasons suggested above. In addition, I think it is fairly obvious that most of the critics and defenders of RE have not really focused on the question of whether RE is an adequate method for characterizing our moral sensibility.[17] As a result, many of the criticisms might not in fact apply to WRE as Rawls thought of it, but that will not be all that important in the larger scheme of things if the criticisms do apply to the way most people conceive of WRE. I suspect most people have not taken the care to distinguish WRE from WrRE and actually have the latter in mind.

Second, having rejected the psychological interpretation of RE favored by Rawls, I want to also reject an interpretation adopted by some of RE's critics. According to this interpretation RE is supposed to provide a definition of moral truth: a moral proposition (MT or CMJ) is true just in case it would be accepted in RE. When combined with the plausible claim that not all inquirers would converge on the same system of beliefs in RE, this interpretation entails some version of moral subjectivism or relativism. I am just going to assume without argument that this interpretation is false. I accept the possibility that the moral view one holds in RE, even WrRE, is false or invalid.

Third, I've just ruled out two prominent views regarding what RE aims to accomplish, but without some idea of what it is supposed to do, it is difficult to know how the method should be evaluated. I'll make two positive assumptions.

First positive assumption: the ultimate aim of RE is to reveal the plain truth about morality. Before leaping to the conclusion that I thereby simply assume the truth of cognitivism and realism and a whole host of controversial—if not downright unfashionable—metaethical "isms," note that I assume RE *aims* to reveal the truth about morality. I do not assume it succeeds. But even more importantly, please bear in mind that I am primarily thinking of *wider* WRE here. This means that one must reflect on the MT that one held in NRE, or even WRE, in connection with one's BTs regarding, for example, meaning, epistemology, and metaphysics—in effect, one must decide what to make of that MT, and successor MTs. Hence, the "truth about morality" that is purportedly revealed might well not be a normative theory taken to have descriptive content that provides an objectively true account of some strand in the fabric of reality. In the extreme case, in WrRE one might view the overall best MT one was able to work out moving from WRE to WrRE as a bunch of hooey having the same status as astrology or numerology.

Second positive assumption: Understood as a method that aims to reveal the truth about something, the evaluation of RE is essentially an epistemological project. I've already assumed that the method is not guaranteed to succeed in providing the truth simply because the truth is defined as what's accepted in WrRE, but the view RE leads one to accept as the truth about morality had better have some sufficiently impressive epistemological credentials. I'm purposefully being a little bit vague here. Why not simply say that RE is a method of justification, and hence that it succeeds just in case the theory of morality it produces (be it normative and/or metaethical) is in fact justified? I'm not comfortable saying this because "justification" has become such a problematic term. Does it imply the "deontological" evaluation of belief—believing what one ought or should or what one has a right to believe? Is such evaluation illegitimate because it implies a kind of voluntary control over belief that we just do not have? Is justification something necessary for knowledge? Is it to be understood in terms of reliable truth production? Must one have some sort of access to whatever it is that justifies one's belief? And the questions go on and on.

Obviously the controversies surrounding justification and the consequent confusion provide one pretty good reason to avoid posing the question about the acceptability of RE in terms of "justification." But suppose the problems regarding justification could be resolved; suppose justification just is X. It still would not be a good idea to pose the question about the acceptability of RE exclusively in terms of justification because this would make the question too narrow. If they have done nothing else, the debates about justification have called attention to the fact that there are a number of interesting, epistemically valuable qualities. Here are just a few examples: being produced by a reliable process of belief formation, being produced by properly functioning cognitive mechanisms, being part of a coherent system of beliefs, being based on an appropriately truth conducive ground, being based on such a ground that one can also see to be such a ground, and being produced by the exercise of intellectual virtue. Regardless of which, if any, of these qualities turns out to be justification, many of them will remain significant. Hence, the question regarding the acceptability of RE would not be exhausted by considering only justification. It might be that RE fails to produce justified beliefs, but it does produce beliefs with some other sufficiently impressive epistemic status or statuses for RE to be acceptable. On the other hand, even if RE guaranteed justification, depending upon what justification is, we might not be satisfied with that. And that's why I was vague and claimed only that the evaluation of RE turns on whether it can yield "sufficiently impressive epistemological credentials." I wanted to leave it open for now what these might be.[18]

Intuitionism

It is not surprising that one of the first charges lodged against RE was that it is a form of intuitionism. The charge may not seem as grave as when it was originally made since intuitionism has enjoyed something of a comeback in recent years,[19] but those who lodged the objection took it to be a very serious matter.

According to the objectors, RE merely systematizes CMJs, which are treated as moral intuitions even though advocates of RE do not come out and claim that these judgments are self-evident or direct apprehensions of moral truths or make any of the other kinds of claims for these "intuitions" that old-fashioned intuitionists might have made. A truly adequate treatment of this objection should begin with accounts of what real intuitions are and what it is to treat something as an intuition (even though it might not be a real intuition). But unfortunately such accounts would take up more space than I have. So perhaps the following will suffice: The root idea of an intuition is something that one can just see to be true. So an intuitive belief would be spontaneous in the sense that consideration of the proposition believed is sufficient for one's belief to have a high epistemological status. Once formed, intuitive beliefs would then be taken for granted in one's reasoning or theory construction, providing grounds for generalizations or abstractions, counterexamples to principles, etc. The charge that CMJs are being treated *as if* they are intuitions, therefore, amounts to the charge that these are spontaneous beliefs that then play a privileged role in one's inquiry.

In his defense of RE, Daniels responds to the intuitionism charge by pointing to the revisability of CMJs. He concedes that NRE might fairly be classified as a sophisticated form of intuitionism, but not WRE:

> In seeking wide reflective equilibrium, we are constantly making plausibility judgments about which of our considered moral judgments we should revise in light of theoretical considerations at all levels. No one type of considered moral judgment is held immune to revision. . . .
>
> Wide reflective equilibrium keeps us from taking considered moral judgments at face value, however much they may be treated as starting points in our theory construction. Rather, they are always subjected to exhaustive review and are "tested," as are the moral principles, against a relevant body of theory. At every point, we are forced to assess their acceptability relative to theories that incorporate them and relative to alternative theories incorporating different considered moral judgments. (Daniels 1979, 267)

It is important that Daniels is not making a simple argument here: intuitions cannot be revised, CMJs can be revised, hence they are not intuitions. He recognizes that intuitions are subject to some revision. So the argument turns on how much revision of CMJs WRE allows. While I certainly agree with Daniels that WRE allows for a lot of revision of CMJs, I do not agree that this revisability is sufficient to rebut the charge of intuitionism. Employing the notation used above, it is certainly the case that the elements of CMJ_1 are not treated as intuitions in anything like a traditional sense, since it is possible, even if unlikely, that none of the judgments in this set will be elements of CMJ_{WRE}. If these judgments (the elements of CMJ_1) can all be rejected, then they obviously do not enjoy a very privileged role in one's inquiry.[20] But what about the elements of CMJ_{WRE}? Are these not serving as intuitions that ground one's moral system in WRE? One may not have used all of them along the way to attaining WRE, but it does not follow from that that they do not play a determinative or sustaining role once one is in WRE. If you want to know why someone holds MT_{WRE}, a large part of the explanation will be provided by the judgments in CMJ_{WRE}, and many of these judgments will be held because they seem to be true on their own and not because they were inferred from any other beliefs. The idea here is that one does not have the intuitions at the start of one's inquiry—not all of them anyway—but that they emerge along the way and function as intuitions in one's final system of beliefs. Let's use the labels *end state intuition* and *end state intuitionism* for this possibility and label the more standard idea *opening state intuitionism*.

Daniels could easily deny that *all* the elements of CMJ_{WRE} necessarily function even as end state intuitions. For some of the elements of CMJ_{WRE} will have been included to conform with certain elements of MT_{WRE} or BT_{WRE}. These elements of CMJ_{WRE} will have replaced elements of earlier sets of CMJs that seemed less likely to be true to S than the relevant elements of MT_{WRE} or BT_{WRE}. Such elements of CMJ_{WRE} would be dependent elements within WRE, included because they were inferred, so they would not be elements that determine the shape of this system; hence, they would not even be end state intuitions.

Unfortunately for friends of WRE who dislike intuitionism, this consideration still does not show that the method of WRE is not a form of end state intuitionism. It only shows that not all the elements of CMJ_{WRE} would necessarily be end state intuitions (Note here that it is *possible* that their CMJs might always seem more likely to be true to some inquirers than anything with which they conflict, so they will attain WRE by revising everything else to conform with their CMJ_{WRE}. But such inquirers, we are supposing, would be very rare.). What then could be serving as end state intuitions in WRE? The intuitions are those elements of the system of beliefs, *of whatever type*, that seemed sufficiently likely to be true to S on their own, and not as a result of any inference from any other beliefs in <CMJ_{WRE}, MT_{WRE}, BT_{WRE}>. It is these beliefs that determine the shape of <CMJ_{WRE}, MT_{WRE}, BT_{WRE}>. The fact that some of these beliefs might be elements of MT_{WRE} or BT_{WRE} does not change the fact that they are functioning as end state intuitions, i.e., that they are held simply because they seem true to the inquirer and not because of any inference and they play a role in determining the shape of S's WRE. Now of course it is highly unlikely that end state intuitions will do all the work determining the shape of an inquirer's state of RE, especially in the case of WrRE, since some BTs will probably be supported empirically. But I am supposing that if one's view is in part determined by intuitions, that's enough for intuitionism. Since it is highly unlikely that the set of S's end state intuitions will be the same as CMJ_{WRE}, MT_{WRE}, or BT_{WRE}, let's label this set I_{WRE}, and the corresponding sets in narrow and wider reflective equilibrium I_{NRE} and I_{WrRE}.

It is worth noting that two inquirers might end up agreeing about <CMJ_{WRE}, MT_{WRE}, BT_{WRE}>, but differ with respect to I_{WRE}. That is just to say that they would make all the same CMJs, and hold the same MT and BTs, but different things would seem true to them apart from any inferences. They would share the same overall system of beliefs, but different things within that system would be serving as premises and conclusions for the two inquirers. Hence, a more exact representation of a persons' point of WRE is provided by <CMJ_{WRE}, MT_{WRE}, BT_{WRE}, I_{WRE}>. Similar points hold for NRE and WrRE.

Daniels might respond that I have ignored the fact that CMJs, along with MTs, are, as he put it in the passage quoted above, revised because of "theoretical considerations" and "tested against a body of theory." Of course, if some element of CMJ_{WRE} is maintained because it is inferred from some theory in MT_{WRE} or BT_{WRE}, then it is not going to be an element of I_{WRE}. But even if many or all the elements of CMJ_{WRE} are held for such reasons, it hardly follows that I_{WRE} will be empty. The relevant theories must have come from some place. In some cases the theory will be a principle that is held because it seems true to S on its own, and in such a case the principle could be an element of I_{WRE} itself. In other cases, there will be reasons for the theory, perhaps reasons supporting these reasons, and so on. But eventually there will be some things that seem true to S on their own, and these will provide the elements of I_{WRE}. This is enough to sustain the charge, or in my view observation, that RE, including WRE, is a form of intuitionism.

Moreover, it is all but guaranteed that it will be a form of *moral* intuitionism, since it is highly unlikely, if not impossible, that there be no moral beliefs that are elements of I_{WRE}. Indeed, when providing his characterization of wide reflective equilibrium, Daniels (1979) himself recognized that the BTs involved in WRE would probably have moral or normative elements, and so to secure the claim that some additional leverage is attained by moving to WRE, he explicitly required that such BTs be supported by CMJs that are distinct from those in CMJ_{NRE}. Presumably they will also not be elements of CMJ_{WRE}.[21]

Now it may be possible for one to end up with a view in WrRE that cannot be characterized as a form of moral intuitionism. After all, as we have already seen, a person might end up holding no moral beliefs at all in WrRE because she has come to adopt an extreme form of moral skepticism. But if S does hold moral beliefs in WrRE, it would be surprising if no moral beliefs were elements of I_{WrRE}, since this would require that S holds all the elements of CMJ_{WrRE} and MT_{WrRE} for reasons that are ultimately and entirely nonmoral, and that would be some feat.

The classic objection and its hip contemporary descendants

Our consideration of the charge that RE is a form of intuitionism puts us in a position to state succinctly the classic objection that this method has faced almost from the moment Rawls proposed it. The moral view S accepts in WRE is determined by I_{WRE}. Hence, the method of WRE would be acceptable only if the elements of I_{WRE} were trustworthy. In particular, since we are talking about WRE here, S will hold a normative moral theory. Remember, strictly understood, there are not the resources in WRE to shift into metaethics and adopt an extreme form of moral skepticism in WRE. So the specifically moral elements of I_{WRE} will be playing a crucial role. Hence, the method of WRE would be acceptable only if the specifically moral elements of I_{WRE} were epistemically trustworthy. But there is no reason to think that these elements are trustworthy, so the method of WRE is not acceptable.

The first question to ask about this objection concerns the sense of trustworthiness that is in play. The most straightforward approach would adopt a reliabilist interpretation: being trustworthy is being sufficiently likely to be true. Rather than fretting about it, let's just adopt this interpretation. There is an immediate response to the objection: Why think WRE would be acceptable only if we have reason to think that the moral elements of I_{WRE} are likely to be true? Why wouldn't it be good enough if these elements are in fact likely to be true, even if we cannot produce *reasons* for thinking that they are? The issue here is similar to one that comes up in connection with the familiar debate between internalists and externalists in epistemology. Epistemological internalists demand that we have some reason for thinking that the grounds of our beliefs are reliable. Externalists respond that it is good enough if our grounds are in fact reliable and point out that accepting the internalists' demand is a fairly sure route to skepticism.[22]

An alternative response championed by Daniels (1979, section III) accepts, putting things in my terms, that some reason must be provided for trusting the moral elements of I_{WRE}, but pleads that one should not expect to be able to provide such a reason prior to attaining a WRE or independently of one's system of beliefs in WRE. Rather, a significant part of a system of beliefs in WRE will be an account of the reliability of the elements of I_{WRE}, most particularly the moral elements. This reply fits very nicely with a coherence approach in epistemology insofar as it eschews the demand for a prior or independent showing that some elements of the system are reliable in favor of the demand that this showing be internal to the system itself.

There is a great deal more to be said about both of these lines of response. Perhaps, in the end, one of them can succeed in rebutting the objection. But we should note that the responses face a serious hurdle. There seem to be concrete reasons to be suspicious of our moral judgments, reasons that would apply to the moral elements of I_{WRE}. Back in the day, when nearly all philosophy was, as the saying goes, "armchair" philosophy, reason for suspicion was provided by the obvious fact that there is a fair amount of disagreement about morality, and most troublingly, disagreement among individuals who seem to be perfectly reasonable, well informed, decent people. Perhaps the extent of such disagreement tends to be exaggerated, but there is clearly enough of it to provide grounds at least for *prima facie* doubts about one's moral judgments. But now psychologists and even neuroscientists have weighed in with studies of how we form moral judgments, and some philosophers have taken up their results to cast even more doubt on the reliability of our moral judgments, and specifically our moral intuitions.

Much of the empirical research is downright fascinating, but I do not think the details really matter that much for the line of argument I wish to develop. Nevertheless, I'll mention a couple of examples that have received a considerable amount of attention just to provide a taste.

Jonathan Haidt and colleagues wanted to investigate whether there are cross-cultural differences between the degrees to which perceived harm and strong emotional reactions such as disgust affect moral judgments. They presented stories, about people doing disgusting things that caused no harm, to subjects from different socioeconomic classes in Philadelphia in the USA and Recife and Porto Alegre in Brazil. They elicited the subjects' judgments and probed whether they made a distinctively moral evaluation, whether they perceived harms, whether they were bothered by the action, etc. Here are two of their stories:

> *Dog*: A family's dog was killed by a car in front of their house. They had heard that dog meat was delicious, so they cut up the dog's body and cooked it and ate it for dinner.
>
> *Chicken*: A man goes to the supermarket once a week and buys a dead chicken. But before cooking the chicken, he has sexual intercourse with it. Then he cooks it and eats it (Haidt et al. 1993, 617.)

Haidt and his colleagues found that there were indeed cross-cultural differences, with subjects who were more "westernized" or from a higher socioeconomic class tending to make moral judgments that corresponded to perceived harms while other subjects made moral judgments that were more influenced by emotions, specifically disgust. They closed their discussion section by considering things a model of moral judgment should do: "1. Place less emphasis on the role of harm", "2. Place more emphasis on the role of the emotions" as well as "3. Place more emphasis on the role of culture'.[23]

Joshua Greene and colleagues conducted fMRI brain scans of subjects while the subjects were forming judgments about various trolley cases and related hypothetical examples.[24] Bottom line: the scans purported to show that when we make moral judgments about trolley type examples that *disapprove* of an action that minimizes the number of deaths, as in the case described above where a fat man was pushed onto the tracks to save five people, parts of the brain associated with emotion are active. But these areas of the brain are not as active when we make judgments approving of actions that minimize the number of deaths, as in the standard trolley case. Haidt's hypothesis to explain this result is that strong emotions are triggered by harms done to others in an up close and personal way, and that these emotions override the result of more consequentialist reasoning of the kind that determines our moral judgments about cases where the harm is not up close and personal.

Why should such empirical findings be taken to show that our intuitive moral judgments are unreliable? Berker (2009) identifies several arguments. The simplest of these might be the most influential: the research shows that emotions are involved in the production of some moral intuitions; hence these intuitions are unreliable. A better argument takes as its key premise the claim that the research shows our moral intuitions can be determined by morally irrelevant factors, such as whether we find an action disgusting or whether it involves an up close and personal harm or a harm done beyond arms' length.[25]

As I said above, while the research is fascinating and might suggest lots of different ideas about moral judgment, including the thought that moral intuitions are not very reliable, the details are not all that important for the defense of RE I would like to offer. The main reason for this is that I want to defend WrRE. And any reasons for doubting some or all of the moral elements of the predecessors to I_{WrRE} that might be provided by psychologists or neuroscientists are simply more material that S must incorporate into her system of belief in WrRE.

I suppose this would be the worst case for normative ethics: the empirical research entails that all of our intuitive moral judgments are mistaken. Suppose the data provided by the research seems much more likely to be true to S than any of her intuitive moral judgments, and that she follows the arguments from the data and has no doubts about them. So, S excises all normative moral beliefs from her overall system. She ends up accepting no moral theory; she makes no moral judgments. She only has beliefs *about* morality, e.g., that all the moral judgments she previously made were mistaken and that all the moral judgments other people make are mistaken. Does it follow that S would have abandoned the method of WrRE? Not at all—she would have done exactly what that method dictates.

But of course, I have just described the worst case scenario for normative ethics. I do not think the empirical research puts those of us who do have moral beliefs in anywhere near the worst case.[26] What the research does provide us with is a great deal to think about and reconcile with our intuitive moral judgments.

Even Peter Singer (2005), a long-time critic of RE who seeks to make philosophical use of Greene's fMRI results as well as research from psychology and evolutionary theory, does not attempt to discredit all of morality. He holds, as Greene himself does, that the empirical findings can be used *differentially* to discredit the intuitive moral judgments that provide counterexamples to consequentialism. He goes on to urge more generally that rather than relying on particular intuitive moral judgments it is better to work from principles that are "rationally defensible." Here's how he closes his paper:

> In the light of the best scientific understanding of ethics, we face a choice. We can take the view that our moral intuitions and judgments are and always will be emotionally based intuitive responses, and reason can do no more than build the best possible case for a decision already made on nonrational grounds. That approach leads to a form of moral skepticism, although one still compatible with advocating our emotionally based moral values and encouraging clear thinking about them. Alternatively, we might attempt the ambitious task of separating those moral judgments that we owe to our evolutionary and cultural history, from those that have a rational basis. This is a large and difficult task. Even to specify in what sense a moral judgment can have a rational basis is not easy. Nevertheless, it seems to me worth attempting, for it is the only way to avoid moral skepticism. (2005, 351)

I'm nowhere near as sure as Singer is about what the best science *shows* regarding ethics, nor am I sure that the position he rejects leads to moral skepticism or that the course he advocates is the only way of avoiding such skepticism. What I am sure of, and what I think should be completely obvious, is that the perfectly sensible approach Singer proposes *conforms* to WrRE. And in spite of framing large parts of his discussion as a criticism of RE, Singer admitted as much at a couple of points earlier in his paper. For example, he writes:

> A defender of the idea of reflective equilibrium might say that these arguments against giving weight to certain intuitions can themselves, on the model of "wide reflective equilibrium," be part of the process of achieving equilibrium between a theory and our considered moral judgments. The arguments would then lead us to reject judgments that we might otherwise retain, and so end up with a different normative theory. (2005, 348–9)

But he concludes with something of a sneer, "making the model of 'reflective equilibrium' as all-embracing as this may make it salvageable, but only at the cost of making it close to vacuous" (349). Well, we'll see about that sneer in the next section. For now, I'm happy enough to have found him admitting even grudgingly to something that few critics of RE have seen, i.e., that their own positions actually conform to WRE or WrRE rather than constituting alternatives.

But wait a minute, someone might object, while the position Singer outlines might be subsumed under WrRE, suppose some S sticks with some of her particular moral intuitions that seem very likely to be true and constructs some "rationalization" of the empirical findings so as to preserve the moral judgments. Wouldn't this fit the model of WrRE? That does not seem good. And don't we still need to say *something* about the reliability of the judgments in I_{WrRE}?

My answers to these two objections turn on the same point. Rather than seeking to defend WrRE in terms of reliability, I think it must be defended as a rational method, and indeed, the only rational method.[27] Boiled down to its essence, WrRE directs one to leave nothing out of consideration and to believe what seems likely to be true upon due consideration. So let's think about the case envisioned just above by my objector. If S indeed has reached a state of WrRE, something like the following will have occurred. She will have given due consideration to the moral judgments in I_{WrRE} as well as everything that might count against them and, in particular, the empirical research that, when given what we are supposing is the most natural interpretation, conflicts with the reliability of some of these judgments. But upon reflection, that interpretation that we think is most natural seems less likely to be true to S than the elements in I_{WrRE} with which it conflicts. Instead there will be some alternative interpretation of the research that S accepts. We might call that interpretation a "rationalization," but all things considered, this interpretation will have to seem more likely to be true to S than the interpretation we favor. In such circumstances, I submit that S would believe exactly what it is subjectively rational for her to believe. She would be believing what seems right to her, after thoroughly considering everything that is relevant. To believe anything else would be subjectively irrational. It would be to believe something that seems less likely to be true rather than what seems more likely to be true and to do so for no reason that she credits.[28]

Admittedly, what it is rational for a person to believe in this sense might be mistaken, it might be unreliable, and it might be downright bizarre. And we could probably come up with more bad things a belief that is subjectively rational might be. But none of that would change the fact that the belief would be subjectively rational. And insofar as one is evaluating a philosophical method of inquiry, it is uniquely important that the method be a subjectively rational one.

Two serious objections and a response to one of them

I want to close by considering two objections to WrRE that I consider very significant. The first has to do with the fact that WrRE is an idealization, and I'm sorry to say that I do not have a very good answer to it. The second objection is significant, in my opinion, largely because of the answer.

I noted above that all the versions of RE that I have presented are idealizations. It just is not humanly possible to pursue a philosophical inquiry all the way to a state of WrRE. But the defense of WrRE I offered applies to this unattainable ideal state. If one were in that state, one's beliefs would be rational and having come to that state, believing anything else would be irrational. But what does that have to do with the way real people should engage in a philosophical inquiry? Suppose I realize that two things I believe are in conflict. One is a moral principle, the other a judgment about a hypothetical example. I try to consider everything that might be relevant. In the end, it seems to me that the particular judgment is more likely to be true, so I dump the principle and try to formulate a better one. Was this a sensible procedure, or should I be doing something entirely different? Perhaps I should ignore all my particular judgments and try to work only with the moral principles that seem best (remember, Singer would have me do something like this.) Maybe the revision I made to the principle would be rational if I had considered everything that might be relevant, and the particular judgment still seemed most likely to be true. And maybe it would be irrational to try to proceed while ignoring all my particular moral judgments if after duly reflecting on everything, some of these judgments would seem very likely to be true. But what do these facts about what it would be rational and irrational to do if I had considered everything show about what I should really do, when I have come nowhere near this ideal? I'm just not sure how to respond. When there is a worthy but practically unattainable ideal, it seems reasonable to think one should nevertheless do one's best to approach the ideal. That's the best I can do, but even I see it isn't much.

The second objection is really just an elaboration of the observation by Singer that I interpreted as sneering. If I am right, WrRE is so wide that it becomes hard to imagine what one might rationally do in the way of a philosophical inquiry into morality that would not count as employing the method. Even the sternest critics of the method turn out to be following it. But rather than signaling the triumph of this method, isn't this feature a cause for concern? Can WrRE be of any significance at all if it is just about impossible not to follow it without doing something that's clearly irrational? Isn't the method then, as Singer remarked, "vacuous"?

I believe the method is deeply significant because it lays bare a fact that many would prefer not to face. That fact concerns I_{WrRE}. Since there is no avoiding the method, there is no avoiding this set of beliefs, judgments, principles, and what have you. The set will likely have different elements for different inquirers. But for each inquirer there will be some things that he or she believes simply because they seem true. I realize that this is a sweeping claim and that I have offered no argument for it—nor will I here—but I am firmly convinced that it is true. And I think that readers who do not already accept this claim need only start reflecting on some moral claim they believe, or something they believe about morality, and if they are persistent and thorough and do not sweep any assumptions under the rug, they will quickly uncover some things that they believe simply because they seem true upon reflection.

So I_{WrRE} is not going to be empty for any inquirer. And be they many or few, grand or humble, the elements of this set will play a crucial role in determining the rest of the system of beliefs that inquirer would hold if he or she pursued a philosophical inquiry into morality through to its conclusion, which would be a state of WrRE. In a sense, then, whether we're armchair speculators or close followers of science, to some significant extent the shape of our entire system of beliefs about morality is determined by nothing but how things seem to us.[29] I believe that those who are sympathetic to RE are willing to live with this fact, while its critics seek to avoid it.[30]

Bibliography

Alston, William. (2005), *Beyond Justification*. Ithaca, NY: Cornell University Press.

Audi, Robert. (2004), *The Good in the Right*. Princeton, NJ: Princeton University Press.

Bealer, George. (1998), "Intuition and the Autonomy of Philosophy," in Michael DePaul and William Ramsey (eds.), *Rethinking Intuition*. Lanham, MD: Rowman & Littlefield, 201–39.

Berker, Selim. (2009), "The Normative Insignificance of Neuroscience." *Philosophy & Public Affairs* 37, 293–329.

BonJour, Laurence. (1985), *The Structure of Empirical Knowledge*. Cambridge, MA: Harvard University Press.

—. (2002), "Internalism and Externalism," in Paul K. Moser (ed.), *The Oxford Handbook of Epistemology*. Oxford: Oxford University Press.

Brandt, Richard. (1979), *A Theory of the Good and the Right*. Oxford: Clarendon Press.

Daniels, Norman. (1979), "Wide Reflective Equilibrium and Theory Acceptance in Ethics." *The Journal of Philosophy* 76, 256–82.

—. (1980), "On Some Methods of Ethics and Linguistics." *Philosophical Studies* 37, 21–36.

DePaul, Michael. (1987), "Two Conceptions of Coherence Methods in Ethics." *Mind* 96, 463–81.

—. (1988), "Naïveté and Corruption in Moral Inquiry." *Philosophy and Phenomenological Research* 48, 619–35.

—. (1993), *Balance and Refinement: Beyond Coherence Methods of Moral Inquiry*. London: Routledge.

—. (1998), "Why Bother with Reflective Equilibrium," in Michael DePaul and William Ramsey (eds.), *Rethinking Intuition*. Lanham, MD: Rowman & Littlefield, 293–309.

—. (ed.) (2001), *Resurrecting Old-Fashioned Foundationalism*. Lanham, MD: Rowman & Littlefield.

Foley, Richard. (1987), *The Theory of Epistemic Rationality*. Cambridge, MA: Harvard University Press.

—. (1993), *Working Without a Net: A Study of Egocentric Rationality*. Oxford: Oxford University Press.

Goldman, Alvin, and Pust, Joel. (1998), "Philosophical Theory and Intuitional Evidence," in Michael DePaul and William Ramsey (eds.), *Rethinking Intuition*. Lanham, MD: Rowman & Littlefield, 179–97.

Greene, Joshua D., Sommerville, R. B., Nystrom, L. E., Darley, J. M. and Cohen, J. D. (2001), "An fMRI Investigation of Emotional Engagement in Moral Judgment," *Science* 293, 2105–8.

Greene, Joshua D., Nystrom, L. E., Engell, A. D., Darley, J. M. and Cohen, J. D. (2004), "The Neural Bases of Cognitive Conflict and Control in Moral Judgment," *Neuron* 44, 389–400.

Greene, Joshua D., Morelli, S. A., Lowenberg, K., Nystrom, L. E. and Cohen, J. D. (2008), "Cognitive Load Selectively Interferes with Utilitarian Moral Judgment," *Cognition* 107, 1144–54.

Haidt, Jonathan, Koller, S. H. and Dias, M. G. (1993), "Affect, Culture, and Morality, or Is It Wrong to Eat Your Dog," *Journal of Personality and Social Psychology* 65, 613–28.

Huemer, Michael. (2005), *Ethical Intuitionism*. New York: Palgrave Macmillan.

Leopold, Aldo. (1949), *A Sand County Almanac and Sketches Here and There*. Oxford: Oxford University Press.

Rawls, John. (1951), "Outline of a Decision Procedure for Ethics," *Philosophical Review* 60, 177–97.

—. (1971), *A Theory of Justice*. Cambridge, MA: Harvard University Press.

—. (1974–1975), "The Independence of Moral Theory," *Proceedings and Addresses of the American Philosophical Association* 48, 5–22.

Shafer-Landau, Russ. (2003), *Moral Realism*. Oxford: Oxford University Press.

Singer, Peter. (1974), "Sidgwick and Reflective Equilibrium," *Monist* 58, 490–517.

—. (2005), "Ethics and Intuitions," *The Journal of Ethics* 9, 331–52.

Timmons, Mark. (2008), "Toward a Sentimentalist Deontology," in Walter Sinnott-Armstrong (ed.), *Moral Psychology, Volume 3, The Neuroscience of Morality: Emotion, Brain Disorders, and Development*. Cambridge, MA: Bradford Books, 93–104.

Important Technical Terms in Ethics

Guide to Authors:

DB = Daniel Boisvert
JB = John Brunero
SM = Sean McKeever
RSL = Russ Shafer-Landau
EW = Eric Wiland

Axiology. Axiology is the field of philosophy devoted to the study of value. A comprehensive axiology would account not only for moral value but also (in so far as they are distinct from moral value) for aesthetic, environmental, and intellectual values. Despite deep and abiding disagreement about the metaphysics of value, philosophers work with a familiar range of distinctions between types of value. It is common to distinguish something being valuable as an end from its being instrumentally valuable (valuable as a means). Something is valuable as an end when it's value is not explained by the fact that it promotes some further valuable result. This distinction allows that something might be both valuable as an end and valuable as a means. For example, in *The Republic*, Plato famously claims that justice is both good for its own sake and good for its consequences. Many philosophers (though not all) draw a distinction between being valuable as an end and being intrinsically valuable. Something is intrinsically valuable when the explanation of its value is to be found entirely in its intrinsic properties. By contrast, an object has conditional value when it's value is conditional upon some nonintrinsic feature. Instrumental value is, thus, one type of conditional value. One important possibility is that something might be good as an end while also being only conditionally valuable. For example, many philosophers agree that happiness is good as an end, but disagree about whether it is unconditionally valuable. Axiology also typically addresses the relationship between the value of wholes and the values of the parts that comprise them. Some philosophers hold that the value of a whole must be equal to the sum of the values of its parts while others claim that "organic unities" are possible, i.e. wholes whose value departs from the value of the sum of their parts. (SM)

Cognitivism and Noncognitivism. The debate between cognitivists and noncognitivists is a debate within metaethics. Such debates concern the status of morality—and in this particular case, the status of moral claims. Cognitivists and noncognitivists disagree in their answers to two central questions about the semantics and pragmatics of moral discourse: (1) are moral claims truth-apt (i.e., capable of being true or false)? And (2) do competent speakers ordinarily intend to make factual assertions and speak the truth when making moral judgments?

Cognitivists answer both questions affirmatively. Cognitivists see moral discourse, in this way at least, as perfectly continuous with nonmoral, factual discourse. When we say, for instance, that genocide is immoral, we are attributing a certain feature—immorality—to the subject of the sentence (genocide). The claim we make is true if genocide really has this feature, and false if it does not.

Noncognitivists answer both questions in the negative. They deny that we are trying to speak the truth when making moral claims. Rather, we are (depending on the specific noncognitivist view in question) giving vent to our emotions, prescribing some course of action, or expressing a commitment to live according to certain plans or rules. None of these kinds of speech act is truth-apt; if, for instance, my condemnation of genocide amounts to saying: "Genocide—arggh!" or "Don't perpetrate genocide!", then I am not saying anything that could be true (or false).

Cognitivism, too, can take a variety of forms. Cognitivism per se takes no stand on how truth-conditions of moral claims are fixed—cognitivist theories span the range from error theories, to relativist views that make moral truth dependent on personal or social opinion, to divine command views and the whole gamut of moral realist views (see also "Expressivism"). (RSL)

Constructivism. Constructivism is a family of metaethical views that endorse the claim that there is moral truth that is in some way constructed from responses or attitudes. The basic idea can be understood by means of an example. Suppose we agree on a moral norm that prohibits us from hurting others without any good reason. And just assume that no more basic or general moral rule explains this one—that this prohibition on gratuitously hurting others is a basic moral rule. We can then ask: does anything make this moral rule correct?

Constructivists will answer affirmatively. What makes this rule correct (if it is) is the fact that some duly specified individual (or group of individuals) would endorse the rule. If constructivism is correct, then this rule, like all other basic moral rules, is correct only because it is authorized or endorsed by the right kind of judge(s) or "constructor(s)." Constructivists differ widely on who the appropriate constructors are: each person (individual relativism), each society (cultural relativism), reasonable and fair people seeking to agree on rules to govern social life (contractarianism), etc.

One of the more prominent versions of constructivism is the ideal observer theory. This theory (which itself admits of variation) says that moral truths are those that reflect the responses of ideal observers. Different ideal observer theories can be developed, depending on what counts as ideal conditions of judgment. Standard attributes include possession of full nonmoral or factual information, perfect instrumental rationality, and emotional equilibrium.

One way to see the essence of constructivism is to consider its contrast with moral realism. Suppose again that the prohibition on gratuitous harm is a fundamental moral rule. Both realists and constructivists can agree that ideal observers will endorse this rule. But realists will say that ideal observers endorse the rule because it is correct. Being ideal, such observers will always land on the truth. But this truth, if realists are right, is antecedent to the endorsement of ideal observers. Constructivists disagree. They will say that the rule is correct only because ideal observers (or, on other versions of constructivism, other appropriately positioned constructors) endorse it—prior to such endorsement, nothing is right or wrong (see also "Realism, Moral"). (RSL)

Contractarianism and Contractualism. Normative social contract theory identifies the origin or content of moral norms in a contract among parties. Contractarianism specifically holds that moral norms are those that would maximize the joint interests of the contracting parties and, consequently, that each party would be rationally justified in adopting those norms in order to maximize its own self-interest. Contractarianism is thus grounded in the rational self-interest of contracting parties. Hobbes and David Gauthier offer respective historical and contemporary versions of contractarianism, which should be distinguished from contractualism, another strain of normative social contract theory historically associated with Rousseau and Kant. Contractualism is grounded in the equal moral status of persons, which in turn is grounded in a person's capacity for rational autonomous agency. Thus, whereas contractarianism views each party as maximizing its own interests, contractualism views each party as promoting its own interests in a way that can be publicly justified to others. Some contractualists, such as John Rawls, hold that norms are justified when they are agreeable to all parties under appropriate conditions, while others, such as T. M. Scanlon, hold that norms are justified when they cannot be reasonably rejected by any party under appropriate conditions. Contractarian and contractualist ethical theories are often combined with corresponding political theories according to which an authority derives its legitimacy through the consent of the governed. (DB)

Decision Theory, Game Theory. Decision theory is, at its foundation, an interdisciplinary approach to the study of rational agency. It purports to offer an account of how ideally rational agents would choose among alternative actions that might achieve their goals. This account is also frequently thought to provide normative standards for how imperfectly rational agents, such as normal human beings, rationally should pursue their goals. Decision theory eschews a substantive account of what is good for an agent to pursue (the agent's utility) and instead constructs the agent's utility out of his preferences. Decision theory, in its modern development, rests on proofs which show that utility scales can be constructed for any agent whose preferences satisfy certain formal coherence constraints, such as being transitive. A relatively few constraints suffice for the construction of an ordinal utility scale (one that ranks outcomes simply from better to worse); somewhat more complex and controversial conditions must be satisfied in order to construct a cardinal utility scale (one that additionally represents how much better one outcome is than another). Also relevant to rational choice is what the agent believes about the state of the world. For example, if one is considering whether to fish in the Yellowstone River, it is relevant how important it is to catch fish for that person (a fact about the agent's utility) and also what one thinks of the Yellowstone—whether it is stocked with fish for certain, stocked with fish with some probability, or utterly uncertain whether it is populated with fish. Because it views rational choice as relative to belief, the development of decision theory has been closely tied to probability theory and also to accounts of how agents ought rationally to revise their beliefs in the light of new information. Game theory rests on the same foundation as decision theory, but it addresses cases involving more than one agent in which one agent's success at achieving his goals is dependent upon the rational choices that another agent will make in pursuing his own goals. Though decision theory and game theory were originally developed to model rational decision-making, many of the tools of decision and game theory have been deployed to model scenarios (such as gene frequency in evolution) that do not obviously involve any rationality at all. (SM)

Deontological Ethics. Deontological ethics refers to a class of ethical theories which hold that certain actions are right or wrong in themselves, regardless of the good or bad consequences yielded by those actions. For instance, actions such as torturing innocent people, killing for fun, and making false promises are often thought to be wrong in themselves even when performing these actions would bring about better consequences than any other alternative (though some deontologists do think these actions could be permissible at some higher threshold, as when, say, one must make a false promise to save a million lives). Act-consequentialists disagree. They think that these actions are not wrong when performing them would bring about better consequences than any other alternative.

The most famous deontologist is Immanuel Kant. In presenting the first formulation of his categorical imperative (often called the "Formula of Universal Law"), Kant argues that a maxim—that is, roughly, a description of someone's action and the purpose for which, and circumstances in which, it is done—is morally impermissible if one cannot will at the same time that it becomes a universal law. Consider, for example, my maxim of making a false promise to escape a difficult situation. Kant argues that if everyone were making false promises to escape difficult situations, no one would believe the promises of anyone else. So, we cannot even *think* of a world in which there is such a practice as universal false promising. For that reason, I am unable to will that my maxim of making a false promise to escape a difficult situation becomes a universal law, and so the maxim is morally impermissible (see also "Imperatives, Categorical and Hypothetical"). (JB)

Dilemmas, Moral. An agent faces a moral dilemma when (i) the agent has compelling moral obligations to perform different acts in the same situation, (ii) none of the obligations clearly overrides the others, and (iii) the agent cannot perform more than one of these alternatives. The result is that the agent appears doomed to moral failure and to its characteristic, sometimes agonizing, moral phenomenology. Sartre famously writes of such a dilemma faced by a student deciding whether to join the Free French in WWII as a means of avenging his brother's earlier death at the hands of German aggressors, or to remain at home to care for his ailing mother, recognizing that he is the only thing left that gives meaning to his mother's life. Two of the more common sources of moral dilemmas are those in which (i) role-related norms conflict with each other, as when a person has both a physician-related obligation to spend more time at the office to care for an increasing number of ill patients and a parental obligation to spend more time at home to care in other ways for her children, or when (ii) role-related norms conflict with general norms, as when a counselor has both a professional obligation to help her patient by, in part, maintaining the confidentiality of patient-client communication and a general obligation to protect an innocent third party from the slight, but relatively certain, harm that the patient intends to cause by spreading a false rumor about the third party. (DB)

Divine Command Theory. This view holds that morally obligatory actions are morally obligatory because they have been commanded by God, and morally wrong actions are morally wrong because they have been forbidden by God's commands, and morally permissible actions are morally permissible because God has neither commanded that they be performed, nor commanded that they not be performed. In this way, deontological morality depends directly on the commands of God, unlike divine will theories which maintain that moral obligations depend directly on the will of God. Though God's commands are expressions of God's will, not everything willed by God is commanded by God. The label "theological voluntarism" has been attached to the class of philosophical views which hold that morality either directly or indirectly depends on the will of God. Divine Command Theory is thus a specific version of theological voluntarism.

One well-known objection to Divine Command Theory comes from Plato's dialogue *Euthyphro*. Consider the following variation on a question Socrates asks in that dialogue: Is helping the needy morally obligatory because God commanded it, or did God command it because it is morally obligatory to help the needy? The first option is unattractive: it seems that helping the needy would be morally obligatory even if God had not commanded us to do so. (And it seems that if God had commanded us to kill innocent children instead, it would not follow that it is morally obligatory to do so.) Of course, if God exists, God would not fail to command us to help the needy (and would not command us to kill innocent children instead). But, why not? Presumably, there is a reason *why* God would command us to help the needy—after all, a perfect being would not issue arbitrary commands, but would instead issue commands for good reasons—but then *those reasons*, and not the fact that God issues the command, would explain why it is morally obligatory to help the needy. Divine command theory might then be false, and we might instead be inclined toward the second option: God commanded us to help the needy because helping the needy is morally obligatory. (JB)

Doctrine of Double Effect. Your actions have many effects (or consequences). Nearly everyone thinks that the moral value of what you do can depend upon whether you *foresee* some of its bad consequences. A more controversial issue is whether, apart from issues of foresight, the moral value of an action can depend upon whether you *intend* some of its bad consequences. According to the Doctrine of Double Effect (DDE), your action is permissible only if 1) the act itself is good or indifferent, 2) any bad effects are not intended, 3) the good effects are not produced by the bad effects, and 4) the good effects outweigh the bad ones. So, acting with the intention to bring about bad consequences can be worse than so acting merely foreseeing the same bad consequences.

It is important to ward off a common misunderstanding of DDE. DDE does not state that the moral value of an action *never* depends upon merely foreseen effects. Nearly all proponents of DDE think that merely foreseen effects matter too: the good effects must be sufficiently good to justify the foreseen bad effects, and there must be no better way to produce these good effects.

But DDE holds that some types of actions (e.g., torture, killing an innocent person, etc.) are always morally problematic. Some proponents of DDE think that one should *never* intend to act in these ways, either as an end or as a means. Other proponents think that, while one's intentions *do* make a moral difference, extreme consequences might justify actions that are usually wrong; for example, while it might be wrong to kill one innocent person in order to save five, it might be not be wrong in order to save five thousand (see also "Deontological Ethics"). (EW)

Duty. As a general term, "duty" names what one is required or obligated to do, though it is common to refer to specific and discrete duties. As a deontic concept, duty is a modal concept; it is used to express what one—in some sense—*must* do. Duty is not an exclusively moral concept. We speak freely of legal, familial, and professional duties without presuming that these must be moral duties. Moral philosophers, of course, disagree about just what our duties are. Nevertheless, it has been common to classify duties into different types. Many allow that an agent may have multiple and conflicting moral duties. To label the idea of duties that are real even if it might not be best all things considered to fulfill them (because one has a conflicting and more weighty duty to do something else), W. D. Ross introduced the term "prima facie duty"; some prefer the term "pro tanto duty." Prima facie duty is to be contrasted with what is one's duty all things considered. It is also commonly thought that certain duties—though genuinely required—leave an agent with considerable discretion as to precisely how the duty is discharged. For example, one might have a duty to help the needy but yet need to decide for oneself precisely how to help. Because the agent retains discretion, it is not true that every case of not helping is a failure to do something that is required. Many philosophers follow Kant in calling such duties "imperfect." Imperfect duties are to be contrasted with perfect duties which specify types of conduct that must always be done (or avoided). The contrast between perfect and imperfect duties is not a matter of stringency; imperfect duties may be every bit as serious as perfect ones. The contrast, instead, concerns the content of what is required. Finally, supererogatory action is action that is morally good but that, in some sense, goes beyond what is or could be required as a matter of duty. (SM)

Egoism. Psychological egoism is a psychological theory about human motivations. It says that all intentional actions are done either exclusively or primarily from a motive of self-interest. Though beneficent action is compatible with such a theory, the existence of altruistic motivation is not. If psychological egoism is true, then while we may often help others, we do so, always, from ultimately self-interested motives.

Ethical egoism is the view that an action is morally required just because it best promotes one's self-interest. According to ethical egoism, our only basic moral duty is to ourselves—to make our lives the best they can be. Though we may have specific duties to others, that is only because fulfilling such duties will best promote our own well-being. Whenever our interests clash with those of others, morality requires us to give ourselves priority.

Psychological egoism often purports to be an empirical hypothesis. But if it is, then it seems falsified by the large amount of data that indicates the existence of altruistic motivation. Of course this data does not admit of only one interpretation. But the large amount of evidence, both from testimony and behavior, and extensive work in social psychology, that points to the existence of at least occasional altruistic motivation, makes vindicating psychological egoism a very tall order.

One of the appeals of ethical egoism is that it solves the perennial "Why-be-moral?" question. If ethical egoists are right, then morality will never conflict with self-interest. And if we assume that we always have at least some good reason to advance our own interests, then, if ethical egoism is correct, we will always have some good reason to adhere to morality's commands.

The biggest problem for ethical egoists is to show why our own interests always take priority over the interests of others. Even if we are morally allowed to give our interests some preference over the interests of others, such a radical demotion of the importance of others' interests requires explanation. (RSL)

Error Theory. Moral error theory is really a family of metaethical theories that share a central feature. Each error theory claims that there is a central presupposition at the heart of morality, and that this presupposition is false. Where error theories differ from one another is in the central error they assign to moral thought. But whatever it is, this error is said to be so basic to the entire moral enterprise as to thoroughly infect our moral thoughts and practices.

Error theorists are cognitivists—they believe that moral claims are intended to state the truth. The problem, according to error theorists, is that there is no moral truth to be recorded by our moral judgments. Thus all moral judgments are untrue.

Though in principle there could be a very large number of different error theories, each alleging the existence of a different fundamental error in moral thought or judgment, in practice error theorists have focused on two related features of moral thought that are claimed to be deeply mistaken: the (sometimes implicit) assumption of morality's objectivity, and the existence of categorical reasons for action that are supplied by moral requirements. All error theorists deny the objectivity of morality, and all deny the existence of categorical reasons—reasons for action that apply to moral agents regardless of whether obedience to such reasons advances the goals or interests of an agent.

Thus there are two basic ways of trying to resist an error theoretic diagnosis of moral thought. First, one might deny that moral discourse really is committed to categorical reasons, or to the objectivity of its central standards. Or, second, one might accept that moral thought presupposes these commitments, but then try to vindicate them (see also "Reasons, Moral"). (RSL)

Experience Machine. What matters to you? A plausible first answer is that you care about having pleasant experiences and avoiding unpleasant ones. But is that really the *only* thing that intrinsically matters to you?

To see whether it is, imagine a machine that can give you any experience you would like, an Experience Machine. This machine can stimulate your brain to make you think that you are writing a wonderful piece of music, or telling a hilarious joke to an appreciative audience, or successfully befriending the person on whom you have a crush . . . anything! If you are attached to the machine, then you will believe that the experience you are undergoing is real.

Now, assuming that the machine works exactly as advertised, would you choose to plug into it for a few years? Or for your entire life? Robert Nozick, who concocted this question, guessed that you would not. He identified three reasons not to opt for a life of pleasant hallucinations. First, you probably want to really *do* certain things, not just think that you are doing them. Second, you probably want to really *be* a certain kind of person—and not the kind who is completely passively programmed by a machine. Third, you probably want to interact with reality, not with just a simulation of reality.

The lesson from thinking about the Experience Machine is supposed to be that we do not value only pleasure. Most of us think that hedonism—the view that pleasure is the only intrinsically good thing—is false. Thinking about why a life on the Experience Machine would be less than ideal can uncover what else we really think is important (see also "Hedonism"). (EW)

Expressivism. According to expressivists, moral terms do not serve to denote moral properties, except, perhaps, in some deflationary sense. This is not a matter of failure of reference as is the case when a term such as "unicorn" turns out not to refer to any actual object. Instead, according to expressivists, moral terms are not in the business of referring. Moral terms serve, instead, to express a speaker's desire-like attitudes. Someone who says sincerely that it is morally right to love your neighbor is expressing a distinctive kind of approval of neighbor-loving. Their use of the term "right" does not serve primarily to attribute a property (rightness) to neighbor loving. Though it is difficult to pin down just what it means to "express" a desire-like attitude, expressivists are agreed that someone who says it is morally right to love your neighbor is not merely *describing* herself as having a desire. In that case she would be expressing a belief about her own psychology, and a view of this sort would be categorized as subjectivism, not expressivism. Expressivists would seem to be committed to holding that typical declarative moral sentences are not truth-apt. This implication must be treated with caution, however, since some of the most influential contemporary versions of expressivism endorse a deflationary, as opposed to a correspondence, theory of truth and claim that moral sentences are truth apt in this deflationary sense. Expressivists are perennially challenged to explain the apparent (or presumed) objectivity of moral distinctions, and contemporary versions of expressivism represent a sophisticated effort to do this. Expressivism is often thought to have an upper hand when explaining the apparent (or presumed) intimate connection between sincere moral judgment and motivation, a connection that is often labeled "motivational internalism" (see also "Cognitivism and Non-Cognitivism," "Motivational Internalism, Externalism"). (SM)

Fact-Value Distinction. The fact-value distinction is the intuitive distinction between the way the world is and the way it ought to be. It is a metaphysical distinction, though it is often articulated in epistemological terms. It is often claimed, for example, that values cannot be inferred from facts, or that one cannot derive an "ought" from an "is," or that no prescription follows solely from a description. The distinction is typically considered to be that between different kinds of facts, properties, or judgments—for example, that moral facts are different in kind from nonmoral facts, or that moral properties cannot be reduced to natural properties, or that moral judgments are products of feelings or attitudes, while factual judgments are products of belief. The fact-value distinction is often supposed to have an important methodological upshot, namely that ethical inquiry is importantly different from scientific inquiry. For while, it is commonly alleged, the observations and verdicts of science are purely descriptive, ethical verdicts are prescriptive, and nothing prescriptive follows solely from the descriptive. (DB)

Hedonism. This is the view that (i) pleasure—and nothing else—is intrinsically good, and (ii) pain—and nothing else—is intrinsically bad. There is a variety of views of what constitutes pleasure and pain, but all hedonists agree that pleasures and pains are essentially mental, so that if any two people shared identical mental states, they would experience the same amount and kind of pleasure and pain.

Some critics have raised the so-called *paradox of hedonism* as an objection to this theory. The paradox is this: those who set out with the aim of gaining pleasure are often frustrated as a result of this aim. Pleasure more often comes to those who value other things than pleasure—say, a loving family life, or challenging work, etc. While this last claim may well be true, the paradox fails to undermine hedonism. For it may be that pleasure is the only thing that is intrinsically good, even if it is not always rational to directly aim to acquire what is intrinsically valuable.

A more telling criticism of hedonism stems from the fact that if hedonism is true, then two people experiencing the same degree of pleasure are having experiences of equal value. But if one person's pleasure is based on a false belief—say, that his acquaintances treasure him, when in fact they despise him—then such pleasure seems either valueless or less valuable than the same pleasure when it is based on a true belief.

Hedonism is also criticized for failing to allow for the intrinsic value of other things—such as autonomy, virtue, and knowledge (see also "Experience Machine"). (RSL)

Imperatives, Categorical and Hypothetical. These are two kinds of commands distinguished by Immanuel Kant, who argued that the requirements of morality are best understood as categorical imperatives. Note that one need not accept Kant's deontological ethics in order to accept this claim; many consequentialists also agree with Kant that the requirements of morality are best understood as categorical imperatives.

Hypothetical imperatives are commands addressed to some agent to intend the necessary means to her ends. For instance, "If you intend to go to graduate school, intend to take the GRE" is a hypothetical imperative. Here, the command addressed to an agent to intend to take the GRE is one which would be withdrawn upon the discovery that she has no intention to go to graduate school (nor any other ends served by taking the GRE). It might be that this particular person has no reason to take the GRE.

Categorical imperatives differ in two ways. First, categorical imperatives, like "Do not lie" and "Do not steal," are commands that would *not* be withdrawn upon the discovery that an agent has no end that would be served by complying with these commands. Second, there is a reason for all rational agents, regardless of the specific intentions they have, to comply with these commands. However, as Philippa Foot has argued, this second feature of categorical imperatives doesn't follow from the first. Consider, for instance, the rules of a club, or the requirements of etiquette. Although these rules and requirements would not be withdrawn upon the discovery that someone has no ends that would be served by complying with them, surely these rules and requirements are not such that there is a reason for all rational agents to comply with them (see also "Deontological Ethics"). (JB)

Incommensurability. To claim that two values are incommensurable is to deny the possibility of certain comparisons between them. On one strong view, two values, A & B, are incommensurable when A is not greater than B in value, B is not greater than A in value, and yet A and B are not equal in value. It is controversial whether any values are incommensurable in this sense. Commonly proffered examples of such incommensurability involve prospective objects of choice whose value involves many dimensions or aspects. Think, for example, of trying to compare the value of two very different career paths. On a more relaxed view, two values are incommensurable so long as they are not equal in value and one cannot measure the degree to which one is better than another. In that case, the value of having friends and the value of being well-dressed might be incommensurable, even if having friends is more valuable. Or, more seriously, Kantians will typically claim that the value of human dignity is greater than the value of happiness, but they reject any common scale that would specify precisely how much more valuable human dignity is. In so far as philosophers agree that certain values are incommensurable, there is yet disagreement about whether this incommensurability is primarily a reflection of the indeterminacy inherent in language, the limitations on human knowledge, or the underlying metaphysics of value. (SM)

Intuitionism. "Intuitionism" has both a narrower and a wider sense. In its narrower meaning, intuitionism is an epistemological view that asserts the existence of self-evident moral propositions. When we believe such propositions on the basis of adequately understanding them, then we are justified in our belief. We can be justified in holding such beliefs even if we do not infer them from other justified beliefs.

One reason that intuitionism is appealing is because it allows us to stop a regress of justification—one that insists that any justified belief be justified by reference to other beliefs. Given a Humean principle that we cannot derive an ought from an is, it follows that any inferential justification of moral beliefs must come from other moral (or normative) beliefs. But unless this chain of justification goes on forever, or loops back onto itself, then if there are any justified moral beliefs at all, at least one—and probably many more—must be noninferentially justified. Intuitionists believe that self-evident moral propositions fit this bill.

Intuitionism in its wider meaning—sometimes known as *rational intuitionism*—is a normative ethical theory that has two parts: an intuitionist moral epistemology, just described, and a commitment to a plurality of fundamental, nonderivative moral rules whose truth can be intuited—i.e., known noninferentially. W. D. Ross's ethic of prima facie duties is perhaps the best-known version of intuitionism thus understood (see also "Pluralism, Moral"). (RSL)

Justice. Justice is the moral requirement, applicable both to individuals and institutions, to distribute benefits and burdens in a fair manner—that is, according to the relevant moral reasons. This is meant as a statement of the *concept* of justice. Various specific *conceptions* of justice will further specify what those relevant moral reasons are, and thus what is involved in distributing benefits and burdens in a "fair manner."

The moral requirement of justice is applicable in several domains. For instance, retributive justice is justice applied to criminal offenders, and requires that states punish offenders just when, and to the extent that, they deserve punishment. And distributive justice is justice applied to the distribution of various social and economic goods (money, education, opportunities, etc.) in a society. Philosophers also discuss international justice, intergenerational justice, justice in warfare, justice in the family, and justice in other domains as well.

Most discussion, however, is focused on distributive justice, responding to issues brought to the forefront with the publication of *A Theory of Justice* by John Rawls in 1971. In that book, Rawls defends a particular conception of justice centered around two principles applicable to the basic structure of society. According to the first principle, justice requires that every person have an equal right to basic liberties (including liberties to vote, freedom of speech, freedom from arbitrary arrest, and others). According to the second principle, justice requires that there be fair equality of opportunity, and that any social and economic inequalities be such that they benefit the least well off in society. (JB)

Moral Luck. Imagine two students each trying to murder her professor. One succeeds, and the other fails. It seems correct to blame or punish the successful murderer more strongly than the would-be murderer, even if the reason for the difference in result is purely a matter of luck. But it is also plausible that a person is morally assessable only for what is within her control—call this the Control Principle.

Thus we face the paradox known as moral luck. Resultant luck, as in this example, is just one form of moral luck. A second form is circumstantial luck, where moral assessability depends upon what decisions one happens to face. For example, we blame those who cooperate with evil regimes more strongly than those who merely would have cooperated had they been faced with such a decision. A third form is constitutive luck, where the things that affect our moral characters—our genes, our upbringing, and our educational opportunities—lie largely beyond our control. Even though we know that life has dealt some people an unfair hand, we still morally assess them for who they are.

So, there appears to be a tension between the thought that we are appropriate objects of moral assessment despite the fact that we do not completely control our influences, circumstances, and effects, and the thought embodied by the Control Principle. In the face of this tension, some reject the Control Principle, while others think we should radically revise the way we make particular moral assessments. And Thomas Nagel, known for articulating the varieties of moral luck, concludes that "the problem has no solution." (EW)

Motivational Internalism, Externalism. Motivational internalism is the view that, necessarily, an agent sincerely holds a moral judgment about her own prospective actions only if that agent is motivated to some extent to act in accordance with it. Thus, if motivational internalism is true, then there is a necessary connection between sincere moral judgments and motivation. Motivational externalists deny this, and argue that there are only contingent connections between our moral judgments and our motivations.

Motivational internalism is important because of its role in a classic noncognitivist argument. If we assume the truth of motivational internalism, and also assume the Humean claim that no motivational state can be true or false, then it turns out that moral judgments are not truth-apt.

Motivational internalists argue that those who are entirely indifferent to what look like their own moral judgments are either really being insincere, or are not really issuing moral judgments at all. They may be using moral vocabulary, but doing so only ironically, or in some other way that shows that theirs is not a real moral judgment, but only a kind of mimicry.

Motivational externalists, by contrast, often rely on the possibility of the amoralist to bolster their case. Amoralists are those who really believe that certain actions are morally right or wrong, but who are entirely indifferent to the moral claims they hold. If amoralism is a possibility, then there is after all no necessary connection between sincere moral judgment and motivation. Externalists have appealed to the apparent conceivability of amoralists to substantiate the claim that there are only contingent connections between sincere moral judgments and motivation (see also "Cognitivism and Non-Cognitivism"). (RSL)

Natural Law Theory. Natural laws are the universal and unchanging moral laws prescribed to us by God and accessible to our human reason. On St. Thomas Aquinas's view, these natural laws are expressions of God's plan for our world. Natural laws thus differ from positive laws—that is, the laws "posited" by legislatures, courts, or other governmental bodies possessing the authority to create laws. Within the philosophy of law, natural law theory is a view about the relationship between natural laws and positive laws. According to natural law theory, for something to count as a genuine law, it is not enough that it be passed by an appropriately constituted governmental body, promulgated to the citizens, and so forth; it also must not disagree with natural laws.

On Aquinas's view, if a positive law disagrees in some way with natural laws, "it is no longer a law, but a corruption of law" (*Summa Theologiea* Part I–II, qu.95, a.2). He argues that when a law is unjust, it loses its validity as a law, and thus loses its claim to be obeyed (though we may still have other good reasons for obeying it, such as a need to preserve social stability).

Contemporary versions of natural law theory, which depart to some extent from Aquinas's views, have been put forth by Lon Fuller, John Finnis, and others. All are united in their rejection of the legal positivist's "separability thesis"—roughly, the thesis that the matter of a law's existence and the matter of its morality are entirely separable matters. (JB)

Naturalism, Ethical, and Ethical Nonnaturalism. The debate between ethical naturalists and nonnaturalists is a debate about the metaphysics of moral properties (or facts, truths, etc.). Ethical naturalists believe that moral properties are natural ones; nonnaturalists deny this.

Much, of course, depends on what is meant by "natural" in this context. There is no uniform agreement on this matter. Most writers follow G. E. Moore, who understood natural facts as those whose discovery is the proper subject matter of the natural and social sciences. Neither Moore himself nor anyone writing after him thought of this conception as fully illuminating. The basic idea, though, is that we have such areas of inquiry as physics, chemistry, engineering, and psychology as central cases of the sciences. Ethical naturalists view ethics as in principle on a par with these disciplines—studying empirically confirmable phenomena through largely a posteriori methods of investigation. If ethical naturalists are correct, moral features of the world are causally efficacious, can impinge on our senses in ways that enable us to know them, and are metaphysically unmysterious.

Ethical naturalism is animated in almost every case by a commitment to *metaphysical naturalism*—the view that all the facts there are, are natural ones. Ethical nonnaturalists reject this view. They insist that ethics is not a science itself; nor are its findings identical to or in any other way reducible to those of the sciences. There is not only a conceptual divide separating the ought from the is—there is also a metaphysical and epistemological divide. According to ethical nonnaturalists, moral facts are not scientific ones; nor are moral facts knowable by means of empirical confirmation.

Supernaturalist views are a species of ethical nonnaturalism. Supernaturalists reject both ethical and metaphysical naturalism, and endorse the existence of a being who is unconstrained by natural laws and whose nature or actions is essential to the content and rational authority of moral norms (see also "Realism, Moral"). (RSL)

Nihilism. Moral nihilism is the metaphysical view that there are no moral facts or properties. No person is good, bad, or evil; no action is right, wrong, or morally permissible. What appear to be distinctively moral facts or properties are actually the projection into the world of one's antecedently held values. There are two main strains of nihilism. Error theory, such as that advocated by J. L. Mackie, holds that since there are no moral properties, nothing can be as morally described, and, therefore, all sentences used to make moral assertions are literally false. On this view, "Lying is wrong" is comparable to "Lying is common among ghosts." Both describe acts of lying, but since there are no moral properties or ghosts, nothing can be truly described as *being wrong* or *being common among ghosts*, and, consequently, both sentences are literally false. Noncognitivism, such as that advocated by A. J. Ayer, holds that since there are no moral facts, moral sentences ought not be viewed as describing such facts, but, rather, as *expressing* a speaker's attitudes. On this view, "Lying is wrong" is comparable to "Lying—boo!". Neither describes acts of lying; rather, both express a speaker's negative attitude towards lying and, consequently, may not even be truth-evaluable. Nihilism is radically at odds with common sense. Nevertheless, its supporters typically suggest that it is the best explanation for the widespread, perhaps intractable, moral disagreement among individuals, cultures, and societies, and for the typical positive correlation between an individual's moral judgments and his or her corresponding, and characteristic, attitudes and motivations (see also "Error Theory", "Cognitivism and Non-Cognitivism"). (DB)

Open Question Argument. An open question is one whose answer is not self-evident to competent language users and, therefore, is "open" for serious discussion. For example, (1) but not (2) is open:

(1) John is a bachelor, but will he marry?
(2) John is a bachelor, but is he married?

G. E. Moore famously used this notion of an open question to argue that moral properties must be simple and nonnatural. According to Moore, moral properties cannot be complex properties, since for every pair consisting of a moral predicate "is M" (e.g., "is wrong") and a nonmoral predicate "is N" that picks out a complex property (e.g., "fails to maximize happiness") every instance of (3) or (4) would be an open question:

(3) Φ-ing is N, but is it M?
(4) Φ-ing is M, but is it N?

For example, "Lying fails to maximize happiness, but is it wrong?" does not have a self-evident answer and, consequently, is an open question. Thus, Moore concluded, moral properties must be simple. Similarly, Moore claimed that for every pair consisting of a moral predicate and a nonmoral predicate that picks out a natural property (e.g., "is pleasurable") every instance of (3) would be open. For example, "Engaging in premarital intercourse is pleasurable, but is it good?" is open. Thus, Moore concluded that moral properties must be nonnatural. The assumption driving Moore's Open Question Argument is the following:

> If any question of the form "φ is P, but is it P_1?" is open then P and P_1 pick out different properties.

As developments in later twentieth-century philosophy would show, there are uncontroversial counterexamples to this assumption. For example, "This is water, but is it H_2O?" is clearly open—its answer required millennia of scientific discovery to determine—but "is water" and "is H_2O" pick out the same property. (DB)

Particularism, Moral. Moral particularism names a family of views that take a negative attitude towards moral principles. Particularism insists that moral distinctions are real and knowable and is thereby distinguished from nihilism and skepticism. What particularism denies is that moral distinctions are well captured or explained in terms of principles. Instead, particularism emphasizes the degree to which subtle differences in context can affect what is good or right in a given case. While sometimes allowing that principles can play a valuable role in deliberation about and assessment of moral conduct, particularists have been keen to emphasize the limitations and dangers of excessive or blind reliance on rules. Particularism is commonly associated with holism about reasons. According to holism, a fact which is a reason in one case may be no reason at all, or even a reason in the other direction, in another case. "Generalism" is the label most commonly given to those who defend a robust place for moral principles. Some philosophers accept generalism because of a prior commitment to some specific moral principle. Others, inspired by Hare, see some level of principled generality as part of the logic of moral language. Others think only generalism can offer a satisfactory account of moral knowledge. (SM)

Pluralism, Moral. According to moral pluralism there is a plurality of fundamental moral values—including duties and obligations—and these cannot be fully reconciled. Moral pluralists thus typically see moral conflict as endemic to morality itself and not attributable entirely to our limited knowledge or parochial interests. For example, one might think that mercy and justice are each compelling values and that no fully clear eyed view could ever remove entirely the genuine moral conflict that can arise between them in a given case. Moral pluralism need not be anti-systematic or anti-theoretical. W. D. Ross's system of prima facie duties provides one well-known example of how a pluralistic view can be worked out. Moral pluralism should be distinguished from moral relativism. Like moral pluralism, moral relativism emphasizes the potential for moral disagreement and conflict, but derives this from a general thesis about value, that value is relative to a valuer. Conflicting values arise from the diverse viewpoints of valuers. For example, according to cultural relativism, it is arguably really cultures that are plural and any plurality of values is (contingently) derived from the differing viewpoints of cultures. For moral pluralists, by contrast, moral conflict is due to the substance of the specific values themselves, not simply to a more general thesis about the nature of value (see also "Duty", "Relativism, Moral"). (SM)

Realism, Moral. Moral realism is a cognitivist metaethical view according to which some moral propositions are true, and true in a special way. Moral realism says that moral truths are stance-independent: when moral propositions are true, they are so not because of the attitudes taken by any human being (actual or ideal) towards their content.

Think for a moment about the basic moral rules, whatever they are. Moral realists insist that such rules are correct *not* because of having been endorsed or ratified as such. Like realists about other domains, moral realists think of the basic (moral) rules as ones that are correct in a way that is conceptually and explanatorily prior to anyone's allegiance to or discovery of them. Scientific or logic realists, for instance, think of the fundamental scientific or logical laws as existing prior to our awareness of them. Such rules are not simply a summary of rules that we have found useful or efficient to rely on. Rather, we have found them useful and efficient, if we have, because of their truth. If moral realists are correct, then the same features apply to the basic rules of morality.

Suppose that some moral claims are true. And suppose, quite fancifully, that there were people who were morally infallible—they could never be morally mistaken. Moral realists claim that such infallibility is a matter of perfectly detecting the truth that obtains independently of the judgments of such infallible people. Moral claims are not made true by the attitudes we take towards them. Rather, if moral realism is correct, then even those who are perfectly morally reliable are gaining access to moral truths not of their own (or any other human being's) making.

Moral realism comes in two primary varieties: ethical naturalism and ethical nonnaturalism (see also "Naturalism, Ethical and Ethical Nonnaturalism"). (RSL)

Reasons, Moral. Moral reasons are considerations or features of a situation that, morally speaking, count in favor or against some action or attitude. At least five distinct but related questions arise about moral reasons. (1) What distinguishes moral from nonmoral reasons? That is, what makes a feature of a situation morally relevant? That someone is able to do the job, but not that he has blue eyes, is (plausibly) a morally relevant consideration when deciding whom to promote; what makes the former, but not the latter, morally relevant? (2) How are moral reasons recognized, and how ought they be recognized? For example, do we, or ought we to, recognize features as morally relevant because they elicit characteristic emotional responses? Or because we reason, or ought to reason, that actions with those features (e.g., that a particular act would cause unnecessary pain) are instances of a more general act-type (e.g., acts that we would not want done to ourselves)? (3) How are moral reasons to be weighed? If insulting someone is pleasant for the one insulting, but unpleasant for the person being insulted, the latter counts more against insulting than the former counts in favor of insulting. Why? (4) Do moral reasons always override nonmoral reasons? That is, do we always have decisive reason to do what is morally obligatory (or permissible) and to avoid doing what is morally wrong? Or do we sometimes, or even often, have sufficient reason to do what is morally wrong and avoid doing what is morally obligatory (or permissible)? (5) Do moral reasons necessarily motivate? Suppose that complimenting someone would raise that person's spirits, but that such a consideration would not at all motivate an agent, either as the agent is or as she would be with an improved subjective motivational set. According to *existence internalism*, a consideration counts as a moral reason for an agent only if it would motivate that agent as she actually is, or perhaps, as she would be with an improved subjective motivational set, and, therefore, it would hold that raising the person's spirits would not constitute a moral reason for the agent to offer a compliment. *Existence externalism* holds that a consideration may count as a moral reason for an agent even if the consideration would leave the agent unmoved, and, therefore, would hold that raising the person's spirits may constitute a reason for the agent to offer a compliment. (DB)

Reflective Equilibrium. Reflective equilibrium is a method of reasoning that continually tests for the mutual consistency of a complex structure of beliefs, revising the set of beliefs as necessary to retain or restore consistency (sometimes reflective equilibrium is understood instead as the complex mental state that would result from ideal use of the method). For example, consider a person who believes that one ought never to engage in homosexual behavior, a belief she holds as a consequence of a more general background belief that one ought to engage in sexual behavior only to procreate. When pressed, she recognizes her additional belief that it is morally permissible for a married heterosexual couple that cannot have children to engage in sexual activity, and, consequently, relinquishes the belief that one ought to engage in sexual behavior only to procreate. At this point, she might then also relinquish the belief that one ought never to engage in homosexual behavior, or, alternatively, she might consistently retain that more particular belief as a result of recognizing other background beliefs, for example, her beliefs that homosexual behavior is unnatural and that one ought never to engage in unnatural behavior. Revision may continue were she to recognize still other background beliefs, for example, that wearing glasses to improve one's vision is unnatural but also morally unobjectionable, and so on. Reflective equilibrium, which gained prominence in political and ethical theory in the 1970s, when John Rawls advocated and defended the method in his landmark *A Theory of Justice*, is sometimes advocated as a kind of coherence theory of justification. Among the more important objections to coherence theories, and to reflective equilibrium in particular, is that it gives evidentiary weight to one's beliefs or intuitions merely because one has them. But, it is argued, no evidentiary weight should be given to such beliefs or intuitions, since they are often the products of enculturation. (DB)

Relativism, Moral. Moral relativism is a family of views advocating that certain important moral phenomena apply "locally" to individuals or groups, rather than "universally" to everyone at all times. There are three main types of moral relativism. Descriptive relativism holds that different groups or societies *accept* different moral norms. As a descriptive thesis, it merely concerns the moral norms that different groups or societies have in fact accepted and denies that a single set of moral norms has been accepted by all persons at all times. Normative relativism holds that there *are* different moral norms for different groups or societies. It thus denies that a single set of moral norms binds all persons at all times. There are two sorts of normative relativism. Individual normative relativism holds that an individual is bound by the set of moral norms that he or she accepts. Cultural normative relativism holds that an individual is bound by the set of moral norms accepted by his or her culture. Metaethical relativism holds that moral beliefs or claims can be *true for* some subset of individuals but *false for* a different subset. It thus denies that moral claims are true or false (full-stop). (DB)

Rights. Rights are entitlements one has to engage in certain activities, or to have certain states of affairs obtain. Some examples of rights mentioned in various well-known political declarations include the right to vote, the right to speak freely, the right to be free from arbitrary arrest, the right to a fair trial, the right to life, and the right not to be subject to torture. Philosophers distinguish between moral rights (those entitlements we have according to morality) and legal rights (those entitlements we have as a matter of law). Earlier political theorists, most notably John Locke, spoke of "natural" rights, which are a kind of moral right we have in virtue of our nature. Locke argued that governments must not violate certain natural rights in order to be legitimate. Others, including Jeremy Bentham, argued that such talk of natural rights was both nonsensical and politically dangerous.

There is a contemporary philosophical debate about the function of rights. "Interest theorists" believe that rights function to protect important interests, while "will theorists" believe that rights function to provide the right-holder with sovereignty in a certain domain. Will theorists have trouble explaining the existence of certain rights that do not seem to provide for sovereignty (such as the rights of animals who are incapable of sovereignty, and unalienable rights, which one is not at liberty to waive), while interest theorists have trouble explaining the existence of rights that do not seem to promote the right-holder's interests, but promote instead the interests of some third party (as when I have a right to your carrying out your promise to me to do something that benefits someone else, not me). (JB)

Sentimentalism, Moral. Moral sentimentalism is the view that sentiment, rather than rationality, is the locus of significant moral phenomena. Sentimentalism is most closely associated with the eighteenth-century moral theories of the Third Earl of Shaftesbury, Francis Hutcheson, David Hume, and Adam Smith, and is appropriately contrasted with Kantian, or rationalist, moral theories. There are at least four specific kinds of sentimentalism. Normative Sentimentalism holds that sentiment, rather than rationality, is the source of justified moral norms. For example, some forms of care and virtue ethics ground moral norms in the notion of a good person, where a good person is one who acts from particular sorts of sentiments, such as the right kind of caring attitude. Descriptive Sentimentalism holds that sentiments (e.g., sympathy) or other noncognitive attitudes (e.g., disgust), rather than rationality, are the source of moral judgments (e.g., the judgment that some action is wrong). It thus holds that moral judgments are the product of sentiments rather than of a rational process. Noncognitivism, which might otherwise be called Constitutive Sentimentalism, holds that sentiments or other noncognitive attitudes are not merely the source of moral judgments, but actually *constitute* moral judgments, rather than, or in addition to, ordinary descriptive beliefs. On such a view, to think that some particular action is wrong *is* (say) to disapprove of such actions. Noncognitivists typically espouse expressivism, or what might otherwise be called Linguistic Sentimentalism, which holds that sentiments, rather than or in addition to ordinary beliefs, are what are expressed by utterances of moral sentences. A sentimentalist moral theory can package any and all of the different sentimentalisms. A complete sentimentalist theory will also provide an adequate theory of the sentiments themselves, explaining, for example, their ontology and that which distinguishes moral sentiments from nonmoral ones (see also "Expressivism"). (DB)

Subjectivism. Subjectivism holds that moral claims are reports or descriptions of oneself as being in particular sorts of mental states and, consequently, that the truth conditions for moral sentences require their speakers to be in those states. For example, to claim that lying is wrong is to report oneself as (say) disapproving of lying and, consequently, that "Lying is wrong" is true if and only if, and because, its speaker disapproves of lying. Thus, on such a subjectivist view, "Lying is wrong" and "I disapprove of lying" would have the same truth conditions and, therefore, the same meaning. Subjectivism should be distinguished from both expressivism and metaethical relativism. For according to expressivism, moral claims do not report a speaker's mental states, but, rather, express them, much like "Boo!" expresses, rather than reports, an unfavorable attitude. Metaethical relativism, unlike subjectivism, holds that no moral sentence is true or false, full-stop, but rather that all are true *for* or false *for* some individual(s) or group(s). Currently, there are few, if any, advocates for subjectivism. Its fatal flaw is thought to be its speaker-relativity, which implies that everyday moral disagreement and criticism is actually impossible. For subjectivism makes it impossible to use "Lying is not wrong" to disagree with someone who utters "Lying is wrong," just as it would be impossible to use "I do not disapprove of lying" to disagree or criticize someone who uses "I disapprove of lying" (see also "Expressivism", "Relativism, Moral"). (DB)

Supervenience. As a general matter, supervenience is a relation of dependence between two classes of properties. One set of properties, A, supervenes on another set, B, just in case it is impossible for two items to differ with respect to their A-properties without differing in respect of their B-properties. Supervenience is a weaker relation than identity since it is compatible with differences in B-properties giving rise to no difference in A-properties. Specific supervenience theses have been explored in many areas of philosophy. For example, mental properties are commonly thought to supervene on physical properties.

In metaethics, moral properties are widely agreed to supervene on natural (or descriptively characterized) properties. If this is right then it would not be possible, for example, for one person to be morally good but another person morally bad unless there were some difference between the natural properties of the two individuals. Likewise, it is not possible for one action to be right but another wrong unless there is some natural difference between them. Supervenience, however, says nothing about what natural properties might make a moral difference.

With only rare exception, contemporary metaethicists accept supervenience. The important disputes have been about how to properly formulate supervenience and how to explain its truth. Even those who deny the existence of moral properties, such as expressivists, accept supervenience while urging that it be understood as a constraint on the apt use of moral concepts. Someone who deploys moral concepts in a way that flouts supervenience betrays a lack of competence with those concepts, even though moral concepts, according to the expressivist, do not serve to pick out moral properties (see also "Expressivism"). (SM)

Utilitarianism. Utilitarianism is a family of consequentialist theories. As their name implies, consequentialist theories make consequences the determinative feature of moral assessment. The basic idea behind such theories is this: once we have determined what is intrinsically valuable, the rightness of actions depends on how well those actions (or rules prescribing those actions) advance what is intrinsically valuable.

There are two primary forms of utilitarianism: *act* and *rule*. Act utilitarians determine whether an action is morally required on the basis of that action's utility, i.e., on how good its results are. Rule utilitarians make this determination based on whether the action conforms to an ideal social rule. A rule is an ideal social rule just because general acceptance of it would yield results that are as least as good as the results that would accrue through general acceptance of any competing rule.

Standardly, utilitarianism in both forms is a maximizing doctrine. Thus act utilitarianism is ordinarily formulated as the view according to which an action is morally obligatory just because, of all options available at a given time, that action maximized the amount of intrinsic value. Rule utilitarianism is often defined as the view according to which actions are morally required just because they are permitted by rules, general acceptance of which would maximize intrinsically good results.

There are problems with standard, maximizing views—most notably, that they seem to demand too much of us, that they sanction injustice, and that they make it nearly impossible (especially on act utilitarianism) to know in advance whether our acts are right or wrong.

Recently, an alternative to maximizing has been developed, largely as a way to address these problems. The alternative is known as *satisficing*, which replaces the maximizing idea in both act and rule utilitarianism with the notion of generating a satisfactory (rather than the greatest possible) amount of intrinsic value.

There is a worry. Suppose actions are right just because they yield a satisfactory amount of goodness, rather than the greatest possible amount in the circumstances. How much goodness is satisfactory? Answering this question remains an outstanding problem for satisficers. (RSL)

Veil of Ignorance. The veil of ignorance is a metaphor used by John Rawls to represent the distinction between those reasons that are relevant and those that are irrelevant to the moral legitimacy of a particular set of basic principles of justice. For Rawls, the veil of ignorance is one important part of a more general metaphor, the Original Position, which represents the equal status of moral persons, as grounded in rational autonomous agency. A description of the Original Position is a description of the fair conditions under which a just social contract can be reached. The Original Position places individuals in the role of representatives whose task, constrained by the veil of ignorance—that is, constrained by the use of only morally relevant reasons and, thereby, constrained to be impartial—is to come to agreement on the basic principles that will be used to structure the resulting society. What someone does not know when "behind the veil of ignorance"—particular facts about himself or others, such as socioeconomic status, race, education, wealth, and talents; particular facts about his society and its history, such as which social classes constitute the powerful or the subjugated, and the historical facts leading to that power structure—represents morally irrelevant reasons. What someone does know when behind the veil—general facts about human behavior and propensities, such as that people are rationally self-interested and somewhat altruistic; general scientific, sociological, or economic facts, such as that societies are often in states of moderate scarcity and that primary social goods are necessary to live according to one's conception of a good life—represents morally relevant reasons. Rawls argues that since the Original Position provides conditions that are procedurally fair to all parties, so too would the principles agreed upon in those conditions be fair, and this sense of fair basic principles is the sense in which a social contract containing them would be just. (DB)

Virtue Ethics. Many different things are meant by the term *virtue ethics*. Central, though, is the thought that the virtues (excellent character traits) occupy a *primary* place in ethical theory. Other approaches acknowledge the existence of virtues too, but they relegate the notion of virtue to a secondary status. For example, a utilitarian might regard as virtues whichever character traits dispose a person to maximize happiness. Likewise, a deontologist might regard as virtues just those traits that dispose one to obey one's independently specifiable duties.

A traditional virtue ethicist, however, insists that the value of virtues cannot be reduced to the value of outcomes or actions. They are often motivated by the thought that ethics itself is not codifiable, and so no finite list of the value of outcomes or of duties could accurately capture the ethical. Many go even farther, arguing that the ethical value of outcomes and actions themselves depends upon virtue. For example, some claim that happiness is neither fully comprehensible nor attainable except from the perspective of a virtuous person (John McDowell). Others argue that right actions are constituted by what a virtuous person acting in character would do (Rosalind Hursthouse).

Character traits—good or otherwise—are sources of not only action, but also motivation, emotion, feeling, and pleasure. And so a virtuous person not only acts well, but also has appropriate motivations, emotions, and thoughts. Thus it can be difficult to determine whether someone has or lacks a particular character trait, and we should be reluctant to describe others as virtuous based upon scant behavioral evidence.

Virtue ethicists disagree with one another about whether there is only one virtue (Socrates, the Stoics) or whether there are multiple virtues: in *The Republic* Plato recognizes the distinct virtues of justice, courage, moderation, and wisdom (the cardinal virtues); later Aristotle adds others, including generosity, magnanimity, wit, and friendliness. Even so, Aristotle argued that the many virtues though distinct were inseparable—a person cannot have one virtue without having all the others too. (EW)

Weakness of Will. In Plato's *Apology*, Socrates plausibly claims that "no one errs willingly." Sure, people often act badly, but why would anyone *deliberately* screw up? Yet we also are all too familiar with the similarly plausible thought that a person can know not to do something, and, alas, intentionally do it all the same. Sometimes it seems a person's will is weak.

Why, then, would anyone think that weakness of will (in ancient Greek, *akrasia*) is impossible? It is no mystery why people—knowing all the risks and consequences—play dangerous sports, eat fatty food, use illicit drugs, and watch American Idol (though usually not all at the same time). There are good reasons both to do and not to do these things. Yet it is puzzling how to understand things if you judge that all things considered it is *best* for you not to watch American Idol, and then watch it anyway. Pedestrian cases like this seem different from cases of addiction or compulsion, such as when an unwilling heroin addict nevertheless shoots up. They also seem different from most cases when a person thoughtfully changes her mind about what is best to do. Most cases of acting against your best judgment are not like that: pedestrian failures are failures of will, rather than of addiction or compulsion.

Still, philosophers are vexed to describe plausibly what is going on in these cases. A minority concludes that *akrasia*, as described above, really is impossible; most think that it is possible but always irrational to err willingly; a third group believes that *akrasia* is not only possible but sometimes even rational, such as when a person (e.g., Huck Finn) violates his mistaken conscience. (EW)

Part I

Central Topics in Ethics

1 Moral Realism

Terence Cuneo

Stated in rough and ready fashion, moral realism is the view that there are objective moral facts. Moral realists believe, then, that in addition to ordinary "descriptive facts" such as *that it is presently raining in Seattle,* there are moral facts such as *that torturing someone simply for fun is wrong*. Some philosophers find moral realism so plausible that they claim to be unable to furnish positive arguments in its favor. Who in their right mind, after all, would deny that torturing merely for fun is wrong? According to these philosophers, the best realists can do is to reiterate how plausible their position is and explain why none of the arguments against it works. Other philosophers, by contrast, are not so impressed by the appearance that there are moral facts; they find moral realism positively exotic. For what type of thing, these philosophers wonder, would a moral fact be and where could we find it? If these philosophers are right, there are plenty of reasons to believe that moral facts would be very strange were they to exist. Among other things, were such facts to exist, then there would be "demands floating around in the world waiting to be perceived by moral agents."[1] And that would be very strange. Moral facts would be so strange, these philosophers argue, that we should try hard to find alternatives to admitting them into our best metaethical theories.

When viewed in this light, it can be difficult to see how to move the debate between realists and their rivals forward; the debate looks like little more than a clash of different philosophical temperaments. Realists appear to be impressed by the commonsensical appearances, while their rivals are not (or they believe that realists have misdescribed these appearances). Still, small steps forward are better than none. At the very least, it is natural to hope that each side in this debate can find common ground to frame their disagreement and better articulate the most powerful considerations for their view. My aim in this essay is to take a few small steps forward by outlining a case for moral realism. In presenting this case, my aim is not to present individual arguments for moral realism. Rather, it is to explore a general *strategy* used to argue for the view, which includes various claims about how we ought to understand the debate between realists and their rivals.

But we cannot rush into these matters headlong. To have the case for realism before us, we need first to understand better what moral realists believe. So, I shall set for myself two tasks. The first is to present a version of generic moral realism, which is acceptable to most who identify themselves as realists. The second is to present what I will call the realist's master strategy. While this strategy is rarely explicitly articulated by realists, it is, I believe, one that realists often presuppose when arguing for their view.

Generic Moral Realism

Our overarching project is to consider the case for moral realism. This project, however, runs the risk of not getting off the ground, for philosophers lump a huge variety of views under the heading of moral realism—views that disagree with one another in important ways.[2] I see little hope of bringing order to this state of affairs. So, I shall resort to identifying three core commitments that those who call themselves realists ordinarily accept. Any position that accepts these core commitments is a version of what I shall call *generic moral realism*. The case I will present for moral realism, then, is one for generic moral realism.

The first claim embraced by moral realists concerns the nature of moral thought and discourse. It says:

> Ordinary moral thought and discourse, by and large, purport to represent moral reality.[3]

The guiding idea behind this claim is that ordinary moral thought and discourse are like mathematical, theological, and external world thought and discourse. They purport to represent or be about a distinct subject matter. In the case of mathematics, that subject matter includes numbers. In the case of theological discourse, it includes God. In the case of morality, its target subject matter includes such things as the wrongness of actions and the goodness of agents.

To get a better idea of what realists believe about moral thought and discourse, consider a paradigmatic moral sentence such as "Oliver North's lying to Congress is wrong." According to realists, in the ordinary case, by uttering this sentence, an agent says (or predicates) of North's action that it is wrong. On the assumption that moral discourse expresses moral thoughts, it follows that moral thought and discourse are not a species of make-believe. To say that North's behavior is wrong is not to pretend to believe that what North did is wrong. Nor, for that matter, is it simply to express an attitude of disgust or disapprobation toward North. Of course by claiming that ordinary moral thought and discourse are not simply expressions of attitudes of disgust or disapprobation, realists needn't deny that they are typically accompanied by the expressions of such attitudes. Indeed, some realists have claimed exactly this.[4]

The claim that ordinary moral thought and discourse purport to represent moral reality is, however, compatible with none of it being such that it actually succeeds in doing so. It is, then, compatible with moral thought and discourse being massively mistaken. So, to the first claim about the function of moral thought and discourse, moral realists add this second claim:

> Some ordinary moral thought and discourse actually represent moral reality.

It is this second claim that distinguishes realists from error theorists, who believe that moral thought and discourse purport to represent moral reality but fail to do so.[5] If we understand truth in terms of accurate representation, the difference between realists and error theorists is (roughly) this: error theorists hold that the contents of moral thought and discourse are untrue. Realists, by contrast, do not.

If, however, ordinary moral thought and discourse sometime succeed in representing moral reality, it follows that there is a moral reality to represent. Moral realists often talk of this reality as a realm of moral facts. According to this approach, the sentence "Oliver North's lying to congress is wrong" accurately represents moral reality just in case it is a fact *that North's lying to congress is wrong*. Talk of there being moral facts raises questions in the minds of some philosophers. For our purposes, however, we needn't worry about the best way to characterize their nature. We can think of moral facts as those things that are the object of moral knowledge (if any such knowledge there be). As such, they might be things having moral properties, moral states of affairs that obtain, or true moral propositions. In any event, once we identify moral reality with a realm of moral facts, we can see that realists are committed to this third thesis:

> Moral facts exist.

This last claim lies at the heart of moral realism, as realism about morality is fundamentally a claim about what there is. It is also the most controversial of the realists' claims. By this I mean not simply that it is the claim about which moral antirealists are most suspicious. I also mean that the issue of how to understand it is the subject of deep disagreements among realists themselves, for realists disagree about how we should think of such facts.

On this occasion, I won't bother to dive into the controversies that divide realist views from one another. I shall simply note that they tend to cluster around two main issues. The first is whether moral facts are mind-independent in the sense that they are not imparted to the world in virtue of our having (or being such that we would, under ideal conditions, have) attitudes of various sorts—such as valuing—toward aspects of nonmoral reality. Traditionally, realists have rejected the claim that moral facts are mind-dependent in this sense, claiming that some acts are wrong regardless of the attitudes we have (or would, in ideal conditions have) toward them. But more recently some philosophers have defended views according to which moral facts are mind-dependent in a robust sense, claiming that some of these views are versions of moral realism.[6] As I have formulated it, generic moral realism is compatible with such response-dependent accounts of moral facts (although, in a moment, we shall see that not all positions which view moral facts as mind-dependent in this way count as versions of moral realism).

The second issue about which realists disagree is whether moral facts are "natural" or whether they belong to a sui generis nonnatural realm. This debate between moral naturalists and nonnaturalists has proven difficult to resolve, mostly because there are no accepted criteria for what renders a fact natural or nonnatural. The intuitive idea, however, is that natural facts are those which form the subject matter of the natural sciences, while nonnatural facts are those which do not. As their name indicates, moral naturalists believe that moral facts are natural. Hence, they have been eager to defend the claim that moral facts play naturalistically respectable explanatory roles, such as causally explaining nonmoral facts in the world. They have also tended to defend the claim that moral reasons behave like other naturalistically acceptable reasons, such as prudential reasons, in this sense: whether or not a moral fact, such as the fact that North acted wrongly, provides a reason to act depends on the desires we have (or would have if we deliberated correctly). Moral reasons, according to these naturalists, are Humean or internal.[7]

Nonnaturalists, for their part, have rejected the naturalist approach. While not suspicious of science or the claim that moral facts are realized in ordinary natural facts, they are wary of the idea that science can shed much light on the nature of morality. Suppose, for example, we were to discover that we are genetically disposed to aggressive behavior. According to nonnaturalists, this would not as such make a moral difference. For we are rational agents who can step back from our desires and inclinations, asking whether we should act upon them. If so, the discoveries of the empirical sciences have moral significance, say nonnaturalists, primarily by way of becoming input for ethical deliberation.[8] Moreover, nonnaturalists typically claim, we shouldn't expect moral facts to causally explain anything. Rather, if nonnaturalists are correct, moral facts are the sorts of thing that *justify* or *favor* various types of responses on our part—where these are not causal but irreducibly normative relations. Finally, nonnaturalists have tended to believe that some moral reasons apply to agents regardless of the desires they might happen to have (or would have if they deliberated correctly). They are not Humean but categorical or external reasons.[9]

As I say, I won't try to resolve the issues that divide naturalists from nonnaturalists on this occasion. I shall simply assume that generic moral realism is neutral with regard to them, being compatible with both moral naturalism and nonnaturalism. It will be remembered, however, that when I initially presented what moral realists believe, I claimed that they hold not simply that moral facts exist, but also that they are objective. So far, I have said little about what this qualification means. Let me close this section by saying something about it.

According to moral realists, moral thought and discourse purport to represent a distinctively moral realm. The predicative component of moral beliefs purports to be about not such things as numbers or trees, but the wrongness of actions and the goodness of agents. If this is right, not anything could count as a moral fact (anymore than anything could count as a number or a tree). For there are conceptual constraints on what could count as a moral fact. What might these constraints be? We can get a feel for their nature by considering stock moral truisms, such as the following:

It is wrong to lie simply because one doesn't feel like telling the truth.

It is wrong to slander another simply because it makes one feel better.

It is wrong to torture someone simply because she has inconvenienced you.

Stock moral truisms such as these indicate that moral properties such as *being wrong* are intimately connected with actions that undercut human well-being or express deep disrespect toward fellow human beings. Torture, for example, is an activity that, in a particularly egregious way, tends to destroy its victim. Slander is an activity that tends not only to rupture harmonious human relations, but also to express profound disrespect for its object. By contrast, moral properties such as *being right* are intimately connected with actions that tend to foster human well-being or express adequate respect toward others. Treating others with fairness and decency is, for example, morally right. For treating others in this way tends to promote the well-being of others, treating them as objects that deserve our respect.[10]

There are subtleties about how to understand the connections between well-being and moral properties that needn't concern us here. More important for present purposes is to note that realists tend to hold that a constraint on a good metaethical theory is that it vindicates truisms such as those listed above. The claims that express them must come out neither untrue nor merely contingently true. If this is right, we now have a way (although certainly not the only way) to understand the realists' claim that moral facts are objective. Moral facts are objective in the sense that the stock moral truisms provide objective constraints on what could count as a moral fact.

This point has theoretical importance. For, if it is right, not every view which claims that there are moral facts is a realist position. Consider, for example, a subjectivist view which says that actions are right for an agent simply because she approves of it. Subjectivism fails to comport with the stock moral truisms, as an agent could approve of just about anything and, hence, just about anything could be right, including torturing for mere pleasure. It follows that subjectivism is not a realist view. Or consider a relativist view according to which right actions for a particular group are those that are approved by that group. Relativism also fails to comport with the stock moral truisms, for groups could approve of just about anything and, hence, just about anything could be right, including recreational torture on a selective basis. Relativism no more than subjectivism is, then, a version of moral realism. So, while generic moral realism is a fairly capacious position, it is not so liberal as to imply that any view which claims that there are moral facts is thereby a version of moral realism.

The Core Moral Data

To this point, our attention has been on preliminary matters. Our project has been to identify, well enough for present purposes, the type of view that realists have wished to defend. Our next task is to present what I earlier called the realist's master strategy. By presenting this strategy, the hope is to provide an alternative to two tendencies that dominate contemporary metaethical discussion.

The first tendency is to discuss various metaethical issues piecemeal, treating certain types of considerations as if they decisively support one or another metaethical view. In recent defenses of expressivism, for example, philosophers such as Simon Blackburn and Allan Gibbard maintain that "expressivism has to be correct" because it alone offers us a satisfactory account of the intimate connection between moral judgments and moral motivation. The assumption seems to be that as long as expressivism nicely explains this particular set of data and its rivals do not, then this is enough to make it the view to beat.[11] The second rather different tendency is for philosophers to assume that theirs is the default position with little or no argument. This tendency is particularly pronounced among realists. Those sympathetic with realism often assume that as long as they can defend their position from objections, little more needs to be said in favor of it, as theirs is the default metaethical position.[12]

Both of these approaches strike me as mistaken. In the first place, we should not lose sight of the fact that philosophy is inherently a comparative enterprise. This means that, if a view fares particularly well or poorly along a given dimension of theory evaluation, this is typically not enough to vindicate or discredit it. We ordinarily need to assess theories along multiple dimensions. Moreover, we need to be not only as articulate as possible about the criteria we use to assess a particular theory, but also to have in mind the data that our theories should accommodate. Such matters, of course, are subject to debate; realists and antirealists often disagree about that which a good metaethical position should explain. But it is worth noting that the issues that metaethical theories are designed to address are not primarily philosophers' inventions. They are ordinarily rooted in lived moral experience. Let us, then, begin with the data that realists maintain that any good metaethical theory should accommodate.

Consider a situation of the following sort:

> A colleague of yours has just given birth to a child. To ease the burden on your colleague and her family, other colleagues have assembled a group of people to provide meals for them. You have signed up to provide a meal on a particular date. Several weeks pass and you receive a phone call to the effect that you are supposed to provide a meal for your colleague this evening. You, however, have forgotten all about this. In fact, you have made plans to see a show with your spouse this evening, which would provide some much desired time together. Upon hearing that you are expected to provide a meal this evening, you race through some practical reasoning. Your colleague and her family, you reckon, probably won't go hungry tonight if you don't provide a meal; no doubt they have food in the freezer they could use. That, you further speculate, might make it permissible to provide a meal some other night, when doing so would be more convenient. But after running through a number of such scenarios, it strikes you that, while there are alibis available, you should cancel your plans and prepare a meal for your colleague and her family. Given that you have made a previous commitment to provide a meal, this is what the situation demands. And so you judge this is what you ought to do.

Scenarios such as this, I trust, will seem familiar to us all. Realists maintain that it is worth paying close attention to their characteristics.

In the first place, your experience has phenomenological dimensions of which to take note.[13] According to the description offered, you experience the situation at hand as *calling for* or *demanding* a certain type of response. This demand, moreover, is experienced as not emanating from you but from elements of the situation itself, in particular, from the fact that you have committed yourself to provide a meal. The demand in question, moreover, feels very different from the demands of appetite, as in the case in which you smell freshly baked cookies and find them "calling your name." Furthermore, it feels very different from a flight of imagination in which you resolve to pretend to treat your environment in a certain way, treating it as if it demands a certain response. To use some philosophical jargon, your experience has moral presentational content, which is different from that of the cases just described.

In the second place, when you step back and assess your situation, you are capable of reasoning about it. Most importantly, this reasoning is such that, when engaging in it, you realize that not any old response to your situation will do. There appears to be a correct way to respond to your situation and, thus, that you can make a mistake about what you should do. In this regard, your experience feels rather different from a case in which you and a friend are comparing the merits of opera. While you appreciate the technical prowess required to perform it well, we can imagine the genre totally fails to move you. While both of you disagree about the merits of opera, you also agree that it would be a stretch to say that one of you has the correct response; you acknowledge that both of you might simply be "wired" to appreciate different things.

At any rate, in the moral case, it is in virtue of there being a response that seems correct that you find yourself "coming down" on a verdict about how the world is: it demands a certain type of response on your part. This verdict, moreover, has the tell-tale marks of being a genuine belief. It appears to be about what the situation demands and is thus a way of categorizing the world. The content of such a judgment, furthermore, is such that it can enter into further inferences and various sorts of logical constructions such as conditional statements. Moreover, it can be said to be true and the object of knowledge in what seem to be perfectly straightforward uses of these terms. In these respects, your judgment is very different from mental states that are not beliefs, such as those that merely express a question or disgust. Questions cannot be the antecedents or consequents of conditional statements. Expressions of disgust such as "Damn!" cannot be true or false.

Finally, if we take yet another step away from the experience itself, we can consider the modal profile of its content. Imagine, for example, someone were to play devil's advocate with you, querying: Why should you bother preparing food for your colleague? Why not lie and wash your hands of the situation? Or, for that matter, instead of delivering freshly cooked food, why not send a slanderous letter? Or, more drastically still, why not prepare to torture your colleague because of the inconvenience she's caused you? In response, you could appeal to what we earlier called stock moral truisms, such as the following:

> It is wrong to lie simply because one doesn't feel like telling the truth.
>
> It is wrong to slander another simply because it makes one feel better.
>
> It is wrong to torture another simply because she has inconvenienced you.

We saw earlier that, according to realists, principles such as these appear to be truisms or obvious necessary truths which anyone who is competent with their constituent concepts can know. Indeed, they function like what Wittgenstein in *On Certainty* called "framework propositions" and what Thomas Reid called "principles of common sense." If someone were to deny them, this would be evidence that that person lacked competence with moral concepts, was not of sound mind, was joking, deeply confused, in the grip of a badly mistaken theory, or the like.[14] That is why, according to realists, we do not find any appreciable disagreement about their truth among competent moral agents. Only the deranged and those pressing the limits of philosophical inquiry call them into question.

In any event, it is because the stock moral truisms have this sort of modal status that certain types of response to the questions raised above seem wrongheaded. Someone, let's imagine, raises the question about why you shouldn't torture your colleague because of the inconvenience she's caused you. On the face of things, it would be totally inappropriate to draw comparisons with etiquette, answering "Well, that's just the way we do things around here. There's really no deep difference between moral principles prohibiting torture and principles of etiquette such as 'Always place a fork to the left of a plate.'" Moreover, on the face of things, it would be similarly inappropriate to say that the property *being wrong* is like *being esteemed* since whether an action is wrong is fixed entirely by the affective attitudes we happen to have toward that action. If the stock moral truisms are to be believed, this could not be so. Even if our attitudes toward torture were to change and we were to discover that many of us relish the experience, this would make no difference with respect to its wrongness. The stock moral truisms, according to what we said earlier, set the limits as to what could count as a moral fact.

The phenomenology of moral experience, the conviction that the conclusions of practical reasoning can be mistaken, the doxastic character of moral judgments, and the modal profile of moral principles: these, according to realists, are among the most important data that a good metaethical theory should take into consideration. For ease of reference, let us refer to them as the *core moral data*. Having identified the core moral data, we must now turn our attention to the more difficult issue of what to make of them. How, then, should a metaethical theory assess the core moral data?

Evaluating the Core Moral Data

According to the realist's master strategy, the core data should be assessed according to three criteria. Let us call them the Reidian, explanatory, and simplicity criteria respectively.

What I shall call the *Reidian criterion* is a natural extension of the approach taken toward theory evaluation by the eighteenth-century Scots philosopher Thomas Reid.[15] A good way to understand the Reidian approach is to begin with the notion of a *doxastic practice* ("doxa" = Greek for belief). For present purposes, think of a doxastic practice as a type of social practice into which we are inducted—often as small children—that yields a certain range of outputs. The activities that constitute such a practice typically include: being introduced to concepts of a certain range and instructed in their proper employment; deploying these concepts to form judgments of certain kinds and engaging in methods of evaluating them; and, being introduced to various methods of attention and inquiry and instructed in their proper employment. The outputs of a practice are the judgments formed as a result of engaging in those activities just described.

A good example of a doxastic practice is the perceptual practice. At a young age, most of us are inducted into this practice by being introduced to concepts such as 'being a tree' and being instructed in their proper employment. Along the way, we develop other skills, such as being able to discriminate some types of trees from others. As a result, we form perceptual judgments of various sorts, which are the output of this practice.

Of course the perceptual doxastic practice is only one among many such practices into which we are inducted. Among others, there is the memorial practice (the practice of forming and evaluating memory judgments) and the introspective practice (the practice of forming and evaluating introspective judgments). Of special interest for our purposes is that doxastic practice which I shall call the *moral practice*. Like the perceptual practice, the moral practice is best thought of as being comprised of various activities that yield a variety of doxastic outputs. These activities include being introduced to moral concepts, such as 'being wrong,' and instructed in their proper employment; deploying these concepts to form moral judgments; and, being introduced to practices of attention and inquiry into moral matters and instructed in their proper employment. In the ordinary case, engaging in these activities yields a variety of moral judgments that concern the moral status of various acts, character traits, and policies.

The Reidian criterion offers us a method for assessing doxastic practices such as the moral practice. It tells us that if a given doxastic practice is socially well-established over time, deeply entrenched (in the limit case being unavoidable for all practical purposes), endowed with sophisticated methods of evaluation of its outputs, and such that its outputs are not massively and systematically inconsistent with each other and those of other doxastic practices in good working order, then (all else being equal) we should maintain that that practice is reliable. There is a strong presumption in favor of believing that it yields a preponderance of judgments that are true.

I shall say more about what favors accepting the Reidian criterion as a mode of theory evaluation in a moment. For now, let us turn to the second criterion of theory assessment, what I called the *explanatory criterion*. The explanatory criterion tells us that a theory should be explanatorily adequate in the following ways.

In the first place, a theory should endeavor to accommodate the full range of core data, not ignoring crucial elements that need to be explained. Second, it should offer us a satisfactory explanation of the data in this sense: it should endeavor to account for the actual data and not some other phenomenon, which might be closely related; there should be no switching the subject. And, third, for any range of data that we wish to accommodate in a given theory, an adequate theory must have the resources to explain this data in such a way that it fits well with our best account of what the world is like (or explain why this data needs no explanation) at least as well as or better than rival theories.

It is worth elaborating on this last point. The explanatory criterion, it will be noted, does not say that, for a given range of data that deserves to be explained, a good theory must actually furnish an explanation of it. For that would be too strong a claim. After all, until fairly recently, we did not have much of an understanding of how perception works. However, the fact that we lacked this understanding did not count significantly against the assumption that there is a world that is accurately represented by our perceptual judgments. So, to be plausible, the explanatory criterion must be understood to say that a theory that endeavors to explain a given range of data must, in principle, be able to furnish an explanation of that data which fits well enough with our best account of what the world is like (or satisfactorily explain why no such explanation is necessary) at least as well as or better than rival theories. If this is right, a theory that endeavors to explain some range of data should avoid positing entities which are such that, given our best understanding of the world, we would have powerful reason to believe that that theory could not satisfactorily account for that data.

To illustrate, consider the problem of free will. Many claim to experience a significant range of their actions as being free. That is, they experience these actions as being not coerced or the inevitable result of the past. Rather, they experience these actions as being up to them; they could have chosen to perform or not perform them. Many philosophers admit that this is how things seem to many of us. Some also claim that so-called compatibilist views, which understand freedom to be compatible with determinism, fail to explain the actual data; they, in effect, switch the subject using the term "freedom" to refer to something else. These same philosophers argue, however, that we could not be free in any robust sense, for this would be incompatible with our best understanding of the laws of nature and the workings of the brain.[16] Cases such as this help us to recognize that, for any range of data that we wish to accommodate in a given theory, a theory might lack the resources to explain them in such a way that fits well with our best account of what the world is like. Although the outputs of a doxastic practice in good working order may, at the outset of inquiry, deserve the benefit of the doubt, this status can be defeated by considerations such as these.

As one might imagine, there are questions about the explanatory criterion which a fuller treatment of it would have to address, such as what it is for a view to be able, in principle, to explain a given range of data. On this occasion, I shall have to rush past such matters, heading instead for the third criterion for theory evaluation, which I referred to earlier as the *simplicity criterion*.

According to the simplicity criterion, a theory that endeavors to explain a range of data should be parsimonious. Or more accurately put, since theory evaluation is an inherently comparative exercise, it should be at least as or more parsimonious than rival theories, other things being equal. And what is it for a theory to be more parsimonious than rival theories? There is no easy answer to this question. For our purposes, I propose the following answer. Suppose we think of a theory as a conjunction of propositions, many of which carry existential commitments, such as the commitment to certain types of entities and entities of those types. Given this understanding of what a theory is, we can say that (roughly speaking) theory A is more parsimonious than theory B regarding some subject matter if and only if A includes fewer conjuncts (which are themselves not probabilistically supported by some other conjuncts of the theory) than B.

Most philosophers have thought that, all else being equal, we should prefer simpler theories. The present formulation of what it is for a theory to be parsimonious gives us some idea why. The reason why we should prefer simpler theories is that the more one's theory says, the more likely it is that it will say something false. This much we can explain by appeal to the probability calculus. For, all else being equal, every new conjunct one adds to a theory drives down its prior probability (which is roughly, the probability of that theory independent of the data that we endeavor to explain).[17]

This account of the simplicity criterion raises delicate questions that I am going to have to ignore on this occasion. There is, however, one matter that needs to be addressed, which is this: if what I have said so far is correct, we should evaluate metaethical theories according to the Reidian, explanatory, and simplicity criteria. One might wonder, however, whether these three criteria deserve to be weighted equally. To this question, realists tend to answer "no." The Reidian criterion, according to realists, enjoys priority of a certain type. We can see this by comparing it to the simplicity criterion.

Consider a radically solipsist position, such as that introduced by Descartes at the beginning of his *Meditations*. According to this view, there exists exactly one person and his mental states and events. Suppose, for illustration's sake, we were to embrace this position because it is more parsimonious than the alternatives. Rather than posit an external world inhabited by an untold number of types of entities and entities of those types, it posits only one substance: the agent himself and his various modifications. Cartesian solipsism, we can agree, is more parsimonious than commonsense realism about the external world. A full and accurate statement of it would include far fewer propositions than commonsense realism.

And yet solipsism is a crazy position. It cannot be, then, that we should weight the simplicity criterion more heavily than the Reidian one. For if we did, then we would have decent reasons to embrace positions such as Cartesian solipsism, which we do not. Nor, for that matter, should we weight the Reidian and simplicity criteria equally. For this suggests that, at the outset of inquiry, we should hold that commonsense realism and Cartesian solipsism are roughly on par, all else being equal. But, at the outset of inquiry, we should not believe this. To the contrary, commonsense realism is the default position, the position to beat.

If this is right, the simplicity criterion has a theoretical role to play in the assessment of theories. But the role it should play is something like that of a tiebreaker. If two theories do roughly an equally good job of explaining core data, which are the outputs of a doxastic practice in good working order, then we should prefer the simpler one, all else being equal.[18]

Let me now return to a point I raised earlier, which concerns the reasons why we should employ the Reidian criterion as a mode of theory evaluation. The way in which the Cartesian solipsist employs the simplicity criterion, we have seen, yields bizarre results. This, I have claimed, indicates what the proper theoretical role of the simplicity criterion is. But the fact that Cartesian solipsism is a crazy position is not the primary problem with it. Rather—and this is a point that Reid himself pressed—the primary problem is that the Cartesian solipsist works with a double standard.

To see this, let us suppose that in order to engage in theory evaluation we must take some sources of evidence as reliable, such as the deliverances of reason. In addition to trusting reason, the solipsist also takes the reports of introspection to be reliable. That is why he takes himself to exist, to have a nature of a certain kind, and to experience sense data of various sorts. But the solipsist disregards other basic sources of evidence, such as that provided by perception. Perception, the solipsist says, offers us a radically mistaken account of what the world is like. It is difficult, however, to see why the solipsist says this. Both our introspective and perceptual judgments are the outputs of doxastic practices that have a very similar profile: they are well-established over time, deeply entrenched (indeed, practically inescapable), have sophisticated methods of evaluation, and yield outputs that, while not infallibly accurate, are not massively inconsistent. The primary problem with the solipsist view, then, is not that it is a crazy view, but that it is infected by arbitrary partiality.

If this is right, realists tend to take the Reidian criterion seriously not because they are intent on defending common sense at nearly all costs. Rather, they do so for the following two reasons. First, in order to engage in theory evaluation, we must trust the outputs of some well-established doxastic practices. A failure to do so would result in the inability to engage in theory evaluation at all. Second, good theories cannot operate with a double standard. They cannot arbitrarily take the outputs of some doxastic practices in good working order seriously, such as the deliverances of reason and introspection, while discounting others in good working order, such as the deliverances of perception. This does not, I should add, imply that doxastic practices cannot be reliable to different degrees. They can. It would, however, be a mistake to infer that, given two doxastic practices in good working order, we should dismiss the outputs of one if they do not enjoy the same impressive epistemic status as the outputs of the other. If, for example, the perceptual practice has a particularly impressive standing, this would not give us reason to dismiss the memorial practice because it is, on the whole, somewhat less reliable.

The Realist's Master Strategy

In the last two sections, we explored the issues of what data a metaethical theory should accommodate and how it should do so. Having done this, we are now in a position to state the realist's master strategy.

The strategy instructs us to start with the core moral data. With this data in hand, we then evaluate a particular metaethical theory by determining how well it accommodates this data vis-à-vis its rivals according to the Reidian, explanatory, and simplicity criteria. According to realists, their view scores extremely well according to the Reidian criterion. When evaluated along this dimension of theory assessment, realists claim that their view fares better than any of its rivals—in some cases, significantly better. Moreover, realists add, their position does well enough according to both the explanatory and simplicity criteria. In some cases, realists claim, it actually fares better than its rivals; in other cases, it fares at least (or nearly) as well. On the whole, realists conclude, their view emerges as the strongest overall metaethical position—at least at the outset of theory evaluation.[19]

Let us now explore this strategy in more detail, beginning with the realists' claims about how their view fares according to the Reidian criterion. We've seen that, according to the realists, any decent metaethical view must take the core moral data seriously, neither ignoring nor explaining the data away. Recall that this data includes the phenomenology of moral experience, the character of moral reasoning, the nature of moral judgment, and the modal profile of the contents of moral judgments—moral judgments, we saw earlier, being the outputs of the moral practice.

What are the credentials of the moral practice? Well, this practice is well-established over time. Moral thinking is not a recent development in the history of humankind. Moreover, it is deeply entrenched. In fact, moral thinking is so deeply entrenched that, for all practical purposes, it is inescapable; try as we might, most of us cannot avoid forming moral judgments. This point is typically recognized by antirealists. No prominent antirealist position suggests that if we were to find their arguments successful, we should try to stop making moral judgments. Most of us just couldn't do it even if we tried.[20] Furthermore, we also have fairly sophisticated methods for evaluating moral judgments. Of course these methods are not the same as those used to evaluate the outputs of other doxastic practices. Unlike the objects of perceptual judgments, we cannot touch moral facts. And unlike the outputs of memory, we cannot grasp them by introspection. Still, we can evaluate, modify, and correct our moral judgments in various ways.

In the first place, we can do so by consulting the behavior of moral exemplars, who are widely acknowledged as deserving emulation. By considering and emulating their lives, we can ascertain concrete ways in which traits such as being loving and fair are expressed. In so doing, we can identify ways in which our practices of moral judgment can be improved. In some cases, we might see that we need to develop better habits of attention, paying closer attention to aspects of situations that are often overlooked. In other cases, we might recognize that we need to develop better habits of assessment, such as stepping back from controversial or explosive situations to gain increased critical distance. In this regard, evaluating moral behavior is rather like evaluating a good musical or athletic performance: to assess it, we look toward those who do it well.

In addition, we can engage in what J. S. Mill called "experiments in living," thereby discerning whether certain patterns of conduct are inimical to the well-being of others or subtly disrespectful.[21] For example, we might take it upon ourselves to live among a historically persecuted group to discern whether certain social policies, which are designed to help them, actually tend to erode the self-respect of those affected.

We can, third, systemize our moral judgments by bringing them into (wide) reflective equilibrium, ascertaining how well they cohere with other moral and nonmoral judgments. In this case, we often have to bring concrete moral experience into equilibrium with abstract moral principles that we endorse by engaging in thought experiments and abstract moral reasoning.

Fourth, we can exercise our capacity to discern whether our moral judgments imply absurd or repugnant conclusions. For example, just as we can evaluate Cartesian solipsism by noting its deeply counterintuitive consequences, we can also assess a moral position by drawing out its repugnant implications, such as the consequence that it provides reason to believe that we ought to engage in such activities as harvesting organs from innocent and healthy people.

The moral practice, then, includes various strategies that agents can employ to determine whether moral judgments are well-formed. Realists emphasize, finally, that a significant range of these judgments—such as those that express the stock moral truisms and their direct implications—are not subject to massive and systemic disagreement. To the contrary, one finds almost no disagreement about whether they are true among competent participants in the moral practice. Of course realists recognize that there is substantial disagreement about other moral matters, such as whether it is permissible to eat animals or to perform elective abortions. And they recognize that moral theorists disagree about what makes actions wrong. But, realists claim, the sort of convergence we find about the stock moral truisms and their direct implications blocks the charge that the disagreement regarding first-order moral matters is sufficiently widespread and recalcitrant that it calls into question the reliability of the moral practice.

For suppose we were to compare the moral practice to paradigmatically unreliable doxastic practices such as extrasensory perception (ESP), aura reading, and sooth-saying. The differences between these practices and the moral practice would be manifest. Practices such as ESP, after all, have very poor track records. We know that over time, for example, they yield massively inconsistent outputs. There is, furthermore, no analogue in these practices to the stock moral truisms—apparently necessary truths such that, were a person to deny them, we would worry about her mental well-being. If this is right, realists claim, the amount of first-order moral disagreement that we actually encounter is not nearly sufficient to give us reason to believe that the moral practice is similar in the relevant respects to paradigmatically unreliable doxastic practices such as ESP.

Some critics of realism concede that first-order moral disagreement is not itself sufficient to throw doubt on the reliability of the moral practice. But, they maintain, deeply entrenched disagreement among moral theorists about what renders actions right or wrong is (at least when it is combined with the actual amount of first-order disagreement).[22] Realists reply to this charge by noting that disagreement among moral theorists is the wrong sort of thing to drive an argument for antirealism.[23] Consider the following comparison: most of us agree that there are ordinary living material things such as plants and animals. Those familiar with contemporary metaphysics know, however, that there is widespread disagreement among its practitioners about what (if anything) accounts for the fact that a given range of matter composes a plant or an animal. It would be a mistake, realists claim, to conclude that disagreement of this sort provides much evidence for believing there are no plants and animals.

In sum, realists claim that their view rates very highly according to the Reidian criterion, since their view implies that we ought (all else being equal) to take the outputs of the moral practice as being reliably formed. But many philosophers worry that, even if this were true, realism fares poorly according to the explanatory and simplicity criteria. In response, realists maintain that, while their view may not rate quite as well according to these criteria as some antirealist views, it nevertheless rates well enough. The only way to make this case, however, is actually to compare realism with some of its main rivals. So, in what remains, let us compare one prominent moral antirealist view with generic moral realism.

A Rival View: The Error Theory

The antirealist position that I would like to consider is the error theory of morality, which is defended by philosophers such as J. L. Mackie and Richard Joyce.[24] According to the error theory:

> Ordinary moral thought and discourse purport, by and large, to represent moral facts. But they fail to do so, as there are none. In this respect, ordinary moral thought and discourse are deeply and systematically mistaken.

Realists maintain that the error theory should be rejected.

The primary reason is that the error theory fares very poorly according to the Reidian criterion. The problem is not simply that, according to the error theory, our moral experience systematically misleads, presenting our environment in such a way that there are moral facts when there are none. It is also that error theorists reject propositions that look like obvious necessary truths. For consider, once again, stock moral truisms, such as:

> It is wrong to lie simply because one doesn't feel like telling the truth.
>
> It is wrong to slander another simply because it makes one feel better.
>
> It is wrong to torture another simply because she has inconvenienced you.

Error theorists maintain that propositions such as these are untrue: they are either false or rest on false presuppositions (and, hence, are neither true nor false). On the plausible assumption that a reliably formed belief must be the deliverance of a reliable belief-forming faculty or method, error theorists are committed to the further claim that none of our moral beliefs is reliably formed. Error theorists, then, are radical moral skeptics. The Reidian criterion, however, implies that skepticism such as this should be rejected, all else being equal. More precisely, it implies that, at the outset of theory evaluation, we have strong pro tanto reason to hold that beliefs which express the stock moral truisms (and their direct applications) are reliable, as they are the output of a doxastic practice in good working order. However, under the present interpretation, error theorists reject this claim regarding the reliability of our moral beliefs. They maintain that, at the outset of theory evaluation, beliefs that express the stock moral truisms enjoy no greater theoretical standing than beliefs that reject them. Accordingly, their view fails the Reidian criterion.[25]

Let us dig into the error theory more deeply. Thoroughgoing moral skepticism is a radical position, as it implies that beliefs that look obviously true are not. It is natural to wonder why error theorists accept it. In the most prominent recent defense of the error theory, Richard Joyce relies almost exclusively on one argument, which we can call:

The categoricity argument

(1) Necessarily, if there are moral facts, then there are categorical reasons—reasons to act that apply to an agent regardless of whether acting in that way satisfies his desires.
(2) There are no categorical reasons.
(3) So, there are no moral facts.

For our purposes, we needn't enter into the issue as to why Joyce believes we should accept (2). Suffice it to say that realists have vigorously contended that the arguments offered for (2) are defective. Russ Shafer-Landau, for example, has maintained that Joyce's argument simply presupposes a Humean or internalist view of reasons, which many realists reject.[26] More interesting for our purposes is the justification Joyce offers for (1). Joyce claims that we should accept (1) because it is a deeply entrenched feature of ordinary moral experience, a conceptual truth. Nothing, Joyce says, could count as a moral system which denied (1).[27]

The most interesting feature of Joyce's rationale for (1), for our purposes, is that it takes the appearances of ordinary moral thought and discourse very seriously. When arguing for (1), Joyce asks us to pay close attention to our actual practices of praising, blaming, and holding others accountable. He claims that, when we do so, we can see that we presuppose that moral reasons are categorical. And yet, when it comes to other well-entrenched features of moral experience, such as that there are stock moral truisms, these are taken to be illusory. The stock truisms, however, look like conceptual truths in the sense in which Joyce is interested: nothing could be a moral system that rejected them.

There are, then, these two apparent conceptual truths:

(A) Necessarily, if there are moral facts, then there are categorical reasons.

And:

(B) It is wrong to torture someone simply for fun.

Joyce offers an argument—The Categoricity Argument—that takes (A) as a premise and concludes that (B) is untrue. Realists maintain that, in so doing,

Joyce's position is infected by arbitrary partiality. For it is difficult to see why, if we take the appearances of ordinary moral thought and discourse seriously, we shouldn't proceed in the reverse direction. If we are prepared to follow Joyce and maintain that there are no categorical reasons, then why not offer an argument that takes (B) as a premise and conclude that (A) is false? Since both (A) and (B) are apparent conceptual truths in the sense in which Joyce is interested, it is difficult to see why we should take one of these claims as our starting point rather than the other.

The brief against the error theory so far rests on two claims: first, the view fails the Reidian criterion and, second, it operates with a double standard. In principle, error theorists can reply to this last charge. They might claim that there are principled reasons to reject (B) rather than (A). One reason is that doing so yields a simpler metaethical theory, which makes no commitments to the existence of moral facts. Another reason is that doing so implies that the error theory better satisfies the explanatory criterion. For, by rejecting (B), the error theory can account for the core moral data without taking on the difficult explanatory burdens that realists must. If so, error theorists might claim, it remains an open question whether their view ought to be preferred, on the whole.

Let us consider these replies, beginning with the error theorist's appeal to the simplicity criterion. If the realist's master strategy is correct, the appeal to simplicity in this context is not persuasive for at least two reasons.

First, it is not apparent that the error theory is significantly simpler than realism. We have seen that error theorists such as Mackie and Joyce embrace:

(2) There are no categorical reasons.

But in so doing they do not deny that there are any reasons. To the contrary, they maintain that:

> There are Humean reasons—reasons to act that apply to an agent because acting in that way would satisfy her desires. Among such reasons are prudential reasons.

Realists, however, can agree with both these claims. For, recall, realists who are moral naturalists tend to believe that:

> All practical reasons, including moral ones, are Humean.

Realists of a naturalistic persuasion, then, can maintain that there is no appreciable sense in which their view is less simple than the error theory.

To this last claim, error theorists have a retort. Even if realists commit themselves only to the existence of Humean reasons, it might be said, their view is not as simple as the error theory. After all, naturalistic realists maintain that there is a category of Humean reasons that error theorists reject, namely, the moral reasons. Accepting one less subspecies of Humean reasons, error theorists might point out, implies that their view is simpler than naturalistic realism.

Realists are likely to consider this last claim as possibly true but innocuous. For, when assessing whether the error theory offers us a simpler account of the core moral data than realism, it is important to recognize the following pair of points.

In the first place, whether error theory offers us a simpler account of the core moral data than realism will depend on whether the error theory can proffer a streamlined explanation of such things as why there appear to be stock moral truisms. Error theorists might offer explanations for these things. But there is no guarantee that these explanations will be particularly simple; they may involve error theorists making extensive (and controversial) theoretical commitments. And, so, there is no guarantee that the error theory will offer a simpler explanation of the core data than realism. In the second place, by claiming that Humean moral reasons exist, realists have not thereby introduced into our ontology a type of entity of which error theorists are suspicious. To say it again, error theorists such as Mackie and Joyce already admit the existence of Humean reasons. At most, then, realists countenance the existence of a subspecies of such reasons that error theorists do not. If this is right, there *might* be a sense in which error theory offers us a moderately simpler account of the core data than realism. But it is difficult to see how such a modest advantage in simplicity could give us reason to reject (B) rather than (A).[28]

I have offered one argument for believing the error theory is not appreciably simpler than realism (canvassing along the way how error theorists might reply to it). I turn now to the second reason to believe that an appeal to simplicity will not help the error theory. According to realists, a good metaethical theory should endeavor to accommodate the full range of core moral data, which include the outputs of the moral practice. Among the core data, however, are beliefs with the following content:

> It is wrong to torture someone simply for fun.

If realists are right, it is not the case that it merely appears that a belief with this content is true, although, given all we reasonably believe, the appearances mislead. Rather, the situation is that, since this belief is the output of a doxastic practice in good working order, we should (all else being equal) take it to be reliably formed. It is innocent until proven guilty.

We saw earlier, however, that a theory gains no credibility if, at the outset of inquiry, it rejects core data of this sort simply in the name of parsimony. Recall Cartesian solipsism once again. The Cartesian solipsist does little to recommend her view by rejecting beliefs such as:

> There are trees, rabbits, and rocks, which are part of a mind-independent external world,

because doing so yields a more parsimonious theory. For appeals to theoretical parsimony, if what we said earlier is correct, play a limited role, which is roughly this: for any range of core data, which is the output of a doxastic practice in good working order, we should prefer the theory that accommodates this data in the more parsimonious way.

Arguably, however, the Cartesian solipsist fails to accommodate the core data. For, in her view, at the outset of theorizing, beliefs such as:

> There are trees, rabbits, and rocks, which are part of a mind-independent external world,

deserve no more credibility than their denial. Similarly, according to realists, error theorists fail to accommodate the core moral data. For, in their view, at the outset of theorizing, beliefs such as:

> It is wrong to torture someone simply for fun,

also deserve no more credibility than their denial. According to realists, by contrast, beliefs such as this deserve the benefit of the doubt. By failing to accord them this status at the outset of theory evaluation, realists maintain that error theorists do not even "get into the explanatory game." For they do not purport to explain what, according to realists, needs to be explained, which, to say it again, is this: that beliefs such as that mentioned above appear to be obviously true and that these appearances deserve to be trusted, all else being equal. If this is right, error theorists cannot legitimately claim that, in virtue of being parsimonious, their view enjoys a theoretical advantage over realism.

We have considered two reasons for believing that an appeal to parsimony is of little help to the error theorist. According to the first, error theory is not appreciably simpler than realism, at least of the naturalistic variety. According to the second, we should prefer the more parsimonious theory only when it actually explains the core data, which the error theory does not. Still, we might reject (B) because doing so better satisfies the explanatory criterion. In this case, error theorists might claim that their view fares better than realism not because realists ignore the core moral data or switch the question. Rather, it is because realism lacks the resources, in principle, to account for the core moral data, such as how beliefs which express the stock moral truisms could be reliably formed.

This last claim would, however, be difficult to defend. Given that we appear able to form reliable beliefs about necessary truths of many sorts, we would need strong reasons to believe it. If realists are right, these reasons have not been forthcoming. Mackie, for example, presents only a bare sketch as to why moral realists could not account for how our moral beliefs are reliably formed. Joyce, by contrast, does not argue for this claim directly. Rather, he devotes nearly all his energies to arguing that realists are committed to (A), which he contends is indefensible. From this he concludes that, since there are no moral facts, moral beliefs which express the stock moral truisms could not be reliably formed.[29]

On this occasion, I wish not to enter into the controversy as to whether there are categorical reasons. Instead, let me note that, when assessing the error theorist's appeal to the explanatory criterion, it is important to keep in mind the dialectic between error theorists and realists. Realists, recall, maintain that error theorists such as Joyce appear to operate with a double standard. According to realists, error theorists take the appearances very seriously by accepting:

(A) Necessarily, if there are moral facts, then there are categorical reasons;

but take equally plausible claims such as:

(B) It is wrong to torture someone simply for fun,

to be illusory. If realists are right, it is not easy to see why those committed to rejecting the existence of categorical reasons should argue from (A) to the rejection of (B) rather than the reverse. In principle, error theorists, we have seen, can reply to this charge. They might claim that there are good reasons to reject (B) rather than (A), since doing so better satisfies the explanatory criterion. But note that error theorists cannot reject (B) on the strength of The Categoricity Argument itself, maintaining that it establishes that realists cannot satisfy the explanatory criterion. For, in the present dialectic, The Categoricity Argument is precisely what realists call into question, charging that the case for its first premise is flawed because it employs a double standard. If this is right, error theorists need to furnish new reasons to believe that claims such as (B) could not be true. These reasons may be forthcoming. But realists will naturally suspect that they will be vulnerable to the sorts of considerations already pressed against the error theory.

Let me summarize: realists contend that the error theory fares poorly according to the Reidian criterion. This is, admittedly, compatible with the error theory being such that it accommodates the core moral data better than realism, on the whole. However, realists contend that, at this point, neither appeals to the simplicity nor the explanatory criterion are sufficient to establish this. Accordingly, realists conclude that their view should be preferred to the error theory, at least at the outset of theory evaluation.

Conclusion

The question we have been pursuing is how to frame and conduct the debate between moral realists and their rivals. Realists, I have claimed, have a strategy they wish to employ. According to this master strategy, we begin by isolating the core moral data that any decent metaethical theory should accommodate. We then evaluate how well a given metaethical view accommodates this data according to the Reidian, explanatory, and simplicity criteria. In our discussion, we put this strategy to work, comparing realism to the error theory. We saw that realists believe that this strategy yields the conclusion that we should prefer their view to the error theory, all else being equal. It is worth emphasizing that this verdict does not imply that realism is true. Nor does it imply that realism is the best position on the whole. If correct, it implies only that realism accommodates the core moral data better than some of its main rivals and, thus, should be preferred to them, all else being equal.

Of necessity our discussion has been programmatic in several respects. In the first place, there are other prominent versions of antirealism, such as expressivism, which we ignored. For all that we said, such views may compare more favorably to realism than the error theory. Second, we bracketed any detailed exploration of positive arguments for and against realism and the available replies to these arguments, focusing instead on a type of strategy that realists employ. As I have just indicated, however, these arguments may be very important, as they may drive up the price tag of a given metaethical view substantially, giving us good reason to reject it. Finally, when presenting the realist's strategy, we glossed over all sorts of subtleties and controversial issues that a more nearly adequate discussion would have to discuss, such as potential problems with formulating and weighting the Reidian, explanatory, and simplicity criteria.

These are not trivial limitations. Still, there are advantages to stepping back from the nitty-gritty give and take of metaethical discussion to consider larger methodological issues. In this case, doing so will have allowed us to see more clearly why realists believe what they do and where their view is most open to challenge.[30]

Bibliography

Adams, Robert. (1999), *Finite and Infinite Goods*. Oxford: Oxford University Press.
Alston, William. (1991), *Perceiving God*. Ithaca, NY: Cornell University Press.
—. (1992), *The Reliability of Sense Perception*. Ithaca, NY: Cornell University Press.
Blackburn, Simon. (1993), *Essays in Quasi-Realism*. Oxford: Oxford University Press.
—. (1998), *Ruling Passions*. Oxford: Oxford University Press.
—. (1999), "Is Objective Moral Justification Possible on a Quasi-realist Foundation?" *Inquiry* 42, 213–28.
Boisvert, Daniel. (2008), "Expressive-Assertivism." *Pacific Philosophical Quarterly* 89, 169–203.
Boyd, Richard. (1988), "How to Be a Moral Realist," in G. Sayre-McCord (ed.) *Essays in Moral Realism*. Ithaca, NY: Cornell University Press, 181–228.
Brink, David. (1989), *Moral Realism and the Foundations of Ethics*. Cambridge: Cambridge University Press.
Copp, David. (1995), *Morality, Normativity, and Society*. Oxford: Oxford University Press.
—. (2001), "Realist-Expressivism: A Neglected Option for Moral Realism." *Social Philosophy and Policy* 18, 1–43.
—. (2008), "Darwinian Skepticism about Moral Realism." *Philosophical Issues* 18, 186–206.
—. (2009), "Realist Expressivism and Conversational Implicature," in R. Shafer-Landau (ed.) *Oxford Studies in Metaethics* 4, 167–202.
Cuneo, Terence. (2007), *The Normative Web: An Argument for Moral Realism*. Oxford: Oxford University Press.
—. (2008), "Moral Realism, Quasirealism, and Skepticism," in J. Greco (ed.) *The Oxford Handbook of Skepticism*. Oxford: Oxford University Press, 176–99.
—. (2011a), "Reidian Metaethics, Part I," *Philosophy Compass* 6, 333–40.
—. (2011b), "Reidian Metaethics, Part II," *Philosophy Compass* 6, 341–9.
—. (2012), "Moral Naturalism and Categorical Reasons," in S. Nuccetelli and G. Seay (eds.) *Ethical Naturalism: Current Debates*. Cambridge: Cambridge University Press, 110-30.
Enoch, David. (2007), "An Outline of an Argument for Robust Metanormative Realism," in R. Shafer-Landau (ed.) *Oxford Studies in Metaethics* 2, 21–50.
—. (2010), "The Epistemological Challenge to Metanormative Realism: How Best to Understand it, and How to Cope with It." *Philosophical Studies* 148, 413–38.
—. (2011), *Taking Morality Seriously: A Defense of Robust Realism*. Oxford: Oxford University Press.
FitzPatrick, William. (2008), "Robust Ethical Realism, Non-Naturalism and Normativity," in R. Shafer-Landau (ed.) *Oxford Studies in Metaethics* 3, 159–206.
—. (2009), "Morality and Evolutionary Biology." *Stanford Encyclopedia of Philosophy*. Available at: http://plato.stanford.edu/entries/morality-biology/.
—. (2010), "Ethical Non-Naturalism and Normative Properties," in M. Brady (ed.) *New Waves in Metaethics*. London: Palgrave, 7–35.
Gibbard, Allan. (1990), *Wise Choices, Apt Feelings*. Cambridge, MA: Harvard University Press.
—. (2003), *Thinking How to Live*. Cambridge, MA: Harvard University Press.

Hare, John. (2003), *God's Call*. Grand Rapids, MI: Eerdmans.
Horgan, Terry and Mark Timmons. (2007), "Moorean Moral Phenomenology," in S. Nuccetelli and G. Seay (eds.) *Themes from G. E. Moore*. Oxford: Oxford University Press, 203–26.
—. (2008), "What Can Moral Phenomenology Tell us about Moral Objectivity?" *Social Philosophy and Policy* 25, 267–300.
Huemer, Michael. (2005), *Ethical Intuitionism*. London: Palgrave.
Jackson, Frank. (1998), *From Metaphysics to Ethics*. Oxford: Oxford University Press.
Joyce, Richard. (2001), *The Myth of Morality*. Cambridge: Cambridge University Press.
—. (2006), *The Evolution of Morality*. Cambridge, MA: MIT Press.
Layman, C. Stephen. (2007), *Letters to Doubting Thomas*. Oxford: Oxford University Press.
Leiter, Brian. (2010), "Moral Skepticism and Moral Disagreement." Available at: http://onthehuman.org/2010/03/moral-skepticism-and-moral-disagreement-developing-an-argument-from-nietzsche/.
Loeb, Don. (2007), "The Argument from Moral Experience." *Ethical Theory and Moral Practice* 10, 469–84.
Mackie, J. L. (1977), *Ethics: Inventing Right and Wrong*. London: Penguin.
Mandelbaum, Maurice. (1955), *The Phenomenology of Moral Experience*. Glencoe, IL: The Free Press.
Mill, J. S. (1978), *On Liberty*. Indianapolis, IN: Hackett.
Miller, Christian. (2009a), "The Conditions of Moral Realism." *The Journal of Philosophical Research* 34, 123–55.
—. (2009b), "Divine Desire Theory and Obligation," in Y. Nagasawa and E. Wielenberg (eds.) *New Waves in Philosophy of Religion*. London: Palgrave Macmillan, 105–24.
Nagel, Thomas. (1986), *The View from Nowhere*. Oxford: Oxford University Press.
Oddie, Graham. (2005), *Value, Reality, and Desire*. Oxford: Oxford University Press.
Olson, Jonas. (2010), "In Defence of Moral Error Theory," in M. Brady (ed.) *New Waves in Metaethics*. London: Palgrave, 62–84.
Parfit, Derek. (2011), *On What Matters*. Oxford: Oxford University Press.
Pereboom, Derk. (2001), *Living without Free Will*. Cambridge: Cambridge University Press.
Railton, Peter. (1986), "Moral Realism." *Philosophical Review* 95, 163–207.
Reid, Thomas. (2002), *Essays on the Intellectual Powers of Man*. Edinburgh: Edinburgh University Press.
Shafer-Landau, Russ. (2003), *Moral Realism: A Defence*. Oxford: Oxford University Press.
—. (2004), "Error Theory and the Possibility of Normative Ethics." *Philosophical Issues* 15, 107–20.
—. (2009), "In Defence of Categorical Reasons." *Proceedings of the Aristotelian Society* 109, 189–206.
Smith, Michael. (1994), *The Moral Problem*. Oxford: Blackwell.
Street, Sharon. (2006), "A Darwinian Dilemma for Moral Realism." *Philosophical Studies* 127, 109–66.

Sturgeon, Nicholas. (1988), "Moral Explanations," in G. Sayre-McCord (ed.) *Essays in Moral Realism*. Ithaca, NY: Cornell University Press, 229–55.
Swinburne, Richard. (1997), *Simplicity as Evidence of Truth*. Milwaukee: Marquette University Press.
Tresan, Jon. (2006), "De Dicto Internalist Cognitivism." *Noûs* 40, 143–65.
Wielenberg, Eric. (2010), "On the Evolutionary Debunking of Morality." *Ethics* 120, 441–64.
Wittgenstein, Ludwig. (1969), *On Certainty*. Eds. G. E. M. Anscombe and G. H. Wright. New York: Harper Torchbooks.
Wolterstorff, Nicholas. (2001), *Thomas Reid and the Story of Epistemology*. Cambridge: Cambridge University Press.
Zagzebski, Linda. (2004), *Divine Motivation Theory*. Cambridge: Cambridge University Press.

2 Ethical Expressivism

Matthew Chrisman

Introduction

Descriptivist theories of meaning hold, roughly, that sentences mean what they do partially in virtue of the parts of reality they can be used to describe. The idea is that a sentence like "The cat is on the mat" means what it does partially in virtue of the fact that it can be used to describe a fact, viz. the fact that the cat is on the mat. Ethical expressivism is a family of metaethical theories about the meaning of ethical sentences.[1] Ethical expressivists tend to agree with the spirit of descriptivism in general but disagree with its application to ethical sentences in particular. Hence, expressivists hold—roughly—that ethical sentences mean what they do in virtue of what they express rather than what they can be used to describe. The basic idea is that although many sentences, when uttered sincerely, express our beliefs about the world, the sincere utterance of ethical sentences expresses some other kind of attitude.

This doctrine is often extended to normative or evaluative sentences more generally, and so we see expressivism defended as a theory of sentences about beauty, reasons, knowledge, etc. Here, however, I will focus only on expressivism as a theory of ethical sentences and leave the scope of the "ethical" up to the reader. There may be other normative or evaluative domains where an expressivist theory is attractive, but they are outside the scope of this chapter.[2]

As we will see, the primary challenge for expressivists is to maintain this contrast between expressive and descriptive sentences while providing plausible articulations of the idea that ethical sentences mean what they do in virtue of what they express. Typically, expressivists argue that we should try to meet this challenge for one or more of the following three reasons. First, the resulting theory will best explain the distinctive *practicality* of ethical discourse. Second, the resulting theory will provide the most plausible way to underwrite intuitions of *supervenience*. Third, this resulting theory will comport with a commitment to a thoroughgoing *naturalistic ontology*.

In what follows, I will first explain what I call the "core expressivist maneuver" and the way it funds these motivations for ethical expressivism. Then I will flesh out the primary challenge expressivists face. In this context, I will briefly discuss some past and contemporary expressivist theories the reader may want to consider further, without attempting to be exhaustive or comprehensive. I will conclude by gesturing towards the sort of expressivist theory I think retains the most promise in light of nearly 75 years of philosophical debate on the topic.

What Is Ethical Expressivism, More Precisely?

The core expressivist maneuver

When we say that something is good or bad, right or wrong, we are evaluating it. Often such evaluations are not ethical, since we are concerned with (say) whether a person is good or bad *for the team*, or whether a colour is the wrong colour *for the dining room*. But often such evaluations are ethical, in that we are concerned with things like whether someone is an ethically good person or whether an action is ethically wrong.

The standard descriptivist way to understand these ethical evaluations is to stress that they are ordinary subject-predicate sentences, and as such should be seen as ascribing some kind of value property—ethical goodness or badness, rightness or wrongness—to things like people, actions, or states of affairs. Expressivists think this is a mistake. They think it is a mistake because they think ethical thought and discourse is legitimate and nonerroneous in spite of the fact that there are no value properties out there in reality, waiting to be described.

In order to argue that the standard descriptivist understanding of ethical evaluations is mistaken, expressivists typically encourage us to begin our metaethical enquiry by asking not about (i) the nature of some kind of supposedly real thing, ethical *value*, but about (ii) the nature of something else we all agree is real, ethical *evaluations*. Then, their answer to question (ii) typically claims some interesting disanalogy between ethical evaluations and descriptions of the world. For example, ethical evaluations are said to express something like an emotion, noncognitive attitude, motivational judgment, or plan—which are all ways of saying that ethical sentences are not straightforward descriptions of reality. If that's right, then any motivation from the ordinary subject-predicate form of ethical evaluations for question (i) appears otiose; for if we think that even though ethical sentences are often in the subject-predicate form they are not descriptions, then we're free to think that ethical discourse is legitimate and nonerroneous in spite of the (putative) nonreality of ethical values.

We might call this change in question and the subsequent answer by disanalogy *the core expressivist maneuver*.[3] We see this very clearly in Gibbard who writes, "'The expressivists' strategy is to change the question. Don't ask directly how to define 'good' . . . [rather] shift the question to focus on judgments: ask, say, what judging that [something] is good consists in" (2003, 6). As a result of this maneuver, expressivists claim there is no theoretical need to recognize ethical values in our ontology. Of course, this is consistent with the objective existence of ethical values. It's just that expressivists think we can explain everything that we want to explain, and leave ethical discourse pretty much just as it is, without ever committing to the existence of ethical values. Then Occam's razor and/or a commitment to a naturalistic ontology supports the avoidance of this commitment.

First Motivation for Expressivism: Practicality of Ethical Discourse

Why should we believe in the proposed disanalogy between ethical evaluations and descriptions of the world? Besides the intuitive idea that ethical evaluations express our feelings, the reason often given and so part of the overall case for accepting expressivism comes from the apparently distinctive practicality of ethical discourse. More specifically, two prominent and popular views—Humeanism about motivating reasons and internalism about ethical judgments—can be combined to argue that ethical sentences are not used to express beliefs in any straightforward way but instead to express something like emotions, desires, noncognitive attitudes, plans, decisions, or practical commitments. If this thought is right, it distinguishes ethical sentences from paradigmatic descriptive sentences, and so supports the core expressivist maneuver. In what follows, I'll describe Humeanism and internalism, explain how their combination is supposed to support the expressivist's needed disanalogy, and briefly mention some complications that arise in the details.

Humeanism about motivation

What mental states lead to someone's acting? A very prominent answer comes from Hume through Davidson (1963/1980), and is articulated most fully by Smith (1987 and 1994, ch. 4) as the "Humean Theory of Motivation". This theory distinguishes between beliefs, which are thought of as cognitive attitudes representing the way the world is, and desires, which are thought of as any conative attitude such as emotion, intention, plan, decision, practical commitment, etc. Then the theory says that motivation to action always requires the cooperation of both a desire for some end and a belief linking the action to the potential achievement of that end. This is sometimes also called the belief-desire psychology of motivation.[4]

Internalism about ethical judgments

Generically, we can say that ethical statements express ethical judgments, where the term "judgment" is meant to refer neutrally to whatever mental state one must have in order to count as being sincere in making the statement; it's the mental state whose expression is guaranteed by sincerity.[5] So far as that goes, we could also say that empirical statements express empirical judgments. However, in that case, all parties to the debate want to view such judgments as beliefs that are cognitive representations of the world, whereas in the ethical case, the nature of the judgments is what is in question.

Expressivists (and others) argue that an answer to this question should be informed by the observation that it would be somewhat strange if a person who made an ethical statement were not at least somewhat disposed to act in a way that accords with the statement when the right sorts of circumstances arise. For example, if your friend tells you that "It is wrong not to help people in need who are right in front of you and easily helped" or "If I see someone in need who is right in front of me and easily helped, the right thing to do in such a case is to help," but, when faced with someone obviously in need and easily helped she showed no propensity at all to help, we would be puzzled. Perhaps, the person is not being sincere, or her motivation to help is outweighed by contrary motivations borne out of greed or fear. Perhaps she is confused about what it means to help someone or doesn't understand the meaning of the word "wrong." If, however, we convince ourselves that none of these explanations is correct, then we would be very puzzled indeed. The same does not seem to be true of empirical descriptions of the world. And this is the important contrast: if someone says, e.g., "It wouldn't cost much to help most people in need" or "The most cost-effective thing to do in cases like these to help," there are no specific motivations we expect the person to have.

This contrast between ethical judgments and descriptive judgments motivates the view called "internalism" or (more precisely) "ethical judgment motivational internalism," which distinguishes the view from "reasons internalism," i.e., the idea that one has a reason to act only if the action will satisfy desire that one actually has or would have under some idealized conditions. (I'll suppress the qualifications in what follows[6]). The thought is that ethical judgments play a special motivational role in the psychology of action. A plausible explanation of this phenomenon is that unlike descriptive beliefs ethical judgments don't need the cooperation of a further conative state to constitute a motivational reason for action. Hence, there is a direct or *internal* connection between ethical judgment and motivation.

Combining Humeanism and internalism

If internalism is correct, then one appears to be faced with two options: Either (i) ethical judgments are a special kind of cognitive representational state that prove Humeanism wrong, because they can motivate action all by themselves without the cooperation of a desire, or (ii) ethical judgments are not properly viewed as cognitive representations of the world and instead should be understood as something conative like an emotion, desire, moral attitude, plan, practical commitment, etc.

Expressivists think that Humeanism is well supported on conceptual and empirical grounds. And they think some version of internalism is very intuitive. So, they adopt (ii) and hold that ethical judgments are conative states of some sort or another. This then funds the disanalogy they need for the core expressivist maneuver. The idea which results is that ordinary descriptive sentences are used to express beliefs, which are understood as cognitive states representing how the world is, but ethical sentences are used to express a desire-like state which serves a different function in the psychology of motivation.

Complications

Some have worried that the argument leading to internalism is plausible when the relevant ethical sentence is about one's own potential actions or about more general matters that bear obviously on one's own potential actions. But not all ethical sentences are like this. Consider these ethical sentences: "It was wrong for the God of the Bible to flood the world" or "Starting a charity is the right thing for billionaires to do" or "Happiness is good." It is far from clear what it means to be disposed to act in their accord. Moreover, whatever that is, it will be near impossible to tell whether someone is indeed so disposed, since any connection between the judgments expressed and actions will be mediated by many other judgments. Because of this, an opponent of expressivism might argue that the observation leading to internalism applies only to certain kinds of ethical sentences and not to all of them. But expressivism is supposed to be a view about *all* ethical sentences. So internalism combined with Humeanism can't really motivate the principal disanalogy needed for the core expressivist maneuver.[7]

A way around this objection is for expressivists to argue that internalism supports the following claim. Having the motivational disposition when applying ethical predicates to one's own potential actions is a necessary condition for understanding the meaning of these predicates, even when they are applied in cases not so obviously linked to motivation.[8] However, going this way does weaken the strength of the internalist intuition, and there may be externalist ways of explaining the motivations that we expect when ethical predicates are applied to one's own potential actions.

Furthermore, some have argued that one can endorse internalism plus Humeanism and yet still think ethical sentences are descriptions of the world. This seems possible as long as one claims that ethical sentences are used to express *both* cognitive beliefs about ethical values *and* conative attitudes. For example, the sentence "Stealing is wrong" might be used to express both the belief that stealing is wrong and a negative attitude towards stealing. Call this view *hybrid descriptivism*.[9] Its proponents can appeal to the expression of a positive or negative attitude to underwrite internalist intuitions within a Humean philosophy of action. But they do so without supporting the expressivist claim that ethical sentences are used to express conative attitudes *rather than cognitive beliefs*. For the hybrid descriptivist claims that they can do both.

Some have found such hybrid descriptivist views attractive because they comport with internalism and Humeanism while clearly supporting the idea that ethical statements have truth-conditions and are truth-apt. As we will see below, most contemporary expressivists think that ethical sentences have truth-conditions and so are truth-apt in some (often "deflationary") sense. So, the possibility of the hybrid view forces some clarity into the debate. In order to be an ethical expressivist, it's not enough to hold that ethical sentences are used to express some conative attitude in some sense. One has to hold that this attitude is part of the semantic content of the sentence; the attitude is not merely something that is conveyed pragmatically.[10]

Second and Third Motivations for Expressivism: Supervenience and Naturalism

Regardless of one's views about action theory and moral psychology, expressivism might seem attractive depending on one's ontological views. There are at least two interconnected reasons for this—intuitions of supervenience and a commitment to naturalism.

Supervenience

If we accept a descriptivist view of ethical language, and we don't think ethical language embodies a massive error or widespread commitment to falsehoods,[11] then we face a question about what in the world our ethical predicates describe. When we say, e.g. "Stealing is wrong," we are, according to descriptivists, describing the act of stealing as having the property of wrongness. But what is the property of wrongness? And, why should we believe that it exists?

This last question is difficult even to begin to answer without some conception of when it's theoretically permitted to accept a property into one's ontology—i.e., to believe that it really exists as "part of the fabric of the universe." Here, many philosophers believe that, at the very least, the properties posited in the course of scientific explanations of natural phenomena are legitimate. These are the natural properties. So, one idea is to attempt to vindicate ethical properties by showing how they reduce to some combination of natural properties. If such a reductionist view is correct, then ethical properties should be just as admissible in our ontology as more obviously permissible natural properties.

Some metaethicists argue that ethical properties do reduce to natural properties.[12] The jury is certainly still out, but the main perceived problem with this idea is that it is very difficult to find the needed reduction either in an analysis of ethical concepts or in a metaphysical account of the nature of ethical properties. Perhaps we will yet discover the desired analytical or metaphysical reduction, but without it descriptivists seem committed to the idea that ethical properties are irreducible, sui generis properties that we must admit into our ontology. That was Moore's antireductionist view, and many contemporary metaethicists think he must have been right about this even if they don't agree with the details of how he argued for his view.[13]

However, expressivists argue that antireductionism about ethical properties offers no plausible explanation of intuitions of supervenience. There has been a lot of debate in metaethics and elsewhere about how best to articulate principles of supervenience,[14] but the basic idea is that there cannot be two circumstances that differ ethically without also differing in some relevant way that is uncontroversially descriptive. For example, if Johnny and Suzy are both trying to decide whether to steal some food, and their circumstances are identical in all relevant descriptive ways, then a principle of ethical supervenience says that it cannot be wrong for Johnny to steal but not wrong for Suzy to do so, or vice versa. That is, if we think Johnny's stealing is wrong, then we must also think either that Suzy's stealing is also wrong or that there is some relevant descriptive difference between their circumstances (e.g., Johnny's family is starving and Suzy is relatively comfortable).

Expressivists argue that their view of ethical judgments as conative attitudes explains and underwrites such intuitions of supervenience. The explanation is that these intuitions reflect a natural consistency constraint on our conative reactions to the way we take the world to be. If, for instance, there are two circumstances that are exactly the same in all relevant descriptive ways, then approving of one while disapproving of the other would be arbitrary. And holding and expressing such arbitrary attitudes would undermine the natural coordinative function of having these attitudes. Hence, over time there would have been pressure towards respecting this consistency constraint in these attitudes. So much so, in fact, that it would have become part of what it is to have such attitudes. According to the expressivist, this manifests itself in the intuitions of supervenience.

In contrast, expressivists argue that antireductionists have no plausible explanation of intuitions of supervenience. If you're an antireductionist, then you think there are ethical properties and they are different from nonethical properties. But if that's true, then it should be at least metaphysically (and perhaps also conceptually) possible for there to be a world (or a situation) which is identical in nonethical properties but not identical in ethical properties. But, expressivists insist that our supervenience intuitions indicate that such a world (or a situation) is not possible; and the antireductionist has no way to explain why this is true, whereas the expressivist thinks he has.[15]

The expressivist's argument here is complex, so let me recap briefly: Concerning the relation between ethical properties and descriptive properties, descriptivists are committed to reductionism or antireductionism. Because of the difficulties with the former, many descriptivists endorse some version of antireductionism. When compared to expressivism, however, antireductionism seems to lack a plausible account of why the ethical seems to supervene on the descriptive. Hence, in this respect, expressivism is supposed to be more attractive than descriptivism. Its theory of the meaning of ethical statements avoids the difficulties with antireductionist descriptivist theories.

Naturalism

Even if one rejects supervenience intuitions as misguided or believes that antireductionists can explain them in the end, there's a second ontological motivation often cited for expressivism. As I said above, most philosophers think that the fact that some property would be posited in the course of accepted scientific explanations of natural phenomena is a good reason to admit it into our ontology. Indeed, many philosophers think such natural properties are the *only* properties we should admit into our ontology. This is one way to formulate the doctrine of naturalism.[16] And expressivists pride themselves on offering a thoroughgoing naturalistic metaethical theory. Among naturalists, then, this turns into an argument for expressivism over descriptivism.

The idea is to force a choice again between three basic kinds of metaethical theory: (i) reductionistist descriptivism, (ii) antireductionist descriptivism, (iii) expressivism.[17] Without a plausible reductionist theory on offer, the first option is eliminated. However, given a choice between the second and third options, expressivists argue that a commitment to naturalism encourages their view over the antireductionist view. This is because antireductionists seem committed to viewing ethical statements as describing the nonnatural properties of things, but naturalists think that there are no such things as nonnatural properties.

However, that commitment generates an important complication. This is because another type of metaethical theory endorsed by those deeply moved by naturalism is error theory.[18] Proponents of this view argue that the three-way choice mentioned above leaves out an important fourth alternative: ethical sentences describe parts of the world as instantiating sui generis ethical properties, but these descriptions uniformly fail, since there are no sui generis ethical properties. Nevertheless one who thinks this could argue that ethical discourse embodies a convenient fiction, which is why we tend to think some ethical sentences are true.[19]

Ethical error theory comports with naturalism just as much as ethical expressivism. The theories differ primarily in their account of the meaning of ethical sentences. Error theorists are descriptivists and so think ethical statements mean what they do in virtue of describing something which isn't the case (though perhaps it involves a convenient fiction). Expressivists are opposed to descriptivism in the ethical case and instead think ethical sentences mean what they do in virtue of the conative attitudes that they can be used to express. So, again we see that its account of the meaning of ethical sentences is crucial to the expressivist position.

Expressivism as a Theory of Meaning: The Primary Challenge

Importantly, all three motivations for expressivism seemed to require not just the vague idea that ethical sentences can be used to express conative attitudes in some way or another. They also required the more specific idea that ethical sentences mean what they do in virtue of the way that they express conative attitudes. Herein lies the main hurdle for the view.[20]

The difficulty is that expressivists are pulled in two different directions in developing their theory of the meaning of ethical sentences. On the one hand, the theory is predicated on drawing some sharp contrast between the meaning of ethical sentences and the meaning of descriptive sentences. On the other hand, ethical sentences function semantically very much like descriptive sentences. Hence, the Holy Grail for expressivists is a theory of the meaning of sentences in general, which allows for a contrast between ethical and descriptive sentences, while explaining the semantic similarities that have become more and more apparent in recent metaethical debate.

In order to evaluate whether this Holy Grail is in sight, I will next describe some of the historical developments of expressivism in light of different aspects of this primary challenge. Using a broad brush, I will paint three successive developments of expressivism: "emotivism," "quasi-realism," and "recent developments" with the hope of giving the reader a sense of the overall trajectory of the debate but not all of its (even important) details.[21]

Emotivism and the Frege-Geach Problem

Original inspirations for expressivism came from Ogden and Richards (1925) and Russell (1935/1961), but it is Ayer (1936/1946) and Stevenson (1937, 1944) who are generally credited with developing the view more fully and putting it onto the philosophical map. In this early form, it was called "emotivism,"[22] and the core idea was that ethical statements are not in the business of stating truths or falsehoods; they are instead expressions of emotion. As such, pure ethical sentences were thought to lack descriptive (or sometimes called "factual") meaning.

But that doesn't mean that emotivists thought that these sentences are completely meaningless. Rather they thought the sentences have "emotive meaning," which is a matter of "the different feelings they are ordinarily taken to express, and also the different responses which they are calculated to provoke" (Ayer 1936/1946, 108) or the "tendency of a word, arising through the history of its usage, to produce (result from) *affective* responses in people. It is the immediate aura of feeling which hovers about a word" (Stevenson 1937, 23, emphasis in the original).

Emotivism draws a stark contrast between ethical sentences and descriptive sentences. However, the starkness of this contrast ultimately makes it implausible as a theory of the meaning of ethical sentences, since it completely ignores the similarities between the semantic function of ethical sentences and descriptive sentences. There are shallow and deep versions of this problem, which we can see by considering one of Ayer's leading examples.

He considers a case where he utters the ethical sentence "Stealing is wrong." About this case, he writes

> I produce a sentence which has no factual meaning—that is, expresses no proposition which can be either true or false. It is as if I had written "Stealing money!!"–where the shape and thickness of the exclamation marks show, by a suitable convention, that a special sort of moral disapproval is the feeling which is being expressed. (ibid., 107)

However, any account which extends these ideas into an account of the meaning of ethical sentences in general will be woefully inadequate to the data of ordinary ethical discourse. The shallow problem is that it's quite obvious that everyday ethical discourse embeds ethical sentences in the truth-predicates. That is, we say things like "What Ayer said about stealing is true, but it'd be false to claim that downloading music off the internet is wrong." In this, ethical sentences seem to work just like descriptive sentences. That is to say that they are *truth-apt*. However, this stands in direct contradiction with the emotivist view.[23] So the emotivist view cannot be the right view of the meaning of ethical sentences.

I say that this problem is shallow because everyone knew about this problem as soon as the emotivist theory was proposed in the late 1930s, but it remained a very popular theory throughout the 1940s, 50s, and 60s. This is because one can chalk up the way ordinary ethical discourse embeds ethical sentences in truth-predicates to a loose use of the truth-predicate, where this does not track with sentences thought to be descriptive of objective facts. It's this sense which inspired Ramsey's (1927) "redundancy theory" of truth, according to which saying that a sentence is true means no more than just saying the sentence.

However attractive that move is, it doesn't address the deep problem of similar semantic function of ethical and descriptive sentences. This was first articulated independently by Searle (1962) and Geach (1965),[24] but since it rests on a point Frege made, it has come to be called the "Frege-Geach Problem." The point made by Frege was that a sentence could occur in one context asserted but in another context unasserted, so we need a notion of the content of a sentence that doesn't depend on whether or not the sentence is asserted (or negated, questioned, assumed, etc.).

This is a problem generated by the idea that the meaning of a whole sentence is a composition of the meaning of its parts and the way they are put together. The assumption that meaning is compositional seems to offer the only plausible explanation of the amazingly quick speed with which humans learn their first language and how we understand novel sentences. However, on the best ways of understanding how semantic compositionality works, we seem to need the idea of some stable content that is contributed by any part of a sentence to the meaning of all of the sentences in which it figures. For, if we have this, then we can think of the meaning of whole sentences as a function of the contents of their parts and the ways these parts are put together according to the compositional rules of the language.

Unfortunately, that much of modern semantics already stands in tension with emotivism. Although he didn't think of it exactly this way, Geach revealed this problem by querying what the emotivist would say about the meaning of a logically complex ethical sentences like

> "If tormenting cats is wrong, then getting little brother to torment cats is wrong."

He grants that the emotivist has an account of the meaning of the logically simple constituents of (1). The sentences "Tormenting cats is wrong" can be said to mean what it does in virtue of the negative moral sentiment it expresses towards tormenting cats; and the sentence "Getting little brother to torment cats is wrong" can be said to mean what it does in virtue of the negative moral sentiment it expresses towards getting little brother to torment cats. However, as Geach shows, those "meanings" cannot be the semantic contents of these simple sentences. Why not? Because negative moral attitudes needn't be expressed at all by an utterance of the logically complex sentence quoted above. This is because one who asserts a conditional—*if p, then q*—can remain neutral about each of its components. Clearly, one could consistently say "If tormenting cats is wrong, then getting little brother to torment cats is wrong" and "Tormenting cats is not wrong."

Geach pressed this point by arguing that emotivism makes a fallacy of equivocation out of what appears to be a clearly valid inference. It holds that the simple sentence "Tormenting cats is wrong" means what it does in virtue of the negative moral attitude it is used to express, but, as we have just seen, it must hold that the antecedent of the conditional "If tormenting cats is wrong, then getting little brother to torment cats is wrong" gets its meaning some other way. This implies that one who infers from these sentences to the obvious conclusion—"Getting little brother to torment cats is wrong"–has equivocated.

Because of this way of pressing the point, many expressivist responses to the Frege-Geach problem have sought to vindicate the inference and ones similar to it. For example, some have claimed that the ethical sentences convey prescriptions of some sort, and there are independently motivated logical constraints on prescriptions, such that one who asserts the simple ethical sentences with the conditionalized ethical sentences is committed to the prescription conveyed by the obvious conclusion.[25] Others have suggested that the conditionalized ethical sentence is used to express a higher-order attitude towards the simultaneous possession of two lower-order attitudes that can be used to make sense of the rational pressure to make the inferences Geach refers to.[26] And still others have developed expressivist accounts on which the content of ethical sentences can be represented as combinations of factual commitments and planning commitments, where the logical constraints on planning help to explain the validity of the inference Geach considered.[27]

I won't go into the complex details of these proposals and rejoinders, as that general line of investigation often seems to me to be blind to the source of the problem.[28] This is the expressivist's need for a plausible explanation of the compositionally stable content of ethical sentences, i.e., whatever is stable in what these sentences contribute to the meaning of the more complex sentences in which they may figure. Everyone agrees that emotivist versions of expressivism fail to provide this. The pertinent question now is whether later versions of expressivism do any better.

Quasi-Realism and the Problem of Creeping Minimalism

As we saw above, some philosophers argue that we should view standard uses of the truth-predicate not as ascribing some property had by all and only true sentences but as playing some other role in our thought and discourse. (Compare this to the way that many philosophers have argued that "exists" shouldn't be viewed as ascribing the property of existence, since then it's unclear what to say about claims of the form "x doesn't exist.") The general idea funds what are called *deflationary theories of truth*.[29] They are called this because they propose to deflate the ontological importance of the truth-predicate. To say "S is true" is not, on these views, to commit to S's possessing the property of truth; it's rather more like just asserting S all by itself.

The advent of deflationary theories of truth has provided inspiration for a new form of ethical expressivism. Recall from above that the shallow problem for emotivism was that it's common for ordinary speakers to embed ethical sentences in the truth-predicate. For example, if Ayer says "Stealing is wrong," I might say "Since Ayer said it, it is true that stealing is wrong." However, strictly speaking the meaningfulness of my statement is incompatible with emotivism since emotivists deny that ethical sentences are truth-apt. Some philosophers chalked that up to loose use of the truth-predicate. But if a deflationary view of truth is correct, then it looks as if the expressivist can say that ethical sentences can be truth-apt, even strictly speaking. This is because claiming that an ethical sentence is true amounts to little more than making the underlying statement. The sentence, "It is true that stealing is wrong" can, according to the deflationist, be used to state that stealing is wrong. And—this is the key—that's a statement to which the expressivist's theory can be applied directly. That is, by saying "It is true that stealing is wrong" in this case I should be seen as expressing a negative attitude towards stealing.

If this is right, it is a powerful idea for two reasons. First, many have thought that the notion of "truth" is conceptually related to notions like "proposition," "belief," and "knowledge," which means that a deflationary theory of truth may be the thin end of the wedge for expressivists to capture and underwrite many of the features of ordinary ethical discourse that tempt some philosophers to descriptivism. That is, expressivists may endorse a form of what Blackburn (1984, 171) dubbed "quasi-realism," while retaining the traditional advantages of expressivism over descriptivism. Second, expressivists can use this quasi-realist maneuver to retool their account of the meaning of ethical statements in a way which potentially overcomes the deeper problem with emotivism brought out by the Frege-Geach problem. In the remainder of this section, I will briefly explain these two ideas and then discuss some of the problems that have been raised for them.

Assuming deflationism is correct,[30] expressivists can say of any ethical sentence that it is true, in the strict and literal sense of "true." In addition to avoiding one of the implausible consequences of emotivism, this also lets them say that ethical sentences express propositions. For one plausible thing to mean by the term "proposition" is that a proposition is whatever is expressed by a truth-apt sentence. So, for example, the sentence "Stealing is wrong" could quite simply be said to express the proposition that stealing is wrong. But if ethical sentences are truth-apt, in a deflationary sense, and so express propositions, in a deflationary sense, there should be little to prevent us from saying that one who sincerely utters an ethical sentence expresses a belief. That is, we might deflate the notion of "expressing a belief" as well, by claiming that to express the belief that p is just to sincerely utter a sentence which expresses the proposition that p. In effect, this collapses beliefs to what I earlier called "judgments." Hence, there would be no difficulty in saying that one who sincerely utters the sentence "Stealing is wrong" has expressed the belief that stealing is wrong. But if we've come so far as recognizing that ethical sentences can be true and hence express propositions, and that one who sincerely utters them can be thought of as expressing a belief in a proposition, we only need to think that some of them are justified to be close to recognizing the possibility of ethical knowledge.

This is both good and bad for the quasi-realist expressivist. It's good for two reasons. First, it's an undeniable feature of ordinary ethical discourse that people ascribe ethical beliefs to themselves and others, which sometimes underwrite ascriptions of ethical knowledge. This has led many to think descriptivism is a presupposition of ordinary ethical discourse. Their idea is that, even if the expressivist can steer the narrow course between realism and error theory when it comes to his account of simple ethical statements, he will be forced to adopt one of these alternative positions when it comes to accounting for ethical truths, beliefs, and knowledge. However, given the possibility of a quasi-realist construal of these things, it looks like the expressivist can avoid this argument against his view and accommodate undeniable features of ordinary ethical discourse.

Second, this idea provides expressivists with an initial response to the deeper problem about the stable content of ethical words and sentences, which Searle and Geach raised for emotivists. Recall that this problem stemmed from the emotivist's inability to explain the compositionally stable content of ethical sentences, which can be embedded in logically complex contexts. However, with the notion of a proposition rehabilitated in broadly deflationary terms, the quasi-realist expressivist can argue that the semantic content of ethical sentences is just like the semantic content of descriptive sentences. "Tormenting cats is wrong" expresses the proposition that tormenting cats is wrong just like "Grass is green" expresses the proposition that grass is green. They each contribute these propositions—deflationarily construed—to the logically complex sentences in which they figure, thus determining the semantic contents of those sentences as a function of the semantic contents of their parts.

I say that this is an "initial" response because the quasi-expressivist will want to insist that this (very minimal) story about semantic content isn't the whole story about meaning. At a deeper level, he wants to say that the meaning of an ethical sentence is still a matter of the conative attitude it can be used to express when it is asserted outright. It's unclear how exactly to incorporate this commitment into the quasi-realist's view, but the basic idea would be to say that ethical beliefs are, at a more fundamental level conative attitudes, whereas nonethical beliefs are cognitive representations of the world.[31]

The need to make this distinction, however, raises a problem for quasi-realist expressivism. The problem is that by using deflationary interpretations of terms like "truth," "proposition," "belief," and "knowledge," it becomes unclear how to articulate this deeper distinction between conative attitudes and cognitive representations of the world. That is, in an attempt to respect the similarities between ordinary ethical discourse and uncontroversially descriptive discourse, especially the way compositional rules seem like they apply uniformly to sentences in both kinds of discourse, the quasi-realist adopts deflationary understandings of all of the standard notions with which we might articulate the semantic distinction between ethical discourse and descriptive discourse. By doing so, however, it may seem to become impossible to tell the difference between a kind of descriptivist who accepts deflationism and an expressivist who accepts deflationism while wanting to insist on some metaethically important semantic distinction between ethical discourse and descriptive discourse.[32]

It is unclear whether this is a fatal problem. Some have suggested nonstandard ways for the expressivist to draw the needed distinction. For example, Dreier (2004), drawing on O'Leary-Hawthorne and Price (1996), Fine (2001), and Gibbard (2003), argues that the distinction can be drawn in terms of what best explains our use of the relevant terms—ethical or descriptive. And, in Chrisman (2008), I have criticized that solution but argued that the distinction can be explained in terms of whether the relevant judgments are best seen as the products of theoretical or practical reasoning.[33]

However, even if one of these solutions works, quasi-realist expressivists may face other problems in their reliance on deflationary construals of the notions of truth, propositions, and belief. For one thing, deflationism is independently very controversial, which means that the viability of quasi-realism depends on the viability of that controversial view. For another thing, the notion of a proposition is used not only to explain the content of a truth-apt sentence but also to explain the content of attitudes like belief, desire, and disapproval, as well as the content of modal operators. It's far from clear that these uses can be deflated in such a way that preserves the quasi-realist's claim to give a uniform semantic analysis of structurally isomorphic pieces of descriptive and ethical discourse while maintaining the underlying difference that is crucial for the core expressivist maneuver. So, in a way, the core semantic problem highlighted by the Frege-Geach problem still poses a challenge for quasi-realist expressivists, even though they can say a lot of plausible things about ethics and semantics that emotivist expressivists could not. It is for reasons like these that nonquasi-realist versions of expressivism have recently begun to emerge. I discuss these next.

Recent Developments

There are many interesting ideas currently under debate for generating new and better versions of expressivism. However, for the sake of space and concreteness, I will discuss only two of them here. Both of these rest on the idea that expressivism will meet the primary challenge facing it only if it proceeds from a completely general account of meaning that leaves room theoretically downstream for the contrast needed for the core expressivist maneuver. More specifically, these views hold that expressivists should start not with the assumption that some areas of discourse are descriptive and argue that ethical discourse differs in being expressive in some important sense. Rather they think expressivists should start with the assumption that *all* sentences get their meaning from what they express. That is, they both suggest that expressivists need an ideationalist theory of meaning, according to which sentences mean what they do in virtue of the state of mind they can be used, according to semantic conventions, to express.[34] However, the two views I will now discuss differ in their application of the general ideationalist framework.

Ridge's ecumenical expressivism

In a series of articles and a book manuscript in progress, Ridge (2006, 2007a, unpublished) defends a hybrid form of expressivism he calls "Ecumenical Expressivism." Above, I mentioned hybrid forms of descriptivism, which claim that ethical sentences are used to express both a conative attitude and a cognitive representation of the world. These counted as forms of descriptivism, however, because the conative attitude is only pragmatically conveyed in some sense, whereas the belief component tracks with the sentence's literal meaning. Ridge holds that both components are determinative of literal meaning, which is what makes his view a (hybrid) form of expressivism. More specifically, he claims that the belief component makes anaphoric reference to the desire component, which is ultimately why the desire component is (partially) determinative of literal meaning.

There are several different ways to work out this idea. But the basic form is this: All sentences mean what they do in virtue of the states of mind conventionally linked to them (this is ideationalism). In the case of ethical sentences, there are two interlocking states of mind conventionally linked to them. First, there's some conative attitude like disapproval. However, this is not disapproval of some specific action, person, state of affairs, etc. Rather it's disapproval of things in general, insofar as they have a particular property—what might be thought of as the descriptive basis of the disapproval. Second, there is some belief which makes suitable anaphoric reference back to the disapproved of property. The meaning of the sentence is a matter of its expressing both the belief and the approval to which it is anaphorically linked.

This is made clearer with an example. For the sentence "Stealing is wrong," Ridge's ecumenical expressivism will say that it means what it does in virtue of conventionally expressing two interlocking states of mind. First, it expresses a conative state like disapproval, but this will be disapproval not directly of stealing but of things insofar as they have some uncontroversially descriptive property F. Second, it also expresses the belief that stealing has property F.[35]

Importantly, Ridge allows that F may vary from speaker to speaker. So, for example, one speaker may disapprove of things insofar as they fail to maximize utility, whereas another speaker may disapprove of things insofar as they violate precepts written in a holy book, and a third speaker may have some complicated mixture of these and other standards for disapproval. This can be thought of as tracking different speaker's moral sensibilities. It also explains why Ridge thinks the conative component is crucial for understanding the meaning of ethical sentences. For if F were the same for everyone, e.g., if it was just the property of violating precepts written in a holy book, then it would be more plausible to think that "Stealing is wrong" just expresses the belief that stealing violates precepts written in a holy book.

The cognitive component is also crucial, for it's what helps Ridge to overcome the problem emotivism had in explaining the content of logically embedded ethical sentences. For example, the ecumenical expressivist can say that the content of Geach's sentence "If tormenting cats is wrong, then getting little brother to torment cats is wrong" is hybrid. Like all ethical sentences, this expresses a conative attitude like disapproval, but it's disapproval of things insofar as they have some property F. And it also expresses the logically complex belief that, if tormenting cats has F, then so does getting little brother to torment cats.

When combined with an account of logical validity given in terms of consistency of beliefs, Ridge argues that he can also use this hybrid expressivist view to explain the validity of Geach's *modus ponens* inference in exactly the same way as he would explain a *modus ponens* inference with only descriptive premises and conclusion. And he does so in a way that doesn't require recourse to the quasi-realist use of deflationist notions of "truth," "proposition," and "belief," which means that his view potentially has more resources to avoid the problems associated with quasi-realism.

It would be unfair and unwise to put objections to Ridge's theory into print before his book is finished. However, let me briefly mention one challenge, which readers may want to explore further. Although ecumenical expressivism has the resources to assign meanings to ethical sentences and descriptive sentences alike, it does not always assign overall content in the same way to sentences with isomorphic syntactical form.

For example, a descriptive sentence like "Stealing is not economically profitable" means what it does, according to ecumenical expressivism, because it expresses the belief that stealing is not economically profitable. By contrast the ethical sentence, "Stealing is not ethically good" means what it does, according to the version of ecumenical expressivism above, because it expresses a conative state like approval of things insofar as they have property F and the belief that stealing is not F. (We might think this sentence expresses disapproval rather than approval, but one could think that stealing is neither good nor bad, and so not disapprove.) This means that, according to Ridge, the logical word "not" functions differently in the two sentences. In the first case, it modifies "economically profitable" in the sentence and then also in the belief expressed by the sentence. Understanding the sentence consists in knowing that it expresses this belief. In the second case, "not" modifies "ethically good" in the sentence but then modifies "F" in the belief expressed by the sentence. Hence, understanding the sentence consists in knowing that it expresses that belief about stealing's not being F.

Of course, these functions are very similar. However, the difference between them means that a child learning the meaning of sentences of the form "x-ing is not G" would have to acquire the ability to tell when the first or second function is appropriate for interpreting any arbitrary sentence which includes a negated predicate. That is, a child would have to be able to tell whether any arbitrary clause of this form is ethical or a descriptive. The same is of course true of clauses and sentences of other grammatical forms as well, since the grammar of ethical clauses and sentences exactly mimics the grammar of uncontroversially descriptive clauses and sentences. So, I think an ecumenical expressivist will have to convince us that language learning children do acquire the ability to distinguish ethical bits of language from descriptive bits of language along with the ability to understand sentences involving negated predicates. Otherwise his claim to have captured the compositionality of meaning, which is crucial to explaining the learnability of language, will be in jeopardy.

Schroeder's proposal

In a series of articles and a recently influential book, Schroeder (2008a, 2008b, 2008c) has discussed the semantic commitments of expressivism in great detail.

Although he himself doesn't endorse any form of expressivism, he develops a new kind of expressivism, which he argues is the best possible kind of non-hybrid[36] expressivism.

This kind of expressivism is one which eschews the idea of descriptive sentences expressing beliefs and ethical sentences expressing something else (even if this something else has a belief component like Ridge thinks). According to Schroeder, the best non-hybrid form of expressivism is one that treats all (declarative) sentences as meaning what they mean in virtue of the mental state they express (this is ideationalism), but he argues that this kind of mental state should be the same nonbelief kind of mental state in all cases. This, Schroeder argues, is the only way a non-hybrid expressivist can give anything approaching a structurally adequate account of the meaning of logically complex sentences.

To see why, consider first an ethical sentence and two variants generated by negation:

(1) Stealing is wrong.
(2) Stealing is not wrong.
(3) Not stealing is wrong.

Most previous expressivists say that sentence (1) means what it does because it expresses something like disapproval of stealing. And on this model, we might say that sentence (3) expresses disapproval of not stealing. But what about sentence (2)? Intuitively, it should be logically inconsistent with (1). Clearly (2) doesn't express approval of stealing—just because you don't disapprove of x, it doesn't mean that you approve of x. A natural but misguided thought is to say that (2) expresses toleration of stealing. The reason this is misguided is that it doesn't explain why (2) is logically inconsistent with (1).[37]

Schroeder notes that descriptivists don't have this problem because they view all three sentences as expressing a single general kind of attitude: belief. Descriptivists will say that it's not the kind of attitude but the content which differentiates the expressive role of these sentences. Sentence (1) expresses the belief that stealing is wrong, sentence (2) expresses the belief that stealing is not wrong, and sentence (3) expresses the belief that not stealing is wrong. And sentences (1) and (2) are inconsistent just in case the beliefs they express are inconsistent, which they are.

Schroeder suggests that the only way expressivists will be able to give a similarly structurally adequate account of the meaning of these three sentences is by following descriptivists in saying that these sentences express some general kind of attitude and letting the contents of this attitude differentiate the expressive role of these sentences. However, the key will be to say that this attitude is different from belief.

According to Schroeder, it doesn't matter exactly what we call this state as long as its not thought of as a cognitive representation of the world. He suggests we dub it *being for*, and the things we can "be for" are characterized with gerunds like *blaming*. Given this much structure, an expressivist can then explain the semantic differences between the three sentences above. Sentence (1) will be said to express the state of being for blaming for stealing, sentence (2) will be said to express the state of being for not blaming for stealing, and sentence (3) will be said to express the state of being for blaming for not stealing. And assuming that the state of being for is like belief and intention in that it is logically inconsistent both to be for x and to be for not x, an expressivist who adopts this structure can explain the meaning of (1) and (2) in a way which underwrites the idea that they are logically inconsistent.

Schroeder argues that this puts the expressivist onto securer footing for explaining the meaning of logically complex ethical sentences. However, it immediately raises a further problem: What should the expressivist say about logically complex sentences which are partially ethical and partially descriptive. For example, what should the expressivist say about a sentence like

(4) Stealing is wrong or stealing maximizes happiness

where, intuitively, the first disjunct is ethical and the second disjunct isn't? The problem here is that (4) doesn't seem to express a state of being for blaming something, nor can the expressivist say it expresses a state of believing something. It's a logically complex composite of both ethical and descriptive elements.

Again, Schroeder points out that descriptivists will have no problem explaining the expressive role of sentences like these. They'll say that (4) expresses a belief with a disjunctive content, viz. that stealing is wrong or stealing maximizes happiness. And again we see descriptivists capturing logical complexity by treating all indicative sentences as expressing a single kind of mental state—belief—with different contents.

Schroeder suggests that the only plausible route for the expressivist is to take a similar tack, but again with a nonrepresentational attitude, such as being for. The details for how this could work are too complex to get into here, but the upshot is that Schroeder argues that expressivists must view *all* indicative sentences—both ethical and descriptive—as expressing states of being for. However, for sentences we'd intuitively think of as descriptive, he suggests that they could be thought of as expressing states of being for, where this is not attached to something like *blaming*, as with ethical sentences, but instead to something like *proceeding as if p is true*.[38]

On the kind of expressivism which Schroeder thinks is the only version of the view to capture logically complex semantic structure in a fully compositional way, both ethical and uncontroversially descriptive sentences are thought to express a state of being for something. And it's differences in the things that one is for which manifest the sort of distinction that expressivists traditionally wanted to draw between ethical and descriptive discourse. *Being for blaming for x* is characteristic of the meaning of ethical sentences, *being for proceeding as if p* is characteristic of the meaning of descriptive sentences, and logically mixed sentences require a logically complex mixture of the things one is for.

I have said that Schroeder proposes this form of expressivism as the best possible form of expressivism, but he himself doesn't endorse it. Why not? He argues that the form of expressivism he develops is the only extant version of expressivism able to explain the meaning of arbitrarily complex sentences of English up to the complexity added by the predicate calculus. However, to do this, it has to take on some very strong commitments about the way language works and, even then, ordinary language—both ethical and descriptive—has far more complexity than this version of expressivism can explain. I'll leave the reader to decide whether he is right, but I can certainly recommend his book as a model of linguistically subtle and aware metaethics. Since expressivism is, after all, a proposal about the meaning of ethical sentences, it would be good if more metaethicists tried to defend expressivism in the context of full awareness of the semantic complexities of our language.

Concluding Remarks

The trajectory of debate about expressivism is one along which expressivists have become more and more aware of linguistic complexity and the sorts of theoretical constraints that drive theory building in semantics. We saw in the discussion of recent developments that both Ridge and Schroeder think that expressivists need to work from within some sort of general ideationalist framework, which nevertheless makes room for a distinction between ethical sentences and descriptive sentences.

I'd like to conclude by very briefly calling the terminus of this trajectory into question. Given the choice between a purely descriptivist framework and an ideationalist framework for explaining meaning, it seems clear that expressivists must choose the latter. Otherwise, the core expressivist maneuver will never get off the ground. However, I think this is a false dichotomy. It leaves out the conceptual-role framework, which philosophers of language such as Harman (1982), Brandom (1994, 2000, 2008), Block (1987, 1993), and Peacocke (1995) have explored in much detail. In this framework, sentences (and subsentential parts) are thought to mean what they do not in virtue of how they describe reality as being and not in virtue of what mental states they conventionally express, but in virtue of their inferential or conceptual connections to other sentences (and subsentential parts). In the philosophy of language, I believe this rather than ideationalism is typically seen as the main competitor to a general descriptivism.[39] This is probably because, although the ideationalist view that pieces of language mean what they do in part because of the mental states they express is probably right, it cannot represent the whole story, since it simply pushes the interesting explanatory question back a level: how do those mental states get the content they have? And here we can see broadly descriptivist and conceptual-role strategies for answering the question about the content of mental states, but one thing we cannot do is try to answer *this* question by appealing to mental states conventionally expressed.

Given this, would it be possible to develop a form of expressivism within a general conceptual-role framework instead of within the general ideationalist framework suggested by Ridge and Schroeder?

Some may object that a necessary condition on any metaethical view's deserving the label "ethical expressivism" is that it say that ethical sentences mean what they do, at least in part, because of the conative attitudes that they express. If that's right, then there couldn't be a conceptual-role version of expressivism, though there may be a view structurally similar to expressivism except for the fact that it has been developed in the conceptual-role framework.[40]

Either way, in addition to the new sorts of expressivism Ridge and Schroeder have recently proposed, I think those interested in the prospects of expressivism should also explore the possibility of developing an analog of ethical expressivism by considering a metaethical application of the conceptual-role approach to meaning. This would involve a view which tried to explain the difference between describing and evaluating in terms of the conceptual role of evaluative language. Thus, we could still pursue the core expressivist maneuver of beginning our metaethical theorizing by asking not about (i) the nature of some kind of supposedly real thing, ethical *value*, but about (ii) the nature of something else we all agree is real, ethical *evaluations*. But the answer to (ii) will turn on a disanalogy in the types of inferential commitments ethical and descriptive sentences help us to make explicit instead of a disanalogy in the types of mental states ethical and descriptive sentences help us to make public. In particular, these types of commitments might be argued to have a different sort of conceptual role from the sorts of commitments carried by descriptive sentences. Perhaps they are commitments to drawing certain conclusions in our practical reasoning about what to do instead of commitments to something's being a part of reality or to drawing certain conclusions in our theoretical reasoning.

This is not the place to develop this idea further. But I mention it in conclusion because I think it's also a place where further metaethical investigation into the prospects of expressivism could be fruitfully pursued.[41]

Works Cited

Acton, H. B. (1936), "The Expletive Theory of Morals." *Analysis* 4, 42–5.
Ayer, A. J. (1936/1946), *Language, Truth and Logic* (2nd edn). London: V. Gollancz ltd.
Baldwin, T. (1985), "Ethical Non-naturalism," in I. Hacking (ed.), *Exercises in Analysis*. Cambridge: Cambridge University Press.
Ball, S. (1988), "Reductionism in Ethics and Science: A Contemporary Look at G.E. Moore's Open-Question Argument." *American Philosophical Quarterly* 25, 197–213.
Bar-On, D. (2004), *Speaking My Mind: Expression and Self-Knowledge*. New York: Oxford University Press.
Bar-On, D. and M. Chrisman (2009), "Ethical Neo-Expressivism." *Oxford Studies in Metaethics* 4: 133–65
Blackburn, S. (1984), *Spreading the Word: Groundings in the Philosophy of Language*. New York: Oxford University Press.
—. (1993), *Essays in Quasi-Realism*. New York: Oxford University Press.
—. (1998), *Ruling Passions: A Theory of Practical Reasoning*. New York: Oxford University Press.
—. (2009), "Truth and *A Priori* Possibility: Egan's Charge Against Quasi-Realism." *Australasian Journal of Philosophy* 87, 201–13.
Block, N. (1987), "Functional Role and Truth Conditions." *Proceedings of the Aristotlean Society*, suppl. volume LXI, 157–83.
—. (1993), "Holism, Hyper-analyticity and Hyper-compositionality." *Philosophical Issues* 3, 37–72.
Boisvert, D. (2008), "Expressive-Assertivism." *Pacific Philosophical Quarterly* 89, 169–203.
Boyd, R. (1988), "How to Be a Moral Realist," in G. Sayre-McCord (ed.), *Essays on Moral Realism*. Ithaca, NY: Cornell University Press.
Brandom, R (1994), *Making it Explicit: Reasoning, Representing, and Discursive Commitment*. Cambridge, MA: Harvard University Press.
—. (2000), *Articulating Reasons: An Introduction to Inferentialism*. Cambridge, MA: Harvard University Press.
—.(2008), *Between Saying and Doing*. Oxford; New York: Oxford University Press.
Brink, D. (1986), "Externalist Moral Realism." *Southern Journal of Philosophy* 24, 23–40.
—. (1989), *Moral Realism and the Foundations of Ethics*. New York: Cambridge University Press.
Brown, C. (2010), "A New and Improved Supervenience Argument for Ethical Descriptivism," in R. Shafer-Landau (ed.), *Oxford Studies in Metaethics*, vol. 6. New York: Oxford University Press.
Chrisman, M. (2008), "Expressivism, Inferentialism, and Saving the Debate." *Philosophy and Phenomenological Research* 77, 334–58.
—. (2009), "Expressivism, Truth, and (Self-)Knowledge." *Philosopher's Imprint* 9, 1–26.
—. (2010), "Expressivism, Inferentialism, and the Theory of Meaning" in M. Brady (ed.), *New Waves in Metaethics*. New York: Palgrave Macmillan.
—. (2013), "Emotivism," in H. LaFollette (ed.), *International Encyclo-pedia of Ethics*. Oxford: Wiley-Blackwell, 1600–1606.
—. (2014), "Attitudinal Expressivism and Logical Pragmatism in Metaethics" in G. Hubbs & D. Lind (eds.), *Pragmatism, Law, and Language*. New York: Routledge.

Copp, D. (2001), "Realist-Expressivism: A Neglected Option for Moral Realism," *Social Philosophy and Policy* 18, 1–43.
Cuneo, T. (2007a), *The Normative Web*. New York: Oxford University Press.
—. (2007b), "Recent Faces of Moral Nonnaturalism," *Philosophy Compass* 2, 850–79.
Dancy, J. (2000), *Practical Reality*. New York: Oxford University Press.
Davidson, D. (1963/1980), "Actions, Reasons, and Causes," *Actions and Events*. Oxford; New York: Oxford University Press.
Davis, W. (2003), *Meaning, Expression, and Thought*. Cambridge: Cambridge University Press.
Dorr, C (2002), "Non-cognitivism and Wishful Thinking." *Noûs* 36, 97–103.
Dreier, J. (2004), "Meta-Ethics and the Problem of Creeping Minimalism." *Philosophical Perspectives* 18, 23–44.
Egan, A. (2007), "Quasi-Realism and Fundamental Moral Error." *Australasian Journal of Philosophy* 85, 205–19.
Enoch, D. (2003), "How Noncognitivists Can Avoid Wishful Thinking." *The Southern Journal of Philosophy* 41, 527–45.
—. (2007), "An Outline of an Argument for Robust Metanormative Realism," in R. Shafer-Landau (ed.), *Oxford Studies in Metaethics*, vol. 2. New York: Oxford University Press.
Field, H. (1986), "The Deflationary Conception of Truth," in G. MacDonald and C. Wright (eds.), *Fact, Science and Morality*. Oxford: Blackwell.
—. (1994), "Disquotational Truth and Factually Defective Discourse," *Philosophical Review* 103 405–52.
Fine, K. (2001), "The Question of Realism." *Philosophers' Imprint* 1, 1–30.
Finlay, S. and Schroeder, M. (2008), "Reasons for Action: Internal vs. External." *The Stanford Encyclopedia of Philosophy* (Fall 2008 Edition). E. N. Zalta (ed.), http://plato.stanford.edu/archives/fall2008/entries/reasons-internal-external.
Finlay, S. (2009), "Oughts and Ends." *Philosophical Studies* 143, 315–40.
Fitzpatrick, W. (2008), "Robust Ethical Realism, Non-Naturalism and Normativity," in R. Shafer-Landau (ed.), *Oxford Studies in Metaethics*, vol. 3. New York: Oxford University Press.
Fodor, J. (1990), *A Theory of Content*. Bradford, MA: MIT Press.
Fodor, J. and Lepore, E. (1991), "Why Meaning (Probably) Isn't Conceptual Role," *Mind and Language* 6(4), 329–43.
Frankena, W. (1939), "The Naturalistic Fallacy." *Mind* 48, 464–77.
Frege, G. (1879), *Begriffsschrift, eine der arithmetischen Nachgebildete Formelsprache des reinen Denkens*. Halle a/S.: L. Nebert.
Geach, P. T. (1965), "Assertion." *The Philosophical Review* 74 (4), 449–65.
Gibbard, A. (1990), *Wise Choices, Apt Feelings: A Theory of Normative Judgment*. Cambridge, MA: Harvard University Press.
—. (2003), *Thinking How to Live*. Cambridge, MA: Harvard University Press.
Grice, H. P. (1957), "Meaning." *The Philosophical Review* 66, 377–88.
Hägerström, A (1953), *Inquiries into the Nature of Law and Morals*. Stockholm: Almqvist & Wiksell.
Hale, B. (1986), "Review: The Compleat Projectivist." *The Philosophical Quarterly* 36, 65–84.

—. (2002), "Review: Can Arboreal Knotwork Help Blackburn out of Frege's Abyss?," *Philosophy and Phenomenological Research* 65, 144–9.
Hare, R. M. (1952), *The Language of Morals*. Oxford: Oxford University Press.
Harman, G. (1982), "Conceptual Role Semantics." *Notre Dame Journal of Formal Logic* 28, 242–56.
Horwich, P. (1990), *Truth*. Oxford: Blackwell.
Horgan, T. and Timmons, M. (2006), "Cognitivist Expressivism," in T. Horgan and M. Timmons (eds.), *Metaethics after Moore*. New York: Oxford University Press.
Hussain, N. and Shah, N. (2006), "Misunderstanding Metaethics: Korsgaard's Rejection of Realism," in R. Shafer-Landau (ed.), *Oxford Studies in Metaethics*, vol. 1. New York: Clarendon Press, 265–94.
Joyce, R. (2001), *The Myth of Morality*. Cambridge: Cambridge University Press.
Kalderon, M. (2005), *Moral Fictionalism*. Oxford: Oxford University Press.
Lenman, J. (2003), "Noncognitivism and Wishfulness." *Ethical Theory and Moral Practice* 6, 265–74.
Locke, J. (1690/1975), *An Essay Concerning Human Understanding*, P. H. Nidditch (ed.). Oxford: Oxford University Press.
Mackie, J. L. (1977), *Ethics: Inventing Right and Wrong*. London: Penguin.
Mandelbaum, M. (1955) *The Phenomenology of Moral Experience*. Glenco, IL: The Free Press.
McGeer, V. (1996), "Is Self-Knowledge an Empirical Problem? Renegotiating the Space of Philosophical Explanation." *Journal of Philosophy* 93, 483–515.
McLaughlin, B. and Bennett, K. (2010), "Supervenience," in E. N. Zalta (ed.), *The Stanford Encyclopedia of Philosophy*, Summer 2010 ed. http://plato.stanford.edu/archives/sum2010/entries/supervenience).
Miller, C. (2008a), "Motivation in Agents." *Nous* 22, 222–66.
—. (2008b), "Motivational Internalism." *Philosophical Studies* 139, 233–55.
—. (2009), "The Conditions of Moral Realism." *The Journal of Philosophical Research* 34, 123–55.
Nagel, T. (1986), *The View from Nowhere*. Oxford: Oxford University Press.
Nolan, D., Restall, G. and West, C. (2005), "Moral Fictionalism Versus the Rest." *Australasian Journal of Philosophy* 83, 307–30.
O'Leary-Hawthorne, J., and Price, H. (1996), "How to Stand Up for Non-Cognitivists." *Australasian Journal of Philosophy* 74, 275–92.
Ogden, C. K. and Richards, I. A. (1925), *The Meaning of Meaning: A Study of the Influence of Language upon Thought and of the Science of Symbolism*. New York: Harcourt, Brace & World, Inc.
Olson, J. (2010), "In Defence of Moral Error Theory," in M. Brady (ed.), *New Waves in Metaethics*. New York: Palgrave Macmillan.
Papineau, D. (2009), "Naturalism," in Edward N. Zalta (ed.), *The Stanford Encyclopedia of Philosophy*, Spring 2009 Edition. http://plato.stanford.edu/archives/spr2009/entries/naturalism).
Parfit, D. (2011), *On What Matters*. Oxford: Oxford University Press.
Peacocke, C. (1995), *A Study of Concepts*. Bradford, MA: MIT Press.
Price, H. (2011), "Expressivism for Two Voices," in J. Knowles and H. Rydenfelt (eds.), *Pragmatism, Science and Naturalism* (Frankfurt am Main: Peter Lang), 87-113.
Quine, W.V. (1970), *Philosophy of Logic*. Englewood Cliffs: Prentice Hall.

Railton, P. (1986), "Moral Realism." *Philosophical Review* 95, 163–207.
—. (1989), "Naturalism and Prescriptivity." *Social Philosophy and Policy* 95, 51–174.
Ramsey, F. P. (1927), "Facts and Propositions." *Proceedings of the Aristotelian Society, Supplementary Volumes* 7, 153–206.
Rea, M. (2002), *World Without Design: The Ontological Consequences of Naturalism*. New York: Oxford University Press.
Ridge, M. (2006), "Ecumenical Expressivism: Finessing Frege." *Ethics* 116, 302–36.
—. (2007a), "Ecumenical Expressivism: The Best of Both Worlds?," in R. Shafer-Landau (ed.), *Oxford Studies in Metaethics*, vol. 2. New York: Oxford University Press, 51–76.
—. (2007b), "Anti-Reductionism and Supervenience." *Journal of Moral Philosophy* 4(3), 330–48.
—. (2008), "Moral Non-Naturalism," in E. N. Zalta (ed.), *Stanford Encyclopedia of Philosophy*, Fall 2008 edn. http://plato.stanford.edu/archives/fall2008/entries/moral-non-naturalism).
—. (unpublished), *Impassioned Belief*.
Rosati, C. (2008), "Moral Motivation," in E. N. Zalta (ed.), *The Stanford Encyclopedia of Philosophy*, Fall 2008 edn. http://plato.stanford.edu/archives/fall2008/entries/moral-motivation).
Ross, W. D. (1939), *Foundations of Ethics; The Gifford Lectures Delivered in the University of Aberdeen, 1935–6*. Oxford: The Clarendon Press.
Russell, B. (1935/1961), *Religion and Science*. New York: Oxford University Press.
Schiffer, S. (1972), *Meaning*. Oxford: Oxford University Press.
Schroeder, M (2008a), *Being For*. New York: Oxford University Press.
—. (2008b), "Expression for Expressivists." *Philosophy and Phenomenological Research* 76, 86–116.
—. (2008c), "How Expressivists Can and Should Solve Their Problem with Negation." *Noûs* 42, 573–99.
—. (2009), "Hybrid Expressivism: Virtues and Vices." *Ethics* 119, 257–309.
—. (2010), *Noncognitivism in Ethics*. New York: Routledge.
Searle, J. R. (1962), "Meaning and Speech Acts." *The Philosophical Review* 71, 423–32.
Sellars, W. (1968), *Science and Metaphysics: Variations on Kantian Themes*. London: Routledge & K. Paul.
Shafer-Landau, R. (2003), *Moral Realism: A Defence*. Oxford: Oxford University Press.
Smith, M. (1987), "The Humean Theory of Motivation." *Mind* 96, 36–61.
—. (1994), *The Moral Problem*. Oxford: Blackwell.
Stevenson, C. L. (1937), "Emotive Meaning of Moral Terms." *Mind* 46, 14–31.
—. (1944), *Ethics and Language*. New Haven: Yale University Press.
Stoljar, D. and Damnjanovic, N. (2009), "The Deflationary Theory of Truth," in E. N. Zalta (ed.), *The Stanford Encyclopedia of Philosophy*, Fall 2009 edn. http://plato.stanford.edu/archives/fall2009/entries/truth-deflationary.
Sturgeon, N. (1985), "Moral Explanations," in D. Copp and D. Zimmerman (eds.), *Morality, Reason, and Truth*. Totowa: Rowman & Littlefield.
—. (2009), "Doubts about the Supervenience of the Ethical," in R. Shafer-Landau (ed.), *Oxford Studies in Metaethics*, vol. 4. New York: Oxford University Press.
Timmons, M. (1999), *Morality without Foundations: A Defense of Ethical Contextualism*. New York: Oxford University Press.
Wittgenstein, L. (1953), *Philosophical Investigations*. Oxford: B. Blackwell.

3 Constructivism and the Error Theory

Hallvard Lillehammer

Introduction

According to the error theory, morality presents itself to us as though it were something to be discovered, but in fact it is not. Morality is something invented, constructed, or made.[1] According to constructivism, morality is something invented, constructed, or made. Thus understood, constructivism and the error theory are close philosophical relatives. Both views assert that morality is a construction. The error theory goes on to say that moral thought also aspires to something more, but does so unsuccessfully. Constructivism stops short of this claim. Which, if any, of these two views should we prefer? That is the question I shall address in this chapter. My answer will be that constructivism has the edge over the error theory in virtue of being committed to less problematic views about the content, truth, and justification of moral claims. I shall not, however, conclude that we ought to believe in constructivism. In order to do that I would have to argue that the claims of the constructivist are more plausible than those of her competitors who claim that morality is neither invented, constructed, or made. That is a task that goes beyond the scope of the present chapter.

Three Marks of Moral Objectivity

It is widely agreed that morality strikes us as objective. It is less widely agreed what moral objectivity amounts to and whether the appearance of objectivity truly reflects what goes on when we make moral judgments. There are at least three marks associated with moral objectivity in contemporary philosophy (cf. Lillehammer 2007, 5–9). The first I call *error*. *Error* requires that agents who make moral claims can be said to do so competently or incompetently. In other words, moral terms have informative conditions of competent application. *Error* is arguably a necessary condition for any kind of objectivity. If there is no sense in which I can be said to go right or wrong in applying moral terms, then there is no point in saying that the claims I make in so doing have any objective aspirations. *Error* is arguably not, however, a sufficient condition for objectivity. This is because the existence of application conditions is a universal feature of any claim we can meaningfully make, subjective or objective.

Consider the following example. Suppose we agree to call an object "blip" if and only if it is such that I convince you to despise it on a Tuesday. Suppose we also stipulate that no genuine blip is to be despised on a Wednesday. Then any object I convince you to despise on a Tuesday is a blip. Furthermore, it is a necessary truth about blips, knowable a priori, that they are not to be despised on a Wednesday. Suppose that on at least one Tuesday I convince you to despise something. Then that something is a blip and ought not to be despised on a Wednesday. So there are blips. So there is a "property" of *blipness*. So there are blip "facts" instantiating those "properties." And so we could go on. Yet in what sense, if any, are blip claims objective? Can we conjure up objective facts and properties by arbitrary stipulation? If *error* were all there was to our idea of objectivity the answer to this question would be an obvious "Yes." Yet this answer is anything but obvious. The problem is that *error* comes too cheaply.[2] Something more than the existence of linguistic terms and their stipulated conditions of application needs to be in play before we can talk about objectivity in any interesting sense.

A second mark of objectivity I call *realism*. The conditions for satisfying this mark of objectivity go beyond *error* and presuppose it. Claims are objective in the realist sense just in case their conditions of correct application are fixed by substantial facts or properties that exist independently of the practice of making those claims and the attitudes of those who make them. In other words, they are mind independent. In this sense, claims about blips are not objective. Were it not for our act of stipulation and the reactive responses it invokes there would be no blips. In the realist sense, it is not appropriate to be an objectivist about blips, even if "blip" has perfectly determinate conditions of application. *Realism* does not come that cheaply, referring as it does to what the world is like "anyway," or independently of our practices and attitudes (cf. Brink 1989, Shafer-Landau 2003, Cuneo 2007, Miller 2009).

Realism is sometimes treated as a sufficient condition for objectivity. Consider the claim that cricket balls move differently if hit on the moon. If true, it is natural to think this obtains regardless of our practices and attitudes. For claims about cricket balls and their physical movement, successful reference to a world of mind-independent facts and properties is exactly what objectivity requires. It is not obviously the same with moral claims. The objective fact that cricket balls move differently if hit on the moon is not normally thought to give anyone a reason to act in one way rather than another unless that person has some particular interest in cricket or the moon. The fact that it is wrong to hit people, on the other hand, is often thought to give everyone at least a defeasible moral reason to act accordingly regardless of their contingent interests. Thus understood, moral claims aspire to be necessarily reason giving in some way that does not apply to other claims that aim to represent the way the world is regardless of our practices and attitudes. If so, *realism* is not a sufficient condition for moral objectivity, even if it is a sufficient condition for the objectivity of claims that have a less intimate relationship to reason and the will. To be sufficient for moral objectivity, realism needs to be supplemented with the claim that moral facts are necessarily reason giving.[3] I return to this issue in my discussion of the error theory below.

Nor is *realism* obviously a necessary condition for moral objectivity. Let us say that a claim is *inescapable* if and only if it meets the condition that no competent agents who genuinely understand it can dismiss it as practically irrelevant to themselves or others without irrationality. In other words, the correctness of that claim renders it necessarily reason giving even for someone who tries to evade it by insisting that he or she has no interest in these kinds of claims. It is a controversial issue whether the claim that morality is necessarily reason giving presupposes that the correctness conditions of moral claims are mind independent. Thus, it might be thought that even if there is no such thing as a mind independent moral reality, morality can make inescapable claims on us in virtue of the fact that a commitment to some moral claims is a necessary feature of sound practical reasoning (cf. Korsgaard 2009). I return to this question in my discussion of both constructivism and the error theory below.

Like *realism* before it, *inescapability* presupposes, but goes beyond *error* in the conditions it imposes for moral objectivity. Consider, once more, the stipulated application conditions for "blip." True, once I explain to someone what these criteria are, he must agree that claims that something or other is a blip are linguistically correct just in case I convince you to despise it on a Tuesday, and that no blip is to be despised on a Wednesday. This does not, however, mean that he must regard these claims as inescapable. He could refuse without mistake to apply the term "blip" at all. He could reasonably remain uninterested in what I manage to convince you to despise on a Tuesday, or indeed on any other day. Indeed, he could reasonably regard our entire practice of blip-talk as ridiculous, stupid, or even wrong. Not so for a wide range of moral claims, for which *inescapability* has sometimes been considered a central part of their objective aspirations. For this reason, *inescapability* has sometimes been considered a sufficient condition for moral objectivity, even if it does not satisfy all the criteria associated with objectivity in areas of thought that have a less intimate relationship to reasons for action and the will.

As we have already seen, any plausible account of morality should be consistent with the idea that moral claims meet the conditions of *error.* In what follows I shall assume that both constructivism and the error theory meet this constraint. Beyond that, different theories differ on which mark of objectivity is considered as more basic to moral claims. As we shall see, the comparative plausibility of different forms of constructivism and the error theory are intimately bound up with this question. In discussing different answers to it, I make two simplifying assumptions. First, I assume that all theories conflicting with constructivism and the error theory are untrue. Thus, I shall not address the question whether or not moral claims really express robustly cognitive states for which the question of correctness or truth can arise (cf. Blackburn 1998, Chrisman [this volume]). I simply assume that they do. Nor shall I seriously discuss, except in passing, the hypothesis that moral truth is best understood in terms of the correspondence of moral claims with a mind independent moral reality (cf. Shafer-Landau 2003, Cuneo [this volume]). I shall mostly assume that they do not. Nothing of what I say below should be thought to depend on the truth of these assumptions, which I make only for the purpose of exposition.

The Moral Error Theory

The idea that moral thought embodies an error has a distinguished history (cf. Broad 1951, Russell 1999, Pigden 2010 for some historical precedents). The most influential statement of the error theory in recent years is due to J. L. Mackie, who sums it up as follows:

> [T]he traditional moral concepts of the ordinary man as well as of the main line of western philosophers are concepts of objective value . . . The claim to objectivity, however ingrained in our language and thought, is not self-validating. It can and should be questioned. But the denial of objective values will have to be put forward . . . as an "error theory," a theory that although most people in making moral judgements implicitly claim . . . to be pointing to something objectively prescriptive, these claims are all false. (Mackie 1977, 35; cf. 48–9)

Thus understood, the error theory is made up of two theses. First, it is a deep fact about moral claims that they aspire to a special kind of objectivity. Second, this aspiration to objectivity is universally mistaken.

In what does the objectivity aspired to by moral claims consist? Mackie's notion of objective prescriptivity can be interpreted in different ways. On a strong reading, objective prescriptivity entails both *realism* and *inescapability*. On this view, moral claims aspire to represent a mind independent moral reality of inescapably reason-giving facts and properties. This strong reading can be denied in at least two ways while maintaining the error theory in some form.

First, objective prescriptivity might be taken to entail *realism* but not *inescapability*. When focused on this combination of commitments the error theory is targeted at certain versions of moral realism, according to which the objectivity of moral claims consists in their sometimes truly representing mind independent moral facts. Mackie seems to deny that there are such facts. Yet his notion of objective prescriptivity goes beyond that to include the idea of a "categorically imperative element" that applies to agents regardless of their desires and the contingent institutions in which they participate (Mackie 1977, 29ff). Thus, at least for Mackie, *inescapability* is an essential feature of the objective prescriptivity to which moral claims aspire.

Second, objective prescriptivity might be taken to entail *inescapability* but not *realism*. Thus understood, the error theory is partly targeted at some versions of Kantian ethics, according to which the objectivity of moral claims differs from other claims by aspiring to objectivity without *realism*. Mackie seems to deny that moral claims are objectively prescriptive in the Kantian sense. Yet his notion of objective prescriptivity goes beyond *inescapability* to include the idea that "if there were objective values, then they would be entities or qualities of a very strange sort, utterly different from anything else in the universe" (Mackie 1977, 38). Thus, at least for Mackie, *realism* is an essential part of the objective prescriptivity to which moral claims aspire.

Why does the error theorist think that moral claims fail to live up to their objective aspirations? There are at least two routes to this conclusion, each corresponding to an attack on *realism* and *inescapability* respectively. First, error theorists often claim that there is no place for mind independent moral facts in our best explanation of morality as a natural phenomenon. This claim plays a crucial role in Mackie's *argument for relativity*, for example, according to which moral disagreement is best explained in nonmoral terms, by supposing that moral belief is a natural function of our contingent human nature and historical circumstances (Mackie 1977, 37). There are at least two ways of taking this claim, one weaker and one stronger. According to the weaker claim, there is no *need* to postulate objective moral values in order to explain why we make the moral claims we do. According to the stronger claim, the very idea of objective value *offends* against both our best theory of the universe, and our best theory of how the universe is known. Both of these claims play a crucial role in Mackie's *argument from queerness*, according to which we have no coherent conception of mind independent objective values that are somehow able to exercise a necessary "pull" on our contingent rational motivations (Mackie 1977, 40).[4] Variations of these arguments have been defended by a number of error theorists in recent years (cf. Garner 1994, Ruse 1995, Joyce 2001).

Second, Mackie argues that the idea of a valid "categorical" and institution-transcendent moral imperative is a fiction. Some moral claims are valid "hypothetically," in virtue to appealing to a preexisting end that their observance would promote. Thus, it might be true that I ought to eat in order to avoid starvation. Other moral claims are valid "categorically," in virtue of being constitutive rules of some kind of contingent human institution. Thus, it might be true that one ought never to drive on a red light (or that no blip should be despised on a Wednesday). Yet no moral claim is valid "categorically" in the sense of being valid and binding on all rational agents, regardless of their ends and institutional or other affiliations. In this debate, the error theorist sides with a long tradition going back at least to Hume, and against a tradition going back at least to Kant (cf. Kant 1981, Hume 1999). In effect, the error theorist is saying that the Kantians are right about the objective aspirations of moral thought but the Humeans are right about the underlying reality. Variations of this argument have also been defended by a number of error theorists in recent years (cf. Joyce 2001, Phillips 2010).

In exactly what sense does the error theorist think that moral claims fail in their objective aspirations? According to Mackie, moral claims are systematically false. A somewhat weaker position is to hold they are not true, but indeterminate or lacking in truth-value. A much stronger position is that they are somehow incoherent. The fine detail need not detain us here (cf. Joyce and Kirchin 2010). We must, however, note that a moral error theorist could admit that ordinary moral claims, however illusory, can at least exhibit the mark of *error*. Thus, a claim can be indeterminate or false without being utterly meaningless. (It might be questioned whether a claim could be genuinely meaningful if it is actually incoherent. I shall not pursue this question further here.) It follows that if there is a metaphysically minimal sense of "true" and "false" that entails nothing more than the existence of recognizable application conditions for moral terms, the error theory is consistent with the idea that some moral claims are "minimally" true. This fact is of more than local significance. There is an influential line of thought in contemporary philosophy of language to the effect that there is nothing more to the idea of truth in any area of thought than what follows from the existence of recognizable application conditions for the terms embodied in that area of thought (cf. Wright 1992, Blackburn 1998). To claim that "P" is true, for example, is not really anything more (subject to minor qualifications) than to claim that P. The predicate "is true" is really a linguistic device for adding emphasis or approval. It does not pick out a property that some claims have and others not, in virtue of their correspondence with nonlinguistic reality. It is natural to think that the truth of the error theory conflicts with this "minimalist" program in the philosophy of language (cf. Wright 1992). Yet this is not obvious. It would take us too far afield to pursue this issue further here (cf. Blackburn 1998, Chrisman [this volume]).

If morality is an illusion, then how did we end up in the grip of it? Although different error theorists have offered different explanations of this otherwise puzzling fact, most of their attempts to diagnose the causes of error are variations on the same theme (cf. Lillehammer 2003). In effect, error theorists claim that the emergence and persistence of our dispositions to make moral claims is explained by the way in which these dispositions have played a variety of coordinating functions during some part of human development or history. Some error theorists have focused primarily on the evolutionary function of moral claims (cf. Ruse 1995). Others have focused more on their historical function (cf. Pigden 2010). Some have focused primarily on the social aspects of coordination (cf. Mackie 1977). Others have focused on the psychological aspects (cf. Joyce 2001). These differences need not concern us here. The basic idea in each case is that certain deep-seated illusions can have staying power if they help enough of us to get along.

What implications does the error theory have for our treatment of moral claims once the mistake embodied in moral thought has been exposed? In fact, there are various options, each of which has had serious defenders among contemporary error theorists. The first option is abolitionism (cf. Garner 1994). According to this view, the correct response to the error theory is to give up making moral claims altogether. The most natural way of understanding abolitionism is as proposing the removal of distinctively moral terms (such as "duty" and "right," etc.) from our vocabulary, and to engage in practical reasoning using only terms that are free from error. Abolitionists are keen to stress that this does not mean giving up on the various ends that moral claims have traditionally served to promote. The abolitionist can continue to care about the fate of his loved ones, or work to promote equality of opportunity or the prevention of climate change. Yet in doing so, he would no longer be describing these issues in substantially moral terms, instead having to present them in some otherwise favorable light, such as serving the collective or individual interests of his interlocutors.

What abolitionism gains by way of purity it loses by way of flexibility. After all, if making untrue claims has stood us in good stead in the past, an abolitionist policy might seem like throwing out the baby with the bathwater. This is the view taken by the moral fictionalist. According to the fictionalist, moral claims can earn their place in our conceptual repertory as a form of practically useful but literally false fiction, or make-believe. There are currently two different versions of this view defended in the literature. According to the revisionist view, we should somehow *adopt* morality as a useful fiction, having discovered that it is an illusion (cf. Joyce 2001). According to the protectionist view, philosophical analysis reveals that morality has played the role of a useful fiction all along (cf. Kalderon 2005; Mackie 1977, 239). The extent to which we should want to go in for morality on either of these terms once the error has been pointed out would presumably depend on the extent to which doing so would conflict with values we hold dear, including the advantages of coordination and our overall commitment to truth, truthfulness, transparency, and so on (cf. Williams 2002). It is a complex empirical question what the practical consequences of a widespread belief in the error theory would be. It would be very optimistic to think the answer would be universally welcome in all historical circumstances. What fictionalism gains by way of flexibility, it may lose by way of wishful thinking.

Revisionary moralism is a third error theoretic option. The revisionary strategy is to reinterpret moral claims so as to avoid any problematically objective aspirations, instead assigning them truth conditions that are compatible with whatever kind of objectivity to which we think they can truly aspire. In this way, much of our existing moral vocabulary could be retained, along with its core pragmatic connotations. So long as enough is preserved to make the result broadly coextensive with the linguistic practice with which we started, there need be no impropriety in describing the result as "morality," or the claims made within it as "moral" (cf. Lewis 2000). Some of Mackie's remarks about the consequences of accepting the error theory might be read as laying the groundwork for a revisionary view along these lines. Thus, Mackie writes:

> [C]ongenial to philosophers . . . would be the attempt systematically to describe our own moral consciousness or some part of it, such as our "sense of justice," to find some set of principles which were themselves fairly acceptable to us and with which, along with their practical consequences and applications, our "intuitive" (but really subjective) detailed moral judgements would be in "reflective equilibrium" . . . This is a legitimate kind of inquiry, but it must not be confused with the superficially similar but in purpose fundamentally different attempt . . . to advance by way of our various "intuitions" to an objective moral truth, a science of conduct. (Mackie 1977, 105)

This claim is revealing in a number of ways. First, it suggests that it is possible to avoid confusion between the (allegedly possible) task of improving our moral commitments and the (allegedly impossible) task of intuiting a domain of objective moral truths. Second, it suggests that it is possible to carry out this "legitimate kind of inquiry" by continuing to use a range of recognizably moral terms, such as "justice," and the like (cf. Mackie 1977, 106–7). This is arguably just what the revisionary moralist calls for. If these are genuine possibilities, the error theoretic path may be open to flexibility without wishful thinking.

At this point, it may be asked whether moral claims really are inextricably committed to a problematic kind of objectivity. Could it instead be that such commitments are contingent features of how moral thought has been conceived of in specific historical circumstances? On the one hand, some error theorists have argued that there are problematic aspirations to objectivity built into the very nature of the moral sensibility we have inherited from our evolutionary ancestors (cf. Ruse 1995, Joyce 2006). On the other hand, philosophers who otherwise share a naturalistic worldview of the kind that most error theorists accept have argued that at least some of the aspirations attributed to moral thought by the error theory are features of a contingent and optional understanding of morality ("the morality system") that belongs to a historically specific worldview such as that which we owe to the great religions and Enlightenment philosophy (Williams 1985; cf. MacIntyre 1984). If this is right, what exactly does it mean to say that moral claims have an erroneous claim to objective prescriptivity "built into them"? Perhaps the objective commitments of moral thought are instead a matter for us to work out in the course of reflecting on morality and its place in the natural and social world? These are troublesome questions to which no conclusive answer can be given here (cf. Kirchin 2010).

Different objections to the error theory take a more or less compromising stance with respect to what moral objectivity consists in. There are at least two ways of rejecting the error theory while accepting *both* that moral thought has genuinely objective aspirations *and* that there are some paradigmatic forms of objectivity to which it cannot truly aspire. The first is taken by moral realists who agree with Mackie that morality is not inescapable, but insist that some moral claims do succeed in truly representing mind independent moral facts (cf. Brink 1989). On this view, it is a mistake to think that moral facts are radically different in kind from the facts postulated by the natural and social sciences. On one way of taking this proposal, to talk about moral rightness and goodness is to talk about what it is for a certain kind of being to live well and in accordance with its nature. Thus, when we talk about what is morally good or bad, for example, we are employing concepts the correct use of which is causally regulated by facts about what does, and does not, benefit human and relevantly similar beings. By analogy, when we talk about what is good or bad for a bird or a tree, for example, we are employing concepts the correct use of which is causally regulated by facts about what does, or does not, benefit a bird or a tree. On this view, the object of morality is to preserve and promote human and other sentient flourishing, a task about which there is nothing illusory as such (cf. Bloomfield 2001). Furthermore, on some versions of this view it is a separate question whether it is always most rational for someone to be interested in their own or anybody else's flourishing (cf. Brink 1989).

One error theoretic reply to this response is to complain that the objectivity it offers is merely a reductionist shadow of the real thing. This reply, however, might be too quick. A common corollary of this form of moral realism is that the reduction of moral facts to natural facts is metaphysical, not conceptual, and therefore knowable only a posteriori. It need therefore be no more difficult in principle to explain our initial sense that something is missing in the naturalist analysis than it is to explain the surprise of someone who discovers for the first time that water is a compound of hydrogen and oxygen (cf. Brink 1989). The issue is controversial (cf. Blackburn 1998).

A second response to the error theory is taken by those who claim that morality is inescapable, but that what moral judgments aspire to, and also succeed in representing, is a mind independent reality of moral facts that are fixed by how moral agents would respond to the world in different circumstances (cf. Wiggins 1988). According to such "response dependent" accounts of morality, the fact that the truth conditions of moral claims are mind dependent does not mean that there are no facts about what is right and wrong, any more than the fact that the truth conditions of claims about the colors are mind dependent means that there are no facts about whether something is red (cf. McDowell 1985).

One error theoretic reply to this view is to admit the possibility of mind dependent truths that are fixed by how subjects would respond to the world in different circumstances (cf. Mackie 1980). The problem is that this idea does not capture the aspirations of moral claims to be truly inescapable. This response is also too quick. The hypothesis that moral truths are mind dependent does not entail that they are therefore anthropocentric or otherwise problematically relative. A moral truth could be mind dependent but also binding on all rational agents. Thus, on one influential version of this view, moral truths are a function of the desires that morally competent agents would converge on in conditions of full rationality, including the desires they would have for the desires of their actual selves (cf. Smith 1994). If there is nothing more to moral truth than what agents would desire in such circumstances, then the rational inescapability of moral truths is guaranteed for anyone who qualifies as a morally competent agent.

One obvious problem with this view has not escaped its proponents (cf. Smith 2010). An a priori, or conceptual, commitment to convergence among all morally competent agents does not entail that such convergence would actually be forthcoming. Furthermore, attempts to describe the constraints on full rationality in terms guaranteed to result in the kind of moral claims to which we are reflectively committed have inevitably been subject to suspicion of vicious circularity (cf. Blackburn 1998, Shafer-Landau 2003). One possible response is to index rational inescapability to contingent facts about our natural sensibility, our ethical upbringing, or our participation in a moral form of life (cf. McDowell 1985). That this approach carries with it an air of relativism has not escaped either its proponents or its critics (cf. McDowell 1998, Lillehammer 2007).

A third response to the error theory has been defended by moral realists who think that moral claims can truly aspire to both *realism* and *inescapability*. One popular way of developing this response is by means of a so-called companions in guilt strategy (cf. Lillehammer 2007). To take one example, it has recently been argued that the objective prescriptivity of moral facts (or facts about moral reasons) is neither more nor less mysterious than the objective prescriptivity of other normative facts, such as epistemic facts (or facts about epistemic reasons). Moral error theorists have not traditionally defended an error theory about epistemic claims. Nor is it clear how they could while also claiming that there are good reasons to believe the moral error theory. If so, the moral error theorist is faced with a dilemma: either claim that there are no epistemic reasons to believe anything, or give up the moral error theory (cf. Cuneo 2007). The crucial question is whether moral and epistemic claims are sufficiently similar for this argument to succeed. Unsurprisingly, there is evidence pointing in both directions.

One the one hand, epistemic reasons are often thought of as reasons relating to which of our beliefs of a given kind, K, make a positive contribution to having true beliefs of kind K. Moral reasons, on the other hand, are one possible instance of K. Thus, we have beliefs not only about morality, but also about mathematics, physics, chemistry, biology, history, psychology, and aesthetics. Each of these domains is a possible instance of K with respect to which we may want to ask the same questions about our epistemic standing. This might be thought to constitute an important structural difference between the ontological classification of epistemic reasons and moral reasons. If an error theory is true for K-facts and there are no (positive) truths about Ks, it is still consistent to suppose we have more reason to believe some K-claims than others, given our available evidence. Thus, you might have more reason to believe that the sun rises in the morning than that it rises in the evening even if it turns out that, on the true theory of the universe, it does neither. By analogy, you might have more reason to believe it is wrong to hit people than that it is not even if it turns out that, on the true theory of morality, it is neither. If so, there can be epistemic facts and epistemic reasons even if there are no moral facts and no moral reasons. To think otherwise would be to make a kind of "category mistake."

On the other hand, it is questionable whether claims about moral and epistemic reasons can be as easily disentangled as this objection assumes (cf. Putnam 2002, Cuneo 2007). On the one hand, some claims about what we have reason to believe might be thought to imply moral or other evaluative claims about how we ought to be. Thus, the virtues of truthfulness and transparency are arguably as moral as they are epistemic. Nor is it obvious that what it is morally right for me to do is entirely independent of what I have good reasons to believe (cf. Jackson 1991). Consider a case where if you throw a cricket ball it will hit me in the throat but all the evidence points the other way. Once more, the issue is controversial. Similar controversies affect other versions of the "companions in guilt" strategy (cf. Lillehammer 2007).

Moral Constructivism

A fourth response to the error theory is to accept the claim that morality is a construction, but not to assert that moral claims are thereby committed to error. This is the view of the moral constructivist.

There is no simple formulation of moral constructivism that easily captures all the views that may be thought to deserve that name. Nevertheless, most forms of constructivism are committed to the following two theses. First, some moral claims are true; or if not robustly true, then objectively valid (I shall drop this qualification from now on). Second, the truth of moral claims is a function of what is either constitutive of, or what can be constructed in, moral reasoning or argument. Thus, insofar as it is acceptable to talk about moral facts or properties, these are facts or properties we, or some idealized version of us, have an essential role in constituting or creating.

Thus understood, constructivism is consistent with the possibility that moral objectivity goes no further than *error*. It therefore does not entail *inescapability*, even though a commitment to *inescapability* has been central to the historically most influential versions of this view (cf. Kant 1981). Thus understood, constructivism is, however, not consistent with *realism*, even if a constructivist could be neutral with respect to whether a commitment to *realism* is embodied in some, or all, ordinary moral claims. I return to the significance of this fact below.[5]

Moral constructivism shares with the response dependent accounts of moral objectivity discussed in the previous section a refusal to accept that moral truths are mind independent. It also shares with such accounts their possible neutrality with respect to the thesis that in order for moral truths to exist they would have to play an indispensable part in the best scientific explanation of our moral beliefs. We have already seen how the absence of moral truths in such explanations plays an important role in Mackie's arguments from *queerness* and *relativity*. A moral constructivist can accept this premise of these error theoretic arguments (cf. Lillehammer 2003, Street 2006). According to the constructivist, what earns moral claims their objective status need not be their *indispensability* in scientific *explanation*. It could also be their *inescapability*, or some otherwise privileged status assigned to them, in moral *deliberation*. It is primarily because we need to make moral claims to think about what to do or be that we have reasons to believe that morality is objective.[6]

There are at least two ways of understanding morality in constructivist terms. Both are deeply rooted in Kant's ethics (cf. Kant 1981), although in most contemporary formulations they are defended independently of Kant's critical philosophy (cf. O'Neill 1988, Ebels-Duggan [this volume], Gert [this volume]).

The first option is to think of moral truths as implicit in our practical reasoning. I shall refer to this view as rationalist constructivism. On this view, the existence of moral truths can be inferred from our decisions to act, at least insofar as we are dealing with genuine decisions to do something for a reason. A constructivist approach along these lines has recently been defended by Christine Korsgaard, who writes:

> [R]espect for humanity is a necessary condition of effective action. It enables you to legislate a law under which you can be genuinely unified, and it is

> only to the extent that you are genuinely unified that your movements can be attributable to you, rather than to forces working in you or on you, and so can be actions. So the moral law is the law of the unified constitution, the law of the person who really can be said to legislate for himself because he is the person who really has a self. It is the law of successful self-constitution. (Korsgaard 2009, 206; cf. Korsgaard 1996)

Korsgaard claims that in order to act for a reason you must bring your action under some generalization, or law. She thinks that this law must be such as to bring the action under a unified conception of yourself as a persisting agent with a distinctive "practical identity" (Korsgaard 2009, 207–12). Formulating a unified conception of oneself can be done only on the basis of reasons that can be universally shared, because "calling a reason 'mine' is just a claim about position. Unless reasons are public, they cannot do their job" (Korsgaard 2009, 206). Appealing to such public reasons commits you to regard those reasons as giving rise to rational constraints on your agency even as they apply to the self-constituting projects of other agents. Effective action therefore commits you to value humanity both in yourself and in others. It follows that some moral claims are rationally inescapable, and therefore objective, in virtue of the fact that they are presupposed by every reasoned attempt to exercise one's agency. The moral claims in question apply merely on the assumption that there are beings who act by exercising their rational capacities. It is in this sense, and not in the sense of denying the genuine "reality" of ethical demands, that morality is said to be a construction (cf. Korsgaard 1996). Similar forms of rationalist constructivism have been defended in recent years by other philosophers with Kantian sympathies (cf. Gewirth 1978, Ebels-Duggan [this volume]).

There are at least four general objections to the rationalist program in ethics (cf. Williams 1985, Blackburn 1998, Enoch 2006). First, it is controversial to what extent, if any, effective rational agency requires a law-like commitment to construct a practical identity that merits the label "a unitary self." True, we are creatures who make plans. Yet the extent to which we are committed to integrate these plans into a unified or coherent story is a contingent matter, and not a necessary presupposition of rational agency as such. Maybe it is a good idea to develop a unified practical identity. But we should be careful about constructing a theory of what agency consists in from a theory of how we think it ought to be exercised. Second, it is controversial to what extent the claim that reasons be universally shared requires us to value humanity in others as well as in ourselves. Perhaps it is true that in order to value my projects I must value my capacity to have projects. Yet as Sidgwick pointed out, it does not follow that I must also value your capacity to have projects, even if I must obviously agree that you have an equally good reason to value either your projects, your capacity to have them, or both (cf. Sidgwick 1907). Third, it is not obvious that in order to value my projects I must value my capacity to have projects. If my end is to no longer have any projects then my valuing of this capacity could seriously get in the way. Thus, not everything presupposed by what is valuable need itself be considered valuable (compare getting rid of a bad hangover). Finally, if I agree to value humanity in others as well as in myself, this tells me very little about what to do, given the vast range of possible practical identities. What these considerations show is that the rationalist program could struggle to meet one, if not two, of the basic desiderata of constructivist theories at the same time. On the one hand, it needs to deliver the conclusion that some moral claims are rationally inescapable. On the other hand, it needs to deliver a non-empty set of substantial and determinate moral claims. The rationalist program threatens to deliver the former only by failing to deliver the latter. Variations on this point have been made by critics of the rationalist program ever since Kant's defense of the view in the eighteenth century (cf. Hegel 1991).

Another way of understanding morality as a construction is to interpret the notion of construction procedurally. Perhaps the most influential formulation of this view in recent years is due to John Rawls, who labels it "Kantian Constructivism" (I will use the label "Procedural Constructivism" in order to distinguish this view from its equally Kantian rationalist cousin (cf. Rawls 1999, Rawls 2000)). Rawls writes:

> Kantian constructivism holds that moral objectivity is to be understood in terms of a suitably constructed point of view that all can accept. Apart from the procedure of constructing the principles of justice, there are no moral facts. Whether certain facts are to be recognized as reasons of right and justice, or how much they are to count, can be ascertained only from within the constructive procedure, that is, from the undertakings of rational agents of construction when suitably represented as free and equal moral persons. (Rawls 1999, 307)

On this version of constructivism, moral facts are defined as the function of a procedure of practical reasoning that presupposes a set of constraints on what counts as legitimate inputs, such as an agreed conception of "free and equal moral persons." The success conditions of this procedure consist in moral claims meeting with universal agreement among reasonable persons. When suitably combined, these features entail a substantial conception of moral objectivity, according to which relevant conclusions are inescapable for all parties as specified in the relevant construction. Analogous versions of procedural constructivism have been defended in recent years by other philosophers influenced by this development of Kant's ideas (cf. Scanlon 1982, Habermas 1996; Street 2008).

Procedural constructivism has a number of attractions compared to its rationalist rival. First, it is indefinitely flexible with respect to the inputs to, and constraints on, procedures of moral construction. A procedural constructivist can frame the procedure by presupposing a set of values regarded as constitutive of agency; intuitively self-evident; reflectively indefeasible; universally accepted; or assumed for the sake of argument, including the values of sentience; individual autonomy; respect for life; or an interest in working out principles with others on terms that nobody so minded could reasonably reject (cf. Scanlon 1998). None of these starting points are incompatible with a fundamentally constructivist outlook. To think otherwise would be to confuse a belief that some claims are fundamental with a belief that those claims are mind independently true.

Likewise, the procedural constructivist can constrain the procedure itself more or less narrowly, by employing principles of formal or instrumental rationality; mutually disinterested utility promotion behind a "veil of ignorance"; transparent and reasoned discussion among persons regarded as "free and equal"; or pursuit of (narrow or wide) reflective equilibrium (cf. Street 2008). Finally, the procedural program is indefinitely flexible with respect to the target truths it aims to construct. Thus, we might construct a specific conception of justice, such as one embodied in some specific society at a given time, leaving a number of other moral or political claims unconstructed (cf. Rawls 1999). Alternatively, we might construct a conception of morality in the "narrow" sense of the obligations owed by one person to another, leaving "wider" conceptions of the moral, such as what is and is not good or reasonable, unconstructed (cf. Scanlon 1998). Or we might construct a conception of what it is for someone to have a reason for action, leaving the relationship of practical reasons thus understood to other conceptions of reason, value, or rationality unconstructed (cf. Street 2008). In each case, the interest of the resulting construction is a function of how strong (or initially controversial) conclusions can be established from how weak (or initially innocuous) premises, by means of a given (and itself potentially constructible) procedure of construction. In this way, different structures of procedural construction can function as heuristic devices by means of which we aim to clarify the rational foundations of a given range of moral or political claims by asking what (and how little) we would have to buy into in order to be committed to them on our own terms. In part because of this inherent flexibility, the procedural program has been thought to speak directly to the practical needs of historically embedded agents who need ways to argue things through with each other in order to live peacefully in conditions of justice (cf. Habermas 1996, Rawls 1999).

Another attraction of the procedural program is its comparative flexibility with respect to the issue of objectivity. Thus, some procedural constructions carry no implications for objectivity beyond *error*. Recall our definition of "blip" in the first section of this chapter. According to this definition, something is a blip if I convince you to despise it on a Tuesday, and no blip is to be despised on a Wednesday. Thus understood, *blipness* is a construction (although the entities falling within the extension of *blipness* need not be). Furthermore, it is a procedural construction (*blipness* being the function of some unspecified process of conviction). Yet blip claims are not in any interesting sense inescapable. There need be nothing wrong with you if you decide that all this talk of blips is just a silly game. Some results of procedural construction are therefore objective neither in the sense of *realism* or *inescapability*. That does not exclude them from being genuine constructions.

Some moral claims, however, are widely thought to aspire to a much less escapable form of objectivity. Any interesting version of procedural constructivism would therefore have to show that moral claims are inescapable in a way that goes beyond *error*. The extent to which this is possible is a function of how much moral content can be generated from how slender a base of initial assumptions and procedural constraints. This is a matter on which there is widespread disagreement. In one sense, however, this need not disturb the procedural constructivist, who could maintain that *inescapability* comes in degrees and may vary from one set of claims to another.[7] Thus, it could be that some basic claims about the moral significance of pleasurable experience, needs, or basic well being, for example, are more strongly inescapable than other claims about "the best life" or the right account of social justice (cf. Wong 2006). In some cases of deep moral conflict, the hope of producing a convincing construction may be slight or even nonexistent. In this case, the procedural constructivist is left with two options. First, he may simply stop and conclude that the attempt to find a rational basis for the moral claims at issue has reached philosophical bedrock. Not every conceivable claim can be derived from a set of more basic premises. Second, he may continue the task of construction, if not by pushing deeper, then by approaching it from a different angle. No doubt, in some cases working towards a construction of a set of disputed claims is paramount to pursuing an unattainable ideal of universal rational agreement. This does not mean it is therefore unreasonable. Aiming at an ideal can be reasonable even in the knowledge that it is unattainable. Some improvements are genuine achievements.

There are at least two ways of interpreting the procedural constructivist program. One is as a description of what ordinary people do when they engage in moral thought. This is an implausible hypothesis, for at least two reasons. First, this is certainly not what most people *take* themselves to be doing when engaging in moral thought. Second, it is also implausible to attribute to all competent moral thought the kind of argumentative structure that would have to be implicit in our thinking if this descriptive hypothesis were correct. As often as not, moral thought is focused on the world around us, the facts of which seem salient as they are, and not in virtue of being derivable from basic premises by means of a process of reasoning. Nor should we assume that ordinary moral thought either would, or should, be transformed by the success of the constructivist program. The extent to which moral philosophy has practical implications for ordinary moral thought is a controversial issue (cf. Dworkin 1996). A more plausible way to think of the constructivist program is as a rational reconstruction of moral thought, by means of which we describe how claims that might otherwise seem ungrounded, controversial, or intractable can be given a comparatively firm and reasonable foundation, regardless of the actual way in which we normally happen to arrive at them.

Thus understood, the constructivist program is largely neutral with respect to the objective aspirations embodied in ordinary moral thought. Perhaps moral claims embody a philosophically problematic commitment to objectivity, or perhaps they do not. A more interesting question for the procedural constructivist is for which of these claims we can give a convincing rational reconstruction. On reflection, this program should be congenial even to the moral error theorist. We have already seen how Mackie, having dismissed the aspirations of moral thought as mistaken, goes on to consider which claims about mutual restraint and assistance can be rationalized by means of a suitable construction. One way to be a moral constructivist is therefore to agree that moral thought embodies erroneous objective aspirations, but then to focus on what to say next. Pure and modest in philosophical intent, this strategy would not, however, come without a cost. A consistent error theoretic constructivist would refuse to believe moral claims (and their negations) that fail to be a consequence of a suitable procedure of construction. Given the objective appearance of much contemporary moral thought, it is far from obvious that this class is empty. Thus, if we find ourselves in deep disagreement over some claim in practical ethics and we are unable to resolve the disagreement by tracing it back to a procedure of construction the credibility of which we can agree on, a consistent constructivist will be committed to judge the matter in question as indeterminate, whatever the pragmatic value of asserting or pretending otherwise.

Another solution is to take no view about the objective aspirations of ordinary moral thought. Thus understood, the constructivist program aims to produce a theoretical underpinning for a wide range of moral claims, whatever their objective credentials. Taking this option is compatible not only with the error theory, but also with the hypothesis that some moral claims exhibit both the marks of *realism* and *inescapability*. Just as an interest in procedural construction is consistent with the error theory, belief in moral realism is consistent with an interest in the heuristic or epistemological potential of procedural construction (cf. Lillehammer 2004). Indeed, an interest in procedural construction might be thought to play a central part in any plausible moral epistemology (cf. Brink 1989). Given the apparently interminable disagreement between moral realists and their opponents, this could be a suitable tribute for constructivists to pay to the neglected virtue of Pyrrhonic indifference (cf. Sinnott-Armstrong 2006).

There are at least four common objections to procedural constructivism. First, it might be objected that the procedural constructivist must implicitly assume what he is trying to explain (cf. Shafer-Landau 2003). Thus, in order to produce a reflectively acceptable construction that yields a range of recognizable moral truths the constructivist must already have independent knowledge of what these truths are. In response to this objection, the constructivist can argue that even though some prior moral beliefs will go into the procedure of construction, this does not entail that the status of these beliefs as knowledge must therefore be independent of the procedure of construction. To think otherwise is to assume that a constructivist account must be reductive, which it need not be.

In reply to this response, a second objection is that any plausible construction is likely to be "gerrymandered" and therefore explanatorily vacuous. Thus, if our confidence in the constraints on construction is no greater than our confidence in the conclusions we hope it will generate, then there is no real sense in which the construction can provide those claims with a rational foundation. This objection, however, would only be successful against versions of procedural constructivism on which the relationship of support between the constraints on construction and the conclusions they generate is intended to be wholly asymmetrical. A procedural constructivist could reject this view, holding that the relations of support between procedural constraints and the conclusions they generate are generally holistic and therefore a matter of explanatory coherence (cf. Rawls 1999, Street 2008).

Third, it has been objected that the nature of the reflective materials of procedural construction envisaged in response to the second objection entail that the upshots of procedural construction are bound to be unduly conservative (cf. Singer 1974). There are at least two possible responses to this objection. The first is that the idea of procedural construction itself does not impose any determinate limit on what goes into procedural construction. Indeed, a concern about undue conservatism can be one reason to choose one version of procedural constructivism over another. The second is that the accusation of undue conservatism may in effect presuppose the existence of independent reasons for thinking that moral truth extends beyond the domain of construction to a mind independent moral reality. To simply assume that this is so is to beg the question against procedural constructivism.

Fourth, it may be objected that procedural constructivism entails an implausible form of moral relativism (cf. Lillehammer 2004). After all, according to the procedural constructivist moral truth is truth within a system. If so, there are as many different moral truths as there are imaginable systems of procedural construction. So moral truth is indefinitely plural. But this claim is absurd, if not morally abhorrent. So procedural constructivism cannot be a satisfactory account of moral truth unless there are independent constraints on the choice of systems of construction. In which case we are back to the first objection that the procedural constructivist must already presuppose what he is trying to explain.

In response to this objection the procedural constructivist has at least two options. The first is to concede that moral truth is indefinitely plural but to point out that this does not imply that we have equally strong reasons to be interested in all imaginable systems of construction. The second is to claim that the criteria for counting something as a genuinely moral system are themselves a function of a reflectively robust procedure of construction, in which case his response is effectively a version of the response to the first objection.

Concluding Remarks

Many contemporary philosophers are sympathetic to the naturalistic worldview that motivates the error theory. Even so, they may be loath to endorse the error theory, not only because the objective aspirations of moral claims might be sufficiently in order as they are, but also because it is arguably negotiable what those aspirations are. By turning to constructivism we can avail ourselves of tools the error theorist needs to make use of anyway, while avoiding the controversial commitments that lend the error theory an initial air of plausibility. Whether in doing so we are best described as placing moral thought on a firm foundation or as changing the subject is a moot point. Is ordinary moral thought like a body of superstition, such as thought about witches apparently was at least until the Enlightenment? Or is it more like a jumbled body of hypotheses, of which some can be dropped on reflection, such as thought about gold is said to have been before the discovery that not everything that looks and feels like gold has the same chemical composition? In answering this question, we do well to be agnostic about whether there is a determinate fact of the matter, hidden within our linguistic competence, concerning which side of the contrast our moral concepts fall. At least sometimes when conceptual problems are settled, we are not only dealing with the question of which side has the true answer. Sometimes it is also a question of who is winning.

References

Ayer, A. J. (1946), *Language, Truth and Logic*, Second Edition. London: Victor Gollancz.

Blackburn, Simon. (1998), *Ruling Passions*. Oxford: Oxford University Press.
Bloomfield, P. (2001), *Moral Reality*. Oxford: Oxford University Press.
Bridges, Douglas. (2009), "Constructive Mathematics." *Stanford Encyclopedia of Philosophy*, http://plato.stanford.edu/entries/mathematics-constructive/. Accessed 31.05/2010.
Brink, D. O. (1989), *Moral Realism and the Foundations of Ethics*. Cambridge: Cambridge University Press.
Broad, C. D. (1951) "Hagerstrom's Account of Sense of Duty and Certain Allied Experiences." *Philosophy* 26, 99–113.
Chrisman, Matthew. (this volume), "Ethical Expressivism," in C. Miller (ed.), *The Continuum Companion to Ethics*.
Cuneo, Terence. (2007), *The Normative Web*. Oxford: Oxford University Press.
—. (this volume), "Moral Realism," in C. Miller (ed.), *The Continuum Companion to Ethics*.
Dworkin, Ronald. (1996). "Objectivity and Truth: You'd Better Believe It." *Philosophy and Public Affairs* 25, 87–139.
Ebels-Duggan, Kyla. (this volume), "Kantian Ethics," in *The Continuum Companion to Ethics*, C. Miller (ed.).
Enoch, David. (2006), "Agency, Schmagency: Why Normativity Won't Come From What Is Constitutive of Action." *The Philosophical Review* 115, 169–98.
—. (2007), "An Outline of an Argument for Robust Metanormative Realism," in R. Shafer-Landau (ed.), *Oxford Studies in Metaethics*, Vol. 2. Oxford: Oxford University Press, 21–50.
Iemhoff, Rosalie. (2008), "Intuitionism in the Philosophy of Mathematics," *Stanford Encyclopedia of Philosophy*, http://plato.stanford.edu/entries/intuitionism/ Accessed 31/05/2010.
Garner, Richard. (1994), *Beyond Morality*. Philadelphia: Temple University Press.
Gert, Joshua. (2007), "Normative Strength and the Balance of Reasons," *Philosophical Review* 116 (4), 533–62.
Gert, Joshua. (this volume), "Morality and Practical Reason," in C. Miller (ed.), *The Continuum Companion to Ethics*.
Gewirth, Alan. (1978), *Reason and Morality*. Chicago: Chicago University Press.
Habermas, Jurgen. (1996), "On The Cognitive Content of Morality." *Proceedings of the Aristotelian Society* 96, 335–58.
Harman, Gilbert. (1977), *The Nature of Morality*. Oxford: Oxford University Press.
Hegel, W. G. F. (1991), *Elements of the Philosophy of Right*, A. W. Wood (ed.). Cambridge: Cambridge University Press.
Hume, David. (1999), *An Inquiry Concerning Human Understanding*, T. L. Beauchamp (ed.). Oxford: Oxford University Press.
Jackson, Frank. (1991), "Decision-theoretic Consequentialism and the Nearest and Dearest Objection." *Ethics* 101, 461–82.
Joyce, Richard. (2001), *The Myth of Morality*. Cambridge: Cambridge University Press.
—. (2006), *The Evolution of Morality*. Cambridge MA: MIT Press.
Joyce, Richard and Kirchin, Simon. (2010), "Introduction," in R. Joyce and S. Kirchin (eds.), *A World Without Values: Essays on John Mackie's Moral Error Theory*. New York: Springer, ix–xxiv.

Kalderon, M. E. (2005), *Moral Fictionalism*. Oxford: Oxford University Press.
Kant, Immanuel. (1981), *Grounding for the Metaphysics of Morals*. Cambridge, MA: Hackett.
Kirchin, Simon. (2010), "A Tension in the Moral Error Theory," in R. Joyce and S. Kirchin (eds.), *A World Without Values: Essays on John Mackie's Moral Error Theory*. New York: Springer, 167–82.
Korsgaard, Christine M. (1996), *The Sources of Normativity*, O. O'Neill (ed.). Cambridge: Cambridge University Press.
—. (2009), *Self-Constitution: Agency, Identity and Integrity*. Oxford: Oxford University Press.
Lewis, D. (2000), "Dispositional Theories of Value," in his *Papers in Ethics and Social Philosophy*. Cambridge: Cambridge University Press, 68–94.
Lillehammer, Hallvard. (2003), "Debunking Morality: Evolutionary Naturalism and Moral Error Theory." *Biology and Philosophy* 18, 567–81.
—. (2004), "Moral Error Theory," *Proceedings of the Aristotelian Society* 104, 93–109.
—. (2007), *Companions in Guilt: Arguments for Ethical Objectivity*. New York: Palgrave Macmillan.
Mackie, J. L. (1977). *Ethics: Inventing Right and Wrong*. Harmondsworth: Penguin.
—. (1980), *Hume's Moral Theory*. London: Routledge Kegan Paul.
MacIntyre, Alistair. (1984), *After Virtue: A Study in Moral Theory*. London: Duckworth.
McDowell, John. (1985), "Values and Secondary Qualities," in T. Honderich (ed.), *Morality and Objectivity*. London: Routledge and Kegan Paul, 110–29.
McDowell, John. (1998), *Mind, Value & Reality*. Cambridge: Harvard University Press.
Miller, Christian. (2009), "The Conditions of Moral Realism." *Journal of Philosophical Research* 34, 123–55.
O'Neill, Onora. (1988), "Constructivisms in Ethics," *Proceedings of the Aristotelian Society* 89, 1–17.
Phillips, David. (2010). "Mackie on Practical Reason," in R. Joyce and S. Kirchin (eds.), *A World Without Values: Essays on John Mackie's Moral Error Theory*. New York: Springer, 87–100.
Pigden, Charles R. (2010), "Nihilism, Nietzsche and the Doppelganger Problem," in R. Joyce and S. Kirchin (eds.), *A World Without Values: Essays on John Mackie's Moral Error Theory*. New York: Springer, 17–34.
Putnam, Hilary. (2002), *The Collapse of the Fact/Value Dichotomy*. Cambridge MA: Harvard University Press.
Rawls, John. (1971), *A Theory of Justice*. Cambridge MA: Harvard University Press.
—. (1999), *Collected Papers*, S. Freeman (ed.), Cambridge MA: Harvard University Press.
—. (2000), *Lectures on the History of Moral Philosophy*. Cambridge MA: Harvard University Press.
Ruse, Michael. (1995), *Evolutionary Naturalism*. London: Routledge.
Russell, Bertrand. (1999), "Is There an Absolute Good?," in C. Pigden (ed.), *Russell on Ethics*. London: Routledge, 119–24.
Scanlon, T. M. (1982), "Contractualism and Utilitarianism," in A. Sen and B. Williams (eds.), *Utilitarianism and Beyond*. Cambridge: Cambridge University Press, 103–28.

—. (1998), *What We Owe to Each Other.* Cambridge MA: Harvard University Press.
Shafer-Landau, Russ. (2003), *Moral Realism: a Defense.* Oxford: Oxford University Press.
Sidgwick, Henry. (1907), *The Methods of Ethics* (seventh edn). London: Macmillan.
Singer, Peter. (1974), "Sidgwick and Reflective Equilibrium." *The Monist* 58, 490–517.
Sinnott-Armstrong, Walter. (2006), *Moral Skepticisms.* Oxford: Oxford University Press.
Smith, Michael. (1994), *The Moral Problem.* Oxford: Basil Blackwell.
—. (2010), "Beyond the Error Theory," in R. Joyce and S. Kirchin (eds.), *A World Without Values: Essays on John Mackie's Moral Error Theory.* New York: Springer, 119–39.
Street, Sharon. (2006), "A Darwinian Dilemma for Realist Theories of Value." *Philosophical Studies* 127, 109–66.
—. (2008), "Constructivism about Reasons." *Oxford Studies in Metaethics* Vol. 3, R. Shafer-Landau (ed.), 207–46.
Wiggins, David. (1988), "Truth, Invention and the Meaning of Life," in G. Sayre-McCord (ed.), *Essays on Moral Realism.* Ithaca: Cornell University Press, 127–65.
Williams, Bernard. (1985), *Ethics and the Limits of Philosophy.* London: Fontana.
—. (2002), *Truth and Truthfulness: An Essay in Genealogy.* Princeton: Princeton University Press.
Wong, David. (2006), *Natural Moralities.* Oxford: Oxford University Press.
Wright, C. (1992), *Truth and Objectivity.* Cambridge: Harvard University Press.

4 Morality and Practical Reason

Joshua Gert

The topic of this chapter is the relation of practical reason—also known as practical rationality—to morality. This topic has long been central to moral theory; the question "Why be moral?" is a perennial starting point for moral philosophy, and one strategy for answering it is to try to show that reason somehow requires moral behavior. Nevertheless, one cannot begin a useful discussion of the topic without first having some idea about what practical reason or rationality is. This chapter therefore begins, in the sections "Practical Reason" and "Practical Reason and Practical Reasons," by laying out some of the views one might take as to the nature of practical reason and reasons for action, and some of the issues that arise once one has decided on a general direction. Once this overview is complete, the next three sections examine some of the ways in which practical reason can be seen as related to morality.

Practical Reason

Historically, practical reason has often been treated as a human *mental faculty*.[1] Understood in this way, an investigation into the nature of practical reason is a psychological or metaphysical investigation, seeking to determine the nature of a certain module or mechanism that plays a distinctive role in the production of intentional human action. A central question here might be: How is it that we reason ourselves to decisions about what to do and act on those decisions? Another important question, when the dominant sense of "reason" is the sense in which it is a mental faculty, is: Can reason produce action on its own, without the help of contingent desires? David Hume famously answered this question in the negative.[2] Kant, on the other hand, answered it positively.[3]

Now, it might be slightly misleading to represent Hume as claiming that the flawless functioning of practical reason cannot, on its own, move us in any particular direction. This is because Hume can be interpreted as holding that the faculty of reason is exclusively concerned with the determination of truth and falsity. And he also holds that mere belief in the truth or falsity of a given proposition can do nothing to produce action, except in conjunction with some contingent desire. Because of this, it is possible to interpret Hume as denying the existence of a faculty of distinctively *practical* reason at all. That is, it is possible to interpret him as holding that there is only a faculty of *theoretical* reason: a faculty that determines what to believe, but not what to desire or to do.

Still, however one interprets Hume, it remains true that he denies that reason can favor any particular action on its own. But even if one agrees with Hume this far, it remains possible to hold that there is an interesting conceptual connection between the faculty of reason and what we ought to do. For example, some contemporary philosophers hold that there is a tight connection between our desires and intentions on the one hand, and our reasoning about what is good and bad, or right or wrong, on the other. Thomas Scanlon, for example, argues that a common and central kind of desire—one he calls "desire in the directed-attention sense"—either is partially constituted by the judgment that something is good, or is caused by such a judgment.[4] And Allan Gibbard has made similar claims about intentions: that they are partially constituted by judgments that the relevant action is best.[5] If one holds such a view, there will be a link between practical reason, understood as a psychological faculty, and the normative notions that are central to ethics. Nevertheless, the link here will not tell us how we ought to act. It will only tell us that there is typically a psychological connection between how we (perhaps falsely) *think we ought* to act, and how we *do* act. If one thinks of practical reason as a faculty, then nothing normative follows from the claim that a person's action was the result of the operation of that faculty—even the unimpeded operation of that faculty.[6]

Although no view of practical reason, thought of merely as a psychological faculty, by itself has normative implications, it is nevertheless a short step from thinking of practical reason as a human faculty, to thinking of practical reason as a set of principles for the *assessment* of that human faculty. That is, we human beings certainly do somehow take in information about the world, make decisions in light of that information, and act on those decisions. Particular instances of this process can be thought of as flawed. Indeed, it makes sense to think of human beings as systematically prone to certain mistakes in reasoning and action: discounting the future too steeply, for example, or thinking that revenge will bring us satisfaction, despite ample evidence that it almost never does. So even the best description of how we actually *do* make and act on decisions will not, by itself, tell us how we *ought* to.[7] For many moral philosophers, the topic of interest when practical reason is discussed is not any actual psychological faculty. Rather, it is the set of principles, sometimes called "principles of practical reason" or "principles of rationality."[8] In this sense, when a philosopher claims that reason requires a certain action, this should not be understood in the *causal* way in which we might take the claim that digestion requires the secretion of bile. Rather, it should be taken in a *normative* way: to mean that if a person acts in some *other* way, then either that person or her action, by that very fact, comes in for criticism in terms of rationality. In general, contemporary discussions of practical rationality take it to be comprised by a set of principles in this way.

If one thinks of rationality in terms of normative assessment in the above way, there is still a very important distinction to be made. First, one might assess an action in terms of principles that specify *the kind of action* we have sufficient reason to perform—the kind of action that our rational faculties are in some sense aiming at. Producing pleasure and avoiding pain, for example, might be thought to be relevant to such an assessment, and a sample principle (though a very implausible one) might be "Rational action is action that produces the greatest balance of pleasure over pain." But clearly the human rational capacity has some inherent limitations, and the agent's position in the world may provide other unavoidable limitations, so that failures to act in accord with such principles need not entail that there was anything that could be regarded as a flaw in the *process* that produced the action. Moreover, there could be a flaw in the processes that produce an action, and yet that action might, by chance, meet the first sort of criteria. So we need a distinction between assessments of *kinds of action,* independently of how they come to be performed—assessments in terms of what is often called "objective rationality"—and assessments that focus on the *mental processes* that lead to action— assessments in terms of what is often called "subjective rationality." There are many accounts of the relation between objective and subjective rationality.[9] Typically objective rationality is taken to be conceptually prior, and subjective rationality is understood in terms of it. In what follows, therefore, I will typically be concerned with objective rationality.

Within the group of philosophers who think of rationality as a set of principles, one very great division is that between those who think of the principles as purely formal ones, and those who think of the principles as substantive: as privileging some ends—such as pleasure, knowledge, or freedom—over others. That is, some philosophers think that it is not contrary to reason to have what most of us would call silly or misguided, or even insane and self-destructive, ends.[10] That is because they do not think the principles of practical reason are in the business of saying what *basic* ends are to be pursued.[11] The core principle of practical reason, on the most bare-bones version of this kind of formal view, is an *instrumental* principle, which directs us merely to take the means to the ends we happen to have, at the moment, in view, or to give up the end. Such a view is not very appealing, since it says nothing at all about other ends that one would take to be important, but that one does not currently have in view. As a result, those who favor formal accounts of practical reason almost always extend the bare-bones formal principle so that it also says something about how to balance the distinct ends one has, given that they cannot all be maximally satisfied and that one has limited resources with which to satisfy them.[12] Such an extension might be summarized in the principle that one should maximize the satisfaction of one's preferences. This view can be modified even further, to take into account the fact that our preferences are sometimes ill-considered, and change with additional reflection on what their satisfaction would actually be like. The resulting principle is the following: rationality requires one to maximize the satisfaction of one's considered preferences. This turns the merely instrumental principle into something like a principle of coherence.

Formal views of the sort just described can become very sophisticated, so that for a preference to count as a "considered preference," it would have to be such that it would survive a kind of reflection that no one ever actually goes through—or even *could* go through. In fact, such a view can make the rationality of one's action depend not on one's actual preferences—whether or not they would pass certain tests—but on preferences that one does not have, but *would* have, if one were—for example—to become fully informed and go through an intensive course of psychotherapy.[13] These modifications to the basic instrumental principle seem to be motivated by a desire for the extensional plausibility of the view. They ensure that it will be very rare for an agent to have a basic set of relevant preferences (which might be counterfactual preferences) such that, for example, it would count as rational for him to sacrifice his future career to satisfy a strong vengeful impulse against a boss who had behaved unjustly.[14] More generally, they seem to be designed to make sure that those actions that qualify as rational on the view will *also* be those actions that—intuitively speaking—make sense and are "worth it" if they involve some kind of sacrifice or harm to the agent.

If one thinks that it is a significant advantage of the more sophisticated versions of the formal or instrumental view, that they allow for a better overlap between rational action and action that "makes sense," then one may be persuaded to abandon the formal view altogether, and adopt a *substantive* view of rationality that more directly tries to capture this notion of making sense.[15] For example, on such a view, certain consequences of action might count as harms: death, pain, injury, loss of freedom, and so on. And other consequences might count as benefits. Rather than grounding rationality in considered preferences, one might instead ground it in these harms and benefits. This is the definitive difference between substantive and formal accounts of practical reason.

Two very simple substantive accounts of practical reason are the egoistic version and the impartial version.[16] The egoistic version holds that the only directly important consequences of action, as far as the rationality of that action are concerned, are those that will ultimately come to the agent as a result of the action. Of course, if the agent cares for some other person, it may be that harm to that person will count as or cause harm to the agent, and will therefore be indirectly important to the rationality of that agent's action. Similarly, if the agent hates some other person, harm to that person may cause or constitute a benefit to the agent. But at bottom, the egoistic version of the simple substantive view looks only to harms and benefits to the agent. Such a view seems to entail that much behavior that is generally regarded as immoral is nevertheless required by reason. In very sharp contrast to this view, the impartial version is in some sense inspired by the intuition that the pleasures and pains, lives and deaths, freedoms and injuries of different people cannot differ in their values *simply* because of the identity of the agent who happens to experience them. This intuition lends support to a view on which the rational action is the one that produces the best overall consequences for everyone affected. On such a view it would be irrational to spend extra cash on a night of entertainment if one could use that same money to produce greater benefits for other people. Since one typically could use the money in this more altruistic way it is probably also true on such a view that going to the movies is typically irrational.

Within the domain of substantive views of practical reason—egoistic, impartial, or some third sort—there is still a further choice to be made.[17] The definitive question of relevance to this choice is: Could there ever be a sufficient reason to act in an irrational way? If this questions strikes one as senseless, or if the answer strikes one as trivially "no," this may be because one takes the principles of practical rationality to be the principles that specify what reasons there are in the first place, and which reasons count as sufficient to justify action. Many philosophers hold this kind of a view, which we can describe as the view that practical reason is the *fundamental normative notion applicable to action*.[18] This means that, as a conceptual matter, there cannot be any possible justification for a violations of the principles of practical rationality: that if those principles require or prohibit a certain action, then that is the end of the road as far as argument goes. It is probably fair to say that the two dominant conceptions of practical reason at present—understanding it in the objective way—are the sophisticated formal view and a nonegoistic substantive view that takes rationality to be the fundamental normative notion.[19]

Practical Reason and Practical Reasons

Up to this point we have been discussing the notion of practical reason largely in terms of a set of principles. But it is also possible to approach the topic in a slightly different way: in terms of discrete considerations that count in favor of, or against, particular actions. These discrete considerations are called "reasons for" and "reasons against" the actions that are open to us. Examples plausibly include the following: the fact that the action will hurt or kill someone, the fact that the action will satisfy a desire of the agent, or the fact that the action will satisfy a desire that the agent would have under ideal conditions. As these three examples suggest, each of the accounts of practical rationality discussed in the section "Practical Reason" can be associated with a distinct account of practical reasons. Sometimes the account of rationality *yields* the associated account of reasons; sometimes the account of rationality *depends on* the associated account of reasons. As an example of the former, consider the sophisticated instrumental view of rationality that tells one to maximize the satisfaction of one's considered desires. Such a view naturally yields a view of reasons as the objects of those very desires. It also yields a view regarding the strength of such reasons: they are given by the strength of those considered desires.[20] On the other hand a view that equates rationality with what we have most substantive reason to do depends on an antecedent view of what reasons are. A surprising number of theorists hold that reasons are in this sense prior to rationality, but then explicitly refuse to offer any positive account of reasons. Scanlon is one such theorist, but so are Jonathan Dancy and Derek Parfit.[21] Other theorists have offered arguments supporting various different accounts of practical reasons.

Most accounts of practical reasons endorse a material conditional claim of roughly the following form:

> There is a reason for agent A to $\varphi \supset$ A would be motivated to some degree to φ if A were *ideal* in certain ways.[22]

This conditional forges a link between *normative* reasons and *motivating* reasons. That is, it forges a link between facts that count in favor of A's φ-ing and facts that could provide A with some motivation to do so. Many theorists wish to preserve a link of this kind, since they think it is essential to the idea of a normative reason that it is the kind of thing that a person could act on. Many theorists hold that the conditional is a consequence of the fact that a consideration counts as a reason for A to φ partly *because* A would be motivated to φ if A were idealized in certain ways. Such theorists are called "internalists." If internalism is correct, it is plausible that different agents will have different reasons for different actions, even when they find themselves in the same external circumstances: a selfish person, for example, might have no reason to help a stranger, while an altruistic person might have a reason. If one endorses the conditional because one understands reasons in this prior-motivation-dependent way, one is a Humean internalist.[23] One might also hold, however, that there are ways of reasoning that would yield certain motives quite regardless of one's motivational starting point. If one endorses the conditional because one understands reasons in this prior-motivation-independent way, one is a Kantian internalist.[24]

There are those who endorse the above conditional, but who do not count as internalists of any kind. These theorists would deny that a consideration counts as a reason *because* it would motivate an ideal agent. Rather, they hold that certain substantive considerations simply count as reasons, and they then say that an agent counts as ideal if that agent is appropriately motivated by reasons. For these theorists, the status of a consideration as a reason depends on something external to the agent, and for this reason they are called "externalists." The possibility of externalism shows that the above conditional can be easily fit into formal, instrumental accounts of practical reason, and also into substantive accounts.

Given that those who endorse both formal and substantive accounts of practical reason can also endorse the above conditional, it may seem that there is no room to deny it. But in fact it is possible. Those who deny it might be called "hyper-externalists." Hyper-externalists hold that certain kinds of reasons are rationally optional: that they provide justification for action, should one choose to act on them, but that they do not exert any kind of rational pressure on choice, and might fail to motivate even a rational agent. Such a view is not very common, but—as will be suggested later—it may offer the best prospects for an appealing account of the relation between practical reason and morality. Here is a way of making such a view a little clearer. Of any given reason, one can ask the following two questions:

(R) How much can this reason rationally require me to sacrifice?
(J) How much can this reason rationally justify me in sacrificing?

A moment's reflection should make it clear that these are not the same question, and that it is at least comprehensible that for some reasons the answer to (J) might be "Quite a lot," while the answer to (R) might be "Not very much." In fact, if we hold that altruistic reasons typically fit this kind of pattern—rationally justifying sacrifices quite a bit more significant than the sacrifices they might rationally require—then we can accommodate commonsense intuitions about the rationality of a much wider class of action than we can if we endorse any other of the views of rationality so far described. For example, we can count it as rational to act in ways that secure benefits for oneself, even if one could have secured greater benefits for other people by acting differently: that is because the prospect of securing those benefits for other people does not *require* much. In this way it becomes rational to go to the movies. But we can also count it as rational to make great sacrifices for the benefit of others, because the prospect of securing those benefits may be able to *justify* a great deal.

The view of practical reasons just described, on which any given reason may play two distinct roles in determining the rationality of an action—a justifying role and a requiring role—departs from all the other views described earlier in that it is a nonmaximizing view of rationality. That is, the other views of rational action entail that for an action to be rational it must maximize some measure, whether of desire-satisfaction, goodness, or something else. Making a distinction between the justifying and requiring roles, on the other hand, undermines this kind of talk.[25] A view that accepts the justifying/requiring distinction will hold that an action's being rational—that is, not irrational—is a matter either of there being no reasons that require one not to perform it, or of there being adequate *justification* for performing it, despite the existence of reasons that would otherwise have required one not to. But even if one has adequate justification—indeed even if one has *more than adequate* justification for making some sacrifice, one need not therefore make it; one is free to choose either way.[26] On a view of this sort, some reasons might serve *only* to justify action, and not to require anything at all. A plausible example might be a reason that involves giving pleasure to a stranger. If such purely justificatory reasons exist, they would support the hyper-externalist position, since even a rational agent might, on some occasions, fail to be motivated by them.

Morality and Instrumental Views of Practical Reason

Let us now turn to morality and its relation to practical reason. Among the various norms that apply to human action, the norms of morality are often regarded as uniquely important in some way. But philosophers have had a hard time explaining precisely what this importance amounts to. One popular way of expressing the unique status of moral norms has been to claim—following Kant—that morality is a source of *categorical* demands. And one popular way of trying to explain what *this* claim amounts to is to distinguish categorical demands, imperatives, or "oughts," from hypothetical ones. A hypothetical imperative is an ought-claim that is valid only on the hypothesis that the agent to whom it is addressed has some particular goal. A plausible example might be "You ought to get on the next train into the city," addressed to someone we take to have the aim of arriving in the city in time for a certain show. If we learn, after having made this claim, that the person no longer wants to see the show, the ought-claim is undermined. Categorical imperatives are not supposed to be goal-dependent in this way. And moral claims certainly seem to fit the bill; the claim that one ought to keep a certain promise cannot be undermined by the counter-claim that one has no goals that would be furthered by doing so. This difference between moral ought-claims and other kinds of ought-claims can seem to be essential—especially if one is antecedently disposed to think of moral norms as uniquely important.

Despite the initial attraction of the above account of the special status of morality, Philippa Foot's seminal paper "Morality as a System of Hypothetical Imperatives" has made it much harder to take categoricity as the defining feature of moral norms.[27] One of her initial points is that many other systems of norms—some of them relatively trivial—seem to be categorical in the same way. A recurrent example in Foot and in subsequent discussions of this issue concerns the rules of etiquette. One such rule might be that one should answer invitations in the third person if they are addressed in that way. A different example might be that one should not wear white after Labor Day.

What Foot's initial point serves to show is that it is easy to mistake a *grammatical* feature of moral imperatives for a *normative* feature. In the face of Foot's initial argument, another attempt to explain the special status of moral norms is to say that they are necessarily reason-giving: indeed that they provide such strong reasons that it is irrational to violate them.[28] Foot, however, thinks that the only source of reasons for a particular agent are the objective interests of that agent (avoiding pain and death, for example), and the subjective desires of that agent (for fame, perhaps, or for the affection of a particular person). Given this conception of reasons, it is certainly plausible that moral norms—at least those norms that commonsense morality sanctions as moral norms—cannot be guaranteed to supply all agents with reasons to follow them.

Foot's suggested solution to the problem of explaining how it is that immoral action is necessarily irrational is to reject the assumption behind the question. That is, Foot's suggestion is that morality may only provide reasons to people who have, as contingent goals, the kinds of things that moral behavior tends to promote: the welfare of other people, strong bonds of trust within a community, and so on. It is no surprise at all that many of us have these goals. Indeed, it is no surprise that for many of us, these goals are sufficiently important that they provide reasons of sufficient strength to justify the kinds of sacrifices that morality sometimes requires. But Foot thinks that for those who happen *not* to have these goals, there may be no reason at all to comply with a clear moral requirement.[29]

Whether or not one agrees with Foot's position, her paper serves to illuminate many important points about the relation between morality and practical reason. One point is that if one holds that an agent's reasons depend heavily on that agent's contingent desires—as Foot does, and as purely formal or instrumental accounts of practical reason do—then it will be extremely hard to show that all agents have reasons to act morally. That is a *theoretical* point. Another is that, as much as we must regret it, it is pretheoretically plausible that there are selfish and powerful people for whom immoral action is neither objectively nor subjectively irrational. Immoral action does not place them at risk of suffering harms, because of their power, and is not contrary to their desires either, since they do not care about other people. That is not a theoretical point, but a *datum* that Foot accepts, and that we ourselves may either want our theory to accommodate, or to explain away.

A point to which Foot does not draw attention, however, but which seems equally to be an implication of her view, is that for some people (call them "bad people") it would be straightforwardly *irrational*—both objectively and subjectively—to behave morally. This is an unfortunate *theoretical* consequence, and not merely an unfortunate fact about human beings that we must regret. At least, that is true if one is thinking of rationality as providing the *fundamental* norms for behavior, since in that case one cannot sincerely recommend morally correct behavior to such a person; one must say—if one is to speak truly about the matter—that the bad person fundamentally ought *not* act in the morally acceptable way. One can avoid this consequence by saying that there are sometimes reasons that are sufficient to justify acting irrationally. This, of course, severs the connection between rationality and reasons—something that Foot herself is presumably reluctant to do. But other philosophers have been less reluctant.[30]

There are a number of ways of trying to respond to Foot's arguments while still holding that an action is required by the principles of rationality if and only if it is uniquely favored by the relevant reasons. One of them is to deny Foot's assumption that the only source of practical reasons is to be found in the objective interests and subjective desires of the agent. That is, one can embrace a substantive view of practical reason that includes, for example, altruistic reasons or reasons with even more explicitly moral content—for example one might hold that promises provide reasons, or that considerations of fairness do. But before moving on to that discussion in the following section, another strategy is worth mentioning. This is to try to argue that *no matter what desires one has*, it will turn out that one has broadly instrumental reasons to behave morally. This very general strategy can be pursued in a variety of ways. Here I present three.

(a) *Optimism about rational motivation*. This view holds that one's reasons are given not by one's actual desires, but by the desires of an idealized version of oneself: a fully informed, maximally reflective and psychologically coherent version. If one is sufficiently optimistic, one might hold that all adult human beings would converge in their end-state desires if they were fully informed, reflective, and maximally coherent in this way. And one might further hold that these end-state desires would include a sufficiently significant complement of altruistic (or other intuitively morally relevant) desires to underwrite reasons that would justify acting in morally required ways. Michael Smith seems inclined to such a view, though as he develops it the result is only that morally required action is always rationally permissible—not that it is always rationally required.[31]

(b) *The Hobbesian model*. Thomas Hobbes provides a model for the second way of arguing that differences in motivational setup do not undermine the claim that we all have sufficient reason to behave morally. Without pretending to be historically faithful to Hobbes in the details, the general idea is that *everyone* will do better if we all observe moral norms than *anyone* will do if no one does. If no one observes moral norms, we have a terrible "state of nature" which is equivalent to a war of all against all, and which it would be worth virtually any sacrifice to exit, no matter what one happens to desire. The only way to get out of this state is to have everyone agree to behave morally. But in individual choice situations in which immoral behavior is maximally advantageous, instrumentally rational people will not behave morally. So it pays to set things up in such a way that there is a coercive apparatus that *makes* it more advantageous to behave morally. Hobbes envisions the state sovereign as such a coercive power. One obvious problem with this strategy is that in individual cases, when circumstances conspire to help the thief, or murderer, the chances of being caught and punished may be so slim that overall, in terms of the formal account of rationality, the rational thing to do will be to steal or kill. David Gauthier is a modern Hobbesian who attempts to get around this problem.[32] He argues that of rationality is a matter of maximizing self-interest by way of *dispositions* to choose, and that the rationality of particular actions is a matter of issuing from such a disposition. On such a view, if it would maximize self-interest to behave in a certain way (say, morally) on the condition that others also do, then it counts as rational to act in that way even in *individual* cases in which it turns out to be more advantageous to violate the agreement. One significant problem with this view is that it depends on our being able to see how other people are disposed to act. The optimal disposition, after all, would be one which leads one to act morally in interactions with people who are also so disposed, but does not lead one to act morally in interactions with people who are not so disposed. Another problem is with the move to a theory of rational action that gives dispositions the foundational role. This theory is controversial, to say the least, since it leads us to say that the uniquely rational choice, in certain circumstances, is one that disadvantages the agent—perhaps with no benefit to anyone.

(c) *Rejecting proportionalism.* A third way of responding to Foot's argument is to deny an assumption that we have so far been accepting as part of the formal, instrumental view: that if an agent's reasons stem from that agent's desires, then the strength of those reasons corresponds to the strength of the relevant desires. Mark Schroeder has rightly pinpointed this assumption—which he calls "proportionalism"—as the source of many of the objections that plague instrumental accounts of practical rationality that take seriously the idea that moral behavior is always rationally permissible.[33] One such objection is that sadistic or "nutty" people will have strong reasons to hurt people or to do nutty things. And the other is that selfish and mean people will have no reason to behave morally. But Schroeder points out that virtually all human beings have an extremely wide range of desires, and that the effects of morally required action can be expected to become very complex when viewed in the long term, so that we cannot say with any confidence that morally required behavior will not serve *some* of the selfish and mean person's ends. Still, if one associates the strength of a reason with the strength of its associated desire, this will not get us what we want: many *strong* reasons for *everyone* to behave morally. The basis of

Schroeder's response to this worry is to say that one reason is stronger than another, not when its associated desire is stronger, but when we have some reason to treat the first reason as more important in our deliberations. This is a second-order reason, but it also stems, on the instrumental view, from our desires. In cases in which second-order reasons fail to determine, on their own, which of two first-order reasons is stronger, we can appeal to even higher-order reasons to adjudicate, and so on. If one is optimistic, one can hold that, viewed in this way, there will be moral reasons of great strength for virtually all agents, no matter whether they are selfish and mean, or generous and kind.[34]

Morality and Substantive Views of Practical Reason

Recall that substantive views of rationality or practical reason are ones according to which certain substantive considerations—as that one's action will cause someone else pain, or will put one at risk oneself of some other substantively-specified harm—provide reasons for and against action, quite independently of the agent's attitude towards them. A substantive account will have little difficulty in explaining why someone who has deep and stable self-destructive desires will count as irrational if he acts on those desires. A formal account will either have to claim that this agent's self-destructive action is perfectly rational, or will have to embrace a modified account on which the desires of the agent provide reasons only when they, or the agent meets certain conditions. For example, a typical modification would say that a desire provides a reason if an *idealized* version of the agent would have it. But even then, the advocate of such a view will have to persuade us that idealization—which must include only such things as increased formal coherence, information, and so on—will transform the desires of the actual imperfect agent into something more "sane." Given the ease with which substantive accounts of practical reason can classify stereotypically crazy behavior as irrational, one might also hope that substantive accounts will have a similar advantage when it comes to classifying stereotypically immoral behavior as irrational as well. As it happens, however, substantive accounts of practical reason have their own set of challenges in providing a persuasive account of the relation of rationality to morality.

One way of ensuring that morally required action is also rationally required is simply to equate morality and practical rationality. Let us consider a popular substantive view of rationality according to which certain substantive features of action—including the consequences they are likely to have, as well as such things as whether the action counts as the breaking or fulfilling of a promise—count as reasons for and against those actions.[35] Such views also typically hold that these reasons come with strength values. Inasmuch as these views represent the rationality of an action as a function of the strengths of the relevant reasons, and inasmuch they hold that this strength can be represented, at least roughly, by a single strength value, they can all be regarded as maximizing views of rationality.[36] Given any choice situation, they will rank the agent's options in terms of the strengths of the reasons that favor and oppose it, and this ranking will typically yield at most a small handful of maximally favored options. All other options will be irrational to a greater or lesser degree.

One general problem with the equation of morally required action with rationally required action is that—as Kant himself stressed—there is a strong connection between the concepts of rational action and the kind of *free* action that imparts full *responsibility*. At least this seems true for *subjective* rationality.[37] Put another way, subjectively irrational action—including paradigmatically compulsive or phobic behavior, or behavior that results from extreme emotion, lack of sleep, and so on—is associated with diminished responsibility. But if we equate morality and rationality, we will thereby be equating extremely immoral action with extremely irrational action. And by doing this, we provide at least a *prima facie* argument that the agent is not to be held fully responsible for his action.[38] And the more egregiously immoral, the less responsible. But this goes against the strong intuitions of many that it is possible to be appropriately held responsible for actions that are extremely immoral. The problem here is even more acute when one realizes that extremely immoral action also seems to justify punishment. Of course Kantians, and other philosophers who equate morality and practical reason, do not see this objection as decisive. But there remains an explanatory burden if one chooses to take this route in order to ensure the rationality of moral behavior.

Another important technical problem for views of the sort that we are considering here is that commonsense morality does not seem to have the structure it would have, if morally required behavior was simply behavior that maximized a measure given by the strengths of the reasons favoring one's options. If it did have that structure, then in cases in which either of two options was morally acceptable, we would have to regard the two options as essentially *tied* with respect to the relevant measure. And in that case, changing the strength of the relevant reasons would turn one of the options into the uniquely required one. But consider any case in which self-defense plausibly provides a justification for the violation of a rule of commonsense morality: say, the rule against harming someone. In such cases, it is morally permissible either to break the rule by defending oneself, or to refuse to do so, and to suffer the consequences at the hands of one's attacker. Now imagine a case in which the harm one could avoid by breaking the rule is slightly greater. In that case, the balance of reasons would tip in favor of harming one's attacker, and one would be morally required to do so. But considerations of self-defense or self-protection simply do not work this way. They cannot morally *require* us to violate rules; they can only morally *justify* us in doing so. It is very hard to see how this feature of reasons of self-protection could be explained if we equate morality and rationality, and if we hold to a substantive maximizing view of rationality.

Another structural feature of commonsense morality is that it includes the category of the supererogatory: actions that are morally good to perform, but not morally wrong to fail to perform. This category is often taken to include making great sacrifices for other people. Consider, then, two cases of such action. In the first, the agent sacrifices his afternoon (say, by testifying in court) in order to save someone from a wrongful imprisonment. In the second, the agent risks his life in order to do the very same thing. Let us suppose that in neither case does the agent have any special duty to the person who is in danger of the being imprisoned. Now, in terms of moral status, the second action seems to be *better* than the first. But how on Earth could the status of an action—here both its moral and rational status, since these are stipulated to be the same thing—be *better* because it is *opposed* by a stronger reason? Of course, one response to these objections from structure is to deny that commonsense morality represents the structure of morality correctly. But this is quite a bullet to bite.

The upshot of this section is that if one adopts a simple substantive account of rationality that equates rational action with action supported by the best or strongest reasons, and one tries to ensure the rationality of moral action by equating morality and rationality, one encounters significant troubles.

Kinds of Moral View

In this section I consider three distinct kinds of moral view, and the problems that arise in trying to provide an account of the relation between morality and practical reason, if one adopts each kind of view. I do this prior to discussing nonmaximizing views of rationality, because the advantages of such a view will be clearer once we have seen some of the difficulties that different kinds of moral view encounter when trying to establish the relation of morally required action to rational action.

The first kind of moral view is contractualism. On a contractualist view, the content of morality is given by the outcome of a certain thought-experiment or counterfactual situation.[39] In the thought-experiment, a set of bargainers must come up with rules for the regulation of conduct that they can all agree to follow, given that others also agree to follow them. It should be fairly clear that some notion of rationality will play a significant role in any account of this sort, since we will need to limit the kind of bargainer who is relevant to the thought-experiment.[40] After all, if we allow *any* kind of person to participate in the imagined bargaining, it is virtually guaranteed that no agreement will emerge. Intuitively speaking, we want to exclude crazy, stupid, or self-destructive people. An additional consideration in favor of this restriction is that the force of the fact that a certain rule would be included in the contract stems in part from the fact that anyone who was *rational* would have agreed to it.

But if we endorse one of the maximizing views of rationality—whether a formal instrumental version, or a substantive version of the sort described in the previous section—then a very significant problem will arise. The problem is that there is no reason to think—and plenty of reason to doubt—that if practical reason uniquely favors agreeing to a certain set of rules *on the condition that others agree to do the same,* then practical reason will also uniquely favor *following* those same rules in every *actual* instance in which they apply. After all, the choice of a set of rules is a very different choice than the choice of a particular action. And the hypothetical situation in which the first choice is made is bound to be very different from the actual situations in which actual agents find themselves. Thus, even if I am rational, and even if I am convinced that in a hypothetical bargaining situation I would agree to a certain set of rules on the condition that other people also agreed, there is no reason to think that it will be rational for me to follow those rules here and now: especially when following them will involve some sacrifice. And if there is any mismatch between what is morally required (what is required by the contract) and what is rational, this means that it will be *irrational* to act morally. Again, if one takes rationality to be the fundamental normative notion, this means that there can be no reason sufficient to justify acting morally, in those situations. But that is an intolerable consequence for most moral theorists.

A second kind of view of morality is designed in a way that guarantees both that there will be reasons to behave in morally required ways, and also that morality is distinct from rationality. This view holds that a certain *subset* of the reasons that determine the rationality of an action count as *moral* reasons.[41] And it holds that the action maximally favored by these reasons counts as morally required. Michael Smith is perhaps the most explicit advocate of this view.[42] But such a view is also held by any theorist who would be willing to agree with the following three claims.

1) Moral status is determined by the balance of moral reasons.
2) Only some reasons count as moral reasons.
3) What one is rationally required to do is determined by the balance of *all* one's reasons.

The advantage of this view is, as has been mentioned, that all morally required action is guaranteed to be favored by reasons. But the disadvantage is that the view also explicitly admits the existence of nonmoral reasons that can compete directly with moral reasons, and that might end up tipping the balance of reasons in favor of immoral action. If one's view of rationality is a maximizing one, this will again virtually guarantee that at least *some* morally required action is irrational. And, if one takes rationality to be fundamental, this means that one simply should not do it: that reasons do not exist of sufficient strength to justify it.

A third kind of view of morality is a consequentialist view, discussed in detail in the chapter on Consequentialism. Such a view involves a list of good and bad consequences, and a ranking of an agent's options for action by reference to those consequences. There are many versions of such a view, depending on whether it is the actual or foreseeable consequences that count, and, in the latter case, on how it is determined that a consequence counts as foreseeable. And of course there are different lists of relevant consequences. More significantly, such a view can evaluate action *directly* in terms of the consequences it will produce, or *indirectly*, by means of a set of rules or principles that themselves are evaluated in terms of their consequences.[43] Direct and indirect consequentialism—sometimes also called act- and rule-consequentialism or extreme and restricted consequentialism—have different relations to rationality.

Advocates of direct consequentialist views are likely to equate morality and rationality, since the alternative entails the existence of direct clashes between what is morally required and what is rationally required. One argument in favor of this position trades on the intuitive plausibility of the following claim: if one is confronted with a choice between producing better or worse consequences, the rational thing to do is to produce the better. Implicit in this claim is that the *location* of an instantiation of some consequence—say, pleasure—does not matter to its relation to the rationality of someone who can choose to produce it or not. That is, it is implicit here that, rationally, I should be just as moved by the prospect of producing some good for myself as by the prospect of producing the same good for another person. If one defends direct utilitarianism in this way, one runs into all the same problems we saw with views that equate morality and rationality. Moreover, this kind of consequentialist morality is much more demanding that commonsense morality, which typically does not require major sacrifices for strangers. It is itself implausible. But to go on to say that such sacrifices are not only morally required, but irrational to fail to perform, is certainly a philosophically heroic position. Some advocates of such views recognize this, and are happy to be seen as offering extremely revisionist views.[44]

Turning now to the relation of indirect versions of consequentialism to rationality, we will encounter the same problems we saw in our discussion of contractualist accounts of morality. This is because the normative content of indirect consequentialist accounts of morality can be seen as the result of a certain version of contractualism. To see this, note that the normative basis for the choice of a set of rules, on an indirect consequentialist view, will be that that particular system of rules will—given certain other stipulations—produce the best consequences. That this is the normative basis of the choice of system suggests that the same kinds of consequences are the basic source of reasons for all choices. And this in turn suggests that rational action is a matter of acting on the strongest reasons, where these reasons are provided by facts about the consequences of one's action.[45] If so, it will certainly be possible to argue that the choice of a certain set of rules would be uniquely rational. But it will also be quite likely that in some particular circumstances—circumstances distinct from those in which one is choosing a set of rules for the regulation of conduct—the uniquely rational action will be something *other than* what is required by these very rules. In such a case, if the relevant view of rationality is maximizing and is taken to be fundamental, we will once again have a situation in which it is irrational to act as morality requires, and in which there is no reason available that could justify moral behavior.

Nonmaximizing View of Rationality

At the end of the section "Practical Reason and Practical Reasons" a nonmaximizing view of practical reason was described. On such a view, the rational status of an action is not determined by adding up the strengths of the reasons that favor and oppose each of the available options, and seeing whether the action is among those that are maximally favored. Rather, the rational status of an action is determined in the following way. If the combined justifying strength of the reasons that favor the action is at least as great as the combined requiring strength of the reasons that oppose it, then it is rationally justified; if not, it is rationally prohibited.[46] Let us consider a version of such a view according to which the justifying strength of a reason does not depend at all on whether the reason is altruistic or self-interested, but according to which it is only self-interested reasons that have any requiring strength. That is:

1) The reason "this action will cause me a great deal of pain over the next two hours" is a reason with significant requiring strength. It requires one not to perform the action unless one has adequate justification.
2) The reason "this action will prevent me from permanently losing my vision" is a reason with significant justifying and requiring strength. It can justify acting against the reason given in (1), and it can require me to act on it unless I have adequate justification not to.
3) The reason "this action will prevent a certain stranger from permanently losing his vision" is a reason with the same justifying strength as that of the reason mentioned in (2), but with no requiring strength at all. It can

justify acting against the reason given in (1), but it cannot require me to act on it, even when I could do so at little or no cost to myself.

Thinking of self-interested and altruistic reasons in this way allows us to classify a very wide range of action as rationally justified. For example, the sacrifices that morality sometimes requires can be rationally justified by reference to benefits for other people. But selfish and immoral behavior will also often count as rationally permissible, since the altruistic reasons that would justify acting in morally better ways do not *require* one to act in those better ways. By allowing that immoral action can count as rational, this kind of view avoids problems about freedom and responsibility that confront views that identify morality with rationality. And, incorporated into a contractualist or a consequentialist view, it can help us avoid the unfortunate implication that some morally required action will be irrational. Let us see why this is.

Consider the contractualist view first, and imagine that all the bargainers are fully-informed and subjectively rational in our nonmaximizing sense. This means that they will never act in ways that will bring them any harm, unless they also think that by doing so they will also produce benefits—to themselves or to someone else—sufficient to justify suffering those harms. Given some other stipulations about the bargaining situation, it is not at all implausible that such people would support a set of rules that was recognizable as our common moral rules.[47] Now, once these same people are envisioned as acting in a more realistic context, their choice situation will be quite different. But whatever rules emerged from the bargaining situation would not require *pointless* sacrifices. And whatever gave these sacrifices their point would provide, on the kind of theory of rationality we are now considering, sufficient justification to make it rationally *permissible* to act morally. The maximizing view of rationality cannot yield this consequence: any difference between what the rules of morality require, and what the reasons one encounters in a particular choice situation require will entail the irrationality of acting morally.

Now consider a consequentialist view according to which one is morally required to choose the act, of those available to one, that will produce the best possible consequences, making no distinction between those who will enjoy or suffer those consequences.[48] Of course such a crude view is implausible. But it is worth seeing how a nonmaximizing view of rationality, of the sort described above, can at least save such a view from some of the problems we saw in the previous section. On such a view of rationality, the morally required action will, plausibly, be rationally permissible. After all, it produces the best consequences, so that even if it requires some personal sacrifice on the part of the agent, that sacrifice will plausibly be justified by the greater benefits to others. But, importantly, since altruistic considerations only rationally *justify* these sacrifices, and do not rationally *require* them, it remains possible to regard moral failures as rationally permissible.[49]

This chapter has described only one version of the nonmaximizing view: one that makes use of a basic distinction between the justifying and requiring roles of practical reasons. But the same kind of effect can be achieved in other ways. Derek Parfit defends a view on which there is a basic distinction between personal and impartial reasons, and on which there is no way to say anything, with any precision at all, about the relative strengths of two reasons of these different kinds.[50] This strategy yields, extensionally, the same kinds of judgments as are achieved by the justifying/requiring distinction. And Joseph Raz argues for the existence of what he calls exclusionary permissions.[51] These are rational permissions to exclude certain reasons from one's deliberations. The existence of such permissions, if they function to allow one to ignore altruistic reasons to a greater or lesser extent, also will allow immoral action to count as rationally permissible while still allowing moral sacrifices to count as rational. Such nonmaximizing views are not the received view, perhaps because they make it inadmissible to talk about the action that is favored by the best, most, or strongest reasons. But, arguably, we will have to give up talking in this simple way if we are to provide an adequate account of the relation between morality and practical reason.[52]

References

Brandt, R. (1998), *A Theory of the Good and the Right*. Amherst, NY: Prometheus.

Brink, D. (1997), "Self-love and Altruism." *Social Philosophy and Policy* 14, 122–57.

Broome, J. (2005), "Does Rationality Give Us Reasons?," *Philosophical Issues*, 15, Normativity, 321–37.

Byron, M. (ed.) (2004), *Satisficing and Maximizing: Moral Theorists on Practical Reason*. Cambridge: Cambridge University Press.

Cullity, G. and B. Gaut. (1997), *Ethics and Practical Reason*. New York: Clarendon Press.

Dancy, J. (2004), *Ethics without Principles*. Oxford: Oxford University Press.

Darwall, S. (1983), *Impartial Reason*. Ithaca: Cornell University Press.

Enoch, D. (2006), "Agency, Shmagency: Why Normativity Won't Come from What Is Constitutive of Action." *Philosophical Review* 115, 169–98.

Foot, P. (2001), *Natural Goodness*. Oxford: Clarendon Press.

—. (1978), "Reasons for action and desires," in *Virtues and Vices*. Oxford: Basil Blackwell, pp. 148–57.

Fumerton, R. (1990), *Reason and Morality: A Defense of the Egocentric Perspective*. Ithaca, NY: Cornell University Press.

Gauthier, D. (1986), *Morals by Agreement*. New York: Oxford University Press.

—. (1967), "Morality and Advantage." *Philosophical Review* 76, 460–75.

Gert, B. (2005), *Morality: Its Nature and Justification*. Oxford: Oxford University Press.
Gert, J. (2008), "Michael Smith and the Rationality of Immoral Action." *The Journal of Ethics* 12, 1–23.
—. (2007), "Normative Strength and the Balance of Reasons." *Philosophical Review* 116, 533-62.
—. (2004), *Brute Rationality: Normativity and Human Action*. Cambridge: Cambridge University Press.
Gibbard, A. (2003), *Thinking How to Live*. Cambridge: Harvard University Press.
—. (1990), *Wise Choices, Apt Feelings*. Cambridge, Harvard University Press.
Goldman, A. (2005), "Reason Internalism." *Philosophy and Phenomenological Research* 71, 505–32.
Hobbes, T. (1994), *Leviathan*. E. Curley (ed.). Indianapolis, Hackett.
Hooker, B. (2000), *Ideal Code, Real World: A Rule-consequentialist Theory of Morality*. Oxford: Oxford University Press.
Hume, D. (1978), *A Treatise of Human Nature*. L. A. Selby-Bigge & P. H. Nidditch (eds.). Oxford: Oxford University Press.
Kagan, S. (1989), *The Limits of Morality*. New York: Clarendon Press.
Kant, I. (1978), *Groundwork of the Metaphysic of Morals*. H. J. Paton (trans.). London: Hutchinson and Co.
Kolodny, N. (2005), "Why be Rational?" *Mind* 114, 509–63.
Korsgaard, C. (1996), *The Sources of Normativity*. O. O'Neill (ed.). Cambridge: Cambridge University Press.
Miller, C. (2008), "Motivational Internalism." *Philosophical Studies* 139, 233–55.
Nagel, T. (1970), *The Possibility of Altruism*. Princeton: Princeton University Press.
Parfit, D. (2011), *On What Matters*. Oxford: Oxford University Press.
—. (1997), "Reasons and Motivation." *Aristotelian Society Supplement* 71, 99–131.
Quinn, W. (1992), "Rationality and the Human Good." *Social Philosophy and Policy* 9, 81–95.
Rawls, J. (1971), *A Theory of Justice*. Cambridge: Harvard University Press.
Raz, J. (1999), *Practical Reason and Norms*. New York: Oxford University Press.
Ripstein, A. (2001), "Preference," in C. Morris and A. Ripstein (eds.), *Practical Rationality and Preference: Essays For David Gauthier*. Cambridge: Cambridge University Press, 37–55.
Scanlon, T. (1998), *What We Owe to Each Other*. Cambridge, MA: Harvard University Press.
Scheffler, S. (1995), *The Rejection of Consequentialism*. Oxford: Clarendon Press.
Schroeder, M. (2007), *Slaves of the Passions*. New York: Oxford University Press.
Shafer-Landau, R. (2003), *Moral Realism: A Defence*. Oxford: Clarendon Press.
Smart, J. J. C. (1956), "Extreme and Restricted Utilitarianism." The Philosophical Quarterly 6, 344–54.
Smart, J.C.C. (1973), "An Outline of a System of Utilitarian Ethics," in Bernard Williams and J.C.C. Smart (eds.), *Utilitarianism: For and Against*. New York: Cambridge University Press, 3–76.
Smith, M. (2002), "Bernard Gert's Complex Hybrid Conception of Rationality," in R. Audi and W. Sinnott-Armstrong (eds.), *Rationality, Rules, and Ideals: Critical*

Essays on Bernard Gert's Moral Theory. Lanham, MD: Rowman and Littlefield, pp. 109–23.
—. (1996), "Normative Reasons and Full Rationality: Reply to Swanton." *Analysis* 56, 160–8.
—. (1994), *The Moral Problem*. Cambridge: Blackwell.
van Roojen, M. (2010), "Moral Rationalism and Rational Amoralism." *Ethics* 120, 495–525.
Wallace, R. J. (2006), *Normativity and the Will: Selected Essays in Moral Psychology and Practical Reason*. New York: Oxford University Press.
Williams, B. (1981), "Internal and External Reasons," in *Moral Luck*, Cambridge: Cambridge University Press, pp. 101–13.
—. (2001), "Postscript: Some Further Notes on Internal and External Reasons," in E. Millgram (ed.), *Varieties of Practical Reasoning*. Cambridge, MA: MIT Press, pp. 91–7.

5 Moral Psychology

Alfred Mele

R. Jay Wallace usefully characterizes philosophical moral psychology as an exploration of

> a variety of psychological phenomena through the unifying prism of a concern for normativity. It studies the psychological conditions for the possibility of binding norms of action; the ways in which moral and other such norms can be internalized and complied with in the lives of agents; and a range of psychological conditions and formations that have implications for the normative assessment of agents and their lives. (2005, 87)

In some contributions to the philosophical literature on moral psychology, close attention is paid to work in scientific psychology; in others, no mention is made of scientific work.

Moral psychology covers a wide range of topics, as Wallace's characterization indicates. This chapter focuses on a pair of topics in moral psychology that are linked to motivation and evaluation: weakness of will and first-person moral ought beliefs. Although weakness of will is not limited to the moral sphere, it does have, in Wallace's words, "implications for the normative assessment of agents and their lives" (2005, 87).

Weakness of Will: Introduction

In Plato's *Protagoras*, Socrates says that the common view about seemingly commonplace intentional actions that clash with agents' beliefs about what it is best to do is that "many people who know what it is best to do are not willing to do it, though it is in their power, but do something else" (352d). In disputing this view, Socrates raises (among other issues) a central question in philosophical work on *akrasia* or weakness of will: Is it possible to perform free, intentional actions that, as one recognizes at the time of action, are contrary to what one judges it best on the whole to do then, the judgment being made from the perspective of one's own values, principles, desires, and beliefs (as opposed, for example, to the evaluative perspective of one's elders or peers)?[1] More briefly, is *strict* akratic action possible (Mele 1987, 7)?

Relevant judgments include judgments in which "best" is relativized to options envisioned by the agent at the time. In instances of strict akratic action, agents do not need to judge that a course of action *A* is the best of all possible courses of action. They may judge that *A* is better than the alternatives they have envisioned—that it is the best of the envisioned options. If, nevertheless, they do not *A* and they instead intentionally and freely pursue one of the envisioned alternatives while recognizing that it clashes with this judgment, they act akratically. (It is useful to have a label for the judgment these agents supposedly act against. I dub it a *decisive judgment*.) Strict akratic action, if it is possible, exhibits at least imperfect self-control.[2]

Aristotle understands *akrasia* and self-control (*enkrateia*) as contrary character traits that fall between vice and virtue (*Nicomachean Ethics* 7.1). In his view, self-control and *akrasia* "are concerned with that which is in excess of the state characteristic of most men; for the [self-controlled] man abides by his resolutions more and the [akratic] man less than most men can" (*Nicomachean Ethics* 1152a25–27). There is a middle ground between self-control and *akrasia*, and not all akratic actions must manifest *akrasia*. Someone who is more self-controlled than most people in a certain sphere may, in a particularly trying situation, succumb to temptation in that sphere against his decisive judgment. If his intentional action is free, he acts akratically—even if his action manifests, not *akrasia*, but an associated imperfection. Similarly, a person with the trait of *akrasia* may occasionally succeed in resisting temptation and act in a self-controlled way. In recent philosophical literature, akratic and self-controlled *actions* have received much more attention than the character traits.

Although, in this chapter, I follow Aristotle in understanding akratic and self-controlled action as two sides of the same coin, I depart from him on a pair of pertinent issues. One is the nature of human beings and, accordingly, the nature of the *self* involved in a proper conception of self-control. The other is the sphere of akratic and self-controlled actions.

Aristotle views the self-controlled agent as a person whose "desiring element" is "obedient" to his "reason" or "rational principle," though less obedient than the virtuous person's (*Nicomachean Ethics* 1102b26–28). A human being "is said to have or not to have self-control according as his reason has or has not the control (*kratein*), on the assumption that this is the man himself" (1168b34–35). Given Aristotle's contention that "reason more than anything else is man" (1178a7; also see 1166a17, 22–23, 1168b27ff., and Plato, *Republic* 588b–592b), his identification of self-control with control by one's "reason" is predictable.

On an alternative, holistic view of human beings of the sort I favor (Mele 1987, 1995, 2003), the self of self-control is identified with the whole human being rather than with reason. Even when one's passions and emotions run counter to one's decisive judgment, they often are not plausibly seen as alien forces. A conception of self-controlled individuals as, roughly, people who characteristically are guided by their decisive judgments even in the face of strong competing motivation does not commit one to viewing emotion, passion, and the like as having no place in the self of self-control. Self-control can be exercised in support of decisive judgments that are based partly on a person's appetites or emotional commitments. In some cases, our decisive judgments may indicate our evaluative ranking of competing *emotions* or *appetites*.

I turn to the second issue. Aristotle limits the sphere of *enkrateia* and *akrasia*, like that of temperance and self-indulgence (*Nicomachean Ethics* 3.10, 7.7), to "pleasures and pains and appetites and aversions arising through touch and taste" (1150a910).[3] However, self-control and *akrasia* have come to be understood much more broadly. Self-control, as it is now conceived, may be exhibited in successful resistance of actual or anticipated temptation in any sphere. Temptations having to do with such things as sexual activity, eating, drinking, and smoking are tied to touch and taste. But we may also be tempted to work less or more than we judge best, to gamble beyond the limits we have set for ourselves, to spend more or less on recreational activities than we believe we should, and so on. Seemingly, we can exercise self-control in overcoming such temptations or akratically succumb to them.

Akratic Action and Free Action

Strict akratic action, again, is free, intentional action that, as the agent recognizes at the time of action, is contrary to his decisive judgment. To the extent that such a judgment derives from one's motivational attitudes, it has a motivational dimension.[4] That helps explain why some philosophers regard strict akratic action as impossible or at least as theoretically perplexing. How, they wonder, can the motivation associated with a judgment of this kind be outweighed by competing motivation, especially when the competing motivational attitudes—or *desires*, broadly construed—have been taken into account in arriving at the judgment? And if it is outweighed, can the agent really be acting freely?

For the purposes of this chapter, it may be assumed (*P1*) that people sometimes act freely and (*P2*) that people sometimes perform intentional actions that they consciously believe at the time of action to be inferior on the whole to another live option—or intentional actions that are contrary to their *V beliefs*, for short. Some compulsive hand-washers or crack cocaine addicts may occasionally confirm *P2*. But acting contrary to one's *V* belief is not sufficient for performing a strict akratic action; the action must be performed freely. Some philosophers argue that strict akratic action is impossible because actions contrary to the agent's *V* beliefs are necessarily unfree (Hare 1963, ch. 5; Pugmire 1982; Socrates in Plato's *Protagoras;* Watson 1977; also see Buss 1997, Tenenbaum 1999, and Wallace 1999).

Assumptions *P1* and *P2* and the following assertion form a consistent triad: (*UF*) All actions contrary to the agent's *V* belief are unfree. How might a philosopher try to defend *UF* while granting *P1* and *P2*? Here is a sketch of one such defense (see Hare 1963, ch. 5 for a similar argument):

Argument A

A1. Having a *V* belief that it is best to *A* now is conceptually sufficient for having an intention to *A* now.

A2. Any agent who intends to *A* now but does not *A* now is unable to *A* now.

A3. Such an agent, because he is unable to *A* now, is compelled to perform—and therefore unfreely performs—whatever pertinent intentional action he now performs.

Premise *A2* is falsified by simple counterexamples. A skilled golfer who intends to sink a short putt may accidentally miss even though he was able to do what he intended. Of course, the failures in alleged strict akratic actions may be importantly different, and it may be claimed that *A2* simply needs to be revised to capture the difference. One likely suggestion is that in alleged strict akratic actions, the failure involves a change of intention—for example, a change from intending to work to intending to play a computer game—whereas the golfer's failure does not. Now, either the change of intention is paired with a corresponding change of belief or it is not. If there is a change of belief that matches the change of intention—for example, a change to believing that it would be better to play a computer game—then the agent does not act contrary to his current *V* belief in executing that intention. But it is assumed that some actions are contrary to their agents' current *V* beliefs, and the skeptic is supposed to be arguing that all such actions are unfree. So suppose that the change of intention is not paired with a corresponding change of belief and the agent's *V* belief persists. Then *A1* is false. It is falsified by an agent who had intended in accordance with a *V* belief but no longer so intends even though the belief persists.

Premise *A1* is in serious trouble anyway, given *P2*. Consider crack addicts or compulsive hand-washers who believe that it is best not to use crack now or not to wash their hands now, but who do so anyway—intentionally and unfreely. If *A1* is true, they are intentionally using crack or washing their hands while intending not to do so. Although this may be conceptually possible—for example, perhaps a commissurotomized agent may intend not to *A* while also intending to *A* and acting on the latter intention—it is a highly implausible hypothesis about representative cases of the kind at issue. A much more plausible hypothesis is that although the troubled agents believe that it would be best not to use crack now or not to wash their hands now, they lack a corresponding intention and instead intend to do what they are doing.

Proposition *A3* also is problematic. Don has been dieting and believes it best to order a fruit salad for lunch today. Unfortunately, he is tempted by several other menu items, including a chilli cheeseburger, a pork steak, and a roast beef sandwich. He orders the burger. Even if Don was unable to order the fruit salad, we would need an argument that he was compelled to order the burger—that, for example, ordering the roast beef sandwich was not a live option.

Gary Watson offers the following argument for *UF* (1977, 336–8):

Argument B

B1. An agent's succumbing to a desire contrary to his *V* belief cannot be explained by his choosing not to resist nor by his making a culpably insufficient effort to resist.

B2. Only one explanation remains: The agent was unable to resist.

So *UF*. All actions contrary to the agent's *V* belief are unfree.

Watson argues that an agent's choosing not to resist cannot explain strict akratic action, for to make such a choice "would be to change" one's *V* belief (337). For example, "The weak drinker's failure to resist her desire to drink is a failure to implement her choice not to drink. To choose not to implement this choice would be to change her original judgment, and the case would no longer be a case of failure to implement a judgment" (336–37). Watson also contends that an insufficient effort cannot be due to a belief that the effort is not worth the trouble, since the belief that it is worth the trouble is implicit in the violated *V* belief (338). Nor, he argues, can the insufficient effort be explained by a misjudgment of "the amount of effort required," for misjudgment is "a different fault from weakness of will" (338).

In some alleged instances of strict akratic action, agents believe that it would be best to *A*, choose accordingly, and then backslide while retaining that belief (Mele 1987, ch. 3). In others, agents with the same *V* belief do not choose accordingly; they do not make the transition from belief to intention (Audi 1979, 191; Davidson 1980, ch. 2; Mele 1992, 228–34; Rorty 1980b). Although Watson has the former kind of case in mind, it is useful to attend to a case of the latter kind (see Mele 2002, 156). Imagine, if you can, that a drinker, Drew, who has had one shot of whiskey and needs to drive home soon, believes that it would be best to switch now to coffee but neither chooses nor intends to do so and intentionally drinks another whiskey. You are not asked to imagine that Drew akratically drinks the second whiskey; it is left open that she drinks it unfreely. If Drew can believe that it would be best not to drink a second whiskey without choosing accordingly, then she can fail "to resist her desire to drink" without there being any failure on her part "to implement her choice not to drink." If she makes no such choice, she does not fail to implement it. And if there is no such failure of implementation, then the reason Watson offers for maintaining that the agent "change[d] her original judgment" is undercut.

A scenario in which an agent does choose in accordance with her *V*-belief is discussed shortly. The plausibility of scenarios of the present sort deserves a bit more attention now. Consider the following story (Mele 2002, 157). On New Year's Eve, Joe, a smoker, is contemplating kicking the habit. Faced with the practical question what to do about his smoking, he is deliberating about what it would be best to do about it. He is convinced that it would be best to quit smoking sometime, but he is unsure whether it would be best to quit soon. Joe is under a lot of pressure at work, and he worries that quitting smoking now might drive him over the edge. Eventually, he judges that it would be best to quit by midnight. But he is not yet settled on quitting. Joe tells his partner, Jill, that he has decided that it would be best to stop smoking, beginning tonight. Jill asks, "Is that your New Year's resolution?" Joe sincerely replies, "Not yet; the next hurdle is to decide to quit. If I do that, I'll have a decent chance of quitting."

This story at least has the appearance of coherence. Seemingly, although Joe decides that it would be best to quit smoking, he may or may not choose (that is, form the intention) to quit. Watson offers no argument for the incoherence of stories of this kind. (I have not claimed that Joe is a free agent.)

If Drew can fail to resist her desire for a second whiskey without changing her belief about what it is best to do, what about Donna, who, like Drew, takes another whiskey despite believing that it would be best to switch now to coffee, but, unlike Drew, chooses to switch now to coffee when she makes her judgment? Watson would say (*W1*) that Donna's "failure to resist her desire to drink [a second whiskey] is a failure to implement her choice not to drink" (*W2a*), that "to choose not to implement this choice [is] to change her original judgment" (*W2b*), that to choose not to resist her desire to drink a second whiskey is to change that judgment, and (*W3*) that Donna's drinking the second whiskey therefore is not a strict akratic action, since it is not contrary to her *V* belief (336–7). Is either *W2a* or *W2b* true? Watson offers no argument for either, and some stories in which analogues of both are false certainly seem coherent.

Here is one such story (from Mele 1987, 25). Alex's friend, Bob, has proposed that they affirm their friendship by becoming blood brothers, since Alex is about to go away to prep school. The ceremony involves the boys' cutting their own right palms with a pocket knife and then shaking hands so that their blood will mix. Alex is averse to cutting himself, but he carefully weighs his reasons for accepting the proposal against his competing reasons (including his aversion) and he judges that it would be best to accept the proposal and to perform the ceremony at once. He chooses, accordingly, to cut his hand with the knife straightaway. Without considering that he may find the task difficult, he grasps the knife and moves it toward his right palm with the intention of drawing blood. However, as he sees the knife come very close to his skin, he intentionally stops, owing significantly to his aversion. He chooses not to implement his original choice just now, and he chooses not to resist his aversion further just now. Alex abandons his original choice. But he has not changed his mind about what it is best to do, and he is upset with himself for chickening out. (Soon, Alex resolves to try again, this time without looking. The second attempt succeeds.)

If this story is incoherent, Watson should explain why. If he were to assent to *A1* (the claim that having a *V* belief that it is best to *A* now is conceptually sufficient for having an intention to *A* now), he could appeal to it here: Because Alex no longer intends to cut his hand straightaway, it would follow that he no longer believes that it would be best to cut it straightaway. But Watson rejects *A1* to accommodate compulsives who act contrary to a *V* belief.

The topic under discussion has been Watson's argument for an element of the first premise of argument *B*. The element is this: (*B1a*). An agent's succumbing to a desire contrary to his better judgment cannot be explained by his choosing not to resist.[5] One may try an alternative defense of this element, arguing that it is illegitimate to explain an alleged akratic action by appealing to a choice not to resist, because such a choice, if free, would itself be an akratic action (see Tenenbaum 1999, 888–9). The thought is that one cannot explain how an akratic action happens by appealing to an akratic action in the explanans. However, this argument cannot support argument *B*. The procedural claim that one cannot explain, *for the reason just cited*, an akratic succumbing to a desire by appealing to an akratic choice not to resist does nothing to support the premise (*B2*) that the only explanation that remains is that the agent was unable to resist; and, of course, the function of *B1* in argument *B* is to support this premise. The procedural claim is compatible with its being the case (1) that something, x, accounts for the agent's akratic choice not to resist, and thereby plays a significant role in accounting for the alleged akratic action at issue; (2) that x and the entire explanatory story are consistent with the agent's being able to resist temptation; and (3) that x is not itself an akratic (overt or mental) action. Various views about what x might be are present in the literature. One such view is sketched in the following section.

Explaining Strict Akratic Action

If we sometimes perform strict akratic actions, why do we do so? In Mele 1987, I defend an answer that rests partly on two theses, both of which I defend there.

1. Decisive judgments normally are formed at least partly on the basis of our evaluation of the "objects" of our desires (that is, the desired items).

2. The motivational force of our desires does not always match our evaluation of the objects of our desires (Santas 1966, Smith 1992, Stocker 1979, Watson 1977).[6]

If both theses are true, it should be unsurprising that sometimes, although we decisively judge it better to *A* than to *B*, we are more strongly motivated to *B* than to *A*. Given how our motivation stacks up, it should also be unsurprising that we *B* rather than *A*.

Thesis 1 is a major plank in a standard conception of practical reasoning. In general, when we reason about what to do, we inquire about what it would be best, or better, or "good enough" to do, not about what we are most strongly motivated to do. When we ask such questions while having conflicting desires, our answers typically rest significantly on our assessments of the objects of our desires—which may be out of line with the motivational force of those desires, if thesis 2 is true.

Thesis 2, as I argue in Mele 1987, is confirmed by common experience and thought experiments and has a foundation in empirical studies. Desire-strength is influenced not only by our evaluation of the objects of desires, but also by such factors as the perceived proximity of prospects for desire-satisfaction, the salience of desired objects in perception or in imagination, and the way we attend to desired objects (Ainslie 1992, Mischel and Ayduk 2004, Rorty 1980a). Factors such as these need not have a matching effect on assessments of desired objects.

A few hours ago, Ed decisively judged it better to *A* than to *B*, but he now has a stronger desire to *B* than to *A*. Two versions of the case merit attention. In one, along with the change in desire strength, there is a change of judgment. For example, last night, after much soul-searching, Ed formed a decisive judgment favoring not eating after-dinner snacks for the rest of the month and desired more strongly to forego them than to indulge himself; but now, a few hours after dinner, Ed's desire for a snack is stronger than his desire for the rewards associated with not snacking, and he decisively judges it better to have a snack than to refrain. In another version of the case, the change in relative desire strength is not accompanied by a change of judgment. Ed retains the decisive judgment favoring not eating after dinner, but he eats anyway. Assuming that Ed eats intentionally and freely, this is a strict akratic action.

Empirical studies of the role of representations of desired objects in impulsive behavior and delay of gratification (reviewed in Mele 1987, 88–93; see Mischel *et al.* 1989 for an overview) provide ample evidence that our representations of desired objects have two important dimensions, a motivational and an informational one. Our decisive judgments may be more sensitive to the informational dimension of our representations than to the motivational dimension, with the result that such judgments sometimes recommend courses of action that are out of line with what we are most strongly motivated to do at the time. If so, strict akratic action is a real possibility—provided that at least some intentional actions that conflict with agents' decisive judgments at the time of action are free actions.

It is a truism that unless a desire of ours is irresistible, it is up to us, in some sense, whether we act on it. Of course, a proper appreciation of the extent of irresistible desires would require an analysis of irresistible desire.[7] It may suffice for present purposes to suggest that, often, when we act against our decisive judgments, we could have used our resources for self-control in effectively resisting temptation. Normal agents apparently can influence the strength of their desires in a wide variety of ways (Ainslie 1992, Mischel and Ayduk 2004, Mischel *et al.* 1989). For example, they can refuse to focus their attention on the attractive aspects of a tempting course of action and concentrate instead on what is to be accomplished by acting as they judge best. They can attempt to augment their motivation for performing the action judged best by promising themselves rewards for doing so. They can picture a desired item as something unattractive—for example, a chocolate pie as a plate of chocolate-coated chewing tobacco—or as something that simply is not arousing. Desires typically do not have immutable strengths, and the plasticity of motivational strength is presupposed by standard conceptions of self-control. Occasionally we *do not* act as we judge best, but it is implausible that, in all such cases, we *cannot* act in accordance with these judgments (Mele 1987, ch. 2; 1995, ch. 3; 2002; Smith 2003.)

I have focused on the nature of akratic action and on how the phenomenon may be explained. As I mentioned, akratic action is not limited by definition to the moral sphere; but, of course, many alleged akratic actions are morally important, and the decisive judgments that agents act against when they act akratically may often rest significantly on moral considerations. The topic of the remainder of this chapter is a related issue about moral ought beliefs.

Internalism about Moral Ought Beliefs: Introduction

How are agents' beliefs that they morally ought to *A* related to motivation to *A*? If we were to discover that moral ought beliefs never help explain actions, we would have little reason to hold that they are motivational in any sense. A plausible presupposition of the question at issue is that sometimes agents act at least partly on the basis of their moral ought beliefs. Consider Joe, who is not a candidate for moral sainthood. A week ago, he agreed to help his uncle clean his house tomorrow afternoon. Today, he is offered a free ticket to his favorite team's game tomorrow afternoon. Joe knows that his uncle is counting on him. He deliberates about whether backing out is morally permissible, and he intends to back out should he determine that it is. However, Joe concludes that he morally ought to help his uncle tomorrow afternoon, as he agreed to do, and he acts accordingly. Joe's helping his uncle may well be explained partly by his feelings for him, but, plausibly, it is also explained partly by his belief that he ought to help. Given the kind of person Joe is, it is very likely that if he had not come to believe that he ought to help his uncle tomorrow, he would not have done so. In the absence of that belief, he probably would have explained his situation to his uncle, asked to be let off the hook, and offered to help next weekend instead. It is plausible that the belief at issue is part of the basis on which Joe decides to help his uncle tomorrow, as he agreed to do. In utterly mundane cases of this kind, first-person moral ought beliefs do seem to help explain intentional actions. They seem to play their *most direct* role in the production of action, the role they play when agents act at least partly *on the basis of* such beliefs.

Cognitivism about first-person moral ought beliefs is the thesis that such beliefs are attitudes with truth-valued content. My topic in this section and the next one is the combination of cognitivism and *internalism* about moral ought beliefs. As Michael Smith reports, an essential feature of internalism is that "it posits some sort of conceptually necessary connection between moral judgment and motivation" (2008, 210). The internalism that concerns me is specifically about first-person moral ought judgments or beliefs. And to simplify exposition further, I limit my attention to *cognitivist* internalism about such beliefs—that is, to the combination of cognitivism and internalism about these beliefs.

Thomas Nagel's discussion of internalism in *The Possibility of Altruism* is frequently cited. He writes:

> Internalism is the view that the presence of a motivation for acting morally is guaranteed by the truth of ethical propositions themselves. On this view the motivation must be so tied to the truth, or meaning, of ethical statements that when in a particular case someone is (or perhaps merely believes that he is) morally required to do something, it follows that he has a motivation for doing it. (1970, 7)

At least two distinct internalistic theses about motivation are discernible here:[8]

1. *Requirement internalism.* "When in a particular case someone is . . . morally required to do something, it follows that he has a motivation for doing it." The presence of this motivation is "guaranteed" by the moral requirement.
2. *Belief internalism.* "When in a particular case someone . . . believes that he is . . . morally required to do something, it follows that he has a motivation for doing it." The presence of this motivation is "guaranteed" by the belief.

Assuming that to have "a motivation" is to be in a motivational *state of mind*, thesis 1 may stand a chance of being true if it expresses the view that having a motivation for *A*-ing is a prerequisite of being morally required to *A*. However, this view is problematic (see Nagel 1970, 13). Presumably, on a cognitivist view, Hitler may have been morally required to release his political prisoners even if he never had "a motivation," in the identified sense, to do so. Thesis 2, on the same reading of "has a motivation," avoids this problem. This thesis does not imply that Hitler's lacking motivation to release his prisoners is inconsistent with his being morally required to release them. I set thesis 1 aside and pursue thesis 2.

I take the term "guaranteed" in both theses to indicate that the companion claim about motivation is to be regarded as a *necessary* truth. Nagel evidently favors *metaphysical* necessity here. He writes: "Human motivation possesses features which are susceptible to metaphysical investigation and which carry some kind of necessity" (1970, 5–6). However, conceptual necessity is a popular option (see Miller 2008, 235). Thesis 2, as I understand it, asserts that, necessarily, anyone who believes himself to be morally required to *A* concurrently "has a motivation" for *A*-ing. This alleged truth rests on the nature of *belief* itself and on the *content* of the belief that one is (oneself) morally required to *A*.

Some Internalist Theses about Moral Ought Beliefs and Some Problems

Here is a concise statement of belief internalism in terms of moral ought beliefs:

O1. Necessarily, any agent who believes at *t* that he morally ought to *A* has motivation at *t* to *A*.[9]

Thesis *O1* leaves it open whether the motivation associated with an agent's belief that he morally ought to *A* is stronger than any competing motivation he has at the time. A proponent of *O1* may consistently believe that agents can act akratically contrary to their first-person moral ought beliefs owing partly to the relative motivational strength of desires that compete with their motivation to *A*. One connection between this chapter's two main topics has now been made explicit.

Thesis *O1* may be compared with an internalist proposal that Michael Smith considers:

O2. It is conceptually necessary that if an agent judges that she morally ought to [*A*] in circumstances C, then she is motivated to [*A*] in C. (Smith 2008, 207).

Smith argues that *O2* "posits a connection between moral judgment and motivation too strong to be credible" (2008, 208); it does not "allow for the possibility of weakness of will as a genuine defect of the will" (211; see 208). On a reading of "*S* is motivated to *A*" that entails "*S A*-s," *O2* precludes weak-willed actions contrary to one's moral ought beliefs. But the expression "is motivated to *A*" in *O2* is open to a more modest reading—"has some motivation to *A*." Having some motivation to *A* is compatible with having—and acting on—motivation to perform an alternative action. In any case, if weak-willed action against a moral ought belief is possible, internalists should leave that possibility open.

Thesis *O1* also apparently leaves it open whether the motivation associated with an agent's belief that he morally ought to *A* is or is not "built into" (Frankena 1958) the belief. It seemingly neither entails nor contradicts the following thesis:

O3. Necessarily, any agent who believes at *t* that he morally ought to *A* has motivation at *t* to *A* and his belief *encompasses* that motivation.

Proponents of *O3* who equate motivation with *desire* are committed to the idea that some beliefs encompass desires. Alleged beliefs that have truth-valued content and encompass desires have been discussed under the label "besire." (The term first appears in Altham 1986, 284–5. Literature on the topic includes Lewis 1988, Price 1989, and Smith 1987, 1994.) David McNaughton (1988, 106–10) explicitly represents first-person moral ought beliefs as being, at once, cognitivist beliefs that one morally ought to *A and* desires to *A*. John McDowell (1978) advances a similar view, with "conceptions" of "how things are" standing in for moral ought beliefs. Also, see David Wiggins 1991, p. 83: "The full moral thought, if you like, is not just a belief. But it is not just a valuation either. The valuation itself can *be* the belief." McDowell (1978, 15–17) attributes a view of this kind to Nagel (in Nagel 1970).

If our moral ought beliefs help explain some of our intentional conduct, theorists should want to understand the most direct explanatory role they play—the role they play when we act at least partly on their basis. Proponents of *O3* seemingly locate that role in the alleged essentially motivation-encompassing character of these beliefs. Is that plausible?

Here are two arguments for *O3* (or a similar thesis).

1. *The argument from moral experience.* (1) Part of what it is to have the (veridical) experience of being morally required to *A* is to apprehend a *reason* to *A*. (2) All reasons for action are motivation encompassing. So (3) having motivation to *A* is internal to the experience of being morally required to *A* (McNaughton 1988, 47–50; also see 23).[10]

2. *The argument from toothlessness*. The truth of *O3* is required by the practical, action-guiding nature of morality. Judgments that one morally ought to *A* are practical judgments—judgments about what to do. As R. M. Hare has put it, "moral judgments, in their central use, have it as their function to guide conduct" (1963, 70). To reject *O3* is to drive a wedge between moral judgments and intentional conduct, thus taking the essentially practical bite out of morality. (Although Hare defends internalism but not cognitivism, the argument from toothlessness is available to noncognitivists and cognitivists alike.)

Some apparent problems for *O3* have been explored in detail by opponents and proponents alike. Apparent problems posed by amoralists, wicked people, and psychopaths are cases in point.[11] Another apparent difficulty is what I have dubbed *the problem of listlessness* (Mele 1996; 2003, ch. 5).[12] It challenges the arguments from moral experience and toothlessness and each of *O1*, *O2*, and *O3*.

Relevant cases of listlessness feature morally good agents, complete with a host of true beliefs about what they morally ought to do. Psychologically devastating tragedies befall them, quashing their motivation to conduct themselves in certain ways. In particular, among the things of which they have long been convinced is that they morally ought to *A*, and they lose all motivation to *A*. To the extent that it is an empirical question whether their belief that they morally ought to *A* must be eliminated in the process (the "must" being nomological rather than logical or metaphysical), it can only be answered by means of careful attention to the human psyche. And it is far from obvious, on empirical grounds, that it is *psychologically impossible* for human victims of severe depression to retain a belief that they morally ought to *A* without having, any longer, motivation to *A*.

Recognizing this, theorists attracted to *O3* may see the question as wholly conceptual or metaphysical—as a question about the essential nature of morality and about what that nature entails about moral ought beliefs. However, they run the risk in so doing of committing themselves to a conception of morality that does not mesh with the psychology of real human beings, a conception that is inconsistent with any actual human being's having first-person moral ought beliefs.

One way to approach an investigation of listlessness involves inventing a psychology for agents that lacks features cognitivist proponents of *O3* require for having first-person moral ought beliefs and then asking whether these agents may have such beliefs even so.[13] (Again, I focus on the combination of cognitivism and internalism.) After you read the following story, please pause to consider whether it seems conceptually possible.

On planet Alpha, beings emerged with a strong genetic predisposition to acquire generic desires to do whatever they morally ought.[14] These beings have no motivation-encompassing beliefs, but they seem, on the whole, to be morally better beings than human Earthlings. Normally, when Alphans judge that they morally ought to do something, a desire to do whatever they morally ought kicks in and helps generate a strong desire to do it. Sometimes, owing to personal tragedies, Alphans temporarily lose all moral motivation even though some of their first-person moral ought beliefs persist. Alphan medical practitioners call this condition moral listlessness. This is their current diagnosis for Eve, who, they claim, continues to believe that she morally ought to help her ailing uncle even though, owing to the very recent loss of her husband and children in a fiery plane crash, she now has no motivation to help him.

Return to the argument from moral experience. Assume that its first premise is true. Then it may be supposed that in having the experience of being morally required to aid her uncle, Eve apprehends a reason to do so. The reason may simply be the fact that she is morally required to help, or the reason may be constituted by the considerations on the basis of which she apprehends this moral requirement.[15] But part of what is at issue, on the assumption that this premise is true, is precisely whether Eve's apprehending the pertinent reason suffices for her having motivation to help. Why cannot her depression be such that although she apprehends a reason to continue helping her uncle, she has no motivation to do so? What proponents of *O1*, *O2*, or *O3* can use here is an argument for the thesis that apprehending a reason for *A*-ing—in precisely the sense of "apprehending a reason" in which it allegedly follows from one's having an experience of being morally required to *A* that one apprehends a reason for *A*-ing—suffices for having motivation to *A*. No argument for this thesis is presented in the argument from moral experience. Even if some analyses of reasons for action treat motivation as an essential constituent of such reasons, this does not provide grounds for confidence that readings of "reason" on which premise 1 of the argument from moral experience is true are readings on which premise 2 is true. For example, Eve believes on some grounds or other that she morally ought to help her uncle; simply calling those grounds "reasons" to help him cannot make it the case that they encompass motivation to help him.

It may be objected that "in the absence of an account of the nature of motivation which shows that it is independent of judging that one has reason to act," what I have just said "looks like a case of *petitio principii* [begging the question]" (Garrard and McNaughton 1998, 49). However, there are excellent grounds for believing that toddlers have motivation-encompassing attitudes, and it is unlikely that they are capable of judging that they have "reason to act" (see Mele 2003, 78). Presumably, such judging requires having a concept of reason for action, and it is implausible that toddlers have such a concept. There is considerable evidence that younger three year-olds tend not to have the concept of belief and that, although the concept of desire emerges earlier, it does not emerge until around the age of two (see Gopnik 1993 for a useful review). Presumably, even if the concept of a reason for action were to have no conceptual ties to the concepts of belief and desire, it would be sufficiently sophisticated to be out of reach of children too young to have proper concepts of belief and desire. (I know of no argument that the concept of a reason for action is simpler or easier to grasp than, for example, the concept of desire or wanting.) Even so, such children act intentionally, and for reasons; so, at least, it is commonly and plausibly thought. And most people happily attribute desires and intentions—motivation-encompassing attitudes—to normal toddlers on the basis of some of their behavior.

If reasons for action are analyzed as complexes of desires for goals and beliefs about means, then in apprehending a reason to help her uncle, Eve apprehends, among other things, a relevant desire of hers—and, hence, *has* such a desire. But this Humean conception of reasons for action is eschewed by typical cognitivist internalists (McDowell 1978, McNaughton 1988, Nagel 1970), who view it as leading either to noncognitivism or (in cognitivists) to externalism. The internalist view at issue is that the apprehension of a moral requirement on oneself itself necessarily encompasses motivation to act accordingly; this apprehension does not depend for its motivational character on a reason that is partially constituted by a desire.

Next on the agenda is the argument from toothlessness. Some versions of this argument would have less clout on planet Alpha than in some other places. As Alphans see it, the great majority of them have a disposition to desire to do whatever they morally ought to do, and they regard themselves as having a practical, action-guiding morality. Except in rare cases, Alphans desire to perform those actions that they apparently believe they morally ought to perform. Typically, then, their ostensible first-person moral ought beliefs—or *M* beliefs, for short—have practical clout.

The Alphans' ostensible *M* beliefs may have no weaker a grip on their behavior than ours have on our behavior. Presumably, like Alphans, we do not always act as we believe we morally ought. We occasionally exhibit moral weakness, it seems; and we may do so even if our own *M* beliefs are uniformly motivation encompassing. In any case, on Alpha, the practical effectiveness of (apparent) moral judgments does not hinge on an alleged metaphysical or conceptual truth that believing that one morally ought to *A* suffices for having motivation to *A*.

In a related vein, no actual human being is *essentially* immune to depression, even in its most severe forms. And if some possible (that is, for us) instances of depression or listlessness are such that people who believe that they morally ought to *A* are devoid of motivation to *A*, then first-person moral ought beliefs do not essentially encompass motivation in actual human beings. No matter what we believe we morally ought to do, we would be devoid of pertinent motivation were we to suffer from listlessness of the kind at issue while holding the belief.

It may be replied that an agent who takes himself to believe that he morally ought to *A* but lacks a *motivation-encompassing* belief that he morally ought to *A* does not have a sufficient grasp of morality to believe what he takes himself to believe. It may be claimed that if he were to understand morality well enough to have beliefs with this content, then, *necessarily*, those beliefs would encompass motivation to *A*. Call this the *proper grasp response*.

One way of filling out this response would be risky for cognitivist proponents of *O3*. Suppose it were claimed that achieving a proper grasp of morality is possible only for beings who already have grasp-promoting desires (e.g., a desire for the well-being of other people), and that this helps explain why, necessarily, anyone who believes that he morally ought to *A* has motivation to *A*. This claim leaves it open that beliefs that one morally ought to *A* do not *encompass* motivation to *A*: such motivation may be wholly external to such beliefs, and *O3* asserts that it is built into them. Advocates of the proper grasp response to attempted counterexamples to *O3* must try to show that, *necessarily*, no agent with a proper grasp of morality is even temporarily a Humean agent with respect to moral motivation—an agent whose *M* beliefs do *not* encompass motivation and whose corresponding motivation derives partly from relevant desires. That is a tall order.

Consider the following thesis:

> *O4*. (1) Necessarily, an agent who is rational at *t* and, at *t*, has no motivation to *A* does not, at *t*, believe that he morally ought to *A*. (2) And, necessarily, if an agent who is rational at *t* believes at *t* that he morally ought to *A*, that belief encompasses motivation to *A*.[16]

Grant proposition 1 here for the sake of argument. Proposition 2 may be viewed as a hypothesis about why proposition 1 is true. But there is an alternative hypothesis about that—namely, that the ought belief is not motivation encompassing and the motivational source of the motivation specifically to *A* lies in some factor that would be absent were the agent not "rational" at the time. The pertinent factor may be, or include, something like the Alphic generic desire. That desire, together with the belief that one morally ought to *A*, may generate a desire to *A*, rather than the belief encompassing motivation to *A*. And, on the assumption that proposition 1 is true, some pertinent desire (e.g., a desire to act for good reasons) may be a constituent of a kind of time-slice rationality that is incompatible with severe listlessness of the sort I have described. Which hypothesis offers a more attractive explanation of the alleged truth of proposition 1?

Derek Parfit distinguishes "substantive" from "procedural" rationality. "To be substantively rational, we must care about certain things, such as our own well-being" (1997, 101). "To be procedurally rational, we must deliberate in certain ways, but we are not required to have any particular desires or aims, such as concern about our own well-being" (101). Proposition 1 in *O4* may be false when the occurrence of "rational" in it is read as "procedurally rational" and true when it is read as "substantively rational." Substantive rationality at a time may be inconsistent with suffering at the time from listlessness of the kind I have described.

Assuming a realistic understanding of the attitudes, the claim that we have beliefs that are, at once, both truth-seeking and motivation-encompassing is at least disputable. Suppose that, as a matter of fact, such beliefs are not in the psychological repertoire of human beings and that somehow this fact were discovered by us. Would we conclude that no human being has ever had a first-person moral ought belief? I doubt it. If, as it turns out, no moral ought beliefs encompass motivation, such beliefs may still contribute to action in conjunction with something like Alphic generic desires, and moral ought beliefs will have practical clout for agents with such desires. Allegiance to a certain conception of morality may naturally lead some theorists to hope that we have motivation-encompassing beliefs. But should that hope be dashed, their allegiance would predictably shift to a modified conception of morality rather than to nihilism. This is an indication that the existence of morality does not *conceptually* or *metaphysically* require that moral ought beliefs of the kind at issue be in the psychological repertoire of moral agents and that morality's existence leaves it open that moral ought beliefs generate moral conduct in conjunction with generic moral desires.

It is an intriguing idea that from putative conceptual or metaphysical truths about the nature of morality (namely, that the existence of morality entails or presupposes *O3* or *O4*) and the premise that some human beings have true beliefs that they morally ought to do certain things, one can deduce the substantive psychological truth that among the mental states of human beings are motivation-encompassing beliefs. This idea is comparable to one sometimes found in discussions of free will: namely, that from a conceptual or metaphysical truth about the nature of free will and the premise that we experience our own freedom, we can deduce that determinism is false (or, in another argument of this form, that determinism is *true*). These arguments for theses about psychological and physical reality are not likely to convince psychologists and physicists. But some philosophers will not be daunted by this; and they may observe, of course, that the second premise (the one affirming the existence of moral ought beliefs, or of veridical experiences of free will) is an empirical one—the arguments are not completely *a priori*. This reinforces my point that cognitivist proponents of *O3* or *O4* put the existence of moral ought beliefs at serious risk. If, as these philosophers claim, the nature of morality is such that no belief is a moral ought belief unless it is both truth-seeking and motivation-encompassing, there is a very real chance that we have never had a moral ought belief. If the constraints that morality's existence places on the psychology of moral beings are less stringent, we are more likely to be—as we believe ourselves to be—beings who have had moral ought beliefs.

I close this section by calling attention to an internalist thesis about moral ought beliefs that is more cautious than the ones identified above:

> *O5*. Necessarily, any agent who believes at *t* that he morally ought to *A* either has motivation at *t* to *A* or is practically irrational at *t*.[17]

Each of *O1*, *O2*, and *O3* asserts that believing at *t* that one morally ought to *A* entails having at *t* motivation to *A*, but *O5* does not. And although *O4* posits motivation-encompassing moral ought beliefs, *O5* does not. Furthermore, if people who suffer from listlessness at a time are practically irrational at that time, *O5* is not undermined by the Alphan thought experiment.

How might *O5* be defended? Michael Smith has suggested that the defense should come in three stages (2008, 214). Here are the three theses to be defended: (1) to believe that an agent morally ought to *A* is to believe that *A* is the alternative open to the agent that "uniquely maximizes value"; (2) to believe that "*p* has value" is to believe that "*p* is something that [I] would want if [I] had a maximally informed and coherent and unified desire set"; (3) "the following combination of belief and lack of desire—someone's believing that she would want that *p*, if she had a maximally informed and coherent and unified desire set, but lacking any desire that *p*—constitutes an instance of practical irrationality in an ordinary sense." Assessing the plausibility of these three theses is way too ambitious a task for this chapter. But I should point out that problems with less cautious versions of internalism have heightened interest in more cautious, restricted versions (see Miller 2008 for a critical review).

Wrapping Things Up

Both philosophical and lay thinking about action include a pair of perspectives on the explanation of intentional actions, a *motivational* and an *intellectual* one (Mele 1995, ch. 2; Pettit and Smith 1993). Central to the motivational perspective is the idea that what agents do when they act intentionally is tightly linked to what they are most strongly motivated to do at the time. This perspective is taken on all intentional actions, independently of the biological species to which the agents belong. If, for instance, cats, dogs, and human beings sometimes act intentionally, the motivational perspective has all three species in its sights. Those who take this perspective believe that, in the case of intentional actions, information about why agents were in the motivational condition they were in at the time of action contributes to our understanding of why they acted as they did.

The intellectual perspective applies only to intellectual beings. Whatever the minimally sufficient conditions for inclusion in the class of intellectual beings may be, practical intellect, as it is normally conceived, is concerned (among other things) with weighing options and coming to conclusions about what it is best, better, or good enough to do. Central to the intellectual perspective is the idea that such conclusions (beliefs) play a significant role in explaining some intentional actions of intellectual beings. Moral considerations seem to play an important role in generating some such conclusions.

It is no accident that the motivational and intellectual perspectives have evolved and survived. They seem to help make sense of our intentional behavior, and a plausible combination is theoretically desirable. Such a combination will include plausible positions on akratic action and on the connection between agents' beliefs that they themselves morally ought to *A* and motivation to *A*. More generally, it will do justice to the intellectual and motivational aspects of our lives and shed light on the important connections between them.[18]

References

Ainslie, G. (1992), *Picoeconomics*. Cambridge: Cambridge University Press.

Altham, J. (1986), "The Legacy of Emotivism,." in G. Macdonald and C. Wright (eds.), *Fact, Science and Morality*. Oxford: Blackwell.

Aristotle. (1915), *Nicomachean Ethics*. Vol. 9 of William Ross (ed.), *The Works of Aristotle*. London: Oxford University Press.

Arpaly, N. (2000), "On Acting Rationally against One's Best Judgment." *Ethics* 110, 488–513.

Audi, R. (1979), "Weakness of Will and Practical Judgment." *Noûs* 13, 173–96.

—. (1997), *Moral Knowledge and Ethical Character*. New York: Oxford University Press.

Bedke, M. (2009), "Moral Judgment Purposivism: Saving Internalism from Amoralism." *Philosophical Studies* 144, 189–209.

Brink, D. (1989), *Moral Realism and the Foundations of Ethics*. Cambridge: Cambridge University Press.

—. (1997), "Moral Motivation." *Ethics* 108, 4–32.

Buss, S. (1997), "Weakness of Will." *Pacific Philosophical Quarterly* 78, 13–44.

Charlton, W. (1988), *Weakness of Will*. Oxford: Basil Blackwell.

Dancy, J. (1993), *Moral Reasons*. Oxford: Blackwell.

Darwall, S. (1983), *Impartial Reason*. Ithaca, NY: Cornell University Press.

—. (1992), "Internalism and Agency." *Philosophical Perspectives* 6, 155–74.

Davidson, D. (1980), *Essays on Actions and Events*. Oxford: Clarendon Press.

Frankena, W. (1958), "Obligation and Motivation in Recent Moral Philosophy," in A. Melden (ed.), *Essays in Moral Philosophy*. Seattle: University of Washington Press.

Garrard, E., and McNaughton, D. (1998), "Mapping Moral Motivation." *Ethical Theory and Moral Practice* 1, 45–59.

Gert, J. and A. Mele. (2005), "Lenman on Externalism and Amoralism: An Interplanetary Exploration." *Philosophia* 32, 275–83.
Gopnik, A. (1993), "How We Know Our Minds: The Illusion of First-Person Knowledge of Intentionality," *Behavioral and Brain Sciences* 16, 1–14.
Gosling, J. (1990), *Weakness of the Will*. London: Routledge.
Hare, R. (1963), *Freedom and Reason*. Oxford: Oxford University Press.
Harman, G. (2004), "Practical Aspects of Theoretical Rationality," in A. Mele and P. Rawling (eds.), *The Oxford Handbook of Rationality*. Oxford: Oxford University Press.
Holton, R. (2009), *Willing, Wanting, Waiting*. Oxford: Oxford University Press.
Kennett, J. and Fine, C. (2008), "Internalism and the Evidence from Psychopaths and 'Acquired Sociopaths'." in W. Sinnott--Armstrong (ed.), *Moral Psychology*, vol. 3. Oxford: Oxford University Press.
Korsgaard, C. (1986), "Skepticism About Practical Reason." *Journal of Philosophy* 83, 5–25.
Lenman, J. (1999), "The Externalist and the Amoralist." *Philosophia* 27, 441–57.
Lewis, D. (1988), "Desire as Belief." *Mind* 97, 323–32.
McDowell, J. (1978), "Are Moral Requirements Hypothetical Imperatives?" *Proceeding of the Aristotelian Society* 52 suppl., 13–29.
McNaughton, D. (1988), *Moral Vision*. Oxford: Basil Blackwell.
Mele, A. (1987), *Irrationality*. New York: Oxford University Press.
—. (1992), *Springs of Action*. New York: Oxford University Press.
—. (1995), *Autonomous Agents*. New York: Oxford University Press.
—. (1996), 'Internalist Moral Cognitivism and Listlessness'. *Ethics* 106, 727–53.
—. (2002), "Akratics and Addicts." *American Philosophical Quarterly* 39, 153–67.
—. (2003), *Motivation and Agency*. New York: Oxford University Press.
—. (2010), "Weakness of Will and *Akrasia*." *Philosophical Studies* 150, 391–404.
—. (2011), "Self-Control in Action," in S. Gallagher (ed.), *Oxford Handbook of the Self*. New York: Oxford University Press, 465–86.
Miller, C. (2008), "Motivational Internalism." *Philosophical Studies* 139, 233–55.
Milo, R. (1984), *Immorality*. Princeton: Princeton University Press.
Mischel, W. and Ayduk, O. (2004), "Willpower in a Cognitive-Affective Processing System," in R. Baumeister and K. Vohs (eds.), *Handbook of Self-Regulation*. New York: Guilford Press.
Mischel, W., Shoda, Y. and Rodriguez, M. (1989), "Delay of Gratification in Children." *Science* 244, 933–8.
Nagel, T. (1970), *The Possibility of Altruism*. Oxford: Oxford University Press.
Parfit, D. (1997), "Reasons and Motivation." *Proceedings of the Aristotelian Society* 71 suppl., 99–130.
Pettit, P. and Smith, M. (1993), "Practical Unreason." *Mind* 102, 53–79.
Plato. (1953a), *Protagoras*. In Benjamin Jowett, trans. *The Dialogues of Plato*. Oxford: Clarendon Press.
—. (1953b), *Republic*. In Benjamin Jowett, trans. *The Dialogues of Plato*. Oxford: Clarendon Press.
Price, H. (1989), "Defending Desire-as-Belief." *Mind* 98, 119–27.
Pugmire, D. (1982), 'Motivated Irrationality'. *Proceedings of the Aristotelian Society* 56, 179–96.

Rorty, A. (1980a), "*Akrasia* and Conflict." *Inquiry* 22, 193–212.
—. (1980b), "Where Does the Akratic Break Take Place?" *Australasian Journal of Philosophy* 58, 333–46.
Roskies, A. (2003), "Are Ethical Judgments Intrinsically Motivational? Lessons from Acquired Sociopathy." *Philosophical Psychology* 16, 51–66.
—. (2008), Internalism and the Evidence from Pathology." in W. Sinnott-Armstrong (ed.), *Moral Psychology*, vol. 3. Oxford: Oxford University Press.
Santas, G. (1966), "Plato's Protagoras and Explanations of Weakness." *Philosophical Review* 75, 3–33.
Smith, M. (1987), "The Humean Theory of Motivation." *Mind* 96, 36–61.
—. (1992), "Valuing: Desiring or Believing?," in D. Charles and K. Lennon (eds.), *Reduction, Explanation, and Realism*. Oxford: Clarendon.
—. (1994), *The Moral Problem*. Oxford: Blackwell.
—. (1996), "The Argument for Internalism: Reply to Miller." *Analysis* 56, 175–84.
—. (2003), "Rational Capacities, or: How to Distinguish Recklessness, Weakness, and Compulsion,." in S. Stroud and C. Tappolet (eds.), *Weakness of Will and Practical Irrationality*. Oxford: Clarendon Press.
—. (2008), 'The Truth About Internalism," in W. Sinnott-Armstrong (ed.), *Moral Psychology*, vol. 3. Oxford: Oxford University Press.
Stocker, M. (1979), "Desiring the Bad." *Journal of Philosophy* 76, 738–53.
Svavarsdottir, S. (1999), "Moral Cognition and Motivation." *Philosophical Review* 108, 161–219.
Tenenbaum, S. (1999), "The Judgment of a Weak Will." *Philosophy and Phenomenological Research* 59, 875–911.
Thalberg, I. (1985), "Questions about Motivational Strength," in E. LePore and B. McLaughlin (eds.), *Actions and Events*. Oxford: Basil Blackwell.
van Roojen, M. (2002), "Humean and Anti-Humean Internalism About Moral Judgements." *Philosophy and Phenomenological Research* 65, 26–49.
Wallace, R. J. (1999), "Three Conceptions of Rational Agency." *Ethical Theory and Moral Practice* 2, 217–42.
—. (2005), "Moral Psychology," in Frank Jackson and Michael Smith (eds.), *The Oxford Handbook of Contemporary Philosophy*. Oxford: Oxford University Press, 86–113
Watson, G. (1977), "Skepticism about Weakness of Will." *Philosophical Review* 86, 316–39.
Wiggins, D. (1991), "Moral Cognitivism, Moral Relativism and Motivating Moral Beliefs." *Proceedings of the Aristotelian Society* 91, 61–85.

6 Morality and Religion

William J. Wainwright

A number of important religious views entail that the ontological and epistemic relations between religion and morality are tighter than most secular thinkers suppose. I will discuss three of them—natural law theory, divine command theory, and divine motivation theory.

Natural Law Theory

Natural law theorists believe that our reason's participation in God's reason enables us to discern what is needed to secure the human good. While revealed laws are necessary for directing us toward our supernatural good, reason alone is a sufficient guide to our earthly good. Both revealed law and the natural law discerned by unaided reason are reflections of God's "eternal law"—the plan of the divine reason or wisdom considered as directing the actions and motions of created beings to their proper end.[1] But the latter is accessible to everyone without supernatural assistance and the former is not.

The most compelling recent formulation of natural law theory is Mark Murphy's.[2] According to Murphy, a fully adequate natural law theory would preserve the general "accessibility of at least the most basic practical principles while offering a tight and distinctive connection between human nature and natural [i.e., moral or ethical] law" (Murphy 2001, 18). What he calls the "real identity thesis" does this. It states that "any state of affairs that theoretical reason grasps as 'x is an aspect of human flourishing' would be correctly grasped by practical reason as 'x is a good worth having,'" and vice versa (Murphy 2001, 19). Neither judgment entails the other, however, and either one of them can be grasped without grasping the other.[3] It is thus possible for someone to grasp the basic principles of commonsense morality without grasping their connection to human flourishing. Nevertheless, because the *contents* falling under the concepts of human flourishing and of goods to be pursued are essentially the same, and the same state of affairs makes both judgments true, once we become aware of the connection "we may be able to use this information to argue in a justifiable way from judgments of one type to judgments of the other type" (Murphy 2001, 20).

The contents in question are "nine basic aspects of well being" which "together . . . exhaust all the fundamental reasons for action." They are "life, knowledge, aesthetic experience, excellence in play and work, excellence in agency, inner peace [largely consisting in the absence of unsatisfied desires and aspirations], friendship and community, religion, and happiness" which Murphy defines as "the successful achievement of a reasonable life plan" (Murphy 2001, 96, 133).[4]

Murphy's natural law theory is the most persuasive known to me. Even so, it shares certain weaknesses with other theories of that type. Consider his account of the basic good of religion, for example.

"Religion" consists in a harmonious alignment between one's own life and a "more-than-human order . . . that can be called, whether univocally or analogically, *personal*" (Murphy 2001, 131–2, his emphasis).[5] Since "human goods are *possibilities* for human fulfillment" (Murphy 2001, 132, my emphasis), those who deny the existence of a higher order will deny that religion is part of the human good. This is no more troublesome, however, than the fact that "radical epistemic skeptics" who deny the possibility of knowledge must deny that knowledge is part of the human good (Murphy 2001, 132).

But even though religion is a basic (i.e., intrinsic or nonderivative) good, it is not a *fundamental* or *foundational* good in the sense that the other basic goods are ordered toward it. For if it were, then if natural law theory is correct, there would have to be a "distinctive human tendency . . . toward subordinating all of the other [basic] goods to the good of religion," i.e., toward regulating the pursuit of all "other goods in terms of what is needed to achieve the religious good" (Murphy 2001, 196). Murphy is skeptical of the claim that we have a tendency to subordinate other goods to the good of religion but not to subordinate the religious good to nonreligious goods. And thinks that even if we did, it is doubtful that it would be best explained by "the thesis that all other basic goods are naturally for the sake of the good of religion" (which carries the implication that "pursuit of the religious good" *should* "be made one's supreme good") (Murphy 2001, 196). For a tendency of the sort in question could be just as easily explained by the less controversial claim that "the other basic goods are more apt to be used as instrumental goods than the religious good is," i.e., by the "fact that the other [basic] goods are (at least apparently) more efficient instruments for bringing about the religious good than the religious good is for bringing about the other goods" (Murphy 2001, 196).

Murphy's arguments at this point illustrate what some would regard as a general weakness of natural law theory, namely, that it focuses on the inclinations of "*fallen*" human nature. That humans as they *are* have little or no tendency to subordinate all other goods to the good of religion entails neither that humans *shouldn't* do so, or that humanity as it was "designed" to be, or at its best, *wouldn't* do so. Thus, our present lack of a tendency to subordinate other goods to the good of religion has little or no obvious relevance. (Note that the view that human nature as it is is deeply flawed isn't peculiar to Augustinian forms of Christianity. All of the so-called higher religions include "a sense that there is *something wrong about us as we naturally stand*" (James 1902, 498, his emphasis). Nor are Augustinian Christians unique in thinking that our inclinations as they stand are radically warped. Advaita Vedantins and Buddhists, for example, would agree that they are.)

The natural law theorist's account of moral obligation is also suspect. Murphy, for instance, suggests that the moral ought be defined as follows: "A morally ought to φ if and only if it is not possible that A, whose practical reasoning is functioning without error, decide to ψ, where ψ-ing and φ-ing are incompatible" (Murphy 2001, 222).[6] But this appears to have the counterintuitive consequence that any prudentially required action is morally obligatory. Suppose, for example, that a specific intellectual and/or physical regimen is a necessary condition of excellence in play, so that without that training it would be impossible to achieve that excellence. If it is, and my practical reasoning is functioning without error, it seems that I can't decide not to train. But if I can't, and Murphy's definition is correct, it follows that I am *morally required* to train. This transforms all prudential obligations into moral obligations, however, and for reasons Kant suggests, it is doubtful that we should do so. For prudential obligations ultimately rest on our desires and inclinations, and are therefore escapable.[7] Moral obligations are not.

A related problem is this. On theories of this type, when human agents are functioning properly, the *ends* of their basic inclinations are good. It follows that (other things being equal) it is *good* to pursue them and that they therefore have a *reason* for doing so. It doesn't follow that they have a *moral obligation* to do so or that they would be doing *wrong* if they didn't. (I wouldn't be doing wrong, for example, if I failed to pursue excellence in play or aesthetic appreciation.)

A further difficulty with natural law theory is this. Natural law theory is often thought to be preferable to more explicitly theistic theories such as divine command theory because it appeals to moral and ethical principles[8] which are inscribed in human nature as such and can therefore provide common ground between theistic moralists, on the one hand, and secular moralists, on the other. There are at least two reasons for believing that this alleged advantage is illusory, however. For one thing, in practice, natural law theory is typically invoked to defend controversial ethical positions (about human sexuality, abortion, suicide, gender relations, and the like) which secular thinkers by and large find rationally unpersuasive. This unsurprisingly arouses the suspicion that appeals to natural law are too often instances of special pleading, unconvincing attempts to find rational grounds for injunctions and prohibitions which would not be embraced unless they had been endorsed by religious authority. For another, natural law theory depends on the concept of proper human function—a notion which has no standing apart from a teleological view of nature and/or a theistic or quasi-theistic understanding of reality. Since there is little reason to expect that the secular moralist qua secular moralist will find these notions compelling the idea that appeals to natural law can provide common ground between religious and secular moral thinkers may be wishful thinking.

The other two accounts of the ontological and epistemic relations between religion and morality are more explicitly theistic. The first of these is divine command theory. Divine command theory is a form of "theological voluntarism"—one of a family of theories which ground moral facts in God's volitional nature. As its name implies, divine command theory roots moral facts in God's commands. Philip Quinn (Quinn 2000) and Mark Murphy (Murphy 1998) ground them in God's antecedent intentions.[9] Others such as Christian Miller (Miller 2009) ground moral facts in God's antecedent preferences or desires.[10]

Divine intention, preference, and desire theories have not been sharply distinguished from divine command theories until quite recently. Partly for that reason, but primarily because of limitations of space, I will focus exclusively on divine command theory in this chapter.

Divine Command Theory

Divine command theory like other forms of theological voluntarism offers two clear advantages. Important strands of the Christian tradition stress God's absolute sovereignty. The emphasis is particularly clear in Augustine, William of Ockham, Martin Luther, and John Calvin. It is an equally important theme in Islam and in Dvaita Vedanta. If God's sovereignty is unlimited and unqualified, as these traditions attest, then there is nothing distinct from God on which he is dependent and nothing distinct from him which is not dependent on him. It would seem to follow that moral facts aren't independent of God. If God is truly sovereign, his will must somehow make them true or constitute the moral facts which they express. For suppose it doesn't, and that God's will is wholly or partly determined by independent standards of value. If it is, then God's activity is not wholly *self*-determined; he is subject to things that exist independently of him.

Indeed, leaving questions of divine dependence aside, the very existence of independent moral and value facts compromises God's sovereignty. For if essences, eternal truths (including moral truths), values, and the like aren't "part" of God or created by him, then God's sovereignty does not extend over all being. So by making moral facts dependent on God's will, divine command theory and other forms of theological voluntarism effectively protect his sovereignty. For theists, this is an important consideration in its favor.

Divine command theory is exposed to powerful objections, however, the most important of which is probably this. Although historically this hasn't always been obvious, divine command theory is, in essence, an account of *deontological* facts, i.e., facts about what is morally obligatory, morally permissible, and morally forbidden. The trouble is that the theory seems to imply that in logically possible worlds in which God fails to exist or commands nothing, such things as promise keeping or fidelity wouldn't be obligatory, and gratuitous cruelty, treachery, and the like wouldn't be forbidden. It seems to many of us, however, that promise keeping and fidelity would be prima facie obligatory in *all* possible circumstances, and that gratuitous cruelty and treachery would be forbidden. Moreover, to make matters worse, divine command theories seem to imply that not only might things like gratuitous cruelty be permitted, they might even be obligatory. For there appear to be logically possible worlds in which God exists and commands us to act cruelly. If there are, and divine command theory is correct, then cruelty is morally obligatory in those worlds. Yet surely one of our most deeply entrenched moral intuitions is that there is *no* possible world in which it would be prima facie obligatory to gratuitously inflict pain on others. In other words, "It is prima facie wrong to inflict gratuitous cruelty on another" appears to be a *necessary* truth.

Divine command theorists who believe that God is self-existent have a response to these objections. God necessarily exists and is such that in any possible world in which creatures like us exist, he commands them not to lie, to protect the innocent, and so on.[11] Robert Adams says that he doesn't "believe that there is a unique set of commands that would be issued by any supremely good God" (Adams 1999, 255). And this is surely correct. A supremely good God might issue one set of ritual commands in one possible world, for example, and another set in another. Yet this admission is fully consistent with claiming that there are some commands that any supremely good God would necessarily issue to beings sufficiently like us. The second table of the Decalogue is, arguably, an example.[12] If moral obligations are best understood as divine commands, then these necessary moral truths can be construed as commands God necessarily issues in the appropriate circumstances.

A second reason why one might want to adopt divine command theory or some other form of theological voluntarism is philosophical. It provides an attractive account of the objectivity of deontological facts.

What conditions must be met if values are to be objective? First, value claims are either true or false. Second, values are universal. If something is prima facie good or right, it is prima facie good or right at all times and places.[13] Third, values aren't products of our desires, interests, or other intentional attitudes.

The goodness of truthfulness or friendship, for example, can't be reduced to the fact that we desire them or would desire them if we were fully informed.

But while these conditions are necessary they aren't sufficient. To be objective in the intended sense, values must also be part of the "furniture of the universe." Goodness and rightness, for example, must be real properties of the things that have them.

J. L. Mackie has persuasively argued that a belief in the objectivity of moral values is embedded in most mainstream Western moral philosophy, and is presupposed in ordinary moral thought and discourse. Mackie himself thinks that moral realism is mistaken. In the first place, value properties, if real, would be "queer" properties, "utterly different from everything else in the universe." Unlike other facts, moral facts would have either "requiredness" or "not-to-be-doneness somehow built into" them, and an objective goodness would have "to-be-pursuedness somehow built into it." Yet how features like these could be related to a thing's natural or empirical features is a total mystery. In the second place, it is unclear how we could *know* these nonnatural features since they don't stand in causal relations to us (Mackie 1977, 38–41).

Mackie's response to these difficulties is to offer an error theory of objective value.[14] But given that an appearance of objectivity is an obvious feature of ordinary moral experience and practice, a belief in the objectivity of values would appear to be the default position. Other things being equal, their apparent objectivity is a good reason for thinking that moral values really *are* objective. So if theists can provide an explanation of moral values which respects the appearance of objectivity, and is at least as good an explanation of their apparent objectivity as Mackie's, then their apparent objectivity is a sufficient reason for preferring the theist's account to Mackie's.

Even if they can do this, though, theists aren't home free. For theistic accounts of the objectivity of moral values have rivals which preserve at least some of the appearances. Two of the most important are naturalism and constructivism.[15]

Naturalism identifies goodness, for instance, with a natural (that is, empirical) property such as pleasure or happiness, or with a cluster of such properties. For example, Richard Boyd identified goodness with what he calls a "homeostatic property cluster"—"things which satisfy important human needs" together with the "homeostatic mechanisms which unify them" (Boyd 1988, 181–228). Boyd doesn't think that "good" *means* "things satisfying important human needs together with the mechanisms which unify them." But he does think that this property cluster *constitutes* goodness, or is what goodness *really is*. (An analogy: "water" doesn't mean "H_2O." Nevertheless, H_2O constitutes water, is what water really is.)

Naturalism has several advantages. Perhaps its most important is that it appears to make moral values robustly objective. In its view, values are ordinary empirical properties (or sets of them). They are thus part of the furniture of the universe, and claims about them are either true or false. Values also appear to be universal in the relevant sense. If goodness is identical with Boyd's homeostatic property cluster, for example, every instance of that property cluster is good regardless of where or when it is found.

Whether naturalism preserves *all* the appearances, however, is doubtful. Mackie has pointed out that moral facts as ordinarily understood have "requiredness" or "not-to-be-doneness" built into them, and that the property (or set of properties) picked out by "goodness" has "to-be pursuedness" built into it. Yet it is difficult to see how purely empirical properties *could* have characteristics like these built into them. Suppose, for instance, that we identify goodness with the set of things which satisfies our more important wants and needs. Given that we *have* wants and needs, we will pursue their satisfaction. But the to-be-pursuedness of the things that satisfy them appears, on this view, to be an artifact of our needs and wants, not an intrinsic feature of the things themselves. If so, then our third criterion of objectivity isn't met; values don't have the necessary independence from our desires and interests.

Constructivists believe that while there *are* moral facts or truths, these facts or truths are the *products* of rational deliberation and choice. For example, John Rawls argued that adequate principles of justice are those which would be chosen under fair conditions by rational agents concerned to maximize their share of such things as "rights and liberties, opportunities and powers, income and wealth," and "a sense of one's own worth" (Rawls 1971, 92). Christine Korsgaard believes that "value is founded in rational nature—in particular in the structure of reflective consciousness." Moral values are bound up with our "practical identity," descriptions under which we value ourselves, "find [our] life to be worth living and [our actions] to be worth undertaking" (Korsgaard 1996, 101, 116).

On views like these, value claims are objective in the sense that they are true or false (or, alternatively, correct or incorrect, reasonable or unreasonable). Whether they meet the other conditions for objectivity is less clear.

Rawls came to admit that his procedures will yield the intuitively "correct" results only when applied to rational agents committed to the values of modern Western liberal democracies.[16] The moral claims supported by the procedures aren't truly universal, then. And critics have accused Korsgaard of paying insufficient attention to the fact that the descriptions under which we value ourselves appear to vary from one person to another and from culture to culture (Cohen 1996, Geuss 1996). If they do, appeals to them won't yield universal moral principles. The fourth condition (viz., that moral values are part of the furniture of the universe) isn't met either. Korsgaard, I think, speaks for all constructivists when she says that the value which "is grounded in . . . the structure of rational consciousness . . . is projected onto the world. So the reflection in question is practical and not theoretical; it is a reflection about what to do, *not reflection about what is to be found in the normative part of the world*" (Korsgaard 1996, 116, my emphases).

By contrast, on a suitably qualified divine command theory, statements of moral obligation meet all four of the conditions that values must satisfy if they are to be considered objective. Since claims that God commands such and such are either true or false, moral claims are true or false. Basic moral values are also universal. God's prohibition of infidelity or murder, for example, extends to all times and places. Furthermore, while God's commands presumably depend on *his* desires, they do not depend on ours. Truth telling, for instance, is prima facie obligatory regardless of what *we* want or desire.[17] Finally, God and his commands are as much part of the furniture of the universe as the stars in their courses or subatomic particles.

The scope of divine command theory is limited, however. While it may explain the objectivity of moral *obligation*, it doesn't obviously account for the objectivity of other values such as the intrinsic goodness of pleasure or knowledge or human love. Our prima facie obligation to avoid inflicting needless pain on others may depend on a divine command as the divine command theorist believes but it is difficult to see how the intrinsic badness of pain could do so. If her account of the objectivity of value is to be complete, then, the divine command theorist must supplement it with a theistic theory of the good. One divine command theorist who has done so is Robert Adams.

Excellence is a property of "persons . . . ; physical objects; some kinds of abstraction (such as poems and mathematical proofs); qualities (such as a beautiful shade of blue); deeds; lives—but not in general of states of affairs." It is an object of *eros* both in "its moments of admiration" and in its moments of pursuit. (The latter is grounded in the former.) Now "the character of our pursuit of excellence, including the character of the things we think are excellent," points in the direction of "a single property or nature" that "would best satisfy the pursuit." "That property or nature," whatever it may be, is what is referred to by "excellence" (Adams 1999, 17, 22). In Adams's view, the nature or property in question is constituted by resemblance to the Good. And because *God* is the Good, excellence is ultimately constituted by resemblance to God.

Why should the Good be identified with God, though? For several reasons, among the most important of which are these. The Good must be personal. Since most important excellences "are excellences of persons, or of qualities or actions or works or lives or stories of persons," and since the excellence of finite things "consists in resembling or imaging" the Good, the Good must be "a person or importantly like a person" (Adams 1999, 42).

It must also be actual. For suppose that it isn't. "Mere possibilities have no standing in the world except as objects of understanding." Now "we [and other finite beings] do not understand the Good itself, in all its perfections." Hence, the Good will have no standing in the world unless God understands it. If God understands it, however, then God exists and "is there as a real being to fill the role of the Good." Assuming that he has the other characteristics needed to fit something for the role of the Good, it is therefore reasonable to identify him with the "objective standard of excellence" (Adams 1999, 44–5).

Views like these are subject to an important objection, however. If we think of God as a person, we can only think of him as "fully and perfectly *exemplifying*" "the order of values," "not as *being* . . . it . . . He will be, so to say, the Great Exemplar" (Maclagen 1961, 88, his emphases). He won't be Goodness itself. The objection, in other words, is that God is a *particular*, and particulars can't be standards.

Furthermore, that God is to be praised and glorified for his goodness is fundamental to theism. But that God is to be praised for his goodness seems to imply that, rather than *being* a standard, God *meets* standards. (We don't praise standards. We praise things for meeting them.)

The distinction between perfect examples and standards is not that sharp, however. Examples are sometimes *prior* to the rules or norms which state that things like the example are good or right, in the sense that the rules or norms are *derived from* the examples. A person, or a pattern of behavior, or a work of art, or a new wine strikes us as exemplary even though it fails to meet existing norms in some respects. Under the impact of the example, we construct new standards or reconstruct old ones. In situations like these, the example is more than a perfect instance of the new or reconstructed norm. It is, in a real sense, its ground or source.

Nor is the priority of the examples in most of these cases purely epistemological. It is not as if, under the impact of the examples, we discover standards that can be stated without reference to them. For, in many of the cases in question, the standards can only be stated in the form "Paintings like this (or behavior like this, or scientific work like this, or . . .) are good or right." The standards, in other words, "make essential reference to one or more individuals" (Alston 1989, 269). It is not clear, then, that there need be anything logically eccentric in suggesting that *God* is both Goodness's perfect exemplar *and* its standard.

Moreover, where the standard *is* a particular, praise or commendation is sometimes in order. Arguably, where particulars function as standards, they do so because they are perfect instances of the class of things being evaluated. Thus, the standard meter bar is (*pace* Wittgenstein) exactly one meter long since it is the same length as itself. If a particular chef's shrimp creoles provide the paradigm for all shrimp creoles, then his creoles are perfect shrimp creoles. Furthermore, while it would be nonsense to praise the rule which states that the chef's creoles provide the paradigm for all shrimp creoles, it is not nonsense to praise the chef's creoles themselves. Even if we do praise things for meeting standards rather than for being standards, it isn't clear that we can't praise the exemplary creoles for their perfect conformity to the rule which states that they are the paradigmatic instances of their class. Similarly, it isn't clear that God's being the standard of goodness is incompatible with praise. Standard examples cannot, of course, fail to match themselves. Whether this precludes praise, however, is doubtful. Classical theists, at least, have no reason to think so. For while they believe that praising God is always in order, they also think that God, being essentially good, cannot fail to meet the appropriate standards.

Note that on Adams's account values, too, meet all four of the conditions they must satisfy if they are to be considered objective. Since claims that things resemble God in the right way are either true or false, value claims are true or false. Values are also universal. If courage, say, or human fidelity faithfully images or resembles God, it does so at all times and places. Nor are the facts of resemblance in which excellence consists dependent on our desires. If visual beauty for instance faithfully images God, it does so whether we admire and desire it or not. Finally, God and the facts of resemblance are part of the "furniture of the universe." That human love resembles God's love, for example, is as objectively real a feature of human love, as a photograph's resemblance to its original or a child's resemblance to its parents. Adams's theory thus saves the appearance of value's objectivity.

A theory like Adams's also dispels Mackie's two main worries. By identifying objective value with resemblance to God, it eliminates, or at least reduces, its ontological "queerness." The existence of objective value is no "queerer" than the existence of God himself. It can also explain our epistemic access to objective value. If theism is true, then it is reasonable to believe that "God causes . . . human beings to regard as excellent approximately those things that are God-like in the relevant way" (He may do so by fashioning their consciences, by endowing them with appropriate emotions and capacities for practical reasoning, by direct revelation, and the like.) If he does, however, "there is a causal and explanatory connection between facts of excellence and beliefs that we may regard as justified about excellence" (Adams 1999, 70). Our epistemic access to objective value thus isn't mysterious.

The theistic justification of moral realism that I have outlined *is* exposed to an important objection, however. If its claims are correct, basic moral facts are *necessary* facts. "Lying is prima facie wrong," for instance, or "Loyalty is a moral excellence" are *necessarily* true, that is, true in all possible worlds. But if they are, divine command theory and theistic theories of the good seem otiose since moral values meet all four criteria for objectivity *just in virtue of their necessity*. Claims about basic values are either necessarily *true* or necessarily *false*. The values in question are also universal. Since propositions expressing basic value facts are necessarily true, they are true in all possible worlds. Our third criterion is met as well. Necessary facts, such as the facts of logic or mathematics, aren't constituted by our willing or desiring them. They thus have the necessary independence of our desires.

Is the fourth criterion met too? It is difficult to see why not. If basic value claims are necessarily true, then the facts that they express are as much part of the structure of reality as the facts of logic and mathematics. If the latter are rightly regarded as objective, then so too are the former. Moreover, value properties are *real* properties of the things that have them. If it is necessarily true that lying is prima facie wrong and that loyalty is a moral excellence, then prima facie wrongness and moral excellence are *essential* properties of lying and loyalty, respectively. And essential properties of a thing are surely *real* properties of it.

The objection is therefore this. There is some reason to think that basic value claims are necessarily true. If they are, their objectivity seems assured, and there is no reason to bring God into the picture. An appeal to theistic metaphysics is thus otiose. Like facts of logic and mathematics, basic value facts are necessary and hence need no further explanation.

There is an important difference between logical or mathematical facts, however, and necessary value facts. The former are logically necessary in the "narrow" sense. Their truth is analytic, a consequence of definitions and logical or syntactic rules. Some necessary truths, though, are *not* analytic. Typical examples are "Nothing is red and green all over," "Nothing is larger than itself," or (more controversially) "No contingent being exists without at least a partial reason for its existence." While propositions like these are true in all possible worlds, their truth can't be deduced from definitions and logical rules. The constraints they impose are *substantive* and not merely *formal. Perhaps* analytic or *narrowly* necessary truths stand in no need of explanation. But synthetic or "*broadly*" necessary truths do. That there is some reason for the existence of contingent beings, for instance, presupposes the world's (partial) intelligibility, and that the world *is* intelligible cries out for explanation. Because necessary moral and ethical truths aren't analytic either, there is more reason to think that they stand in need of explanation than for thinking that the truths of logic and mathematics do.

Erik Wielenberg disagrees. In his view, at least some "ethical states of affairs that obtain necessarily . . . are [simply] brute facts." While they are synthetic, "to ask of such facts, 'where do they come from?' or 'on what foundation do they rest?' is misguided in much the same way that, according to many theists, it is misguided to ask of God 'where does He come from?' or 'on what foundation does He rest?'" (Wielenberg 2009, 26).

The two cases are relevantly dissimilar, however. In the first place, God is essentially causeless but basic moral facts are not. (Since divine command theory isn't obviously incoherent, it appears that we can consistently conceive that basic facts about moral obligation have causes.)

Wielenberg rightly insists that a lack of obvious incoherence isn't sufficient to establish a thing's metaphysical possibility. Nor is the fact that I can imagine it. I can imagine what backwards time travel is like (by reading H. G. Well's *The Time Machine*, for example). Nor is it *obviously* incoherent. Nevertheless, there are plausible arguments purporting to show that backwards time travel *isn't* metaphysically possible. Similarly, even though I can imagine "that there is a stone floating in space with nothing else (including God) in existence" (Wielenberg 2009, 29) and what I imagine isn't obviously incoherent, this is not sufficient to show that God's nonexistence is metaphysically possible and, indeed, the thrust of arguments like Anselm's, Leibniz's, Hartshorne's, and Plantinga's is that it *isn't* metaphysically possible. By contrast, if divine command theory is true, the facts expressed by statements of moral obligation do have causes or distinct grounds. Hence, if divine command theory is possibly true, it is possible that all facts of moral obligation have causes or external grounds, in which case facts of moral obligation are *not* essentially causeless. For the two cases to be genuinely parallel, then, Wielenberg would have to show that there are reasons for thinking that divine command theory isn't metaphysically possible which are at least as strong as the arguments offered by Leibniz and others for the metaphysical impossibility of God's nonexistence. And Wielenberg hasn't done that.

Moreover, classical theists believe that God's existence is not only essentially causeless but also self-explanatory or intrinsically intelligible (though not necessarily intelligible to *us*); if we could grasp God's nature we would see why it is instantiated. The fact that so many modern ethical theorists reject moral realism strongly suggests that the existence of basic moral facts, on the other hand, is *not* self-explanatory or intrinsically intelligible. The cases thus, once again, appear relevantly dissimilar.

So are God's existence and the existence of basic moral facts, on a view like Wielenberg's, equally "brute"? In Wielenberg's sense, yes, for he defines a brute fact as a state of affairs whose obtaining "is not explained by a distinct state of affairs" (Wielenberg 2009, 30). There are at least two other senses of "brute fact," however. In the first, facts are brute if and only if they are contingent but have no explanation. On some views, the existence of the physical cosmos or the obtaining of the basic laws of nature are brute facts in this sense. In the second, facts are brute if and only if they are susceptible of a distinct explanation yet lack one. Since both God's existence and basic moral facts are necessary, neither are brute facts in the first of these two senses. But on the theistic view we are discussing, while God's existence isn't susceptible of a distinct explanation, the existence of facts of basic moral obligation is. The latter, if lacking an external explanation, is thus brute in a way in which the former is not. Moreover, since only facts that are brute in one or the other of these two senses cry out for an explanation, the existence of facts of basic moral obligation on a view like Wielenberg's requires an explanation in a way in which the God of classical theism does not. The two cases, then, aren't really on a par.

Of course divine command theory isn't the only theistic (or religious) game in town. There is another way of both securing God's sovereignty and explaining the existence of objective moral obligations (and other values), and that is to insist that while facts of moral obligation *are* metaphysically dependent on God, they aren't metaphysically dependent on his *commanding or willing* them. They might be metaphysically dependent on his thinking them, for example. Thus W. R. Sorley argues that objectively existing values must exist in either matter or minds. Because he believes they can't exist in matter, he concludes that they must exist in minds. And since finite minds are limited and contingent, he further concludes that they exist in an infinite mind.[18] Or they might be metaphysically dependent on God's being the Supreme Good or standard of value, so that the existence of the standard contributes to the existence of moral obligations but the existence of moral obligations doesn't contribute to the existence of the standard.[19] Or we might embrace Linda Zagzebski's "divine motivation theory."

Divine Motivation Theory

"Divine motivation theory makes the ground of what is morally good and morally right God's motives rather than God's will." Divine motivational states "such as love and compassion . . . [which] are components of God's virtues constitute the metaphysical basis for moral value" (Zagzebski 2004b, 357).

Divine motivation theory is "a virtue theory because" it regards "the moral properties of persons" (namely, virtues and vices) as "more basic than the moral properties of acts and outcomes . . . Outcomes [and acts] get their moral value by their relation to good and bad motivations." Good acts, for example, are the sort of acts which express the good emotional dispositions that are constituents of the virtues (Zagzebski 2004b, 358).[20]

Divine motivation theory is also an "exemplarist" theory in which "the moral properties of persons, acts, and outcomes are defined via an indexical reference to an exemplar of a good person. . . . The paradigmatically good person," however, "is God . . . God's motives are perfectly good and human motives are good in so far as they are like the divine motives as those motives would be expressed in finite and embodied human beings. [Human virtues are good personal traits that] imitate God's virtues" in the sense that they are the way those virtues "would be expressed by human beings in human circumstances" (Zagzebski 2004b, 358).

Zagzebski thinks that divine motivation theory has several advantages over divine command theory, one of the most important of which is this. In divine command theory, "God's own goodness and the rightness of God's own acts . . . are not connected to divine commands because God does not give commands to himself." Divine motivation theory, on the other hand, "has the theoretical advantage of providing a unitary theory of all [moral] evaluative properties, divine as well as human . . . Both divine and human goodness are explained in terms of God's motives, and the goodness of human motives is derived from the goodness of divine motives" (Zagzebski 2004b, 360f).

Whether divine motivation theory is preferable to divine command theory on other counts is another matter. It does seem to do an equally good job of protecting God's sovereignty and independence. If God's motivational states are the metaphysical basis of the goodness or badness of persons and the rightness or wrongness of their actions, then the fact that certain motivational states are good and others bad, and that some human actions are morally right while others are wrong, is not metaphysically independent of God.

On the other hand, the emphasis which Judaism, Christianity, and Islam place on obedience to God seems more at home in a divine command theory than in divine motivation theory considered simply as such. Furthermore, the plausibility of divine motivation theory depends on the plausibility of *virtue* theory. Whether virtue theory can adequately account for our sense of moral *obligation*, though, is controversial. Those sympathetic toward Kantian accounts of moral duty and moral obligation will probably judge that it can't since Kantian ethics doesn't comport well with virtue theory.

Notions of law and moral obligation are central to divine command theory. Virtue theories such as Zagzebski's downplay their importance. She denies that "obligation . . . logically entails law," for example. In her view, our sense of obligation is identical with our felt response to situations in which it noninferentially seems to us that only one response is appropriate ("We must do it") or that a response is clearly inappropriate ("We must not do it"). The moral imperatives experienced by "the Homeric heroes" or the protagonists of the Greek tragedies, for instance, were real but "not the modern one[s] of law." They were, instead, felt compulsions arising from strong emotional responses to the highly specific but existentially fraught situations in which they found themselves. Laws, on the other hand, are no more than

> generalizations of particular obligations and [particular] obligation precedes . . . law. It is true that once we reflect on the nature of a reason for acting in a particular case, then if we are obliged to be consistent, we are obligated to act in a like manner in situations that are suitably similar to the one with which we are confronted . . . It is probably [also] true that if the move from [e.g.] "She is suffering" to "I ought to help her" is an inference, then it uses or [at least] presupposes a general principle or law. (Zagzebski 2004a, 146–9)

What Zagzebski denies, however, is that our obligation *depends* on the possibility of generalizing it, or that when I feel compelled to help a person whom I see suffering, for example, I am typically making an inference.

It is by no means clear, though, that a sense of obligation or duty should be identified with a feeling of compulsion—not even one that the agent has no reason to believe is inappropriate. While the sense of moral obligation typically includes a sense of compulsion, not all examples of legitimate felt compulsion are instances of a sense of moral obligation. The feeling that I can do no other than follow a certain calling, for example (that of an actor, say, or a philosopher, or baseball pitcher), seems qualitatively different from believing or recognizing that it is my *duty* to do so, and acting on that feeling seems qualitatively distinct from acting out of Kantian respect for the moral law. Note too that even though a *recognition* of generalizability may not be "a condition for the obligation to obtain in any particular case" (Zagzebski 2004a, 151), the *possibility* of generalization might be. Moreover, even if my inability to generalize wouldn't eliminate my *feeling* of obligation or compulsion, it might nonetheless eliminate the *obligation itself*, and make it unreasonable for me to continue to *believe* that the object of my feeling really was obligatory.

Nor is Zagzebski clearly correct in claiming that while "value is capable of grounding obligation," "obligation is not capable of grounding value." Why does she think this?

> Obligation generates a regress; good does not . . . That is because when I ask for a justification of obligation—"Why must I do this?"—the answer will always be something that generates the same question: "Why must I do what is right?" "Why must I obey authority?" "Why must I obey a legitimate authority?" This last question can be asked even when the legitimate authority is God. [Good, on the other hand,] does not generate a regress. The goodness of something is . . . [sometimes] explained by the goodness of other things but the idea of an intrinsic good is perfectly coherent and . . . ends any threatened regress . . . The concept of an intrinsic obligation [on the other hand,] is . . . probably senseless. (Zagzebski 2004a, 162–4)

This isn't fully persuasive, however. In the first place, the notion of an intrinsic obligation is *not* clearly senseless. The commands of a drill sergeant, for example, are intrinsically authoritative and this entails that those under his command are intrinsically obligated to obey them. It is true that the intrinsic authoritativeness of the drill sergeant's commands is a function of the roles which he and those under his command occupy. But, similarly, the intrinsic goodness of pleasure or beauty or friendship are functions of their natures.[21] Moreover, obligations arguably *can* ground value. Kant, for instance, claims that the only thing that is unconditionally *good* is the good will, i.e., the will that always chooses the right because it *is* right, that is, morally obligatory.

The most important point, however, is this. It is by no means clear that value as such is capable of generating moral obligation. That something is good, and hence an appropriate object of desire may ground a *hypothetical* imperative; it isn't clear that it can ground a *categorical* one. Again, while the fact that the happiness of others is intrinsically good may give me a *reason* to promote it, it is *not* clearly sufficient to establish a moral obligation to do so.

Divine motivation theory has many merits. It protects God's sovereignty and provides a unified account of moral and ethical values. Moreover, while Zagzebski doesn't explicitly discuss this, divine motivation theory, too, entails moral realism. Since God's character traits are objective features of the universe if God exists, and those traits provide the standard of moral and ethical excellence, the standards of moral and ethical excellence are as much a part of the furniture of the universe as trees, persons, and hydrogen atoms. Divine motivation theory is a virtue theory, however, and it is doubtful that virtue theories provide an adequate account of *moral obligation*. In any case, I have argued that Zagzebski's virtue theory does not.

Note that divine command theories, divine motivation theories, and theistic conceptions of the good are *meta*-theories, explanations of value's ontological status. As such, they are compatible with a wide variety of substantive moral theories. The two currently most popular are (one or more forms of) utilitarianism or consequentialism and Kantianism. Divine command theory can be combined with both.

Divine Command Theory and Utilitarianism

For example, John Gay and William Paley argued that while (1) God's will is the source of moral obligation, (2) *what* God wills is the general happiness. (2) is supported by an appeal to God's nature and activity.

> It is evident from the nature of God, viz, his being infinitely happy in himself . . . and his goodness manifested in his works, that he could have no other design in creating mankind than their happiness; and therefore he wills their happiness; therefore the means of their happiness; therefore that my behavior, as far as it may be the means of the happiness of mankind should be such. (Gay 1731, xix)

When asked how one determines which actions promote or hinder the happiness of humanity, Gay responds, by "experience or reason" (Gay 1731, xx). Paley believes that there are *two* ways of ascertaining God's will, however—by what reason can discover of his designs and dispositions from his works but also by the "express declaration of scripture."

> An ambassador, judging only from what he knows of his sovereign's dispositions, and arguing from what he has observed of his conduct, or is acquainted with his designs, may take his measures in many cases with

> safety; and presume with great probability, how his master would have him act on most occasions that arise; but if he have his commission and instructions in his pocket, it would be strange never to look into them. (Paley 1785, 64–5)

These ways of ascertaining God's will complement each other. Where scriptural "instructions are clear . . . there is an end of all further deliberation."Where they are "silent or dubious," though, a person should "endeavor to supply or explain them by what he has been able to collect from other quarters of his master's general inclination or instructions,"i.e., by direct appeals to utility (Paley 1785, 54–7). Moreover, if God exists, and has expressly declared his will in scripture, it may sometimes be easier to determine his will (and hence, given that God wants us to maximize utility, what maximizes utility) than to independently ascertain the relevant long-range consequences of our actions (Wierenga 1984, 313–14).

But while utility fixes the *content* of morality, it does not determine its obligatory character. What does is God's commands. Gay, for example, believes that the concept of obligation entails the concept of sanctions, and that that in turn entails the idea of something impinging on my happiness as a consequence of my actions. Actions can affect our happiness in four ways, however. By (1) "natural consequence," (2) "as producing the esteem and favor of our fellow creatures, or the contrary," (3) by the penalties or rewards "arising from the authority of the civil magistrate," or (4) "from the authority of God." But because *moral* obligations are, by definition, universal, binding on all people in all circumstances, they can arise only from God. His authority alone can give rise to "a full and complete obligation which will extend to all cases" since only he "can in all cases make a man happy or miserable" (Gay 1731, xvii–xix).[22]

Gay's account of obligation is predicated on his psychological egoism, the belief that each of us is ultimately moved only by what he or she believes will contribute to his or her own happiness. And Paley's view is similar:

> A man is said to be obligated "when he is urged by a violent [i.e., compelling] motive resulting from the command of another" . . . It follows that we can be obliged to nothing but what ourselves are to gain or lose something by; for nothing else can be a violent motive to us . . . if it is asked why I am obliged to keep my word? [for example] the answer will be, because "I am urged to do so by a violent motive," (namely, the expectation of being after this life rewarded, if I do or punished for it, if I do not) resulting from the command of another (namely, God) . . . Therefore, private happiness is our motive, and the will of God our rule. (Paley 1785, 49–52)

The implication of Gay's and Paley's reflections is that there are *two* criteria of virtue. "The will of God is [its] immediate criterion . . . and the happiness of mankind is the criterion of the will of God; and therefore the happiness of mankind may be said to be the criterion of virtue, but once removed" (Gay 1731, xix). Neither criterion is the first principle of *action*, however. On Gay's and Paley's view, we should promote the general happiness because God commands us to. We should do what God commands us to do, however, because doing so will make us happy. Gay and Paley are thus not only psychological egoists, they are also *ethical* egoists.

There are a number of problems with Gay's and Paley's view. For one thing, it is doubtful that psychological egoism is true and, for another, the theistic traditions have nearly unanimously condemned ethical egoism, insisting that self-love or the desire for our own happiness is at best an inferior motive for loving God and doing our duty. Furthermore, Gay's and Paley's view seems to make God, too, a prudential utility maximizer, someone who promotes *our* happiness only because doing so promotes his[23]—a view which is inconsistent with an important strand in at least some theistic thinking, namely, the insistence on God's self-giving love.

In spite of these weaknesses, however, Gay and Paley may be right to insist that God's command is the source of the *obligatoriness* of promoting the general happiness if not of the *goodness* of doing so.[24] Moreover, if God's authority doesn't wholly or even partly rest on his power to make us miserable or happy,[25] then theories like Gay's and Paley's can be stripped of their psychological and ethical egoism without undermining their ability to provide a live option for theists who find utilitarianism independently attractive.

Divine Command Theory and Kantianism

Kantianism may also be compatible with some versions of divine command theory. If basic moral truths are necessarily true, for example, it would appear open for divine command theorists to identify them with Kant's synthetically necessary categorical imperatives.[26] Kant thinks that their content (speak the truth, do justice, and the like) governs the conduct of *all* rational beings, including God. God's will necessarily conforms to them, however, and ours does not. It is therefore appropriate to speak of *duty* or unconditional *obligation* in our case but not in his. Because the wills of finite rational beings with inclinations like ourselves don't necessarily conform to the norms of morality, they appear to us as imperatives, obligations, or constraints. Moreover, in so far as they bear on us, Kant is quite willing to speak of these norms as divine commands: "As soon as anything is recognized as a duty . . . obedience to it is also a divine command." "Religion is (subjectively regarded) the recognition of all duties as divine commands." Just as earthly commonwealths depend for their existence on a legislator, so too "an ethical commonwealth" cannot exist without "a public lawgiver," namely, God conceived of as "the moral ruler of the world" (Kant 1960, 90–1, 142).

How, though, can claims like these be reconciled with Kant's apparent *repudiation* of divine command ethics? He says, for example, that the Bible, or any other purported divine revelation, should be interpreted according to our moral principles, not the other way around. Or that if something were "represented as commanded by God, through a direct manifestation of Him, yet if it flatly contradicts morality, it cannot, despite all appearances be of God (for example, were a father ordered to kill his son who is, so far as he knows, perfectly innocent)" (Kant 1960, 81–2).

R. T. Nuyen suggests that we look at a paper entitled "A New Exposition of the First Principles of Metaphysics" in which Kant distinguished a thing's *ratio essendi* from its *ratio cognoscendi* (Nuyen 1998). A is the *ratio cognoscendi* of B if B is known through A. A is the *ratio essendi* of B if, when "the first is not supplied, the determined thing is not intelligible" (Kant 1929, 220). Or as Nuyen puts it, A is B's *ratio essendi* if it "determines the logical [or metaphysical] grounds for B, or the logical [or metaphysical] connections between B as a subject and its predicates, thus enabling us to understand why [B] is what it is." Thus Kant thinks, "freedom is the *ratio essendi* of the moral law"—it is what makes morality or the moral law possible. Morality or the moral law, however, "is the *ratio cognoscendi* of freedom, that through which we become aware of it" (Nuyen 1998, 448).

Similarly, Nuyen suggests, Kant thinks that while the moral law is the *ratio cognoscendi* of God, God is the *ratio essendi* of the moral law. "The holiness, the universal authority, the binding force of moral laws derives from God's nature itself as a holy, universally authoritative Being capable of commanding obedience." Yet if God really is the ground of the moral law, how can Kant be so sure that no divine command can contradict what we perceive to be the demands of morality? Because, on Kant's view, God is only *known* through the moral law. There is thus no possible world in which we would have reason to believe that God commands what clearly seems to us to be evil (Nuyen 1998, 449, 451).

If the norms are synthetically *necessary*, though, why introduce the notion of commands at all? Why think that commands are needed to explain the norms' obligatory force? For starters, perhaps this. If we were to prescind from divine commands and other sources of authority, then deviations from the norms would still involve departures from what an ideally functioning practical reason would prescribe, with the consequence that one's life would fall short of what it ideally could be. It doesn't follow that one would have failed to discharge one's moral obligations, however. It isn't clear, in other words, why one would be *morally obligated* to follow practical reason's dictates, as distinguished from its being good, or even the best thing, to do so. What, then, is the source of the norms' *prescriptive force*?

Kant rather clearly thinks that at least part of the answer is the moral agent's capacity for self-legislation, i.e., the property the will has of being "a law to itself" (Kant 1959, 59). But Kant also appears to think that "the binding force of moral laws derives from God's nature itself, as a holy, universally authoritative Being capable of commanding obedience." How can these positions be reconciled?

John Hare argues that Kant's final position is that neither we nor God are authors of the moral law in one sense but that we are both its authors in another (Hare 2001). Neither of us is the law's "*creator*," i.e., the source of its content. That is, we don't simply make up or *choose* the law's content, select it by fiat. But both of us are the authors of the law's *obligatoriness*. That is, the law derives its prescriptive character from our "endorsements," although "our contributions" aren't "symmetrical" since "we ordinary moral agents have to see our role as [merely] recapitulating in our own wills the declaration in God's will of our duties . . . For me to will the law autonomously is to declare it my law," i.e., to existentially appropriate it (Hare 2001, 94–6). Whether this resolution is successful, however, is doubtful.

Moral obligations arguably bind us whether we endorse them or not. A person who habitually subordinates moral maxims to his desire for happiness (or power or prestige) when what the former enjoins conflicts with the latter is nonetheless bound by the former:

> We all of us, in Kant's view, start off with our wills subordinate to the evil maxim which tells us to put our happiness first and our duty second. We are thus corrupt in the very ground of our more specific maxims, all of which take their fundamental moral character from this one. Kant is clear [however] that duty [nevertheless] puts us under the good maxim, which reverses the order of incentives, telling us to follow after happiness only so long as the maxims of our actions pass the test of the categorical imperative. (Hare 1996, 53)

The problem, then, is this. If our will is corrupted in the way Kant thinks, then we do *not* endorse the good maxim. So if the latter binds us only in so far as we endorse it, the categorical imperative does *not* bind us. Kant argues that "a seed of goodness remains in us, despite the propensity to evil, and this seed is still pure and uncorrupted, even though we are not"[27] (Hare 1996, 61). But this would resolve Kant's apparent inconsistency[28] only if our possession of this seed involved an implicit endorsement of the good maxim,[29] and it is difficult to see how it could do so if our willing nature is corrupt at its root.[30]

Moreover, Kant's insistence that principles and maxims lack moral authority if they aren't self-legislated seems inconsistent with any standard form of divine command theory. For divine command theorists typically think that God's commands *alone* are sufficient to create moral obligations. If they are, then self-legislation isn't also needed, and Kant is mistaken in thinking that self-legislation is a necessary condition of a principle or law possessing moral authority.

It thus seems that Kantian divine command theorists like John Hare must either reject Kant's autonomy requirement or radically revise divine command theory itself. Both options remain open, however, and so Kantianism, as well as utilitarianism and other forms of consequentialism, comport fairly well with divine command theory.

Other substantive moral theories do not. As we saw in examining Zagzebski, virtue theory is an example. Nevertheless, Aquinas succeeded in seamlessly incorporating Aristotelian virtue theory in a robust theory of Christian ethics,[31] and Zagzebski has shown that a Christian virtue theory coheres nicely with another theistic meta-theory, namely, divine motivation theory.

Can Religious Truths conflict with Rational Morality?

Could divine commands, for example, or authoritative religious teaching such as the Buddha's conflict with what reason demands?

God's commands can't conflict with basic moral truths. For since basic truths of moral obligation are necessarily true, any reasonable divine command theory is committed to the claim that the duties these truths prescribe are *necessarily* commanded by God. Again, since necessary moral truths are of course true, their denials couldn't be countenanced by a God of truth or by an omniscient Buddha.[32]

On the other hand, given that our epistemic faculties are warped by (e.g.) sin (Christianity) or existential ignorance and thirst (Buddhism), and that the Good (God or Nirvana, etc.) transcends our rational capacities, our judgments of reasonableness are inevitably fallible and subject to radical correction. This is especially true, moreover, of our assessments of the relative weights of conflicting prima facie obligations, our judgments of *ultima facie* obligations, and the like. So even though divine command theory, divine motivation theory, and other positions of the sort are compatible with a variety of first-order (substantive) ethical positions, their adoption may lead to claims which can't be justified on (e.g.) utilitarian or Kantian grounds. The absolute proscription of violence in early Christianity and early Buddhism is an example.[33]

Other potential conflicts may be more severe. While radical pacifists are sometimes dismissed as misguided or irrational, few think of them as immoral. The tension between religion and morality would be much greater if God were to require actions which almost all of us would regard as obviously wrong. Yahweh's demand that Abraham sacrifice his son Isaac seems to be just such and example. Note that the problem can't be evaded by denying that the story is historical. Even if it is not, the fact remains that the God in whom Jews, Christians, and Muslims believe is represented in their scriptures as commanding something that seems clearly immoral, and hence as being the sort of God who would be within his *rights* to issue such a command whether he in fact did so or not. The majority of Jewish and Christian commentators have tried to explain away the apparent immorality of God's command and of the act he requires of Abraham.[34] Others have argued that this can't be done so easily.[35]

The mystical strands in the world's major religious traditions provide yet another area of possible conflict. While many like Walter Stace (Stace 1960) believe that mysticism *supports* morality, others such as Arthur Danto (Danto 1972) and Jeffrey Kripal (Kripal 2002) think that it *undercuts* it. Still others believe that some forms of mysticism support morality while others do not.[36] The issue is far from settled, however, and given the important role mysticism plays in the spiritual traditions of both Eastern and Western religions, warrants further investigation.

Bibliography

Adams, R. M. (1996), "The Concept of a Divine Command," in D. Z. Phillips (ed.), *Religion and Morality*. New York: St. Martin's Press.

—. (1999), *Finite and Infinite Goods*. New York and Oxford: Oxford University Press.

—. (2002), "Responses." *Philosophy and Phenomenological Research* 64, 475–90.

Alston, W. P. (1989), "Some Suggestions for Divine Command Theorists," in W. P. Alston, *Divine Nature and Human Language: Essays in Philosophical Theology*. Ithaca, NY: Cornell University Press, 253–73.

Aquinas, T. (1947), *The Summa Theologica*. New York: Benziger Bros.

Boyd, R. (1988), "How to Be a Moral Realist," in R. Sayre-McCord (ed.), *Essays on Moral Realism*. Ithaca, NY: Cornell University Press, 181–228.

Cohen, G. A. (1996), "Reason, Humanity, and the Moral Law," in Onora O'Neill (ed.), *The Sources of Normativity*. Cambridge: Cambridge University Press, 167–88.

Dancy, J. (2004), *Ethics without Principles*. Oxford: Clarendon Press.

Danto, A. (1972), *Mysticism and Morality: Oriental Philosophy and Moral Thought*. New York: Harper Torchbooks.

Evans, S. (2004), *Kierkegaard's Ethics of Love: Divine Commands and Moral Obligations*. New York and London: Oxford University Press.
Finnis, J. (1980), *Natural Law and Natural Rights*. Oxford: Oxford University Press.
Gay, J. A. (1731), " Dissertation Concerning the Fundamental Principle of Virtue or Morality," prefixed to the first edition of Edmund Law's translation of Archbishop King's *Essay on the Origin of Evil*, London (reprinted in New York: Garland, 1978).
Gellman, J. I. (2003), *Abraham! Abraham! Kierkegaard and the Hasidim on the Binding of Isaac*. Aldershot and Burlington, VT: Ashgate.
Guess, R. (1996), "Morality and Identity," in Onora O'Neill (ed.), *The Sources of Normativity*. Cambridge: Cambridge University Press, 189–99.
Hare, J. E. (1996), *The Moral Gap*. Oxford: Clarendon Press.
—. (2001), *God's Call: Moral Realism, God's Commands, and Human Autonomy*. Grand Rapids, MI: Eerdmans.
Huemer, M. (2005), *Ethical Intuitionism*. Basingstoke, Hampshire and New York: Palgrave Macmillan.
James, W. (1902), *The Varieties of Religious Experience*. New York: The Modern Library.
Kant, I. (1929), "A New Exposition of the First Principles of Metaphysical Knowledge," appears as an appendix in F. E. England, *Kant's Conception of God*. London: Allen and Unwin.
—. (1959), *Foundations of the Metaphysics of Morals*, trans. Lewis White Beck. Indianapolis: Bobbs-Merrill.
—. (1960), *Religion within the Limits of Reason Alone*, trans. Theodore M. Greene and Hoyt H. Hudson. New York: Harper Torchbooks.
Kierkegaard, S. (1954), *Fear and Trembling*, trans. Walter Lowrie. Garden City, NY: Doubleday Anchor Books.
Korsgaard, C. (1996), "The Tanner Lectures," in Onora O'Neill (ed.), *The Sources of Normativity*. Cambridge: Cambridge University Press, 1–166.
Kripal, J. J. (2002), "Debating the Mystical as Ethical: An Indological Map," in G. William Barnard and Jeffrey J. Kripal (eds.), *Crossing Boundaries: Essays on the Ethical Status of Mysticism*. New York and London: Seven Bridges Press, 15–69.
Lisska, A. J. (1996), *Aquinas's Theory of Natural Law: An Analytic Reconstruction*. Oxford: Oxford University Press.
Mackie, J. L. (1977), *Ethics: Inventing Right and Wrong*. Harmondsworth, Middlesex: Penguin Books.
Maclagen, W. G. (1961), *The Theological Frontier of Ethics*. New York: Macmillan.
Miller, C. (2009), "Divine Desire Theory and Obligation," in Y. Nagasawa and E. Wielenberg (eds.), *New Waves in Philosophy of Religion*. Basingstoke, Hampshire and New York: Palgrave Macmillan, 105–24.
Moore, G. E. (1903), *Principia Ethica*. Cambridge: Cambridge University Press.
—. (1912), *Ethics*. New York: Oxford University Press.
Murphy, M. M. (1998), "Divine Command, Divine Will, and Moral Obligation." *Faith and Philosophy* 15, 3–27.

—. (2001), *Natural Law and Practical Rationality*. Cambridge: Cambridge University Press.
—. (2002), *An Essay on Divine Authority*. Ithaca, NY: Cornell University Press.
Nuyen, R. T. (1998), "Is Kant a Divine Command Theorist?," *History of Philosophy Quarterly* 15, 441–53.
Paley, W. (1785), *The Principles of Moral and Political Philosophy*. London: printed for R. Faulder.
Porter, J. (1999), *Natural and Divine Law: Reclaiming the Tradition for Christian Ethics*. Grand Rapids, MI: Wm. B. Eerdmans.
Quinn, P. L. (1986), "Moral Obligation, Religious Demand, and Practical Conflict," in Robert Audi and William J. Wainwright (eds.), *Rationality, Religious Belief, and Moral Commitment*. Ithaca, NY: Cornell University Press, 195–212.
—. (1988), "In Adam's fall, we sinned all." *Philosophical Topics* 16, 89–118.
—. (2000), "Divine command theory," in Hugh LaFollette (ed.), *The Blackwell Guide to Ethical Theory*. Malden, MA: Blackwell, 53–73.
Rawls, J. (1971), *A Theory of Justice*. Cambridge: Harvard University Press.
—. (2001), *Justice as Fairness: A Restatement*. Cambridge, MA and London: Harvard University Press.
Shafer-Landau, R. (2003), *Moral Realism: A Defense*. Oxford: Clarendon Press.
Sorley, W. R. (1918), *Moral Values and the Idea of God*. Cambridge: The University Press.
Stace, W. T. (1960), *Mysticism and Philosophy*. Philadelphia: J. B. Lippincott.
Wainwright, W. J. (2005), *Religion and Morality*. Aldershot and Burlington, VT: Ashgate.
Wielenberg, E. J. (2005), *Value and Virtue in a Godless Universe*. Cambridge: Cambridge University Press.
—. (2009), "In Defense of Non-Natural, Non-Theistic Moral Realism." *Faith and Philosophy* 26, 23–41.
Wierenga, E. (1984), "Utilitarianism and Divine Command Theory." *American Philosophical Quarterly* 21, 311–18.
Yearly, L. H. (1990), *Mencius and Aquinas: Theories of Virtue and Conditions of Courage*. Albany: State Universities of New York Press.
Zagzebski, L. T. (2004a), *Divine Motivation Theory*. Cambridge: Cambridge University Press.
—. (2004b), "Religion and Morality," in William J. Wainwright (ed.), *The Oxford Handbook of Philosophy of Religion*. New York: Oxford University Press, 343–64.

7 Consequentialism

Douglas W. Portmore

The defining feature of consequentialism is that it ranks outcomes (the outcomes associated with acts, codes of rules, sets of motives, or something else) and then takes the normative statuses of actions to be some (increasing) function of how those outcomes rank. Little else can be said unequivocally about consequentialism, as consequentialists disagree about most everything else. Consequentialists disagree on whether we should assess the normative statuses of actions directly in terms of how their outcomes rank (act-consequentialism) or indirectly in terms of whether, say, they comply with the code of rules with the highest-ranked associated outcome (rule-consequentialism). They disagree on whether the relevant function is a maximizing one (maximizing consequentialism) or a satisficing one (satisficing consequentialism). And they disagree on whether there is just one ranking of outcomes that is the same for all agents (agent-neutral consequentialism) or potentially different rankings for each agent (agent-relative consequentialism).

As most see it, consequentialism is a theory about the permissibility of actions, but some hold instead that it is a theory about only the comparative moral value of actions (scalar consequentialism). And whereas some hold that consequentialism is committed to ranking outcomes in terms of their impersonal value, others deny this. Even those who agree that outcomes are to be ranked in terms of their impersonal value disagree about whether outcomes are to be ranked in terms of their actual value (objective consequentialism) or their expected value (subjective consequentialism).

Given all this disagreement, there can be no set of necessary and sufficient conditions that captures all the various uses of the term "consequentialism." Instead, as Walter Sinnott-Armstrong (2003) points out, "the term 'consequentialism' seems to be used as a family resemblance term to refer to any descendant of classic utilitarianism that remains close enough to its ancestor in the important respects." And since philosophers disagree as to which are the important respects, there is no agreement on how to define "consequentialism." But even if there is no agreement on how to define "consequentialism," there is, as Sinnott-Armstrong suggests, a paradigm: viz., act-utilitarianism. In this essay, I will start with this paradigm, abstract from it the most traditional version of consequentialism, and then explain how various objections to this traditional version have led philosophers to adopt more nuanced versions of consequentialism.

Act-Utilitarianism and Traditional Act-Consequentialism

As we will soon see, act-utilitarianism is a species of *traditional act-consequentialism*, which holds:

> **TAC** (1.0) S's performing *x* is morally permissible if and only if, and ultimately because, there is no available alternative, *y*, whose outcome ranks higher than *x*'s outcome, and (2.0) *y*'s outcome ranks higher than *x*'s outcome if and only if *y*'s outcome is (impersonally) better than *x*'s outcome.

Or, more simply put, TAC holds:

> S's performing *x* is morally permissible if and only if, and ultimately because, S's performing *x* would maximize the (impersonal) good.

Two aspects of TAC are in need of clarification. First, note that S's performing *x* would maximize the good if and only if there is no available alternative act whose outcome is better than *x*'s outcome. For one, this means that there can be more than one act that would maximize the good, as there can be more than one act that is tied for first place in terms of the production of the good. For another, this means that TAC is not committed to there being a complete ranking of outcomes. Indeed, it may be that some outcomes are incommensurable with others such that they are not better than, worse than, or just as good as the others. Thus, on TAC, an act can be permissible even though there are available alternatives whose outcomes are incommensurable with its outcome. So long as there is no available alternative whose outcome is *better* than its outcome, it will be permissible.

Second, note that, by including the words "and ultimately because" in my formulation of TAC, I am acknowledging that someone could fail to be a traditional act-consequentialist (a TACist) even though she accepts the following bi-conditional:

> **BC** S's performing *x* is morally permissible if and only if S's performing *x* would maximize the (impersonal) good.

Take, for instance, a divine command theorist who accepts not only that S's performing *x* is morally permissible if and only if, and ultimately because, S's performing *x* is not forbidden by God, but also that S's performing *x* is forbidden by God if and only if S's performing *x* would fail to maximize the good. This divine command theorist would accept BC, but she would not, I presume, count as a TACist, for she would deny that, when acts are permissible, they are so *ultimately because* they maximize the good. To deny this is to deny TAC.

Now, act-utilitarianism is a species of TAC, for it is committed to both TAC and the following further claim about what is good. That is, *act-utilitarianism* is committed to the following two claims:

> **AU** (i) S's performing *x* is morally permissible if and only if, and ultimately because, S's performing *x* would maximize the good, and (ii) S's performing *x* would maximize the good if and only if S's performing *x* would maximize aggregate utility.

The aggregate utility that would be produced by an act is the sum of all the utility it would produce minus the sum of all the disutility that it would produce, where utility is a measure of whatever it is that enhances a subject's welfare, and disutility is a measure of whatever it is that diminishes a subject's welfare. The classical utilitarians (e.g., Mill 1861 and Bentham 1789) held that pleasure is the only thing that contributes to a subject's welfare and that pain is the only thing that detracts from a subject's welfare. This view about welfare is known as *hedonism*. Hence, the view according to which both hedonism and act-utilitarianism are true is known as *hedonistic act-utilitarianism* (**HAU**). HAU is perhaps the simplest version of TAC. For this reason, I will often use it to illustrate some of the putative problems with TAC.

Three Objections to Traditional Act-Consequentialism

TAC makes only three claims: (I) that it is never permissible to fail to maximize the good, (II) that it is always permissible to maximize the good, and (III) that if S's performing *x* is morally permissible, it is ultimately because S's performing *x* would maximize the good. This means that there are only three general sorts of objections to TAC, each corresponding to the rejection of one of the above three claims. I will consider these three general objections below.

First objection: It is sometimes permissible to fail to maximize the good.

Agent-Sacrificing Options and the Self-Other Asymmetry:
According to TAC, maximizing the good is always obligatory. According to commonsense morality, by contrast, it is often optional. On commonsense

morality, there is often the moral option either to act so as to make things better overall but worse for oneself (or others) or to act so as to make things better for oneself (or others) but worse overall. These options, which are known as *agent-centered options*, provide agents with the freedom to give their own interests more or less weight than they have from the impersonal perspective. They come in two varieties: *agent-sacrificing options* and *agent-favoring options*. I will consider them in order.

Agent-sacrificing options permit agents to perform suboptimal acts so long as these acts are suboptimal only because they involve producing less good for the agent. The underlying thought is that agents are permitted to make things worse for themselves so long as they do not thereby make things worse for others overall.[1] To illustrate, suppose that Abe is stranded on a deserted island. Given his isolation, what Abe does will affect only himself. Now, suppose that he is presently sitting next to an ant hill and that the ants are starting to bite him. Assume that letting the ants continue to bite him is not what is best for him. What would be best for him is his getting up and collecting coconuts. Of course, since he is the only one affected by his actions, his getting up and collecting coconuts is not only what is best for him but also what is best overall. So, on a traditional act-consequentialist theory such as HAU, it is wrong for Abe to let the ants continue to bite him.

This may seem counterintuitive. Although it is clearly stupid, foolish, and irrational for Abe to let the ants continue to bite him, there does not seem to be anything immoral about his doing so. After all, in doing so, he does not hurt anyone but himself. Of course, it might, in certain circumstances, be immoral for Abe to let the ants bite someone else, but that is someone else. On commonsense morality, there is an asymmetry between the self and others. Whereas there is a *prima facie* obligation to ensure that others enjoy pleasure and avoid pain, there is no such obligation with regard to ourselves.

Given this asymmetry, which is known as the *self-other asymmetry*, we often have the option of sacrificing our own greater utility for sake of promoting others' lesser utility. I can, for instance, permissibly give you my last two aspirins so as to relieve your slightly less severe headache even if that entails my forgoing the opportunity to relieve my slightly more severe headache. But a traditional act-consequentialist theory, such as HAU, entails that it would be wrong for me to do so. For if my taking the aspirins is what would maximize aggregate utility, then that is what I am required to do. On HAU, there is no self-other asymmetry; there is just as much of an obligation to promote one's own utility as to promote anyone else's. Thus, HAU seems objectionable in that it is unable to accommodate agent-sacrificing options and the self-other asymmetry.

To meet this objection, some have proposed revising HAU. Ted Sider (1993), for instance, has proposed that we adopt instead *self-other utilitarianism:*

> **SOU** (1.0) S's performing x is morally permissible if and only if, and ultimately because, there is no available alternative, y, whose outcome ranks higher than x's outcome, and (2.1) y's outcome ranks higher than x's outcome if and only if both (a) y's outcome contains more utility for others (i.e., those other than S) than x's outcome and (b) y's outcome contains more overall utility than x's outcome.

In other words, SOU holds that an act is morally permissible so long as there is no available alternative that produces both more utility for others and more overall utility. SOU thereby allows agents to give their own utility anywhere from no weight at all to the same weight that everyone else's utility has from the impersonal perspective.

SOU accounts for both agent-sacrificing options and the self-other asymmetry. For instance, it accounts for the thought that Abe does no wrong in allowing the ants to bite him, for there is no available alternative whose outcome contains more utility for others. And SOU accounts for the thought that it would be permissible for me to give my last two aspirins to someone else so that she can relieve her less severe headache. This is permissible, because there is no available alternative whose outcome contains *both* more overall utility and more utility for others. There is only an available alternative whose outcome contains more overall utility: the one in which I take the aspirins. But this alternative produces less utility for others.

Agent-Favoring Options:

Although SOU accounts for both agent-sacrificing options and the self-other asymmetry, it fails to account for agent-favoring options. Agent-favoring options permit agents to favor their own interests and, thus, to promote their own utility even when doing so entails doing less to promote the impersonal good. SOU's failure to accommodate agent-favoring options gives rise to what is known as the *demandingness objection*. Theories such as TAC, HAU, and SOU are too demanding in that they imply that agents are morally required to sacrifice their projects, interests, and/or special relationships whenever doing so would maximize the good. According to both HAU and SOU, I am morally required to sacrifice my interest in living in material comfort, to neglect my relationship with my daughter, and to abandon my project of writing a book on consequentialism if I could thereby produce more aggregate utility. Suppose, for instance, that what would maximize utility is my taking all my money and moving to some poor developing nation in Africa, founding a school for the education and empowerment of young women. Assume that this is, of all my options, the one that would produce the most utility. Yet, to perform this option, I must give up living in material comfort, abandon my project of writing a book on consequentialism, and desert my daughter, leaving her to become a ward of the state. Theories such as HAU and SOU imply that I am required to make such sacrifices for the sake of maximizing utility. But many philosophers (such as: Stroud 1998, Hurley 2006, and Portmore 2011) think that this is to demand more from me than can be reasonably demanded of me.

Proponents of utilitarianism might try to respond to this objection by arguing that the problem lies not with HAU (or SOU), but with the sorry state of the world that we live in. That is, they might argue that it is only because we live in a world in which there is so much suffering and hardship that agents like myself are required to make such tremendous sacrifices. But, in fact, this is false. For theories such as HAU and SOU are too demanding even in utopian worlds. To illustrate, imagine that we live in a utopian world in which everyone leads very happy and fulfilled lives. And imagine that my blood contains the makings of some new drug that would make everyone but myself slightly more happy. Suppose, though, that in order to synthesize the drug I would need to sacrifice my life so that scientists could drain out all of my blood. Assume that they need all of my blood at once in order to synthesize the drug. And imagine, for the moment, that we can accurately quantify the resultant changes in people's utilities in terms of *utiles*—a measurement of utility equivalent to the utility in a person's experiencing the mildest of pleasures for the briefest of moments. Assume that if this drug were synthesized and evenly distributed among the remaining population of six billion and one people, each person would get an additional utile. And assume that in laying down my life I would thereby be sacrificing exactly six billion utiles.

In this case, I could produce one extra utile of aggregate utility by sacrificing my life. And so, on HAU and SOU, I am morally required to do so. But to demand that I make such a tremendous sacrifice for the sake of such a miniscule gain in the total aggregate utility (i.e., one utile) is, it seems, to demand more from me than can be reasonably demanded of me. For it seems that I have at least as much reason, all things considered, to refrain from sacrificing my life in this instance. Perhaps, I have some reason to sacrifice my life for the sake of producing one extra utile of utility, but given that a utile is a rather small measure of utility this will not be a very strong reason. Moreover, it seems that I have a strong agent-relative reason to safeguard my own utility by refusing to sacrifice my life. This reason is an agent-relative reason in that it is a reason that is specific to me, and it goes beyond the agent-neutral reason we each have to promote the total aggregate utility. The thought, then, is that although we each have an agent-neutral moral reason to promote the total aggregate utility, we also each have an additional agent-relative nonmoral reason to promote our own utility. And, given this additional reason, we sometimes have sufficient reason, all things considered, to do something that will promote our own utility at the expense of failing to maximize the total aggregate utility. Indeed, many utilitarians (e.g., Singer 1999, Sidgwick 1907) concede as much.

At this point, such utilitarians argue that although utilitarian views such as HAU and SOU demand that we sacrifice more than we have decisive reason, all things considered, to sacrifice, this is no objection to their view. For they claim that it is just a fact about morality that it demands more from us than we have decisive reason, all things considered, to give. And so it is no objection to these views that they exhibit the unreasonable demandingness that is inherent in morality itself. As David Sobel puts it, "What morality asks, we could say, is too much to be the thing the agent has most reason to do all things considered, but not too much to count as what morality asks" (2007, 14).

Critics of utilitarianism argue, though, that in salvaging utilitarianism from the demandingness objection by claiming that moral requirements are not necessarily anything that we have decisive reason, all things considered, to obey, the utilitarian wins the strategic battle only to lose the war. They succeed in defending the high bar that they set for what morality demands of us only by lowering the bar for what reason demands of us by way of our compliance with morality's demands, thereby implausibly marginalizing the role that morality plays in our practical reason and deliberation (Hurley 2006, 705). And other critics argue that this type of defense is wholly misguided, for morality *is*, by necessity, supreme in its rational authority (Portmore 2011).

There is, however, another way of responding to the demandingness objection. We could revise SOU so that it accommodates agent-favoring options. We can do so by adopting *Schefflerian utilitarianism:*

> **SU** (1.0) S's performing *x* is morally permissible if and only if, and ultimately because, there is no available alternative, *y*, whose outcome ranks higher than *x*'s outcome, and (2.2) *y*'s outcome ranks higher than *x*'s outcome if and only if both (a) *y*'s outcome contains more utility for others (i.e., those other than S) than *x*'s outcome and (b*) *y*'s outcome contains more egoistically-adjusted utility than *x*'s outcome, where egoistically-adjusted utility includes everyone's utility but adjusts the overall total by giving S's utility, say, ten times the weight of anyone else's.

In other words, SU holds that an act is morally permissible so long as there is no available alternative that produces both more utility for others and more egoistically-adjusted utility. SU thereby allows agents to give their own utility anywhere from no weight at all to ten times the weight that their utility has from the impersonal perspective.

Since SU allows agents to give their own utility less weight than it has from an impersonal perspective, SU accommodates agent-sacrificing options just as SOU does. But, unlike SOU, SU can also accommodate agent-favoring options and, as we will see below, supererogatory acts as well. To illustrate, consider the

Table 1[2]

x	$U_s(x)$	$U_{-s}(x)$	$U(x)$	$U_{+s}(x)$	deontic status
a_1	7	**10**	17	**80**	merely permissible
a_2	2	**4**	6	**24**	impermissible
a_3	1	**15**	16	**25**	supererogatory[3]
a_4	−1	**20**	19	**10**	supererogatory

case of Edouard, who has the following four mutually exclusive and jointly exhaustive alternatives: a_1, a_2, a_3, and a_4. (To ensure that they are jointly exhaustive, let a_1 be the act of performing something other than a_2, a_3, or a_4.) The consequences of each of these alternatives are laid out in Table 1.

Let $\mathbf{U_s}(x)$ = the utility that would accrue to S if S were to perform x, let $\mathbf{U_{-s}}(x)$ = the utility that would accrue to others if S were to perform x, let $\mathbf{U_{+s}}(x) = U_{-s}(x) + [10 \times U_s(x)]$, and let $\mathbf{U}(x)$ = the overall utility that would be produced if S were to perform x.

Whereas Edouard is, on HAU, obligated to perform a_4, he is, on SU, permitted to perform a_1 instead, which is better for him. Thus, SU permits him to perform a_1 even though his performing a_4 would be both better for others and better in terms of the impersonal good. Edouard has, then, the agent-favoring option of performing a_1 as opposed to a_4. Furthermore, SU accommodates agent-sacrificing options. For instance, Edouard can permissibly choose to perform a_3 as opposed to a_1, thereby providing others with a net benefit of five utiles at a cost of six utiles to himself.

Supererogatory Acts:

Interestingly, SU can also accommodate *supererogatory acts*, acts that go above and beyond the call of duty. This is a plus, as HAU is usually thought to be unable to accommodate supererogatory acts or, at least, unable to accommodate the range of acts that we take to be supererogatory.

An act is supererogatory if and only if it meets the following three conditions: (i) it is morally optional, (ii) it is morally praiseworthy, and (iii) it goes beyond the call of duty.[4] Clearly, HAU can meet the first two conditions. Some acts will be morally optional on HAU, for sometimes there will be more than one available alternative that would maximize utility. And some of these morally optional alternatives will be morally praiseworthy. Suppose, for instance, that Smith has the choice of benefiting himself or Jones and that either way utility will be maximized. If Smith chooses to benefit Jones as opposed to himself, this certainly seems to be a morally praiseworthy choice. Moreover, it is morally optional, since it would maximize utility. So, here is an act that meets the first two conditions for being supererogatory.

What about the third? Does it go beyond the call of duty? Some argue that it does (Harwood 2003, Vessel 2010). They argue that an agent goes beyond the call of duty so long as she does more for others than she is required to do. But we might wonder whether this correctly specifies the relevant sense of going beyond the call of duty. If we hold that going beyond the call of duty amounts only to doing more for others than is required, then we must deny the possibility of supererogation with respect to self-regarding duties. Yet it certainly seems possible to go beyond what such duties require (Kawall 2003, Portmore 2008). For instance, we might think that there is a duty to develop our talents and that this is an imperfect duty that doesn't require that we take advantage of every opportunity to develop our talents, but requires only that we take advantage of a sufficient number of such opportunities. But if this is right, then it is surely possible to go above and beyond our duty to develop our talents, and yet doing so may be of no benefit to anyone besides ourselves.

Consider also that a supererogatory act must involve doing more of whatever there is more moral reason to do. After all, we would not think that perspiring more than is required is supererogatory, because we do not think that there is any moral reason to perspire more than is required. So we should think that doing more for others than is required is supererogatory only if there is more moral reason to do more for others than is required. Yet, on HAU, Smith has no more moral reason to enhance Jones's utility by some amount than to enhance his own utility by that same amount. All that matters on HAU is that utility is maximized, and utility would be maximized either way.

Even if we allow that an agent goes beyond the call of duty so long as she does more for others than is required and, thus, allow that HAU can accommodate certain supererogatory acts, such as Smith's choosing to benefit Jones rather than himself, HAU still cannot accommodate the range of acts that we take to be supererogatory. On HAU, no *optimific act* could ever be supererogatory.[5] Yet, intuitively, many such acts are supererogatory. For instance, Edouard's performing a_4 seems supererogatory. Yet HAU implies that it is obligatory. To illustrate, suppose that Edouard has exactly $3,000 in disposable income each month and, thus, that he can reasonably afford to perform a_1, which involves giving $1,000 a month to charity. By contrast, his performing a_4 involves his giving $3,000 a month to charity, thereby sacrificing everything beyond what is needed for his continued subsistence. Now, his making such a sacrifice would, we will suppose, be optimific in that his donating all of his disposable income to charity would do more good than his spending any of it on himself. Even so, on commonsense morality, this level of sacrifice would be considered supererogatory, not obligatory, as HAU implies.

Worse yet, HAU implies that many intuitively supererogatory acts are actually morally wrong (McConnell 1980). Suppose, for instance, that Smith has just been given the last piece of cherry pie. Since, unlike Jones, cherry pie is Smith's favorite, Smith would enjoy eating the last piece of pie more than Jones would. Suppose, then, that Smith must choose between giving Jones the last piece of pie, thereby enhancing Jones's utility by five utiles, or keeping the last piece for himself, thereby enhancing his own utility by six utiles. In this case, HAU implies that it would be wrong for Smith to choose to benefit Jones instead of himself. Yet, arguably, giving Jones the last piece of pie is supererogatory. To avoid such counterintuitive implications and to accommodate a wider range of supererogatory acts, the act-consequentialist must adopt a view such as SU instead.

So, as we've seen above, one general sort of objection to TAC is that it implausibly holds that it is never permissible to fail to maximize the good. We just considered two instances of this objection: (i) that it is permissible to fail to maximize the good when doing so will make only oneself worse off and (ii) that it is permissible to fail to maximize the good when the alternative would be unreasonably demanding. In the next section, we'll consider a third instance of this general objection: (iii) that it is permissible to fail to maximize the good when one doesn't know what would maximize the good.

Traditional Act-Consequentialism and Not Knowing What Will Maximize the Good:

We rarely know what will maximize the good. Although it is sometimes possible to anticipate the immediate effects of our actions, it is clearly impossible to anticipate all the effects that our actions will have over an indefinite future. And these unforeseen future effects may be truly massive, affecting, perhaps, the identities of people over countless generations (Lenman 2000). Such massive unforeseen effects would likely dwarf whatever immediate effects we do foresee. The upshot of all this is that we are literally clueless as to which of our actions would maximize the good (Lenman 2000). And, given our cluelessness, TAC can be of no practical use in deciding what to do.

At this point, the TACist can point out that this is really no objection to the theory, for TAC provides only a *criterion of rightness* and not a *decision-making procedure* (Bales 1971). Whereas a decision-making procedure must be something that actual agents with limited knowledge and imperfect calculating abilities can use to guide their decisions about what to do, a criterion of rightness does not. A criterion of rightness need only specify the features of actions that determine whether they are right or wrong, and it may turn out that actual agents are often unable to discern whether their actions have these features. So, if TAC is meant to provide only a criterion of rightness, which it is, then it is no objection to it that it fails as an adequate decision-making procedure. To object to TAC, we must deny one of its claims—that is, one of (I)–(III) from the beginning of the section "Three Objections to Traditional Act-Consequentialism."

At this point, the critics of TAC may wish to distinguish between *objective rightness* and *subjective rightness*. Subjectively right (i.e., required) actions are those that we can legitimately expect *actual* agents with limited knowledge and imperfect calculating abilities to perform if acting conscientiously and, thus, are the ones that we can rightfully blame them for failing to perform. Objectively right actions, by contrast, are those that we could legitimately expect only *idealized* agents with full knowledge and perfect calculating abilities to perform if acting conscientiously. Having made this distinction, the critics of TAC can argue that the primary function of an ethical theory is to provide an account of rightness that can be used to guide our practical deliberations and to inform our assessments of blame and praise—that is, to provide an account of subjective rightness. And this, they argue, is something that TAC fails to do. To see why, consider the following example:

> *Mine Shafts:* A hundred miners are trapped underground in one of two mine shafts. Floodwaters are rising, and the miners are in danger of drowning. Carmine can close one of three floodgates. Depending both on which floodgate she closes and on which shaft the miners are in, the results will be one of the following six possibilities:

		The miners are in . . .	
		Shaft A	Shaft B
Carmine closes . . .	Gate 1	Carmine saves 100 lives	Carmine saves zero lives
	Gate 2	Carmine saves zero lives	Carmine saves 100 lives
	Gate 3	Carmine saves 90 lives	Carmine saves 90 lives

Carmine does not know which shaft the miners are in, but she knows all the above as well as the fact that, given her evidence, there is a 50 percent subjective chance that the miners are in Shaft A as well as a 50 percent subjective chance that the miners are in Shaft B. As a matter of fact, though, the miners are in Shaft A. Assume that Carmine is not in any way at fault for her imperfect epistemic position with regard to the location of the miners. And assume that the long-term effects of her actions would be the same regardless of which gate she closes and that Carmine knows this.[6]

Carmine does not know whether it is closing Gate 1 or Gate 2 that would maximize the good, but she knows that there is no chance that closing Gate 3 would maximize the good. In fact, we are told that the miners are in Shaft A, which means that it is closing Gate 1 that would maximize the good. Thus, according to TAC, Carmine is required to close Gate 1. But if we are talking about what Carmine is required to do in the subjective sense—the sense that is suppose to guide her practical deliberations and inform our assessments of blame and praise for her actions, then it is counterintuitive to suppose that Carmine is required to close Gate 1. Indeed, it seems that, in the subjective sense, Carmine should instead close Gate 3. Here, then, is a case in which it seems (subjectively) morally permissible for an agent to fail to maximize the good. And so here we have a genuine objection to TAC, assuming that the primary function of an ethical theory is to provide a criterion of subjective rightness. The objection would be that claim (I)—the claim that it is never permissible to fail to maximize the good—is false, for Carmine should close Gate 3, which fails to maximize the good.

To see why Carmine should, in the subjective sense, close Gate 3 and not Gate 1, recall that Carmine has no idea whether it is closing Gate 1 or Gate 2 that would maximize the good. Thus, we should not expect Carmine, if morally conscientious, to close either one. Doing so would be too risky, carrying the subjective risk of saving no one. In closing Gate 3, by contrast, she ensures that 90 miners will be saved. Given the associated risk, we would blame Carmine for closing Gate 1 even though this is what TAC implies that she is required to do. So, if we are looking for an account of rightness that can be used to guide our practical deliberations and inform our assessments of blame and praise, TAC is not it.

There are at least two ways to respond to this objection. One is to deny that the primary function of an ethical theory is to guide our practical deliberations and inform our assessments of blame and praise. Perhaps, the primary function of ethical theory is instead to figure out what our objective ends should be (e.g., maximizing the good, acting virtuously, or abiding by the Categorical Imperative). This would leave it to decision theory or some other branch of practical philosophy to provide an account of how agents with limited knowledge should make practical decisions given both their normative uncertainty about what their objective ends should be and their nonnormative uncertainty about how best to achieve these ends.[7]

Another way to respond to the above objection is to accept that the primary function of an ethical theory is to provide an account of subjective rightness and try to revise TAC so that it can serve this function. Some (e.g., Jackson 1991) have suggested that the way to do this is to adopt *subjective consequentialism:*

> **SC** (1.0) S's performing *x* is (subjectively) morally permissible if and only if, and ultimately because, there is no available alternative, *y*, whose outcome ranks higher than *x*'s outcome, and (2.3) *y*'s outcome ranks higher than *x*'s outcome if and only if *y*'s outcome is better than *x*'s outcome in terms of expected value.

S maximizes expected value if and only if S maximizes $\sum_i Pr(O_i/A_j) \times V(O_i)$, where *Pr* is S's probability function at the time, *V* is consequentialism's value function,

O_i are the possible outcomes, and A_j are the possible actions (Jackson 1991, 463–4).

But even if SC gets the intuitively correct answer in *Mine Shafts*, it suffers from two significant problems. First, given agents' limited knowledge and imperfect calculating abilities, they are hardly ever in the position to reliably figure out which of the countless alternatives available to them would have the highest expected value over an indefinite future (Feldman 2006). After all, the only reason that SC can be used in *Mine Shafts* to guide Carmine's practical deliberations and to inform our assessments of blame and praise for Carmine's actions is because it was artificially stipulated that the long-term effects of Carmine's actions would be the same regardless of which gate she closes and that she knows this. So although SC might be useful in a few artificial cases like *Mine Shafts*, it is not much of an improvement over TAC in providing action guidance.

Second, SC seems suspect in that it allows for an agent's nonnormative uncertainty, but not for her normative uncertainty, to affect the subjective rightness of her actions. Whereas SC allows that an agent's uncertainty about which act will maximize the good affects the subjective rightness of her actions, it does not allow for her uncertainty as to whether she ought to be seeking to maximize the good to affect the subjective rightness of her actions. This is potentially problematic, for arguably an agent's nonculpable uncertainty with regard to the relevant normative facts (e.g., whether her objective end should be to maximize the good or something else) is just as important in determining what we can legitimately expect her to do and to blame her for not doing as her nonculpable uncertainty with regard to the relevant nonnormative facts is (e.g., whether this or that act will best achieve the objective ends that she ought to be pursuing). And because of this, SC seems to fall prey to a counterexample that is analogous to *Mine Shafts*, only in this example we swap normative uncertainty for nonnormative uncertainty.

I will present the counterexample shortly, but first let me state my assumptions. First, I will assume that although impermissibility does not come in degrees, the moral badness of impermissible acts does. That is, some impermissible acts are morally worse than others. For instance, on TAC, any act that fails to maximize value is impermissible. But it is plausible to suppose that some acts that fail to maximize value are worse than others, as some fall further from the mark of maximal value than others do. Likewise, on Kantianism, any act that violates the Categorical Imperative is impermissible. But it is plausible to suppose that some violations of the Categorical Imperative are morally worse than others. For instance, it seems that violating the Categorical Imperative by killing someone with an otherwise bright future is much worse than violating the Categorical Imperative by telling a relatively harmless lie. Second, I will assume that we can measure the degree to which acts are morally good/bad in terms of their *deontic value*, where the deontic value of a supererogatory act is always positive, the deontic value of an impermissible act is always negative, and the deontic value of a nonsupererogatory optional act is always zero. (Let 'DV(x)' stand for 'the deontic value of x'.) Third, and more controversially, I will assume that we can make inter-theoretic comparisons of deontic value.[8] Fourth and last, I will assume that TAC and Kantianism are accounts of objective rightness. Now, here is the counterexample to SC:

> *Normative Uncertainty:* Norma must choose among the following three mutually exclusive and jointly exhaustive options: a_1, a_2, and a_3. (To ensure that they are jointly exhaustive, let a_3 be the act of doing something other than either a_1 or a_2.) If she does a_1, she will maximize value (not deontic value, but nonmoral value)[9] but violate the Categorical Imperative. If she does a_2, she will abide by the Categorical Imperative but fail to maximize value. And if she does a_3, she will both fail to maximize value and violate the Categorical Imperative. Depending both on which theory of objective rightness is true and on which act she performs, the deontic value of her action will be one of the following:

		The true theory is . . .	
		TAC	Kantianism
	a_1	$DV(a_1) = 0$	$DV(a_1) = -100$
Norma performs . . .	a_2	$DV(a_2) = -100$	$DV(a_2) = 0$
	a_3	$DV(a_3) = -10$	$DV(a_3) = -10$

Norma does not know whether TAC or Kantianism is true, but she knows all the above as well as the fact that, given her evidence, there is a 50 percent subjective chance that TAC is true as well as a 50 percent subjective chance that Kantianism is true. Assume that Norma is not in any way at fault for her imperfect epistemic position with regard to which ethical theory is true. And note that since Norma knows that her performing a_1 is what would maximize value, it follows that Norma's performing a_1 is also what would maximize expected value.

Norma does not know whether it is performing a_1 or a_2 that is morally permissible, but she knows that there is no chance that performing a_3 is morally permissible. Of course, since Norma knows, as stipulated, that her performing a_1 would maximize value, it follows that her performing a_1 would maximize expected value (not expected deontic value, but expected nonmoral value). So, according to SC, Norma is required to perform a_1. But if we are talking about what Norma is required to do in the subjective sense—the sense that is supposed to guide her practical deliberations and inform our assessments of blame and praise for her actions, then it is counterintuitive to suppose that Norma is required to perform a_1. After all, given her ignorance of whether it is TAC or Kantianism that is true, we should expect Norma, if morally conscientious, to perform a_3. For performing either a_1 or a_2 is just too risky. They both carry the subjective risk of performing an act with a deontic value of −100, whereas if she performs a_3, she can be certain that the deontic value of her act will be no worse than −10. Given the associated risk, we would blame Norma for performing a_1 even though this is what SC implies that she is required to do. So, if we are looking for an account of rightness that can be used to guide our practical deliberations and inform our assessments of blame and praise, then SC is not it.

Second objection: It is sometimes impermissible to maximize the good.

Agent-Centered Constraints:

As we saw above, TAC seems too demanding. Interestingly, it seems to be too permissive as well. On TAC, there are no types of acts that are off-limits, not even rape, murder, torture, or genocide. Of course, the TACist can hold that, say, murder is especially bad and, indeed, so bad as to make one murder worse than any number of deaths by natural causes. The TACist can, then, hold that it is impermissible to murder one person even if doing so is necessary to produce a vaccine that would save countless lives. Nevertheless, the TACist must still concede that it would be permissible to commit one murder so as to prevent two other comparable murders. Since no matter how bad murder is, two murders will, other things being equal, be worse than one murder, the TACist must concede that it will be permissible to commit murder so as to minimize the overall commissions of murder. Thus, on TAC, any type of act, no matter how intrinsically bad, will be permitted in those circumstances in which committing one instance of that act-type will minimize overall commissions of that act-type.

This illustrates a more general problem with TAC: it is unable to accommodate *agent-centered constraints.* An agent-centered constraint is a constraint on maximizing the good that it would be wrong to infringe upon even in some circumstances in which doing so would minimize comparable infringements of that constraint.[10] On commonsense morality, there are two types of agent-centered constraints: *agent-centered restrictions* and *special obligations.* Agent-centered restrictions *prohibit* agents from performing certain types of acts (e.g., murder) even in some circumstances in which doing so would minimize comparable commissions of that act-type. Special obligations, by contrast, *require* agents to do certain things (e.g., to keep their promises) even in some circumstances in which their failing to do so would minimize comparable failings of that type. These special obligations often arise as the result of performing certain past acts (e.g., making a promise) but also come with occupying certain roles (e.g., certain professional and familial roles). Since TAC is unable to accommodate these agent-centered constraints, it can seem too permissive. This is the *permissiveness objection.*

If we give credence to the intuitions that ground the permissiveness objection, we might think that TAC must be abandoned for the sake of some version of consequentialism that can accommodate agent-centered constraints. One such version can be obtained by modifying SU, the result being:

> **Mod-SU** (1.0) S's performing *x* is morally permissible if and only if, and ultimately because, there is no available alternative, *y*, whose outcome ranks higher than *x*'s outcome, and (2.4) *y*'s outcome ranks higher than *x*'s outcome if and only if there is no available alternative that would produce both more constraint-adjusted utility and more comprehensively-adjusted utility than *x* would, where the constraint-adjusted utility of an outcome is just the sum of the utility for others, adjusted by multiplying any disutility (or loss of utility) resulting from S's infringement of an agent-centered constraint by 500, and where the comprehensively-adjusted utility of an outcome is just its constraint-adjusted utility added to the product of S's utility times ten.

In other words, Mod-SU holds that an act is morally permissible so long as there is no available alternative that produces both more constraint-adjusted utility and more comprehensively-adjusted utility. Like SU, Mod-SU allows agents to give their own utility anywhere from no weight at all to ten times the weight that everyone else's utility has from the impersonal perspective. But, unlike SU, Mod-SU requires that agents give the disutility caused by their infringements of constraints 500 times the weight that this disutility has from the impersonal perspective.

Mod-SU could easily accommodate a nonabsolute constraint against, say, committing murder.[11] Agents would, other things being equal, be prohibited from committing murder even so as to prevent up to 500 others from each committing some comparable murder. And Mod-SU could easily accommodate a nonabsolute constraint against failing to fulfill the special obligation that parents have to nurture their own children. Parents would, other things being equal, be prohibited from failing to nurture their own children even so as to prevent up to 500 others from each comparably failing to nurture their children. Clearly, then, Mod-SU can accommodate both agent-centered restrictions and special obligations.

Table 2

W_x	. . . , 1, 1, 1, 1, –8, 1, 1, 1, 1, . . .
$W_{\sim x}$	. . . , 1, 1, 1, 1, –2, 1, 1, 1, 1, . . .

Infinite Goodness and the Strong Pareto Principle:
TAC can also seem too permissive in cases in which all the alternatives open to an agent would produce an infinite amount of goodness. Suppose, for instance, that you have the choice either to do *x* or to refrain from doing *x*. If you do *x*, W_x will be the actual world. If you refrain from doing *x*, $W_{\sim x}$ will be the actual world.[12] These two possible worlds are depicted in Table 2. Assume that the two worlds have the same locations of value (e.g., the same people or times) and that they have an infinite number of locations.[13] Thus, the ellipses indicate that the 1's should continue indefinitely in each direction in both W_x and $W_{\sim x}$.

Intuitively, it seems wrong for you to do *x*. Yet if we think that one world can be better than another if and only if the total sum of goodness contained by the one is greater than the total sum of goodness contained by the other, then TAC implies that its permissible to do *x*. After all, the total sum of goodness contained by each of W_x and $W_{\sim x}$ is the same positive infinity. Thus, on the assumption that one world can be better than another if and only if the total sum of goodness contained by the one is greater than the total sum of goodness contained by the other, TAC counterintuitively implies that it is permissible for you do *x*, for $W_{\sim x}$ would, then, be no better than W_x. So, here is another case in which it seems impermissible to maximize the good, for, in this case, it seems impermissible to maximize the good by doing *x*.

One way to defend TAC against this objection is to reject the assumption that one world can be better than another if and only if the total sum of goodness contained by the one is greater than the total sum of goodness contained by the other and to hold instead the *strong pareto principle:* if every location has at least as much goodness in W_i as it does in W_j, and at least one location has more goodness in W_i than it does in W_j, then W_i is better than W_j (Lauwers and Vallentyne 2004). On this principle, $W_{\sim x}$ is better than W_x. Thus, when combined with the strong pareto principle, TAC gets the intuitively correct result, implying that it is impermissible for you to do *x*.

Another response to the objection is to accept the assumption that one world can be better than another if and only if the total sum of goodness contained by the one is greater than the total sum of goodness contained by the other and so accept that we need to replace TAC with something along the lines of the following view, which I call *rational-preference consequentialism:*

RPC (1.0) S's performing *x* is morally permissible if and only if, and ultimately because, there is no available alternative, *y*, whose outcome ranks higher than

> *x*'s outcome, and (2.5) *y*'s outcome ranks higher than *x*'s outcome if and only if S has decisive reason, all things considered, to prefer *y*'s outcome to *x*'s outcome.

RPC ranks alternative outcomes not in terms of their impersonal goodness, but in terms of the agent's (agent-neutral and agent-relative) reasons to prefer each to the others. So, even if $W_{\sim x}$ is not, strictly speaking, better than W_x, it is clear that you ought to prefer $W_{\sim x}$ to W_x. For the fact both that every location has at least as much goodness in $W_{\sim x}$ as it does in W_x and that at least one location has more goodness in $W_{\sim x}$ than it does in W_x would seem to constitute a decisive reason for you to prefer $W_{\sim x}$ to W_x. Thus, RPC implies that it is impermissible for you to maximize the good by doing *x*.

Third objection: It is not the case that if S's performing *x* is morally permissible, it is ultimately because S's performing *x* would maximize the good.

One might accept that S's performing *x* is morally permissible if and only if S's performing *x* would maximize the good but deny that what makes S's performing *x* morally permissible is that S's doing so would maximize the good. Philippa Foot (1985), for instance, holds that it is the other way around: that what makes S's performing *x* an act that would maximize the good is that it is a morally permissible act, for she argues that we have no grasp of the notion of a good state of affairs that is independent of what is required by the virtue of benevolence. And, on her view, benevolence is itself constrained by the other virtues; that is, benevolence comes into play only in choosing among actions that are not ruled out by the practice of the other virtues (such as, justice). Thus, it makes no sense to say that the state of affairs in which you commit one murder is better than the one in which five others each commit murder, for your committing murder, even so as to prevent five others from doing the same, is ruled out by the practice of justice. On Foot's view, then, we can make sense of one state of affairs being better than another only if we see benevolence as requiring us to bring about the one as opposed to the other and, thus, see no other virtue as prohibiting us from doing so. And, therefore, we can have no grasp of one state of affairs being better than another that is independent of our understanding of whether it would be permissible for us to bring about the one as opposed to the other.

Others, though, have questioned this view. For instance, Samuel Scheffler asks: "[D]o we really cease to understand what is meant by 'a better state of affairs' if the question is raised whether infringing a right or telling a lie or treating a particular individual unfairly might perhaps produce a better state of affairs than failing to do so?" (1985, 412). But even if we side with Scheffler on this point, we might think that some of the versions of consequentialism discussed above, such as Mod-SU and RPC, are particularly prone to this sort of Footian worry. On these consequentialist views, the outcomes of actions are not given an agent-neutral ranking in terms of their impersonal goodness, but are instead given an agent-relative ranking in terms of the agent's reasons for preferring each outcome to its alternatives. And it may seem that the correct agent-relative ranking was settled upon on the basis of our intuitions about what it is right and wrong to do. The worry, then, is that insofar "as an agent-relative ordering of all states of affairs from better to worse can be constructed only once we have figured out which actions are right, it cannot serve as a guide to rightness" (van Roojen 2004, 169). Thus, the Footian worry is that these more nuanced versions of "consequentialism" avoid counterintuitive implications only at the cost of abandoning one of consequentialism's core commitments: specifically, the commitment to the idea that the deontic statuses of actions are determined by how their outcomes rank, not vice versa.[14]

Other Responses to These Objections

I have suggested that one move that the TACist can make in response to an objection is to modify TAC so that it avoids the objection. Specifically, I have suggested modifying TAC by modifying the way it ranks outcomes—that is, by modifying (2.0) in the formulation of TAC given at the beginning of the section "Act-Utilitarianism and Traditional Act-Consequentialism." This strategy is called *consequentializing*. The idea is to start with some plausible nonconsequentialist theory that avoids the objection in question and take whatever features that it considers to be relevant to assessing the deontic statuses of actions and incorporate them as features that are relevant to how outcomes rank, thereby generating a consequentialist theory that avoids the objection.[15]

There are, of course, other ways for the TACist to respond to an objection. One is to accept the general conciliatory approach of thinking that TAC must be modified so as to avoid the objection but to modify TAC by modifying its account of how its ranking of outcomes determines the deontic statuses of actions—that is, by modifying (1.0) as opposed to, or in addition to, modifying (2.0) in the above formulation of TAC. Another way for the TACist to respond to an objection is not at all conciliatory and involves discrediting the intuitions on which the objection is based. I will explain both strategies at greater length below.

Modifying (1.0) of TAC

If one takes the intuitions behind the demandingness objection seriously, one might reject TAC and adopt *satisficing consequentialism* in its place:

> **SAT** (1.1) S's performing *x* is morally permissible if and only if, and ultimately because, *x*'s outcome ranks high enough relative to the best available alternative(s), and (2.6) *x*'s outcome ranks high enough relative to the best available alternative(s) if and only if the total amount of (impersonal) goodness contained in *x*'s outcome plus *n* ($n > 0$) is greater than or equal to the total amount of (impersonal) goodness contained within each of the best available alternatives.[16]

SAT can accommodate agent-centered options and supererogatory acts. The problem, though, is that it permits agents to sacrifice their own good for the sake of making things worse for others as well (Bradley 2006). To illustrate, consider the case depicted in Table 3.

Let U(x) = the overall utility that would be produced if S does x, and let us suppose that $n = 80$. Assume that a_1 is the act of your keeping to yourself while you work to complete some important project for your job, that a_2 is the act of your instead dissuading six others from donating money to Oxfam, that a_3 is the act of your instead dissuading seven others from donating money to Oxfam, and that a_4 is the act of your instead dissuading eight others from donating money to Oxfam. Assume that your failure to complete the important project will cost you ten utiles. And assume that for each person that you dissuade from donating money to Oxfam there will be ten fewer utiles of aggregate utility.

SAT implies that it is permissible for you to neglect your work so as to dissuade seven others from donating their money to Oxfam, thereby making things worse not only for you, but also for others. What is worse, SAT implies that it is actually supererogatory for you to neglect your work so as to dissuade six others from donating their money to Oxfam, thereby making things worse not only for you, but also for others. The idea that making a personal sacrifice

Table 3

x	*U(x)*	*deontic status*
a_1	+190	supererogatory and best
a_2	+120	supererogatory
a_3	+110	merely permissible
a_4	+100	impermissible

for the sake of making things worse for others can be permissible and even supererogatory is utterly absurd.

Perhaps, then, the solution to the demandingness objection is to adopt *scalar consequentialism* instead:

> **SCAL** (1.2) S's performing y is morally better than S's performing x if and only if, and ultimately because, y's outcome ranks higher than x's outcome, and (2.0) y's outcome ranks higher than x's outcome if and only if y's outcome is (impersonally) better than x's outcome.[17]

Since SCAL does not provide a criterion for assessing the permissibility of actions but provides only a criterion for assessing the comparative deontic value of alternative acts, SCAL avoids issuing any requirements (or permissions) at all. And by avoiding issuing any demands at all, it certainly avoids the demandingness objection. But it does so at the price of not even providing a criterion of rightness. Thus, SCAL succeeds in avoiding the demandingness objection only at the price of failing to fulfill the function of an ethical theory, which is, it seems, to provide a criterion of rightness.

If we think that this is indeed too high a price to pay, we could instead avoid the demandingness objection, and the permissiveness objection as well, by adopting *rule-consequentialism:*

> **RC** (1.3) S's performing x is morally permissible if and only if, and ultimately because, x is permitted by the code of rules with the highest-ranked associated outcome, and (2.7) the outcome associated with one code of rules ranks higher than the outcome associated with another code of rules if and only if the one is (impersonally) better than the other.[18]

Not very long ago, the consensus was that RC is untenable, the thought being that it either collapses into practical equivalence with TAC or suffers from incoherence. Brad Hooker (2000) has been largely responsible for shattering this consensus. He has shown that if we formulate RC so that it ranks codes of rules in terms of the amount of good that would result from their gaining widespread *acceptance* as opposed to the amount of good that would result from their being universally *complied with*, RC will not collapse into practical equivalence with TAC.

The thought was that RC will collapse into practical equivalence with TAC, because a rule that never permits failing to maximize the good (such as "Take care of your loved ones except when doing otherwise would maximize the good") will always win out over one that sometimes permits failing to maximize the good (such as "Take care of your loved ones"), for the former type of rule would produce more good if universally complied with. So, when formulated in terms of compliance, RC collapses into practical equivalence with TAC.

However, this does not happen when we formulate RC in terms of acceptance. For there are costs associated with getting each new generation to accept a given code of rules, and, thus, the ideal code of rules cannot be too complicated or too demanding or the costs of getting the rules inculcated will exceed the benefits of having them widely accepted. Consider, for instance, that the costs of getting a rule such as "Take care of your loved ones except when doing otherwise would maximize the good" to become widely accepted would be incredibly high given people's natural inclination to favor their loved ones. Thus, when formulated in terms of acceptance, RC avoids the collapse objection by including rules that sometimes permit failing to maximize the good.

However, the worry now is that if RC includes rules that sometimes permit failing to maximize the good, then RC must be guilty of incoherence. After all, it may seem that RC is ultimately committed to the maximization of the good, and it certainly seems incoherent to be committed to the maximization of the good while holding that it is sometimes permissible to fail to maximize the good. However, Hooker (2000) argues that RC is not committed to the maximization of the good. The argument for RC is not that it is the theory that derives from some overarching commitment to the maximization of the good, but that it does a better job of meeting various desiderata (e.g., internal consistency, coherence with our considered moral convictions, etc.) than any other alternative moral theory does.

The dismissive reply

In the above, I have suggested a number of ways that we might modify TAC so as to avoid various objections. Most of these objections stem from certain commonsense intuitions about what it is right and wrong to do in particular cases. Some consequentialists have argued, though, that instead of modifying TAC in response to such objections, we should instead dismiss the intuitions on which these objections are based. The thought is that if TAC conflicts with our commonsense intuitions, then so much the worse for our commonsense intuitions.

Recently, this sort of blusterous response has been given more substance via an appeal to the work of the psychologist Joshua D. Greene. Greene has conducted experiments using functional magnetic resonance imaging that purport to show that emotional neural processes tend to generate characteristically deontological judgments, whereas cognitive neural processes tend to generate characteristically consequentialist judgments. And Peter Singer (2005) and Greene (2003, 2008) have both argued that these empirical findings impugn the credibility of characteristically deontological intuitions without impugning the credibility of characteristically consequentialist intuitions. The empirical findings purport to show that the emotional processes that give rise to characteristically deontological intuitions are tracking whether or not the relevant harm is up-close and personal. And they argue that since this is clearly a morally irrelevant factor, it follows that the emotional processes and the characteristically deontological intuitions that they give rise to should be deemed unreliable. Singer explains:

> If . . . our intuitive responses are due to differences in the emotional pull of situations that involve bringing about someone's death in a close-up, personal way, and bringing about the same person's death in a way that is at a distance, and less personal, why should we believe that there is anything that justifies these responses? . . . For most of our evolutionary history, . . . violence could only be inflicted in an up-close and personal way—by hitting, pushing, strangling, or using a stick or stone as a club. To deal with such situations, we have developed immediate, emotionally based responses to questions involving close, personal interactions with others. The thought of pushing the stranger off the footbridge elicits these emotionally based responses. Throwing a switch that diverts a train that will hit someone bears no resemblance to anything likely to have happened in circumstances in which we and our ancestors lived. . . . But what is the moral salience of the fact that I have killed someone in a way that was possible a million years ago, rather than in a way that became possible only two hundred years ago? I would answer: none. (2005, 347–8)[19]

So Singer and Greene argue that there is good reason to question the reliability of our deontological intuitions: they are tracking what appear to be morally irrelevant factors. But there seems to be no equivalent reason for thinking that the consequentialist factors that our cognitive processes are tracking are likewise morally irrelevant. Indeed, they argue, unlike in the case of our characteristically deontological intuitions, we cannot give an evolutionary debunking of our characteristically consequentialist intuitions. And if all that is right, then perhaps we should reject the deontological intuitions on which the objections to TAC rest rather than reject TAC itself.[20]

Conclusion

Historically, the debate over consequentialism has focused on TAC with consequentialists responding to objections either by abandoning TAC for some other more nuanced version of consequentialism or by attempting to discredit the intuitions on which the objections are based. Consequentialism has thus proved amazingly resilient to the onslaught of criticisms that have been leveled against it. Ultimately, though, whether consequentialism will rule the day depends on what the best version of it is and how this, the best version, compares to the best versions of its nonconsequentialist rivals. Only time will tell.[21]

Bibliography

Arneson, R. (2005), "Sophisticated Rule Consequentialism: Some Simple Objections." *Philosophical Issues* 15, 235–51.
Bales, R. E. (1971), "Act-Utilitarianism: Account of Right-Making Characteristics or Decision-Making Procedure?" *American Philosophical Quarterly* 8, 257–65.
Bentham, J. (1789), *An Introduction to the Principles of Morals and Legislation*, J. Burns and H. L. A. Hart (eds.). London: Athlone Press, 1970.
Berker, S. (2009), "The Normative Insignificance of Neuroscience." *Philosophy & Public Affairs* 37, 293–329.
Bradley, B. (2006), "Against Satisficing Consequentialism." *Utilitas* 18, 97–108.
Bykvist, K. (2003), "Normative Supervenience and Consequentialism." *Utilitas* 15, 27–49.
Dreier, J. (1993), "Structures of Normative Theories." *The Monist* 76, 22–40.
Feldman, F. (2006), "Actual Utility, the Objection from Impracticality, and the Move to Expected Utility." *Philosophical Studies* 129, 49–79.
Foot, P. (1985), "Utilitarianism and the Virtues." *Mind* 94, 196–209.
Greene, J. D. (2008), "The Secret Joke of Kant's Soul," in W. Sinnnott-Armstrong (ed.), *Moral Psychology, Vol. 3: The Neuroscience of Morality: Emotion, Brain Disorders, and Development*. Cambridge, MA: MIT Press, 35–79.
—. (2003), "From Neural "Is" to Moral "Ought": What Are the Moral Implications of Neuroscientific Moral Psychology?" *Nature Reviews Neuroscience* 4, 847–50.
Harwood, S. (2003), "Eleven Objections to Utilitarianism," in L. Pojman (ed.), *Moral Philosophy: A Reader*, 3rd Edition. Indianapolis: Hackett Publishing, 179–92.
Hooker, B. (2000), *Ideal Code, Real World*. Oxford: Clarendon Press.
Hurley, P. (2006), "Does Consequentialism Make Too Many Demands, or None at All?" *Ethics* 116, 680–706.
Jackson, F. (1991), "Decision-Theoretic Consequentialism and the Nearest and Dearest Objection." *Ethics* 101, 461–82.
Kagan, S. and Vallentyne, P. (1997), "Infinite Value and Finitely Additive Value Theory." *The Journal of Philosophy* 94, 5–26.
Kagan, S. (1991), *The Limits of Morality*. Oxford: Oxford University Press.
Kawall, J. (2003), "Self-Regarding Supererogatory Actions." *Journal of Social Philosophy* 34, 487–98.
Lauwers, L. and Vallentyne, P. (2004), "Infinite Utilitarianism: More Is Always Better." *Economics and Philosophy* 20, 307–30.
Lawlor, R. (2009a), *Shades of Goodness: Gradability, Demandingness and the Structure of Moral Theories*. New York: Palgrave Macmillan.
—. (2009b), "The Rejection of Scalar Consequentialism." *Utilitas* 21, 100–16.
Lenman, J. (2000), "Consequentialism and cluelessness." *Philosophy & Public Affairs*, 29, 342–370.
Louise, J. (2004), "Relativity of Value and the Consequentialist Umbrella." *Philosophical Quarterly* 54, 518–36.
McConnell, T. C. (1980), "Utilitarianism and Supererogatory Acts." *Ratio* 22, 36–8.
McNamara, P. (2011). "Supererogation, Inside and Out: Toward an Adequate Scheme for Common-sense Morality." *Oxford Studies in Normative Ethics*, 1, 202–35.
—. (1996), "Making Room for Going beyond the Call." *Mind* 105, 415–50.

Mill, J. S. (1861), *Utilitarianism*, in Roger Crisp (ed.), Oxford: Oxford University Press, 1998.
Norcross, A. (2006), "Reasons without Demands: Rethinking Rightness," in J. Dreier (ed.), *Contemporary Debates in Moral Theory*. Oxford: Blackwell, 5–20.
Parfit, D. (2011), *On What Matters, Volume One*. Oxford: Oxford University Press.
Portmore, D. W. (2011), *Commonsense Consequentialism: Wherein Morality Meets Rationality*. New York: Oxford University Press.
—. (2009a), "Consequentializing." *Philosophy Compass* 4, 329–47.
—. (2009b), "Rule-Consequentialism and Irrelevant Others." *Utilitas* 21, 368–76.
—. (2008), "Are Moral Reasons Morally Overriding?" *Ethical Theory and Moral Practice* 11, 369–88.
Scheffler, S. (1985), "Agent-Centered Restrictions, Rationality, and the Virtues." *Mind* 94, 409–19.
Sepielli, A. (2010), "Normative uncertainty and intertheoretic comparisons," unpublished manuscript.
—. (2009), "What to Do When You Don't Know What to Do." *Oxford Studies in Metaethics* 4, 5–28.
Sider, T. (1993), "Asymmetry and Self-Sacrifice." *Philosophical Studies* 70, 117–32.
Sidgwick, H. (1907), *The Methods of Ethics, Seventh Edition*. London: Macmillan. First Edition 1874.
Singer, P. (2005), "Ethics and Intuitions." *The Journal of Ethics* 9, 331–52.
—. (1999), "A response," in D. Jamieson (ed.), *Singer and His Critics*. Oxford: Blackwell, 269–335.
Sinnott-Armstrong, W. (2003), "Consequentialism." *The Stanford Encyclopedia of Philosophy (Summer 2003 Edition)*, Edward N. Zalta (ed.), http://plato.stanford.edu/archives/sum2003/entries/consequentialism.
Smith, M. (2006), "The Right, the Good and Uncertainty," in T. Horgan and M. Timmons (eds.), *Metaethics after Moore*. Oxford: Oxford University Press, 133–48.
Sobel, D. (2007), "The Impotence of the Demandingness Objection." *Philosophers' Imprint* 7, 1–17.
Stroud, S. (1998), "Moral Overridingness and Moral Theory." *Pacific Philosophical Quarterly* 79, 170–89.
Thomson, J. J. (1990), *The Realm of Rights*. Cambridge, MA: Harvard University Press.
Timmons, M. (2008), "Toward a sentimentalist deontology," in W. Sinnott-Armstrong (ed.), *Moral Psychology, Volume 3: The Neuroscience of Morality: Emotion, Brain Disorders, and Development*. Cambridge, MA: MIT Press, 93–104.
van Roojen, M. (2004), "The Plausibility of Satisficing and the Role of Good in Ordinary Thought," in M. Byron (ed.), *Satisficing and Maximizing*. Cambridge: Cambridge University Press, 1–13.
Vessel, J-P. (2010), "Supererogation for Utilitarianism." *American Philosophical Quarterly*, 47, 299–319.
Zimmerman, M. J. (1996), *The Concept of Moral Obligation*. Cambridge: Cambridge University Press.

8 Kantian Ethics

Kyla Ebels-Duggan

Over the past few decades enormous talent has been brought to bear on developing Kantian approaches to moral theory with the result that Kantianism is now taken to be one among a small handful of live options for fundamental approaches to ethics. No one could hope to do justice to the work of even one of the many moral philosophers reasonably counted as Kantians, much less supply a complete survey of the field. I aim instead to articulate some characteristic Kantian commitments, positions that all or most Kantian moral theorists share, and to say a bit about what makes these positions attractive.[1] In addition to discussing these points of agreement, I hope to help readers understand some of the most important internal disagreements in the field.

We can helpfully, if somewhat artificially, divide contemporary Kantians into two groups: *Kantian Constructivists* draw inspiration from Kant's claim to have articulated a distinctively formal practical theory, and seek to derive substantive practical norms from formal principles of practical reasoning. But many philosophers who are drawn to Kantian ideas doubt that this project can be successfully executed and/or regard it as unnecessary. These form a second category, which we might call *Kantian Realists*. They view the Kantian enterprise as ultimately grounded in a substantive value, usually identified with what Kant calls "humanity," and are more willing to rely on normative claims that they do not purport to derive from the theory's foundational principles.[2]

In the first section of this chapter, "The Good Will and the Motive of Duty," I begin by trying to dispel some points of common misinterpretation of Kant and the Kantian program, arising largely from misreadings of Kant's *Groundwork I*. I regard the positions that I survey in this section as common to most Kantians. In the next section I discuss Kantian Constructivism and its connection with Kant's Formula of Universal Law, focusing primarily on the work of Christine Korsgaard. In the third section I describe some versions of Kantian Realism, a view that downplays the Universal Law and tends to rely more on Kant's Formula of Humanity. The fourth section discusses the application of the Formula of Humanity in normative ethics. I outline some normative commitments that most Kantians share and then discuss differences between Constructivists and Realists over how the formula ought to be applied.

The Good Will and the Motive of Duty

It is now commonplace among Kantian moral theorists to complain that a longstanding exclusive focus on the *Groundwork* produced widely held misinterpretations of the Kantian approach. Kantians have been productively developing the insights in many of Kant's other texts.[3] But one can still approach Kantian ethics through the *Groundwork* while avoiding such pitfalls if one keeps the purpose of the work firmly in mind. Kant's title announces his intention: the book is not intended as a complete ethical theory. Kant does not here lay out his full story about normative ethics, nor does he go into detail about the nature of virtue, or the whole of the human good. These are all topics that he addresses elsewhere, primarily in the *Doctrine of Virtue* and *Religion within the Bounds of Mere Reason*. In the *Groundwork* he conceives his task narrowly as identifying and vindicating the fundamental principle of morality.

Kant announces that he will accomplish the task in two steps. As he describes them these are, first, an analytic project: derive, from the content of our pretheoretical moral concepts, the fundamental moral law. And second, a synthetic project: vindicate the authority of this principle (Kant 1998, 4:392). Kant tells us that the first two sections of the work are dedicated to the analytic task, and that he will defend the purported authority of the moral law only in section III.

He begins the analytic project by looking to the good will, and argues that it is uniquely unconditionally good (4:393–4). But he is less interested in this claim about value than in the epistemic role that thinking about the good will can play in his foundational project. In Kant's view the person of good will, or virtuous person,[4] not only does the morally right thing, but does it for the right reason. So reflection on the good will's motivation should reveal the reasons that are distinctive of moral action and thus illuminate the fundamental moral principle. Kant's idea then is to move from the concept of the virtuous agent to the content of the moral law.

This methodology already presupposes a central Kantian commitment: morality must be first-personal.[5] That is on a Kantian view it is built into the very idea of morality that it must be capable of guiding a person's deliberations about what she ought to do. In order to so much as qualify as a candidate for a moral principle a norm of action must be transparent in the sense that an agent can, and in some sense should, act on it in full knowledge of what she is doing. So the moral principle is the very principle on which the virtuous person acts. This contrasts with certain consequentialist principles that define obligatory actions as those that maximize the value of outcomes, but may admittedly fail to provide guidance in practice due to lack of information and the capacity to calculate these values.[6] It is especially opposed to indirect forms of consequentialism on which the fundamental moral demand is to produce the best outcomes, but it is thought that the best way to achieve this is to direct one's self by some other principle.

Kant elicits the person of good will's principle of action by contrasting her with others who also do the right thing, but for the wrong reasons. That is, these others act on reasons that do not mark them out as virtuous. His first foil is the honest shopkeeper (4:397). The shopkeeper refrains from overcharging his customers. He does so because this is good for business. His actions are permissible, but guided by his own advantage; he would cheat his customers if that would benefit him. Even though the honest shopkeeper does no wrong, Kant denies that he has a good will.

Many readers accept this, but balk at Kant's next example, the "sympathetic" person. The sympathetic person helps others. Kant describes him as "find[ing] an inner satisfaction in spreading joy around [him]" and "tak[ing] delight in the satisfaction of others so far as it is [his] own work" (4:398). Though the sympathetic man clearly acts permissibly, Kant claims that his actions also have no "moral worth." I take this to be a way of denying that the sympathetic person's actions are virtuous, that is motivated in the way that a virtuous person's actions would be. Kant continues with what is perhaps his single most damaging claim for the reputation of Kantian moral theory: should this person sink into a depression that dispels his satisfaction, and yet continue helping from duty alone, *then* his actions would have moral worth and he would display a good will.

Many have read the passage as advancing an implausible and unattractive view of virtuous action. They take it that Kant thinks that anyone who enjoys acting well is really aiming at her own pleasure, and thus that only those who act well begrudgingly display virtue. But contemporary Kantians have defended more attractive interpretations.[7] To see what Kant is really saying, it helps to keep the honest shopkeeper in mind. In refraining from overcharging he does something that is both required morally and in his interest, but Kant describes him as moved by only the latter consideration. It is this stipulation that rules out his action as a distinctively virtuous one. Acting in a way that benefits himself doesn't disqualify him as having a good will, but taking his own interests as his exclusive or overriding reason for action does.

A parallel holds with the sympathetic person. His helpful actions are both the right thing to do and a source of enjoyment for him. But Kant describes him as motivated only by the latter consideration: he responds to the pleasure of helping, not to others' claim on his help. As was true of the honest shopkeeper, we couldn't read this off his action, even if we knew that helping gives him joy.

The problem isn't that he enjoys helping, but rather that he takes his enjoyment as his exclusive or overriding reason for action. And that is not what a good person would do; the virtuous person knows that sometimes she ought to help whether she wants to or not.

It is worth pausing again over the methodology here. It is often said that Kant thinks that the permissibility of an action depends on its motives.[8] Some Kantians may believe this, but Kant's strategy for formulating the fundamental moral principle seems incompatible with the doctrine that permissibility generally tracks an agent's reasons for acting. The whole point of the contrasting characters that Kant introduces is that they act permissibly, or even in ways that are morally required, but do not act for the right reasons.

What then is the distinctive motive that moves the good willed or virtuous person? Kant thinks that it must be the very fact that the action in question is right or required, and this is what he calls the motive of *duty*. The problem with the foils is that this motive is insufficient to move them to action. The shopkeeper does not see his customers as having claim on his honesty, and the sympathetic person does not see those in need as having claim on his help. What disqualifies their actions from having moral worth is not the presence of a nonmoral motive, but the absence or insufficiency of the distinctively moral one.[9] Actions have moral worth when and only when the motive of duty is sufficient to motivate the action. Kant characterizes the foils as acting merely "in accord with duty" but not "from duty." We can understand acting in accord with duty to be acting permissibly and acting from duty to be acting virtuously.[10]

The misreading of Kant's treatment of the sympathetic person has it that one can act from duty only against inclination, but this is a mistake: the virtuous Kantian agent can perfectly well act from duty and in accord with inclination.[11] Kant casts his sympathetic person into a sort of depression not because a melancholy state is necessary for being virtuous, but only because consideration of such a person makes vivid the *possibility* of a motive for doing right besides enjoyment or self-interest.[12]

A lesson that Kant draws from his discussion of these examples is that the good will is not characterized by its purpose (4:399). It is not characterized by what it accomplishes, nor even what it aims to accomplish. The sympathetic man's purpose, what he aims to bring about, remains constant through the change in his emotive state. Both before and after depression settles on him, this purpose is to help others. What changes is his motive for adopting this aim, that is what he takes as giving him reason to adopt it, and thus the principle on which he acts when he provides help. As first described he aims to help because he enjoys doing so, while in his later state he is motivated to help by the fact that he is required to help, that it is his duty.

This Kantian insight is important for two reasons. First, it brings out one of the most important contrasts between Kantians and consequentialists of all sorts. Consequentialists generally hold that the point of action is to produce outcomes and on this view it seems obvious that morality must direct us to produce the best possible outcomes.[13] There is debate among consequentialists about which outcomes are valuable and which principles of action best realize them. But there is a deeper disagreement between all parties to this debate on the one hand and Kantians on the other. Kantians do not think of action primarily as the production of outcomes and instead hold that morality directs us to act on certain principles, or to take certain considerations as reason for action.[14] More on this near the end of the chapter, when I discuss the sense in which "humanity" functions as an end in Kantian moral theory.

The second implication of Kant's refusal to characterize the good will by its purposes is subtler, but just as important. It amounts to a denial of another unattractive position with which Kantians are sometimes saddled, the view that the purpose of the virtuous person is *to do her duty*. Someone who adopts this as her purpose seems guilty of an undue concern with herself, and what some philosophers have named moral fetishism.[15] She does not appear to present an attractive moral ideal. But on Kant's view doing one's duty is *not* the purpose of the virtuous agent. Doing one's duty, as Kantians understand it, is not even the sort of thing that can compete with other purposes, such as helping those in need. The virtuous agent has no distinctive purpose, but rather regards her purposes and the considerations that tell in favor of them in a distinctive way. Again the discussion of the sympathetic person makes this clear. His actions come to have moral worth not because he changes his purpose, for his purpose does not change. What changes is the way that he relates considerations of need to actions of helping, now for the first time seeing the former as generating a claim or, as Kant says, an obligation. Forging this relation is the distinctive function of the Kantian motive of duty.[16]

Kant now has in hand these resources for specifying the principle on which the virtuous person acts: (a) The principle is not characterized by its purpose; it does not direct us to bring about some state of affairs. This is at least one thing that Kant means when he says that the fundamental moral principle cannot be a material principle, but must be formal. (b) It represents actions as required, as necessary to do no matter what our desires or other purposes are. That is, the good will, in acting from duty, represents its action to itself as if it were dictated by an authoritative law. Kant concludes that the good will is moved by the form of law, and so reaches his initial formulation of the Categorical Imperative, his fundamental moral principle: "I ought never to act except in such a way that I could also will that my maxim should become a universal law" (4:402).[17]

Recall Kant's intent in this discussion: he is trying to move from the concept of a good will or virtuous person to the content of the fundamental moral principle. He reaches this content via a thought about the role of the distinctively moral motive, which he calls *duty*. In tracing this development I have tried to dispel three persistent misconceptions of Kantian moral thought. These are (1) that proper motivation is a condition of moral permissibility; (2) that only someone who takes no pleasure in acting as he ought has a good will or counts as virtuous; and (3) that the person of good will acts for the purpose of fulfilling his duty. The rejection of these positions is commonplace and rarely in dispute among moral theorists who consider themselves Kantians. But misreadings persist among critics of Kant and live on in many presentations of his work to students encountering it for the first time, so the corrections bear repeating.

Kantian Constructivism and The Universal Law

In Section II of the *Groundwork* Kant proceeds through several formulations of the fundamental moral principle that he calls the Categorical Imperative. His initial formulation from *Groundwork I*, quoted above, differs only superficially from the first of these, commonly known as the Universal Law Formulation: "act only in accordance with that maxim through which you can at the same time will that it become a universal law" (4:421). The primary division within contemporary Kantian ethics that I mentioned above could be understood as a disagreement about the relative importance and usefulness of this formula, with Kantian Constructivists placing greater emphasis on it and Kantian Realists preferring later formulas, including the formula of Humanity as a End: "So act that you use humanity, whether in your own person or in the person of any other, always at the same time as an end, never merely as a means" (4:429).[18]

The best way into Kantian Constructivism may be through Kant's own characterization of what is distinctive in his theory.[19] In the *Groundwork* he declares:

> "If we look back upon all previous efforts that have ever been made to discover the principle of morality, we need not wonder now why all of them had to fail. It was seen that the human being is bound to laws by his duty, but it never occurred to them that he is subject *only to laws given by himself but still universal . . .* "

and he informs us that he ". . . will therefore call [his] basic [moral] principle the principle of the **autonomy** of the will in contrast with every other . . . " All previous attempts at moral theory, and the principles associated with them, he designates "heteronomy" (4:432–3, emphases in original).

As Kant sees it, there are only two possible strategies for establishing the authority of a purportedly moral principle. One is to appeal to some prior interest of ours. We should care about morality because, for example, it helps us coordinate our social interactions and we want to live together in a harmonious way. But Kant thinks that any such attempt bottoms out in appeals to what *we want.*[20] Whatever such a normative view may have to recommend it, he holds that it is not a proper basis for *moral* theory because of its appeal to inclinations that we could, in principle, lack or lose. The authority of a principle grounded in this way is thus conditional or escapable in a way that Kant supposes moral authority could not be. Kant thinks that such an approach to morality renders us heteronomous, because it leaves us ultimately subject to the inclinations that we happen to have. This sounds like a concern about us, but it is more fundamentally a concern about the inadequacy of the proposed source of the authority of the principle.

Kantian Constructivists likewise regard any theory that begins from the posit of a substantive value or values as relying on a heteronomous source of authority. In positing values, the theory apparently dictates to us something that we must take as reason-giving. Constructivists sometimes complain that any such appeal faces insurmountable metaphysical and epistemic problems, but these issues can be seen as symptoms of a deeper normative problem about how any independent order of value could have legitimate authority to guide our wills. One can question the justification of any such claim to authority, and theories that take these value commitments as a starting point will have no compelling answer. Agents can then regard the purportedly valuable thing as reason-giving only by taking this claim as if on authority. This is so whether the claim to authority is said to be grounded in an independent order of values, as in metaphysical value realism,[21] or in some feature of our psychology or biology, as in variants of Humean and Aristotelian views.[22] And Kant holds that it is equally true even if the purported value is one that we do happen to want.[23] Most Kantian Constructivists think that this sort of undefended appeal to substantive value is the problem that Kant saw with all previous theories, and that this problem is real.

Kantian Constructivists thus think that it is a mistake to regard our practical reasoning as correct insofar as it tracks prior reasons or values. Instead, they reverse this order of priority: reasons and values are established by correct procedures of reasoning. Constructivists are thus voluntarists who take Kant's talk of legislating the moral law to be more than metaphorical. They hold that we create practical norms, reasons, and values through rational willing. Even so, they are not subjectivists or relativists about moral claims. They embrace voluntarism precisely to avoid the problem of contingency in the authority of the moral law that they take Kant to have identified. So Constructivists believe that there are values that are objective in the sense that any rational agent must affirm them, and reasons that have authority to guide anyone capable of action. The great hope of the view is to argue to substantive practical principles—and so to commitments to values or reasons that can provide genuine practical guidance—beginning from premises that are in some sense merely formal. If successful, this Constructivist strategy would cut a middle path between metaphysical realism and subjectivism, avoiding the purported problems of each. The norms that govern us arise from our own commitments, and this renders their metaphysical status and claims to authority unmysterious. But there are some commitments that we cannot avoid, and thus some norms that we must legislate, norms that are not optional or escapable, and are in this sense objective.

Constructivists are often drawn to the Universal Law Formula because it is the most obviously formal of Kant's statements of the Categorical Imperative. One way to accomplish the move from form to substance would be to vindicate Kant's position that application of this principle yields recognizable moral content. Successful execution of this strategy would yield a version of formalism free from the charges of emptiness that have dogged Kantianism at least back to Hegel. It also promises to avoid the problem of heteronomy by providing an argument for the authority of all substantive normative claims that the resulting theory affirms.[24]

Important work by Onora O'Neill and Andrews Reath exemplifies the Constructivist strategy, but Constructivism is today most strongly associated with the work of Christine Korsgaard.[25] As we will see, though Korsgaard is friendlier to the Universal Law Formula than most Kantian Realists are, she believes that in the end Constructivists too must appeal to the Formula of Humanity.[26]

Korsgaard's version of Constructivism starts with the idea that normative concepts name practical problems that we face, and function as placeholders for the answers to these problems (Korsgaard 2008b, 302–26). So, for example, the normative term *justice* can be taken to name the practical problem of how to distribute the benefits and burdens of civil society. The normative term *reason* names the answer to a more general practical problem: determining which considerations should bear on our practical deliberations. Following Rawls, Korsgaard names specific proposals about how to solve the normative problems in question "conceptions."[27] This way of understanding the function of normative concepts lends itself to a plausible account of the place of normativity in the world. As Korsgaard puts it, "if you recognize the problem to be real, to be yours, to be one you have to solve, and the solution to be the only or best one, then the solution is binding upon you" (Korsgaard 2008b, 322).

So far this says nothing about what would make a particular normative conception "best," and is compatible with a realist metaethics, on which a conception is best in virtue of accurately representing mind-independent normative facts. Korsgaard's distinctive and ambitious Constructivist hope goes further, aiming to derive conceptions, contentful practical views, from our normative concepts. This would be to derive the substantive answers to our practical problems from the form of our questions.

Korsgaard views Kant as the originator of this strategy and as applying it in the *Groundwork.* On her view, Kant sees the rational will as facing a problem: it must find a principle on which it can act. It faces the problem of finding a principle because in the situation of deliberation it experiences itself as undetermined by external forces—as Kant says, "negatively free". It thus cannot take its law directly from nature. But it needs some principle since if it tried to act without one it would, in effect, move randomly and so not be recognizable as rational. So the rational will must give itself a law. It must be autonomous, or as Kant says "positively free" (Kant 1998, 4:446). Korsgaard thus reads Kant as arguing that since what it needs is a law, but nothing determines this law's content, the will can rely only on the idea of the form of law. The only principle that it can then adopt without truncating its freedom is that of acting on principles fit to be laws. But this just is the Categorical Imperative in its Universal Law Formula.[28]

No one supposes that the Categorical Imperative provides a mechanical algorithm that delivers all by itself a complete account of what we ought to do in any situation.[29] But if it can be shown to have some attractive content, for instance to rule out some plausibly immoral ways of acting, then the task of deriving moral substance from the form of law would be accomplished. To accomplish this one needs to make sense of Kant's claim that violations of the Categorical Imperative involve us in contradictions. He claims that just as violating a formal principle of theoretical reasoning results in contradictory beliefs, violating the Universal Law Formula results in some sort of contradiction. He identifies two different types of contradiction to which such violations can lead, each corresponding to a type of duty. Narrow or perfect duties are obligations to perform or, more often, omit a particular action. Wide or imperfect duties are obligations to adopt some end, but do not specify exactly what or how much you are to do about it. Maxims that violate narrow duties supposedly cannot even be conceived as a universal law, and generate a so-called *contradiction in conception*. Those that violate wide duties can, Kant thinks, be conceived as universal laws, but cannot be willed as such. These generate a *contradiction in the will* (4:424). Interpretations of Kant's notion of "contradiction" have to make sense of both of these varieties.

Scholars have offered different ways of trying to make sense of this idea of contradiction. Most agree that the procedure for applying the Categorical Imperative must start with the formulation of a proposed maxim. Many hold that a canonical formulation states an act, the end or purpose for which one proposes to do it, and relevant features of the circumstance in which one proposes to act. On this approach, the general form of a maxim is: *I will do Action A in circumstances C in order to achieve Purpose P.*[30] To any such maxim corresponds a universal law: *Everyone who wills purpose P in circumstances C does Action A.* The permissibility test for maxims involves imagining ourselves willing them in a situation in which the corresponding universal law holds. Maxims fail the test of permissibility if this scenario generates some sort of contradiction.

Interpreters diverge in their accounts of the contradiction. Korsgaard's approach, which she calls the *Practical Contradiction Interpretation*, treats a maxim as generating the relevant sort of contradiction if its universalization is practically self-defeating (Korsgaard 1996d).[31] A maxim generates a contradiction in conception, on this view, if universalization undermines its stated purpose. So, for instance, a false promise will not generate its intended effect—Kant's example is to produce some needed cash—if everyone who aims to secure that effect makes false promises.

The Practical Contradiction Interpretation provides a continuous, yet distinct, treatment of contradictions in the will: Forgoing a required end generates a contradiction in the sense that universalization undermines the effectiveness of the will in general. That is, under universalization, our power to pursue ends is diminished. This happens because the required ends are associated with all-purpose means, necessary for almost any discretionary end that we might adopt. For instance, if no one adopts the end of helping others then others' help is not available for my own pursuit of my ends. Since others' help is a very general means, useful for all sorts of ends, its lack constricts my ability to pursue ends generally. Thus a practical contradiction results from combining a principle of nonbeneficence with any end that depends on others' help, or—more importantly—with a general interest in my power to pursue ends. This, according to Korsgaard's Practical Contradiction Interpretation, provides the argument that beneficence is required. This interpretation of the contradiction test is now probably the dominant view, widely regarded as the best hope for making something like Kant's own attempts to derive content from form work.[32]

However the test so conceived faces serious obstacles. It is no accident that its advocates tend to focus on Kant's own example of the lying promise. This and other actions that depend on widely observed conventions while at the same time violating them are easiest to rule out with a practical contradiction test. But the strategy has difficulty dealing with actions the success of which does not depend on conventions. For example, one can apparently accomplish the purpose of killing or hurting someone by treating him violently even if everyone acts on a corresponding maxim.

Korsgaard herself believes that Kant's views must be modified in light of these problems. In *The Sources of Normativity*, she continues to pursue a Constructivist strategy of deriving contentful normative principles from formal starting points, but does not think that the Universal Law Formula alone can serve as this basis. She treats this principle as specifying only what it is to act on a reason: reasons must be universal in form. But she argues that without the scope of universalization specified this principle fails to determine any particular content. So any principle of action, including the egoist principle of doing whatever is most in my interest, and the wanton principle of acting on my strongest present desire, meet this standard. Clearly on this view the formula can no longer be thought to track moral content. Korsgaard maintains that what fixes the scope of the principle are our "practical identities," descriptions under which we value ourselves and find our lives worth living. She regards these self-conceptions as the basic sources of reasons or normativity (Korsgaard 1996h, 100–13).

Since practical identities vary from person to person, so too, on this view, do our reasons for action. But Korsgaard argues that we are all committed to what she calls our identity as human, and thus Kant's Formula of Humanity, "never treat humanity in a person as a mere means, but always at the same time as an end in itself," applies to all. She calls this principle "the moral law," and provides an argument for it inspired by her reading of Kant's own (Kant 1998, 4:428).[33] The point of the argument is to show that, though values exist in the world only because we confer them, rationality demands that if we value anything then we also value humanity. Thus humanity is objectively valuable in the sense that every valuing agent must value it. Korsgaard's argument involves a regress on the conditions for the authority of our practical identities: we can rationally take our practical identities as reason-giving only if we also treat as authoritative our identity as creatures who face the practical problem of deciding what to do, and so need reasons for action. But this just is what Korsgaard understands as our identity as human. The upshot is that if we take ourselves to have any reason at all to act, we are rationally committed to thinking that humanity generates reasons to act.[34]

This argument, if successful, leaves us with the choice between nihilism and acknowledging the authority of the Formula of Humanity. In more recent work Korsgaard goes further, arguing that the moral law is among the constitutive principles of action.[35] This amounts to construction of the moral law from a formal concept of agency. If we are to act at all, we must act in a way that acknowledges the authority of the fundamental moral principle. Thus, though she has lowered her expectations for the Universal Law, Korsgaard continues to seek a comparably thin basis on which to ground her normative theory. She aims thereby to explain and vindicate the inescapable nature of moral authority in a way that is consistent with the autonomy of moral agents.

Kantian Realism

Kantian Constructivism is arguably the most distinctive Kantian program in moral philosophy today, comprising not only a Kantian normative view, but also a tightly associated position that explains the place of normativity in the world, and so answers or displaces metaethical questions. But figured by number of advocates it is probably not the dominant contemporary reception of the Kantian heritage. Many moral theorists attracted to a Kantian approach are less interested in providing a foundational argument for moral authority than in exploring and defending the nuances of Kantian normative ethics. Many think it wiser to begin with the requirement to treat humanity as an end, and regard the normative implications of the Formula of Humanity rather than any argument for it as the core of Kantian ethics.[36] They usually deemphasize the Formula of Universal Law and the idea that there is something distinctively formal in the Kantian approach.[37] This is the approach that I am calling Kantian Realism. (I will use "Realism" in what follows to refer solely to the Kantian variety.)

Paul Guyer advocates a particularly stark version of this view.[38] He identifies freedom as the fundamental value in the Kantian system. He holds that, being fundamental, this value cannot be established by any argument, and so is indemonstrable. But Guyer believes that we nevertheless value freedom above all else. He also supposes that we can characterize freedom without reference to the moral law, and understands this law as commanding us to preserve and promote the conditions for the exercise of freedom.[39] We thus have reason to follow the law because doing so is a means to bringing about our freedom, which we value. On this view, far from being central to Kant's theory, conformity to universal law turns out to have merely instrumental value in promoting an independently valuable end.

Recall that Constructivists regard a theory as providing a satisfactory ground for the authority of morality only if it backs any substantive normative claim with argument, and so avoids appeal to values or norms to which we must defer as if on authority. On this view, arguments that establish the inescapable nature of moral authority provide us with sufficient reason to honor this authority, and so render us properly autonomous. To the extent that Realists share Guyer's view that no defense of the value or values to which they appeal is possible, they have to make sense of Kant's statements about autonomy in some other way. There are several possibilities for doing so. First, and most obviously, if freedom is identical to autonomy, then on Guyer's view it just is the undefended value in question. Second, if Guyer is correct that we value freedom, then the defense of the law rests solely on commitments of the agents that this law purports to govern. Finally, Realists could aim to show that we are bound by the law not just by something that we happen to value, but in virtue of what we are, what is most essential about us.[40]

Allen Wood opts for the third strategy. In treating the value of humanity as foundational, he presents a more paradigmatic version of Kantian Realism. Wood believes that misplaced emphasis on the Formula of Universal Law is responsible for many misinterpretations, and associated criticisms, of Kantian ethics and that the Formula of Humanity is a better candidate as the organizing principle of a Kantian moral system.[41] He holds that any sensible moral theory must appeal to some value to show the point of its prescriptions, and thus rejects the characterization of Kantian ethics as "deontological," where this names a moral theory comprised of rules that are independent of any value that is served by following them. He believes that the Formula of Humanity identifies the value in question. On his view, humanity has objective value that gives obedience to the law its point, and "grounds" all other values, in the sense that anything else that is valuable is so only and ultimately because of its relation to humanity.

With Guyer, Wood affirms a view that he also attributes to Kant: claims about ultimate value, the claim that humanity is objectively valuable among these, are "indemonstrable," not subject to proof.[42] This would seem to leave him no choice but to assert the value of humanity much as Guyer asserts the value of freedom, but Wood significantly tempers his claim of indemonstrability. Wood takes "humanity" to name our capacity to choose and pursue ends. He regards the attribution of objective value to humanity in this sense as a significant and controversial normative thesis. He thus takes the argument that he finds Kant making for it to be important. This argument begins with things that we explicitly acknowledge as valuable and purports to show that the value of humanity is an implicit presupposition of these commitments. The result appears very similar to Korsgaard's regress strategy for demonstrating the value of humanity, and Wood acknowledges his affinity to Korsgaard here.[43]

But Wood strenuously rejects a Constructivist interpretation of both this argument and of Kantian ethics more generally.[44] He thinks that it is inconsistent with Kant's views, and more importantly implausible, to regard the value of humanity as constructed or conferred by our rational activity. This activity, he argues, must respond to prior reasons in order to count as rational, and so could not create the foundational value. Wood thus takes the regress argument to show something quite different: our practical thought and action presume that humanity already *has* value, prior to this activity. This gives us as good a reason as any argument could to accept that this value is real. Thus Wood claims that "Human beings have absolute worth, which belongs to them essentially," and classifies his Kantianism as a version of "metaethical realism" (Wood 2007, 112).

In addition, Wood rejects the idea of deriving practical substance from form. On his view, no formulation of the categorical imperative is meant to provide anything like an algorithm for testing for moral duties and no formal decision procedure can construct the content of morality (70–82). Instead moral laws should be regarded as "natural laws" (113). A moral law is "grounded not in any being's volitions but absolutely, in the nature of things, independently of how any being should choose to look at the matter" (76). In particular, the moral law is to be located in the nature of the rational will, which is essentially governed by and responsive to its norms. It is on this account that Wood regards Kantian ethics as autonomous.[45]

Barbara Herman is the prominent Kantian moral philosopher most difficult to place in one of my two categories. She sounds Constructivist in recent work, when she calls the Categorical Imperative "the law constitutive of the will's own power" (Herman 2007a, 246) and describes the will as a "norm-constituted power" (Herman 2007a, 249).[46] And in an earlier essay she expresses metaethical ambitions associated with Constructivism when she characterizes Kant as cutting a path between naturalism and metaphysical realism (Herman, 1993d).[47] She also claims there that the activity of good willing brings value into the world, that to be a separate person is "being a source of reasons all the way down," and that an autonomous agent is "its own original source of reasons." These are the sorts of Constructivist claims that Wood so adamantly opposes.

Even so, Herman's substantial contributions to Kantian moral theory are arguably more Realist in spirit. She explicitly rejected the label "deontological" well before Wood did (Herman 1993c),[48] and resists the idea that formal or procedural constraints on reasoning could determine what we must do. She is concerned to explicate the Categorical Imperative in such a way that it reveals not just *that* but also *why* certain actions are forbidden and others are required, and takes a theory of value to be indispensable to this.[49] For all of these reasons she does not find the Universal Law formula especially useful. She prefers the Formula of Humanity, which invokes the relevant value and to her mind provides needed interpretation of the first formula.[50]

Herman is not primarily concerned with the metaethics of this value. She takes a greater interest in understanding how it properly guides our moral thought and has probably done more than anyone to develop an attractive and plausible account of Kantian moral psychology and the role that the Categorical Imperative plays in it. She thinks that no contradiction test yields well-defined duties or conclusions about what we must do all by itself, but that such a test can generate what she calls "deliberative presumptions." It reveals of some actions that we may not do them simply for the reason that they serve some end of ours. These actions require special justification to rebut the presumption. For example, we may not tell lies merely to advance our own interests. This is not the same as claiming that there is an absolute prohibition on lying. Rather if you are considering lying there is a burden on you to determine what morally relevant feature of the situation would place it outside of the normal prohibition. Once deliberative presumptions are in place they serve as inputs to practical reasoning. They govern which courses of action present themselves to the agent as live options for consideration, and which she regards as morally ambiguous and calling for further thought. In the normal course of action, an agent governed by the Categorical Imperative acts without explicit reflection and has no occurrent thought of the fundamental moral principle at all.[51] But the principle nevertheless plays an important governing or structuring role for her.

Kantian Constructivists and Kantian Realists differ in important ways over matters traditionally classified as metaethical. But the Formula of Humanity is an important point of agreement for those of both types. Constructivists hold out hope that the value of humanity can be constructed and thus vindicated through formal procedures of reasoning, but all share the convictions that humanity is of value, and that this value plays a pivotal role in normative ethics.[52] Constructivists would thus join Realists in rejecting the idea that Kantian ethics is deontological, at least in the sense meant by Herman and Wood. All reject the picture of the Kantian agent as acting on principles of duty, to the exclusion of considerations about value. This is a striking and important result, since Kantian ethics has traditionally been cited as the primary exemplar of a deontological theory. It seems that, with few exceptions, only opponents of a Kantian approach now accept this characterization.

Kantian Normative Ethics

Self-identified Kantians almost unanimously understand the Formula of Humanity as the basis of a normative theory that is different from and superior to any version of consequentialism.[53] Kantians and consequentialists often differ over what is most fundamentally of value. For most Kantians, the value for the sake of which we act when we act morally is that of humanity. With some variation in details, the dominant view is that "humanity" refers to our capacity to choose and pursue ends, that is to our agency.[54] By contrast many consequentialists take pleasure or well-being to be the value at the root of their ethical theory. This difference leads to two contrasting ways of conceiving of persons. For Kantians, the moral attitude of respect is owed to others conceived as agents, while consequentialists sometimes seem to be committed to viewing people primarily as sites of pleasure or loci of well-being. But this difference over what is valuable is only a tendency. In principle consequentialists can accept the Kantian characterization of the value. The deeper difference between the two views is a difference in structure, a disagreement over the proper response to value.

Sometimes this disagreement is cast as one about the relative priority of the right or the good. There are ways of interpreting the question of priority that make this accurate, but the difference is better located in the role that the foundational value plays. Though nearly all Kantians affirm the importance of the value of humanity, they almost unanimously reject the exclusively teleological treatment of value characteristic of most consequential views. I have already suggested that consequentialists treat action primarily as a means to the production of value. This is most clearly true of act-consequentialists, but insofar as they trace reasons to outcomes, all varieties of consequentialism share in this conception. Kantians understand the value of humanity in a completely different way. Kant claims that humanity is an *existent* end, thus not one that calls for being produced (4:437).[55] Moreover, Kantians hold that humanity has dignity rather than price. That is, it is not simply something of very great value to be placed high on a scale with other values, but rather a value of a different kind, incommensurate with others. It cannot be traded off against other values, and on most versions of the view not even with other instances of itself.[56] The value of humanity calls not for production or maximization, but rather for respect.[57] Respect requires recognizing certain entitlements that others have in virtue of their humanity and acting in ways that honor these entitlements. Most Kantians acknowledge entitlements of two kinds, giving rise to two categories of duties towards others: negative duties of noninterference with people's pursuit of their ends, and some sort of positive duties. Some theorists construe the latter primarily as duties to contribute to the ends of others, while others stress contributing to the development of others' agency and the creation and maintenance of the social conditions necessary for this.[58]

This Kantian approach captures widely shared moral convictions that many consequentialists struggle to vindicate. In virtue of our dignity, we each have rights that may not be violated, even in the interest of the greater good. This fits with pretheoretical convictions that many people hold, especially when the good in question is understood as pleasure or the satisfaction of preferences considered just as such. Most people will agree, for example, that no one should be thrown to the lions merely to provide the pleasures of entertainment to any number of people. Act-consequentialists have the most difficult time vindicating these beliefs. While other sorts of consequentialists may be able to fix up their approach to avoid denying them, they follow easily from the most central aspects of Kantian normative theory.

What are often called agent-centered obligations and entitlements also find a natural place in a Kantian scheme. If I make a promise my obligation, at least prima facie, is to keep the promise. Even if breaking my own promise would bring it about that several other people would keep theirs, this does not seem to make it permissible, much less obligatory, to do so. Kantians can easily account for this: when I make the promise I entitle the promisee to my performance, and this entitlement on her part corresponds to an obligation on mine. I have a prima facie obligation to the person to whom I made the promise, and I am not responsible for seeing to it that others keep their promises, at least not in any simple or straightforward way. A consequentialist who treats all value as to-be-produced has more difficulty with agent-centered restrictions like promise-keeping, since she must apparently base the obligation to keep a promise on producing the good outcome of a promise fulfilled. On this view it is hard to resist the idea that bringing about the keeping of more promises rather than fewer is to be preferred.

Finally, since Kantians understand our obligations towards others in terms of the ends that they choose rather than what they might like, want, or even benefit from, Kantianism is strongly anti-paternalist. Kantians tend towards the view that, at least among competent adults, each person's entitlement to make his or her own choices is limited only by the similar entitlements of others, even if this will result in choices that are mistaken or ill-advised. This commitment to a protected sphere of freedom for each individual is the basis of a Kantian approach to political philosophy, one that yields a liberal theory that many people find attractive.[59] But Kantians also tend to privilege respect for others' choices over concern for their well-being even in personal contexts.[60]

Despite wide agreement on the content and attractiveness of these implications of the Formula of Humanity, Kantians disagree about exactly how the formula is to be applied, including precisely what respect for humanity requires and how to realize it. These disagreements to some extent track and even recapitulate the divide between Constructivists and Realists described above.

Korsgaard is interested in giving an account of respect for humanity that allows the Formula of Humanity to yield practical conclusions without reliance on further normative judgments. On her view we respect humanity just in case we allow others to act only for ends that they set. She believes that to meet this standard we must act only in ways that make possible the actual consent of those affected by our actions. This appears to rule out deceptive use of others' agency: when I give you false information about the ends to which your action contributes, I eliminate the opportunity for you to consent to the ends that you actually further.[61] Korsgaard believes that a similar argument will rule out the use of force and coercion (Korsgaard 1996a, 106–32).[62] It is important to Korsgaard that it would be *impossible*, not merely irrational or unreasonable, for you to consent to these interactions. The latter view would require the sort of further normative judgment that she hopes to avoid.

By contrast Kantian Realists are more likely to regard the idea of respect for humanity as framing the questions that we must raise about our actions, while acknowledging that the answers will appeal to further substantive moral judgments. Wood advocates this view most clearly. He thinks that any practical conclusion drawn from the Formula of Humanity must also rely on an intermediate premise claiming that the action being considered is incompatible with or required by respect. For instance, if lying is incompatible with the Formula of Humanity, this is because it is a substantive truth that lying violates respect for humanity. Such premises cannot be derived from the Formula of Humanity, but rather are independent convictions about the meanings of our actions and the demands of respect. Since people might have different such convictions even those who sincerely agree that the Formula of Humanity ought to govern their actions might differ irresolvably over how they ought to act. Realists are committed to thinking that, when these disagreements are genuine, at least one of the parties to them is objectively mistaken though there is nothing like an algorithm for determining which it is. However, Wood also points out that the truth of the intermediate premises will vary with the background conditions, so that a particular way of treating a person may be genuinely respectful in one cultural moment, and disrespectful in another (Wood 1998).[63]

Herman concurs that the final outcomes of our deliberations require substantive normative judgments about how best to take account of all of the claims that are relevant to our actions. No formal test will reliably guide us all the way to the answers about what we ought to do. She emphasizes that a full story about how we are to treat others depends on contingent facts about our vulnerabilities to one another. These include the vulnerabilities of human beings as such, such as our need for accurate information and susceptibility to false belief. But they also include the particular vulnerabilities of particular people fully situated.[64] Moreover, because our situations are constantly shifting, Herman views moral knowledge as "dynamic" and never complete (Herman 1993d).[65] As the circumstances of human life evolve so will the needs of our agency and our potential power over and susceptibility to one another. We have every reason to suppose that this will change how we must act, so the task of moral deliberation is ongoing.

The more Realist interpretation of the Formula of Humanity reveals the affinity between Kantian ethics and certain contractualist approaches, such as that of T. M. Scanlon (Scanlon 1998).[66] Scanlon argues that the fundamental moral requirement is, roughly, to avoid treating others in ways that they could reasonably reject.[67] In Scanlon's view his contractualist principle characterizes moral wrongness, but its application depends on what sort of treatment it would be reasonable to reject in any given case. He believes that there is no formal or procedural way to settle this; a judgment that rejection is reasonable is an irreducibly substantive normative judgment. While he does not lean explicitly on the Kantian apparatus, the question of what each of those affected by our action could reasonably demand of us is recognizably Kantian, and is naturally read as articulating a conception of respect. Scanlon also rejects moral reasoning that is fundamentally aggregative, and in this way acknowledges what Kant calls the dignity of the individual. These similarities result in massive, arguably complete, overlap between the normative commitments of Scanlon's contractualism and those of many self-identified Kantians.

Scanlon vindicates the authority of his principle by appeal to the substantive value of the relationship that it defines, which he calls the relationship of mutual recognition. He holds that such relationships are valuable, but that people can fail to recognize this. Such a person would, on Scanlon's view, be making a mistake about value, but he would not necessarily be subject to any internal, formal contradictions. In this, Scanlon's theory is, at least by Kantian Constructivist lights, heteronomous. This is a designation that Scanlon gladly accepts (Scanlon 1998, 6) but it is not clear that all Kantian Realists would agree that his theory should be so described. If we understand the contractualist formula as an interpretation of the requirement to respect humanity, then Scanlon's contractualism may be autonomous in whatever sense Kantian Realism is (Scanlon 1998).[68]

Conclusion

I have tried to strike the dominant themes, both of agreement and difference, in contemporary Kantian moral theory. I began with some widely held correctives to misreadings of the moral psychology that Kant surveys in *Groundwork I*, and then discussed in some detail contemporary treatments of two of the formulae of the Categorical Imperative that he articulates in *Groundwork II*. But my treatment of Kantian normative theory has been very abbreviated. And though I have had much to say about autonomy in passing I have not explicitly discussed Kant's Formula of Autonomy, nor so much as mentioned the Formula of the Kingdom of Ends. I have said very little about the foundational project of justification or vindication that Kant pursues in *Groundwork III*, made only the briefest mention of his political theory, and none at all of his concern to integrate a practical role for our interest in happiness and the connection of this to his religious views and philosophy of history. All of these are important themes in Kant's own work and that of contemporary Kantians. The positions treated here are no more than a starting point for understanding the resources of a Kantian approach to moral theory.[69]

Bibliography

Anderson, E. (1993), *Value in Ethics and Economics*. Cambridge, MA: Harvard University Press.

Baron, M. (1995), *Kantian Ethics Almost without Apology*. Ithaca, NY: Cornell University Press.

—. (1997), Kantian Ethics. *Three Methods of Ethics*. Malden, MA: Blackwell, 3–91.

Bennett, J. (1974), "The Conscience of Huckleberry Finn." *Philosophy*, 49, 123–34.

Cummiskey, D. (1996), *Kantian Consequentialism*. New York: Oxford University Press.

Darwall, S. L. (2006), *The Second-Person Standpoint: Morality, Respect, and Accountability*. Cambridge, MA: Harvard University Press.

Dean, R. (1996), "What Should We Treat as an End in Itself?" *Pacific Philosophical Quarterly* 77, 268–88.

—. (2006), *The Value of Humanity in Kant's Moral Theory.* New York: Oxford University Press.

Denis, L. (2007), "Kant's Formula of the End in Itself: Some Recent Debates." *Philosophy Compass* 2, 244–57.

Ebels-Duggan, K. (2008), "Against Beneficence: A Normative Account of Love." *Ethics*,119, 142–70.

—. (2009), "Moral Community: Escaping the Ethical State of Nature." *Philosophers' Imprint* 9, 1–19.

Frierson, P. R. (2003), *Freedom and Anthropology in Kant's Moral Philosophy.* New York: Cambridge University Press.

Guyer, P. (1996), "The Value of Agency." *Ethics* 106, 404–23.

—. (1998), "The Possibility of the Categorical Imperative," in P. Guyer (ed.), *Kant's Groundwork of the Metaphysics of Morals.* Lanham, MD: Rowman and Littlefield.

—. (2000), "Kant's Morality of Law and Morality of Freedom," *Kant on Freedom, Law, and Happiness.* New York: Cambridge University Press, 129–71.

Hare, J. E. (1996), *The Moral Gap : Kantian Ethics, Human Limits, and God's Assistance.* New York: Oxford University Press.

Hare, R. M. (1981), *Moral Thinking.* New York: Oxford University Press.

Herman, B. (1993a), "Agency, Attachment and Difference." *The Practice of Moral Judgment.* Cambridge, MA: Harvard University Press.

—. (1993b), "Integrity and Impartiality." *The Practice of Moral Judgment.* Cambridge, MA: Harvard University Press.

—. (1993c), "Leaving Deontology Behind." *The Practice of Moral Judgment.* Cambridge, MA: Harvard University Press.

—. (1993d), "Moral Deliberation and the Derivation of Duties." *The Practice of Moral Judgment.* Cambridge, MA: Harvard University Press.

—. (1993e), "Mutual Aid and Respect for Persons." *The Practice of Moral Judgment.* Cambridge, MA: Harvard University Press.

—. (1993f), "On the Value of Acting from the Motive of Duty." *The Practice of Moral Judgment.* Cambridge, MA: Harvard University Press.

—. (1993g), "The Practice of Moral Judgment." *The Practice of Moral Judgment.* Cambridge, MA: Harvard University Press.

—. (2007a), *Moral Literacy* Cambridge, MA: Harvard University Press.

—. (2007b), "Obligatory Ends." *Moral Literacy.* Cambridge, MA: Harvard University Press, 254–75.

Hill, T. E. (1991), *Autonomy and Self-Respect.* New York: Cambridge University Press.

—. (1992a), "Humanity as and End in Itself." *Dignity and Practical Reason.* Ithaca, NY: Cornell University Press.

—. (1992b), "Making Exceptions without Abandoning the Principle: or How a Kantian Might Think about Terrorism." *Dignity and Practical Reason.* Ithaca, NY: Cornell University Press.

—. (2006), "Kantian Normative Ethics", in D. Copp (ed.), *The Oxford Handbook of Ethical Theory.* New York: Oxford University Press.

Kant, I. (1971), *Education.* Ann Arbor, MI: University of Michigan Press.

—. (1996), *The Metaphysics of Morals.* New York: Cambridge University Press.

—. (1998), *Groundwork of the Metaphysics of Morals.* New York: Cambridge University Press.
—. (2001), *Religion and Rational Theology* New York: Cambridge University Press.
—. (2006), *Anthropology from a Pragmatic Point of View* New York: Cambridge University Press.
Korsgaard, C. M. (1996a), *Creating the Kingdom of Ends.* New York: Cambridge.
—. (1996b), "From Duty and for the Sake of the Noble: Kant and Aristotle on Morally Good Action," in S. P. Engstrom and J. Whiting (eds.), *Aristotle, Kant, and the Stoics: Rethinking Happiness and Duty.* New York: Cambridge University Press, 203–36.
—. (1996c), "Kant's Formula of Humanity." *Creating the Kingdom of Ends.* New York: Cambridge University Press, 106–32.
—. (1996d), "Kant's Formula of Universal Law." *Creating the Kingdom of Ends.* New York: Cambridge University Press, 77–105.
—. (1996e), "Morality as Freedom." *Creating the Kingdom of Ends.* New York, 159–87.
—. (1996f), "The Reasons We Can Share." *Creating the Kingdom of Ends.* New York: Cambridge University Press, 275–310.
—. (1996g), "The Right to Lie: Kant on Dealing with Evil." *Creating the Kingdom of Ends.* New York: Cambridge University Press.
—. (1996h), *The Sources of Normativity.* Cambridge; New York: Cambridge University Press.
—. (1999), "Self-Constitution in the Ethics of Plato and Kant." *Journal of Ethics* 3, 1–29.
—. (2008a), "Realism and Constructivism in Twentieth-Century Moral Philosophy." *The Constitution of Agency.* New York: Oxford University Press, 302–26.
—. (2008b), *The Constitution of Agency : Essays on Practical Reason and Moral Psychology.* Oxford; New York: Oxford University Press.
—. (2009), *Self-Constitution : Agency, Identity, and Integrity.* New York: Oxford University Press.
Langton, R. (2007), "Objective and Unconditioned Value." *Philosophical Review* 116, 157–85.
Markovits, J. (2010), "Acting for the Right Reasons." *Philosophical Review* 119, 201–42.
Martin, A. M. (2006), "How to Argue for the Value of Humanity." *Pacific Philosophical Quarterly* 87, 96–125.
Mill, J. S. (1998), *Utilitarianism.* New York: Oxford University Press.
O'neill, O. (1989a), "Between Consenting Adults." *Constructions of Reason.* New York: Cambridge University Press.
—. (1989b), "Consistency in Action." *Constructions of Reason.* New York: Cambridge University Press.
—. (1989c), *Constructions of Reason : Explorations of Kant's Practical Philosophy.* New York: Cambridge University Press.
—. (1999), "Universal Laws and Ends in Themselves." *Constructions of Reason.* New York: Cambridge.
Pallikkathayil, J. (2010), "Deriving Morality from Politics: Rethinking the Formula of Humanity." *Ethics* 121, 116–47.
Parfit, D. (2011), *On What Matters.* New York: Oxford University Press.

Paton, H. J. (1958), *The Categorical Imperative.* London, UK: Hutchison.
Pettit, P. (1997), "The Consequentialist Perspective." *Three Methods of Ethics.* Malden, MA: Blackwell, 93–174.
Rawls, J. (1971), *A Theory of Justice.* Cambridge, MA: Harvard University Press.
—. (2000), *Lectures on the History of Moral Philosophy.* Cambridge, MA: Harvard University Press.
—. (2001), "Kantian Constructivism in Moral Theory," in S. Freeman (ed.), *Collected Papers.* Cambridge, MA: Harvard University Press, 303–58.
Reath, A. (2003), "Value and Law in Kant's Moral Theory." *Ethics* 114, 127–55.
—. (2006), *Agency and Autonomy in Kant's Moral Theory.* New York: Oxford University Press.
Ridge, M. (2009), "Consequentialist Kantianism." *Philosophical Perspectives* 23, 421–38.
Ripstein, A. (2009), *Force and Freedom : Kant's Legal and Political Philosophy.* Cambridge, MA: Harvard University Press.
Scanlon, T. (1998), *What We Owe to Each Other.* Cambridge, MA: Harvard University Press.
—. (2008), *Moral Dimensions : Permissibility, Meaning, Blame.* Cambridge, MA: Harvard University Press.
Schapiro, T. (1999), What is a Child? *Ethics*, 109, 715–38.
Smith, M. (1994), *The Moral Problem* Cambridge, MA: Blackwell.
Sussman, D. (2003), "The Authority of Humanity." *Ethics* 113, 350–66.
Timmerman, J. (2006), "Value without Regress: Kant's 'Formula of Humanity' Revisited." *European Journal of Philosophy* 14, 69–93.
Timmons, M. (2002), *Kant's Metaphysics of Morals: Interpretative Essays.* New York: Oxford University Press.
Uleman, J. K. (2010), *An Introduction to Kant's Moral Philosophy.* New York: Cambridge University Press.
Velleman, J. D. (2006a), "Love as a Moral Emotion." *Self to Self.* New York: Cambridge University Press.
—. (2006b), "The Voice of Conscience." *Self to Self: Selected Essays.* Cambridge: Cambridge University Press, 110–28.
Williams, B. (1981), "Persons, Character, and Morality." *Moral Luck.* New York: Cambridge University Press.
—. (1985), *Ethics and the Limits of Philosophy.* Cambridge, MA: Harvard University Press.
Wolf, S. (1982), "Moral Saints." *Journal of Philosophy* 79, 419–39.
Wood, A. W. (1970), *Kant's Moral Religion.* Ithaca, NY: Cornell University Press.
—. (1978), *Kant's Rational Theology.* Ithaca, NY: Cornell University Press.
—. (1991), "Unsocial Sociability: The Anthropological Basis of Kantian Ethics." *Philosophical Topics* 19, 325–51.
—. (1998), "Humanity as an End in Itself," in P. Guyer (ed.), *Kant's Groundwork of the Metaphysics of Morals.* Lanham, MD: Rowman and Littlefield.
—. (1999), *Kant's Ethical Thought.* New York: Cambridge.
—. (2007), *Kantian Ethics.* New York: Cambridge University Press.

9 Virtue Ethics

Christine Swanton

Part I. Virtue Ethics

Introduction

Part I of this article discusses the nature of virtue ethics as a type of normative ethical theory, alongside primarily consequentialism and Kantianism. However, since the virtue concepts are central to all types of virtue ethics, attention also needs to be paid to the notion of virtue as an excellence of character, and related notions such as the virtue concepts as applied to actions (e.g., kind act). Part II discusses the notion of virtue as an excellence of character, while Part III further elucidates the nature of virtue ethics by considering a number of central but selected issues, such as the notion of virtuous action and virtue ethical conceptions of right action. Needless to say not all of interest can be treated here.

Virtue ethics is a family of moral theories where the notion of virtuous character, and virtue concepts in general, as opposed to for example consequences of action, or duty, are seen as central in moral theorizing. In this way a distinctive form of moral theory is provided. Virtue ethics has been distinguished from virtue theory (Driver 2001). The latter type of theory (such as trait consequentialism) provides accounts of the nature of virtue without necessarily being virtue ethical. For virtue (as opposed to, e.g., consequences) may not be sufficiently central for a virtue theory to qualify as being a species of virtue ethics. What counts as "sufficiently central" can be a matter of interesting debate, for example, debate about the nature of Kant's virtue theory (Hill 2008, Johnson 2008). Because virtue is in various ways central to their substantive views, virtue ethicists give distinctive accounts of important topics in moral theory—for example, applied ethics (Hursthouse 1987, 1991, 2006, 2007), objectivity, and demandingness (Swanton 2003, 2009), and our obligations to strangers (Slote 2001, 2007).[1]

Though an ancient type of moral theory, until relatively recently virtue ethics has been accorded little attention in the modern era. Ancient virtue ethics, like all virtue ethical theories, focuses attention on the virtues and vices of character since these are deemed essential to the living of a good life. Since this seems a sensible view why the neglect of virtue ethics? Ironically, given that Hume, the greatest British moral philosopher, is now often interpreted as a form of virtue ethicist (see the section "Response-Dependent Virtue Ethics"), a prime reason for the neglect of virtue ethics in the British tradition has been the dominant interpretation of Hume as some form of metaethical subjectivist and, on the normative front, a proto-utilitarian. Much of British substantive moral philosophy has been focused on the development of utilitarianism, a kind of theory according to which consequences of action are central in moral evaluation.

In the United States there was another reason for the continued invisibility or even hostility towards virtue ethics. Here, Kant-inspired duty-based or deontological theories of ethics have held sway. The Kantian turn of modern analytic ethics took the form of what has been called The Moral Law folk theory (Johnson 1993, 191) according to which moral reasoning takes the form of deductive reasoning where particular cases are subsumed under universal moral principles. This development, exemplified by the work of Donagan (1997), is also not conducive to taking virtue ethics seriously. For although virtue ethicists countenance the existence of moral rules (what Hursthouse (1999) calls the V-rules, such as "Be kind," "Be courageous," "Be generous," "Be just," "Be caring"), which may at times (contrary to many characterizations of virtue ethics (Hill 2008, 32)) constitute stringent duties even in contexts of family and friendship, those rules do not characteristically lend themselves to The Moral Law deductive model (see the section "Skepticism about Character").

The resurgence of interest in virtue ethics began with attention to Aristotle as an inspirational source rather than with the writings of Hume or Nietzsche, for whom virtue is also central in their moral theorizing. Anscombe (1958) is widely credited with beginning that revival with her insistence that "it would be a great improvement if instead of 'morally wrong,' one always named a genus such as 'untruthful,' 'unchaste,' 'unjust' " (p. 10). In other words, moral thought should deploy the "thick" virtue and vice concepts rather than focus on the "thin" concepts. Not surprisingly perhaps, given the provenance of renewed interest and subsequent developments, virtue ethics has often been *defined* in terms of eudaimonistic virtue ethics, the ethics of the ancient Greeks. Although this type of virtue ethics has several forms, we limit our attention to a currently influential Aristotelian version.

Eudaimonistic virtue ethics

Eudaimonistic virtue ethics may be characterized by a central problematic: the yoking together of two conceptions of virtue. According to one, virtues make one good *as* a human being (the good qua human); according to the other they are characteristically good *for* one as a human being. As Hursthouse (1999) puts it, the task for a eudaimonist is to integrate what she calls "Plato's requirement on the virtues," namely

(1) "The virtues benefit their possessor."
(2) "The virtues make their possessor a good human being" (167).

The concept which effects the connection between the good qua and the good for humans is *eudaimonia* (literally being well spirited, but often translated as happiness or flourishing). For Aristotle it is a necessary though not sufficient condition of *eudaimonia* that one possesses and exercises the virtues in a life of rational activity. Severe misfortune, or a sufficiently serious lack of "external goods" such as money or power, can prevent the attainment of *eudaimonia* (Annas 1993). The Stoics invoke a stronger connection between *eudaimonia* and virtue (Becker 1998, Annas 2005, Brennan 2005).

Two major challenges to be faced by modern versions of neo-Aristotelian virtue ethics will be briefly discussed. The first is this. Properties which make their possessors good human beings are supposedly able to be determined from within a framework of what Foot (2001) calls "natural goodness." In general, natural goodness determines what is defective in human beings, and we are defective if we do not possess and exercise the virtues. What is defective is relative to the organism's characteristic modes of development and flourishing. These characteristic modes provide natural norms: for example Asperger's syndrome affects deleteriously one's functioning as a human social animal, as does borderline personality. The challenge is to understand the relationship between natural norms and defect so that we can on that basis form an account of virtue and vice. For example, not all deviations from the norm badly affect an organism's development and flourishing: indeed some may benefit. Such deviations would not count as defects.[2] On the other hand some quite prevalent abnormalities caused by, e.g., environmental deprivations or harms may count as defects.

Furthermore what counts as a defect is often a matter of interpretation.[3] Even if on one level of understanding not having the use of one's limbs, for example, is a defect; on other levels of understanding the claim is an insult. For the nature of the lives of the disabled is a matter of interpretation. Indeed Hacker-Wright states that something like this claim is needed to rebut the objection that the thesis of natural goodness is committed to "deeming disabled human beings to be defective" (2009, 317).

Interpretation is also needed to serve another characteristic mode of human functioning, giving our lives *meaning*. As McDowell points out, the naturalism of virtue ethics cannot be seen as fully analogous to a naturalism which claims that humans need virtues for their lives to go well in the way wolves "need a certain sort of cooperativeness if their life is to go well" (1995, 151). We as humans are in a position to reflect on our lives and to conceive them as having purpose or meaning as agents and not just as knowers (1995, 152). In particular, a rational human is able to conceive of a purpose or meaning other than what is good for it as a species, namely what is good or right for him or her to do or be (1995, 153). It may thus be argued, for example, that the lives of the disabled may derive meaning from a more positive way of interpreting disability, and the life of a creative person derives meaning from her quite personal creative endeavors. That we are beings who give our lives meaning or significance by, e.g., our projects, narratives, or descriptions appropriate to a larger whole (such as a role) is an idea emphasized in the continental tradition (see further van Hooft 2006) and also by MacIntyre (1982).

The question then arises: how does the claim that we are interpretative beings fit with the idea of natural goodness, and how do we make room for the idea of bad interpretations? Consider three possible interpretations of disability:

(i) Disability is a defect that should be eradicated by the kind of eugenics envisaged and practiced by the Nazis.
(ii) There are no disabilities; there are no handicaps: rather people are "challenged" in all kinds of ways.
(iii) We should "call a spade a spade": disabilities are disabilities but we should be both tolerant of and positive towards people with disabilities.

To avoid counting (i) as a possible interpretation that is ethically acceptable, we need an account of what counts as an ethically acceptable interpretation. It is not always clear how debates about whether interpretations are pernicious or self-serving, whether they conceal, sanitize, or exaggerate, are resolvable from within a framework of "natural goodness."

A second challenge is effecting a connection between a trait being a virtue and its necessarily being good for its possessor (Swanton 2003). According to Foot:

> In most cases we speak of what each member of the species needs to be and do in order that *it* should flourish. But of course what is needed may be needed in a group like cooperation in a pack, or obedience to a leader, and what a member is or does may advantage others rather than himself. (Foot 2001, p. 33n, emphasis hers)

The problem arises: how does this point gel with the "Platonic requirement on the virtues"? How can it be the case that in human society virtues must be characteristically good for the possessor if they are to count as virtues at all? We too need to cooperate, and we too need to obey leaders in authority if chaos is not to develop in business and other contexts. The eudaimonist, it would seem, needs to give an indirect account of the status of traits as virtues; for example the point and function of justice as a virtue is not that it benefits the agent, but that it demands respect for persons and their entitlements. Yet according to the first "Platonic requirement on virtue," it is not a virtue unless it characteristically benefits its possessor.

It is a controversial issue whether or not these and other challenges for the currently dominant form of virtue ethics can be met; however there are options for virtue ethics other than eudaimonism, as we illustrate in the next section.

Response-dependent virtue ethics

A genre of virtue ethics that has not to date been as salient as eudaimonism is what we might call response-dependent virtue ethics. A major source for such an understanding of virtue ethics is the sentimentalist tradition, most notably represented by David Hume. Hume is increasingly being interpreted as having a virtue ethical normative ethics; indeed on surface inspection this is a natural interpretation since virtue and vice feature so prominently in his moral theorizing. Taylor goes so far as to say that "Hume's moral philosophy may plausibly be construed as a version of virtue ethics," for "among the central concepts of his theory are character, virtue and vice, rather than rules, duty, and obligation" (2006, 276). Yet there are obstacles to reading Hume as a virtue ethicist, most notably what Cohon calls *"the common reading"* (2008, 12, emphasis hers) that Hume embraces a form of noncognitivist subjectivism not normally thought congenial to virtue ethical interpretations. However as Pigden (2009) and others have noted, reading Hume as a kind of moral sense theorist in a manner nowadays described as a response-dependent theorist is arguably compatible with a type of virtue ethical interpretation.

For Hume (1978) basic moral emotions and capacities, notably benevolence and (benevolent) empathy, are conditions of our having a sense that can properly be called a *moral* sense. Without such a sense there would be no moral properties. In short Hume is a response-dependence theorist insofar as he believes that a virtue or a vice is a power in an object (575) to elicit relevant responses in the observer or contemplator of that virtue (or vice). To have the *sense* of virtue (where virtue as opposed to vice is contemplated) "is nothing but to *feel* a satisfaction of a particular kind from the contemplation of a character" (471, emphasis his). Those feelings for Hume are sentiments of approbation as a form of pleasure or pain, more specifically the pleasure of a "fainter and more imperceptible love" (614).

In brief we can think of Hume's response-dependence theory of morality as a three part theory.

(1) The moral sense and thereby the conditions of possessing a moral sense are necessary for the moral world to be intelligible as a moral world. The sentiments constituting the moral sense arise from a virtue's power to give rise to them in suitably constituted subjects. It may be thought that the moral sense could be a form of love of vice and hatred of virtue, but it is important to note that for Hume the moral sense by definition is relative to common and usual human nature. That nature for Hume is one where benevolence is "original" in the sense of being part of our very frame and constitution. Benevolence and the capacity for sympathy so that benevolence can be extended well beyond our immediate circle, are the cornerstone of ethics for Hume, and are the fundamental conditions of a sense of virtue being a moral sense (Swanton 2007).

(2) For Hume not all those with a moral sense have an authoritative moral sense: it is wrong therefore to understand a virtue as something that *anyone* approves. For him there are a number of conditions that need to be satisfied for a moral sense to be authoritative, conditions such as possessing a general point of view, doxastic virtue, and an undistorted imagination (Swanton 2007, Taylor 2006).

(3) For Hume the moral sense is necessary but not sufficient for accurate claims about the status of traits as virtues, for cooperation of the "reason of the understanding" (which gives us knowledge of causal relations) is also necessary for accurate determinations (1975, 137). There can be reasonable but mistaken views about for example "tendencies" of traits in certain kinds of conditions; truth may not be attained even by those with an authoritative moral sense.

The main challenge for Hume's virtue ethics is to explain what he calls the "natural fittingness" of traits to be appreciated as virtues by an authoritative moral sense, and what counts as a moral sense being (sufficiently) authoritative. We need an account of the relation between Hume's criteria of virtue (such as the tendencies of traits to the happiness of mankind) and the response-dependent character of the metaethics of his virtue ethics. For Hume, there are two broad causes of approbation of traits as virtues (1978, 589–90). On his moral sense theory these types of cause suggest two broad criteria of virtue, the application of which yields virtues conforming to his well-known taxonomy of traits "useful" or "agreeable" to self or other. These criteria are:

A trait is a virtue if it tends to the happiness of mankind.

> A trait is a virtue if it has properties, not reducible to consequences for happiness, which make it naturally fitting that its "species or appearance" causes "this immediate taste or sentiment" which itself causes approbation. (1978, 589)

A fascinating project is to account for features which, for Hume, make qualified judges of virtue approve of traits for reasons other than their tendencies for the "good of mankind." Assuming Hume's account allows for the existence of such virtue, Hume could be read as a virtue ethical theorist as opposed to a virtue consequentialist (Crisp 2005).

Part II. Virtue

Excellence of character

A virtue is a good, excellent, or admirable character trait. As such, it does not consist solely in tendencies to right behavior. It also incorporates the emotional, motivational, and ratiocinative dispositions of the agent. It is a commonplace in virtue ethics that part of excellence in character is being sensitive to circumstance. Practical wisdom, discernment, and situational appreciation are features much emphasized as qualities of virtuous agents. A dissenting voice is Slote (2001). According to him a virtue is an admirable trait of character, and one is admirable through having and acting from admirable motives, even if not wisdom. (Such a view is more associated with Hume's precursors e.g. the Third Earl of Shaftesbury and Francis Hutcheson, than with classical virtue theory). Indeed for Aristotle (1976) not only do the virtuous necessarily have practical wisdom but practical wisdom requires virtue, since one cannot have proper discernment if one does not possess the right motivational and emotional dispositions.

A perennial question in discussions of excellence of character (virtue) is whether there is a distinction between virtue as an excellence and self-control as a supposedly inferior state. For Aristotle (1976), if an agent possesses the various dispositions constituting virtue, then she will be in a state of harmony. For example, the field (domain of concern) of the virtue of temperance with respect to food is eating. People with the virtue not only reason well with respect to such factors as how much to eat, when, where, and with whom, for example, they also have fine motives and affective states. They will not eat to impress, to avoid punishment, to punish themselves and so on. Further, they will not have to overcome temptation; their desires will be in harmony with their reason.

By apparent contrast, Kant (1996) focuses on weakness and other imperfection when he argues that virtue is, or at least presupposes, strength of will.

"Virtue is . . . the moral strength of a human being's will in fulfilling his duty . . . " (164). However, we should not assume from this that virtue for Kant is one and the same thing as overcoming temptation, whereas for Aristotle it is something quite different: a state of harmony. On the contrary, Kant claims that virtue is something unattainable, so in the real human world we focus on areas of imperfection (where our inclinations are unruly). Indeed we may be entitled to praise people as virtuous when they show moral strength of will in areas of imperfection. Despite this, we have a duty to improve in those areas by cultivating relevant emotions and desires, such as the duty to cultivate our sympathetic feelings, so that the "obstacles" furnished through our inclinations are lessened. "Virtue is always *in progress* . . . It is always in progress because, considered *objectively*, it is an ideal and unattainable, while yet constant approximation to it is a duty" (167, emphasis his). Because it "has a subjective basis in human nature" and is therefore "affected by inclinations" it can "never settle down in peace and quiet with its maxims adopted once and for all but, if it is not rising, is unavoidably sinking" (167). To avoid the sinking, we must constantly work on our feelings, and in this Kant sides with Aristotle.

The question then arises as to whether virtue should be seen as an idealized state, or simply as a (sufficiently) good (and not necessarily excellent) character trait. On the latter view, a person has a virtue if she possesses the relevant dispositions to a sufficient degree with respect to a sufficiently large part of the domain of the virtue, and she is tempted to act contrary to virtue only under relative duress or unusually tempting circumstances. We do not demand total harmony in all circumstances relevant to the field or domain of a virtue for a person to be described as possessing that virtue.[4] On this view, virtue in real human agents should be seen as a threshold or what Dan Russell (2009) calls a *satis* concept: that is one can be said to be virtuous if one is virtuous enough. Where the threshold is set is not determinate, and will vary according to context. As Russell claims, virtue is also a vague concept (114).

Virtue and stages of life

An analysis of character must accommodate the fact that the kindness of an individual, for example, is something that evolves in a developmental process of upbringing, by overcoming vicissitudes such as inner conflict, and through responsiveness to social norms and change. Should virtue be therefore seen as a state achievable only in maturity, or even as an idealized condition? On this view a virtue is not just a personal excellence (for even a child can have personal excellences) but an excellence of *character* arguably requiring features such as wisdom that can only be attained (if at all) with experience, in adulthood or even in old age (as in Confucian thought). That orthodoxy has however come under challenge, with the idea that virtues may be relative to stages of life, including childhood. Slote claims that "various facts about human life and development make it plausible to regard certain personal traits as virtues or excellences only in relation to some particular period of life, rather than as virtues, or excellences, *tout court*" (1983, 39). Welchman disputes the view that "prior to one's mature realization of one's potential character, one either has no character at all or a character not truly one's own" (2005, 143). In her 2005, she makes the following points:

1. The process of growth and education is continuous, and does not end in a state of maturity: ". . . the educational process is one of continual reorganizing, reconstructing and transforming."[5]
2. Childhood is a phase of human development and is not a lack or imperfection.
3. An understanding of a virtue proper as a "stable realization of a mature human disposition" threatens the process of change and growth, for (on that understanding) "traits fostering continual change threaten our virtues" (150).
4. Children have virtues specific to that stage of life: they are not mere precursors of virtue.

If the orthodox view is to be retained, then 4 must be rejected. Furthermore, if we accept 1 and 2, as I do, then we must resolve the apparent tension between the idea that a virtue is a stable mature state and the claim that, to be a virtue, a trait must not foster rigidity.

It may seem that views in developmental psychology such as Erik Erikson's developmental account of "basic virtue" favor Welchman's view, by supporting 4. However, Erikson's (2000) view suggests that his basic virtues are psychological "unifying strengths," necessary for the development of virtue proper, but not wholly constitutive of it. Each has "its time of ascendance and [developmental] crisis, yet each persists throughout life" (211). These basic virtues (in developmental sequence) are hope, will, purpose, competence, fidelity, love, care, and wisdom. For example basic trust gives rise to hope, as opposed to a view of the world characterized by basic mistrust. Industriousness, which requires purposiveness, can arise only where the individual is capable of producing things and of manifesting creativity. But if his life is already characterized by basic mistrust and lack of hope, shame, and (self) doubt, "the brother of shame" (Erikson 1963, 253) this development will be stymied. As unifying strengths, the "basic virtues" should not be contrasted with vices, but rather with weaknesses whose symptoms are "disorder, dysfunction, disintegration, anomie" (211).

It is clear that some of these strengths, such as "will," are not themselves character traits, but their preconditions. They are psychological properties described in a way which highlights the developmental sequence of these building blocks, as well as the obstacles that need to be resolved, in the various developmental stages. It is consistent with Erikson's view, then, that maturity is necessary for virtues proper, but that these must be based on the various unifying strengths which, along with virtues proper, continue to develop throughout life. The view that maturity is necessary for virtue proper is consistent with a claim that virtues can have analogues of personal excellence in children. For example, patience can exist at the "novice stage" in children, expressible by basic emotional orientation (suitable for children) and appreciation of basic rules and instructions such as "Don't rush," "Sit quietly," and "Wait for Mum to come to the table before starting your dinner." Though close analogues of adult patience would be unseemly in a child, it is still clear that some rudimentary underpinning must be instilled.

Erikson's developmental theory on the progress of virtue is also consistent with 1 above. Like Kant, he warns against seeing a basic virtue as an achievement "secured once and for all at a given state" (Erikson 1963, 273). Because of this, the idea of virtue as a stable trait needs to be consistent with the view that rigidity is a vice. Stability, or the need for it, is taken to excess. But there is a corresponding vice or set of vices—a boredom driven need for excitement and constant change, or a perfectionistic need for continual change due to permanent dissatisfaction with the status quo.

To conclude: the basic strengths and potentialities for the development of virtue proper arise in developmental sequence, and are not virtues proper. Virtue is a mature state, contrasted with excellences in children. Nonetheless virtue should also be understood as a dynamic state. The possession of virtue is compatible with a constant process of what Nietzsche would call "overcoming" (even for the best of us) as opposed to being a once and for all achievement.[6] "Perfect" virtue, as Kant claims, is unattainable in a lifetime.

Skepticism about character

It is a central tenet of virtue ethics that in this actual world, some people are properly describable as e.g., kind, reliable, courageous, and so on, where these qualities are character traits. Appeal to such traits plays a major role in the explanation of behavior. However this view has come into question as the "situationist critique" of the belief that character traits exist, at least as conceived in Aristotelian virtue ethics, and arguably common sense. Here they are regarded as reliable, relatively unified, robust dispositions to feel, reason, and act in certain sorts of ways, dispositions that are operative in wide ranges of conditions and circumstance. This critique is based on the following alleged fact:

> Behavioural variation across a population owes more to situational differences than dispositional differences among persons. Individual dispositional differences are not as strongly behaviourally individuating as we might have supposed. (Doris 1998, 507)

Much has been written about the implications of this critique for the attribution of traits, and its implications for virtue ethics (for example Harman 2000, Athanassoulis 2000, Doris 1998, 2002, Merritt 2000, Sreenivasan 2002, Kamtekar 2004, Adams 2006, and Miller 2009). I shall not review this large literature here, but simply offer some necessary background in order to draw some implications of psychological attribution theory. According to this theory, there are three major types of attributions: internal factors such as traits or motives, external factors, and extenuating circumstances. In the situationist critique it is standardly assumed that virtue ethicists are committed to the claim that character traits are "global" in the sense that, e.g., persons with the trait of honesty would behave honestly "in a wide variety of different honesty-relevant eliciting conditions (taking exams, testifying, talking to a spouse . . .) as well as in repeated instances of the same conditions (i.e., many exams taken over multiple years)" (Miller 2009, 147). However this conception of character as involving consistency of *behavior* should not blind us to the distinction between the three types of attribution where traits are deemed to be in a suitable sense internal (as is standardly believed in virtue ethics). In particular, character is determined by such factors as dispositions of emotion and feeling, what the agent is disposed to recognize as reasons for action, the agent's ends, the agent's wisdom, and the agent's strength of purpose and other strengths, all of which are "internal" dispositional factors not reducible to patterns of behavior.

There is a second potential problem with the idea of deploying the notion of "global trait" to the idea of character in the situationist critique. The innumerable situations in which people are honest are rendered invisible, for these forms of honesty do not call for explanation (see further the discussion of default reasons in the section "Virtue and Reasons for Action"). It is not the case that Joe Bloggs merely steals occasionally from his friends (the odd cashmere jersey, the expensive aftershave); he never does. It is not that he occasionally embezzles money from his employer, or burgles houses, or fakes C.V.'s; he never does. The fact that Joe never does these things does not call for explanation. However on a fateful night he committed an indiscretion, leading to an affair and occasional untruthful interactions with his spouse. The affair does call for explanation. Joleen, Joe's sister, is exactly like Joe except that she has never had an illicit affair, but through fear, has been less than truthful to her doctor. Joleen who is rather like her friend Alice, is unlike her in finding social lies distasteful. Joleen and Alice too perform innumerable honest but unnoticed acts and omissions as part of their daily lives, but have limited areas of noticeable weakness. Given that virtue is a *satis* and vague concept, people will reasonably disagree about where the threshold of virtue is to be set from case to case. What is to count as satisfying the standards for possessing a virtue as a "global" trait is fuzzy and contextually determined. However, if we recognize the myriad forms of honesty which do not call for explanation, we will see that Joe, Joleen, and Alice, along with numerous others, are a very long way from Hume's "sensible knave" whose life is structured by dishonest ends, whose motives are dishonest, and who has none of the emotions characterizing an honest person. It is reasonable to think they possess honesty as a global trait.

According to attribution theory, "almost all behaviour is the product of both the person and the situation" (Gross and McIlveen 2000, 448). In different kinds of situations however, either personal or situational factors are explanatorily salient. Our tendency to be selective, and not to analyse the full range of explanatory factors, leads to a variety of explanatory biases, including both the "fundamental attribution error" where personal factors are exaggerated (Ross 1977), *and* a tendency to overestimate situational factors when people "are alerted to the possibility that behavior may be influenced by environmental constraints" (Gross and McIlveen, 2000, 449).

To illustrate the workings of attribution theory, consider the example of a student Peter being late for a tutorial.[7] One cannot infer from Peter's lateness that it is attributable to a personal trait (unreliability). It may be attributable to a motive (e.g., a desire to discombobulate the tutor) or to an emotion (fear that he will be shown up in class as a result of being ill-prepared). Alternatively, it may be attributable to external factors (such as the previous class routinely going over time), or extenuating circumstances (such as the tutorial's location being unexpectedly changed, and to a place that is unfamiliar to Peter). Trait attribution (in this case unreliability) is likely warranted under the following conditions: there is "low consensus" (other students are not late), "high consistency" (Peter is always or generally late for this tutorial), and "low distinctiveness" (Peter is usually late for other appointments). The dimension of distinctiveness is important for working out whether there is a character trait involved. If the student is reliable in other areas we do not claim that he is an unreliable character. Having a tendency to be late for a tutorial in ethics would not in ordinary parlance be regarded as a *character* trait.

Virtue ethics is not committed to a claim that character traits are routinely explanatory of behavior even where there is a high degree of virtue. Indeed, were such explanations too dominant, there would be a case for attributing the vice of rigidity, where there would be insufficient situational appreciation. Consider the case of the ethics tutorial again. Imagine that the previous (very important) class is routinely late, and there is a general understanding that students attending that class would be late for their (not very important) tutorial. But Joe, a member of the routinely late class, is nonetheless never late for his tutorial. Though punctuality is a virtue (being a species of reliability) we may attribute to Joe the vice of punctuality to excess, due to rigidity. The vice would be attributed on the grounds of low consensus (other relevant students are late), high consistency (Joe is never late for this tutorial), and low distinctiveness (Joe is obsessively punctual in a range of circumstances). What we would expect if Joe was virtuous in this area (and he is contrary to fact late) would be an explanation of his behavior (being late) *not* in terms of traits, but in terms of external circumstances.

External circumstances may make what appears to be nonvirtuous behavior not in fact contrary to virtue on closer analysis. One would expect a compassionate person to vary his behavior according to the number of potential helpers and situational ambiguity. Thus what may appear to be unhelpful behavior may not, in the situation, be incompatible with the presence of a general virtue of helpfulness, even though the situation as such is a "helpfulness-relevant eliciting condition." Furthermore a sophisticated account of helpfulness as a *virtue* will recognize a problem of helpfulness to excess where helpfulness may be incompatible with a solid sense of self. Finally virtuously helpful people may behave differently and virtuously in the same situation. As Kant (1996) recognized, the virtue of beneficence has "latitude": a degree of personal discretion in how or whether to be helpful or beneficent in a wide range of circumstances.

Given the expected prevalence of explanation in terms of situational factors in the presence of virtue, whence the scepticism about traits? It may be based on the so-called fundamental attribution error (Ross 1977), but this error has no tendency of itself to cast doubt on the existence of traits. We cannot infer, for example, that the trait of compassion does not exist because situational factors explain participants' uncompassionate *behavior* in such experiments as the Milgram (1963) experiments. For note the point made above that character is a complex of dispositions of feelings, motives, and so forth. Consider a participant who exhibits uncompassionate *behavior*. It is quite possible that the behavior has high distinctiveness: in a wide range of circumstances he would not exhibit lack of compassion. In the Milgram experiments this hypothesis has plausibility: many of those administering what they supposed to be electric shocks "reported and manifested intense strain and anguish" (Milgram 1963, 376). We would not expect a trait explanation to be applicable unless the subject was callous (the noncompassionate behavior had low distinctiveness).

Part III. Issues in Virtue Ethics

Virtue and reasons for action

We turn now to the relation between virtue, situation, and moral reasons for action. A live debate both within and outside virtue ethics is the relation between situational discernment and moral principles. We have noted that virtue ethics can admit the existence of "virtue rules" ("V-rules"). The V-rules provide reasons for action unlike bare appeals to the "thin" concepts such as the rightness of an act (Dancy 2000, 2004). The question for virtue ethics is: What is the status of reasons for action such as the action's kindness, and in particular are they expressible as moral principles that are either decisive (such that the kindness of an act guarantees its rightness), or *pro tanto* (such that the kindness of an act *always* has positive moral valence) at least in specifiable theoretically privileged cases (Lance and Little 2006)? In short does virtue ethics need moral principles if it is to be a theory which allows for the use of reasons in ethics?

According to radical particularists, notably Dancy (2004), the "thick" moral concepts as applied to acts such as the act's kindness or justness do not or need not always have invariant valence (whether positive, negative, or indifferent). This is due to the holism of reasons, at least in the ethical domain. Despite the attractiveness of such a position from the point of view of an Aristotelian emphasis on the situational discernment of *phronesis* (practical wisdom) and *nous* (intuition), there has been stubborn resistance to radical particularism (henceforth particularism). This resistance is brought about by the thought that reasons require generality, and without such generality neither ethical learning nor predictability could occur (Hooker 2000). Reasons on the particularist view, it is claimed, cannot be intelligible as reasons; they cannot *serve* as reasons to justify actions. One just has to see the situation as a whole to grasp the rightness of an act.

I myself believe that the resources of the particularist position have not yet been fully deployed to rebut this widespread charge. In the remainder of this section I show how such deployment, in conjunction with attention to virtue ethics, can overcome the objection that particularists cannot use notions such as the kindness or justness of acts to serve as reasons for action in justificatory and learning contexts. I do not have space here to show how such a theory can be coupled with a view of rational deliberation and action.[8]

There is one kind of generalization apparently downplayed by Dancy that is at the heart of a virtue ethical particularism. This is supplied by the notion of a default reason introduced in Dancy, 1993 (26, 103, 230). A default reason is a reason that is "set up to be a reason in advance" (Dancy 2004, 112). Virtue and vice terms as applied to acts (such as "kind," "just," and "generous") are paradigm cases of such reasons: the generosity or justness of an act has positive valence unless "switched off if the circumstances so conspire" (Dancy 2004, 113). As Dancy claims, a default reason is not an invariant reason (113) in any generally describable type of circumstance.

Dancy believes that the idea of a default reason is a "bit thin," suggesting that it does not do much work. However on my view such reasons can be heavy hitting. This is indeed suggested by Dancy's claim that "... where the justness of an action counts in favour of doing it, there is nothing to explain; in that sense this is what we should expect to happen" (2004, 113). For the claim raises the question: "*Why* is there nothing to explain?" Answering that question within the context of a virtue ethics, for example, shows how and why default reasons are default reasons. In the first place answering the question "Why is there nothing to explain?" when the justness of an act counts in its favour, engages the resources of substantive moral theory. For example, if an unsophisticated Nietzschean were to say the justness of an act is a default reason *against* doing something, because justice is expressive of a weak commitment to equality, one might reply by engaging that person in a discussion of Nietzsche's texts (*On The Genealogy of Morality* and others) where Nietzsche discusses justice, calls it that great and rare virtue, and distinguishes justice as a virtue from correlative vices. Such vices are "scientific fairness" (which *is* expressive of a weak commitment to [the wrong sorts of] equality) and rigorous punitivism (expressive of cruelty).

A full explanation of the nature of the default status of justness as a reason for action, then, involves a deep-level understanding of the evaluative point of justice—that feature which unifies the disparate "shapeless" descriptive characteristics which constitute the "resultance base" of justice. This comprises the features in virtue of which acts (for example) are just (Dancy 1993, Williams 1995b). In virtue ethics the evaluative point of a concept such as just and kind is determined not just by those familiar with their deployment in the users' culture (which appears to be Williams's 1995a view), for there may be widespread vice in a culture, but by virtuous agents in various kinds of context.

To the reply that such sophisticated discussions hardly provide a context of *learning* that the justness of acts provides a default reason *in favour* of them (let alone a strong one), one might argue that ethical concepts are prototype concepts, mastery of which is gained not by mastery of invariant reasons but by (in early learning contexts) knowledge of paradigms, by articulating basic emotional experiences, by inculcation into mothers' knees rules, and so on (Johnson 1993, Churchland 1989). With increasing sophistication and experience such prototypes are imaginatively extended into novel, difficult, and specialized contexts through sensitive description where morally salient properties are highlighted, through narrative expressing situational embeddedness, and through metaphor. For example understanding love through the metaphors of bonds and ties helps one appreciate the psychology of attachment as central to love, and that love does not necessarily track value, and nor does its virtuousness as Hume saw so clearly. Such imaginative extensions can themselves be justified at a deep level by reasoned discussion about the point and function of, for example, justice in good institutions and a good life: a life importantly constituted by the inhabiting of roles, by possessing a narrative shape, and by being culturally and historically situated. None of this requires that the justness of acts must be understood as an invariant reason in favor of performing it, if we are to live as rational moral agents.

Indeed the particularist model of the nature of ethical concepts gels well both with the notion of default reasons and also with connectionist understandings of cognition. Though Dancy does not deploy the notion of a default reason in his (1999) discussion of learning the difference between right and wrong on a particularist model of reasons, he provides in that article an account of the connectionist model of mastery of an ethical concept such as "kind" which can be understood as a model for default reasons. Consider a connectionist machine which is such that "if we fire the nodes for action and kind alone, the node for right will fire strongly . . . " (1999, 11). The machine would agree that:

> . . . a kind action is right, in the sense that if we only fire the kindness node, the rightness node is fired as well. But it would not agree that a kind action is always *pro tanto* right [even granted it operates with a model of *pro tanto* rightness], since it might be that when exposed to the kind action of wiping the torturer's brow, the rightness node does not fire at all (12).

This is exactly how default reasons operate.

It should be noted, however, that when the evaluative point of kindness is grasped we can appreciate that kindness is a default reason that is strongly positive: that is, in the real world it is rare that the rightness node does not fire when the kindness node does. Indeed Dancy (2000, 2004) goes as far as to say that the positive default status of justice is so strong that it may not even be possible to imagine the justness of an act counting against that action.[9] By contrast, the positive default status of "loyal" is weaker and more controversial. This is reflected by disagreement at a deep level about the evaluative point of loyalty, and its putative incompatibility with other (alleged) very important goods (Keller 2007).

We can now see how potentially powerful is the notion of a default reason when combined with a substantive virtue ethics. For a virtue ethical particularist, who understands *why* the justness of an act is a strongly positive default reason in favour of performing it, why the loyalty of an act is not a strongly positive default reason in favour of performing it, and so on, is in an excellent position to justify her claims that in *this* case the default status of justness as a reason has not been "switched off," and in *that* case the default status of loyalty (or kindness) as a reason has been switched off. Justifications in the light of subtle understandings of the evaluative points of loyalty, justice, and so on, including their relation to other virtues (and vices), sophisticated understandings of the nature of the world, and insight into and knowledge of the particularities of the case before her, display her mastery of the relevant concepts. Pervasive unpredictability is avoided and in her hands particularist reasons can serve as reasons.

Virtuous action and right action

In virtue ethics right action is understood as virtuous action in one or other understandings of that notion. The idea of "virtuous action" is not at all clear: indeed it is multiply ambiguous with at least four salient meanings. Each of these is associated with a distinctive conception of right action in virtue ethics. We discuss each in turn.

(1) "Virtuous action" may mean "Action properly subsumable under a thick 'virtue' concept as applied to action, such as 'kind act,' 'just act,' 'honest act.'"

For some philosophers, an action properly described as, e.g., "kind" or "just" is an act that is right, because unless it was right it could not be genuinely just or kind. This position has difficulties, because as we saw above the thick concepts have descriptive resultance bases, descriptive properties in virtue of which an act is, for example, honest. As a result, it is impossible to describe a lie as honest even if it is overall right; it is impossible to describe a violation of a rule of justice as "just" even if (one might think) the violation is overall right on the grounds of its consequences.

(2) "Virtuous action" may mean "Action that expresses or proceeds from virtue or at least a virtuous or admirable motive; or more weakly action that does not express or proceed from a vice or a vicious or deplorable motive."

In *The Nicomachean Ethics* (Book 2 [iv]) Aristotle distinguishes between senses (1) and (2) of "virtuous action" by distinguishing between a just act and an act performed in the way a virtuously just person would perform it. In modern virtue ethics someone who ties rightness to the virtuousness or absence of viciousness of inner states is Slote. For him, a necessary and sufficient condition of wrong action is that it reflects, exhibits, or expresses an absence of "fully developed empathic concern for (or caring about) others on the part of the agent." (Slote 2007, 31; for thorough critical discussion see Russell 2009)

(3) "Virtuous action" may mean "Action that would be performed by a virtuous agent acting characteristically."

Such an account of virtuous action rules out as virtuous certain uncharacteristic actions of virtuous agents, such as those performed by virtuous agents acting in the grip of a tragic dilemma (Hursthouse 1999), and those of virtuous agents having uncharacteristic lapses. This third notion also counts as virtuous some actions which are not performed by virtuous agents let alone express virtue. One such account of right action is the following:

> An act is right iff it is what a virtuous agent would characteristically (i.e., acting in character) do in the circumstances. (Hursthouse 1996, 22)

There is an issue of whether this definition gives an account of what makes actions right or merely tells us what is common to right actions (van Zyl 2013, Crisp 2010, 25). Since what *makes* actions right are such things as benefiting friends and repaying debts, it seems that the definition merely tells us what is common to right actions. Notice though that for Hursthouse what it is for an agent to act "virtuously" or "well" (1999, Chapter 6) requires much stronger conditions, such as acting for the right reasons, and from the right states.

Assessing this view of rightness is not straightforward since it is not clear what counts as a virtuous agent. If rightness should be understood in terms of *success* in attaining practical truth/correctness, it might be argued (Swanton 2003) that real-life virtuous agents may be wrong even though aiming at practical truth and possessing *phronesis* (practical wisdom). However the above definition of rightness may relate not to real virtue but to virtue understood as a model concept. Perhaps the idea of a virtuous agent should be seen as part of what Russell (2009) calls model discourse. This is "discourse not about *things*, but about a certain *model* of things" (136, emphasis his). Note that since the discourse is not about things it is not about (real) exemplars of virtue either. Note also that though on this model an ideally virtuous agent could be said to have perfect practical wisdom, such wisdom, even perfected, does not embrace all forms of specialist knowledge (for the acquiring of which as Aristotle notes even the virtuous have to consult experts), and certainly is not a nonhuman omniscience. On the assumption that model virtue pertains to idealized humans and not nonhumans, even idealized virtuous humans can get things wrong, albeit in a way that is not blameworthy.

(4) "Virtuous action" may mean "Action that hits the targets of relevant virtues."

This sense of virtuous action is suggested by Aristotle's distinction between *aiming* at the "mean" which virtuous agents do, and success in hitting it (1976). As Aristotle notes this is often difficult since there are many ways of failing to hit it. A virtue ethics understands "hitting the mean" as hitting the targets of virtue. The target of a virtue is determined by its point and function in relation to its field or domain of concern. Given that the "mean" has many aspects, including getting things right in relation to such features as manner and feeling or emotion, getting things right is complex. In different contexts different features will be salient; furthermore some virtues, like benevolence, will have as their main target success in relation to external features such as consequences for welfare, while others such as caring may focus more on other external features such as right manner, and on targets internal to the agent such as properly caring motivation or attitude (Swanton 2003).

The notion of right action suggested by the fourth sense of virtuous action is this: an action is right if and only if it hits the targets of relevant virtues. This conception of rightness is an abstractly formulated account of what makes actions right, since the targets of virtues are the right-making features. Once we have a conception of the targets of various virtues (and such conceptions will be controversial, more or less rich, and have various theoretical provenances) we have a substantive account of what makes actions right and not merely an account of what is common to right actions.[10]

This conception of rightness allows for the possibility of (real-life) virtuous agents getting things wrong, even though they are characteristically the rule and the measure of rightness as Aristotle (1976) suggests, for they characteristically see things aright. It also raises the question of whether the targets of the virtues can conflict with each other, an issue concerning the unity of the virtues which I do not have space to discuss here.[11]

A problem for the above "target-centered" view is that it apparently leaves open the possibility that some actions which are to be done are not "right" for they are not the target of any virtue. Some virtue ethical views countenance but a limited range of virtues. I argue against that view in Swanton (2003) and elsewhere, siding with Nietzsche and Hume, not to mention novelists such as Jane Austen who admit a very rich array of character traits. Note also that, as Aristotle claims (1976), some virtues do not have names.

Secondly, it appears the self-improving actions of the nonvirtuous may be right without hitting the target of a virtue.[12] However such actions can be understood as exemplifying a virtue of self-improvement within a dynamic conception of virtue as an excellence, the attainment of which, as noted in the section "Excellence of Character," is never a once and for all achievement. This virtue is being well disposed in relation to the field of improving oneself (Swanton 2009). Some actions could thus be seen as right insofar as they hit the target of that virtue.

Grounds of virtue

An issue in virtue ethics is whether or not the features which make traits virtues are at a basic level pluralistic. In a eudaimonistic virtue ethics, agent flourishing grounds all the virtues. This should not be understood in a foundationalist way as if one could provide a conception of flourishing entirely independent of virtue (Hursthouse 1999). We might illustrate the point with pleasure. In a flourishing life pleasure has a proper place: as Aristotle claims pleasure is a good (1976). We might express this point by saying that the default status of the value of pleasure is strongly positive. However even though pleasure is a good in this sense, its goodness "without qualification" (as Aristotle (1976) puts it) is not entirely independent of virtue. That is, for a virtue ethicist, pleasure does not always have positive moral valence; indeed its default status as a good is switched off in the case of sadistic pleasure. In this respect virtue ethicists differ from axiologists such as Hurka (2001).

A virtue ethicist of a more pluralistic persuasion would reject flourishing as the only ground of virtue. I shall discuss four possible grounds of virtue: value, status, bonds, and the good for, calling the virtues so grounded, value-based, status-based, bond-based, and flourishing-based. Again it should be noted that these "grounds" of virtue should not be seen as foundational. Where a virtue is status-based, for example, we should not assume that all status is somehow a good or valuable, and that virtues are traits respecting or honoring such independently understood goods or values. For many status properties such as caste are thoroughly infused with vice and are not respected in status-based virtue. We briefly distinguish and discuss value, status, bond, and flourishing-based virtue.

Value-based virtues. A thing is valuable insofar as it is worthy of, e.g., creation, appreciation, maintenance, preservation. Value-based virtues are associated with promoting, enhancing, or maintaining such valuable things, appreciating them or creating them. For example environmental virtue aimed at sustaining and preserving rock formations, beaches, or species is of this kind. Moral and indeed physical courage in particular is aimed at promoting, for example, valuable causes such as reducing whaling. The appreciation of value is manifested in what might be called virtues of connoisseurship. The refined and cultured person whom Hume (1978, 335) describes as the person of "an elevate disposition" is the sort who can take joy in, for example, landscapes, sunsets, and art. Virtues of creativity express the creative nature of human beings, and assuming such virtue is aimed at bringing into being valuable objects, these can also be regarded as value-based virtues distinct from those value-based virtues directed at enhancing and sustaining existing valuable objects, or appreciating valuable objects.

Status-based virtues. These include justice, fidelity, obedience, (appropriate) deference, consideration, and politeness. The status properties in virtue of which different forms of respect are owed are many and varied. In justice, respect is owed to a person on the basis of her status as someone who has a due, whether contractual or otherwise. She may be someone who is not to be violated (in respect of property rights for example), or as someone who is owed. In fidelity, respect is owed to a person in virtue of her status as someone to whom a promise has been made, and whether or not the promise is to be kept does not depend on the value of the outcomes of keeping it. In obedience, respect is owed (in the form of more or less formal requirements of obedience) in virtue of a person's status as having authority over you, and her authority to give orders or instructions. Within limits that authority is dependent on authority structures and not on the value or merits of the office-holder. In appropriate deference, respect (of sometimes conventional forms) is owed to a person in virtue of some special social status she has (e.g., queen, or elder). That respect is expressed in specific ways legitimized by the relevant culture, and sanctioned by morality in general. For not all social status properties (such as certain caste properties, status as a slave) can be so sanctioned. In consideration or politeness respect is owed to a person simply because she is a person with feelings and sensitivities (to, e.g., humiliation and offence). Though such respect is owed by virtue of universal properties shared by humans, there will be legitimate cultural variation in how these virtues are manifested in forms of politeness and etiquette.

Bond-based virtues. These are the various virtues of love and amity. They are expressive of our nature as creatures who form bonds, the fundamental need for which is well attested by psychological theories such as attachment theory (Bowlby 1969, Gerhardt 2004). Virtuous expressions of bonds are not reducible to promoting another's welfare, nor are they reducible to value-based virtues. As Hume (1978) saw, strength of bond manifested in a virtue of friendship, for example, does not necessarily coincide with the merits of the person to whom one is bonded:

> When we have contracted a habitude and intimacy with any person; tho' in frequenting his company we have not been able to discover any very valuable quality, of which he is possess'd; yet we cannot forbear preferring him to strangers, of whose superior merit we are fully convinc'd. (Hume 1978, 352)

Virtues of intimacy and affection are virtues whose proper expression is not primarily, if at all, a matter of value recognition or responsiveness.

The virtuous expression of bonds would be defective too if they were entirely directed at the welfare of the person with whom one has a bond with no concern for the *expression* of affection or intimacy. Nonetheless, as Hume (1978) saw, many forms of love, notably love of a parent for her child, are causally connected with benevolence and beneficence: desire for another's good. Those desires are at the heart of the flourishing-based virtues of benevolence.

Flourishing-based virtues. These are aimed at the good of beings or systems having a good, such as sentient beings and ecosystems. Although we would consider persons possessing the bond-based virtues to have a concern for the welfare of those to whom they are bonded, the flourishing-based virtues are not necessarily associated with love or even amity. Charity is one such virtue. Nor should we confuse the flourishing-based virtues with the value-based virtues. As Foot (1985) points out, benevolence is a virtue that is not as such responsive to valuable properties, let alone the "value" of states of affairs (inasmuch as that notion makes sense, which it does not for Foot). Rather it is a virtue responsive to what is good *for* sentient beings, that is, their flourishing.

Virtue ethics, then, is a family of theories in which the virtue and vice concepts occupy a central theoretical role, but that leaves room for multiple views on the grounds of virtue, the nature of right action, and the nature of virtue itself as an excellent, good, or admirable character trait.[13]

Bibliography

Adams, Robert Merihew. (2006), *A Theory of Virtue: Excellence as Being for the Good*. Oxford: Oxford University Press.

Annas, Julia. (1993), *The Morality of Happiness*. New York: Oxford University Press.

—.(2005), "Virtue Ethics: What Kind of Naturalism," in Stephen M. Gardiner (ed.), *Virtue Ethics Old and New*. Ithaca: Cornell University Press.

Anscombe, G. E. M. (1958), "Modern Moral Philosophy". *Philosophy* 33, 1–19.

Aristotle. (1976), *The Nicomachean Ethics*. Trans. J. A. K. Thomson, revised H. Tredennick. Harmondsworth: Penguin.

Athanassoulis, Nafsika. (2000), "A Response to Harman: Virtue Ethics and Character Traits." *Proceedings of the Aristotelian Society, New Series* 100, 215–21.

Becker, Lawrence. (1998), *A New Stoicism*. Princeton: Princeton University Press.

Bowlby, John. (1969), *Attachment*. London: Pelican.

Brennan, Tad. (2005), *The Stoic Life*. Oxford: Oxford University Press.

Churchland, Paul. (1989), *A Neurocomputational Perspective: The Nature of Mind and the Structure of Science*. Cambridge, MA: MIT Press.

Cohon, Rachel. (2008), *Hume's Morality: Feeling and Fabrication*. Oxford: Oxford University Press.

Crisp, Roger. (2005), "Hume on Virtue, Utility, and Morality," in Stephen M. Gardiner (ed.), *Virtue Ethics, Old and New*. Ithaca: Cornell University Press, 294–336.

—. (2010), "Virtue Ethics and Virtue Epistemology." *Metaphilosophy* 41, 22–40.

Dancy, Jonathan. (1993), *Moral Reasons*. Oxford: Blackwell.

—. (1999), "Can a Particularist Learn the Difference between Right and Wrong?," in Klaus Brinkman (ed.), *The Proceedings of the Twentieth World Congress of Philosophy Vol 1 Ethics*. Bowling Green: Philosophy Documentation Center, 59–72.

—. (2000), *Practical Reality*. Oxford: Oxford University Press.

—.(2004), *Ethics without Principles*. Oxford: Clarendon Press.

Das, Ramon. (2003), "Virtue Ethics and Right Action." *Australasian Journal of Philosophy* 81, 324–39.

Dewey, John. (1944), *Democracy and Education: An Introduction to the Philosophy of Education*. New York: The Free Press.

Donagan, Alan. (1997), *The Theory of Morality*. Chicago: Chicago University Press.

Doris, John M. (1998), "Persons, situations, and virtue ethics." *Noûs* 32, 504–30.

—. (2002), *Lack of Character: Personality and Moral Behaviour*. Cambridge: Cambridge University Press.

Driver, Julia. (2001), *Uneasy Virtue*. Cambridge: Cambridge University Press.
Erikson, Erik. (1963), *Childhood and Society*. New York: W.W. Norton.
—. (2000), (from) *Insight and Responsibility*, in Robert Coles (ed.), *The Erik Erikson Reader*. New York: W.W. Norton.
Foot, Philippa. (1985), "Utilitarianism and the virtues." *Mind* 94, 196–209.
—. (2001), *Natural Goodness*. Oxford: Clarendon Press.
Gerhardt, Sue. (2004), *Why Love Matters: How Affection Shapes a Baby's Brain*. London: Routledge.
Gross, Richard and McIlveen Rob. (2000), *Psychology: A New Introduction*. London: Hodder and Stoughton.
Hacker-Wright, John. (2009), "What Is Natural about Foot's Ethical Naturalism?" *Ratio New Series* 22, 308–21.
Harman, Gilbert. (2000), "The Nonexistence of Character Traits." *Proceedings of the Aristotelian Society New Series* 100, 223–6.
Hill, Thomas E. Jr. (2008), "Kantian Virtue and 'Virtue Ethics,'" in Monika Betzler (ed.), *Kant's Ethics of Virtue*. Berlin: Walter de Gruyter, 29–59.
Hooker, Brad. (2000), "Moral particularism—wrong and bad," in Brad Hooker and Margaret Little (eds.), *Moral Particularism*. Oxford: Clarendon Press, 1–23.
Hume, David. (1975), *Enquiries Concerning Human Understanding and Concerning the Principles of Morals*, 3rd edn., ed. P. H. Nidditch. Oxford: Clarendon Press.
—. (1978), *A Treatise of Human Nature*, ed. L. A.Selby-Bigge. Oxford: Clarendon Press.
Hurka, Thomas. (2001), *Virtue, Vice, and Value*. Oxford: Oxford University Press.
Hursthouse, Rosalind. (1987), *Beginning Lives*. Oxford: Blackwell.
—. (1991), "Virtue Theory and Abortion." *Philosophy and Public Affairs* 20, 223–46.
— (1996), "Normative Virtue Ethics," in R. Crisp (ed.), *How Should One Live? Essays on the Virtues*. Oxford: Clarendon Press, 19–36.
—. (1999), *On Virtue Ethics*. Oxford: Oxford University Press.
—. (2000), *Ethics, Humans and Other Animals: An Introduction with Readings*. London: Routledge.
—. (2006), "Applying Virtue Ethics to Our Treatment of the Other Animals," in Jennifer Welchman (ed.), *The Practice of Virtue: Classic and Contemporary Readings in Virtue Ethics*. Indianapolis: Hackett, 136–55.
—. (2007), "Environmental Virtue Ethics," in Rebecca L. Walker and Philip J. Ivanhoe (eds.), *Working Virtue: Virtue Ethics and Contemporary Moral Problems*. Oxford: Clarendon Press, 155–71.
Johnson, Mark. (1993), *Moral Imagination: Implications of Cognitive Science for Ethics*. Chicago: University of Chicago Press.
Johnson, Robert N. (2003), "Virtue and right," *Ethics* 113, 810–34.
—. (2008), "Was Kant a Virtue Ethicist?" in Monika Betzler (ed.), *Kant's Ethics of Virtue*. Berlin: Walter de Gruyter, 61–76.
Kamtekar, R. (2004), "Situationism and Virtue Ethics on the Content of Our Character." *Ethics* 114, 458–91.
Kant, Immanuel. (1996), *Metaphysics of Morals*. Mary Gregor (ed. and trans.). Cambridge: Cambridge University Press.
Keller, Simon. (2007), *The Limits of Loyalty*. Cambridge: Cambridge University Press.

Lance, Mark Norris, and Little, Margaret Olivia. (2006), "Defending Moral Particularism," in James Dreier (ed.), *Contemporary Debates in Moral Theory*. Oxford: Blackwell, 305–21.

MacIntyre, Alasdair. (1982), *After Virtue*. London: Duckworth.

McDowell, John. (1995), "Two Sorts of Naturalism," in Rosalind Hursthouse, Gavin Lawrence and Warren Quinn (eds.), *Virtues and Reasons*. Oxford: Clarendon Press, 149–79.

Merritt, Maria. (2000), "Virtue Ethics and Situationist Personality Psychology." *Ethical Theory and Moral Practice* 3, 365–83.

Milgram, Stanley. (1963), "Behavioural Study of Obedience." *Journal of Abnormal and Social Psychology* 67, 371–8.

Miller, Christian. (2009), "Social Psychology, Mood, and Helping: Mixed Results for Virtue Ethics." *Journal of Ethics* 13, 145–73.

Pigden, Charles R. (2009), "If Not Non-Cognitivism, Then What?," in Charles R. Pigden (ed.), *Hume on Motivation and Virtue*. Basingstoke: Palgrave Macmillan.

Ross, Lee. (1977), "The Intuitive Psychologist and His Shortcomings," in L. Berkowitz (ed.), *Advances in Experimental Social Psychology*. Volume 10. New York: Academic, 173–220.

Russell, Daniel C. (2009), *Practical Intelligence and the Virtues*. Oxford: Oxford University Press.

Slote, Michael. (1983), "Relative Virtues," in Michael Slote (ed.), *Goods and Virtues*. Oxford: Clarendon Press.

—.(2001), *Morals from Motives*. Oxford: Oxford University Press.

— (2007), *The Ethics of Care and Empathy*. London: Routledge.

Sreenivasan, Gopal. (2002), "Errors about errors: virtue theory and trait attribution." *Mind* 100, 47–68.

Stohr, Karen E. (2003), "Moral Cacophany: When Continence Is a Virtue." *The Journal of Ethics*7, 339–63.

Swanton, Christine. (2003), *Virtue Ethics: A Pluralistic View*. Oxford: Oxford University Press.

—. (2005), "Nietzschean Virtue Ethics," in Stephen M. Gardiner (ed.), *Virtue Ethics, Old and New*. Ithaca: Cornell University Press, 179–92.

— (2007), "Can Hume Be Read as a Virtue Ethicist?" *Hume Studies* 33, 91–113.

—. (2009), "Virtue Ethics and the Problem of Demandingness," in Timothy Chappell (ed.), *The Problem of Moral Demandingness: New Philosophical Essays*. Basingstoke: Palgrave Macmillan, 104–22.

—. (2013), "The Definition of Virtue Ethics," in Daniel Russell (ed.), *Cambridge Companion to Virtue Ethics*. Cambridge: Cambridge University Press, 315–338.

Taylor, Jacqueline. (2006), "Virtue and the Evaluation of Character," in Saul Traiger (ed.), *The Blackwell Guide to Hume's Treatise*. Oxford: Blackwell, 276–95.

Van Hooft, Stan. (2006), *Understanding Virtue Ethics*. Chesham: Acumen.

Van Zyl, Liezl. (2013), "Virtue Ethics and Right Action," in Daniel Russell (ed.), *Cambridge Companion to Virtue Ethics*. Cambridge: Cambridge University Press, 172–196.

Welchman, Jennifer. (2005), "Virtue Ethics and Human Development: A Pragmatic Approach," in Stephen M. Gardiner (ed.), *Virtue Ethics, Old and New*. Ithaca: Cornell University Press, 142–55.

Williams, Bernard. (1995a), "Evolution, Ethics, and the Representation Problem," in Bernard Williams (ed.), *Making Sense of Humanity and Other Philosophical Papers 1982–1993*. Cambridge: Cambridge University Press, 100–10.
—. (1995b), "Replies," in J. E. J. Altham and Ross Harrison (eds.), *World, Mind, and Ethics: Essays on the Ethical Philosophy of Bernard Williams*. Cambridge: Cambridge University Press, 185–225.

10 Feminist Ethics

Anita Superson

The past few decades have witnessed a significant contribution of feminism to traditional moral theory. Feminists have critiqued traditional moral theories, modified some of them to accommodate feminist concerns, and used some of their insights to make feminist points. They have introduced new topics, including the harms and wrongdoings associated with sexism and oppression, that had not previously received attention. They have examined the connection between oppression and people's psychology and moral character and actions. And they have shed new light on traditional issues in metaethics, including the internalism-externalism debate, moral epistemology, moral relativism, and moral skepticism. In tackling these issues, feminists have questioned traditional or male issues, concerns, and experiences as the norm.

None of this is to say that feminist ethics endorses a "woman's way" of doing ethics, or a female way of reasoning, or even gender essentialism—the view that "all women, in virtue of being women, share a common gendered subjectivity"—as some early work on the ethic of care may have suggested (Calhoun 2004, 8). For the most part, feminists dismiss this genderization of traits, and distinguish feminine ethics, which might endorse such tenets, from feminist ethics, which has as its aim ending the oppression of women. In connection with this aim, feminist ethics is concerned with the most fundamental issues in ethics—respect, equality, autonomy, and justice. It brings to light the ways in which these values, for women, have played out and should play out in ethics.

Normative Ethics

Feminist critiques of traditional moral theories

Feminist critiques of traditional moral theories have been multifarious. Among these are that traditional theories ignore issues that are of particular interest to women because of their direct impact on women's lives—including their bodies and their social situation—and that they thereby falsely dichotomize a public and private sphere; they explicitly or implicitly endorse harmful sexist stereotypes about women; they do not address social issues such as oppression, or perhaps even do not exclude its being morally permissible; and they ignore or downplay the role of emotions and play up the role of reason because of the historical association of emotions with women and reason with men. To illustrate these complaints, we can take as our focus the moral theories of Aristotle, Thomas Hobbes, and Immanuel Kant.

Nancy Tuana traces Aristotle's view about men's and women's moral capacities to their biological differences (Tuana 1992). According to Tuana, for Aristotle, heat "concocts" matter, and the more heat an animal is able to generate, the more developed it will be (Tuana 1992, 23). Since women generate less heat than men, as evidenced by the abundance of female semen, or, menses, in comparison to lesser male semen that has been concentrated by heat, women are "mutilated" males who are both physically and intellectually weaker than men (Tuana 1992, 24–6). Tuana notes that although Aristotle allows that free women are superior to male slaves, since slaves possess no deliberative faculty at all (Tuana 1992, 28, citing Aristotle, *Politics* 1260a 12–14), free women, due to their lesser degree of heat, are still by nature inferior to free men both in their psychology and in their intellect. Tuana notes that for Aristotle, woman's imperfect deliberative faculty requires that she be ruled by a man—either her husband or her master (Tuana 1992, 28, citing Aristotle, *Politics* 1254b 6–14). Aristotle associates women with passion; women need the guidance of a superior deliberator who can guide her on proper action. According to Aristotle's virtue ethics, one should follow the dictates of reason, aiming for the mean between two extremes, such as acting courageously rather than in a foolhardy or cowardly way. Since women are not perfect deliberators who are ruled by reason and can thus follow the doctrine of the mean, they must of necessity be ruled and are excluded from the realm of practical wisdom, which involves reasoned arguments designed to identify right from wrong (Tuana 1992, 29; Aristotle, *Politics* 1277b 26–27). At best, Aristotle allows women to be virtuous in a sense: "a free woman becomes virtuous by placing herself in obedience to a virtuous man" (Tuana 1992, 29; Aristotle, *Politics* 1260a 20–23). This is very different from the virtue a free man can have, which is commanding. Tuana notes that Aristotle correlates these differences in the sexes with a household division of labor, relegating women to be bearers and nurturers of children and companions to their husbands (Tuana 1992, 29; Aristotle, *Politics* 1277b26). Thus we see in Aristotle the gendered dichotomy between reason and emotion, the public-private distinction, and the grounding of sexist stereotypes. Tuana believes that these views make Aristotle's moral theory inherently sexist.

Hobbes's moral theory, and the liberal contractarian tradition at large, has also come under feminist critique. Like Aristotle, Hobbes emphasizes reason or rationality over emotionality, but defines reason in terms of maximizing the satisfaction of one's own interests. Rationality, that is, requires that one pursue one's good or self-interest as defined by oneself and measured in terms of one's interests or, for contemporary Hobbesians, preferences for states of affairs. Hobbes believes that persons have only instrumental value, their value lying with their rational nature, or, the expectation that they will benefit others in interactions: "The value, or worth of a man, is as of all other things, his price" (Hobbes 1651 and 1962, 73). Morality comes about for self-interest based contractarians like Hobbes because each person expects to do better for himself in a system where he sometimes is called upon to make sacrifices to his own self-interest, and where others make similar sacrifices. Only then, but not when each acts for his immediate self-interest, can we expect to attain security, peace, and the material benefits of cooperation. Self-interest grounds the rationality of a hypothetical bargainer's "laying down" some of the rights or privileges he has in the State of Nature (Hobbes 1651 and 1962, 105). Rationality requires that each bargainer sacrifice as little as possible, just enough to gain and make participation in the system provide an expectation of self-benefit.

Alison Jaggar discusses four main feminist criticisms of the Hobbesian scheme that inform feminist revisionist moral theory to date. First, it is developed in a context of a dualistic metaphysics that favors the mind over the body, which encourages both political solipsism and political skepticism (Jaggar 1983, 40). Political solipsism, one of the starting points of social contract theory, is the assumption that humans are essentially solitary, having needs and interests separate or even in opposition to those of others, which Jaggar believes is at odds with human biology (Jaggar 1983, 41). Political skepticism is skepticism about whether we can justify establishing a political institution that promotes any specific conception of human well-being and fulfillment (Jaggar 1983, 41). In order to protect autonomy and one's own authority regarding one's needs and desires, liberals favor neutrality in institutions regarding the ends of human life, when, according to Jaggar, they ought to take as their starting point the biological needs that all humans have in common. Second, "abstract individualism," which Jaggar defines as "the assumption that the essential human characteristics are properties of individuals and are given independently of any particular social context," is questionable because research shows that most if not all of the cognitive and emotional differences between the sexes are the result of differing experiences, and that a person's desires and interests are heavily influenced by her social context (Jaggar 1983, 42). Third, the model of the egoistic rational agent is suspect: it fails to acknowledge that persons can be mistaken about their own desires due to sexist social conditioning, and it neither speaks to women's experiences that are more about altruism than egoism, nor can serve as the basis for political theory which requires communitarian values (Jaggar 1983, 44–5). Finally, the liberal individual, abstracted from particularities and primarily rational in nature, that is present in the model is male-biased because it perpetuates both the association of men with reason and women with emotion, and a sexual division of labor in which men dominate the intellectual, public sphere, and women, the private sphere, and makes it easy to ignore varying needs, particularly biological ones, that women have (Jaggar 1983, 46–7).

Nancy Tuana criticizes Kant's moral theory because it downplays the significance of emotion while associating emotion with women, and reason with men, and because it excludes women from full participation in morality. Tuana reads Kant as saying that a person must be completely divorced from inclination in order for the person's act to have moral worth (Tuana 1992, 58). This view, though standard, has been disputed by Barbara Herman, who understands Kant's view to be that inclination may be present in morally required acts (and is normally present in acts that are morally permissible), but that the moral motive, or acting for the sake of duty, is necessary for the agent's act to have moral worth (Herman 1981, 359–66). That is, the agent must act for the sake of duty even if he also has motives that circumstantially issue in morally right action, in order for his act to have moral worth. Nor need the agent have to fight off inclination that conflicts with duty for his act to have moral worth, as is the case with the person who loves his enemy even when he does not fight off an aversion to him (Kant 1785 and 1981, 11, AKA 398). Herman's point is that the object of the agent's motive, not conflict between inclination and duty, is what determines whether a person's right act has moral worth. On either Herman's or Tuana's reading, it is clear that Kant favors reason over emotion or inclination, since acting for the sake of duty is the rational motive one must have for one's act to have moral worth. The significance of this point for feminism is that Kant believes that women are more emotional than men, attributing to women "a strong inborn feeling for all that is beautiful, elegant, and decorated," and "many sympathetic sensations, goodheartedness, and compassion" (Tuana 1992, 62). Tuana notes that while Kant's view that women are more emotional than men does not entail that woman's moral capacity is not the same as man's, his view that women are less rational than men does (Tuana 1992, 62). Kant argues that women's understanding is "beautiful," while men's is "noble." He excludes women from "deep meditation and a long-sustained reflection" (Tuana 1992, 62, citing Kant 1960, 78). He believes that in acting morally women are guided not by a sense of duty but by their belief that acting wickedly is ugly. Moreover, Kant applies this description only to "civilized" women, or European bourgeoisie women particularly from England and France; non-European women—and men—are not sufficiently developed, he believed, to possess even a beautiful understanding, and so are incapable of acting morally (Tuana 1992, 62–3).

Not only does Kant's view reflect sexist stereotypes, it is at odds with the fundamental tenets of his moral theory. Kant believed that morality should be "derived from the universal concept of a rational being in general," because moral laws should be binding on all rational beings (Tuana 1992, 59). Morality is the business of humans, who have the capacity for rationality, but not animals, who act from instinct. In brief, any rational being could come up with the Categorical Imperative and apply any maxim to it to figure out the content of our duties. Kant contradicts himself when he claims on the one hand that morality is derived from the concept of a rational being in general, applying to all rational beings or all of humanity, but on the other hand, that women do not act on principle but on inclination—women follow beautiful virtue, not genuine, noble virtue, so they are incapable of following the Categorical Imperative (Tuana 1992, 63). Thus Kant's universal principle is not universal after all, unless, Tuana notes, Kant excludes women as rational. But Tuana cites a passage where Kant explicitly claims that woman is a rational being: "It [nature] provided the man with greater strength than the woman in order to bring them together into the most intimate *physical* union, which, insofar as they are still *rational* beings too, it orders to the end most important to it, the preservation of the species" (Tuana 1992, 65, citing Kant 1974, 169). Another inconsistency in Kant's theory lies with the Formula of Humanity, which states that one ought to "act in such a way that you treat humanity, whether in your own person or in the person of another, always at the same time as an end and never simply as a means" (Kant 1785 and 1981, 36), and Kant's view that women should be educated not in the development of their rational capacities, but to fit them into "their appropriate social roles: wives and mothers" (Tuana 1992, 65). Kant's reason for the latter is that educating women in their rational capacities would "weaken their charms with which she exercises her great power over the other sex" (Tuana 1992, 66). Tuana understands Kant to mean that educating women this way would inhibit man's development and improvement and refinement of society, which suggests that women are to be treated merely as a means to the ends of men and society at large, contra the second formulation of the Categorical Imperative. Kant succumbs to this inconsistency not because he believes, as Aristotle does, that women are incapable of rationality, but because of his views about the social roles they should inhabit (Tuana 1992, 67).

Oppression

Feminists have critiqued traditional moral theory not only for what it emphasizes, but for what it leaves out. One major oversight is any discussion of oppression, particularly women's oppression, John Stuart Mill's *The Subjection of Women* being one exception. Most feminists understand oppression to be systematic harm done to a group of people in virtue of certain, typically unchangeable, features shared by members of the group. The fact of women's oppression is the subcontext of all feminist critique of traditional moral theory;

the suggestions feminists have made for improving moral theory are offered with the aim of ending women's oppression. While traditional moral theory focuses on persons as individuals, how they should act and the characters they should develop, and typically ignores the role of socialization and institutions and practices on action and character, feminists have examined the ways in which oppressive systems affect a person's character, actions, and desires, and question whether and to what extent a person who undergoes oppressive socialization is responsible for her or his actions. Oppression, then, is central not only to feminist normative theory, but to feminist moral psychology as well. Feminists also examine the ways in which traditional moral theories might, by not addressing oppression, countenance it, or at least fail to aim for its demise.

Since oppression plays such a central role in feminist critique, feminists have explained and analyzed the notion of oppression. Marilyn Frye's early but classic paper analyzes oppression as systematic, interrelated forces that jointly function to keep a social group subordinate, just as a birdcage traps a bird, with each line of the cage representing a factor that contributes to a group's oppression (Frye 1983). Only a macroscopic view of all the lines on the cage and their interconnections enables us to see why a bird cannot escape or that a group is oppressed, though too often we take a microscopic view, seeing just one line on the cage. Frye argues that oppression is an objective fact, independent of people's intentions and beliefs, and is determined by context. Alison Bailey analyzes privilege as the flipside of oppression; indeed, for each oppressed group, there is a corresponding privileged group (Bailey 1998). Bailey defines privilege in a narrow sense to be unearned assets or benefits conferred systematically to almost all members of a privileged group, functioning like a wild card in a poker game that can be used in many circumstances (e.g., white persons' being able to buy bandages matching their skin color, and not having to speak for their race when they exhibit a faulty character trait).[1] For Bailey, all privilege is advantageous, but not all advantages are privileges. Privilege is mostly invisible to its bearers; much feminist analysis of issues such as sexual harassment, abortion, and rape reveals the way that privilege embedded in practices and institutions sustains women's oppression.

More recently, Ann Cudd has offered a comprehensive analysis of oppression, which she locates in stereotyping, or generalizations we form about individuals and the groups to which they belong, coupled with violence. Cudd defines oppression as "an institutionally structured harm perpetrated on groups by other groups using direct and indirect material and psychological forces that violate justice" (Cudd 2006, 26). The material forces of oppression are violence and economic deprivation (Cudd 2006, 85). For violence to count as a force of oppression, it must operate systematically, causing harm to one social group and harming its direct victim(s), while benefiting another social group (e.g., sexual assault and domestic violence). Obviously violence is direct when it is intended to physically harm a person through application of physical force (Cudd 2006, 86), but it is indirect when it threatens future violence, especially when the threat is never spoken about as such, but persons' behavior is attributed to their genuine preferences (e.g., women's staying indoors is attributed to their being timid rather than fear of threat of rape). The forces of economic oppression, the other material force of oppression, are both direct, as when men earn 141 percent of what women earn, and indirect, as in "oppression by choice," including the ways in which women willingly contribute to their own oppression by becoming stay-at-home mothers because it is economically rational for them rather than their partners to raise their children, even though their doing so perpetuates the stereotype of women as unreliable wage workers. The psychological forces that sustain oppression and are key to its longevity include both direct forms such as terror, humiliation and degradation, and objectification, and indirect forms such as false consciousness and deformed desires, the latter of which Cudd believes are the most damaging and enduring forces of oppression because they can obstruct a person's recognition of her own oppression and because fighting them is painful if not harmful (Cudd 2006, 183).[2] Feminists aim to show how these elements of oppression play out in moral theory.

Feminist modifications of traditional moral theories

Feminists have suggested a variety of ways to improve the state of moral theory in light of the problems they have identified with traditional moral theory. These range from introducing and developing a new moral theory, the ethic of care, to taking a traditional theory in an entirely new direction, to fixing up a traditional theory when the problems feminists have identified are not inherent to it, to borrowing useful concepts from traditional theory and employing them for feminist ends. Underlying all of these suggestions is the goal of eradicating women's oppression.

The Ethic of Care

Perhaps the most well-known feminist response to traditional moral theory has been the development of a new moral theory, the ethic of care, spawned by Carol Gilligan's work in moral psychology, the conclusion of which was that for the most part, females employ what she called "the care perspective," which emphasizes care, situatedness, preserving relations, and satisfying needs, while males employ "the justice perspective," which emphasizes justice, abstraction, and rule-following (Gilligan 1982). The emotion of care governs action with intimates, particularly the mother-child relationship, in the so-called private sphere to which (at least white, middle class) women have been relegated, and by bringing it into moral theory, moral theory will be certain to include women's experiences.

Focusing on care and caring relations makes us see persons in terms of their particularities and their needs, rather than as abstract independent individuals divorced from their needs, whose history is unknown and irrelevant to morality, and whose value is merely instrumental. Thus the ethic of care aims to defeat most of the objections feminists have raised about traditional moral theories.

Annette Baier suggests that feminists not completely abandon traditional moral theory, but borrow from it in developing the ethic of care. She notices similarities between the ethic of care and David Hume's moral theory, referring to Hume as the "woman's moral theorist" (Baier 1987). The commonalities include the fact that Hume makes morality a matter of cultivating character traits directed at peace of mind and integrity, that he takes sympathy, or the heart's responses to particular persons, to be the fundamental moral capacity, that he emphasizes convention rather than rules in determining moral rightness, and that he emphasizes relations between unequals and builds his moral theory on the bond between parents and their children.

In spite of the feminist interest in the ethic of care, there has been a great deal of feminist critique of it. For starters, feminists have criticized Gilligan's theory for perpetuating sexist stereotypes (Tronto 1987 and 1993), for inaccuracies and false conclusions about differences in male and female moral reasoning (Walker 1984 and 1993; Greeno and Maccoby 1986 and 1993), for concerns about sample size and characterizations (Luria 1986 and 1993), and for invoking generalizations that can be used to support racist views (Moody-Adams 1991, 199). The ethic of care itself has been criticized for being merely a *feminine*, but not a *feminist*, moral theory. A feminine ethic includes the experiences and intuitions of women, though it need not aim at ending women's oppression; the salient feature of a feminist ethic, though, is that it aims to end women's oppression. One issue is that care, notwithstanding its status as a natural, positive sentiment, is a motive that women experience mainly in connection with their being in a position of exploitation, given that our society is premised on dominance and subordination. Thus valorizing or centralizing care in a moral theory will not aid in overcoming women's oppression but may even perpetuate it. In addition, the ethic of care is founded on care in the unequal mother-child relationship that might never be reciprocated, which not only overlooks the needs of one party, but creates expectations of unidirectional caring from all females (Hoagland 1991, 251, 254). Further, the theory does not acknowledge the tension many mothers feel between tenderness and resentment (Hoagland 1991, 253, 254, and 256). Feminists worry that the kind of caring enjoined by the ethic of care is also problematic: men's caring has to do with protection and material forms of help that men provide and control such as a paycheck and material goods for their family, while women's caring found in emotional work has to do with admitting dependency and sharing or losing control, thereby contributing to their own oppression (Friedman 1993, 175, 177). Some argue that women's caring makes mothers lose touch with or suppress their own needs and judge themselves solely in terms of the success of their children, leading to a denial of self and autonomy (Blum et. al. 1973–4, 231–2, 235, and 239). Others worry that women's caring is not virtuous when it is really misplaced gratitude to men who have the power to abuse them or exchange "protection" for care (Card 1993, 216). When considered jointly, these objections challenge whether the ethic of care is fair to women and promotes their equality and autonomy.

Some feminists have responded by developing the ethic of care in ways that maintain the centrality of care but do not sustain women's oppression. Eva Feder Kittay takes up what she calls "the dependency critique," which is a feminist critique of equality that charges that conceptions of society as an association of equals are misguided because they mask inequitable dependencies such as those found in infancy, childhood, old age, illness, and disability (Kittay 1999, xi). Kittay notes that both persons who are in dependent stages in life, and those who have to put aside their interests when caring for dependents, do not enter into competition for the goods of social cooperation on equal terms with others. This burden of care for dependents, though not inherently gendered, historically has fallen disproportionately on women, and even the ones who have escaped traditional caring roles have needed the services of other women for their dependency work. Kittay argues that in order to achieve equality for all, the wider community should accept responsibility for the care of dependents and support of caregivers (Kittay 1999, 182).

Taking Traditional Theory in a New Direction

A clear example of taking a traditional moral theory in a new direction in line with feminist aims is the recent development of feminist virtue ethics. Traditional virtue ethics such as Aristotle's theory focuses on character development and the connection between moral goodness and the good life. Robin Dillon argues that there should not be a feminist virtue ethics, since the focus for feminist ethics is not just or mainly with individuals and the development of their character and how they should act to live a good life, but with individuals as members of social groups organized around power (Dillon 2012). Instead, Dillon argues for replacing standard virtue theory with what she calls "critical character theory," that is based on the recognition that oppression can operate on and through character. Oppression can damage character and one's opportunity for living a good life, and can shape character in ways that affect whether persons living in oppressive systems resist or maintain, intentionally or not, such systems. The goal of critical character theory, Dillon notes, is to aim to dismantle unjust hierarchies of power both for and through the liberation of character: it makes central women's oppression and examines character development, appraisals of character, and treatments of virtue and vice in terms of women's oppression and with an eye toward making the world one in which women and men are treated equally and with respect (Dillon 2012). Questions asked in traditional virtue theory about whether a certain character trait is good, which, for traditional virtue ethics, is determined independently of its connection to oppression, should be re-focused into questions about whether it helps the agent to resist oppression or aids the agent in contributing to oppression. Critical character theory also pays attention to vice in both the oppressed and the privileged, and its connection to oppression, which has been largely ignored in traditional virtue theory. Attention to vice is important because moral theory can be used to enable people to improve their characters, to resist or live with oppression, to determine how to act and with whom, and to ameliorate the forces that distort characters by vice (Dillon 2012).

Lisa Tessman discusses what she terms "burdened virtues," virtues that privileged persons have that actually stand in the way of their own flourishing and thus make them morally damaged (Tessman 2001). Due to their experiences of privilege, privileged persons might not develop certain self-regarding traits, including the habits of hard work, the capacity to value fully the fruits of one's labor, and even courage. Although they can develop other-regarding traits, they may direct them only toward other privileged persons (Tessman 2005, 68). Tessman argues that the privileged may suffer various different vices of domination: batterers and rapists and those who terrorize racial minorities exhibit cruelty, indifference, contempt, and arrogance (Tessman 2005, 54). But others who merely participate in oppression may suffer what she calls "ordinary vices of domination," including callousness, greed, self-centeredness, dishonesty, and cowardice, in addition to, perhaps, lacking compassion, generosity, cooperativeness, and openness to appreciating others (Tessman 2005, 55). Tessman acknowledges that oppression can also prevent the oppressed from flourishing and living the good life, thereby making them morally damaged. This happens when the oppressed internalize their oppression to the extent that it impedes their developing appropriate levels of confidence (Tessman 2005, 56), or when they internalize stereotypes of oppression (e.g., that women's value lies with their capacity to nurture and care for others) and then become *too* other-directed, and exhibit servility (Tessman 2005, 65).

Modifying Traditional Theories: Feminist Contractarianism

In spite of the many feminist critiques of traditional moral theory, some feminists argue that some traditional moral theories, with some tweaking, can actually serve feminist aims. One example is Jean Hampton's Kantian contractarianism, developed in light of feminist objections to both the ethic of care and Hobbesian contractarianism (Hampton, 2002). Hampton argues that feminists should make the motive of self-interest, rather than the motive of care, central to their moral theory because without it women are likely to lose themselves in slavish action. They will become like Amy, a girl that Carol Gilligan describes in her case study on gendered moral reasoning (Hampton 2002, 338–9, citing Gilligan 1982, 35–6). Amy reasons from the perspective of care, understanding morality to be a matter of responding to others' needs, not hurting others, and being in service to them. Since Amy always places others' needs before her own, and is not able firmly to assert herself or let her own interests count, she loses herself in moral dilemmas, bordering on outright servility (Hampton 2002, 340). Jake, in contrast, a representative male reasoner in Gilligan's study (Hampton 2002, 339, citing Gilligan 1982, 46), reasons from the justice perspective, understanding morality as a set of traffic rules that amount to pursuing one's own interests without interfering with the interests of others. Jake believes that his own self ought to come first, and is insensitive to others' needs. Hampton does not laud either character as morally exemplary, but believes that Amy suffers more than Jake because she is highly exploitable. Thus Hampton argues against the ethic of care on the grounds that it is likely to align itself with gendered social roles for men and women, and thus lead to the exploitation of women.

Hampton favors contractarianism for the reason that it enjoins a person to be prompted by self-interest in putting forward claims with other potential contractors to the hypothetical bargain from which morality is derived. Rationality requires that each Hobbesian hypothetical bargainer not make or keep contracts that do not provide an expectation of benefit to him. Amy needs to recognize her interests and assert them in her moral dealings with others. In order to make sure that contractarianism includes the interests of all, particularly the disenfranchised such as Amy-types with whom others might not expect to benefit, Hampton argues that contractarians assume, with Kant, that all persons have intrinsic value (Hampton 2002, 344–5). Thus all persons come to the bargaining scheme having intrinsic value that must be respected, and then, with this assumption in place, each can assert her legitimate interests and insist on her own worth. Hampton intends for her revised version of Hobbesian contractarianism to apply to private relationships, where each party can ask, "Given the fact that we are in this relationship, could both of us reasonably accept the distribution of costs and benefits . . . if it were the subject of an informed, unforced agreement in which we think of ourselves as motivated solely by self-interest?" (Hampton 2002, 351). Hampton's contractarianism aims to end women's oppression by disallowing exploitation.

Traditional Concepts Applied to Feminist Aims

Intrinsic Value

Some feminists have neither abandoned traditional moral theory, nor modified it wholesale, but have demonstrated its usefulness for feminist aims by employing some of its concepts and ideas in feminist analyses of moral issues.

Foremost among traditional concepts is Kant's notion of intrinsic value, the value that all persons have in virtue of their capacity for rationality, which is evidenced by their having interests and desires, and making plans and setting goals, making them deserving of respect and the kind of beings who are not to be treated merely as means to an end. The notion of intrinsic value has played a role in many feminist critiques of certain kinds of treatment of women. I argue that a violation of the "facts about humanity" (i.e., that humans are deserving of respect in virtue of their capacity for rationality) lies at the root of sexist forms of immorality (Superson 2004). I argue that social privilege fosters the development of arrogance, self-interest, and failure to accept responsibility in the privileged, and that these traits can cause the agent to engage in sexist forms of immorality that in turn function to maintain his privilege. One example of sexist immorality is that of a conscientiously wicked person, who, according to Stanley Benn, governs his actions by a primary goal or principle that can reasonably be seen as good but does so "at the cost of a callous insensitivity to evil done by the way" (Benn 1985, 801). That is, he endorses and follows a seemingly good principle, and follows it insensitively even when it leads to bad. An example is an employer who subscribes to the seemingly fair and neutral principle, "Justice means giving each what he deserves," who ends up knowingly favoring men in hiring, because (he knows or should know that) men but not women are encouraged to develop traits needed for traditionally male jobs (Superson 2004, 41). The employer fails to accord women due respect as persons who have equal intrinsic value to men by denying them opportunities readily granted to men. Since he knows or should know that the principle he endorses advantages men at the expense of women, his continued endorsement of it is arrogant and self-centered.

Violations of intrinsic value occur not just in sexist, immoral actions, but in systems and practices as well. Jean Hampton analyzes the wrongness of rape—both the act and the practice—in terms of violation of the intrinsic value of women. Hampton defines a moral injury such as rape as a wrongful action that is disrespectful of a person's value as a person (Hampton 1999, 123). A moral injury conveys the (erroneous) view that the wrongdoer is superior in value or worth to the one he wrongs: a wife abuser in his abusive acts sends the message that his wife has the value of chattel, while a rapist in the act of rape sends the message that his victim is even lower than chattel, a mere object to be used at the rapist's discretion (Hampton 1999, 134–5). Indeed, Hampton argues, rape goes further in sending this message to all women, not just the direct victim: "As a woman, you are the kind of human being who is subject to the mastery of people of my kind," and that "Your kind isn't the equal in worth of my kind" (Hampton 1999, 135). Hampton, though, agrees with Kant that a person's value cannot actually ever be lowered, though it can be "diminished," or have the appearance of being lowered (Hampton 1999, 128).[3]

Sexual objectification is widely discussed by feminists, most of whom employ a Kantian analysis of it even if they do not identify it as such. Sandra Bartky describes sexual objectification as occurring when a person's sexual parts or sexual functions are separated out from the rest of her personality and reduced to the status of mere instruments or else regarded as if they are capable of representing her (Bartky 1979 and 1990b, 26). A sex object, then, is one who is seen in terms of her sexual parts or functions. The victim of catcalls, for example, is made to see herself as her harassers see her, as less than a whole person but as a mere part or body (Bartky 1979 and 1990b, 27).

Clelia Anderson and Yolanda Estes offer a Kantian analysis of prostitution, according to which the prostitute must pretend to her client that she is a woman with subjectivity because the client wants a "woman-thing, mind and soul," a willing slave (Anderson and Estes 1998). The prostitute's job is to acknowledge her client's subjectivity in the form of his sexual desires, and to disassociate herself from her sexual activity, which in reality she cannot do. In their sexual encounter, both the prostitute and her client try to use the other as a mere means to an end, but the bodily nature of the encounter forces them to recognize their mutual humanity: "each walks away having given up more of themselves than was agreed to in the bargain"(Anderson and Estes 1998, 158). Although the prostitute is never actually objectified, her client treats her as if she were an object. The wrongness of prostitution, according to Anderson and Estes, is the attempt to lower the prostitute's value as a person by appropriating her body without concern for its subjectivity (Anderson and Estes 1998, 153).

Not all feminists find objectification in the Kantian sense to be problematic. Martha Nussbaum argues that while there are bad forms of objectification that violate Kantian norms, including treating someone as a tool for one's purposes (instrumentality), treating someone as lacking in self-determination (denial of autonomy), treating someone as lacking in agency (inertness), and treating someone as one whose experiences and feelings need not be taken into account (denial of subjectivity), there are also acceptable forms of objectification (Nussbaum, 1999c). Nussbaum argues that good, fun sex can involve surrender of autonomy and subjectivity, and identification of the other with his or her genitalia in a nondehumanizing way that actually, contrary to Kant's views, makes the person be "seen more fully as the human individual she is" (Nussbaum 1999c, 230). This kind of objectification is not morally problematic, Nussbaum argues, because it takes place in the context of mutual respect and rough social equality and enormous trust (Nussbaum 1999c, 230).

Rae Langton, through the issue of pornography, challenges Nussbaum's Kantian analysis of objectification (Langton 2009). Langton expands Nussbaum's list of the ways in which a person can be objectified to include, most importantly, treating a person as silent or as lacking the capacity to speak. The central idea for Langton in treating a person as an object is to treat her or him as something lacking in subjectivity and autonomy (Langton 2009, 231). But Langton explains that instrumentality does not entail autonomy-denial construed as nonattribution of autonomy, since a rapist may treat his victim merely as a means while attributing autonomy to her—he seeks to violate her autonomy, after all (Langton 2009, 234–5). However, instrumentality may entail autonomy-denial construed as autonomy-violation. Langton applies her notion of objectification to the case of the pornographic film starring Linda Lovelace, who is supposed to represent a character, both fictional and real, as autonomously choosing a life satisfying her insatiable desire for throat sex. Langton argues that Lovelace was not treated autonomously, *tout court*, because she was made to look like she chose to be objectified, while in reality, she was forced through violence, rape, and death threats to act the way her pimp and husband, Charles Traynor, told her to act. She was silenced. In agreement with Hampton's analysis of rape, Langton argues that when the kind of sex portrayed in this film is seen as autonomously chosen by women, all women's autonomy is denied and they are silenced. Thus pornography objectifies even as it affirms autonomy (Langton 2009, 240).

Autonomy

Autonomy is a central theme in both traditional ethical theories and in feminist theory. Indeed, it is one of the most frequently and hotly debated topics in feminism, as it figures into many issues that are of great concern to feminists, such as abortion, rape, and sexual harassment, as well as self-determination in the face of patriarchal socialization. Arguably, the main feminist complaint about sexist behavior and systematic oppression is their denial of women's autonomy. As we have seen, feminists have challenged the individualistic model of the autonomous agent as a rational chooser seeking to maximize good, if not without interference from others, then in complete isolation from them. They also charge that this model depicts the autonomous agent as knowing what it wants and being able to subject its desires to critical self-reflection (Friedman 1997, 40, 42). According to Catriona Mackenzie and Natalie Stoljar, many feminist theorists regard the concept of autonomy with suspicion because it "is inherently masculinist, that it is inextricably bound up with masculine character ideals, with assumptions about selfhood and agency that are metaphysically, epistemologically, and ethically problematic from a feminist perspective, and with political traditions that historically have been hostile to women's interests and freedom" (Mackenzie and Stoljar 2000, 3). Underlying the many feminist critiques of the traditional notion of autonomy, which Mackenzie and Stoljar classify as symbolic critiques, metaphysical critiques, care critiques, postmodernist critiques, and diversity critiques, is the charge that individual autonomy is fundamentally individualistic and rationalistic (Mackenzie and Stoljar 2000, 6–12 and 3).

In response to these varied critiques, some feminists have reconstrued the concept of autonomy as "relational autonomy." Mackenzie and Stoljar define "relational autonomy" as an "umbrella term" of perspectives of autonomy which have in common that "persons are socially embedded and that agents' identities are formed within the context of social relationships and shaped by a complex of intersecting social determinants, such as race, class, gender, and ethnicity" (Mackenzie and Stoljar 2000, 4). Mackenzie and Stoljar are quick to point out that many feminists, themselves included, do not deny the individualistic nature of autonomy: the phrase "individual autonomy" implies that agents are separate entities with a capacity for autonomy (Mackenzie and Stoljar 2000, 8). Rather, feminist critiques of traditional autonomy emphasize that the characteristics and capacities of the self need to be analyzed with attention to the rich and complex social and historical contexts in which agents are embedded, viewing the agent as both an emotional, embodied, desiring, creative, feeling creature, and as a rational creature who is psychically internally and socially differentiated from others (Mackenzie and Stoljar 2000, 21).

Among the most significant contributions of relational autonomy theorists is their insight that oppressive socialization can impede an agent's autonomy in (1) the formation of the agent's beliefs and desires, (2) the agent's capacities for self-reflection and self-direction, and (3) the agent's ability to act on her desires or to make autonomous choices (Mackenzie and Stoljar 2000, 22). I will discuss each of these points in turn.

Most feminists acknowledge that oppressive socialization leads to women's having deformed desires (e.g., Bartky 1982 and 1990a, Nussbaum 1999a, Benson 2000, Superson 2005, Cudd 2006). Natalie Stoljar argues that procedural accounts of autonomy, which make no assessment of the content of a person's desires, values, beliefs, and emotional attitudes, but determine autonomy solely on the basis of whether the agent subjects her motivations and actions to the appropriate kind of critical reflection (Mackenzie and Stoljar 2000, 13–14), cannot explain what she calls "the feminist intuition," the view that preferences influenced by oppressive norms of femininity cannot be autonomous (Stoljar 2000, 95). Rather, what is needed is a strong substantive account of autonomy, since this kind of account recognizes that agents adopt norms of femininity and sexual agency that are false, and criticizes these norms and the desires and values formed in their wake for interfering with the agent's autonomy. Stoljar focuses on Kristin Luker's study of women who take contraceptive risks and adopt norms about pregnancy and motherhood that are false and criticizable from a feminist perspective. These women count as autonomous on various procedural accounts of autonomy since they pass various procedural tests. These include: they weigh the costs and benefits of using contraception and take the risk based on their preferences grounded in patriarchal norms; they are not self-deceived in the formation of their desires though they are influenced by these norms; their beliefs and desires are internally consistent though they might be ambivalent about their desires; their first-order desire to take a contraceptive risk is endorsed by their second-order volition or norm about pregnancy and motherhood; and they bargain over oppressive norms and resistance to them (Stoljar 2000, 102–3, 105–7). Stoljar favors a substantive account of autonomy which assesses the content of an agent's desires, rather than whether the agent subjects her desires to some procedure, and argues that since the women in Luker's study have internalized oppressive norms, they lack the capacity to perceive the norms as false, and the desires from which these norms emanate impede their autonomy (Stoljar 2000, 109).

A second way that oppressive socialization can impede an agent's autonomy is by affecting her capacity for self-reflection and self-direction. Andrea Westlund defends a procedural account of autonomy that addresses how this may happen, though she argues that an agent who is influenced this way can still be autonomous (Westlund 2003). Westlund offers a "dialogical" account of autonomy, according to which an autonomous person has an attitude of responsibility for her commitments, and more deeply, for her self, and is prepared both to engage in a dialogue with herself and (perhaps hypothetical) others with differing viewpoints (external critical perspectives), and to offer justificatory reasons for why she has the desires and action-guiding commitments that she has. In order to examine whether deference is compatible with autonomy, Westlund takes up two characters, the first of which is Thomas Hill's Deferential Wife (DW), who tends not to form her own interests, but when she does, she counts them as less important than her husband's (Hill 1973 and 1995). Westlund argues that the DW fails to be answerable to her critics, since she fails to internalize the relationship of holding and being held answerable for her action-guiding commitments. The DW cannot give answers to why she ranks her husband's preferences higher than her own, merely treating the fact that he has preferences and desires as a conclusive reason for her to act in deference to them. Her imperviousness to her critics' questioning shows that she is tightly gripped by her commitments. She fails to be autonomous because she is not self-responsible in the sense of being her own representative, speaking for herself and holding herself answerable to her own commitments. Westlund contrasts the DW with "AF," the extreme anti-feminist, who gives proper uptake to the question, "Why be so deferential?," but who offers a rather unsophisticated response grounded in her religious beliefs (e.g., the Bible tells her to be subservient to her husband). Westlund argues that "AF's engagement in justificatory dialogue releases us from the sort of uncertainty we feel in the DW's case just insofar as it convincingly demonstrates that AF functions as her own representative" (Westlund

2003, 513). If AF is really self-responsible, she will distinguish herself from her husband as separately and ultimately answerable for her action-guiding commitments by being disposed to take up further challenges of her principle of deference, and by not giving pat responses. Even if we disagree with her reasons, she counts as autonomous if she exhibits an openness to justificatory dialogue. The larger conclusion to draw is that women who undergo oppressive socialization and internalization of oppressive norms such as those relating to deference can still be autonomous if they exhibit genuine dialogical responsiveness to the demand for justification for their beliefs and desires. This procedure, not the content of their desires, determines whether they are autonomous.

A third way that oppressive socialization can compromise an agent's autonomy is by affecting the agent's ability to act on her desires or to make autonomous choices. Uma Narayan addresses the topic of whether agents who have desires deformed by patriarchy can nonetheless have the ability to act on their desires or make autonomous choices (Narayan 2002). Narayan takes as her case study Sufi Pirzada Muslim women who are expected "to veil" (including wearing a burqua). She believes that they have a mix of desires that are deformed by patriarchy (e.g., a desire to maintain their reputation) and desires that are not so deformed (e.g., a desire not to veil because it is uncomfortable and risks injury), and have external constraints on their liberty as well (e.g., economic and political implications of not veiling), but that in the face of both these internal and external constraints "bargain" with patriarchy and do what they believe is best for themselves. Their agency is not completely pulverized by patriarchy since they have the capacity for critical reflection or resistance to patriarchal norms (Narayan 2002, 422). Narayan rejects Marilyn Friedman's more restrictive account of autonomy on two grounds: (1) that it requires that the level of coercion, manipulation, and deception be insignificant, and (2) that there be significant and morally acceptable alternatives from which to choose (Narayan 2002, 428–9). Narayan argues that a person can make clear choices even in the absence of acceptable alternatives, which is a reason to respect the person's choices rather than not count them as real. Narayan favors a liberal view of autonomy, according to which a person is autonomous as long as she is a "normal adult" with no serious cognitive or emotional impairments and is not subject to literal or outright coercion from others (Narayan 2002, 429). Thus on her account, deformed desires do not threaten the agent's autonomy because, despite her choices being constrained by patriarchy, she can still make genuine, reflective choices within these constraints, exhibit active moral agency, and be self-directing. Narayan acknowledges that sometimes the starkness of patriarchal constraints actually enhances the agent's critical abilities, causing her to face head on the conflict in her desires and to choose in ways that are at odds with patriarchy.

Moral Psychology

Moral psychology concerns issues relating to the motivation of moral action, including how we see or fail to see moral issues, why we act or fail to act morally, and whether and to what extent we are responsible for our actions. Feminist moral psychology concentrates on these same issues, but in connection to the oppression of women. It examines the ways in which oppression can affect the psychology and subsequent actions of both women and men. One major contribution of feminism is the examination of desires deformed by patriarchy, including how they are brought about (Elster 1983, Nussbaum 1999a, Bartky 1982 and 1990a); whether and to what extent they impede the agent's autonomy (see "Autonomy," previous section); and how having them and other forms of psychological oppression can help sustain the oppression of a group (Cudd 2006, Bartky 1979 and 1990b). Feminist moral psychology also examines the ways in which oppression—specifically, a morally corrupt society in general and particular kinds of male socialization—cultivates sexist attitudes and behaviors in men (Thomas 1996, May 1998b, May 1998a). Finally, feminist moral psychology is concerned with the notion of responsibility in connection with oppression. It examines whether the oppressed are responsible for contributing to their own oppression by not resisting it (Superson 1993, Hay 2005, Cudd 2006), whether being a member of an oppressed group mitigates one's responsibility for wrongdoings linked to oppressive socialization (Benson 2000, Superson 2010), and whether being a member of a dominant group implicates one—and to what it extent—for the harms of oppression ("collective responsibility") (Friedman and May 1985, Calhoun 1989, Moody-Adams 1994, May and Strikwerda 1999, Superson 2004). For an in-depth discussion of these and related issues, see Superson, 2009a.

Metaethics

Internalism-externalism debate

Broadly stated, internalism is the view that there is a necessary connection between two concepts, typically reasons, motives, obligations, and moral judgments; externalism is the denial of the necessity claim. According to one version of internalism, sometimes labeled "motivational internalism," "there is a (conceptually or logically) necessary connection between moral judgment and motivation such that, for any case in which an agent is motivated to act by her moral judgment, it is this moral judgment itself that generates the motivation in question" (Shafer-Landau and Cuneo 2007, 225–6). Further qualifications have been made to this thesis. David Brink contrasts what he calls "agent internalism," the view that in virtue of the concept of morality, moral obligations (or moral reasons, if obligations and reasons are necessarily connected) necessarily motivate the agent to act morally, with what he calls "appraiser internalism," the view that it is in virtue of the concept of morality that moral belief or moral judgment provides the appraiser with a motive (or reason) for action (Brink 1986, 27). The key difference is that agent internalism is objective, tying motivation to a moral consideration of anyone's recognition of her obligation or reason, while appraiser internalism is subjective in the sense that it links the appraiser's motives to her beliefs or judgments about moral considerations independent of whether the beliefs or judgments are correct or justifiable. Michael Smith defends a version of internalism that he calls "the practicality requirement," according to which "If an agent judges that it is right for her to φ in circumstances C, then either she is motivated to φ in C or she is practically irrational" (Smith 1994 and 2007, 232). Smith believes that "for an agent to judge that she ought to act in a certain way just is for her to judge that an ideally rational version of herself would desire to act in that way" (Shafer-Landau and Cuneo 2007, 227). An agent who failed to be motivated by her moral judgments suffers some irrationality such as weakness of will or compulsion (Smith 1994 and 2007, 240).

Some feminists have raised problems with motivational internalism as a conceptual thesis. Peggy DesAutels explores the possibility of an agent's having a moral commitment to the ethic of care yet failing to follow through on it even when the agent is competent and does not ignore her moral commitments. DesAutels's project is to ask whether there is empirical evidence that would cast doubt on internalism as a purely conceptual thesis about what it means to make a moral judgment. DesAutels argues that sexism, in the form of unrecognized psychological habits or subtle social influences, often makes even a morally competent agent who does not ignore her moral commitments fail to follow through (DesAutels 2004, 69). Although she is not clear on this point, DesAutels seems to suggest that the agent does not follow through because she lacks the appropriate motivation as required by motivational internalism. One factor that can influence an agent's following through on her moral commitments is moral oblivion. DesAutels argues that an agent can be "somewhat aware" of a morally relevant feature of an act, or of her moral demands, but fail to attend *fully* to that feature or the demand itself, as when she allows deeply entrenched stereotypes to block her noticing the needs of others (DesAutels 2004, 74–5). Another factor that can influence whether an agent follows through on her moral commitments is social influence. DesAutels has in mind a case where an agent is aware that a situation *might* call for a moral response, but is unsure and does not respond. An example is when an agent feels social pressure to conform to the attitudes and inactions of others around her, as when 38 people failed to intervene to help Kitty Genovese when she was stabbed repeatedly over a

30-minute period (DesAutels 2004, 75–6). Being only "somewhat aware" of a moral demand, or being uncertain of a moral demand, can fail to entail motivation, and hence, action, even in morally competent agents.

James Lindemann Nelson argues that internalists about moral judgments and motivation fail to capture the notion that an agent's judgment might come in varying degrees of confidence in the correctness of the judgment or the exigency of the values involved (Nelson 2004, 84). Rather than an all-or-nothing connection, which is the standard depiction of motivational internalism, Nelson takes internalism and externalism to be points on a scale reflecting the relationship between an agent and the moral understandings she takes to be authoritative. On the traditional view of motivational internalism, if one acts immorally because one is not appropriately motivated, one simply must not have believed the relevant moral judgment. Nelson rejects this view in favor of the view that internalism reflects the degrees to which a person grasps moral beliefs and to which she acts on these beliefs. On Nelson's account, if one lacks a strong sense of what one ought to do, this need not mean that one completely lacks an authentic belief about what one ought to do. Nelson's account is sensitive to the fact that a person's own moral beliefs and reasons may not be consistent with those held widely in her society, especially when it is a sexist one. Thus a person might truly believe that her society takes something to be morally required, but not be fully motivated by her society's moral requirements because they dictate sexist behavior. Nelson's suggestion sheds doubt on internalism as a thesis about a conceptual connection between belief and motivation, or at least means that it should be clarified to say that a low degree of confidence will match a low degree of motivation, rather than be presented as an all-or-nothing thesis.

I employ the case of the Deferential Wife (DW) to question the motivational internalist claim advocated by philosophers such as Michael Smith, that if a person fails to be motivated by her moral judgment, she must be irrational (Superson 2009, 151–8). The DW, like many women who are victims of oppressive socialization, is confused about her worth as a person, which prevents her from being motivated by a moral judgment that one ought to be self-respecting. I argue that it may be the case that agents like the DW reason correctly (are rational), understand what it means to have intrinsic worth as a person, see that if a person has intrinsic worth she would respect herself, but get the facts wrong in their own case due to their circumstances. These circumstances include patriarchal socialization that can make an agent fail to see her own worth as a person. Judging the DW to be irrational, as this kind of motivational internalism does when there is a failure of motivation, is at odds with feminist aims, for it blames victims of bad circumstances for a failure in rationality when their failure to be motivated by a moral judgment is more plausibly explained by bad circumstances. There is nothing wrong with the DW's reasoning—she responds correctly to the facts as she sees them—so it is wrong to impugn her rationality.

Moral epistemology

Margaret Little showcases the contribution of the ethic of care to moral epistemology, examining the role of emotion and desire in acquiring moral knowledge (Little 1995 and 2007). Little challenges the traditional "bureaucratic model," according to which reason determines moral verdicts which it passes on to motivation which in turn issues in the appropriate response. This view is prominent because of the belief that moral judgments should correct biases introduced by sentiment, though Little suspects (in agreement with Nancy Tuana, above) that the "lesser" role assigned to emotions has its roots in emotion's historical association with women. Little's view, in contrast, is that the agent's having certain desires and emotions, particularly caring about people, is a necessary condition for seeing what morality requires in the first place (Little 1995 and 2007, 421). When we care about a person, we have the right background disposition for morally relevant features to come into our consciousness; we are receptive to the particularities of a person, listen to their narrative, and respect the person as a responsible subject. Only then do we know what is morally called for (Little 1995 and 2007, 424). Little argues that a person who has merely an intellectual comprehension of the moral landscape, and yet never responds appropriately (e.g., one who sees that certain things are painful and knows what pain is, yet does not see pain as evil), has a clouded perception, much like the person who uses the term "green" correctly but has never seen the color and so lacks the concept of "green" (Little 1995 and 2007, 427). The moral case is even worse, Little argues, because a person who lacks the appropriate emotions just will not get morality right. This is because nonmoral terms cannot completely explain morality (e.g., they cannot explain the different kinds of cruelty), and because whether a feature plays a role in determining an act's moral status is dependent, in a way that cannot be codified, on other relevant features (e.g., an act's being fun may be a reason to do it, but it is also the feature that makes hunting animals problematic) (Little 1995 and 2007, 428). Since affect is necessary for seeing the moral landscape, it may get us to moral truths, and is consistent with moral realism (Little 1995 and 2007, 431).

Moral relativism

There are two main feminist points of view on the issue of moral relativism, the view that moral truths are relative to the culture, or even to a given individual

(individual moral relativism) endorsing them. One is the worry about judging other cultures, particularly, judging women's behavior in other cultures, especially when similar judgments are not made about one's own cultural practices. Since women throughout history have been judged according to patriarchal standards, some feminists believe that we should refrain from judging women's behavior and imposing standards of the good on women. Since moral relativism has been associated with tolerance (erroneously, since relativism does not entail tolerance), this has led some feminists to favor it over moral realism, the view that there are universal moral truths. An opposing feminist view is that there is—indeed, there must be, for the sake of ending women's oppression—absolute truth in ethics, or, moral truths that hold for all persons at all times—so judgment of practices in any culture that are harmful to women is in order.

Uma Narayan examines the issue of judging other cultures, and might implicitly endorse moral relativism, though she does not take a stand on this issue (Narayan, 2002; see "Autonomy" above). Narayan accuses Western feminists of judging, without basis, women in the Sufi Pirzada community of Old Delhi who veil, to be either the dupes of patriarchy, who have only desires deformed by patriarchy, or the prisoners of patriarchy, who have extreme restrictions on their liberty, and thus a compromised agency. Narayan believes that the real story, which she knows from conversation with veiling women, is that they are bargainers with patriarchy, who have both deformed and nondeformed desires, and in the context of limitations on their liberty autonomously choose to veil. Narayan urges Western feminists to compare them to Western women who would not go out in public without makeup or with their hairy legs uncovered (Narayan 2002, 421). She worries that Western feminists overemphasize constraints and underemphasize choice in cultures other than their own, while doing the opposite when it comes to their own culture, and then concluding that "Western liberal contexts" are more empowering for women's agency and choices than other cultural contexts (Narayan 2002, 424–5). Narayan argues that we not judge veiling women according to Western standards of the good because their choices are more complex than we might believe, and because it is wrong to impose Western standards of value on others who are competent and autonomous in judging what is best for them. Although Narayan does not explicitly endorse moral relativism, she seems to reject absolute standards of value, or at least to suggest that we define them with a lot more latitude than Western feminists are wont to do.

Martha Nussbaum argues against feminists like Narayan who believe that it is condescending to judge women in developing countries who have their own view of what is good (Nussbaum 1999b). Nussbaum argues that the practice of female genital mutilation, or FGM, is objectively harmful to women both physically (e.g., repeated infections, painful intercourse, and obstructed labor and delivery) and because it destroys a fundamental human capacity to have pleasurable sex. FGM is a much worse practice than the Western practice of women's conforming to beauty standards, since, among other reasons, it involves physical force typically used against very young girls who have no chance to select an alternative, is irreversible, and is practiced on females whose autonomy may be limited by illiteracy, economic dependence, intimidation, and the like (Nussbaum 1999b, 123–4). Nussbaum endorses an objective standard of the good according to which we can judge other cultures, thereby rejecting moral relativism.

Susan Moller Okin casts the issue of multiculturalism—the claim that minority cultures should be protected by special rights (e.g., to polygamous marriage) or the right to be left alone in a liberal society—in terms of respect for diversity versus equality and other feminist norms (Okin 2004). Okin argues that feminists should be skeptical of multiculturalism because it is at odds with the basic tenets of feminism, that "women should not be disadvantaged by their sex, that they should be recognized as having human dignity equal to that of men, and that they should have the opportunity to live as fulfilling and as freely chosen lives as men can" (Okin 2004, 392). Cases that multiculturalists use to support their view typically are ones concerning the private sphere of our sexual and reproductive lives, and have a much greater impact on the lives of women than men, given women's association with the private sphere and the fact that the practices at issue are about men's control of women's lives (e.g., polygamy in Judaism, Islam, and by the Mormons, and pressuring a rape victim to marry her rapist in Latin America, rural Southeast Asia, and parts of West Africa) (Okin 2004, 195–6). Underlying these kinds of practices, and the recent legal "cultural defense" appeals in criminal cases, Okin argues, is the view that women are not human beings of equal worth to men, but are men's subordinates whose main or sole function is to serve men sexually and domestically (Okin 2004, 198). Okin concludes that minority group rights might actually contribute to women's oppression. Since she endorses an objective standard of value consistent with feminist aims, she rejects moral relativism cloaked in the guise of multiculturalism.

Louise Antony argues that feminists should not give up (objective, universal) truth at all, because one of the goals of feminism is to be able to tell the truth about women's lives and experiences, and that truth is needed to be able to assert that discrimination, misogynist violence, and the denial of each of these are facts or statements about the way the world actually is (Antony 2002, 116). Antony argues that any theory that rejects the notion of truth "deprives [itself] of any conceptual tools for distinguishing the grounds of a statement's truth from the explanation of a statement's acceptance" (Antony 2002, 115). Although her concern is epistemology, her point applies generally to feminism at large: there exist objective values without which feminist aims cannot be served.

Alison Jaggar aims to harmonize respect for cultural difference and moral objectivity (Jaggar 2004). Jaggar agrees that it is difficult and dangerous to critique another culture from an external perspective, but she believes that such critique is possible and at times warranted. She argues that while it is good for disenfranchised persons to seek support in groups with others of their kind, if the assumptions and ideologies of such groups go unchallenged, the groups face the dangers of inspiring dogmatism, excluding dissenters and those who are different, denial of autonomy, intellectual dishonesty and self-deception, elitism, and partialism. They also risk being seen as cult-like by outsiders (Jaggar 2004, 239–41). Jaggar argues that such closed communities should open their basic commitments to external scrutiny, implying that there are objective values. Jaggar believes that feminists too should subject their own beliefs and assumptions to intracultural critique so they do not fall prey to imperial arrogance and insistence on their own norms, which can happen when wealthier and more powerful groups appeal to cultural relativism (Jaggar 2004, 246). Jaggar notes that many non-Westerners have supported feminist aims, and that these groups should serve as a source for a global feminist discourse (Jaggar 2004, 242–3).

Moral skepticism

One kind of moral skepticism is "practical skepticism," or, skepticism about the rationality of acting morally. As tradition has it, the skeptic of this kind adopts a theory of practical reason according to which rational action is action that maximizes the agent's expected utility, or, the satisfaction of the agent's desires, interests, or preferences. The challenge of the moralist is to show, according to the skeptic, that every morally required action is rationally required, even when morality and self-interest conflict.

Some feminists, particularly those working within the framework of the ethic of care, have implicitly or explicitly suggested that we jettison the project of defeating the skeptic. Some have argued that the notion of reason could never be neutral, given its historical association with maleness and the view that it is supposed to control unruly "female" emotion (Lloyd 1984, Held 1990). Skepticism about reason in general extends to skepticism about reason backing morally required action. Nel Noddings rejects both moral truths and the project of justifying the rationality of adopting a moral disposition rather than of acting morally: since moral statements are not truths, she claims, they cannot be justified in the way facts are, and so there is no justification for taking the moral point of view (Noddings 1984, 50). When it comes to defeating skepticism about morally required actions, Noddings rejects the traditional approach because it aims at justification rather than motivation, which, she believes, should be central in moral theory (Noddings 1984, 95). Noddings is a care ethicist who grounds morality on the feeling of care, in particular, a person's remembrance of being cared for as a child and of caring, which forms an "ethical ideal" (Noddings 1984, 92). Care, in the case of interactions with close relatives, is a universally accessible and natural feeling (Noddings 1984, 104). Why act in morally required ways towards these people? The answer is because you love them and naturally do care for them. When it comes to strangers, a feeling of obligation arises when the agent realizes that caring is superior to other forms of relatedness, and that a caring response will enhance the agent's ethical ideal: one acts morally because one is or wants to be a moral person (Noddings 1984, 83, 50). In essence, Noddings gives an explanatory reason, not a justificatory reason, for acting morally, thereby rejecting the traditional project of skepticism.

Other feminists work within the paradigm of the traditional skeptical project, but argue for an alternative model of practical reason to that of expected utility theory. Sara Ruddick argues that mothers engage in "maternal thinking," which involves a unity of reflection, judgment, and emotion, and is neither responsive to preferences or interests nor requires the maximization of their satisfaction, but is instead responsive to demands the mother tries to satisfy for the development of a child who is acceptable to society (Ruddick 1986, 341; Hampton 1992, 222–3). But Jean Hampton argues that Ruddick's view of rational action is consistent with the expected utility theory. Hampton believes that the demands to which a mother responds might be best understood as other-regarding preferences whose mutual satisfaction may not be possible very often, as when a mother has to choose between getting up in the middle of the night to answer her baby's cries instead of enjoying a peaceful sleep (Hampton 1992, 222).

I argue for redefining the traditional view of the skeptic to capture more immoralities than self-interest when it is at odds with morality, particularly versions of sexist behavior or behavior that in some way perpetuates women's oppression, including sexist forms of malignant wickedness (doing evil for its own sake), moral indifference (knowing what it is for an act to be wrong but failing to have the appropriate negative attitude toward it due to lack of concern for others' interests), moral negligence (failing, due to ignorance, to act in accord with one's own moral principles), and even benefiting in an undeserved way from an oppressive system (Superson 2009b). A defeat of the traditional skeptic that justifies acting in morally required ways rather than self-interestedly when these are opposed leaves open the rational status of these other, non-self-interested forms of immorality. Since feminists want it to be shown that all behaviors contributing to women's oppression are irrational, they must redefine the skeptic's position such that a successful defeat would show this. I argue for redefining it in terms of privilege, which underlies all sexist immoralities. By "privilege" I mean that a person favors his interests and reasons over others and their reasons by failing to respect their intrinsic worth as persons, which is inconsistent. Thus the skeptic holds the view that rationality requires favoring one's interests and reasons over those of others. Even though the privilege model is not grounded in a theory of practical reason, it has several advantages: it does not beg the question in favor of morality by assuming the skeptic endorses moral reasons, it captures the notion that value and reasons have to do with the satisfaction of a person's desires or pleasure, it expresses the idea of advantaging oneself but in a richer way than mere self-interest, and it has a rational basis, the principle of consistency (Superson 2009b, 122). To defeat the skeptic, then, moralists need to show that rationality requires, on grounds of consistency, that one not disrespect others' humanity by privileging oneself and one's reasons over another and her reasons.[4]

Bibliography

Anderson, Clelia Smyth and Estes, Yolanda. (1998), "The Myth of the Happy Hooker: Kantian Moral Reflections on a Phenomenology of Prostitution," in Stanley G. French, Wanda Teays, and Laura M. Purdy (eds.), *Violence against Women: Philosophical Perspectives*. Ithaca, NY: Cornell University Press, 152–8.

Aristotle. (1984), *Politics*, in Jonathan Barnes (ed.), *The Complete Works of Aristotle*. Princeton, NJ: Princeton University Press.

Baier, Annette C. (1987), "Hume, the Women's Moral Theorist?" in Eva Feder Kittay and Diana T. Meyers (eds.), *Women and Moral Theory*. Savage, MD: Rowman & Littlefield Publishers, Inc., 37–55.

Bailey, Alison. (1998), "Privilege: Expanding on Marilyn Frye's 'Oppression'." *Journal of Social Philosophy* 29 (3), 104–19.

Bartky, Sandra. (1990a), "Narcissism, Femininity, and Alienation," in Sandra Lee Bartky (ed.), *Femininity and Domination: Studies in the Phenomenology of Oppression*. New York: Routledge. Reprinted from *Social Theory and Practice*, 1982, 33–44.

—. (1990b), "On Psychological Oppression," in Sandra Lee Bartky (ed.), *Femininity and Domination: Studies in the Phenomenology of Oppression*. New York: Routledge. Reprinted from *Philosophy and Women*, Wadsworth Publishing, 1979, 22–32.

Benn, Stanley I. (1985), "Wickedness." *Ethics* 95, 795–810.

Benson, Paul. (2000), "Feeling Crazy: Self-Worth and the Social Character of Responsibility," in Catriona MacKenzie and Natalie Stoljar (eds.), *Relational Autonomy: Feminist Perspectives on Autonomy, Agency, and the Social Self*. New York: Oxford University Press.

Blum, Larry, Homiak, Marcia, Housman, Judy and Scheman, Naomi. (1973–1974), "Altruism and Women's Oppression." *The Philosophical Forum: Special Issue on Women & Philosophy* 5 (1 & 2) (Fall-Winter), 222–47.

Brink, David. (1986), "Externalist Moral Realism." *Southern Journal of Philosophy* 24 supp., 23–41.

Calhoun, Cheshire. (1989), "Responsibility and Reproach." *Ethics* 99 (2), 389–406.

—. (2004), "Introduction," in Cheshire Calhoun (ed.), *Setting the Moral Compass: Essays by Women Philosophers*. New York: Oxford University Press, 3–19.

Card, Claudia. (1993), "Gender and Moral Luck," in Owen J. Flanagan and Amelie Oksenberg Rorty (eds.), *Identity, Character, and Morality: Essays in Moral Psychology*. Bradford, MA: MIT University Press, 199–218.

Cudd, Ann E. (2006), *Analyzing Oppression*. New York: Oxford University Press.

DesAutels, Peggy. (2004), "Moral Mindfulness," in Peggy DesAutels and Margaret Urban Walker (eds.), *Moral Psychology: Feminist Ethics and Social Theory*. Lanham, MD: Rowman & Littlefield Publishers, Inc, 69–81.

Dillon, Robin S. (2012) "Critical Character Theory: Toward a Feminist Perspective on 'Vice' (and 'Virtue')," in Sharon L. Crasnow and Anita M. Superson (eds.), *Out from the Shadows: Analytical Feminist Contributions to Traditional Philosophy*. New York: Oxford University Press.

Dworkin, Andrea. (1987), *Intercourse*. New York: Free Press.

Elster, Jon. (1983), "Sour Grapes," in Jon Elster (ed.), *Sour Grapes: Studies in the Subversion of Rationality*. New York: Cambridge University Press, 109–40.

Friedman, Marilyn. (1993), "Liberating Care," in Marilyn Freidman (ed.), *What Are Friends For*. Ithaca, NY: Cornell University Press, 142–83.

—. (1997), "Autonomy and Social Relationships: Rethinking the Feminist Critique," in Diana Tietjens Meyers (ed.), *Feminists Rethink the Self*. Boulder, CO: Westview Press, 40–61.

Friedman, Marilyn and Larry May. (1985), "Harming Women as a Group." *Social Theory and Practice* 11, 207–34.

Frye, Marilyn. (1983), "Oppression," in *The Politics of Reality: Essays in Feminist Theory*. Trumansburg, NY: Crossing, 1–16.

Gauthier, David. (1986), *Morals by Agreement*. New York: Oxford University Press.

Gilligan, Carol. (1982), *In a Different Voice: Psychological Theory and Women's Development*. Cambridge, MA: Harvard University Press.

Greeno, Catherine G. and Maccoby, Eleanor E. (1993), "How Different Is the 'Different Voice'?" in Mary Jeanne Larrabee (ed.), *An Ethic of Care: Feminist and Interdisciplinary Perspectives*. New York: Routledge, 193–8. Originally published in *Signs: Journal of Women in Culture and Society* 11 (1986), 310–16.

Griffin, Susan. (1981), "Rape: the All-American Crime," in Mary Vetterling-Braggin, Frederick A. Elliston, and Jane English (eds.), *Feminism and Philosophy*. Totowa, NJ: Littlefield, Adams & Co., 313–2. Originally published in *Ramparts*, September 1971, 26–35.

Hampton, Jean. (1992), "Rethinking Reason." *American Philosophical Quarterly* 29 (3), 219–36.

—. (1996), "On Instrumental Rationality," in J.B. Schneewind (ed.), *Reason, Ethics, and Society: Themes from Kurt Baier, with His Responses*, Chicago: Open Court, 84–116.

—. (1999), "Defining Wrong and Defining Rape," in Keith Burgess-Jackson (ed.), *A Most Detestable Crime*. New York: Oxford University Press, 118–56.

—. (2002), "Feminist Contractarianism," in Louise M. Antony and Charlotte E. Witt (eds.), *A Mind of One's Own: Feminist Essays on Reason and Objectivity*, 2nd ed., Boulder, CO: Westview Press, 337–68.

Hay, Carol. (2005), "Whether to Ignore Them and Spin: Moral Obligations to Resist Sexual Harassment." *Hypatia: A Journal of Feminist Philosophy*. Special Issue on *Analytical Feminism* 20(4), 94–108.

Held, Virginia. (1990), "Feminist Transformations of Moral Theory." *Philosophy and Phenomenological Research* 1, 321–44.

Herman, Barbara. (1981), "On the Value of Acting from the Motive of Duty." *Philosophical Review* 90(3), 359–82.

Hill, Thomas E., Jr. (1995), "Servility and Self-Respect," in Robin S. Dillon (ed.), *Dignity, Character, and Self-Respect*. New York: Routledge, 76–92. Reprinted from *The Monist* 57 (1973).

Hoagland, Sarah Lucia. (1991), "Some Thoughts about 'Caring'," in Claudia Card (ed.), *Feminist Ethics*. Lawrence, KS: University of Kansas Press, 246–63.

Hobbes, Thomas. 1962, *Leviathan*. Ed. Michael Oakeshott. New York: Collier Books (originally published 1651).

Jaggar, Alison M. (1983), *Feminist Politics and Human Nature*. Totowa, NJ: Rowman & Allanheld, Publishers.

—. (2004), "Globalizing Feminist Ethics," in Cheshire Calhoun (ed.), *Setting the Moral Compass: Essays by Women Philosophers*. New York: Oxford University Press, 233–55.

Kant, Immanuel. (1960), *Observations on the Feeling of the Beautiful and Sublime*. Trans. John Goldthwait. Berkeley, CA: University of California Press.

—. (1974), *Anthropologie from a Pragmatic Point of View*. Trans. Mary J. Gregor. The Hague, Netherlands: Martinus Nijhoff.

—. (1981), *Grounding for the Metaphysics of Morals*. Trans. James W. Ellington. Indianapolis: Hackett (originally published 1785).

Kittay, Eva Feder. (1999), *Love's Labor: Essays on Women, Equality, and Dependency*. New York: Routledge.

Langton, Rae. (2009), "Autonomy-Denial in Objectification," in Rae Langton (ed.), *Sexual Solipsism: Philosophical Essays on Pornography and Objectification*. New York: Oxford University Press.

Little, Margaret Olivia. (2007), "Seeing and Caring: The Role of Affect in Feminist Moral Epistemology," in Russ Shafer-Landau and Terence Cuneo (eds.), *Foundations of Ethics: An Anthology*. Malden, MA: Blackwell Publishing, 420–32. Reprinted from *Hypatia* 10(3) (Summer 1995), 117–37.

Lloyd, Genevieve. (1984), *The Man of Reason: "Male" and "Female" in Western Philosophy*. Minneapolis, MN: University of Minnesota Press.

Luria, Zella. (1993), "A Methodological Critique," in Mary Jeanne Larrabee (ed.), *An Ethic of Care: Feminist and Interdisciplinary Perspectives*. New York, Routledge, 199–203. Reprinted from *Signs: Journal of Women in Culture and Society* 11 (1986), 321–4.

Mackenzie, Catriona and Stoljar, Natalie. (2000), "Introduction: Autonomy Refigured," in Catriona Mackenzie and Natalie Stoljar (eds.), *Relational Autonomy: Feminist Perspectives on Autonomy, Agency, and the Social Self*. New York: Oxford University Press, 3–31.

MacIntosh, Peggy. (2000), "White Privilege and Male Privilege: A Personal Account of Coming to See Correspondences through Work in Women's Studies," in Anne Minas (ed.), *Gender Basics: Feminist Perspectives on Women and Men*, 2nd ed. Belmont, CA: Wadsworth, 30–8.

May, Larry. (1998a), "Sexual Harassment and Solidarity," in Larry May (ed.), *Masculinity and Morality*. Ithaca, NY: Cornell University Press, 98–115.
—. (1998b), "Socialization and Separatism," in Larry May (ed.), *Masculinity and Morality*. Ithaca, NY: Cornell University Press, 116–34.
May, Larry and Strikwerda, Robert. (1999), "Men in Groups: Collective Responsibility for Rape," in Christine Koggel (ed.), *Moral Issues in Global Perspectives*. Peterborough, Ontario, Canada: Broadview Press, 721–32. Reprinted from *Hypatia* 9 (2) (1994), 134–51.
Mill, John Stuart. (1986), *The Subjection of Women*. Buffalo, NY: Prometheus Books (originally published in 1861).
Moody-Adams, Michele M. (1991), "Gender and the Complexity of Moral Voices," in Claudia Card (ed.), *Feminist Ethics*. Lawrence, KS: University Press of Kansas, 195–212.
—. (1994), "Culture, Responsibility, and Affected Ignorance." *Ethics* 104(2) (January), 291–309.
—. (2004), "The Idea of Moral Progress," in Cheshire Calhoun (ed.), *Setting the Moral Compass: Essays by Women Philosophers*. New York: Oxford University Press, 256–72. Reprinted from *Metaphilosophy* 30 (July 1999).
Narayan, Uma. (2002), "Minds of Their Own: Choices, Autonomy, Cultural Practices, and Other Women," in Louise M. Antony and Charlotte E. Witt (eds.), *A Mind of One's Own: Feminist Essays on Reason and Objectivity*, 2nd ed. Boulder, CO: Westview Press, 418–32.
Nelson, James Lindemann. (2004), "The Social Situation of Sincerity: Austen's *Emma* and Lovibond's *Ethical Formation*," in Peggy DesAutels and Margaret Urban Walker (eds.), *Moral Psychology: Feminist Ethics and Social Theory*. Lanham, MD: Rowman & Littlefield Publishers, Inc., 83–98.
Noddings, Nel. (1984), *Caring: A Feminine Approach to Ethics and Moral Education*. Berkeley, CA: University of California Press.
Nussbaum, Martha C. (1999a), "American Women," in Martha C. Nussbaum (ed.), *Sex and Social Justice*. New York: Oxford University Press, 130–53.
—. (1999b), "Judging Other Cultures: The Case of Genital Mutilation," in Martha C. Nussbaum (ed.), *Sex and Social Justice*. New York: Oxford University Press, 118–29.
—. (1999c), "Objectification," in Martha C. Nussbaum (ed.), *Sex and Social Justice*. New York: Oxford University Press, 213–39.
Okin, Susan Moller. (2004), "Is Multiculturalism Bad for Women?," in Amy R. Baehr (ed.), *Varieties of Feminist Liberalism*. Lanham, MD: Rowman & Littlefield Publishers, Inc., 191–205.
Ruddick, Sara. (1986), "Maternal Thinking," in Marilyn Pearsall (ed.), *Women and Values: Readings in Recent Feminist Philosophy*. Belmont, CA: Wadsworth, 340–51.
Shafer-Landau, Russ and Cuneo, Terence, (eds.). (2007), *Foundations of Ethics: An Anthology*. Malden, MA: Blackwell Publishing.
Smith, Michael. (2007), "The Externalist Challenge," in Russ Shafer-Landau and Terence Cuneo (eds.), *Foundations of Ethics: An Anthology*. Malden, MA: Blackwell Publishing, 231–42. Reprinted from *The Moral Problem* (Oxford: Blackwell, 1994).
Stoljar, Natalie. (2000), "Autonomy and the Feminist Intuition," in Catriona Mackenzie and Natalie Stoljar (eds.), *Relational Autonomy: Feminist Perspectives on*

Autonomy, Agency, and the Social Self. New York: Oxford University Press, 94–123.
Superson, Anita M. (1993), "Right-Wing Women: Causes, Choices, and Blaming the Victim." *Journal of Social Philosophy* 73(14), 453–66.
—. (2004), "Privilege, Immorality, and Responsibility for Attending to the 'Facts about Humanity'." *Journal of Social Philosophy* 35(91), 34–55.
—. (2005), "Deformed Desires and Informed Desire Tests." *Hypatia A Journal of Feminist Philosophy* 20(4), 109–26.
—. (2009a), "Feminist Moral Psychology." In *Stanford Encyclopedia of Philosophy*, *http://plato.stanford.edu/contents.html*.
—. (2009b), *The Moral Skeptic*. New York: Oxford University Press.
—. (2010), "The Deferential Wife Revisited: Agency and Moral Responsibility." *Hypatia: A Journal of Feminist Philosophy* 25(2), 253–75. (On-line version at *http://onlinelibrary.wiley.com/journal/123318804/articletext)*
Tessman, Lisa. (2001), "Critical Virtue Ethics: Understanding Oppression as Morally Damaging," in Peggy DesAutels and Joanne Waugh (eds.), *Feminists Doing Ethics*. Lanham, MD: Rowman & Littlefield Publishers, Inc., 79–99.
—. (2005), *Burdened Virtues: Virtue Ethics for Liberatory Struggles*. New York: Oxford University Press.
Thomas, Laurence. (1996), "Becoming an Evil Society." *Political Theory* 24(92), 271–94.
Tronto, Joan. (1993), "Beyond Gender Difference to a Theory of Care," in Mary Jeanne Larrabee (ed.), *An Ethic of Care: Feminist and Interdisciplinary Perspectives*. New York: Routledge, 240–57. Reprinted from *Signs: Journal of Women in Culture and Society* 12 (1987), 644–63.
Tuana, Nancy. (1992), *Woman and the History of Philosophy*. New York: Paragon House.
Walker, Lawrence J. (1993), "Sex Differences in the Development of Moral Reasoning: A Critical Review," in Mary Jeanne Larrabee (ed.), *An Ethic of Care: Feminist and Interdisciplinary Perspectives*. New York: Routledge, 157–76. Reprinted from *Child Development* 55 (1984), 677–91.
Westlund, Andrea C. (2003), "Selflessness and Responsibility for Self: Is Deference Compatible with Autonomy?" *The Philosophical Review* 112 (4) (October 2003), 483–523.

Part II

New Directions in Ethics

11 Moral Particularism

Pekka Väyrynen

Moral particularism, as it figures in the past few decades of moral philosophy, is not a single sharply defined position, but a family of views, united by an opposition to giving moral principles a fundamental or important role in morality.[1] As such, particularism challenges the project of ambitious moral theory in the traditional style of Kant, Mill, and virtually every other major figure in the history of moral philosophy. *Moral generalism* is, likewise, a family of views, united by the thought that moral principles do play some such important role.

This chapter first distinguishes two central roles which moral principles have traditionally been asked to play in moral theory and three different forms which opposition to principles playing either of those roles has taken in recent literature. It then surveys some of the leading arguments for and against thinking that principles play these central roles.

Two Roles of Principles: Standards and Guides

What it means to deny that principles play some important role in morality depends on what a moral principle is. Some important features of principles seem clear. Principles by their very nature involve some kind of generality, and a specifically moral principle presumably must deploy a moral concept. If a moral principle is to be something that can be thought about, accepted, doubted, or denied, it must also be a proposition or at least expressible as one.

An account of what a moral principle is should not, however, require any specific normative content. For instance, consequentialists and nonconsequentialists in normative ethics can all be generalists. Philosophers otherwise as diverse as Plato, Aquinas, Kant, Mill, Sidgwick, Moore, Ross, Hare, and Rawls debate whether the morally right thing to do is what brings about the best outcome available, but agree that whatever the morally right thing to do may be, it can be captured in general principles.

Nor should an account of what a moral principle is require any specific metaethical account of moral propositions or their subject matter. For instance,

Mill, Moore, and Hare have significant differences regarding the semantics, metaphysics, and epistemology of morality. In semantics, for example, Hare holds the expressivist view that moral principles express general prescriptions or other noncognitive attitudes (perhaps in a propositional guise), whereas Mill and Moore hold the cognitivist view that moral principles are in the business of capturing general moral facts. But they all count as generalists in virtue of accepting some or other form of utilitarianism as the fundamental principle of morality.

These two points illustrate how the generalism-particularism debate concerns the structure of morality more than its specific normative content or metaethical foundations.

Looking at the roles which moral theorists have asked principles to play in morality provides a grip on what the sort of moral principles over which generalists and particularists disagree would need to be like. Moral theories can be thought of as having both a *theoretical* and a *practical* function. First, moral theories, like theories in general, aim to *explain* certain phenomena. Those who take morality seriously wish to understand not merely what things are morally right and wrong, good and bad, just and unjust, but also *why* they are so. Second, moral theories aim to *guide action*. Those who take morality seriously wish to figure out what things are right and wrong, beneficial and harmful, cruel and kind, before action, not only in hindsight.[2] What generalists and particularists dispute is whether general principles serve any fundamental theoretical or practical function in morality beyond functioning merely as useful rules of thumb. Let us now consider these two roles in more detail.

Principles might play an important theoretical role in morality by explaining why things have the moral features they do. These are not "brute" facts: the moral features of things "result" from other, typically nonmoral, features; for instance, some wrong actions are wrong in virtue of involving lying, others because they cause pain, and so on.[3] One thing that principles can claim to do is to provide a general connection between a given moral feature and the features or conditions in virtue of which things have it. To count as genuine principles, such "standards" for the correct application of moral concepts must have *modal* and *explanatory* implications.[4]

Genuine moral standards have modal implications because they must support counterfactual conditionals ("If P were the case, then Q would be the case"); moreover, at least fundamental or nonderivative principles are usually regarded as necessary, not contingent. If a claim like "It is wrong to harm others" were correct merely as a summary of actual past harmings, it would not support the counterfactual "If I were to harm another person, that would be wrong." If the former claim were also a necessary moral principle, it would entail something logically yet stronger, namely that harming others is wrong in all possible worlds.

Some moral claims which have the requisite modal character can be accepted on all hands. If "murder" were defined or analyzed as "wrongful killing," then "Murder is wrong" would be a trivial analytic truth which no one, particularists included, need deny.[5] Similarly, some necessary moral truths, such as "Any action that is not permissible is wrong," are uninformative and not material for an interesting debate. But the generalism-particularism debate should leave it open whether some moral truths might be substantive and yet analytic. Particularists would protest if told that some such principle as Kant's fundamental Categorical Imperative is true, irrespective of whether it were held to be an analytic truth. Similar neutrality applies to the epistemic status of principles. Many (though not all) generalists and particularists agree that basic moral knowledge is a priori. That gives one way to explain how we can have moral knowledge of hypothetical cases and come to know whether what we are considering doing is right or wrong before doing it.[6] But particularists would protest if told that some such principle as the principle of utility is true, irrespective of whether it were held to be knowable a priori.

Other moral claims which have the requisite modal character fail to be explanatory. Consider the widely accepted claim that the moral "supervenes" on the nonmoral.[7] This is to say that no two objects can differ in any moral respect without some nonmoral difference between the objects or the broader world(s) they inhabit. Assume that moral nihilism is false: some things are right and wrong, good and bad, and so on. And take a right action and an exhaustive description of the world in which it occurs (including the action itself). On these assumptions, supervenience entails that, necessarily, any action that is just like this one is also right. Particularists need not oppose necessary "supervenience functions" of this sort. An exhaustive description of a right act will include many facts which are irrelevant to whether it is right, such as having been done east of Hollywood. (Such a description may also be too complex to be a possible object of thought to cognitively limited humans). By contrast, a genuine principle should refer only to features which are directly relevant to whether the moral feature in question obtains.[8]

Principles understood as standards come in two kinds, corresponding to a distinction between "contributory" and "overall" moral claims.[9] Some moral claims concern a contribution of some factor to the moral character of a particular action or situation, whereas others express an overall moral assessment which is a function of all the various contributions. A principle may advance either sort of claim. Claims about moral reasons, as claims about what considerations count in favor or against what actions or attitudes, are one example of contributory claims. Another are pro tanto moral claims to the effect that something is right or wrong, or good or bad, or what one has reason to do or not do, *so far as* its being of a particular kind (promise-keeping, truth-telling, killing, etc.) goes. A prominent example of pro tanto moral claims are what W. D. Ross calls "prima facie" duties.[10] This distinction is required because individual contributory claims rarely determine what one ought to do all things considered. Reasons can be opposed (most things have some features that count in their favor but others that count against them) and outweighed (considerations on one side are stronger than those on the other).

Overall moral assessment is determined jointly by the various morally relevant factors. The way such factors combine in different contexts to do this is clearly quite complex. Consider, as but one example, conflicts between the duty to keep one's promises and the duty to help others. Sometimes, when a promise is trivial but the potential benefits to others are great, the right thing to do overall may be to break the promise. But sometimes, when a lot is at stake in the promise but the potential benefits to others are minor, the right thing to do overall may be to keep the promise. In either case, the balance of reasons may shift yet again depending on whether any further morally relevant factors are in play and their importance. This may not happen in any straightforwardly additive fashion.[11]

Contributory and overall principles play importantly different roles in the generalism-particularism debate. Many otherwise different classical moral theorists—Bentham, Mill, and Kant alike—agree that it is possible to spell out what one ought to do all things considered in general principles, despite all the complexity in how such facts are determined. Others, such as Ross and his plurality of "prima facie" duties, argue that while it is possible to specify principles determining how individual nonmoral features of circumstances contribute to their overall moral nature, the way these contributory factors combine to determine overall moral assessment is much too complex and sensitive to context to be captured by anything worth calling principles.

In contrast to both camps, contemporary particularists argue that the ways in which the nonmoral features of particular circumstances combine to make something morally relevant in the first place and determine its valence as morally positive or negative (and not merely to determine its weight relative to other relevant factors) is too complex and sensitive to context to be captured even in principles concerning how morality works at the contributory level, let alone in principles concerning how it works at the level of overall moral assessment. This argument will be discussed below as the "argument from holism." The point for now is that debates about whether there are overall or merely contributory principles are typically classified as family disputes within generalism, whereas particularists are united by their opposition to principles of both kinds.[12]

Turning now to the practical function of morality, principles might play an important practical role by providing guidance for moral reasoning, decision, and action in the face of moral novelty, uncertainty, and difficulty. A principle counts as a valuable "guide" if people—or, at least, conscientious moral agents who care about living up to the demands of morality can more reliably act in morally valuable ways and avoid immoral actions with its assistance than without it.[13] A reliable guide for "acting well" in this sense need not be an "algorithmic" decision procedure which will achieve this goal without fail and can be applied to particular cases without any further exercise of judgment.[14] Judgment is necessary (though fallible) even in the application of both the moral and nonmoral concepts which figure in principles. (To use a famous example by H. L. A. Hart, does a war-memorial statue of a Jeep count as a "vehicle" with respect to the rule "No vehicles in the park"?) This is especially clear with principles that require varied implementation in different cases (such as "Teachers should set work which is adjusted to each student's level of ability").[15] As we will see, particularists nonetheless argue that, even allowing the need for judgment, relying on principles in deliberation is often a hindrance to acting well.

Particularists' opposition to moral principles does not extend to everything one could decide to call a principle. They can accept principles understood as rules of thumb or other heuristic aides for deliberation. For instance, they can grant that how past situations have turned out morally could be summarized in true generalizations which may be useful as one input to future deliberations. Such summary generalizations will lack the requisite modal and explanatory implications. They are also in principle dispensable in deliberation. Hence they make no claim to play a fundamental theoretical or practical role.

Three Forms of Particularism

We have seen that particularism is defined by opposition to general principles concerning the contributory and the overall. There are three main forms which opposition to principles—whether as theoretical standards, or as practical guides, or both—may take within an antinihilist agreement that some substantive moral claims are correct and knowable. One is that there *are no* true or valid moral principles. The second, an evidential variant of the first, is that there is *no good evidence* for the existence of true or valid moral principles.

The third option is that morality *in no way depends* on the existence of moral principles. A leading particularist, Jonathan Dancy, puts this idea as follows: "The possibility of moral thought and judgment do not depend upon the provision of a suitable supply of moral principles."[16] This position is logically weaker than the first two: it can allow that morality displays some patterns that can be captured in principles, while denying that morality must be so or that anything in morality hangs on it.

In the course of the debate, some particularists have moved towards the third form of particularism.[17] What exactly it says turns on what kind of relation of dependence is at issue and what "moral thought and judgment" is taken to cover.[18] Many generalists allow that there can be moral agents who do not accept or even implicitly rely on moral principles, just as many particularists allow that some agents (however mistakenly) follow principles. What these generalists would claim is not that such agents are incapable of engaging in moral thought and judgment, but that they are unlikely to get their moral judgments reliably right.

The third position counts as a form of particularism about standards so long as it denies that particular moral facts depend for their existence, or moral judgments for their correctness, on principles. And it counts as a form of particularism about guides so long as it denies that reliable moral guidance or the practical accessibility of moral truths depends on principles. These claims do not require that the very conditions of moral thought and judgment depend on principles. But if they are correct, principles will still have a hard time playing any fundamental role in explaining, or guiding us to, particular moral facts.

Arguments for and against Particularism

Let us now review some main arguments that have been offered for and against moral particularism, beginning with the theoretical role of principles. Consider first those particularists who claim that there are no true principles or no good evidence for their existence. Generalists could settle their debate with those particularists in one of two ways.

One strategy is to try to establish some specific moral principle. But this strategy is not likely to provide a distinctive or swift resolution to debates about particularism. Historical and contemporary normative ethics already contain ample discussion of the merits of various specific principles. To any particular candidate, a particularist could reply that the spirit of generalism requires a supply of principles to cover the whole of morality. So establishing one specific principle helps the generalist cause only if it is an overarching overall principle like the principle of utility or Kant's Categorical Imperative. But one thing that the long-standing debates in normative ethics have made clear is that although any overarching overall principle which purports to be substantive and explanatory will be highly controversial, such principles also often prove to be resourceful in dealing with putative counterexamples.

A different strategy is to pursue some general considerations which are relevant to the role of principles in morality, whatever their specific content. Some argue that morality requires some principles, whatever their specific content, on the basis of metaethical claims to the effect that competence with moral concepts, and therefore their deployment in genuine moral judgments, requires at least an implicit or tacit grasp of some moral principles.[19] This implies that there are some explanatory principles which are conceptual truths, even if it is difficult to work out what they are or we are incompetent in doing so. Hence its plausibility depends on the prospects for substantive and yet conceptual moral truths (to which generalism as such has no particular commitment, as noted earlier), its response to G. E. Moore's "Open Question Argument,"[20] and more.

The most prominent argument for particularism also appeals to a general claim that bears on the role of principles in morality. This is known as the argument from "holism." The holism at issue concerns an important kind of context-sensitivity of morality, and reasons for action generally, which bears on the theoretical role of principles in explaining particular moral facts. According to holism about reasons for action, a consideration that is a reason to φ in one set of circumstances may be no reason at all, or even a reason not to φ, in some different set of circumstances. Contrary to "atomism" about reasons, it is not part of what it is to be a reason for action that if something is a reason to φ in a particular context, then there is something that is a reason to φ in every other context.[21] Analogous holisms can be formulated for other contributory notions, such as right-making and good-making factors. One example is that although actions which cause pleasure are often the better for it, they are in no way better when they bring pleasure to a sadist delighting in his victim's pain; another is that even if the fact that I promised to do something is often a reason to do it, that fact may be no reason at all when the promise was given under duress or fraud.[22] Particularists argue that if reasons are contextually variable in the way that holism implies, then general principles are too blunt an instrument to capture their behavior across contexts. Generalists have taken issue with this argument with respect both to its soundness, contesting holism, and to its validity.

Some generalists argue that holism is false because morality is based on some factors which are or generate invariable reasons. Perhaps, for instance, morality is based on virtues and vices, and these give rise to invariable reasons. The idea would be that whether an action is right or good is determined by whether it is generous, courageous, just, and so on, and if something is generous, courageous, just, and so on, that is invariably a reason to do it. This view can grant to holists that considerations such as lying might have variable moral import; perhaps not all lies need involve dishonesty, which is the real and invariable reason why lying is wrong, when it is.[23] In reply, some particularists deny that specific virtues and vices are invariably relevant in the same way (perhaps actions can sometimes be worse for being honest or considerate), whereas others limit holism to nonmoral considerations.[24]

Other arguments against holism target the distinction that holism requires between considerations that are reasons (e.g., that I promised) and other features of the broader context which can be relevant to whether some consideration is a reason without themselves being reasons. Reasons are thus distinguished from "defeaters," whose presence makes something that would in their absence have been a reason not be one (perhaps, for example, that my promise was given under duress), and from "enablers," whose presence is required to make something that would in their absence not have been a reason be one (such as that what I promised to do is itself morally permissible).[25] Reasons can be variable in the way holism requires only if they depend on further background conditions which may vary by context.

Some generalists object that the examples in support of holism are ineffective because they specify reasons incompletely. Full reasons for action include the background conditions which holism classifies as defeaters or enablers.[26] Thus the reason for me to fix your bike is not simply that I promised; it is that I made an uncoerced and informed promise to fix your bike, and fixing your bike is not itself morally impermissible, and so on for any other relevant features of the background context. If reasons are composed in this inclusive way, it becomes less plausible that what is a reason in one context may be no reason at all or even an opposite reason in a different context. But this debate fast becomes difficult to track, because both sides rely on different judgments about what exactly is the reason in a particular case in the first place; hence the debate cannot be settled by examples alone.[27] Those judgments may also be unreliable in predictable ways, and hence a poor basis for arguments either way.[28]

Other generalists object to a claim which some particularists associate with holism, namely that *any* consideration whatever can be a reason, given suitable circumstances.[29] This threatens to "flatten the moral landscape" by jettisoning the strong intuition that considerations like killing, infliction of pain, and truth-telling have a greater and deeper moral import than considerations like shoelace color or hair parting. Some particularists seek to capture this difference by arguing that some considerations, "default" reasons, need no enablers and hence are reasons unless some defeater prevents them from being so, whereas others, "non-default" reasons, are not reasons unless enabled by some features of the context.[30] Issues in this debate include which of the various possible notions of a default reason (e.g., pragmatic, epistemic, and metaphysical) particularism needs, which of these notions are plausible, and whether particularism offers the best account of any plausible default reasons that there might be.[31]

A different response to the argument from holism is to argue that holism is compatible with generalism and hence does not support particularism even if true. A common claim here is that principles concerning moral reasons can incorporate as part of their content the very contextual variability of reasons which follows from holism.[32] Principles can make reference not only to features which provide reasons but also, in some or other fashion, to contextual features like defeaters and enablers. For instance, one could endorse a principle like "Necessarily, that an action promotes pleasure is a reason to do it, unless the pleasure is sadistic." This specifies the fact that an action promotes pleasure as a reason for doing it and the condition that the pleasure is not sadistic as something which must obtain in any particular case in order for the fact that an action promotes pleasure to be a reason to do it.

One particularist reply to this objection is that the argument from holism is indirect. Although holism is compatible with generalism, particularism provides a better explanation of holism. Given holism, it would be a mere "cosmic accident," rather than anything supporting the dependence of morality on principles, if reasons behaved in a way that can be captured in general principles.[33] How exactly such an indirect argument is to be understood is a complicated issue.[34] Some generalists offer accounts of moral principles according to which the best overall explanation of particular moral facts under holism still relies on principles.[35] Others argue, on more epistemological grounds, that the way in which enablers, defeaters, and all the other distinctions and complications on which holism insists work out in reasoning can in fact be predicted and explained by general and independently plausible principles.[36]

The force of these objections to the validity of the argument from holism depends less on the extent to which morality is context-sensitive than on what exactly is required by all the other conditions for being a principle. Thus an increasingly active topic of discussion is whether general principles can capture all the context-sensitivity which they must capture to accommodate holism and still retain the requisite modal implications, count as appropriately explanatory of particular moral facts, and so on.

The argument from holism remains a central focus of debates about particularism because discussions of it bear on a wide range of important further issues. One is whether genuine principles must hold without exception or may include some kind of hedges. Generalists can try to accommodate holism in two different ways depending on this issue.

One strategy is to pursue "unhedged" principles which enumerate the potential defeaters and enablers. The idea is that it is possible to complete a list of the requisite qualifications and exceptions, thus arriving at least at contributory principles which hold without exception.[37] An example might be that the fact that one promised to do something will always be a reason to do it, provided that the promise was informed and uncoerced, requires nothing morally impermissible, has not been canceled by the promisee, and _____ (where the blank stands for all the further relevant features, whatever they may be).[38]

The success of this strategy requires that the list of the potential defeaters and enablers is finite. This claim has been defended by arguments from moral epistemology. One is that if knowledge of what is morally right and wrong in particular cases is possible (as particularists agree it is), then the idea that moral facts are not brute can be used to support generalism.[39] If the moral features of things result from their other features (such as that they are cases of lying, killing, and so on), then moral knowledge in particular cases requires appropriate sensitivity to these underlying features. Under holism this requires sensitivity not only to considerations which are reasons but also to the absence of various potential defeaters and the presence of various enablers, defeaters for defeaters, and the like. Unless there were only finitely many factors for moral standards to list and for us to check, cognitively limited beings like us humans could not have moral knowledge, since we could not reliably judge whether various considerations are undefeated reasons.[40] But more remains to be said about why epistemological considerations should constrain the complexity of moral facts.

A different strategy is to allow that the list of potential exceptions and qualifications might be open-ended and not fully specifiable, but argue that general moral claims which are hedged in some way need not thereby fall short of other requirements on principles.[41] To be sure, certain ways of hedging principles do trivialize them. If "Breaking promises is wrong, other things being equal" amounted merely to "Breaking promises is wrong, except when it is not," it could not explain when or why breaking promises is wrong. But many philosophers accept that the special sciences, such as biology and psychology, feature genuine laws which permit exceptions. Some argue that the same is true of morality: such claims as "In suitable conditions, lying is wrong" or "All else equal, pain is bad" can state principles even if there is nothing wrong with some lies or nothing bad about some instances of pain, so long as their hedge clauses can be given substantive content. This grants to particularists that substantive moral generalities may be subject to exceptions, but not that there are no genuine principles.

The success of this strategy requires an account of how hedged principles can be explanatory if they permit exceptions and how grasping them can improve our reliability in detecting reasons, defeaters, enablers, and the like. On this score, some take the "unexceptional" cases where pain is bad, lying wrong, etc., as basic and argue that exceptions can then be explained in terms of deviations from them.[42] But explanation might run deeper: just as the moral status of an action (as right or wrong, for instance) requires explanation in terms of its other features, why those other features contribute to its moral status as they do might itself require explanation; these might not be brute facts either. For instance, if some government policy is bad because it increases the inequality of well-being, perhaps there should also be some explanation of why such inequality has negative moral significance in the first place. (One might coherently wonder why inequality is not morally irrelevant instead.) Such an explanation might well turn on features which are not manifested by all instances of inequality. For instance, perhaps unequal distributions of well-being are bad when and because of some such deeper moral flaws as that they are unfair or not to everyone's benefit. Exceptional cases might then be explained in the same stroke by the absence of the very same features whose presence explains why inequality is bad, when it is. Perhaps inequality as such is not bad when those who have less are worse off through a fault or choice of their own (in which case the inequality is not unfair) or when it makes everyone better off than they would otherwise be. Some generalists argue that the best account of this kind of explanation delivers principles which incorporate the common explanatory basis of both moral reasons and their enabling and defeating conditions.[43] More remains to be said here as well. For instance, how the notion of explanation is best understood in ethics remains controversial.[44]

Let us now turn to arguments concerning principles in their practical role as guides. Some of these are corollaries of theoretical considerations such as the argument from holism. If moral reasons were context-sensitive in some way that principles cannot capture, then relying on principles for guidance might be more likely than not to make agents go morally astray. It might, for instance, encourage the thought that if a consideration was a reason to φ in one case, then it will be a reason to φ in others, whereas if holism is true, the consideration *can* make a moral difference in other cases, too, but is not guaranteed to matter.[45] Generalism is, however, hurt by this argument only if it is incompatible with holism.

A different worry is that even if principles can capture holism, they might be able to do so only by becoming too complex to be adequate guides. But, again, the roles of principles as standards and as guides are distinct.[46] A rule that is too simple to be accurate and explanatory with respect to all actual and possible cases in its scope might still be a valuable guide precisely if it oversimplifies in useful ways, even if it also sometimes leads to error.[47] For instance, "Killing is wrong" can be a reliable heuristic guide in the actual world even if what is fundamentally wrong with killing is some more specific feature not possessed by all killings and even if most killings are permissible in hypothetical Mad Max worlds.

Other particularist arguments are more directly practical. Some particularists claim that relying on principles tends to direct our attention only to the features which already figure in our principles and we may thus miss morally relevant features which we would have noticed, had we only given the details and nuances of the particular case the kind of attentive examination which particularists think can be sufficient for reliably acting well. So they claim that, at least in imperfect humans, relying on principles instead of cultivating the kind of moral sensitivity that marks the virtuous person easily breeds moral laziness, rigidity, or narrow-mindedness. They recommend "principle abstinence" as an antidote.[48]

Some generalists respond that principles are more useful than anything particularism offers in ensuring the benefits of interpersonal assurance, coordination, and the like.[49] Others respond, more directly to the point of the objection, that principles may be able to provide reliable guidance even if their guidance is fallible and does not take the form of a rigid checklist of considerations. Generalists can agree that the kinds of sensitivity to reasons and skill of judgment on which particularists insist is necessary (though perhaps not sufficient) for acting well, and they can accommodate the evidence from cognitive science that people's moral decisions are often not consciously based on principles.[50] Acceptance of principles might instead be best understood as informing and shaping one's responsiveness to reasons and bringing with it a commitment to further cultivating moral sensitivity and judgment.

One challenge to particularists is to explain how we are able to learn from moral experience, as we plainly are, if not by coming to grasp generally applicable principles. The typical reply is that experience can inform our judgments in new cases by telling us what sorts of features *can* be morally relevant and what sort of relevance these various features *can* have in different cases. But getting from such information to accurate judgments of particular cases would seem to be quite complicated under particularism. So the worry arises whether particularists can offer valuable guidance to that multitude of us who are still trying to refine our moral sensitivities and judgment and advance on our path towards practical wisdom.

Particularists regard describing someone as "a person of principle" as criticism, not praise. But relying on principles which are more than mere rules of thumb for guidance need not mean dogmatism, rigidity, or narrow-mindedness. As a view about the structure of morality, generalism has no commitment to any particular substantive view about the content of the correct moral principles. Thus it need not recommend people to adhere dogmatically to the principles they accept and close their minds to moral improvement.

Fundamentalists and fanatics aside, many people are uncertain about at least some of the moral views they hold and regard some others as capable of refinement and improvement. Generalists no less than particularists can acknowledge that our actual moral outlooks are works in progress and that resolving uncertainty, error, and disagreements about particular moral principles requires thinking hard about a wide range of notoriously difficult and controversial concrete moral problems. Both can agree that the best remedy for poor moral judgment is better moral judgment. But as with sex education, so with moral principles: teaching abstinence may well not be the best policy.[51]

References

Berker, Selim. (2007), "Particular Reasons." *Ethics* 118, 109–39.

Crisp, Roger. (2000), "Particularizing Particularism," in Hooker and Little (2000), 23–47.

Cullity, Garrett. (2002), "Particularism and Presumptive Reasons." *Proceedings of the Aristotelian Society*, supplementary volume 76, 169–90.

Dancy, Jonathan. (1993), *Moral Reasons*. Oxford: Blackwell.

—. (2000), "The Particularist's Progress," in Hooker and Little (2000), 130–56.

—. (2004), *Ethics without Principles*. Oxford: Clarendon Press.

Dworkin, Gerald. (1995), "Unprincipled Ethics." *Midwest Studies in Philosophy* 20, 224–39.
Gert, Bernard. (1998), *Morality: Its Nature and Justification.* Oxford: Oxford University Press.
Hooker, Brad. (2000), "Moral Particularism: Wrong and Bad," in Hooker and Little (2000), 1–22.
—. (2008), "Particularism and the Real World," in Lance, Potrĉ, and Strahovnik (2008), 12–30.
Hooker, Brad and Little, Margaret (eds.). (2000), *Moral Particularism.* Oxford: Clarendon Press.
Horty, John F. (2007), "Reasons as Defaults." *Philosophers' Imprint* 7 (3), http://www.philosophersimprint.org/007003.
Jackson, Frank, Pettit, Philip, and Smith, Michael. (2000), "Ethical Particularism and Patterns," in Hooker and Little (2000), 79–99.
Kagan, Shelly. (1988), "The Additive Fallacy." *Ethics* 99, 5–31.
Lance, Mark, and Little, Margaret. (2006a), "Particularism and Anti-Theory," in David Copp (ed.), *The Oxford Handbook of Ethical Theory.* Oxford: Oxford University Press, 567–94.
—. (2006b), "Defending Moral Particularism," in James Dreier (ed.), *Contemporary Debates in Moral Theory.* Oxford: Blackwell, 305–21.
—. (2007), "Where the Laws Are," in Russ Shafer-Landau (ed.), *Oxford Studies in Metaethics*, vol. 2. Oxford: Oxford University Press, 49–71.
Lance, Mark, Potrĉ, Matjaž, and Strahovnik, Vojko (eds.). (2008), *Challenging Moral Particularism.* London: Routledge.
Leibowitz, Uri. (2009), "A Defence of a Particularist Research Programme." *Ethical Theory and Moral Practice* 12, 181–99.
—. (2011), "Scientific Explanation and Moral Explanation." *Noûs* 45, 472–503.
Little, Margaret. (2000), "Moral Generalities Revisited," in Hooker and Little (2000), 276–304.
McDowell, John. (1979), "Virtue and Reason." *The Monist* 62, 331–50.
McKeever, Sean, and Ridge, Michael. (2005), "What Does Holism Have to Do with Moral Particularism?" *Ratio* 18, 93–103.
—. (2006), *Principled Ethics: Generalism as a Regulative Ideal.* Oxford: Clarendon Press.
McLaughlin, Brian, and Bennett, Karen. (2008), "Supervenience." *The Stanford Encyclopedia of Philosophy (Fall 2008 Edition)*, ed. Edward N. Zalta, http://plato.stanford.edu/archives/fall2008/entries/supervenience.
McNaughton, David. (1988), *Moral Vision.* Oxford: Blackwell.
McNaughton, David, and Rawling, Piers. (2000), "Unprincipled Ethics," in Hooker and Little (2000), 256–75.
Moore, G. E. (1903/1993), *Principia Ethica*, revised edition, ed. Thomas Baldwin. Cambridge: Cambridge University Press.
O'Neill, Onora. (1996), *Towards Justice and Virtue.* Cambridge: Cambridge University Press.
Peacocke, Christopher. (2004), "Moral Rationalism." *Journal of Philosophy* 101, 499–526.
Pietroski, Paul. (1993), "Prima Facie Obligations, *Ceteris Paribus* Laws in Moral Theory." *Ethics* 103, 489–515.

Raz, Joseph. (2000), "The Truth in Particularism," in Hooker and Little (2000), 48–78.
—. (2006), "The Trouble with Particularism (Dancy's Version)." *Mind* 115, 99–120.
Robinson, Luke. (2006), "Moral Holism, Moral Generalism, and Moral Dispositionalism." *Mind* 115, 331–60.
Ross, W. D. (1930), *The Right and the Good*. Oxford: Clarendon Press.
Schroeder, Mark. (2009), "A Matter of Principle." *Noûs* 43, 568–80.
—. (2011), "Holism, Weight, and Undercutting." *Noûs* 45, 328–44.
Strandberg, Caj. (2008), "Particularism and Supervenience," in Russ Shafer-Landau (ed.), *Oxford Studies in Metaethics*, vol. 3. Oxford: Oxford University Press, 129–58.
Stratton-Lake, Philip. (2000), *Kant, Duty, and Moral Worth*. London: Routledge.
Sunstein, Cass. (2005), "Moral Heuristics." *Behavioral and Brain Sciences* 28, 531–42.
Väyrynen, Pekka. (2004), "Particularism and Default Reasons." *Ethical Theory and Moral Practice* 7, 53–79.
—. (2006), "Moral Generalism: Enjoy in Moderation." *Ethics* 116, 707–41.
—. (2008), "Usable Moral Principles," in Lance, Potrĉ, and Strahovnik (2008), 75–106.
—. (2009a), "Normative Appeals to the Natural." *Philosophy and Phenomenological Research* 79, 279–314.
—. (2009b), "A Theory of Hedged Moral Principles," in Russ Shafer-Landau (ed.), *Oxford Studies in Metaethics*, vol. 4. Oxford: Oxford University Press, 91–132.

12 Experimental Ethics

Thomas Nadelhoffer and Walter Sinnott-Armstrong

Experimental ethics involves performing or citing experiments in order to explore issues in metaethics, moral theory, and applied ethics.. The contrasting method is a priori reflection or "armchair speculation," as critics call it. However, experimental moral philosophers probably could not entirely avoid a priori reflection, and they need not do so, because experiments can complement reflection. Experimental moral philosophers often use experiments not to replace traditional philosophical reflection but, instead, to confirm or raise doubts about reflections by themselves or others.

In drawing philosophical lessons from empirical results, experimental moral philosophers do not have to commit the dreaded "naturalistic fallacy" (Moore) or try to jump the chasm between "is" and "ought" (Hume), because they can admit either that experimental results provide evidence but do not entail normative conclusions or that normative premises are needed to supplement experimental results before reaching any normative conclusion. Experiments can also be used to test empirical assumptions of ethical or metaethical theories and to determine whether humans are able to comply with the standards of various moral theories. In those cases, empirical findings are used only to challenge a normative claim by challenging its presuppositions and not to support any positive normative conclusion.

As a general method, experimental ethics can be applied to a wide variety of issues in substantive moral theory (such as whether demanding forms of consequentialism are defensible), practical ethics (such as which patients understand their choices when they consent to medical procedures), moral semantics (such as whether moral speakers take themselves to be referring to real or objective moral facts or properties), and the nature of morality (such as its function as revealed by its evolution). We will focus on only three topics that have been central to experimental ethics: moral intuitions, moral internalism, and virtue.

Moral Intuitions, Emotion, and Framing

Moral philosophers have deployed and worried about moral intuitions since ancient Greece (see Stratton-Lake 2003). Moral psychologists began to study moral intuitions with strict experimental methods only in the late twentieth century. Whether these two groups are talking about the same thing depends on what they count as a moral intuition.

The term "moral intuition" is used in many ways. (1) Some moral philosophers and psychologists use it to refer to moral seemings—that is, reactions with moral content that may or may not be endorsed or believed (Tolhurst 1998). In this use, a person might be said to have a moral intuition of wrongness when she feels guilty even if she does not believe that she did anything wrong and even if she rejects her feelings of guilt as unjustified or even irrational. (2) Others restrict the term "moral intuition" to moral beliefs, and they count any immediate (or direct or noninference-based) moral belief as a moral intuition. Moral intuitions then include (but are not limited to) moral beliefs that one holds momentarily and gives up easily. (3) Still others include an immediate moral belief in the class of moral intuitions only if it has additional nonepistemic features, such as resulting from reflection or being stable and strong in the sense of resisting change and counterevidence (see, for example, Audi 2004 on reflection). (4) Some philosophers add that real moral intuitions must have certain epistemic properties, such as truth, probability, or justification.

To study moral intuitions of this fourth kind (4), researchers would need to determine which moral beliefs are true, probable, or justified. To study moral intuitions of the third kind (3), experimenters would need to determine how long and how strongly their subjects hold the tested moral beliefs. Most experimental ethicists avoid these difficulties by studying only moral intuitions of the first two kinds. Hence, we will use the term "moral intuition" in the second way (2) to refer to any immediate (that is, direct or noninference-based) moral belief (and then immediate moral reactions that fall short of moral beliefs can be called "moral seemings").

Various models of moral intuitions have been proposed by psychologists as well as philosophers. One "Rawlsian" model claims that perception of an act, situation, or story triggers unconscious computations that produce a moral judgment that in turn leads to emotional reactions. This model is sometimes developed as a "linguistic analogy," which claims a universal moral grammar much like the universal grammar postulated by Chomsky for natural languages (see Harman 1999a, Dwyer 1999, Mikhail 2007 and 2011, and Hauser et al. 2008). The main evidence for this model is drawn from surveys of responses to moral conflicts.

A competing "Humean" model claims that perception of an act, situation, or story causes emotional responses that then in turn produce moral intuitions.

Emotion is supposed to be a cause rather than an effect of moral judgment. Haidt has championed this model, using correlational studies (e.g., Haidt 1993) and manipulations of emotions by hypnosis or environment (e.g., Wheatley and Haidt 2005, Schnall et al. 2008, and Valdesolo and DeSteno 2006). Additional evidence for the causal role of emotion comes from patient studies (Koenigs et al. 2007, Ciaramelli et al. 2007, and Mendez et al. 2005; for a critical response, see Huebner et al. 2009.)

The third model combines emotion and reasoning into a dual-process model. This model has been championed by Joshua Greene. on the basis of fMRI experiments (2001, 2004, 2008a) and cognitive load studies (2008b). This model upends traditional philosophical classifications, because Kant claims that moral judgments are (or could or should be) based on pure reason, and consequentialism developed out of a sentimentalist tradition, but characteristically Kantian or deontological judgments are tied to brain areas associated with emotion, and consequence-based judgments are tied to brain areas associated with more "rational" processes, such as working memory. (For critical responses, see Berker 2009 and Kamm 2009.) More specifically, Greene argued that "personal" moral dilemmas, which usually lead to deontological moral judgments, evoke certain emotions that function as alarms to prevent or oppose decisions to seek the best consequences. This dual-process model can be refined by replacing Greene's distinction between personal and impersonal dilemmas with some more precise account of what triggers "emotional" processes and what triggers "rational" processes behind moral judgments (e.g., Schaich Borg et al. 2006, Sinnott-Armstrong et al. 2008c, and Greene et al. 2009).

These three models agree that moral intuitions do not result from conscious moral reasoning (though other moral beliefs still might result from conscious moral reasoning). All three models are also compatible with the claim that some moral intuitions are innate (see Sripada 2008 and Prinz 2008). They also agree that emotion has some place in moral life. What these models disagree about is the causal role of emotion in relation to either computation or reasoning.

A major problem in this debate is the lack of a clear line between emotion and reason. Emotions guide both practical and theoretical reasoning by indicating salience and directing attention. As a result, people whose emotions are distorted usually also have deficits in reasoning (Damasio 1994). Conversely, people need to gather information about a situation or action, even if only unconsciously, before emotionally reacting to it. Thus, reasoning depends on emotion, and emotion depends on reasoning or at least cognition.

It is also not clear why it matters whether moral judgments rest on emotion. Some assume that moral judgments are less objective or reliable if they are based on emotion. However, emotions can be reliable indicators of objective features of the world (Allman and Woodward 2008). When people have experienced enough danger such that their feelings of fear have become conditioned responses to dangerous situations, their fear can be evidence that a situation really is dangerous. If there are objective moral facts, then it is not clear why other emotions could not become reliable indicators of those moral facts in the same way as, with training and experience, fear can be a reliable indicator of danger. Of course, emotions are not always perfectly reliable indicators of objective truth (either danger or moral facts), but neither is reasoning.

In our view, what really matters to moral epistemology is not reason or emotion but, instead, reliability. Whether the processes that produce moral intuitions are reliable is relevant to whether (and, if so, how) people are epistemically justified in trusting those moral intuitions. The problem is that moral psychologists cannot directly study reliability without an independent test of which moral belief-forming processes are reliable, which requires controversial moral assumptions. A solution may be to turn from reliability to unreliability. Although moral theorists do not agree on which moral judgments are true or reliable, they usually do agree that moral judgments are unreliable to the extent that moral beliefs are subject to framing effects, including effects of the order in which moral problems are encountered (A-B-C versus C-B-A), irrelevant wording changes ("the five die" rather than "the five are not saved"), and grammatical person ("It would be morally wrong for me to do this act in these circumstances" instead of "It would be morally wrong for you or him to do this same act in these same circumstances") (see Sinnott-Armstrong 2008b and Nadelhoffer and Feltz 2008). Thus, experimental philosophy can more directly address the issues that matter by studying when, how, and how much various moral judgments are subject to framing effects.

Moral Internalism and Psychopathy

A second issue that occupies experimental ethicists is the relation between moral judgments and motivation. Many philosophers hold that motivational force is a defining feature of moral judgments that helps to distinguish moral beliefs from their nonnormative counterparts. (See the chapter by Mele in this volume on moral psychology.) The belief that Atlanta is south of Nashville need not by itself motivate you to do anything. In contrast, if you sincerely believe that you are morally obligated to help a child, then it is supposed to follow somehow that you are motivated to help the child.

Internalists claim that there is an internal relation between a moral judgment about an act and motivation or reason to do or not do that act. We will focus on versions that make claims about motivation rather than about reasons to act.

Even with that specification, the metaphor of an internal relation can be cashed out in many ways:

> (SI) It is conceptually necessary that, if a moral agent believes that she morally ought to *A* in circumstances *C*, then she will be *overridingly* motivated to *A* in circumstances *C*.
>
> (MI) It is conceptually necessary that, if a moral agent believes that she morally ought to *A* in circumstances *C*, then she will be *defeasibly* motivated to *A* in circumstances *C*.
>
> (WI) It is conceptually necessary that, if a moral agent believes that she morally ought to *A* in circumstances *C*, then she will be *defeasibly* motivated to *A* in circumstances *C*, unless she is *irrational* or *abnormal*.

Externalists of various kinds reject all or some of these theses and argue, instead, that the relation between morality and motivation is conceptually contingent (for even more distinctions among kinds of internalism, see Miller 2008 and Sinnott-Armstrong 2009).

The strongest version of internalism (SI) was endorsed by Socrates, who (according to Plato) said, "If a man knows good and bad, nothing can force him to act contrary to the good" (Plato 1961, 352a–353b). To ensure moral action, the motivation tied to moral belief must override other motivations that might tempt the agent to act contrary to what the agent judges to be morally good or obligatory. Unfortunately, SI seems to exclude weakness of will—that is, acting contrary to one's judgment of what one morally ought to do—as well as acting on a strong self-interested motivation that overrides a weaker motivation to be moral. Because acts of these sorts seem common, almost all contemporary internalists reject SI in favor of some weaker thesis (but see Hare 1963, ch. 5).

The moderate version of internalism (MI) claims that moral beliefs necessarily motivate moral agents at least to some defeasible degree. Since MI allows conflicting motivations to be stronger than any motivation tied to moral belief, MI is compatible with weakness of will. Nonetheless, MI is still not compatible with the reality or even conceptual possibility of amoralism—i.e., individuals who are sometimes entirely unmotivated by their moral beliefs.

The weakest version of internalism (WI) can allow even total amoralism by declaring it irrational or abnormal (cf. Smith 1994). But then WI might seem to allow too much. Critics (such as Roskies 2003) charge that WI does not really exclude anything, since any moral agent who is not motivated at all by moral beliefs could be declared irrational or abnormal on that very basis. If so, WI would seem to lack specific content, at least until its defenders provide an independent test of rationality or normality. The same problem is supposed to arise for moral internalists who qualify their claims with a "ceteris paribus" clause

(Kennett and Fine 2008, 174). They can always stave off empirical objections by saying that the ceteris are not paribus, so to speak, but they need to show why this move is not ad hoc (for discussion of attempts to solve this problem, see Miller 2008).

If SI is too strong to be plausible and WI is too weak to be interesting, as critics claim, then it makes sense (like Goldilocks) to focus on MI. One way to test MI experimentally is to ask common folk whether amoralism is possible. If most people see amoralism as possible, then their concept of moral judgment would seem not to necessarily imply moral motivation, as MI claims. Nichols (2004) conducted this experiment and the results seem to speak against MI.

Another approach is to look for actual cases of amoralism. Roskies (2003) describes patients with frontal lobe damage who display what is sometimes described as "acquired sociopathy." The symptoms are much more severe when the frontal lobe damage occurs early in life. Another plausible example, which will be our focus, is psychopaths (who typically do not have frontal lobe damage). Psychopaths refute MI if, but only if, (a) they hold moral beliefs but (b) they lack any motivation to act according to their moral beliefs.

Motivation is often revealed by behavior. Psychopaths are stunningly aggressive, predatory, and recidivistic (see Hare 1993, Blair et al. 2005). Although less than 1 percent of the population is thought to be afflicted with psychopathy, researchers estimate that psychopathic individuals could nevertheless be responsible for around 30–40 percent of violent crime. Their acts, thus, suggest a lack of motivation to be moral. This impression is confirmed by personality tests. The diagnostic traits of psychopathy, according to the official Psychopathy Checklist-Revised, suggest that psychopaths are prone to glibness, self-grandiosity, pathological lying, manipulativeness, remorselessness, shallow affect, refusal to take responsibility, parasitic lifestyle, poor behavior controls, sexual promiscuity, multiple marital relationships, lack of realistic goals, impulsivity, early behavior problems, and criminal versatility. Directly relevant here is their callousness and deficits in empathy and guilt or remorse for harming others. This clinical picture seems to suggest that psychopaths lack motivation to be moral.

The next question is whether psychopaths make genuine moral judgments. Several studies have found that moral judgments endorsed by psychopaths are not significantly different than moral judgments made by normal controls and by nonpsychopathic prisoners on Kohlberg-style moral reasoning tasks (Link et al. 1977, O'Kane et al. 1996) and standard batteries of moral dilemmas as well as rankings of the seriousness of crimes (Cima et al. 2010, Schaich Borg and Sinnott-Armstrong 2013). These experimental findings provide some evidence that psychopaths make moral judgments much like nonpsychopaths.

Other research, however, suggests that psychopaths might merely be mouthing words that they do not really appreciate. As Kennett and Fine put it, "the supposed moral judgments of psychopaths are rightly understood in the inverted comma sense" (2008, 178). This view is supported by a variety of studies. First, psychopaths tend to consider themselves to be "above the rules"—i.e., they tend not to think that moral and legal norms apply to them (Chandler and Moran 1990). Second, when reasoning about real-world rather than merely hypothetical moral dilemmas, psychopaths appeal far more often than normals to the moral legitimacy of their own needs and interests (Trevethan and Walker 1989). Third, psychopaths seem to misunderstand moral concepts. In one striking example, "When asked if he experienced remorse over a murder he'd committed, one young inmate told us, 'Yeah, sure, I feel remorse.' Pressed further, he said that he 'didn't feel bad inside about it'" (Hare 1993, 41). Finally, recent neural studies have found that, when making moral judgments, psychopaths use brain areas (the temporoparietal junction or TPJ) that are associated with ascribing beliefs to others (Harenski et al. 2010), suggesting that psychopaths are reporting what they think that others think, rather than what they themselves think, about morality.

One prominent issue is whether psychopaths distinguish authority-dependent conventional norms from authority-independent moral norms. Normal four-year-old children do so, but Blair (1995, 1997) found that psychopaths and prepsychopaths failed to draw this distinction. These results have, however, been thrown into doubt by recent retesting (Aharoni et al. 2012). Overall, then, the experimental evidence conflicts and does not yet settle the issue of whether psychopaths make real moral judgments.

Moreover, even if psychopaths do have genuine moral beliefs, it is also not clear that they lack all motivation to be moral. When exposed to pictures of distress cues (such as a picture of a group of crying adults or a close-up of a crying face), psychopaths demonstrated significant galvanic skin responses even though their responses were much reduced compared to nonpsychopaths (Blair 1997). This finding suggests that some or even all psychopaths might retain at least some emotion and maybe motivation to be moral. If so, they cannot refute moderate internalism (MI), at least until we learn more about the worst cases.

Virtue Ethics and Situationist Psychology

A third use of experiments in ethics concerns not metaethics but normative moral theory. This example shows how scientific research can raise doubts about empirical presuppositions of substantive moral theories.

Consequentialist and deontological theories have dominated substantive moral philosophy in recent centuries, but many philosophers and students are dissatisfied with these alternatives. Critics charge that both approaches are psychologically unrealistic in part because common folk rarely, if ever, calculate utilities or appeal to categorical principles when they make moral judgments or decisions (Anscombe 1958, Flanagan 1991). In contrast, we commonly assess people's behavior in terms of character traits, such as when we call agents and their acts honest, courageous, generous, kind, and just or dishonest, cowardly, stingy, malicious, and unfair. We typically praise and reward those who display virtues, and we typically condemn and sometimes punish those who exemplify vices. Virtue ethics aims to capture this aspect of our everyday moral practices (see the chapter in this volume by Swanton on virtue ethics).

On most views, virtues are understood as character traits that make agents more likely to do the right acts and have the right emotions in the right circumstances for the right reasons. In addition, Aristotle asserts that, once an agent acquires virtuous character traits, these traits are "firm and unchangeable" (Aristotle 1984, 1105b1). This claim implies that, although virtues are not sufficient by themselves for moral behavior, truly virtuous individuals will do what is right when they have the ability and opportunity, no matter how costly or difficult it might be (Aristotle 1984, 1105a88–b10).

Such virtue theories, thus, depend on some form of dispositional moral psychology whereby what you do is usually largely a matter of your character traits. This assumption is attractive at least initially. However, some critics question this presupposition on the basis of experimental evidence (Harman 1999b, 2000 and Doris 1998, 2002; cf. Flanagan 1991 who was the first to reveal this tension). On this skeptical view, situational stimuli affect our acts much more than virtue ethicists suppose. Some skeptics go so far as to deny the existence of any robust and stable character traits.

To get a feel for the sorts of experiments behind this "Situationist Challenge," consider the surprising results reported in Isen and Levin (1972). Subjects were random pedestrians in San Francisco and Philadelphia who stopped to use a public payphone. Whereas some subjects found a dime that had been planted in the phone booth by researchers, other subjects found nothing. When subjects left the phone booth, a female confederate of the researchers dropped an armful of papers, and researchers recorded whether or not the individuals leaving the phone booth stopped to help. The results were clear: The subjects who found a dime were 22 times more likely to help than were the subjects who did not find a dime. It was shocking that something as insignificant as a dime—which gave agents no more reason to help and which agents would deny affected their actions—had such a pronounced effect on people's moral behavior.

It is even more astounding that these results appear to be representative rather than anomalous. Other studies have shown that our moral behavior is sensitive to situational factors such (a) the level of ambient noise (Mathews and Cannon 1975), (b) how many people happen to be standing around (Latané and Darley 1970), (c) whether the person telling us to do something morally suspect happens to be wearing a lab coat (Milgram 1974), (d) whether we are in a hurry

(Darley and Batson 1973), (e) whether we are asked to play the role of prison guards (Zimbardo 2007), and (f) whether we have recently been primed to think about a ghost (Bering et al. 2005), about achievement goals (Bargh and Chartrand 1999), or about equality and loyalty (Hertel and Kerr 2000). In each of these studies and more, morally extraneous features of the situation have a stark effect on people's moral behavior. The gathering data is supposed to suggest that situation trumps character often enough to motivate skepticism about whether there are robust and stable character traits of the kind that virtue ethics seems to presuppose.

Virtue theorists have not taken the situationist challenge lightly. To meet it, virtue theorists as well as others who believe in robust and stable character traits adopt various strategies (Hursthouse 2000, Merritt 2000, Sreenivasan 2002, Miller 2003 and 2009, Swanton 2003, Kamtekar 2004, Annas 2005, Sabini and Silver 2005, Russell 2009, and Snow 2009). Here are some popular retorts:

1. Empirical Issues: Many situationist studies have sample sizes too small to support generalization, none of them observes people's behaviors across situations as needed to test whether character is cross-situational, and some attempted replications have failed (Miller 2009).
2. The Rarity Response: All that situationist data show is how genuinely difficult and rare it is to be a virtuous agent, but a truly virtuous agent still would have helped regardless of whether or not she found a dime, etc.
3. The Immunization Hope: We can use situationist experiments to shield ourselves from the encroachment of morally irrelevant situational factors, so that we will become better equipped to enable our moral dispositions to guide our actions.
4. The Libelous Reply: Characterological skeptics misrepresent virtue theories and misunderstand how traditional virtue ethics conceives of character.
5. The Revisionist Rejoinder: Although experimental data puts serious pressure on classical versions of virtue ethics, virtue theorists can still offer revised versions of virtue ethics that are better equipped to deal with the situationist challenge (see, e.g., Merritt 2000 and Driver 2001 on nonclassical accounts of virtue).

It is controversial which, if any, of these strategies works. Nonetheless, it is clear that experiments revealing the situational roots of behavior have led many virtue theorists to reform or supplement both ancient and contemporary accounts of virtue.

One potential reform is worth highlighting. Situationism does not challenge the picture of virtues as character traits but, rather, the Aristotelian claim that virtuous (and vicious) character traits are robust and cross-situational. A neat solution would be to understand character traits not as simple dispositions to be analyzed by conditionals but, instead, as patterns of probabilities over various kinds of situations (compare Fleeson 2001). Even if nobody has perfect virtue (or vice), some people are still more likely than others to do the right thing more often in more sorts of circumstances. This probabilistic model is compatible with all of the situationist evidence, which reveals only trends in groups. It also allows degrees of virtue and vice, as well as improvement or deterioration over time, and it brings virtue theory in line with the tendency of science to find probabilities on multiple dimensions. Experiments can, thus, help to make philosophical ethics more realistic and precise without sacrificing its main goals.

Conclusions

There are, of course, many other uses of experiments in ethics. However, the three cases that we discussed here are enough to illustrate a general point—namely, how hard it can be to bridge the gap between experiments and philosophical views and methods. Empirical data by themselves are unlikely to settle classic philosophical issues conclusively. Still, as we learn more about framing effects, psychopathy, and situational effects on decision-making, we are often forced to rethink our philosophical assumptions., sometimes in fundamental ways. Even if the fields remain distinct, philosophical theories need to be compatible with the best available scientific evidence. Experiments can and should thereby constrain moral philosophy even if experiments do not replace ethics.

References

Aharoni, A., Sinnott-Armstrong, W. and Kiehl, K. (2012), "Can Psychopathic Offenders Discern Moral Wrongs? A New Look at the Moral/Conventional Distinction." *Journal of Abnormal Psychology* 121 (2), 484–497.

Allman, J. and Woodward, J. (2008), "What Are Moral Intuitions and Why Should We Care about Them? A Neurobiological Perspective." *Philosophical Issues* 18(1), 164–85.

Annas, J. (2005), "Comments on John Doris' *Lack of Character*." *Philosophy and Phenomenological Research* 73, 636–47.

Anscombe, G. E. M. (1958), "Modern Moral Philosophy." *Philosophy* 33, 1–19.

Aristotle. (1984), *Nichomachean Ethics*. In *The Complete Works of Aristotle*, J. Barnes (ed.). Princeton: Princeton University Press.

Audi, R. (2004), *The Good in the Right: A Theory of Intuition and Intrinsic Value*. Princeton: Princeton University Press.

Bargh, J. A. and Chartrand, T. L. (1999), "The Unbearable Automaticity of Being." *American Psychologist* 57 (7), 462–79.

Bering, J. M., McLeod, K. and Shackelford, T. K. (2005), "Reasoning about Dead Agents Reveals Possible Adaptive Trends." *Human Nature* 16, 360–81.

Berker, S. (2009), "The Normative Insignificance of Neuroscience." *Philosophy & Public Affairs* 37, 293–329.

Blair, R. J. R. (1995), "A Cognitive Developmental Approach to Morality: Investigating the Psychopath." *Cognition* 57, 1–29.

—. (1997), "Moral Reasoning in the Child with Psychopathic Tendencies." *Personality and Individual Differences* 22, 731–9.

Blair, J., Mitchell, D. and Blair, K. (2005), *The Psychopath: Emotion and the Brain*. New York: Wiley-Blackwell.

Chandler, M. and Moran, T. (1990), "Psychopathy and Moral Development: A Comparative Study of Delinquent and Nondelinquent Youth." *Development and Psychopathology* 2, 227–46.

Ciaramelli, E., Muccioli, M., Làdavas, E. and di Pellegrino, G. (2007), "Selective Deficit in Personal Moral Judgment Following Damage to Ventromedial Prefrontal Cortex." *Social Cognitive and Affective Neuroscience* 2(2), 84–92.

Cima, M., Tonnaer, F. and Hauser, M. D. (2010), "Psychopaths Know Right from Wrong but Don't Care." *Social Cognitive Affective Neuroscience* 5, 59-67.

Darley, J. M. and Batson, C. D. (1973), "From Jerusalem to Jericho: A Study of Situational and Dispositional Variables in Helping Behavior." *Journal of Personality and Social Psychology* 27, 100–8.

Doris, J. (1998), "Persons, Situations, and Virtue Ethics." *Nous* 32(4), 504–30.

—. (2002), *Lack of Character: Personality and Moral Behavior*. Cambridge: Cambridge University Press.

Driver, J. (2001), *Uneasy Virtue*. Cambridge: Cambridge University Press.

Dwyer, S. (1999), "Moral Competence," in Kumiko Murasugi and Robert Stainton (eds.), *Philosophy and Linguistics*. Boulder, CO: Westview Press, 169–90.

Flanagan, O. (1991), *Varieties of Moral Personality: Ethics and Psychological Realism*. Cambridge MA: Harvard University Press.

Fleeson, W. (2001), "Toward a Structure- and Process-Integrated View of Personality: Traits as Density Distributions of States." *Journal of Personality and Social Psychology* 80, 1011–27.

Greene. J. D. (2008a), "The Secret Joke of Kant's Soul". In Sinnott-Armstrong 2008a, 3, 35–79.

Greene, J. D., Cushman, F. A., D., Stewart, L. E., Lowenberg, K., Nystrom, L. E. and Cohen, J. D. (2009), "Pushing Moral Buttons: The Interaction between Personal Force and Intention in Moral Judgment." *Cognition* 111(3), 364–71.

Greene, J. D., Morelli, S. A., Lowenberg, K., Nystrom, L. E. and Cohen, J. D. (2008b), "Cognitive Load Selectively Interferes with Utilitarian Moral Judgment." *Cognition* 107(3), 1144–54.

Greene, J. D., Nystrom, L. E., Engell, A. D., Darley, J. M. and Cohen, J. D. (2004), "The Neural Bases of Cognitive Conflict and Control in Moral Judgment." *Neuron* 44, 389–400.

Greene, J. D., Sommerville, R. B., Nystrom, L. E., Darley, J. M. and Cohen, J. D. (2001), "An fMRI Investigation of Emotional Engagement in Moral Judgment." *Science* 293, 2105–8.

Haidt, J., Koller, S. H. and Dias, M. G. (1993), "Affect, Culture, and Morality, or Is It Wrong to Eat Your Dog?" *Journal of Personality and Social Psychology* 65, 613–28.

Hare, R. D. (1993), *Without Conscience: The Disturbing World of Psychopaths Among Us*. New York: Atria.

Hare, R. M. (1963), *Freedom and Reason*. Oxford: Clarendon Press.
Harenski, C. L., Harenski, K. A., Shane, M. S. and Kiehl, K. A. (2010), "Aberrant Neural Processing of Moral Violations in Criminal Psychopaths." *Journal of Abnormal Psychology* 119(4), 863-874.
Harman, G. (1999a), "Moral Philosophy and Linguistics,". in K. Brinkmann (ed.), *Proceedings of the 20th World Conference of Philosophy: Vol. 1: Ethics*, 107–15. Bowling Green, OH: Philosophy Documentation Center.
—. (1999b), "Moral Philosophy Meets Social Psychology: Virtue Ethics and the Fundamental Attribution Error." *Proceedings of the Aristotelian Society* 99, 315–31.
—. (2000), "The Nonexistence of Character Traits." *Proceedings of the Aristotelian Society* 100, 223–6.
Hauser, M., Young, L. and Cushman, F. (2008), "Reviving Rawls' Linguistic Analogy: Operative Principles and the Causal Structure of Moral Action." In Sinnott-Armstrong 2008a, 2, 107–43.
Hertel, G. and Kerr, N. L. (2000), "Priming In-Group Favoritism: The Impact of Normative Scripts in the Minimal Group Paradigm." *Journal of Experimental Social Psychology* 37(4), 316–24.
Huebner, B., Dwyer, S. and Hauser, M. D. (2009), "The Role of Emotion in Moral Psychology." *Trends in Cognitive Science* 13(1), 1–6.
Hursthouse, R. (2000), *On Virtue Ethics*. New York: Oxford University Press.
Isen, A. M. and Levin, P. F. (1972), "Effect of Feeling Good on Helping: Cookies and Kindness." *Journal of Personality and Social Psychology* 21, 384–8.
Kamm, F. (2009), "Neuroscience and Moral Reasoning: A Note on Recent Research." *Philosophy & Public Affairs* 37, 330–45.
Kamtekar, R. (2004), "Situationism and Virtue Ethics on the Content of Our Character." *Ethics* 114, 458–91.
Kennett, J. and Fine, C. (2008), "Internalism and the Evidence from Psychopaths and 'Acquired Sociopaths.'" In Sinnott-Armstrong 2008a, 3, 173–90.
Koenigs, M., Young, L., Adolphs, R., Tranel, D., Cushman, F., Hauser, M. and Damasio, A. (2007), "Damage to the Prefrontal Cortex Increases Utilitarian Moral Judgments." *Nature* 446, 908–11.
Latané, B. and Darley, J. (1970), *The Unresponsive Bystander: Why Doesn't he Help?* New York: Appleton-Century Crofts.
Link, N., Sherer, S. E. and Byrne, P. N. (1977), "Moral Judgment and Moral Conduct in the Psychopath." *The Canadian Psychiatric Association Journal / La Revue de l'Association des Psychiatres du Canada* 22(7), 341–6.
Mathews, K. E. and Cannon, L. K. (1975), "Environmental Noise Level as a Determinant of Helping Behavior." *Journal of Personality and Social Psychology* 32, 571–7.
Mendez, M. F., Anderson, E. and Shapira, J. S. (2005), "An Investigation of Moral Judgment in Frontotemporal Dementia." *Cognitive Behavioral Neurology* 18(4), 193–7.
Merritt, M. (2000), "Virtue Ethics and Situationist Personality Psychology." *Ethical Theory and Moral Practice* 3, 365–83.
Mikhail, J. (2007), "Universal Moral Grammar: Theory, Evidence, and the Future." *Trends in Cognitive Science* 11, 143–52.
—. (2011), *Elements of Moral Cognition: Rawls' Linguistic Analogy and the Cognitive Science of Moral and Legal Judgment*. Cambridge: Cambridge University Press.

Milgram, S. (1974), *Obedience to Authority*. New York: Harper and Row.
Miller, C. (2003), "Social Psychology and Virtue Ethics." *The Journal of Ethics* 7, 365–92.
—. (2008), "Motivational Internalism." *Philosophical Studies* 139, 233–55.
—. (2009), "Social Psychology, Mood, and Helping: Mixed Results for Virtue Ethics." *The Journal of Ethics*, Special Issue on Situationism 13, 145–73.
Nadelhoffer, T. and Feltz, A. (2008), "The Actor-Observer Bias and Moral Intuitions." *Neuroethics* 1(2), 133–44.
Nichols, S. (2004), *Sentimental Rules: On the Natural Foundations of Moral Judgment*. New York: Oxford University Press.
O'Kane, A., Fawcett, D. and Blackburn, R. (1996), "Psychopathy and Moral Reasoning: Comparison of Two Classifications." *Personality & Individual Differences* 20, 505–14.
Plato. (1961), *Protagoras*. In E. Hamilton and H. Cairns (eds.), *The Collected Dialogues of Plato*. Princeton: Princeton University Press.
Prinz, J. (2008), "Is Morality Innate?" In Sinnott-Armstrong 2008a, 1, 367–406.
Roskies, A. (2003), "Are Ethical Judgments Intrinsically Motivational? Lessons from 'Acquired Sociopathy.'" *Philosophical Psychology* 16(1), 51–66.
Russell, D. C. (2009), *Practical Intelligence and the Virtues*. New York: Oxford University Press.
Sabini, J. and Silver, M. (2005), "Lack of Character? Situationism Critiqued." *Ethics* 115, 535–62.
Schaich Borg, J., Hynes, C., Grafton, S. and Sinnott-Armstrong, W. (2006), "Consequences, Action, and Intention as Factors in Moral Judgments: An fMRI Investigation." *Journal of Cognitive Neuroscience* 18(5), 803–17.
Schaich Borg, J. and Sinnott-Armstrong, W. (2013), "Do Psychopaths Make Moral Judgments?" in K. Kiehl and W. Sinnott-Armstrong (eds.), *Handbook on Psychopathy and Law*. New York: Oxford University Press, 107–128.
Schnall, S., Haidt, J., Clore, G. and Jordan, A. (2008), "Disgust as Embodied Moral Judgment." *Personality and Social Psychology Bulletin* 34, 1096–109.
Sinnott-Armstrong, W. (ed.). (2008a), *Moral Psychology*, 3 Volumes. Cambridge: MIT Press.
—. (2008b), "Framing Moral Intuitions". In Sinnott-Armstrong 2008a, 2, 47–76.
Sinnott-Armstrong, W., Mallon, R., McCoy, T. and Hull, J. (2008c), "Intention, Temporal Order, and Moral Judgments." *Mind & Language* 23(1), 90–106.
Sinnott-Armstrong, W. (2009), "Mackie's Internalisms," in R. Joyce and S. Kirchin (eds.), *A World Without Values: Essays on John Mackie's Moral Error Theory*. Dordrecht: Springer, 55–70.
Smith, M. (1994), *The Moral Problem*. Oxford: Blackwell.
Snow, N. E. (2009), *Virtue as Social Intelligence: An Empirically Grounded Theory*. New York: Routledge.
Sreenivasan, G. (2002), "Errors about Errors: Virtue Theory and Trait Attribution." *Mind*, 111, 47–68.
Sripada, C. (2008), "Nativism and Moral Psychology." In Sinnott-Armstrong 2008a, 1, 319–43.
Stratton-Lake, P. (ed). (2003), *Ethical Intuitionism: Re-evaluations*. New York: Oxford University Press.
Swanton, C. (2003), *Virtue Ethics: A Pluralistic View*. New York: Oxford University Press.

Tolhurst, W. (1998), "Seemings." *American Philosophical Quarterly 35*, 293–302.

Trevethan, S. D. and Walker, L. J. (1989), "Hypothetical versus Real-Life Moral Reasoning among Psychopathic and Delinquent Youth." *Development and Psychopathology* 1, 91–103.

Valdesolo, P. and DeSteno, D. (2006), "Manipulations of Emotional Context Shape Moral Judgments." *Psychological Science* 17(6), 476–7.

Wheatley, T. and Haidt, J. (2005), "Hypnotic Disgust Makes Moral Judgments More Severe." *Psychological Science* 16, 780–4.

Zimbardo, P. G. (2007), *The Lucifer Effect: Understanding How Good People Turn Evil*. New York: Random House.

13 Biology, Evolution, and Ethics

William FitzPatrick

Several decades have now passed since E. O. Wilson first suggested that "the time has come for ethics to be removed temporarily from the hands of the philosophers and biologicized" (Wilson 1975, 562). He was writing in the context of the emergence of sociobiology—the study of social organization and behavior in animals, including humans, from the perspective of genetics and evolutionary biology. The idea was that once we accept that natural selection has shaped not only the physiologies of organisms but also complex patterns of social behavior in animals ranging from ants to chimpanzees, it is natural to suppose that there have been similar evolutionary influences on human nature as well: we should expect the human brain and mind to have been shaped by selection pressures to perform in ways that were adaptive in ancestral environments, by way of evolved "social instincts." This then opens the door to rethinking the explanation of patterns of human emotion, cognition, and behavior traditionally studied by other disciplines (Wilson 1978). In particular, we might wonder whether many phenomena commonly grouped under the heading of "morality" can be freshly illuminated by approaching them from an evolutionary perspective.

Wilson's theme of "biologicizing" the study of human social life is forcefully echoed by contemporary evolutionary psychologists, who view a wide array of psychological traits—including those involving *moral* feeling, judgment, and reasoning—as culturally conditioned products of evolution through natural selection. Why, after all, do human beings possess and exercise psychological capacities for moral judgment and motivation, which appear to be no less universal than our capacity for language acquisition? Why do we have emotions such as sympathy, parental love, jealousy, resentment, blame, and guilt, and make judgments condemning incest, unfairness, cheating, and in-group harming, or praising loyalty, reliability, and cooperation? The suggestion is that these things all stem ultimately from *psychological adaptations*—dedicated ("domain specific") psychological modules or mechanisms or "programs" that originally emerged as adaptations for solving problems of social exchange faced by our Pleistocene ancestors, though they may or may not remain adaptive in current environments (Barkow et al. 1992, Buss 2005; but for critiques of evolutionary psychology, see also Coyne 2000, Buller 2005 and Richardson 2007).

The excitement over this way of understanding "morality" has led to many claims—much celebrated in the popular media—about the evolution, nature, explanation, and status of morality, often with the suggestion (following Wilson) that new scientifically grounded insights are supplanting earlier pretensions to insight about morality from the philosophical tradition. It is far from clear, however, whether or to what extent this is so, and the matter cannot properly be assessed without first distinguishing the many issues at play and the complex relations among them. We will therefore begin the first section with some clarifications about the meaning of "morality" and the different questions that can be raised about it. In the second section we will distinguish various scientific explanatory projects and positions, going on in the third and fourth sections to explore the interface between some of these scientific projects and issues in moral philosophy. Importantly, we will see that some scientific explanatory projects address matters that in fact turn partly on issues in moral philosophy that remain far from settled. This means that it is misleading to represent the conclusions of these projects as purely "scientific" unless they are carefully qualified and limited. Sweeping conclusions about evolutionary *explanations of our moral beliefs*, for example, actually rely implicitly on highly controversial philosophical assumptions. We will then conclude with a critical look at a dominant trend in much of the work at the intersection of the sciences and moral philosophy, whereby appeals are made to allegedly independent, scientific results to underwrite deflationary philosophical accounts of morality, such as moral subjectivism, skepticism or nihilism. If the points in the third and fourth sections are correct, such deflationary arguments have less real scientific support than their proponents take them to have.

What Do We Mean By "Morality"?

A recent headline on CNN.com posed the question: "Can morality be changed magnetically?" (Landau 2010). To a philosopher, such a question is liable to come across at first as a jarring category mistake. Moral philosophers are accustomed to asking such questions as: "does morality require that we make large sacrifices to aid distant strangers?" (i.e., "are we morally obligated to do so?"), or "are there objective truths in morality—such as the fact that slavery is wrong?" To speak this way is to use "morality" in the *normative sense*, where "morality" refers (roughly) to the *set of norms or ideals* that *ought* to be adopted concerning the fundamentals of *how we should live* (understood broadly to include not just how we should act, but also how we should be and what we should value), where these norms or ideals are related to the assessment of persons or their lives as good or bad as such. Obviously morality in this sense, if it exists at all, is not the sort of thing that might be affected by magnetism![1]

The CNN story was clearly referring to something quite different in speaking of "morality," which is of interest to scientists: it was using "morality" to refer to certain *empirical phenomena for which we might seek causal explanations*. In this case, scientists were exploring whether people's patterns of moral judgment are affected by transcranial magnetic stimulation. We might likewise inquire into "the evolution of morality," seeking causal explanations for such phenomena as our coming to have a capacity for moral judgment, or tendencies to make certain judgments or to behave in certain ways. When scientists ask such questions, they're asking about morality in the *empirical sense*.

A second clarification concerns morality in the empirical sense: what empirical phenomena, exactly, count as falling under the heading of "morality" for scientific purposes? Many traits, such as cooperative patterns of behavior or sympathetic and altruistic emotions, are often spoken of loosely as "moral." Strictly speaking, however, they belong to morality only insofar as they are relevantly associated with the phenomenon of *moral judgment*, which is the key concept (Joyce 2006, Prinz 2008). The richly cooperative behavior of bees, for example, does not fall under the category of morality, and the prosocial emotions of more psychologically complex animals are at most part of proto-morality that may be part of explaining the origins of morality but shouldn't be conflated with it. Morality is most usefully conceived as a range of phenomena connected in one way or another with moral judgment, such that inquiry into morality in the empirical sense is inquiry into what made moral judgment possible in the first place, what causal influences have shaped it, and how it in turn affects a variety of emotions and behaviors, which latter we may then properly call "moral" in the empirical sense.[2]

For example, the mere disposition to develop a sexual aversion toward close kin does not *itself* count as a "moral" disposition: it is not yet part of "morality" in the empirical sense. But we might come to the conclusion that this disposition is a psychological adaptation that explains "moral sentiments relating to incest" by influencing emotionally laden moral *judgments* about incest; and these in turn influence behavior, perhaps in combination with other adaptations for "regulat[ing] the sexual behavior of one's kin," all mediated by cultural inputs (Lieberman 2008, 165). This would now count as part of explaining morality in the empirical sense. And the same goes for structurally similar explanations for the praising of family loyalty, for example, and resulting altruistic behavior toward kin, among many other phenomena.

Now a central question we need to consider is how scientific explanatory projects concerning morality in the *empirical* sense are related to philosophical projects concerning morality in the *normative* sense. For example, might the existence of knowable *truths* about morality in the *normative* sense make a difference to the proper *explanation* of certain aspects of morality in the *empirical* sense, such as explaining why we have some of the moral beliefs we have, and so act as we do? If there are moral truths or facts, as many philosophers believe, such as the fact that racial discrimination is wrong, and you believe that racial discrimination is wrong because you've *grasped* that fact, then how does this bear on scientific attempts to explain your beliefs by appeal to the kinds of causal factors scientists consider, such as evolutionary influences? We will take that up after looking more closely at the different kinds of scientific explanatory projects.

Explaining Morality in the Empirical Sense: Capacities and Content

It is no surprise that scientists approach "morality," like other explananda in science, as a set of empirical phenomena to be causally explained with scientific tools. And this approach is warranted for *some* explanatory projects in this area: namely, those dealing with the emergence of basic mental *capacities* relevant to moral judgment—in particular, the human capacity for *normative guidance* (Gibbard 1990; Kitcher 2006a, 2006b; Joyce 2006, ch. 2; Korsgaard 2006; Bratman 2007). How did human beings come to have the capacity to grasp and to accept norms of social interaction and response, to make normative judgments and to be motivated by them? And more specifically, in connection with *morality*, how did this capacity emerge with respect to norms of behavior tied to norms for sentiments such as blame, resentment, and guilt, so that one could be motivated, for example, not to commit an act of violence against another member of one's group by the thought that it would be *wrong* and the sense that one would be *blameworthy* if one did it?

It seems clear enough that these questions call for a causal story of a scientific sort. In fact, since we're evolved creatures, it seems clear that there will be *some* sort of evolutionary explanation for the emergence of such capacities. But there are different possibilities here: a complex capacity may itself be an *adaptation*—a trait that was selected for in ancestral environments because its exercise increased the reproductive success of its possessors, differentially propagating the alleles that give rise to it—or it may instead be a *by-product* of other adaptations. The capacity to play jazz piano is obviously not itself an adaptation, but a by-product of other adaptations, such as manual dexterity and other traits that are themselves either adaptations or again by-products of adaptations, such as a capacity for musical intelligence, all combined with cultural inputs. So, we might ask: Is the general capacity for moral judgment and motivation *itself* an adaptation, selected for because of its adaptive effects? Or is it simply a by-product of more basic adaptations, such as the capacity for language acquisition, rule following, grasping of authority relations, and so on, such that there was never selection specifically for the capacity to make moral judgments?[3]

Here we have an issue that *can* plausibly be investigated by scientists independently of the traditional concerns of moral philosophers—just as scientists can investigate the causal origins of the capacities that enable us to do math without engaging the mathematical concerns of number theorists. The same applies to the closely related question whether the basic capacity for moral judgment is *innate* or not, with capacity (or faculty) *nativists* claiming it is (Dwyer 2008) and *antinativists* denying this (Prinz 2008). This would just be the same question as before if a trait's being an adaptation were essential to its being innate, and some take it that way. But we might instead have a conception of innateness whereby it is sufficient for a trait's being innate that it is a consistent and stable feature of the evolved package such that it will be manifested in normal development in virtually any cultural context—never mind whether it was itself selected for. In this sense, an underlying "competence for morality" (in the psychologists' sense) might be innate, as opposed to a contingent cultural construction, even if it is not itself an adaptation.

The most common view, however, is that it is an adaptation, perhaps stemming originally from a limited altruistic trait enabling beneficial participation in small coalitions, followed by the evolution of a more stable capacity for normative guidance through internalized social norms and enforcement mechanisms; after this, it developed into a robust capacity for acceptance of linguistically infused norms in the context of social discourse. All of this, the idea goes, was selected for by virtue of its promoting social coordination and making possible cooperative projects in larger groups with more reliable conformity, enhancing fitness in ancestral humans (Gibbard 1990; Kitcher 2006a, 2006b).

Things get more interesting as we move beyond the basic capacities for normative guidance and moral judgment. Many scientists have argued for the innateness of particular aspects of moral competence—a kind of innate "Universal Moral Grammar" analogous to the Universal Grammar posited by linguists to make sense of language acquisition and the underlying commonalities among languages (Mikhail 2008, Hauser et al., 2008). Children across cultures "possess an elaborate system of natural jurisprudence and an ability to compute mental representations of human acts in legally cognizable terms" (Mikhail 2008, 354–5). They are capable from a very early age, and with little explicit instruction, of distinguishing between moral and merely conventional violations, or intended effects and accidents, or mistakes of fact and mistakes of principle; and they're sensitive to issues involving negligence and restitution, proportionality in punishment, mitigating factors, and procedural fairness. These data, combined with a "poverty of the stimulus" argument, suggest the existence of *innate predispositions* to employ certain concepts and distinctions in moral judgment.

To the extent that these innate predispositions involve capacities, this claim would still fall under *capacity* nativism. But there are also suggestions of *content* nativism here. Content nativism holds that there are innate structures that reliably affect the content of moral norms and judgments across varying cultural inputs (Sripada 2008). Consider, for example, intuitions about procedural and/or distributive fairness, or the greater exculpatory force of mistakes of *fact* over mistakes of *principle*, or the greater moral significance of harm that is *done* over that of harm that is *allowed*, or the greater moral significance of harm that is *intended as a means or end* over that of harm that is merely *foreseen*. If these too are partly innate, as many claim for similar reasons, then the *content* of many of our moral judgments may be influenced by innate dispositions as well.

If there are culturally invariant or universal general moral norms regulating harm, sexual behavior, and distributive fairness, for example, this would provide support for a strong form of content nativism where the innate structure directly provides such content for moral norms.[4] Evidence of significant variation even with respect to such matters, however, might suggest a less robust influence, giving a more significant role to cultural inputs. Perhaps the universal existence of norms regulating physical violence supports an innateness claim about moral content at this very general level of description, but given the complex variation in the actual content of such norms across societies, most of the content of actual norms may best be explained by appeal to cultural inputs. What is innate may thus be just weak "biases" that make norms with certain contents more or less likely to emerge and be transmitted (Sripada 2008). Or again, there is well-known variation in moral norms between cultures with a collectivist conception of society and cultures embracing a more individualistic conception, which would suggest that norms are not innate at that level of description, and what is innate is instead something more general, such as the tendency for people to converge on the prevailing norms of their society (Dwyer 2008, 412).

Just where to draw the lines between innate contributions and cultural inputs is a matter of ongoing investigation and debate. We turn now, however, to critical questions about the strength and scope of the conclusions that may be drawn from the scientific considerations.

Evolutionary Causes and Moral Reasons

As noted earlier, it is natural for scientists to approach "morality" in the empirical sense as a set of empirical phenomena fully amenable to causal explanation using scientific tools, just like other things scientists investigate. But while this is unproblematic when it comes to basic moral *capacities*, things are more complicated when we move to explaining moral *content*. Even though moral beliefs, feelings and behavior are also empirical phenomena, we cannot just assume that they are fully amenable to scientific causal explanation. The first step to seeing why not is to notice that moral *beliefs*—as well as emotions and actions based on them—are things for which people possess and offer *reasons*, not merely causes, just as we do in other domains.

Imagine, for example, that you encounter a teenager tormenting a neighbor with Down syndrome, and you respond with moral indignation and intervene to stop it. You will not regard your emotional and behavioral response as something for which there is merely a set of causes, as you might for a startle response or a reflex kick. If asked why you felt and acted the way you did, you will cite the *reasons* why you believed the teenager's behavior to be morally deplorable—that it was cruel, for example, imposing undeserved pain and suffering on a person; and you take these reasons to *justify* the claim that his behavior was wrong and likewise to *justify* your anger and intervention. So our explanation of your moral belief, feeling, and behavior will (absent any special reason to doubt your sincerity or to suspect that you are deceived about your reasons) be a *reason-giving explanation* rather than a *merely causal* explanation.

This is no different from the way we treat beliefs in other domains: in explaining your mathematical belief that there is an infinite set of prime numbers, or your scientific belief that there is no such thing as absolute rest, we typically offer a reason-giving explanation citing your reasons for your belief, rather than merely independent causes—at least *absent* any reason to suspect that your belief is simply the result of hypnosis or brainwashing, say. When people believe things for which they offer *justifying reasons*,[5] whether these are beliefs based on mathematical arguments they've seen, or on evidence and theory they've found compelling, or on values or principles they hold, the default is to appeal to the reasons they give in explaining why they believe what they do: their beliefs are typically explained by the fact that *they took the reasons they cite as providing support for those beliefs*, which then likewise explains behavior based on those beliefs.

Now suppose for a moment that in addition to there being truths of mathematics and physics there are also *moral truths*: just as the claims about prime numbers or absolute rest are true, for the reasons we give for believing them, so too perhaps the claims that it is wrong to torment mentally disabled people, or to keep slaves, or to molest children, are likewise *true*, for roughly the reasons we give for believing them. This is a position widely (though by no means universally) shared by both philosophers and the general public, and *if* it's correct then a natural *explanation* for why people have certain moral beliefs—along with associated feelings and behaviors—is that they believe these things *for the reasons they give*, which are the reasons why they are in fact *true*. We believe tormenting people with disabilities to be wrong, it seems, because it *is* wrong and *as* morally mature and decent people *we recognize that fact*, as indicated by our reason-giving explanation of our belief, which constitutes a sound *justification* for that belief. In that case, the proper explanation for our belief (and related emotions and behaviors) will be one that essentially makes reference to the *truth* of what is believed (i.e., to the fact in question), just as in the case of other beliefs: you believe (let us suppose) there is an infinite number of primes because there *is* and, being familiar with Euclid's argument, you *recognize* that fact.

The crucial point, then, is that the very possibility that the above holds for at least some moral beliefs is enough to show that scientists cannot simply *assume* that moral beliefs across the board are susceptible to explanations invoking biological, psychological and sociological causal influences that operate *independently of the possible truth of the content* in question—such as appeals to psychological adaptations that cause us to come to certain moral opinions, just as other adaptations cause us to crave fats, simply because of what was once biologically adaptive. To approach "the explanation of morality" in that way would be in effect just to *assume* implicitly that metaethical nihilism is true and there are no moral truths at all, or at least that moral skepticism is true and that we are systematically incapable of ever knowing such truths; for only if that is so can it safely be assumed that our moral beliefs can generally be explained by scientific appeals to causal influences as such, as opposed to at least some being explained in terms of people's grasping relevant truths or facts, which they believe for good reasons, just as with beliefs in other domains. But metaethical nihilism and skepticism are of course (contentious) *philosophical* claims, not scientific results or even issues that scientists as such engage with.[6]

This means that if scientists wish to draw general explanatory conclusions about our moral beliefs, feelings, and behaviors across the board—proposing to tell us why we believe what we do and act as we do in the moral sphere, or "where our moral beliefs come from"—then they should acknowledge explicitly that their project is not a purely scientific one, but is predicated on a controversial philosophical doctrine they have done nothing to establish but are simply assuming in their methodology; moreoever, they should acknowledge that if that philosophical doctrine turns out to be mistaken, then the "scientific" explanations offered for many moral beliefs may be as far off base as analogous evolutionary explanations for why we believe what we do about algebraic topology or particle physics would be.[7]

A better position for scientists to take would be to remain *neutral* on the philosophical issues, such as whether there are knowable, objective moral truths, and to scale back their explanatory claims about moral content accordingly. Rather than claiming without qualification to be explaining our moral beliefs or feelings and related behavior, they would offer only modest claims about plausible evolutionary influences on at least *some* moral beliefs (etc.), leaving it open whether this provides a complete or only a *partial* explanation of these beliefs, and whether there are other beliefs that are independent of such influences altogether. Perhaps our moral belief that we have a strong obligation to care for our children, for example, is indeed influenced, and so partly explained, by feelings of parental love stemming from a psychological adaptation that evolved for obvious biological reasons. But this is entirely compatible with there *also* being a genuine obligation to care for one's children, which we've come to understand through moral reflection and which therefore also partly explains our belief. In other words, there may be *overdetermination* in many cases, where there are both evolutionary causal influences on belief (as explored by scientists) and *good reasons* for holding those beliefs (as explored by philosophers). There may be both native and nonnative contributions to content for certain moral beliefs, and illuminating the former in no way precludes construing the latter in terms of the acquisition of moral knowledge.

In some cases, of course, the scientific explanation may be complete in itself. For example, many traditional moral beliefs embodying racism, homophobia, rigid gender roles, blind submission to authority, and tribalism may well be explained simply by appeal to evolutionary influences and cultural conditioning. This will be plausible where the beliefs are either held unreflectively or the reflection is itself strongly under the influence of evolutionary or other distorting causes, and it is dubious that the beliefs have genuine merit, as in the case of the common belief that homosexuality is morally evil. In other cases, however—particularly (though not necessarily) where moral beliefs are arrived at through careful and informed moral reflection, within serious cultural traditions of systematic and critical moral inquiry—moral beliefs may not be shaped by specific evolutionary influences at all, any more than reasoned beliefs about algebraic topology or general relativity are. After all,

> humans somehow have managed to redeploy and leverage their limited, partial, human-scale psychologies to develop shared inquiry, experimental procedures, technologies and norms of logic and evidence that have resulted in genuine scientific knowledge and responsiveness to the force of logic. . . . possibilities [that] were not foreclosed by the imperfections and partiality of the faculties we inherited. (Railton 2010)

Since this clearly happens in other domains of inquiry, why should it not be expected to happen in moral inquiry as well (FitzPatrick 2008)?

If it does, then at least some moral beliefs may be simply a result of grasping moral truths through *autonomous moral reflection* analogous to the kind of reflection and reasoning we carry out in other spheres. "Autonomous" reflection here refers to exercises of our cognitive capacities that follow norms and standards appropriate to the subject matter in question (whether mathematics, the sciences, or morality), free of direct shaping by specific evolutionary influences such as adaptations for favoring one's group (Nagel 1979). The moral beliefs we arrive at in this way may even go against the grain of whatever specific evolutionary influences there are—e.g., if we come to the view that we have an obligation to make local sacrifices in order to respect the rights of distant and nonthreatening (perhaps not yet even existing) strangers, despite contrary evolved tendencies to favor one's in-group and to limit altruism toward nonreciprocating outsiders.

In sum, insofar as the philosophical issues remain open, all of the above possibilities remain open for moral beliefs or judgments: it can't be assumed that a single model of explanation applies, and there may be limits to what can be explained scientifically. Even if it turns out that nihilism is correct and there are no moral truths at all, so that the only explanations of our moral beliefs are those appealing to causal factors having nothing to do with moral truth, there may remain significant limits to *evolutionary* explanations in particular. Suppose moral judgments are merely expressions of attitudes, commitments, or acceptance of norms, and are not straightforwardly truth-assessable: it remains possible that our moral judgments are still at least sometimes the result of autonomous redeployments of our (evolved) faculties rather than simply results of thinking along the ruts laid down for us by our evolutionary history and modified by similarly influenced cultural developments. One needn't believe in real moral truths in order to believe that autonomous reflection may still result in innovative moral content and standards that transcend specific evolutionary influences.

Doubts about Autonomous Moral Reflection and Judgment

These worries about the limits of scientific, and especially evolutionary, explanations of moral content might be mitigated if we had good scientific reason to believe that autonomous applications of human intelligence are somehow either impossible or virtually never found in the moral domain, despite being so robust in other domains of inquiry. Perhaps we rarely, if ever, have the moral beliefs we do for the reasons we give for them: they are simply *caused* by evolved emotional responses and the *reasons* we cite and defend as good reasons for thinking these beliefs to be true are just fabricated *post hoc rationalizations* (Haidt 2001). Or perhaps we do often believe what we believe for the reasons we give, but the proper explanation for *why we take* these considerations to *be* reasons favoring these beliefs is a merely causal one appealing to evolutionary influences with cultural window dressing, rather than lying in the fact that they *really are good reasons* for believing the things in question.

Both of these "debunking" models of moral judgment and justification are in fact plausible for *some* moral beliefs: even the staunchest moral realist—who posits the existence of moral truths that are robustly independent of our moral beliefs and attitudes, our conceptual schemes, and our particular stances—will need some such causal models to explain cases of erroneous moral judgment.[8] The question is whether we have any good reason for thinking that such accounts apply quite generally to *all* moral beliefs—not merely to unreflective condemnations of interracial marriage, say, but equally to considered and well-defended judgments about basic human rights or obligations to distant future generations.

It is highly doubtful that the scientific data give us any reason to accept such strong deflationary claims about moral judgment or belief. While there is good evidence that many moral judgments occur quickly, without moral reflection and reasoning taking place on the spot, this is consistent with their nonetheless being informed by background reflection and reasoning, which give rise to standing moral beliefs for which our reason-giving explanations are accurate—beliefs that enable us often to respond to particular cases without the need for fresh reasoning (Pizarro and Bloom 2003). Nor does the fact that we sometimes find it hard to articulate a rationale for a quick moral judgment show that the response is merely emotion-driven as opposed to being a cognitive response to objective normative features of the situation—for the same situation might arise for a chess master whose grasping that a certain move is best outruns her ability on the spot to articulate exactly why (Kamm 2007). And even if it's true that moral reflection and reasoning, where it does occur, is often distorted by evolved emotional influences, whether this is so for a given case can be decided only by looking at that case carefully and determining whether this provides a better explanation for that reasoning and judgment than alternatives, such as the explanation that the reasoning and judgment are in fact *morally plausible*. This itself requires critical *moral* reflection, and so isn't something that can be settled within the scientific work as such. And this means that the scientific work, while highlighting ways in which evolved emotional dispositions may sometimes determine moral judgment, cannot by itself settle when or how often this is happening.[9]

Evolutionary Explanations and Evolutionary Metaethics

All of this has significant implications not only for the scientific explanatory projects themselves but also for philosophical projects that involve appeals to scientific results about morality in the empirical sense. It has been argued, for example, that in light of our best understanding of evolutionary biology, moral realism (in the sense clarified below) turns out to saddle us with moral skepticism, and is therefore implausible (Street 2006). The argument goes roughly as follows, beginning with a very strong claim of *content nativism*:

(i) "Evolutionary forces have played a tremendous role in shaping the content of human evaluative attitudes." That is, "our system of evaluative judgments is thoroughly saturated with evolutionary influence," through the pervasive shaping of relevant psychological dispositions by natural selection in ancestral environments (Street 2006, 109, 114).
(ii) According to credible evolutionary accounts, natural selection would have shaped our psychological dispositions simply in ways that favored whatever variations best contributed to the biological fitness of our hunter-gatherer ancestors, ultimately promoting their reproductive success over peers with other variations (Street 2006, pp. 127ff, Joyce 2006, 131, 184).
(iii) So the contents of our evaluative attitudes thoroughly reflect this shaping of our psychologies by natural selection based on what promoted differential reproductive success by our hunter-gatherer ancestors.
(iv) Thus, even if there were moral truths of the sort realists posit—i.e., truths that are both *independent* of our evaluative attitudes (rather than being merely functions of them) and *not reducible* to truths about what would maximize reproductive success in hunter-gatherers in ancestral environments—we have no reason to suppose that our evaluative attitudes and underlying psychological dispositions would tend to *track* those truths; the pervasive evolutionary influences on our evaluative faculties and attitudes would just constitute a *distorting* influence on the project of trying to grasp such independent moral truths.[10]
(v) Therefore, if the realist account of moral truth were correct, then we would have no reason to suppose that our moral judgments are even approximately true, given their pervasive "shaping" and "saturation" by evolutionary influences. Moral realism thus leads to moral *skepticism*, which undermines the attraction of realism (what good are objective moral truths if we cannot know them?). If we want to avoid moral skepticism, we should abandon moral realism.[11]

The crucial question to raise about this argument, however, is why we should believe the first premise to begin with.[12] We have seen that it is not established by the sciences. In order to get such a strong claim we would have to supplement the scientific evidence for *some* evolutionary influence with the further, very strong assumption that we cannot or at least do not exercise autonomous reflection and thought in the moral domain as we plainly do in other domains.[13] And once again it is far from clear that we have any reason to believe that, especially if we have *not already* rejected moral realism (and the possibility of our having grasped independent moral facts) to begin with—a rejection that obviously cannot be presupposed by this argument against moral realism without just begging the question.

Again, we might be pushed toward discounting autonomous moral reflection if it could be shown that whatever moral reflection and reasoning we engage in is limited merely to assessing "thoroughly contaminated" evaluative beliefs using "tools of rational reflection [that are] equally contaminated" (Street 2006, 124). But this claim is based upon the very premise in question (premise [i]): the tools of reflection are allegedly thoroughly contaminated *because of* the "tremendous" evolutionary influence on the content of "our" moral judgments across the board; yet our question was why we should believe the latter to begin with. Until we are given independent reason to discount the power of moral reflection so radically, treating it as nothing more than using some rotten apples to judge other rotten apples, we have no reason to dismiss the possibility of autonomous moral reflection, and therefore no reason to accept premise (i) and its claim of pervasive "saturation" of our moral beliefs with evolutionary influence. The argument would persuade one of a deflationary picture of morality only if one *started out* with such a picture in the first place.[14]

Conclusion

Nothing has been said here to show that there *are* in fact objective moral truths, or that some of our moral beliefs are best explained as apprehensions of such truths, as the realist maintains. The point has been simply that this is a deep and live philosophical issue, and that how things stand in this regard makes a difference to scientific projects aimed at explaining why human beings have the moral beliefs, feelings, and behavioral patterns we do: although these are empirical phenomena, they may often not be explicable through a purely scientific approach.

This may seem a surprising result, but if it does, this is likely because those engaged in scientific inquiry into morality in the *empirical* sense tend to isolate this project from reflection on morality in the *normative* sense and from their own moral commitments as moral agents. If one began by thinking about one's own commitment to the proposition that racial discrimination is wrong, for example, and why one accepts this proposition and thinks that others should too, it would be harder to slip into the assumption that the way to explain moral beliefs across the board is by scientific appeal to merely causal influences rather than by philosophical appeal to justifying reasons. The whole matter might then better be seen in all its complexity, perhaps slowing the rush to deflate morality in the name of scientific progress.[15]

References

Barkow, J. H., Cosmides, L. and Tooby, J. (1992), *The Adapted Mind: Evolutionary Psychology and the Generation of Culture*. New York: Oxford University Press.

Bratman, M. (2007), *Structures of Agency*. Oxford: Oxford University Press.

Buller, D. J. (2005), *Adapting Minds: Evolutionary Psychology and the Persistent Quest for Human Nature*. Cambridge, MA: MIT Press.

Buss, D. M. ed., (2005), *Handbook of Evolutionary Psychology*. Hoboken, NJ: John Wiley & Sons.

Copp, D. (2008), "Darwinian Skepticism about Moral Realism." *Philosophical Issues* 18 (1), 186–206.

Coyne, J. A. (2000), "Of Vice and Men." *The New Republic* 222(14), 27–34.

Dwyer, S. (2008), "How Not to Argue that Morality Isn't Innate: Comments on Prinz," in Sinnott-Armstrong, W. (ed.) (2008a), 407–18.

Enoch, D. (2010), "The Epistemological Challenge to Metanormative Realism: How Best to Understand It, and How to Cope with It." *Philosophical Studies* 148, 413–38.

FitzPatrick, W. (2008), "Morality and Evolutionary Biology." in Zalta, E. N. (ed.), *Stanford Encyclopedia of Philosophy*: http://plato.stanford.edu/archives/win2008/entries/morality-biology/ .

—. (2009), "Recent Work on Ethical Realism." *Analysis Reviews* 69(4), 746–60.

Gibbard, A. (1990), *Wise Choices, Apt Feelings*. Cambridge, MA: Harvard University Press.

Haidt, J. (2001), "The Emotional Dog and Its Rational Tail: A Social Intuitionist Approach to Moral Judgment." *Psychological Review* 108(4), 814–34.

Haidt, J. and Bjorklund, Fredrik. (2008), "Social Intuitionists Answer Six Questions about Moral Psychology," in Sinnott-Armstrong, W., (ed.) (2008b), 181–217.

Hauser, M., Young L. and Cushman, F. (2008), "Reviving Rawls's Linguistic Analogy: Operative Principles and the Causal Structure of Moral Actions," in Sinnott-Armstrong, W. (ed.) (2008b), 107–44.

Joyce, R. (2006), *The Evolution of Morality*. Cambridge, MA: MIT Press.

Kamm, F. (2007), *Intricate Ethics: Rights, Responsibilities, and Permissible Harm*. Oxford: Oxford University Press.

Kitcher, P. (2006a), "Biology and Ethics," in Copp, D. (ed.), *The Oxford Handbook of Ethical Theory*. Oxford: Oxford University Press, 163–85.

—. (2006b), "Between Fragile Altruism and Morality: Evolution and the Emergence of Normative Guidance," in G. Boniolo and G. DeAnna (eds.), *Evolutionary Ethics and Contemporary Biology*. Cambridge: Cambridge University Press, 159–77.

Korsgaard, C. (2006), "Morality and the Distinctiveness of Human Action," in de Waal, F., *Primates and Philosophers: How Morality Evolved*. Princeton: Princeton University Press, 98–119.

Landau, E. (2010), "Can Morality Be Changed Magnetically?," CNN.com, March 30, http://pagingdrgupta.blogs.cnn.com/2010/03/30/can-morality-be-changed-magnetically/

Lieberman, D. (2008), "Moral Sentiments Relating to Incest: Discerning Adaptations from By-Products," in Sinnott-Armstrong (2008a), 165–90.

Mikhail, J. (2008), "The Poverty of the Moral Stimulus," in Sinnott-Armstrong (2008a), 353–9.

Miller, C. (2009), "The Conditions of Moral Realism." *The Journal of Philosophical Research* 34 123–55.

Nagel, T. (1979), "Ethics without Biology," in *Mortal Questions*. Cambridge: Cambridge University Press, 142–6.

Parfit, D. (1997), "Reasons and Motivation," *Proceedings of the Aristotelian Society*, Supp. Vol. 71, 99–130.

Pizarro, D. and Bloom, P. (2003), "The Intelligence of the Moral Intuitions: Comments on Haidt (2001)." *Psychological Review* 110(1), 193–6.

Prinz, J. (2008), "Is Morality Innate?," in Sinnott-Armstrong (2008a), 367–406.

Railton, P. (2010), "Moral Camouflage or Moral Monkeys?," in *The New York Times*, "The Stone," July 18: http://opinionator.blogs.nytimes.com/2010/07/18/moral-camouflage-or-moral-monkeys/

Richardson, R. C. (2007), *Evolutionary Psychology as Maladapted Psychology*. Cambridge, MA: MIT Press.

Ruse, M. (1986), *Taking Darwin Seriously*. New York: Blackwell.

Sinnott-Armstrong, W. ed. (2008a), *Moral Psychology, Vol. 1: The Evolution of Morality: Adaptations and Innateness*. Cambridge, MA: MIT Press.

— ed. (2008b), *Moral Psychology, Vol. 2: The Cognitive Science of Morality: Intuition and Diversity*. Cambridge, MA: MIT Press.

Sripada, C. S. (2008), "Nativism and Moral Psychology: Three Models of the Innate Structure that Shapes the Contents of Moral Norms," in Sinnott-Armstrong, W. (ed.) (2008a), 319–44.

Street, S. (2006), "A Darwinian Dilemma for Realist Theories of Value," *Philosophical Studies* 127, 109–66.

Wielenberg, E. (2010), "On the Evolutionary Debunking of Morality." *Ethics* 120, 441–64.

Wilson, E. O. (1975), *Sociobiology: The New Synthesis*. Cambridge, MA: Harvard University Press.

— (1978), *On Human Nature*. Cambridge, MA: Harvard University Press.

Part III

Additional Resources

Resources for the Fields of Metaethics and Normative Theory

Christian B. Miller

Note: The sections below do not include resources relevant to applied ethics.

Selected Centers and Institutes Related to Ethics

Brandeis University International Center for Ethics, Justice and Public Life
http://www.brandeis.edu/ethics/
California State University Bakersfield Kegley Institute of Ethics
http://www.cs.csubak.edu/~donna/kie/
Cardiff University Centre for Ethics, Law and Society
http://www.ccels.cardiff.ac.uk/
Dartmouth College Ethics Institute
http://www.dartmouth.edu/~ethics/index.html
Duke University Kenan Institute for Ethics
http://kenan.ethics.duke.edu/
Emory Center for Ethics
http://ethics.emory.edu/index.html
Ethics Resource Center
http://www.ethics.org/
European Center for Ethics
http://www.kuleuven.be/oce/index.php
Harvard University Edmond J. Safra Foundation Center for Ethics
http://www.ethics.harvard.edu/
Indiana University Poynter Center for the Study of Ethics and American Institutions
http://www.indiana.edu/~poynter/
Institute for Global Ethics
http://www.globalethics.org/
Oxford Centre for Ethics and Philosophy of Law
http://users.ox.ac.uk/~lawf0081/cepl/?path=/cepl/
Princeton University Center for Human Values
http://uchv.princeton.edu/
Southern Methodist University Center for Ethics and Public Responsibility
http://smu.edu/ethicscenter/about/default.asp

Stanford University Center for Advanced Study in Behavioral Sciences
http://www.casbs.org/index.php?act=page&id=2
Stetson University Institute for Christian Ethics
http://www2.stetson.edu/~ljguenth/group/
St. James Ethics Centre (Sydney, Australia)
http://www.ethics.org.au/
Tulane Center for Ethics and Public Affairs
http://murphy.tulane.edu/center/
University of Colorado at Boulder Center for Values & Social Policy
http://www.colorado.edu/philosophy/center/
University of Idaho Center for Ethics
http://www.educ.uidaho.edu/center_for_ethics/
University of Miami Law School Center for Ethics and Public Service
http://www.law.miami.edu/ceps/index.php
University of Notre Dame Center for Ethics and Culture
https://sites.google.com/a/nd.edu/the-notre-dame-center-for-ethics-and-culture/
University of San Diego Values Institute
http://www.sandiego.edu/cas/phil/affiliations/Values_Institute.php
University of St. Andrews Centre for Ethics, Philosophy and Public Affairs
http://www.st-andrews.ac.uk/ceppa/
University of Tampa Center for Ethics
http://www.ut.edu/landingtemplate.aspx?id=11594&terms=center%20for%20ethics&fragment=&SearchType=&terms=center%20for%20ethics
University of Toronto Centre for Ethics
http://www.ethics.utoronto.ca/index.php
Utah Valley University Center for the Study of Ethics
http://www.uvu.edu/ethics/
Vanderbilt University Center for Ethics
http://www.vanderbilt.edu/CenterforEthics/index.html
Western Michigan University Center for the Study of Ethics in Society
http://www.wmich.edu/ethics/

Research Fellowships Specifically Pertaining to Ethics Research

Harvard University Edmond J. Safra Foundation Center for Ethics Faculty Fellowships
http://www.ethics.harvard.edu/
Princeton University Center for Human Values Visiting Fellowships
http://uchv.princeton.edu/
Stanford University Center for Advanced Study in Behavioral Sciences
http://www.casbs.org/index.php?act=page&id=2
Tulane Center for Ethics and Public Affairs Faculty Fellowships
http://murphy.tulane.edu/center/faculty-fellowships.php
University of St. Andrews Centre for Ethics, Philosophy and Public Affairs Visiting Research Fellowships
http://www.st-andrews.ac.uk/ceppa/research.html

University of Toronto Visiting Faculty Fellowships
http://www.ethics.utoronto.ca/index.php?id=16
Utah Valley University Center for the Study of Ethics
http://www.uvu.edu/ethics/

Ethics Societies

Association for Feminist Ethics and Social Theory
http://www.afeast.org/
British Society for Ethical Theory
http://www.bset.org.uk/
International Society for Utilitarian Studies
http://www.ucl.ac.uk/Bentham-Project/info/isus1.htm
Moral Psychology Research Group
http://www.moralpsychology.net/group/
North American Society for Social Philosophy
http://www.pitt.edu/~nassp/nassp.html
Society for Empirical Ethics
http://spinner.cofc.edu/~see/SEE_home_page.htm?referrer=webcluster&
Society for Ethics
http://www2.gsu.edu/~phljac/society.html

Research Projects on Topics in Ethics

The Character Project (Wake Forest University)
http://thecharacterproject.com/
Defining Wisdom (University of Chicago)
http://wisdomresearch.org/
Knowing in Religion and Morality (Purdue University)
http://www.cla.purdue.edu/phil/knowing//index.html
Science of Generosity Project (University of Notre Dame)
http://generosityresearch.nd.edu/
Science of Virtues Project (University of Chicago)
http://scienceofvirtues.org/default.aspx

Some Helpful Websites with Ethics Content

Bibliography of Metaethics (James Lenman)
http://www.lenmanethicsbibliography.group.shef.ac.uk/Bib.htm
EpistemeLinks
http://www.epistemelinks.com/index.aspx
Ethics Updates
http://ethics.sandiego.edu/

Glossary of Common Terms in Ethical Theory (Robert Johnson)
http://web.missouri.edu/~johnsonrn/eterms.html
Guide to Philosophy on the Internet
http://www.earlham.edu/~peters/gpi/index.htm
Internet Encyclopedia of Philosophy
http://www.iep.utm.edu/
JSTOR
http://www.jstor.org/
Noesis (online search engine)
http://hippias.evansville.edu/
Online Papers in Philosophy (David Chalmers)
http://consc.net/people.html
Philosopher's Index
http://philinfo.org/
The Philosopher's Magazine
http://www.philosophersnet.com/
The Philosophical Calendar
http://www.crvp.org/Philosophical_Calendar/index.html
Philosophy Around the Web
http://users.ox.ac.uk/~worc0337/phil_index.html
Philosophy News Service
http://www.philosophynews.com/
Philosophy Now
http://www.philosophynow.org/
PhilPapers: Online Research in Philosophy
http://philpapers.org/
Routledge Encyclopedia of Philosophy
http://www.rep.routledge.com/
Stanford Encyclopedia of Philosophy
http://plato.stanford.edu/

Some Leading Blogs with Ethics Related Discussions

Brainethics
http://brainethics.org/
Ethics Etc.
http://ethics-etc.com/
Experimental Philosophy
http://experimentalphilosophy.typepad.com/
Flickers of Freedom
http://agencyandresponsibility.typepad.com/flickers-of-freedom/
Janus Blog (Virtue Ethics)
http://janusblog.squarespace.com/
PEA Soup (Philosophy, Ethics, and Academia)
http://peasoup.typepad.com/peasoup/

Philosophy of Action
http://www.philosophyofaction.com/
The Situationist
http://thesituationist.wordpress.com/
Unideal Observers
http://bgethics.blogspot.com/

Regular Conferences

Arizona Workshop in Normative Ethics
http://www.mctimmons.com/home.html
British Society for Ethical Theory Annual Conference
http://www.bset.org.uk/
Conference on Value Inquiry (2010)
http://philosophy.siuc.edu/CALLFORPAPERS.htm
Felician College Ethics Conference
http://faculty.felician.edu/khawajai/
International Social Philosophy Conference
http://www.pitt.edu/~nassp/ISPConference.htm
International Society for Utilitarian Studies
http://www.ucl.ac.uk/Bentham-Project/info/isus1.htm
New Orleans Workshop on Agency and Responsibility
http://murphy.tulane.edu/events/conferences-symposia/1888.php
Northwestern University Society for Ethical Theory and Political Philosophy
http://www.philosophy.northwestern.edu/conferences/moralpolitical/
Rocky Mountain Ethics Congress
http://www.colorado.edu/philosophy/center/rome.shtml
St. Louis Annual Conference on Reasons and Rationality
http://umsl.edu/~slacrr/index.html
Wisconsin Metaethics Workshop
http://sites.google.com/site/shaferlandau/home

Selected Print Journals Related to Ethics

Annual Review of Law and Ethics
http://www.str2.jura.uni-erlangen.de/hruschka/JRE/
Cultural Values
http://www.blackwellpublishing.com/journal.asp?ref=1362-5179
Ethical Perspectives
http://www.ethical-perspectives.be/
Ethical Theory and Moral Practice
http://www.springerlink.com/content/102880/
Ethics
http://www.journals.uchicago.edu/toc/et/current

Ethics and Behavior
http://www.tandf.co.uk/journals/titles/10508422.asp
Ethics and Education
http://www.tandf.co.uk/journals/titles/17449642.asp
Ethics and International Affairs
http://www.carnegiecouncil.org/resources/journal/index.html
International Journal of Politics and Ethics
http://www.ijpe.blogspot.com/
Journal of Ethics
http://www.springer.com/sociology/applied+ethics/journal/10892
Journal of Global Ethics
http://www.tandf.co.uk/journals/titles/17449626.asp
Journal of Happiness Studies
http://www.springer.com/social+sciences/well-being/journal/10902
Journal of Moral Education
http://www.tandf.co.uk/journals/titles/03057240.asp
Journal of Moral Philosophy
http://www.brill.nl/jmp
Journal of Religious Ethics
http://www.blackwellpublishing.com/journal.asp?ref=0384-9694
Journal of Social Philosophy
http://www.wiley.com/bw/journal.asp?ref=0047-2786
Journal of Value Inquiry
http://www.springer.com/philosophy/ontology/journal/10790
Notre Dame Journal of Law, Ethics, & Public Policy
http://www.nd.edu/~ndlaw/jlepp/
Philosophy and Public Affairs
http://www.wiley.com/bw/journal.asp?ref=0048-3915&site=1
Public Affairs Quarterly
http://www.press.uillinois.edu/journals/paq.html
Reason Papers: A Journal of Interdisciplinary Normative Studies
http://www.reasonpapers.com/
Res Publica: A Journal of Moral, Legal and Social Philosophy
http://www.springer.com/philosophy/value+theory/journal/11158
Studies in Christian Ethics
http://sce.sagepub.com/
Utilitas
http://journals.cambridge.org/action/displayJournal?jid=UTI
Vera Lex (Journal of the International Natural Law Society)
http://web.pace.edu/press/VeraLex.html

Electronic Journals Related to Ethics

BEARS (Brown Electronic Article Review Service)
http://www.brown.edu/Departments/Philosophy/bears/homepage.html

Ethic@: An International Journal for Moral Philosophy
http://www.cfh.ufsc.br/ethic@/
Issues in Ethics
http://www.scu.edu/ethics/publications/iie/
Journal of Buddhist Ethics
http://blogs.dickinson.edu/buddhistethics/
Journal of Ethics and Social Philosophy
http://www.jesp.org/
Studies in the History of Ethics
http://www.historyofethics.org/

Classic Works in Ethics Online

Akamac E-Text Links
http://www.cpm.ehime-u.ac.jp/AkamacHomePage/Akamac_E-text_Links/Akamac_E-text_Links.html
Christian Classics Ethereal Library
http://www.ccel.org/
EpistemeLinks
http://www.epistemelinks.com/Main/MainText.aspx
Ethics Updates
http://ethics.sandiego.edu/resources/books/books.asp
Humanities Text Initiative
http://www.hti.umich.edu/
Online Books Page
http://onlinebooks.library.upenn.edu/
Philosophy Research Base
http://www.erraticimpact.com/names_index.htm

Other

Intercollegiate Ethics Bowl
http://www.indiana.edu/~appe/ethicsbowl.html

Selected Works in Contemporary Metaethics and Normative Theory

Christian B. Miller

Note: This list is intended to be a helpful resource for those interested in digging deeper into metaethics and normative theory. It focuses mainly on familiar and influential pieces, with a few recent works added as well. The list dates back to the beginning of the twentieth century, but makes no attempt at being exhaustive. My apologies in advance for any glaring omissions.

Metaethics

Biology, Evolution, and Ethics

Axelrod, R. (1984), *The Evolution of Cooperation*. New York: Basic Books.
Barkow, J. H., Cosmides, L. and Tooby, J. (1992), *The Adapted Mind: Evolutionary Psychology and the Generation of Culture*. New York: Oxford University Press.
Boniolo, G. and DeAnna, G. (eds.) (2006), *Evolutionary Ethics and Contemporary Biology*. Cambridge: Cambridge University Press.
Buller, D. J. (2005), *Adapting Minds: Evolutionary Psychology and the Persistent Quest for Human Nature*. Cambridge: MIT Press.
Casebeer, W. (2003), *Natural Ethical Facts: Evolution, Connectionism, and Moral Cognition*. Cambridge: MIT Press.
Copp, D. (2008), "Darwinian Skepticism about Moral Realism," *Philosophical Issues* 18, 186–206.
Dawkins, R. (1982), *The Extended Phenotype*. New York: Oxford University Press.
—.(1989), *The Selfish Gene*. Oxford: Oxford University Press.
de Waal, F. (1996), *Good Natured: The Origins of Right and Wrong in Humans and Other Animals*. Cambridge: Harvard University Press.
—.(2006), *Primates and Philosophers*. Princeton: Princeton University Press.
Diamond, J. (1992), *The Third Chimpanzee: The Evolution and Future of the Human Animal*. New York: Harper Collins.
FitzPatrick, W. (2000), *Teleology and the Norms of Nature*. New York: Garland.
Foot, P. (2001), *Natural Goodness*. Oxford: Oxford University Press.

Gibbard, A. (1990), *Wise Choices, Apt Feelings*. Cambridge: Harvard University Press.
Haidt, J. (2001), "The Emotional Dog and Its Rational Tail: A Social Intuitionist Approach to Moral Judgment," *Psychological Review* 108, 814–34.
Hauser, M. (2006), *Moral Minds: How Nature Designed Our Universal Sense of Right and Wrong*. New York: Harper Collins.
Joyce, R. (2006), *The Evolution of Morality*. Cambridge: MIT Press.
Nagel, T. (1979), "Ethics without Biology," in *Mortal Questions*. Cambridge: Cambridge University Press, 142–6.
Katz, L. (ed.) (2000), *Evolutionary Origins of Morality: Cross Disciplinary Perspectives*. Thorverton, Exeter: Imprint Academic.
Kitcher, P. (1985), *Vaulting Ambition*. Cambridge: MIT Press.
—. (1993), "The Evolution of Human Altruism," *The Journal of Philosophy* 90, 497–516.
Maynard Smith, J. (1982), *Evolution and the Theory of Games*. Cambridge: Cambridge University Press.
McDowell, J. (1995), "Two Sorts of Naturalism," in *Virtues and Reasons*. R. Hursthouse, G. Lawrence, and W. Quinn (eds.). Oxford: Oxford University Press, 149–80.
Nichols, S. (2004), *Sentimental Rules: On the Natural Foundations of Moral Judgment*. Oxford: Oxford University Press.
Pinker, S. (1997), *How the Mind Works*. New York: Norton.
Pizarro, D. and Bloom, P. (2003), 'The Intelligence of the Moral Intuitions: Comments on Haidt (2001)," *Psychological Review* 110, 193–6.
Rachels, J. (1990), *Created from Animals: The Moral Implications of Darwinism*. Oxford: Oxford University Press.
Richardson, R. (2007). *Evolutionary Psychology as Maladapted Psychology*. Cambridge: MIT Press.
Rottschaefer, W. (1998). *The Biology and Psychology of Moral Agency*. Cambridge: Cambridge University Press.
Ruse, M. (1986), *Taking Darwin Seriously*. New York: Blackwell.
—. (1988), "Evolutionary Ethics: Healthy Prospect or Last Infirmity?," *Canadian Journal of Philosophy*, Supp. Vol. 14, 27–73.
Sinnott-Armstrong, W. (ed.) (2008), *Moral Psychology*, Volumes 1, 2, 3. Cambridge: MIT Press.
Sober, E. (ed.) (1994), *Conceptual Issues in Evolutionary Ethics*. 2nd ed. Cambridge: MIT Press.
Sober, E. and Wilson, D. S. (1998), *Unto Others: The Evolution and Psychology of Unselfish Behavior*. Cambridge: Harvard University Press.
Street, S. (2006), "A Darwinian Dilemma for Realist Theories of Value," *Philosophical Studies* 127, 109–66.
Thompson, M. (1995), "The Representation of Life," in *Virtues and Reasons*. R. Hursthouse, G. Lawrence, and W. Quinn (eds.). Oxford: Oxford University Press, 247–96.
Tooby, J. and Cosmides, L. (2005), "Conceptual Foundations of Evolutionary Psychology," in *The Handbook of Evolutionary Psychology*. D. Buss (ed.). Hoboken: Wiley, 5–67.
Trivers, R. (1971), "The Evolution of Reciprocal Altruism," *Quarterly Review of Biology*, 46, 35–57.

Wielenberg, E. (2010), "On the Evolutionary Debunking of Morality," *Ethics* 120, 441–64.
Wilson, E. O. (1975), *Sociobiology: The New Synthesis*. Cambridge: Harvard University Press.
— (1978), *On Human Nature*. Cambridge: Harvard University Press.
Wilson, J. Q. (1993), *The Moral Sense*. New York: The Free Press.
Wright, R. (1994), *The Moral Animal: The New Science of Evolutionary Psychology*. New York: Pantheon.

Constructivism

Copp, D. (1995), *Morality, Normativity, and Society*. Oxford: Oxford University Press.
Firth, R. (1952), "Ethical Absolutism and the Ideal Observer," *Philosophy and Phenomenological Research* 12, 317–45.
Harman, G. (1977), *The Nature of Morality*. Oxford: Oxford University Press.
—. (2000), *Explaining Value and Other Essays in Moral Philosophy*. New York: Oxford University Press.
Harman, G. and Thomson, J. J. (1996), *Moral Relativism and Moral Objectivism*. Oxford: Blackwell.
Johnston, M. (1989), "Dispositional Theories of Value," *Proceedings of the Aristotelian Society*, 62, 139–74.
Korsgaard, C. (1996), *The Sources of Normativity*. O. O'Neill (ed.), Cambridge: Cambridge University Press.
—. (2009), *Self-Constitution: Agency, Identity and Integrity*. Oxford: Oxford University Press.
Lewis, D. (1989), "Dispositional Theories of Value," in *Papers in Ethics and Social Philosophy*. Cambridge: Cambridge University Press, 68–94.
O'Neill, O. (1988), "Constructivisms in Ethics," *Proceedings of the Aristotelian Society* 89, 1–17.
Rawls, J. (2001), "Kantian Constructivism in Moral Theory," in *Collected Papers*. S. Freeman (ed.). Cambridge: Harvard University Press, 303–58.
Smith, M. (1989), "Dispositional Theories of Value," *Proceedings of the Aristotelian Society* Supplementary Volume. 89–111.
—. (1994), *The Moral Problem*. Oxford: Blackwell.
Timmons, M. (1999), *Morality without Foundations: A Defense of Ethical Contextualism*. New York: Oxford University Press.
Wiggins, D. (1988), "Truth, Invention and the Meaning of Life," in *Essays on Moral Realism*. G. Sayre-McCord (ed.). Ithaca: Cornell University Press, 127–65.
Wong, D. (1986), *Moral Relativity*. Berkeley: University of California Press.
—. (2006), *Natural Moralities*. Oxford: Oxford University Press.

Error Theory

Joyce, R. (2001), *The Myth of Morality*. Cambridge: Cambridge University Press.
—. (2006), *The Evolution of Morality*. Cambridge: MIT Press.

Joyce, R., and Kirchin, S. (eds.) (2010), *A World without Values: Essays on John Mackie's Moral Error Theory*. New York: Springer.
Kalderon, M. (2005), *Moral Fictionalism*. Oxford: Oxford University Press.
Mackie, J. L. (1977), *Ethics: Inventing Right and Wrong*. London: Penguin.
Nolan, D., Restall, G. and West, C. (2005), "Moral Fictionalism versus the Rest," *Australasian Journal of Philosophy* 83, 307–30.
Olson, J. (2010), "In Defence of Moral Error Theory," in *New Waves in Metaethics*. M. Brady (ed.). New York: Palgrave Macmillan.
Wielenberg, E. (2010), "On the Evolutionary Debunking of Morality," *Ethics* 120, 441–64.

Moral Methodology, Formulation of Positions, and Moral Epistemology

Audi, R. (1997), *Moral Knowledge and Ethical Character*. New York: Oxford University Press.
—. (2004), *The Good in the Right: A Theory of Intuition and Intrinsic Value*. Princeton: Princeton University Press.
Daniels, N. (1979), "Wide Reflective Equilibrium and Theory Acceptance in Ethics," in *Morality, Reason, and Truth*. D. Copp and D. Zimmerman (eds.). Totowa: Rowman & Allanheld.
DePaul, M. (1993), *Balance and Refinement: Beyond Coherence Methods of Moral Inquiry*. London: Routledge.
DePaul, M. and W. Ramsey (eds.) (1998), *Rethinking Intuition*. Lanham: Rowman & Littlefield.
Dreier, J. (2004), "Meta-Ethics and the Problem of Creeping Minimalism," *Philosophical Perspectives*, 18, 23–44.
Fine, K. (2001), "The Question of Realism," *Philosophers' Imprint* 1, 1–30.
Huemer, M. (2008), *Ethical Intuitionism*. London: Macmillan.
Little, M. (1997), "Virtue as Knowledge: Objections from Philosophy of Mind," *Noûs* 31, 59–79.
Mandelbaum, M. (1955), *The Phenomenology of Moral Experience*. Glencoe: The Free Press.
McNaughton, D. (1988), *Moral Vision*. Oxford: Basil Blackwell.
Miller, C. (2009), "The Conditions of Moral Realism," *The Journal of Philosophical Research* 34, 123–55.
Rawls, J. (1951), "Outline of a Decision Procedure for Ethics," *Philosophical Review* 60, 177–97.
—. (1971), *A Theory of Justice*. Cambridge: Harvard University Press.
—. (1974–75), "The Independence of Moral Theory," *Proceedings and Addresses of the American Philosophical Association* 48, 5–22.
Sayre-McCord, G. (1988), "Introduction: The Many Moral Realisms," in *Essays on Moral Realism*. G. Sayre-McCord (ed.). Ithaca: Cornell University Press, 1–23.
Sidgwick, H. (1907), *The Methods of Ethics*. Seventh Edition. London: Macmillan.
Sinnott-Armstrong, W. (2006), *Moral Skepticisms*. Oxford: Oxford University Press.

Stratton-Lake, P. (ed.) (2003), *Ethical Intuitionism: Re-evaluations*. New York: Oxford University Press.
Superson, A. (2009), *The Moral Skeptic*. New York: Oxford University Press.
Wright, C. (1992), *Truth and Objectivity*. Cambridge: Harvard University Press.

Moral Psychology

Arpaly, N. (2000), "On Acting Rationally against One's Best Judgment," *Ethics* 110, 488–513.
Audi, R. (1997), *Moral Knowledge and Ethical Character*. New York: Oxford University Press.
Berker, S. (2009), "The Normative Insignificance of Neuroscience," *Philosophy & Public Affairs* 37, 293–329.
Brink, D. (1986), "Externalist Moral Realism," *Southern Journal of Philosophy* 24, 23–40.
Charlton, W. (1988), *Weakness of Will*. Oxford: Basil Blackwell.
Copp, D. and D. Sobel (2001), "Against Direction of Fit Accounts of Belief and Desire," *Analysis* 61, 44–53.
Dancy, J. (2000), *Practical Reality*. New York: Oxford University Press.
Davidson, D. (1980), *Essays on Actions and Events*. Oxford: Clarendon Press.
Doris, J. (2002), *Lack of Character: Personality and Moral Behavior*. Cambridge: Cambridge University Press.
Flanagan, O. (1991), *Varieties of Moral Personality: Ethics and Psychological Realism*. Cambridge, MA: Harvard University Press.
Frankena, W. (1958), "Obligation and Motivation in Recent Moral Philosophy," in *Essays in Moral Philosophy*. A. Melden (ed.). Seattle: University of Washington Press.
Frankfurt, H. (1988), *The Importance of What We Care About*. Cambridge: Cambridge University Press.
Garrard, E., and McNaughton D. (1998), "Mapping Moral Motivation", *Ethical Theory and Moral Practice* 1, 45–59.
Gosling, J. (1990), *Weakness of the Will*. London: Routledge.
Harman, G. (1999), "Moral Philosophy meets Social Psychology: Virtue Ethics and the Fundamental Attribution Error," *Proceedings of the Aristotelian Society* 99, 315–331.
Holton, R. (2009) *Willing, Wanting, Waiting*. Oxford: Oxford University Press.
Knobe, J. and Nichols S. (eds.) (2008). *Experimental Philosophy*. New York: Oxford University Press.
Korsgaard, C. (1986), "Skepticism about Practical Reason," *The Journal of Philosophy* 83, 5–25.
Lewis, D. (1988), "Desire as Belief," *Mind* 97, 323–32.
Mandelbaum, M. (1955), *The Phenomenology of Moral Experience*. Glenco, IL: The Free Press.
Mele, A. (1987), *Irrationality*. New York: Oxford University Press.
—. *Springs of Action*. New York: Oxford University Press.
—. *Autonomous Agents*. New York: Oxford University Press.
—. "Internalist Moral Cognitivism and Listlessness", *Ethics* 106, 727–53.
— *Motivation and Agency*. New York: Oxford University Press.

Miller, C. (2008), "Motivation in Agents," *Noûs* 22, 222–66.
—. (2008), "Motivational Internalism," *Philosophical Studies* 139, 233–55.
Milo, R. (1984), *Immorality*. Princeton: Princeton University Press.
Nichols, S. (2004), *Sentimental Rules: On the Natural Foundations of Moral Judgment*. New York: Oxford University Press.
Pettit, P. and M. Smith (1993), "Practical Unreason," *Mind* 102, 53–79.
Price, H. (1989), "Defending Desire-as-Belief," *Mind* 98, 119–27.
Prinz, J. (2008), *The Emotional Construction of Morals*. New York: Oxford University Press.
Rottschaefer, W. (1998), *The Biology and Psychology of Moral Agency*. Cambridge: Cambridge University Press.
Schroeder, T. (2004), *Three Faces of Desire*. Oxford: Oxford University Press.
Sinnott-Armstrong, W. (ed.) (2008), *Moral Psychology*. Volumes 1, 2, 3. Cambridge: MIT Press.
Smith, M. (1994), *The Moral Problem*. Oxford: Blackwell.
Stocker, M. (1976), "The Schizophrenia of Modern Ethical Theories," *The Journal of Philosophy* 73, 453–66.
—. (1979), "Desiring the Bad," *The Journal of Philosophy* 76, 738–53.
Svavarsdottir, S. (1999), "Moral Cognition and Motivation," *Philosophical Review* 108, 161–219.
Tresan, J. (2006), "De Dicto Internalist Cognitivism," *Noûs* 40, 143–65.
Wallace, R. (2006), *Normativity and the Will: Selected Essays on Moral Psychology and Practical Reason*. New York: Oxford University Press.
Watson, G. (1977), "Skepticism about Weakness of Will," *Philosophical Review* 86, 316–39.

Moral Realism

Bloomfield, P. (2001), *Moral Reality*. New York: Oxford University Press.
Boyd, R. (1988), "How to Be a Moral Realist," in *Essays on Moral Realism*. G. Sayre-McCord (ed.). Ithaca, NY: Cornell University Press.
Brink, D. (1989), *Moral Realism and the Foundations of Ethics*. New York: Cambridge University Press.
Cuneo, T. (2007), *The Normative Web*. New York: Oxford University Press.
Dancy, J. (1993), *Moral Reasons*. Oxford: Blackwell.
Enoch, D. (2011), *Taking Morality Seriously: A Defense of Robust Realism*. Oxford: Oxford University Press.
FitzPatrick, W. (2008), "Robust Ethical Realism, Non-Naturalism and Normativity," in *Oxford Studies in Metaethics*. R. Shafer-Landau (ed.). Volume 3. Oxford: Oxford University Press, 159–206.
Frankena, W. (1939), "The Naturalistic Fallacy," *Mind* 48, 464–77.
Harman, G. and Thomson J. J. (1996), *Moral Relativism and Moral Objectivism*. Oxford: Blackwell.
Jackson, F. (1998), *From Metaphysics to Ethics*. Oxford: Oxford University Press.
McDowell, J. (1985), "Values and Secondary Qualities," in *Morality and Objectivity*. T. Honderich (ed.). London: Routledge and Kegan Paul, 110–29.

— (1998), *Mind, Value & Reality*. Cambridge: Harvard University Press.
McNaughton, D. (1988), *Moral Vision*. Oxford: Basil Blackwell.
Moore, G. E. (1903), *Principia Ethica*, Revised Edition. Cambridge: Cambridge University Press.
Nagel, T. (1986), *The View from Nowhere*. Oxford: Oxford University Press.
Parfit, D. (2011), *On What Matters*. Oxford: Oxford University Press.
Platts, M. (1979), "Moral Reality," in *Ways of Meaning*. London: Routledge and Kegan Paul.
Railton, P. (1986), "Moral Realism," *Philosophical Review* 95, 163–207.
Ross, W. D. (1930), *The Right and the Good*. Oxford: Oxford University Press.
Sayre-McCord, G. (ed.) (1988), *Essays on Moral Realism*. Ithaca: Cornell University Press
Shafer-Landau, R. (2003), *Moral Realism: A Defence*. Oxford: Oxford University Press.
Street, S. (2006), "A Darwinian Dilemma for Realist Theories of Value," *Philosophical Studies* 127, 109–66.
Sturgeon, N. (1985), 'Moral Explanations', in *Morality, Reason, and Truth*. D. Copp and D. Zimmerman (eds.). Totowa: Rowman & Littlefield.
Wielenberg, E. (2010), "On the Evolutionary Debunking of Morality," *Ethics* 120, 441–64.

Noncognitivism and Expressivism

Altham, J. (1986), "The Legacy of Emotivism," in *Fact, Science and Morality*. G. Macdonald and C. Wright (eds.). Oxford: Blackwell.
Ayer, A. J. (1936/1946), *Language, Truth and Logic*. Second Edition. London: V. Gollancz ltd.
Blackburn, S. (1984), *Spreading the Word: Groundings in the Philosophy of Language*. New York: Oxford University Press.
—. (1993), *Essays in Quasi-Realism*. New York: Oxford University Press.
—. (1998), *Ruling Passions: A Theory of Practical Reasoning*. New York: Oxford University Press.
Copp, D. (2001), "Realist-Expressivism: A Neglected Option for Moral Realism," *Social Philosophy and Policy* 18, 1–43.
Gibbard, A. (1990), *Wise Choices, Apt Feelings: A Theory of Normative Judgment*. Cambridge, MA: Harvard University Press.
—. (2003), *Thinking How to Live*. Cambridge, MA: Harvard University Press.
Geach, P. T. (1965), "Assertion," *The Philosophical Review* 74 (4), 449–65.
Hare, R. M. (1952), *The Language of Morals*. Oxford: Oxford University Press.
Schroeder, M. (2008), *Being For*. New York: Oxford University Press.
—. (2010), *Noncognitivism in Ethics*. New York: Routledge.
Searle, J. (1962), "Meaning and Speech Acts," *The Philosophical Review* 71, 423–32.
Stevenson, C. L. (1937), "The Emotive Meaning of Moral Terms," *Mind* 46, 14–31.
—. (1944), *Ethics and Language*. New Haven: Yale University Press.

Practical Reason, Practical Reasons, and Practical Reasoning

Audi, R. (2005), *Practical Reasoning and Ethical Decision*. Second Edition. London: Routledge.
Brandt, R. (1998), *A Theory of the Good and the Right*. Amherst, NY: Prometheus.
Bratman, M. (2007), *Structures of Agency: Essays*. Oxford: Oxford University Press.
Broome, J. (2005), "Does Rationality Give Us Reasons?," *Philosophical Issues* 15, Normativity, 321–37.
Byron M. (ed.) (2004), *Satisficing and Maximizing: Moral Theorists on Practical Reason*. Cambridge: Cambridge University Press.
Cullity, G, and Gaut. B. (1997), *Ethics and Practical Reason*. New York: Clarendon Press.
Dancy, J. (2004), *Ethics without Principles*. Oxford: Oxford University Press.
Darwall, S. (1983), *Impartial Reason*. Ithaca: Cornell University Press.
Enoch, D. (2006), "Agency, Shmagency: Why Normativity Won't Come from What is Constitutive of Action," *Philosophical Review* 115, 169–98.
Gert, B. (2005), *Morality: Its Nature and Justification*. Oxford: Oxford University Press.
Gert, J. (2004), *Brute Rationality: Normativity and Human Action*. Cambridge: Cambridge University Press.
Kolodny, N. (2005), 'Why be Rational?' *Mind* 114, 509–63.
Korsgaard, C. (1996), *The Sources of Normativity*. O. O'Neill (ed.). Cambridge: Cambridge University Press.
Millgram, E. (1997), *Practical Induction*. Harvard: Harvard University Press.
—. (ed.) (2001), *Varieties of Practical Reasoning*. Cambridge: MIT Press.
Nagel, T. (1970), *The Possibility of Altruism*. Princeton: Princeton University Press.
Parfit, D. (1997), "Reasons and Motivation," *Aristotelian Society Supplement* 71, 99–131.
—. (2011), *On What Matters*. Oxford: Oxford University Press.
Raz, J. (1999), *Practical Reason and Norms*. New York: Oxford University Press.
Richardson, H. (1994), *Practical Reasoning about Final Ends*. Cambridge: Cambridge University Press.
Russell, D. (2009), *Practical Intelligence and the Virtues*. New York: Oxford University Press.
Schmidtz, D. (1995), *Rational Choice and Moral Agency*. Princeton: Princeton University Press.
Schroeder, M. (2007), *Slaves of the Passions*. New York: Oxford University Press.
Setiya, K. (2007), *Reasons without Rationalism*. Princeton: Princeton University Press.
van Roojen, M. (2010), "Moral Rationalism and Rational Amoralism," *Ethics* 120, 495–525.
Velleman, J. (2000), *The Possibility of Practical Reason*. Oxford: Oxford University Press.
Wallace, R. (2006), *Normativity and the Will: Selected Essays in Moral Psychology and Practical Reason*. New York: Oxford University Press.
Williams, B. (1981), "Internal and External Reasons," in *Moral Luck*, Cambridge: Cambridge University Press, 101–13.
—. (2001), "Postscript: Some Further Notes on Internal and External Reasons," in *Varieties of Practical Reasoning*. E. Millgram (ed.). Cambridge: MIT Press, 91–7.

Normative Theory

Consequentialism

Adams, R. (1976), "Motive Utilitarianism," *The Journal of Philosophy* 73, 467–81.
Bennett, J. (1995), *The Act Itself*. New York: Oxford University Press.
Brandt, R. (1979), *A Theory of the Good and the Right*. New York: Oxford University Press.
—. (1992), *Morality, Utilitarianism, and Rights*. Cambridge: Cambridge University Press.
Brink, D. (1989), *Moral Realism and the Foundations of Ethics*. New York: Cambridge University Press.
Broome, J. (1991), *Weighing Goods*. Oxford: Basil Blackwell.
Cummiskey, D. (1996), *Kantian Consequentialism*. New York: Oxford University Press.
Driver, J. (2001), *Uneasy Virtue*. Cambridge: Cambridge University Press.
Feldman, F. (1997), *Utilitarianism, Hedonism, and Desert*. New York: Cambridge University Press.
Foot, P. (1985), "Utilitarianism and the Virtues," *Mind* 94, 196–209.
Griffin, J. (1986), *Well-Being*. Oxford: Clarendon Press.
Hare, R. M. (1981), *Moral Thinking*. Oxford: Clarendon Press.
Harsanyi, J. C. (1977), "Morality and the Theory of Rational Behavior," *Social Research* 44, 623–56.
Hooker, B. (2000), *Ideal Code, Real World: A Rule-Consequentialist Theory of Morality*. Oxford: Oxford University Press.
Hospers, J. (1961), "Rule-Utilitarianism," in *Human Conduct: An Introduction to the Problem of Ethics*. Reprinted in *Moral Philosophy: A Reader*. Louis P. Pojman (ed.). Indianapolis: Hackett Publishing Company, 2003.
Hurley, P. (2009). *Beyond Consequentialism*. New York: Oxford University Press.
Hurka, T. (2003), *Virtue, Vice, and Value*. New York: Oxford University Press.
Jackson, F. (1991), "Decision-Theoretic Consequentialism and the Nearest and Dearest Objection," *Ethics* 101, 461–82.
Kagan, S. (1989), *The Limits of Morality*. New York: Clarendon Press.
Kagan, S. and Vallentyne P. (1997), "Infinite Value and Finitely Additive Value Theory," *The Journal of Philosophy* 94, 5–26.
Lenman, J. (2000), "Consequentialism and Cluelessness," *Philosophy & Public Affairs* 29, 342–70.
Lyons, D. (1965), *Forms and Limits of Utilitarianism*. Oxford: Clarendon Press.
Mulgan, T. (2001), *The Demands of Consequentialism*. Oxford: Oxford University Press.
Murphy, L. (2000), *Moral Demands in Nonideal Theory*. New York: Oxford University Press.
Parfit, D. (1986), *Reasons and Persons*. Oxford: Oxford University Press.
Portmore, D. (2011), *Commonsense Consequentialism: Wherein Morality Meets Rationality*. New York: Oxford University Press.
Railton, P. (2003), *Facts, Values, and Norms: Essays toward a Morality of Consequence*. Cambridge: Cambridge University Press.

Regan, D. (1980), *Utilitarianism and Cooperation*. Oxford: Clarendon Press.
Scanlon, T. (1982), "Contractualism and Utilitarianism," in Sen and Williams (1982).
Scheffler, S. (1995), *The Rejection of Consequentialism*. Oxford: Clarendon Press.
Sen, A. and Williams B. (1982), *Utilitarianism and Beyond*. Cambridge: Cambridge University Press.
Sidgwick, H. (1907), *The Methods of Ethics*. Seventh Edition. London: Macmillan.
Singer, P. (1993), *Practical Ethics*. Second Edition. Cambridge: Cambridge University Press.
Slote, M. (1984), "Satisficing Consequentialism," *Proceedings of the Aristotelian Society* 58, 139–63.
Smart, J. J. C. (1956), "Extreme and Restricted Utilitarianism," *The Philosophical Quarterly* 6, 344–54.
Smart, J. J. C. and Williams B. (1973), *Utilitarianism: For and against*. Cambridge: Cambridge University Press.
Thomson, J. J. (1976), "Killing, Letting Die, and the Trolley Problem," *The Monist* 59, 204–17.
Unger, P. (1996), *Living High and Letting Die*. New York: Oxford University Press.
Williams, B. (1981), "Persons, Character, and Morality", in *Moral Luck*. Cambridge: Cambridge University Press.

Ethical Concepts

Adams, R. (1999), *Finite and Infinite Goods: A Framework for Ethics*. New York: Oxford University Press.
Anderson, E. (1993), *Value in Ethics and Economics*. Cambridge, MA: Harvard University Press.
Annas, J. (1993), *The Morality of Happiness*. New York and Oxford: Oxford University Press.
Audi, R. (2004), *The Good in the Right: A Theory of Intuition and Intrinsic Value*. Princeton: Princeton University Press.
Feldman, F. (2004), *Pleasure and the Good Life: Concerning the Nature, Varieties, and Plausibility of Hedonism*. New York: Oxford University Press.
Griffin, J. (1986), *Well-Being*. Oxford: Clarendon Press.
—. (1996), *Value Judgement: Improving our Ethical Beliefs*. Oxford: Clarendon Press.
Hurka, T. (2003), *Virtue, Vice, and Value*. New York: Oxford University Press.
Kraut, R. (2007), *What is Good and Why: The Ethics of Well-Being*. Harvard: Harvard University Press.
Sinnott-Armstrong, W. (1988), *Moral Dilemmas*. Oxford: Basil Blackwell.
Williams, B. (1985), *Ethics and the Limits of Philosophy*. Cambridge: Harvard University Press.
Zimmerman, M. J. (1996), *The Concept of Moral Obligation*. Cambridge: Cambridge University Press.

Feminist and Care Ethics

Antony, L. and Witt C. (eds.) (2002), *A Mind of One's Own: Feminist Essays on Reason and Objectivity*. Second Edition. Boulder: Westview Press.
Calhoun, C. (ed.) (2004), *Setting the Moral Compass: Essays by Women Philosophers*. New York: Oxford University Press.
Card, C. (ed.) (1991), *Feminist Ethics*. Lawrence: University Press of Kansas.
—. (1993), "Gender and Moral Luck," in *Identity, Character, and Morality: Essays in Moral Psychology*. Owen J. Flanagan and Amelie Oksenberg Rorty (eds.). Cambridge: MIT Press, 199–218.
Cudd, A. (2006), *Analyzing Oppression*. New York: Oxford University Press.
DesAutels, P. and Walker M. (2004), *Moral Psychology: Feminist Ethics and Social Theory*. Lanham: Rowman & Littlefield.
Dworkin, A. (1987), *Intercourse*. New York: Free Press.
Friedman, M. (1993), "Liberating Care," in *What Are Friends for*. Marilyn Freidman (ed.). Ithaca: Cornell University Press, 142–83.
Frye, M. (1983), *The Politics of Reality: Essays in Feminist Theory*. Trumansburg: Crossing, 1–16.
Gilligan, C. (1982), *In a Different Voice: Psychological Theory and Women's Development*. Cambridge: Harvard University Press.
Held, V. (1990), "Feminist Transformations of Moral Theory," *Philosophy and Phenomenological Research* 1, 321–44.
Hoagland, S. (1991), "Some Thoughts about 'Caring'," in *Feminist Ethics*. Claudia Card (ed.). Lawrence: University of Kansas Press, 246–63.
Jaggar, A. (1983), *Feminist Politics and Human Nature*. Totowa: Rowman & Allanheld, Publishers.
Kittay, E. (1999), *Love's Labor: Essays on Women, Equality, and Dependency*. New York: Routledge.
Langton, R. (2009), *Sexual Solipsism: Philosophical Essays on Pornography and Objectification*. New York: Oxford University Press.
Little, M. (2007), "Seeing and Caring: The Role of Affect in Feminist Moral Epistemology," in *Foundations of Ethics: An Anthology*. Russ Shafer-Landau and Terence Cuneo (eds.). Malden: Blackwell Publishing, 420–32.
Mackenzie, C. and Stoljar N. (eds.) (2000), *Relational Autonomy: Feminist Perspectives on Autonomy, Agency, and the Social Self*. New York: Oxford University Press.
May, L. (1998), *Masculinity and Morality*. Ithaca: Cornell University Press.
Noddings, N. (1984), *Caring: A Feminine Approach to Ethics and Moral Education*. Berkeley: University of California Press.
Nussbaum, M. (ed.) (1999), *Sex and Social Justice*. New York: Oxford University Press.
—. (2000), *Women and Human Development: The Capabilities Approach*. New York: Cambridge University Press.
Okin, S. (2004), "Is Multiculturalism Bad for Women?" in *Varieties of Feminist Liberalism*. Amy R. Baehr (ed.). Lanham: Rowman & Littlefield, 191–205.
Superson, A. (2009), *The Moral Skeptic*. New York: Oxford University Press.
Tessman, L. (2005), *Burdened Virtues: Virtue Ethics for Liberatory Struggles*. New York: Oxford University Press.

Tronto, J. (1993), "Beyond Gender Difference to a Theory of Care," in *An Ethic of Care: Feminist and Interdisciplinary Perspectives*. Mary Jeanne Larrabee (ed.). New York: Routledge, 240–57.

Walker, M. (1998), *Moral Understandings: A Feminist Study in Ethics*. New York: Routledge.

Westlund, A. (2003), "Selflessness and Responsibility for Self: Is Deference Compatible with Autonomy?" *The Philosophical Review* 112, 483–523.

Kantian Ethics, Contractarianism, and, Contractualism

Baron, M. (1995), *Kantian Ethics Almost without Apology*. Ithaca: Cornell University Press.

Bennett, J. (1974), "The Conscience of Huckleberry Finn," *Philosophy* 49, 123–34.

Cummiskey, D. (1996), *Kantian Consequentialism*. New York: Oxford University Press.

Darwall, S. (2006), *The Second-Person Standpoint: Morality, Respect, and Accountability*. Cambridge: Harvard University Press.

Dean, R. (2006), *The Value of Humanity in Kant's Moral Theory*. New York: Oxford University Press.

Donagan, A. (1977), *The Theory of Morality*. Chicago: University of Chicago Press.

Frierson, P. (2003), *Freedom and Anthropology in Kant's Moral Philosophy*. New York: Cambridge University Press.

Gauthier, D. (1986), *Morals by Agreement*. New York: Oxford University Press.

Gert, B. (2005), *Morality: Its Nature and Justification*. Revised Edition. New York: Oxford University Press.

Gewirth, A. (1978), *Reason and Morality*. Chicago: University of Chicago Press.

Guyer, P. (ed.) (1998), *Kant's Groundwork of the Metaphysics of Morals*. Lanham: Rowman and Littlefield.

—. (2000), *Kant on Freedom, Law, and Happiness*. New York: Cambridge University Press.

Hare, J. (1996), *The Moral Gap : Kantian Ethics, Human Limits, and God's Assistance*. New York: Oxford University Press.

Herman, B. (1993), *The Practice of Moral Judgment*. Cambridge: Harvard University Press.

Hill, T. (1991), *Autonomy and Self-respect*. New York: Cambridge University Press.

—. (1992), *Dignity and Practical Reason*. Ithaca: Cornell University Press.

Korsgaard, C. (1996), *Creating the Kingdom of Ends*. New York: Cambridge University Press.

—. (1996), *The Sources of Normativity*. Cambridge: Cambridge University Press.

—. (2008), *The Constitution of Agency: Essays on Practical Reason and Moral Psychology*. Oxford: Oxford University Press.

—. (2009), *Self-Constitution: Agency, Identity, and Integrity*. New York: Oxford University Press.

Louden, R. (2000), *Kant's Impure Ethics*. New York: Oxford University Press.

Markovits, J. (2010), "Acting for the Right Reasons," *Philosophical Review* 119, 201–42.

Nagel, T. (1991), *Equality and Partiality*. Oxford: Oxford University Press.
O'Neill, O. (1989), *Constructions of Reason: Explorations of Kant's Practical Philosophy*. New York: Cambridge University Press.
—. (1996), *Towards Justice and Virtue*. Cambridge: Cambridge University Press.
Parfit, D. (1986), *Reasons and Persons*. Oxford: Oxford University Press.
Paton, H. J. (1958), *The Categorical Imperative*. London: Hutchison.
Rawls, J. (1971), *A Theory of Justice*. Cambridge: Harvard University Press.
—. (1993), *Political Liberalism*. New York: Columbia University Press.
—. (2000), *Lectures on the History of Moral Philosophy*. Cambridge: Harvard University Press.
Reath, A. (2006), *Agency and Autonomy in Kant's Moral Theory*. New York: Oxford University Press.
Ross, D. (1954), *Kant's Ethical Theory*. Oxford: Clarendon Press.
Scanlon, T. (1982), "Contractualism and Utilitarianism, in *Utilitarianism and Beyond*. A. Sen and B. Williams (eds.). Cambridge: Cambridge University Press, 103–28.
—. (1998), *What We Owe to Each Other*. Cambridge MA: Harvard University Press.
—. (2008), *Moral Dimensions: Permissibility, Meaning, Blame*. Cambridge: Harvard University Press.
Sherman, N. (1998), *Making a Necessity of Virtue*. New York: Cambridge University Press.
Stratton-Lake, P. (2000), *Kant, Duty, and Moral Worth*. London: Routledge.
Timmons, M. (ed.) (2002), *Kant's Metaphysics of Morals: Interpretative Essays*. New York: Oxford University Press.
Vallentyne, P. (ed.) (1991), *Contractarianism and Rational Choice*. Cambridge: Cambridge University Press.
Velleman, J. (2006), *Self to Self: Selected Essays*. Cambridge: Cambridge University Press.
Williams, B. (1985), *Ethics and the Limits of Philosophy*. Cambridge: Harvard University Press.
Wolf, S. (1982), "Moral Saints," *The Journal of Philosophy* 79, 419–39.
Wood, A. (1999), *Kant's Ethical Thought*. New York: Cambridge University Press.
—. (2007), *Kantian Ethics*. New York: Cambridge University Press.

Moral Pluralism and Particularism

Audi, R. (2004), *The Good in the Right: A Theory of Intuition and Intrinsic Value*. Princeton: Princeton University Press.
Dancy, J. (1993), *Moral Reasons*. Oxford: Blackwell.
—. (2004), *Ethics without Principles*. Oxford: Oxford University Press.
Hooker, B. and Little M. (eds.) (2000), *Moral Particularism*. Oxford: Clarendon Press.
Kagan, S. (1988), "The Additive Fallacy," *Ethics* 99, 5–31.
Lance, M., Potrĉ M., and Strahovnik V. (eds.) (2008), *Challenging Moral Particularism*. London: Routledge.
McDowell, J. (1979), "Virtue and Reason," *The Monist* 62, 331–50.
McKeever, S. and Ridge M. (2006), *Principled Ethics: Generalism as a Regulative Ideal*. Oxford: Clarendon Press.

McNaughton, D. (1988), *Moral Vision*. Oxford: Blackwell.
—. (1996), "An Unconnected Heap of Duties?," *Philosophical Quarterly* 46, 433–47.
Murdoch, I. (1970), *The Sovereignty of Good*. Oxford: Blackwell.
Ross, W. D. (1930), *The Right and the Good*. Oxford: Clarendon Press.
—. (1939), *Foundations of Ethics*. Oxford: The Clarendon Press.
Stratton-Lake, P. (ed.). (2003), *Ethical Intuitionism: Re-evaluations*. New York: Oxford University Press.
Väyrynen, P. (2006), "Moral Generalism: Enjoy in Moderation," *Ethics* 116, 707–41.
Wiggins, D. (1987), *Needs, Values, Truth*. Oxford, Blackwell.

Natural Law Theory

Braybrooke, D. (2001), *Natural Law Modernized*. Toronto: University of Toronto Press.
Finnis, J. (1980), *Natural Law and Natural Rights*. Oxford: Oxford University Press.
—. (1998), *Aquinas: Moral, Political, and Legal Theory*. Oxford: Oxford University Press.
George, R. (ed.) (1996), *Natural Law, Liberalism, and Morality*. Oxford: Oxford University Press.
Gomez-Lobo, A. (2002), *Morality and the Human Goods: An Introduction to Natural Law Ethics*. Washington: Georgetown University Press.
Haakonssen, K. (1996), *Natural Law and Moral Philosophy: From Grotius to the Scottish Enlightenment*. Cambridge: Cambridge University Press.
Kaczor, C. (2002), *Proportionalism and the Natural Law Tradition*. Washington: Catholic University of America Press.
Lisska, A. (1996), *Aquinas's Theory of Natural Law: An Analytic Reconstruction*. Oxford: Oxford University Press.
Murphy, M. (2001), *Natural Law and Practical Rationality*. Cambridge: Cambridge University Press.
Oderberg, D. and Chappell T. (eds.) (2004), *Human Values: New Essays on Ethics and Natural Law*. New York: Palgrave.
Porter, J. (2005), *Nature as Reason: A Thomistic Theory of the Natural Law*. Grand Rapids: Eerdmans.
—. (1999), *Natural and Divine Law: Reclaiming the Tradition for Christian Ethics*. Grand Rapids: Wm. B. Eerdmans.
Striker, G. (1986), "Origins of the Concept of Natural Law," *Proceedings of the Boston Area Colloquium in Ancient Philosophy* 2, 79–94.

Structure of Ethical Theories

Dreier, J. (1993), "Structures of Normative Theories," *The Monist* 76, 22–40.
Kagan, S. (1992), "The Structure of Normative Ethics," *Philosophical Perspectives* 6, 223–42.
— (1998), *Normative Ethics*. Boulder: Westview Press.

Timmons, M. (2002), *Moral Theory: An Introduction*. Lanham: Rowman and Littlefield Publishers.

Theological Voluntarism

Adams, R. (1987), *The Virtue of Faith and Other Essays in Philosophical Theology*. Oxford: Oxford University Press.
—. (1999), *Finite and Infinite Goods: A Framework for Ethics*. New York: Oxford University Press.
Alston, W. (1989), "Some Suggestions for Divine Command Theorists," in *Divine Nature and Human Language: Essays in Philosophical Theology*. W. Alston (ed.). Ithaca: Cornell University Press, 253–73.
Audi, R. and Wainwright W. (eds.) (1986), *Rationality, Religious Belief, and Moral Commitment*. Ithaca: Cornell University Press.
Beaty, M. (ed.) (1990), *Christian Theism and the Problems of Philosophy*. Notre Dame: University of Notre Dame Press.
Chandler, J. (1985), "Divine Command Theories and the Appeal to Love," *American Philosophical Quarterly* 22, 231–39.
Evans, S. (2004), *Kierkegaard's Ethics of Love: Divine Commands and Moral Obligations*. New York: Oxford University Press.
Hare, J. (1996), *The Moral Gap*. Oxford: Clarendon Press.
—. (2001), *God's Call: Moral Realism, God's Commands, and Human Autonomy*. Grand Rapids: Eerdmans.
Idziak, J. (ed.) (1979), *Divine Command Morality*. New York: Edwin Mellen.
Miller, C. (2009), "Divine Desire Theory and Obligation," in *New Waves in Philosophy of Religion*. Y. Nagasawa and E. Wielenberg (eds.). Basingstoke: Palgrave Macmillan, 105–124.
Murphy, M. (1998), "Divine Command, Divine Will, and Moral Obligation," *Faith and Philosophy* 15, 3–27.
—. (2002), *An Essay on Divine Authority*. Ithaca: Cornell University Press.
Quinn, P. (1978), *Divine Commands and Moral Requirements*. Oxford: Oxford University Press.
—. (2000), "Divine Command Theory," in *The Blackwell Guide to Ethical Theory*. H. LaFollette (ed.). Malden: Blackwell, 53–73.
—. (2006), *Essays in the Philosophy of Religion*. C. Miller (ed.). Oxford: Oxford University Press.
Wainwright, W. (2005), *Religion and Morality*. Aldershot: Ashgate.
Wielenberg, E. (2005), *Value and Virtue in a Godless Universe*. Cambridge: Cambridge University Press.
—. (2009), "In Defense of Non-Natural, Non-Theistic Moral Realism," *Faith and Philosophy* 26, 23–41.
Wierenga, E. (1983), "A Defensible Divine Command Theory," *Noûs* 17, 387–407.
—. (1984), "Utilitarianism and Divine Command Theory," *American Philosophical Quarterly* 21, 311–18.
Zagzebski, L. (2004), *Divine Motivation Theory*. Cambridge: Cambridge University Press.

Virtue Ethics

Adams, R. (2006), *A Theory of Virtue: Excellence as Being for the Good*. Oxford: Oxford University Press.
Annas, J. (1993), *The Morality of Happiness*. New York: Oxford University Press.
Anscombe, G. E. M. (1958), "Modern Moral Philosophy," *Philosophy* 33, 1–19.
Audi, R. (1995), "Acting from Virtue," *Mind* 104, 449–71.
Badhwar, N. (1996), "The Limited Unity of Virtue," *Noûs*, 30, 306–29.
Chappell, T. (ed.) (2006), *Values and Virtues*. Oxford: Oxford University Press.
Crisp, R. (ed.), (1996), *How Should One Live?* Oxford: Clarendon Press.
Crisp, R. and Slote M. (eds.) (1997), *Virtue Ethics*. Oxford: Oxford University Press.
Dent, N. (1984), *The Moral Psychology of the Virtues*. Cambridge: Cambridge University Press.
Doris, J. (2002), *Lack of Character: Personality and Moral Behavior*. Cambridge: Cambridge University Press.
Driver, J. (2001), *Uneasy Virtue*. Cambridge: Cambridge University Press.
Flanagan, O. and Rorty A. (eds.) (1990), *Identity, Character and Morality*. Cambridge: MIT Press.
Foot, P. (1978), *Virtues and Vices*. Oxford: Blackwell.
—. (1985), "Utilitarianism and the Virtues," *Mind* 94, 196–209.
—. (2001), *Natural Goodness*. Oxford: Clarendon Press.
Gardiner, S. (ed.) (2005), *Virtue Ethics Old and New*. Ithaca: Cornell University Press.
Geach, P. (1977), *The Virtues*. Cambridge: Cambridge University Press.
Harman, G. (1999), "Moral Philosophy Meets Social Psychology: Virtue Ethics and the Fundamental Attribution Error," *Proceedings of the Aristotelian Society* 99, 315–31.
Hudson, S. (1986), *Human Character and Morality*. Boston: Routledge & Kegan Paul.
Hurka, T. (2003), *Virtue, Vice, and Value*. New York: Oxford University Press.
Hursthouse R. (1987), *Beginning Lives*. Oxford: Blackwell.
—. (1991), "Virtue theory and abortion," *Philosophy and Public Affairs* 20, 223–46.
—. (2000), *On Virtue Ethics*. New York: Oxford University Press.
Johnson R. (2003), "Virtue and Right," *Ethics* 113, 810–34.
Kamtekar, R. (2004), "Situationism and Virtue Ethics on the Content of our Character," *Ethics* 114, 458–91.
MacIntyre, A. (1984), *After Virtue: A Study in Moral Theory*. London: Duckworth.
McDowell, J. (1995), "Two Sorts of Naturalism", in *Virtues and Reasons*. R. Hursthouse, G. Lawrence, and W. Quinn (eds.). Oxford: Oxford University Press, 149–80.
Merritt, M. (2000), "Virtue Ethics and Situationist Personality Psychology," *Ethical Theory and Moral Practice* 3, 365–83.
Miller, C. (2010), "Character Traits, Social Psychology, and Impediments to Helping Behavior," *Journal of Ethics and Social Philosophy* 5, 1–36.
Nussbaum, M. (1988), "Non-Relative Virtues: An Aristotelian Approach," in *Midwest Studies in Philosophy Vol. XIII Ethical Theory: Character and Virtue*. P. French, T. Uehling, Jr., and H. Wettstein (eds.). Notre Dame: University of Notre Dame Press, 32–53.
Oakley, J. (1996), "Varieties of Virtue Ethics," *Ratio* 9, 128–52.

Pincoffs, E. (1971), "Quandary Ethics," *Mind* 80, 552–71.
Russell, D. (2009), *Practical Intelligence and the Virtues*. Oxford: Oxford University Press.
— (ed.), *Cambridge Companion to Virtue Ethics*. Cambridge: Cambridge University Press.
Sherman, N. (1998), *Making a Necessity of Virtue*. New York: Cambridge University Press.
Slote, M. (ed.) (1983), *Goods and Virtues*. Oxford: Clarendon Press.
—. (2001), *Morals from Motives*. Oxford: Oxford University Press.
Sreenivasan, G. (2002), "Errors about Errors: Virtue Theory and Trait Attribution," *Mind* 100, 47–68.
Stocker, M. (1976), "The Schizophrenia of Modern Ethical Theories," *The Journal of Philosophy* 14, 453–66.
Swanton, C. (2003), *Virtue Ethics: A Pluralistic View*. New York: Oxford University Press.
Taylor, G. (2006), *Deadly Vices*. Oxford: Oxford University Press.
Tessman, L. (2005), *Burdened Virtues: Virtue Ethics for Liberatory Struggles*. New York: Oxford University Press.
Walker, R. and P. Ivanhoe (eds.) (2007), *Working Virtue: Virtue Ethics and Contemporary Moral Problems*. Oxford: Clarendon Press.
Williams, B. (1981), *Moral Luck*. Cambridge: Cambridge University Press.
—. (1985), *Ethics and the Limits of Philosophy*. Cambridge: Harvard University Press.
—. (1995), *Making Sense of Humanity and Other Philosophical Papers 1982–1993*. Cambridge: Cambridge University Press
Zagzebski, L. (1996), *Virtues of the Mind*. Cambridge: Cambridge University Press.

Notes

Overview of Contemporary Metaethics and Normative Ethical Theory

1 I am understanding the "evaluative" broadly so that it even includes "ought" and "should" statements—intuitively, these statements can be said to evaluate a given action, typically in relation to its compliance with relevant norms.
2 Copp 2006, 4.
3 Darwall 1998, 5, emphasis removed.
4 Deigh 2010, 7.
5 Deigh 2010, 10.
6 See Hinman 2008, 15–6; Pojman and Fieser 2009, 7–8, and Rachels 2010, 13.
7 See, e.g., Williams 1985.
8 Or more precisely, something that is intrinsically good or that eliminates or prevents something that is intrinsically bad.
9 See Timmons 2002, 9 and Pojman and Fieser 2009, 48.
10 Although in legal and political contexts, we may be using "justice" more as a deontological concept. Thanks to Jason Baldwin for pointing this out to me.
11 See, e.g., Audi 2009.
12 See, e.g., Zagzebski 1996.
13 Darwall 1998, 7–8 and Timmons 2002, 4–6.
14 As noted, though, this claim can be challenged. With respect to some normative fact or property, for instance, it might be difficult to arrive at a specification of the (ultimate) underlying facts or properties without appealing in some way to a normative consideration.
15 Moore 1903.
16 What follows assumes, purely for the sake of simplicity, that the normative property is directly based on a nonnormative property, rather than another normative one. For related discussion of the grounding of normative properties, see Brink 1989, 156–61; Dancy 1993, 73–9; and Shafer-Landau 2003, 73–8.
17 Compare Deigh 2010, 7. Some philosophers understand "morality" to only encompass the deontological realm of moral obligations, while the "ethical" extends more widely to include the axiological and characterological too (Williams 1985). As noted in the text, I do not follow this practice.
18 There may not be a sharp divide but rather more of a continuum between normative ethical theory, applied ethics, and metaethics. See Kagan 1998, 2–7.
19 Although there are well-known exceptions. Certain utilitarians from Mill onwards, for instance, have wanted to loosen the relationship between their theoretical accounts

of moral obligation and their practical decision procedures, as we will see in more detail in the final section of this chapter.

20 Darwall 1998, 8.

21 Hinman 2008, 20–1.

22 See, e.g., Timmons 2002, 3–6.

23 For more on methodology in moral theorizing, see Michael DePaul's chapter.

24 Although matters are sometimes not as straightforward as this familiar characterization suggests. For instance, sometimes first-order moral claims are used in objections against the adoption of a particular metaethical view, such as moral relativism or the error theory. In addition, certain metaethical positions may commit their advocates to affirming or denying certain first-order moral claims. For relevant discussion of this last point, see Fantl 2006. Thanks to both Jason Baldwin and Terence Cuneo here.

25 For related discussion, see also Sturgeon 1986; Brink 1989, ch. 8; and Darwall 1998, 12–13.

26 This section draws upon the more detailed discussion in Miller 2007, 2009a.

27 For extensive references to advocates of each of these six theses, see my 2007.

28 Some realists take the mere existence of X to be sufficient for the truth of realism about X. Others argue that some further condition beyond mere existence is necessary, but reject the claim that this condition has anything to do with dependence relations involving human beings. So even this rough statement of the metaphysical thesis is not uncontroversial.

29 Thus Michael Devitt holds that according to realism, "tokens of most current common-sense and scientific physical types objectively exist independently of the mental" (Devitt 1991, 23).

30 Geoffrey Sayre-McCord writes that, "realism involves embracing just two theses: (1) the claims in question, when literally construed, are literally true or false, and (2) some are literally true. Nothing more" (Sayre-McCord 1988, 5). Admittedly it is a bit hard to reconcile this claim with what he writes a few pages later, namely that "for the most part, realism is a matter of metaphysics, not semantics" (7). See also his 1991, 157.

31 According to Paul Horwich, the "essence" of realism concerns "how it is possible for us to know of the existence of certain facts given our ordinary conception of their nature" (Horwich 1998, 55). Similarly he writes that, "anti-realism is the view that our common-sense conception of what we know is incoherent: the supposed character of facts of a certain type cannot be reconciled with our capacity to discover them" (Ibid., 56). Later Horwich also gives the nonequivalent but still epistemic formulation of realism according to which realism is concerned with "the *justifiability* of believing in facts that exist independently of thought or experience" (Ibid., 57, emphasis mine).

32 For James Griffin, "realism about a kind of thing is the view that things of that kind must appear in the best account of what happens in the world" (Griffin 1996, 61).

33 Hilary Putnam claims that for the realist, "the world consists of some fixed totality of mind-independent objects. There is exactly one true and complete description of 'the way the world is.' Truth involves some sort of correspondence relation between words or thought-signs and external things and sets of things" (Putnam 1981, 49).

34 Gideon Rosen, for instance, at times flirts with quietism when he makes remarks such as the following: "[w]e *sense* that there is a heady metaphysical thesis at stake in these debates over realism . . . But after a point, when every attempt to say just what the issue is has come up empty, we have no real choice but to conclude that despite all the wonderful, suggestive imagery, there is ultimately nothing in the neighborhood to discuss" (Rosen 1994, 279, emphasis his).

35 See my 2007.

36 Even if this God figures centrally into the objectively best explanation of various facts about the world, this is simply parasitic on the more fundamental matter of his objective metaphysical existence.
37 For arguments against alternative accounts of objectivity, see my 2007.
38 An intentional attitude "pertains" to X insofar as a token of that attitude has (a representation of) X as part of its content. So one of my beliefs "pertains" to unicorns if, for instance, I believe that unicorns do not exist.
39 A more refined version of (ii) would also require lack of counterfactual dependence on conceptual schemes as well as intentional attitudes, but I ignore such complications here.
40 I have omitted positions in moral epistemology and methodology, such as intuitionism and reflective equilibrium. These are discussed at length in the chapter by Michael DePaul. Similarly I have omitted positions in moral psychology on the motivational power of moral judgments (motivational internalism and externalism), and on the nature of moral reasons (reasons internalism and externalism). The first debate is addressed at length both in the chapter by Alfred Mele on moral psychology and in the chapter by Thomas Nadelhoffer and Walter Sinnott-Armstrong on experimental ethics. The second debate is discussed at length by Joshua Gert in the chapter on morality and practical reason.
41 For references to these various statements of cognitivism and noncognitivism, see my 2009a.
42 I use "noncognitivism" as synonymous with "expressivism," "projectivism," and "nonfactualism." In a more systematic treatment, we would need to distinguish expressivism/projectivism as merely one form of noncognitivism (to be contrasted, say, with R. M. Hare's prescriptivism). Noncognitivism in turn would be classified as merely one among several forms of nonfactualism. But such complications can be left aside for our purposes here.
43 See Ayer 1936.
44 Given that noncognitivism avoids metaphysical claims about moral properties, it seems to be neutral about the truth of moral realism. So on my view technically speaking *moral noncognitivism does not entail moral antirealism*. And *moral realism does not entail moral cognitivism*. But many find these to be highly controversial claims, and I do not want to stress them in the text above in the context of what is supposed to be an introduction to ethics. For challenges to these claims, as well as actual views which seem to combine noncognitivism with moral realism, see my 2009a. For more on noncognitivism in general, see the chapter by Matthew Chrisman.

Admittedly, noncognitivists may employ certain arguments in order to motivate their view which *themselves* have metaphysical implications about the existence of moral facts. But just because some of the arguments used to argue for this position have metaphysical implications, it does not follow that the position itself does. Similarly, cognitivism could in theory be supported with arguments having either realist or antirealist metaphysical implications. But cognitivism by itself is neutral on metaphysical issues about the existence and nature of moral facts, and the same holds for noncognitivism. Thus it is only the formulations of various metaethical positions that we are concerned with in this chapter, not the arguments used to support them.
45 Mackie 1977. For a leading contemporary error theory, see Joyce 2001. See also the chapter by Hallvard Lillehammer.
46 Hence it follows on my taxonomy that a moral error theory, as such, is compatible with both moral realism and moral antirealism. This is another controversial claim that, as in endnote 44, I have chosen to not stress in the main text.
47 For more, see the chapter by Hallvard Lillehammer.
48 Rawls 1971, ch. one.

49 1995, 299. See also Smith 1989, 110.
50 Lewis 1989.
51 Firth 1952.
52 Wright 1992. So for something like justice, the "ideally suited" class of respondents on Rawls' view would be free and rational persons of the kind briefly described in (iii).
53 Wright 1992, 108.
54 For more on moral realism, see the chapter by Terence Cuneo.
55 See Brink 1989, 22, 156–9; Darwall 1998, 27–8; Shafer-Landau 2003, ch. 3; and Sturgeon 2006, 92. On an alternative account of the divide, the central claim of moral naturalism is that moral properties are reducible to nonmoral properties. But these nonmoral properties do not have to be subject to empirical investigation, and so can be supernatural or Platonic. Moral nonnaturalists, on the other hand, would reject the reductive claim (Pigden 1991). On still a third framework, the moral naturalist must hold that moral properties are identical to descriptive properties which are investigable empirically in the sciences (and so may not be nonreductively constituted by descriptive properties).
56 For leading statements of each view, see Jackson 1998 for moral functionalism and Brink 1989 for Cornell realism. For clarification of their differences, see in particular Jackson 1998, 144–5.
57 See Adams 1999.
58 See, e.g., Shafer-Landau 2003; FitzPatrick 2008; and Enoch 2011.
59 Two approaches which are noticeably absent from this section are Simon Blackburn's quasi-realism and the various minimalist approaches to moral truth and facthood. I summarize these views at length and apply the taxonomy developed in (R+) to each of them in my 2009a.
60 For more on what follows, see Kagan 1992, 1998.
61 Other labels for agent-centered constraints include "side-constraints," "deontological restrictions," and "agent-relative prohibitions."
62 Other labels for agent-centered options include "agent-relative permissions" and "agent-centered prerogatives."
63 A third feature of ordinary morality often mentioned along with constraints and options are special obligations, which we have in virtue of our personal environment and history. Examples might include a promise to a dying relative to honor her will, or a commitment to lovingly raise one's child. I have omitted special obligations from the above for three reasons: (i) to keep the taxonomy as simple as possible, (ii) because it is not apparent that they contribute any additional conceptual clarity to the divisions between the leading positions in ethical theory beyond what is captured by thinking in terms of options and constraints, and (iii) any special obligation that does not involve maximizing the good, may just be an instance of an agent-centered constraint, since the failure to live up to such an obligation would be morally forbidden, even if violating the obligation could bring about more good in the world (in other words, there would be an agent-centered constraint against failing to satisfy such a special obligation).
64 Note that this is only one strategy for dividing up the conceptual landscape. Another is to use the agent-relative versus agent-neutral distinction (e.g., Dreier 1993; McNaughton and Rawling 2006). A more common strategy is to distinguish in various ways between teleological and deontological theories (e.g., Brink 1989, ch. 8; Deigh 2010, ch. 1). See also Kagan 1992, 1998. Limitations of space prevent a (likely tedious) assessment of the relevant strengths and weaknesses of different strategies.
65 See, e.g., Mill 1998.
66 Bentham 1948.

67 Mill 1998.
68 See also endnote 19 and the relevant text.
69 For an overview, see Batson 1991.
70 Similarly ethical egoists could hold views which focus initially, not on actions or rules, but rather on motives, character traits, or institutions. See Kagan 1998, 204–5.
71 2002, 230, 4:429 emphasis removed.
72 Hill 2006, 490.
73 2002, 231, 4:430 emphasis removed.
74 2002, 194, 4:392.
75 For an overview of the debate about this topic, see Hill 2006, especially footnote 2. For a presentation of the second formulation which is in line with the above, see Timmons 2002, 160–1 and Audi 2004, ch. 3. For more on Kantian ethics in general, see the chapter by Kyla Ebels-Duggan.
76 A different version of RU could hold that the utility associated with actual *compliance* with the rules needs to be considered instead of mere acceptance of them. Still another version would mention *universal* acceptance rather than general acceptance. For these various distinctions, see Hooker 2000, ch. 3.
77 Hooker 2000, 32. Technically speaking, Hooker uses the concept of expected *well-being*, which is intended to be neutral between competing accounts of the good including utility.
78 See, e.g., Hospers 1961.
79 See Adams 1999.
80 See Murphy 1998.
81 See Miller 2009b, 2009c.
82 See Zagzebski 2004.
83 See Miller 2009b, 2009c.
84 See, e.g., Quinn 2000.
85 For more on theological voluntarism, see the chapter by William Wainwright.
86 1993, 20.
87 For more detailed discussion, see Timmons 2002, ch. 8 and Audi 2004. The formulation in (i) may need some fine-tuning if we also accept the existence of moral dilemmas.
88 For related discussion, see Audi 2004 and McNaughton and Rawling 2006.
89 Ross 1930, 27, 41.
90 For related discussion, see McNaughton and Rawling 2006, 446.
91 Brink 1989.
92 Ibid., 231–6.
93 Ibid., 264.
94 For a hybrid pluralist view which accepts options without constraints, see McNaughton and Rawling 2006.
95 Moore 1903.
96 Dancy 1993, 61.
97 A weaker version of holism would just limit it to the valance of a consideration, rather than both its valance and relevance. For more on holism, see the chapter on particularism by Pekka Väyrynen.
98 For helpful overviews of particularism, see Dancy 1993, 2004; Hooker and Little 2000; Timmons 2002, ch. 10; and Lance and Little 2006. It is worth noting that particularists disagree about the scope of their holism—some claim it applies to all normative features, whereas others make exceptions, say for thick ethical properties (McNaughton and Rawling 2000).
99 Compare Oakley 1996, 129 and Hursthouse 1999, 28.

100 Indeed, there may even be versions of virtue ethics which simply deny that there is any grounding relation at all between the virtues and either one or several more fundamental morally relevant features. Such views would then stand outside of the entire taxonomy we have used to unpack the differences between normative ethical theories. Thanks to Terence Cuneo here for calling this to my attention.
101 For one interesting attempt to carve out a conceptually distinct, neo-Aristotelian virtue ethical theory, see Oakley 1996. For much more on virtue ethics, see the chapter by Christine Swanton.
102 Many thanks to Jason Baldwin and Terence Cuneo for extremely careful and helpful comments which greatly improved the chapter.

Methodological Issues

1 Rawls, 1971, 51. Although Rawls' claim that Sidgwick employed reflective equilibrium is vigorously contested in Singer 1974.
2 The proposition that murder is wrong is a good example of a trivial moral proposition. It is trivial since murder just is wrongful killing. While many people might think it is obviously true, the proposition that killing in self-defense is not wrong is not trivial as is indicated by the fact that the denial of this proposition is not contradictory.
3 I must acknowledge that my presentation of RE is heavily indebted to the excellent work done by Norman Daniels, especially his 1979. For more on the filtering of IMJs to obtain CMJs, and in particular for doubts about the significance and even legitimacy of this filtering see DePaul 1993, 17–18.
4 I'll use "S" to designate an inquirer employing RE throughout this chapter.
5 When I refer to moral beliefs or beliefs in moral propositions here and below I do not mean to take any stand or beg any questions in the cognitivism versus noncognitivism debate. I mean no more than that moral judgments seem upon quick introspection like other beliefs, we typically report them with declarative sentences like other beliefs, sometimes even using "belief," etc. I think all sides to the cognitivism/noncognitivism debate could agree.
6 To be explicit, capitals with a subscript, e.g., "CMJ_n," names a set of beliefs. Small case with a subscript, e.g., "cmj_n" or "mt_1," strictly speaking, refers to a belief, i.e., a mental state or propositional attitude. However, I will often also use this notation to refer to the object of the corresponding belief. I do not think any confusion results, and always inserting "the object of" makes the prose tedious.
7 This is perhaps the most common view. In his influential early criticism of RE, Richard Brandt (1979, chapter 1) explicitly interprets RE in this way.
8 Daniels often frames RE in these terms, e.g., "we are constantly making plausibility judgments about which of our considered moral judgments we should revise . . . " (1979, 267).
9 See, e.g., George Bealer (1998, 207–214) and Michael Huemer (2005, 99ff.).
10 It is worth noting that "p seems more likely to be true than q to S" is ambiguous between "the degree to which p seems true to S is greater than the degree to which q seems true" and "the proposition that p is more likely to be true than q seems true to S." In some cases it may well be the latter that determines revisions in RE.
11 Rawls makes this point explicitly in his earlier seminal paper on the decision procedure for ethics (1951), which he claims to be following when he describes reflective equilibrium in his (1971).

12 I have considerable sympathy with the worry that such a judgment would have to be an element of CMJ_{NRE} already. See DePaul, 1993, 20–2. But I am here trying to articulate Daniels' conception of the transition to WRE, and I think he would classify this judgment as a BT.
13 For more on radical versus conservative reflective equilibrium see DePaul 1987.
14 For more on this addition to the standard conception of RE see my 1993, chapter 4, or 1988.
15 One prominent example is provided by Peter Singer's (2005) effort to attack the sorts of anti utilitarian CMJs many people form about certain versions of trolley cases, thereby lending support to a utilitarian MT. For an excellent presentation and criticism of this kind of argument, along with the empirical research on which it relies, see Berker (2009). I will have more to say about these matters in section III.C.
16 There are, however, prominent exceptions. Goldman and Pust (1998) seek to defend the use of intuitions in philosophy in general, including in particular epistemology, by arguing that philosophers use intuitions as evidence for and against analyses of concepts. Since concepts are mental or psychological entities that play a role in determining the intuitive judgments we make, it is legitimate to use these judgments as evidence for or against accounts of those concepts.
17 There are exceptions, e.g., Daniels 1980 which criticizes Rawls' suggestion that moral inquiry via RE is similar to the efforts of linguists to construct a grammar.
18 For more on epistemic justification and the idea that there are a number of distinct concepts of epistemic evaluation, see Alston 2005.
19 Cf. Shafer-Landau 2003, Audi 2004, and Huemer 2005.
20 Although as Christian Miller has reminded me, it is the case that these elements might be functioning as intuitions in a more contemporary sense. Contemporary intuitionists (see previous note) agree with traditional intuitionists that intuitions are justified noninferentially. But they tend to think they are only prima facie justified. Hence, the fact that an element of CMJ_1 is revised would not show that it did not have this status, since it could have been revised because it's prima facie justification was defeated.
21 See note 12 above for reservations about this element of Daniels' view of WRE.
22 See BonJour 2002 or the essays by Richard Fumerton, Laurence BonJour, John Pollock and Richard Fumerton in DePaul 2001.
23 Haidt et al., 625–6. I have removed italics. In the original, each was followed by a brief comment.
24 Cf. Greene et al. 2001, Greene et al. 2004 and Greene et al. 2008.
25 Berker thinks the first few arguments he identifies, including the one that claims moral intuitions are unreliable simply because emotions are involved in their production, are clearly bad. Indeed, he calls this argument in particular a "howler." But he criticizes even the best argument, the one that proceeds from the premise that some of moral intuitions are determined by morally irrelevant factors.
26 In addition to Berker 2009, for more cautious assessments of what the science might show see also Timmons 2008.
27 See my 1998 for a fuller presentation of this defense.
28 Richard Foley had done the most to explore the subjective sense of rationality I am here employing. See his 1987 and 1993.
29 But what about coherence, I can here someone objecting. Let me hint at a response by citing BonJour (1985), who did the most thorough job of actually trying to work out a coherence theory of justification (for empirical beliefs) that I am aware of. Spontaneous beliefs, i.e., beliefs not formed as a result of inference from other beliefs, played a crucial role in his account. Since he was interested in empirical justification, these would have been perceptual beliefs. He did not, of course, claim that such beliefs are

foundationally justified; he held that they would be justified because within the larger coherent system arguments would be developed for the reliability of these cognitively spontaneous beliefs. But the important point for my purposes is that he recognized that there would be spontaneous beliefs and that they would play a crucial role in determining the coherent system of empirical beliefs that one accepts. I think that any plausible version of coherentism will share this feature.

30 Many thanks to Christian Miller for helpful comments on an earlier version of this chapter.

Moral Realism

1 Nagel (1986) is a philosopher who belongs to the first group; Mackie (1977) is one who belongs to the second. The quotation comes from Joyce (2006), 174. He is quoting W. D. Casebeer.

2 Miller (2009a) offers an overview of what different philosophers say on the matter.

3 Here and elsewhere, I use the term "represent" as a success term. To represent is to accurately represent. I should also note that throughout this essay I attribute to realists positions of various sorts. Unless the context indicates otherwise, these attributions are probably best read as being implicitly normative: the positions in question are those that, in my judgment, realists should accept.

4 See, for example, Boisvert (2008), Copp (2001) and (2009), Hare (2003), and Tressan (2006).

5 It also distinguishes realism from certain versions of expressivism, such as that defended by Blackburn (1999) and Gibbard (2003), which hold that there are moral facts but that there is no interesting sense in which moral thought and discourse represent them. Cuneo (2007) and (2008) explore these views in more detail. See also note 11.

6 See Smith (1994), Ch. 5 and Jackson (1998), Ch. 6, for example. Under a natural interpretation, Smith claims that moral reasons are determined by what an idealized version of oneself would want oneself to want.

7 Copp (1995), Boyd (1988), Brink (1989), Jackson (1998), Railton (1986), and Sturgeon (1988) defend moral naturalism. To be clear, naturalists do not claim that whether it is wrong for an agent to perform an action depends on her desires. Rather, they claim that whether the wrongness of an action favors certain kinds of responses on our part depends on the desires that we have (or would have if we deliberated correctly).

8 FitzPatrick (2008), 173.

9 Enoch (2007) and (2011), FitzPatrick (2008) and (2010), Huemer (2005), Oddie (2005), Parfit (2011), and Shafer-Landau (2003) defend moral nonnaturalism. According to the characterization offered above, supernaturalist views such as those defended by Adams (1999), Miller (2009b), and Zagzebski (2004) would also count as versions of nonnaturalism.

10 I have stated the stock moral truisms in such a way that they do not have any qualifications attached to them. One might believe, however, that most of them should be understood to have implicit ceteris paribus riders attached to them, since there might be extraordinary circumstances in which, say, lying simply because one doesn't feel like telling the truth is okay. Under this interpretation, most of the stock truisms are ceteris paribus norms, which, if true, are necessarily so. Understanding the truisms in this way is compatible with the overarching argument I wish to make.

11 See Blackburn (1998) and Gibbard (2003), Introduction. The quotation comes from Blackburn (1998), 70. Roughly put, metaethical expressivism is the position that

moral judgments express not moral propositional content that purports to represent moral reality, but nonrepresentational states such as attitudes of approbation or disapprobation.

12 Loeb (2007) develops this challenge. It was reading Loeb's essay that impressed upon me the importance of thinking about methodological issues in metaethics. Much of what I say here (and in Cuneo 2011a and 2011b) is an attempt to address the challenges he raises to realism in his essay.

13 The classic text here is Mandelbaum (1955). Horgan and Timmons (2007) and (2008) explore the issue of moral experience with subtlety. Horgan and Timmons, I should add, defend expressivism, arguing that it can accommodate the relevant data. In this sense, I am borrowing the terms of the debate from those who defend moral antirealism.

14 See Wittgenstein (1969) and Reid (2002). Wolterstorff (2001), Ch. IX explores the similarities between their views.

15 See Reid (2002). Those familiar with Alston (1991) and (1992) will recognize my debt to Alston's appropriation of Reid, although my gloss on the notion of a doxastic practice differs from Alston's. Cuneo (2011a) and (2011b) explore Reid's own formulation of the Reidian criterion as applied to metaethics.

16 See, for example, Pereboom (2001).

17 For helpful discussions, see Swinburne (1997) and Layman (2007).

18 "What about the explanatory criterion?" you may wonder. Does the Reidian criterion deserve to be weighted more heavily than it? In principle, realists could say different things on this matter.

19 There is, then, a sense in which realists hold that their view is the one to beat, the default position. But it is important not to freight this claim with too much significance. For when realists claim that theirs is the default position, this is probably best understood to mean simply that their view does a better job than rival views accommodating the core moral data.

20 One problem is that moral evaluations seem intimately intertwined with other sorts of evaluations, such as epistemic and prudential ones. For discussion, see Cuneo (2007), Ch. 2.

21 See Mill (1978).

22 See, for example, the discussion of Leiter (2010) at: http://onthehuman.org/2010/03/moral-skepticism-and-moral-disagreement-developing-an-argument-from-nietzsche/.

23 An implication of Parfit (2011) is that critics of realism exaggerate the degree of disagreement among moral theorists. Moral theorists, according to Parfit, have actually tended to converge on important issues in normative ethics.

24 See Mackie (1977) and Joyce (2001) and (2006). Olson (2010) defends the view as well. See also the chapter dedicated to constructivism and error theory in this volume.

25 There is a different way to interpret the error theory, according to which error theorists claim that their view *satisfies* the Reidian criterion. According to this interpretation, error theorists agree that, at the outset of theorizing, we should take beliefs that express the stock moral truisms as reliably formed, all else being equal. They simply contend that the presumption in favor of their reliability is defeated, since we have powerful reasons to believe that realism fares rather poorly according to the explanatory and simplicity criteria. In my judgment, this is not what error theorists such as Mackie and Joyce claim. While these philosophers agree that the core moral data in some sense support realism, they do not say that we should, at the outset of theorizing, take the moral practice to be reliable. However that may be, much of what I say about the error theory in the text should apply (with some fairly minor modifications), *mutatis mutandis* to a version of the error theory which claims that it satisfies the Reidian criterion.

26 See Shafer-Landau (2004) and (2009). In Cuneo (2007) Ch. 7, I argue that Joyce's argument works with an inadequate account of explanation.
27 See Joyce (2001), 43, 177.
28 I develop this response at more length in Cuneo (2012). Among other things, I assess Joyce's charge that moral naturalists do not defend anything worth calling a moral system, arguing that this is incorrect. A worry that one might raise is that the strategy under consideration is not available to realists who believe that moral reasons are categorical. Strictly speaking, this may be correct. But realists who believe that moral reasons are categorical can still maintain that the error theorist's methodology is arbitrarily partial. They might say that since there is no more reason to reject premise (1) of The Categoricity Argument rather than the stock moral truisms, we should reject the argument's second premise.
29 This is true of Joyce (2001), at least. That said, Street (2006) and Joyce (2006) do argue for the claim that moral beliefs are not reliably formed, although Street is not an error theorist and does not reject the stock moral truisms. For responses, see Copp (2008), Enoch (2010), FitzPatrick (2009), Wielenberg (2010) and Parfit (2011).
30 Tyler Doggett, Steve Layman, Don Loeb, Christian Miller, Russ Shafer-Landau, Andrew Reisner, Sarah Stroud, Christine Tappolet, and an audience at the University of Montreal offered helpful feedback on an earlier version of this essay. They have my thanks.

Ethical Expressivism

1 This family includes the early "emotivist" theories of Ayer (1936/1946) and Stevenson (1937, 1944), the later "quasi-realist" theories of Blackburn (1984, 1993, 1998), Gibbard (1990, 2003), and Timmons (1999), Horgan and Timmons (2006) as well as a recent "ecumenical expressivist" theory under development by Ridge (2006, 2007a, unpublished) and a nondescriptive semantics for ethical terms sketched in some detail (but not endorsed) by Schroeder (2008a). There are also strong family resemblances between these theories and the "prescriptivism" of Hare (1952), as well as some aspects of the pragmatist-inspired "inferentialism" of Sellars (1968, ch. 7).
2 There are also at least two other families of philosophical theories going under the moniker "expressivism" which are not versions of expressivism as it is usually conceived in metaethics. First is the expressivist account of avowals inspired by Wittgenstein (1953, 89), which highlights the expressivist role of avowals to explain the asymmetry between statements of one's own present mental states (e.g., "I am sad") and third-personal statements about the mental states of others (e.g., "Johnny is sad"). See McGeer (1996) and Bar-On (2004) more subtle contemporary developments of this expressivist idea; and see Chrisman (2009) for comparison to metaethical expressivism. The second is a view in the philosophy of logic inspired by the early work of Frege (1879). The thought is that logical symbols like "$\neg$" and "$\supset$" help us to express commitments that we can otherwise only manifest in practice. See Brandom (1994, 2000) and Chrisman (2010) for more discussion. Price (2011) argues that ethical expressivism could benefit from taking on some of the theoretical resources of Brandom's sort of logical expressivism. In particular it could explain how to extend the basic expressivist idea to other areas of discourse such as modal or probabilistic. Here, I am mostly ignoring this possibility but I will come back to it briefly at the end. See also Chrisman (2014) for more discussion.
3 Note that this is different from what Schroeder (2008a, 18, 56–60; 2010, 70–6) calls the "basic expressivist maneuver." This is to argue that ethical and descriptive language

are on a par in expressing mental states, which purports to get them off the hook of explaining *how* sentences express mental states, since it is an explanatory burden that everyone faces. Schroeder argues that this maneuver is mistaken.

4 This theory is prominent but also controversial. See Miller (2008a) for an extensive critique and references to other critics.

5 This use of the term "judgment," which is pervasive in metaethics can be confusing. One reason it can be confusing is that it's also somewhat common to use the term to refer to the speech-act performed by uttering an ethical sentence with comprehension. This, however, is what I am calling an ethical "statement" (which I am thinking of as the utterance of an ethical sentence with comprehension). Another reason the usage can be confusing is that it's common in the debates about the metaphysics of mind to view judgments as active or nonstative in a way that contrasts with states of mind such as beliefs and desires. Furthermore, judgments so construed are often thought to be paradigmatically *cognitive*, in that they involve reasoning and the aim of truth rather than anything like conative reacting. I think that is the more proper way to use the term "judgment"; however, here I will conform to the standard usage in metaethics which I've articulated in the main text above.

6 Compare Rosati (2008) and Miller (2008b) for a more detailed discussion of various versions of motivational internalism, and see Finlay and Schroeder (2008) for a detailed discussion of reasons internalism.

7 Some also object that there are counterexamples to the internalism which is premised in this argument. For example, psychopaths or extremely depressed people might be able to make sincere ethical statements even about their own potential actions and yet not be at all motivated. Debate about the sense in which this is possible is complex. See Miller (2008b) and Bar-On and Chrisman (2009) for further discussion

8 See the distinction Mandelbaum (1955, 127) makes between "direct" and "removed" judgments of moral obligation. Horgan and Timmons (2006) follow him and offer a subtle discussion of the phenomenology of both of these kinds of judgments.

9 Prominent defenders of something like this idea include Copp (2001) and Boisvert (2008); see also the useful discussion in Schroeder (2009).

10 Below I'll briefly discuss hybrid versions of expressivism which meet this constraint while remaining expressivist in an interesting sense.

11 Here, I am ignoring the options of error theory and fictionalism, which would embrace attribution of error or commitment to falsehoods in ordinary moral discourse. Expressivists typically see those views as implausibly radical in their ethical judgments, whereas proponents of those views typically see expressivists as implausibly radical in their philosophy of language. I also encourage the reader to consult the essay by Lillehammer on error theory and constructivism in this volume in order to make your own comparison.

12 See Sturgeon (1985), Brink (1986, 1989), Railton (1986, 1989), Boyd (1988), Finlay (2009).

13 Nagel (1986, ch. 8), Dancy (2000), Shafer-Landau (2003, ch. 3), Enoch (2007), Cuneo (2007a), Fitzpatrick (2008), Parfit (2011, ch. 29). See also Cuneo (2007b) for useful discussion and other references.

14 The details matter for the strength of this argument. So I advise the reader to consider more detailed treatments of moral supervenience, such as McLaughlin and Bennett (2010), Blackburn (1992, ch. 7), Ridge (2007b), Sturgeon (2009), Brown (2010).

15 Blackburn (1992, ch. 7), Ridge (2007b).

16 See Papineau (2009) for a helpful introduction. Once we begin to ask what a natural phenomenon is, it can be very difficult to specify naturalism precisely and its implications for classical philosophical debates are up for grabs. See Rea (2002) for a critique of naturalism along these lines.

17 Constructivism is sometimes seen as an alternative. However, see Hussain and Shah (2006) for an argument that there are constructivist versions of each of these options, which would mean that it doesn't represent a genuine alternative to them.
18 Mackie (1977, ch. 1) is the canonical source, but see also Hägerström (1953), Olson (2010).
19 Joyce (2001), Kalderon (2005), Nolan et. al. (2005).
20 There are two other prominent objections to the view that I won't have the space to discuss fully. First, Dorr (2002) argued that expressivism licenses inferences from desires to beliefs, which constitutes an objectionable form of wishful thinking. See Lenman (2003), Enoch (2003), for discussion and response. Second, Egan (2007) argues that some forms of expressivism which are otherwise attractive cannot fully capture the phenomenon of "fundamental moral error," that is error in ethical view where one is internally coherent and could not correct the error by any change that one would antecedently endorse as an improvement in overall view. The problem, Egan argues, is that an expressivist can recognize this possibility in someone else, but not in himself, which commits proponents of the view to "unpardonable smugness." See Blackburn (2009) for discussion and response.
21 Schroeder, 2010 is an excellent book-length treatment of many more of the important details.
22 See Chrisman (2013) for more discussion of the history of emotivism.
23 There's a complication here that I am glossing over. Ayer distinguishes between two ways of using ethical sentences. First, they are used to make statements about what is acceptable or unacceptable to the moral sense of a particular community. As such, he'd agree that they are descriptive. Second, they are used as "normative ethical symbols" (op. cit., 106). This is the standard use within normative ethical theory and part of ordinary moralizing. Similarly, Stevenson suggests (op. cit., 24–6) that ethical sentences have truth-conditions, but he argues that these sentences are not used in ethical discourse to assert that these truth conditions obtain.
24 But see also Acton (1936) and Ross (1939, ch. 2.2) for anticipation of the idea.
25 Hare (1952, chs. 1–3)
26 See Blackburn (1984; 1993, ch. 10). For criticism see Hale (1986, 2002) and Schroeder (2008c; 2010, ch. 6).
27 This is Gibbard's strategy (1990, ch. 5; 2003, chs. 3–4).
28 A good discussion of the various proposals expressivists have made and problems with them can be found in Schroeder (2010).
29 Prominent defenders include Ramsey (1927), Quine (1970), Field (1986, 1994), Horwich (1990). For a useful introduction and further discussion, see Stoljar and Damnjanovic (2009).
30 This is by no means a trivial assumption, but it is outside the scope of this essay to evaluate the viability of this theory of truth. See Stoljar and Damnjanovic (2009) for discussion. In light of the controversy, we must see defending deflationism as a potential cost of quasi-realist expressivism.
31 Blackburn (1998, 73), Gibbard (2003, 179–84).
32 Compare Dreier (2004).
33 See also Miller (2009).
34 This ties in with a tradition in the philosophy of language stemming from Locke (1690/1975) and with more contemporary expression in Grice (1957), Schiffer (1972), and Davis (2003).
35 For the structure of the view, it doesn't matter exactly what F is. In his original paper on this, Ridge suggests that it would have to do with what different types of advisers would approve or disapprove of. However, in more recent work, he suggests that it has to do with what does or doesn't meet various kinds of standards.

36 In the book, Schroeder simply assumes that non-hybrid forms of expressivism are at issue. He discusses many different kinds of hybrid expressivism in his 2009.
37 As Schroeder (2008c) points out, one can of course *stipulate* that toleration is logically inconsistent with disapproval. But this doesn't explain why they are, and it undermines a natural ideationalist account of the meaning of "not."
38 As it turns out, Schroeder argues, a descriptive sentence like "Stealing maximizes happiness" cannot be analyzed as expressing an attitude of being for proceeding as if stealing maximizes happiness, because this generates intuitively incorrect contents for its negation. This leads him to develop what he calls a "biforcated attitude semantics." I encourage the interested reader to consult chs. 7–10 of his 2008a for more discussion.
39 See for example Fodor (1990), Fodor and Lepore (1991).
40 I sketch and motivate this idea in more detail in Chrisman (2010).
41 I'd like to thank J. Adam Carter, Raymond Critch, Graham Hubbs, Michael Ridge, Mark Schroeder and Christian Miller for helpful feedback on earlier drafts of this chapter.

Constructivism and the Error Theory

1 The term "morality" can be used in at least three different ways. First, morality can be thought of as comprising the institutions, practices, and attitudes that social scientists refer to in speaking of human moralities. Second, morality can be thought of as comprising the objects (propositional or otherwise) of the attitudes that form part of morality in the first sense. Third, morality can be thought of as whatever in the world the objects of moral attitudes answer to and that explains their correctness, meaning, or significance. When the moral error theorist says that morality is a construction, he can be interpreted as claiming either that there is nothing to the idea of morality in the third sense or that insofar as there is, this is best explained in terms of the attitudes that form part of morality in the first sense (cf. Mackie 1977, 1980; Blackburn 1998).
2 In fact, *error* comes so cheaply that it fails to rule out anything but the crudest form of noncognitivism. Perhaps this view might be attributed to some forms of classical emotivism (cf. Ayer 1946). It is not, however, attributable to most forms of contemporary expressivism (cf. Blackburn 1998; Chrisman [this volume])
3 The idea that moral claims are necessarily reason giving is a defining feature of moral rationalism. It is controversial both whether rationalism is a plausible account of morality and if so, whether it is compatible with a strong form of moral realism (cf. Smith 1994, Shafer-Landau 2003, Korsgaard 2009). I return to the plausibility of moral rationalism in the section on moral constructivism.
4 There is a large literature on how to interpret the idea of facts having "has-to-be-pursuedness" built into them, and the extent to which this entails an implausible form of the "motivational internalist" thesis that there is a necessary connection between moral judgment and moral motivation. The issue is controversial (cf. Brink 1989, Smith 1994, Joyce and Kirchin 2010).
5 An important relative of moral constructivism elsewhere in philosophy is constructivism about mathematics. Thus, mathematical constructivists do not deny that some mathematical claims are true. What they deny is that mathematical truth extends beyond what we can mathematically construct, by which is meant that we can decide on those truths by means of a certain kind of proof (cf. Bridges 2009, Iemhoff 2008). One controversial implication of mathematical constructivism is the refusal to affirm the Law of the Excluded Middle (A or not-A) where no proof currently exists for either the truth of a statement or its negation. The most obvious implication of this

refusal is that we may have to accept a significant range of objective indeterminacy where proof runs out. Moral constructivists are committed to accepting an analogous form of objective indeterminacy in ethics.

6 For a recent attempt to make alternative use of the deliberative inescapability of moral claims in an argument for moral realism, see Enoch 2007.

7 Some forms of moral relativism can be interpreted as versions of moral constructivism as defined at the outset of this section. Thus, Gilbert Harman accounts for the truth of moral claims in terms of certain (largely implicit) agreements among actively participating members of a given society (Harman 1977). David Wong moves beyond Harman's relativism to draw a distinction between moral claims the truth of which obtains relative to a given society and other (more basic and general) moral claims the truth of which may apply to any society (Wong 2006, cf. Scanlon 1998).

Morality and Practical Reason

1 Kant (1978); Hume (1978); See also Korsgaard (1996) and Wallace (2006).

2 Hume (1978), 413–16; As Broome (2005) rightly points out, this does not entail that there is nothing to be said against a given desire or action—only that reason, as a faculty, is not going to say it.

3 Kant (1978), 60–2.

4 Scanlon (1998), 18, 23–4, 33–5, 56–7.

5 Gibbard (2003), p. 215.

6 It is possible to read Korsgaard (1996) as denying this. She seems in some places to hold that practical reason is the capacity to step back from our desires and endorse them, and that one's endorsement of a desire is what actually provides one with a normative reason. See Korsgaard (1996), 94, 99 n. 8, 108, 256–7.

7 For criticisms of attempts to extract normative implications from the nature of human agency, see Enoch (2006).

8 Kolodny (2005); Broome (2005).

9 Brandt (1998), 72–3; Rawls (1971), 417; Gibbard (1990), 18–19; Raz (1999), 22; Cullity and Gaut (1997), p. 2.

10 Williams (1981).

11 They can tell us what *derivative* ends are to be pursued: those ends that are necessary in the pursuit of our basic ends.

12 Hume has been "credited" with the extreme view. Most modern Humeans, including Williams (1981) and Brandt (1998), have moved towards the amended view in one way or another.

13 This is Brandt's (1998) suggestion.

14 Something certainly needs to be done to ensure this, if rationality is to count as the fundamental normative notion applying to action. See Quinn (1992).

15 See Ripstein (2001).

16 Smart (1956) seems to defend the impartial substantive view, and Fumerton (1990) the egoistic. Hobbes (1994) is commonly taken as a representative of the egoistic view, but this interpretation is of doubtful accuracy. Brink (1997) defends a kind of egoism, but his eudaimonistic conception of self-interest is sufficiently different from what one might call "selfishness" that it is also not entirely clear whether he should be regarded as an egoist.

17 One "third sort" of view is a blend of the egoistic and impartial views. Parfit (2011) seems to defend such a view, on which substantive impartial and egoistic reasons

both figure in overall rational status, but on which they are only imprecisely comparable. Scanlon (1998) and Dancy (2004) also seem fairly explicit in their acceptance of both impartial and agent-relative objective reasons.

18 See Gert (2004), Chapter 1 for a discussion of this notion of fundamentality. For statements endorsing this view of rationality, see Darwall (1983), 215–6; Nagel (1970), 1–9; Gibbard (1990), p. 49.

19 Thomas Scanlon reserves the term "irrational" for a kind of subjective inconsistency of normative judgment and action: acting against one's judgment is the only kind of action Scanlon is willing to call "irrational." But it is probably best simply to think of "rationality" and "practical reason" as technical philosophical terms, and to think of Scanlon as having appropriated the term "irrational" as a label for one specific kind of mental malfunction: *one* form of *subjective* irrationality. Scanlon uses the phrase "what we have most reason to do" as a label for what we have been describing with the phrase "objectively rational."

20 Smith (1996).

21 Scanlon (1998), p. 17; Dancy (2004), p. 29; Parfit (2011), chapter 1.

22 Some theorists would replace the conditional with a biconditional. Bernard Williams, whose 1981 initiated contemporary discussion of the link between normative reasons and motivation, seems to regard the counterfactual motivation only as a necessary condition, and is agnostic about its sufficiency. See Williams (2001). See also Parfit (1997), p. 100.

23 Williams (1981) and Goldman (2005) are representatives of this category.

24 Korsgaard (1996) is an example. Smith (1994) is also, arguably, another, since he seems to hold that mechanisms that push our beliefs and desires into maximal coherence would yield a uniform set of basic desires.

25 There are also satisficing versions of the other views: versions that claim that rationality is a matter of getting *close enough* to maximizing the relevant measure. But such views still need to make sense of maximizing talk.

26 I provide much more detailed discussion of this idea in Gert (2007).

27 Foot (1978).

28 This position is called "moral rationalism." Defenders include van Roojen (2010) and Shafer-Landau (2003). Together with the conditional discussed in the previous section moral rationalism entails that under suitable conditions any agent will have some motivation to act as she is morally required to act. This thesis is closely related to the thesis of moral judgment internalism: the view that under suitable conditions any agent will have some motivation to act as she judges she is morally required to act. See Miller (2008).

29 At least, this is what she thought when she wrote Foot (1978). She has since changed her views. See Foot (2001).

30 Kolodny (2005). This is a consequence of his taking "rationality" to mean only "subjective rationality."

31 Smith (2002). Smith is explicit about this limitation, and takes it to be an advantage of his view. Indeed, he takes it to be a requirement on any adequate joint view of rationality and morality that immoral behavior sometimes be rationally permissible. A common and understandable misreading of Smith interprets him as holding that it is always irrational to behave immorally. But see Gert (2008).

32 Gauthier (1967, 1986).

33 Schroeder (2007).

34 Possibly a great deal of optimism is required here, since Schroeder does not provide any real argument that moral reasons will turn out to be sufficiently strong to make morally required behavior rationally permissible in all cases.

35 It is possible to regard Kant as having another sort of substantive view of rationality, and as equating rationality with morality. See the chapter on Kantian ethics.
36 Such views can also be modified to take a *satisficing* form, on which they hold that in order to be rational, an action must come *close enough* to being maximally supported by reasons. Such views avoid some of the problems about to be discussed, but involve other difficulties. See the papers in Byron (2004).
37 Subjective rationality is more plausibly identified with morality than objective rationality. The objective rational status of an action might often be impossible for the agent to determine, but it is a common and plausible view that the moral status of an action can always be determined by any moral agent.
38 It must be admitted that some forms of subjective irrationality need not diminish responsibility, and in some cases one's state of irrationality is itself something for which one can be held responsible (say, because one took too many hallucinogens). Still, cases in which the problem is a constitutional incapacity to be motivated by the reasons that rationally require an action *do* seem to diminish responsibility. That is what is going on in cases of phobias or compulsions.
39 Gauthier (1986); Scanlon (1998).
40 Possibly it will be the notion of subjective rationality. But typically the bargainers are regarded as fully informed, which minimizes the difference between objective and subjective rationality.
41 It is common to equate moral reasons with altruistic reasons, or at least to think of all altruistic reasons as moral reasons. But in fact the bulk of immoral action is done for the sake of other people: lying to get one's child into a good school, allowing a friend to copy one's homework. And of course a great deal of the most immoral action is done for the sake of one's country. These examples suggests both that the equation of morality and altruism is a mistake, and that the making of this mistake may be part of what allows people to justify altruistic immoral action to themselves.
42 Smith (1994).
43 Brandt (1998); Hooker (2000).
44 Smart (1956); Kagan (1989).
45 This objection is a variation of a well-known worry that rule-consequentialism collapses into act-consequentialism. See Smart (1973), 11–12. For some responses see Hooker (2000), 93–9.
46 Given the equation of "failing/omitting to φ is rationally prohibited" with "φ-ing is rationally required," this formula also explains when an action is rationally required.
47 Gert (2005) develops a detailed view of this sort.
48 This is a direct consequentialist view. Given that indirect consequentialism can be seen as having the same normative content as a certain contractualist position, the argument of the previous paragraph can be taken as showing how the nonmaximizing view of rationality can help indirect consequentialism avoid the same problem.
49 This view has some connection with the moral view described in Scheffler (1995). However, Scheffler's view is a rejection of maximizing consequentialism, while the view described here is only a rejection that what is morally required by such a view is also rationally required.
50 Parfit (2011).
51 Raz (1999), 89–95.
52 Many thanks to Christian Miller both for inviting me to contribute to this volume, and for extensive and very useful written comments.

Moral Psychology

1. Richard Holton argues that *akrasia* and weakness of will are very different things (2009, ch. 4). See Mele, 2010 for a reply.
2. A feature of paradigmatic strict akratic actions that typically is taken for granted and rarely made explicit is that the judgments with which they conflict are *rationally* formed. In virtue of their clashing with the agent's rationally formed decisive judgment, such actions are subjectively irrational (to some degree, if not without qualification). There is a failure of coherence in the agent of a kind directly relevant to assessments of the agent's rationality. On failures of coherence, see Arpaly, 2000 and Harman, 2004.
3 For other restrictive features of Aristotle's notion of *enkrateia*, see Charlton, 1988, 35–41.
4 This is not to say that motivation is built into the judgment itself.
5 This premise has another element, (*B1b*): An agent's succumbing to a desire contrary to his better judgment cannot be explained by his making a culpably insufficient effort to resist. Again, Watson claims that an insufficient effort cannot be explained by a misjudgment of "the amount of effort required", because misjudgment is "a different fault from weakness of will" (338). In Mele, 1987 (25–7), I argue that misjudgment and weakness may be combined in an explanation of an action contrary to one's better judgment.
6 For opposition to the idea that desires vary in motivational strength, see Charlton, 1988; Gosling, 1990; and Thalberg, 1985. For a reply to the opposition, see Mele, 2003, ch. 7.
7 See Mele, 1992, ch. 5, for an analysis of irresistible desire.
8 See Darwall on "existence" and "judgment" internalism (1983, 54; 1992, 155).
9 Having motivation at *t* to *A* must be distinguished from having motivation to *A* at *t*. I have motivation today to finish this chapter within six weeks, but I have no motivation today to finish this chapter today.
10 Some philosophers distinguish between normative and motivating reasons for action and others reject the distinction (see Mele, 2003, ch. 3, for discussion). Premise 2 is about all reasons for action, not just a species thereof.
11 See Bedke, 2009; Brink, 1989, 46–50, 59–60, 83–6; 1997; Dancy, 1993, 3–6; Kennett and Fine, 2008; Lenman, 1999; McNaughton, 1988, ch. 9; Miller, 2008; Milo, 1984, chs. 6 and 7; Roskies, 2003, 2008; Stocker, 1979; Svavarsdottir, 1999; van Roojen, 2002.
12 Also see Bedke, 2009; Dancy, 1993, 23–6; Gert and Mele, 2005; Lenman, 1999; Smith, 1994, 120–4, 135, 154–5; Stocker, 1979, 744–6.
13 The following story is a short version of one told in Mele, 1996 and 2003, ch. 5.
14 Michael Smith contends that people motivated by a generic desire of this kind have "a fetish or moral vice" (1994, 75; also see 76 and Smith 1996, 181–3). For a reply, see Mele, 2003, 124–5.
15 Eve Garrard and David McNaughton favor the second construal of "reason" (1998, 53–4).
16 For an influential brand of internalism that emphasizes rationality, see Korsgaard, 1986. For instructive criticism of a version of internalism that is geared specifically to rational agents, see Audi, 1997, ch. 10.
17 Compare *O5* with "WMI" in Smith, 2008, p. 211.
18 Parts of this chapter derive from Mele, 2002, 2003, and 2011. I am grateful to Christian Miller for comments on a draft of this chapter. This chapter was made possible through the support of a grant from the John Templeton Foundation. The opinions expressed in this chapter are my own and do not necessarily reflect the views of the John Templeton Foundation.

Morality and Religion

1 Cf. Aquinas, 1947, I II, q. 93, a. 1.
2 Other recent formulations of interest include John Finnis, 1980; Anthony J. Liska, 1996; and Jean Porter, 1999.
3 Cf. "I am in my study" and "William J. Wainwright is in his study." Since neither entails the other, I can grasp the first without grasping the second, and grasp the second without grasping the first. (I might, for example, forget who I am.)
4 Happiness so-defined "has something in common with Aristotle's *eudaimonia*, on the one hand, and Rawls's . . . life plan on the other" (Murphy 2001, 133–4). It differs from the former in that the plan or structure which orders the nine basic goods is not objectively given but *chosen*. Because basic goods are incommensurable, no hierarchical ranking of them is objectively (i.e., independently of our desires and preferences) better or worse than any other. It differs from the latter in that the goods which are ordered *are* objectively given.
5 This is plausible only if "personal" is construed *very* broadly so as to encompass non-theistic religions like Buddhism or Jainism as well as theistic religions such as Christianity, Islam, or Vaishnavism.
6 Thus, on Murphy's view, "John morally ought to speak the truth to Sally" is roughly equivalent to: "It is not possible for John to lie to Sally without committing an error of practical reason."
7 If not by us, then by rational beings with different basic desires and inclinations.
8 All moral principles are ethical principles but not all ethical principles are moral principles. For not all ethical principles express obligations. For example, emotional dispositions such as sympathy or actions "that go beyond the call of duty" can be ethically desirable without being obligatory.
9 God's antecedent intentions should be distinguished from his consequent intentions. The relevant antecedent intentions are [roughly] what God intends persons to do in the particular situations in which they find themselves considered in abstraction from the wider context in which the actions he antecedently intends them to perform occur. God's consequent intentions are what he intends persons to do all things considered.
10 For a critical look at divine will theories see Robert Adams (Adams 1996, and Adams 2002, 982–4).
11 So, strictly speaking, what is necessarily true in worlds in which there are no appropriate recipients of a divine command to protect the innocent, say (because no rational creatures exist in it or because, in those worlds, innocents can't be harmed) is that if there *were* beings like us, God would command them to protect the innocent, and hence they *would* have an obligation to do so.
12 The second table of the Decalogue comprises the last six of the Ten Commandments.
13 *Pace* moral particularists such as Jonathan Dancy (Dancy 2004) who argue that there are no significant or useful general moral principles. For a discussion of this view see Pekka Väyrynen's chapter on moral particularism in this volume.
14 Mackie argues that the belief in the objectivity of moral values can be explained by the mind's "propensity" to spread itself on external objects' (Hume), i.e., by our projecting our attitudes on to their objects; by our tendency to reverse "the direction of dependence" between desires and goodness, "making the desire depend upon the goodness, instead of the goodness on the desire"; by our unconsciously suppressing the fact that statements of moral obligation are implicitly hypothetical (asserting that so-and-so should be done if we or others want such-and-such); by "the persistence of a belief in something like divine law when the belief in the divine legislator has

faded out"; and the like (Mackie 1977, 42–6). For more on error theory see note 15 below.

15 See the chapters in this volume by Terence Cuneo on moral realism and by Hallvard Lillehammer on constructivism and the error theory. A third alternative to divine command theory might be called "secular non-naturalism." Its most famous protagonist is probably G. E. Moore who advocated a view of this sort in the first half of the twentieth century (see Moore 1903 and 1912). Moore's brand of nonrealism fell into disfavor in the second half of the last century but is currently involving something of a revival. See, e.g., Russ Shafer-Landau (Shafer-Landau 2003, especially chapters 3, 4, and 11) and Michael Huemer (Huemer 2005). Another recent advocate is Erik Wielenberg (Wielenberg 2005). Wielenberg's attack on theistic theories like mine will be discussed below.

16 That is the clear implication of Rawls remarks in Rawls, 2001. See, e.g., p. 5.

17 Kant thought that grounding moral precepts in desires would subject morality to the fluctuations and variations of desire, and thus undercut its universality and inescapability. But if God *necessarily* exists, *necessarily* prizes truth telling, and as a result, *necessarily* commands it, then the moral rightness of truth telling isn't hostage to the potential fluctuations or variations of *anyone's* desires (either ours *or* God's). So a divine command theory which incorporates these claims isn't exposed to Kant's objection.

18 See Sorley, 1918. For a critique of Sorley. see Wainwright, 2005, 54–7.

19 That is, one might think that in the absence of objective values there could be no objective obligations. There could be no objective obligation to keep our promises or to promote the happiness of others, for example, if (e.g.) promise keeping or the happiness of others weren't objectively good. On the other hand, it is by no means obvious that the existence of objective values entails the existence of objective obligations.

20 For more on virtue theory see the chapter by Christine Swanton on virtue ethics in this volume.

21 There is this difference between the case of God and that of the drill sergeant. The roles of drill sergeant and person under his command are extrinsic to those who occupy them. In God's case, the roles aren't extrinsic. God's position of authority is intrinsic to him (i.e., he is essentially such that any beings he might create would be subject to his authority) and we, in turn, are essentially his subjects.

22 Including those in which, my wrong having escaped detection, I am not exposed to any adverse natural, social, or civic consequences.

23 If they had thought that God wasn't ultimately motivated by his own happiness, they would have surely recognized that they owed us an explanation of why human and divine motivations are so different. There is no evidence that they did, however.

24 There is no suggestion in either Gay or Paley that the goodness of happiness isn't intrinsic or that, whether God commands it or not, the pursuit of happiness isn't a good thing.

25 Some divine command theorists derive his authority from the fact that he has created us and bestowed so many benefits upon us. Others derive it from his superlative goodness. Still others believe that the commands of a perfect being would be intrinsically authoritative. For a critique of the claim that God's commands can be intrinsically authoritative, see Murphy, 2002, chapter 3. For a response to Murphy's critique see Wainwright, 2005, 136–41.

26 Cf. Kant, 1959: "One should only act on maxims which one can will to be universal laws," "One should only act on maxims which respect people's status as ends in themselves," and (derivatively) maxims that pass these tests, e.g., "If one has made a promise, one ought to keep it."

27 Cf. Kant, 1960, 23–4 and 41–2.
28 Between "Principles bind us only if we endorse them" and "The good principle binds us even though we do not in fact endorse it because our wills are corrupt at their root."
29 I.e., an *actual* endorsement. That the good seed involves the *potentiality* of an endorsement isn't sufficient.
30 For a good discussion of Kant's views on "original sin," see Quinn, 1988, 89–118.
31 Aquinas, 1947, II II, qq. 1–170. Virtue theory coheres nicely with some other religious worldviews as well. For an interesting comparison of Aquinas's and Mencius's virtue theories see Yearly, 1990.
32 Though cf. the Mahayana doctrine of "skillful means," according to which the Buddha is not interested in the truth of his teachings but only in his teaching's spiritual helpfulness.
33 For more on this possibility see Wainwright, 2005, chapter 9.
34 For several recent examples see Stephen Evans, 2004, chapter 13; Jerome Gellman, 2003; and Robert Adams, 1999, chapter 12, and Adams, 2002, 984–7.
35 Most famously, Soren Kierkegaard (Kierkegaard, 1954). For defenses of Kierkegaard see Quinn, 1986 and 2000, and Wainwright, 2005, chapter 10.
36 See, for example, Wainwright, 2005, chapter 11.

Consequentialism

1 Some might hold that there is sometimes, on commonsense morality, an option to act so as to make things worse both for oneself and for others. Whether this is plausible or not depends on whether there is, on commonsense morality, a pro tanto moral reason to promote the impersonal good, as Shelly Kagan (1991) has argued. (A pro tanto moral reason is one that has genuine weight such that it generates an obligation in the absence of countervailing reasons.)
2 The third and fifth columns appear in boldface type, for these are the two columns that, on SU, are most salient to determining moral permissibility.
3 I'm assuming that, although it wasn't explicitly stated above, SU includes the following claim: S's performing x is supererogatory if and only if, and ultimately because, there is a permissible alternative, y, whose outcome contains less utility for others (i.e., those other than S) than x's outcome.
4 I would actually prefer to do away with condition (ii)–see Portmore (2011). That is, I prefer to let the term "supererogatory" denote the pretheoretic notion of going above and beyond the call of duty (i.e., that of doing more than one has to), and an act can go above and beyond the call of duty without being praiseworthy, as where the agent performs such an act with a bad motive—see McNamara (2011). If we were to let the term "supererogatory" refer to the pretheoretical notion of exceeding the minimum that morality demands, as I would prefer, we would be following McNamara (1996). Nevertheless, I include condition (ii) here, for many philosophers take it to be a necessary condition for an act's being supererogatory.
5 An act is optimific if and only if its outcome outranks that of every other available alternative.
6 I borrow this example, with some minor revisions, from Derek Parfit (2011).
7 Michael Smith (2006) defends such a view.
8 See Sepielli (2009, 2010) for a defense of this controversial assumption as well as some suggestions about how this might be done.
9 Whereas only acts can be *morally* good and bad and, thus, have deontic value, states of affairs (such as the state of affairs in which people experience more pleasure) can

have nonmoral value—that is, value, *simpliciter*. The deontic value of an act is a measure of how much moral reason there is to perform that act.

10 If there is a constraint against performing a certain act-type, then any commission of an act of that type constitutes an *infringement* of that constraint. But not all infringements of a constraint are wrong. All and only those infringements that are wrong constitute *violations* of that constraint. I follow Thomson (1990, 122) and Zimmerman (1996, 181) in making this terminological distinction.

Constraints needn't be absolute. It may be permissible to infringe upon a constraint if enough good is at stake, and it may be permissible to infringe upon a constraint if doing so would prevent a sufficient number of comparable infringements of that constraint.

11 If we want Mod-SU to include an absolute constraint against committing murder, we need only replace "500" with "∞" in Mod-SU.

12 I will assume that for each act alternative there is some determinate fact as to what the world would be like were she to perform that alternative. This assumption is sometimes called *counterfactual determinism*—see, e.g., Bykvist (2003, 30). Although this assumption is controversial, nothing that I will say here hangs on it. I make the assumption only for the sake of simplifying the presentation. If counterfactual determinism is false, then instead of correlating each alternative with a unique possible world, we will need to correlate each alternative with a probability distribution over the set of possible worlds that might be actualized if S were to perform that alternative.

13 This example is borrowed with minor modifications from Kagan and Vallentyne (1997).

14 For a response to this objection, see Portmore (2009a, 2011).

15 See, for instance, Dreier (1993), Portmore (2009a, 2011), and Louise (2004).

16 This is modeled on Ben Bradley's formulation of comparative level satisficing consequentialism—see Bradley (2006, 101).

17 For a defense of this view, see Norcross (2006). For a critique of this view, see Lawlor (2009a, 2009b) and Portmore (2011).

18 What outcome is associated with a given code of rules will depend on how rule-consequentialism is formulated. It may be the outcome that would result from universal compliance with it or from widespread acceptance of it or from something else. For a defense of rule-consequentialism, see Hooker (2000). For criticisms of rule-consequentialism, see Arneson (2005) and Portmore (2009b).

19 Those unfamiliar with the cases involving switching the train (or trolley) from one track to another and pushing the fat man off the footbridge should see http://www.youtube.com/watch?v=Fs0E69krO_Q.

20 For responses to these sorts of arguments by Greene and Singer, see Berker (2009) and Timmons (2008).

21 For helpful comments on an earlier draft, I thank Christian Miller.

Kantian Ethics

1 Both of these goals are served by contrasting the Kantian approach to a consequentialist alternative. Rawls, in describing his own theory as Kantian, helpfully said " . . . the adjective 'Kantian' expresses analogy, not identity; it means roughly that a doctrine sufficiently resembles Kant's in fundamental enough respects so that it is far closer to his view than to the other traditional moral conceptions that are appropriate for use as benchmarks for comparison." Rawls, 2001, 303–58. On many points,

especially within normative ethics, consequentialism is the most relevant benchmark, and many Kantians are motivated by the perceived need to articulate an alternative to this approach. Even the opposition to consequentialism, though, fails to serve as either a necessary or sufficient feature of Kantians, since many nonconsequentialists are not Kantians and some scholars argue that Kant's own commitments yield a consequentialist normative theory. For the latter see the classic Hare, 1981, along with Cummiskey, 1996, and Ridge, 2009.

2 Jennifer Uleman draws a similar distinction, placing herself firmly in the latter camp, in Uleman, 2010, p. 3.

3 Foremost among these is Kant, 1996. Timmons, 2002 provides an excellent sampling of recent work on this text. On *Religion within the Bounds of Mere Reason* found in Kant, 2001, see, for example Wood, 1970; Wood, 1978; and Hare, 1996. On *Anthropology from a Pragmatic Point of View* (Kant 2006), see Frierson, 2003. And on *Education* see Schapiro, 1999.

Perhaps surprisingly, when Kantians complain of a myopic focus on the *Groundwork*, it is usually not ignorance of *The Critique of Practical Reason* that bothers them. This text does not figure prominently in Kantian efforts to correct misconstruals of the approach, though Kantian Realists sometimes invoke the *fact of reason* argument as evidence that Kantians should not try to derive a substantial moral principle from formal starting points. See, e.g. Guyer, 2000, p. 109.

4 Kant does not use the language of "virtue" in the *Groundwork*, but most contemporary Kantian moral theorists would regard "virtuous person" as synonymous with "person of good will." I view this as a helpful translation out of Kant's technical vocabulary into more familiar terms, and believe that it is consistent with Kant's later explicit discussions of virtue.

5 But compare Darwall, 2006 who argues that the first-person standpoint provides an insufficient basis for morality. He believes that the materials for an argument vindicating morality are only to be found in contexts of interpersonal interaction that he calls "second-personal." I comment further on the relations between Darwall's view and those of other Kantians below.

6 See Portmore, in this volume.

7 Among the best are Herman, 1993f and Korsgaard, 1996b. See also Korsgaard's introduction to Kant, 1998, p. 252.

8 See, for example, Scanlon, 2008, 37–88.

9 There is an additional complication involving counterfactuals of competing motives that I am glossing over here. Suppose that the moral motive is sufficient to motivate the action given the agent's current state, but wouldn't have been if the countertemptation had been stronger. In the *Religion* (Kant 2001), Kant holds that this shows that the agent's fundamental maxim is not the moral maxim. This puts pressure on Kant to say that even an action like this has no moral worth. On this view few, if any actions, would qualify as morally worthy, but that seems consistent with the pessimistic view of human nature that Kant advances in the *Religion*. In any case, this strong position and the details of the moral psychology behind it are not required for the simpler point being made in the *Groundwork*.

10 Cf. O'Neill, 1989b, p. 86.

11 Someone might wonder about the case in which someone is motivated both by duty and by inclination. There are many ways to spell out what is going on in this kind of case, each of which a Kantian would treat somewhat differently. But what is most important to Kant, especially in the *Groundwork*, is that the good will is sufficiently motivated by duty. Cooperating motives might be present, but they are not necessary. One of the best treatments of the moral psychology of the *Groundwork* is Herman, 1993f.

In later writings Kant lays out a moral psychology on which we are always motivated by both duty and inclination, or what he there calls "self-love." The question is which of these two principles of action we treat as fundamental, and as conditioning the other. Do we fulfill our obligations just in case doing so is compatible with our inclinations, or do we act on inclination just in case doing so is compatible with fulfilling our obligations? See Kant, 2001, 6:36–7.

12 So Kant says that "certain subjective limitations and hindrances . . . far from concealing [the good will] and making it unrecognizable, rather bring it out by contrast and make it shine forth all the more brightly." Kant, 1998, 4:397. On Kant's interest in the sympathetic man as primarily epistemic, compare Rawls, 2000, p. 179.

13 Cf. Korsgaard, 1996f, 275–310, and see, Pettit, 1997, 129ff.

14 Cf. Baron, 1997.

15 See Smith, 1994; and compare Williams, 1985, chapters 8 and 9; and Wolf, 1982.

16 I believe that a failure to appreciate this distinctive function is behind the criticisms of purportedly Kantian moral psychology in e.g., Bennett, 1974; Williams, 1981; and Markovits, 2010. For more discussion of the motive of duty in Kantian ethics see Baron, 1995, 79, 419–39. I discuss Barbara Herman's treatment of related issues below.

17 For clarity, I capitalize "Categorical Imperative" when this refers to the fundamental moral principle. More particular principles of action may be called "categorical imperatives" in a derivative sense, and Kant himself uses the terminology this way (e.g., 4:414).

18 Though it is oversimplifying to associate Constructivism with the Universal Law Formula and Realism with the Formula of Humanity, it is certainly true that constructivists are interested in Kant's distinctive *formalism* whereas Realists usually are not. As a result, Constructivists tend to have considerably more interest in the Universal Law Formula than do Realists, who sometimes treat it as little more than an unfortunate and misleading distraction.

19 In what follows I mean "Constructivists" to refer only to the Kantian variety. Very different theories are sometimes labeled with the same term, but I do not explore the connections, if any, between these theories and Kantian Constructivism here. See Lillehammer, in this volume.

20 In fact he at least sometimes seems to think that they must all bottom out in our interest in our own pleasure. Contemporary Kantians rarely defend this aspect of his view.

21 See Cuneo, in this volume.

22 Kant's common objection to these two very different types of moral theory is an important point of emphasis for Rawls. See for example Rawls, 2000, pp 226–30.

23 e.g., Kant, 1998, 4:453.

24 For discussion of the relationship between what I am calling Kantian Constructivism and Rawls' Kantian Constructivism see n. 40.

25 See O'Neill, 1989c especially "Consistency in Action," and "Universal Laws and Ends-in-Themselves."

Reath develops a detailed Constructivist account of rational agents as legislators of the moral law. He uses this notion to illuminate the connection between the universalizability constraint stated in the Formula of Universal Law and the autonomy of moral agents, arguing that the Universal Law is the constitutive principle of autonomous, and so authoritative, willing. See his essays "Legislating the Moral Law," "Autonomy of the Will as the Foundation of Morality," and "Legislating for a Realm of Ends," all collected in Reath, 2006.

Darwall, 2006 presents a new strategy for vindicating the authority of morality that I think should also be regarded as Constructivist. Darwall argues that the idea of "the second person standpoint," "the perspective that you and I take up when we make and acknowledge claims on one another's conduct and will" (p. 3) is an essential element of any plausible Constructivist argument for the authority of morality. His idea is to move from what we might understand as formal features of second personal interactions to the substantive vindication of the authority of the Categorical Imperative, or something like it. The account of the grounds of our duties to others that I give in Ebels-Duggan, 2009 is in some ways similar.

26 In early work Korsgaard (1996d) seemed to think that the Universal Law could yield substantive moral norms all by itself. This work is the paradigmatic instance of the connection between Constructivism and the Universal Law, and remains a—perhaps even the—leading interpretation of the Universal Law Formula. Korsgaard has, as I discuss below, moved progressively away from this emphasis on the Universal Law. But one might nevertheless think that developing the Universal Law into a contradiction test remains the best hope for the Constructivist program.

27 The concept/conception distinction is introduced by Rawls in Rawls, 1971, Section 9.

28 Korsgaard is here interpreting the opening part of *Groundwork* III, 4:446–47. Along with Korsgaard, 2008a, 302–26, see Korsgaard, 1996e; and Korsgaard, 1996h, 92–8.

29 Even on the most optimistic views about what work the formal principle can accomplish there is still need for sensitivity to context and the exercise of judgment. For instance, one needs moral sensitivity to know what sorts of situations raise moral questions and so call for moral reasoning. This is a point that is emphasized by both O'Neill, 1999 and Herman, 1993d and Herman, 1993g. Compare Rawls, 2000, 161–6. Additionally it seems that on any view at least the contradiction in will test will require judgment in application. For example, on Rawls' view about how to apply the contradiction in will test we need judgment to determine what should count as our "true needs." See Rawls, 2000, pp 172–5.

30 See, among others, Rawls, 2000, p. 168; Hill, 2006, p. 482; and Korsgaard, 2008a, p. 219. Rawls adds the clause "unless Z" to the end. Hill adds "from the motive M." It is noteworthy that the maxims that Kant himself employs in his examples do not adhere to this form.

31 Velleman, 2006b develops a different version of the practical contradiction interpretation, one that understands "universalizing" a maxim to mean making it common knowledge among all rational agents.

32 Its primary competitor is the Logical Contradiction Interpretation, on which the maxim becomes logically impossible in the situation of universalization. This interpretation is favored by some of Kant's language, but seems too narrow. Less popular is the Teleological Contradiction Interpretation that holds that the contradiction is between the agent's purposes and those of nature. This interpretation was favored by Paton, 1958 and has the advantage of ruling out violent actions. But it faces both the external problem of depending on a teleology of nature and the internal problem of apparently making no use of universalization. I am not aware of anyone who advocates this reading today.

33 For a helpful critical discussion of this argument see Langton, 2007.

34 Dean, 2006, Ch. 6, argues for a particular reading of this argument. For alternative ways of understanding Kant's argument that humanity is the unique end-in-itself, see Sussman, 2003; and Martin, 2006.

35 See Korsgaard, 1999 and Korsgaard, 2009.

36 For example, Wood, 2007 writes: "We may have to face the fact that the mere *claim* that human beings have absolute worth as ends in themselves may in the end be more compelling all by itself than any argument that Kant or anyone else could ever offer for it" p. 89 (Wood's emphasis). Wood nevertheless thinks that Kant does

provide an argument for this claim, one that does all that any argument for a foundational value could be expected to do. More on Wood's view below.

37 On the relations among the formulations of the Categorical Imperative see Wood, 1999; Guyer, 1998; O'Neill, 1989a; Wood, 2007.

38 See Guyer, 2000. For a helpful critique of Guyer's view see Reath, 2003. For another clear statement of Kantian Realism see Langton, 2007.

39 Cf. Guyer, 1996, p. 407.

40 Unsurprisingly given his pivotal role in the development of contemporary Kantian ethical theory, Rawls' thought contains aspects of both Constructivism and Realism. In Rawls, 2000, he lays fairly heavy stress on the Universal Law Formula, or more exactly on the closely related Law of Nature Formula. He holds that the other Formulae add nothing to its content and moreover that the Categorical Imperative procedure implicit in the Law of Nature Formula in some way specifies the content of these later formulae (182–3). He regards this procedure as prior in authority to any contentful principle; a principle counts as authoritative just in case it is the outcome of this procedure, properly applied. He claims that the procedure yields plausible moral content in its positive and negative results, and claims most strongly, that all norms to which we are legitimately subject can be seen as resulting from this procedure (e.g., 206 and 244). He nevertheless takes it to yield objective moral principles (163). He endorses the priority of right, meaning by this that the goodness of all things depends on meeting the substantive conditions imposed by the formal requirements of the procedure in question (156, 226, 230).

On the other hand, Rawls flatly denies that any such procedure is adequate for generating the whole content of a reasonable moral doctrine (163). He says that the Categorical Imperative procedure itself is not constructed but simply laid out. He also supposes that it simply systematizes ideas and commitments already implicit in our everyday practical thought, and so neither purports to answer skeptical questions nor stands in need of justification (239). He stresses the role of moral feeling in Kantian theory, especially the fact that we find his conceptions of freedom and the Kingdom or Realm of Ends attractive, and so motivating (148, 213). And he says of his own exposition of Kant: "I have played down the role of the *a priori* and the formal . . . I believe that the downplayed elements are not at the heart of his doctrine" (275).

Rawls' affinity with each of the sides of the division that I have identified in contemporary Kantianism is encapsulated in the fact that while he attributes to Kant an original doctrine that he calls "constructivism" (273), he is clear that "not everything can be constructed" (240). Rawls' version of Kantian Constructivism moves from a certain conception of ourselves—as reasonable and rational—and our relations to one another—as free and equal— to the substantive claims of morality (e.g. 239, and cf. Rawls, 2001). Rawls does not defend the authority of this self-conception, but treats it as given. Notably the conception seems to include substantive moral content, especially in its element of "reasonableness." This suggests that Rawls is not after the strong version of autonomy that the most ambitious Constructivists attempt to secure. Rather he regards morality as autonomous insofar as it is based on a self-conception that we in fact have (237).

41 See Wood, 1998, especially p.165; and Wood, 1999, ch. 4, especially 111, 141 and 147. Wood regards the Formula of Autonomy, along with the Formula of the Realm of Ends which he understands as a variant, as better still. He takes seriously Kant's claim that it is this formula that presents "a complete determination" (Kant, 1998, 4:436) of the moral law. See Wood, 2007, Chapter 4, especially 80–4.

42 Wood, 1998, p. 173 and Wood, 1999, p. 114.

43 Wood, 1998, p. 174. Martin, 2006 also links Wood's argument to Korsgaard's.

44 See Wood, 2007, especially chapters 4–6.

45 Wood, 1998, 121–2, acknowledges that his reading of the sense in which moral agents legislate the law to themselves is deflationary and will be regarded by many as disappointing. But he thinks that any theorist must choose between rendering the law subjective and arbitrary by emphasizing self-legislation, or understanding self-legislation as a metaphor. He holds that the choice for the latter is an easy one (106–11).

A distinctive theme of Wood's development of a Kantian program that I lack space to discuss is the importance of the moral law as a source of noncomparative, thus noncompetitive, bases of self-worth. It follows from the claim that humanity is of absolute worth that each person is of equal worth, but Wood finds in Kant a concern about the human tendency to locate our worth elsewhere, in things that bear comparison and make some of us more valuable than others. Examples are our wealth, talents, or social status. This tendency underlies all of the vices explicitly recognized by Kant and Wood claims that "it is no exaggeration to say that Kant even regards [comparative conceptions of self-worth] as the sole and exclusive ground of all moral evil," Wood, 1999, p 135. This insight is the basis of Wood's development of Kant's notion of our "unsocial sociability." See Wood, 1999 Chapters 8 and 9; and Wood, 1991.

46 And cf. Herman, 2007b. Herman strikes Realist notes in Herman, 1993d, 149 and 134.

47 I take Herman to mean by "naturalism" Humean or more generally empiricist theories, and by "realism" rationalist theories of the sort advocated by Clarke and Price. Simon Blackburn would be a contemporary representative of the former, and Thomas Scanlon and Derek Parfit contemporary representatives of the latter.

48 Herman characterizes the deontology that she is concerned to reject as "the subordination of all considerations of value to principles of right or duty" (p. 210).

49 In particular she wants an account that can make the regulative role of morality in our practical reasoning intelligible to us and provide guidance for deliberation in difficult practical circumstances. See Herman, 1993c. She strikes similar themes about the role of the Categorical Imperative in Kantian moral thought in Herman, 1993d, and to a lesser extent in Herman, 1993e.

50 As she puts it the value "lies behind all of the formulations of the CI, both as the condition of their possibility *and* as the source of moral content," Herman, 1993g, n. 12, emphasis in original.

Like Kant himself, Herman talks about the value in several different ways. Sometimes she adopts Kant's language of the good will as in Herman, 1993c, p. 209, or transposes this to good willing as in Herman, 1993d, p. 154, while in Herman, 1993c, p. 213 she refers to the value of rationality, and in Herman, 1993d simply agency. Sometimes she even uses the Rawlsian term "separateness" of agents to mark out what is supposed to be of value. See Herman, 1993c, 212–13.

51 This view corrects the version of Kantian moral psychology on which Bernard Williams relies in his famous "one thought too many" argument.

52 Cf. Kant's claim that the later formulae serve to "bring an idea of reason closer to intuition . . . and thereby to feeling." Kant, 1998, 4:436. As many theorists note, Kant himself relies most heavily on the Formula of Humanity when he works out normative principles in Kant, 1996.

53 Thomas Hill has been especially focused on working out the normative implications of the Categorical Imperative, and has made valuable contributions in his Kantian analysis of issues in "applied" ethics, including terrorism (Hill, 1992b), servility, suicide, and affirmative action (Hill, 1991).

54 For versions of the capacity view see Korsgaard, 1996c; Wood, 1998; Hill, 1992a; and Rawls, 2000. For opposing interpretations see Dean, 1996, who argues that "humanity" should be identified with the good will; Timmerman, 2006, who argues that "humanity" should be identified with each rational being; Martin, 2006, who argues

that "humanity" should be identified with autonomous beings. For a helpful summary of all of this literature see Denis, 2007.

55 Wood, 1998, emphasizes this point.

56 Hill argues that Kant holds that we may not trade off some instantiations of values having dignity with others, so that, for example, we may not kill one person solely as a means to saving the lives of any number of others (Hill, 1992a). This makes vivid the anticonsequentialist implications of Kant's approach. Following Mill, 1998, 55–9, consequentialists could acknowledge qualitative differences among values. But it is difficult to see how a consequentialist view that eschewed any trade-offs among values could work.

Hill also believes that many will find Kant's unyielding position implausible absent the hope that Kant founded on his religious thought. I think that he is at least right to suppose that Kant's religious work is motivated in part by a perceived need to deal with consequentialist intuitions about improving the state of the world.

57 Anderson, 1993 provides an account of the many ways that value can appropriately figure in our practical reasoning. Cf. Scanlon, 1998, 78–107.

58 The different interpretations of positive duties seem to track, again roughly, the Constructivist/Realist divide. Korsgaard (1996c, 127-8 and 1996h, 132-45) emphasizes contribution and discusses related themes in Korsgaard, 1996f. Herman takes it that respect for agency requires that we support the development and protection of individual agents' capacities for practical reasoning and, as a part of this, contribute to the establishment and maintenance of social structures that make such development possible for all. She does not treat the promotion of others' particular ends as central. See Herman, 1993e. In more recent work she develops her thinking about moral education, but also tends more towards a contribution view. See Herman, 2007a, Chapters 4, 5, 6, 9 and 11.

Kant also believes that we have significant duties to ourselves. Contemporary Kantians have focused less on these, and are less unified in their treatment, though Herman discusses the duty to develop one's talents in a fair amount of detail in Herman, 2007b.

59 For a recent systematic treatment of Kant's own political theory see Ripstein, 2009.

60 For my own treatment of this see Ebels-Duggan, 2008. For an alternative Kantian account of love see Velleman, 2006a.

61 Herman makes a similar argument against deception in Herman, 1993c.

62 See also O'Neill's similar argument in O'Neill, 1989a. For a critique of Korsgaard's and O'Neill's argument against the permissibility of coercion see Pallikkathayil, 2010.

Note that I discuss here only what Korsgaard takes respect for humanity to require. In at least one article she suggests that, in nonideal circumstances, we sometimes have sufficient reason to depart from treating humanity as an end. See Korsgaard, 1996g.

63 And cf. Wood, 2007, 81–2. For a similar reading defended by a Constructivist see Dean, 2006, Chapter 7.

64 In this Herman is responding to a criticism of Kantian ethics as overly abstract, one now classic statement of which is found in Williams, 1981. Compare Herman, 1993b and Herman, 1993a.

65 This is a theme that Herman has developed considerably in more recent work. See "Can Virtue Be Taught? The Problem of New Moral Facts," "Training to Autonomy," "Moral Improvisation," and "Responsibility and Moral Competence," all in Herman, 2007a.

66 Scanlon himself denies that he is a Kantian in "How I am Not a Kantian," in Parfit, 2011. But the view from which he is concerned to distinguish himself is really Kantian Constructivism, not Kantianism broadly construed. Scanlon also opposes Kantian themes in Chapter 3 of Scanlon, 2008, where he rejects the idea that treating someone as an end rather than a mere means is of fundamental moral importance.

67 Scanlon's full formula reads: "an act is wrong if its performance under the circumstances would be disallowed by any set of principles for the general regulation of behavior that no one could reasonably reject as a basis for informed, unforced general agreement." Scanlon, 1998, p. 153.
68 It is also not clear that all Kantian Constructivists would affirm this. Darwall argues that his second-personal moral theory provides a foundation for Scanlon's contractualism (Darwall, 2006, Chapter 12), and that autonomy is a presupposition of the second-person standpoint (Chapter 10). I suggest above (n. 25) that Darwall's theory is best understood as a version of Kantian Constructivism.
69 My thanks to Ryan W. Davis, Jon Garthoff, and Adrienne Martin, whose comments and advice resulted in substantial improvements in this essay.

Virtue Ethics

1 For more on the definition of virtue ethics see Swanton (2013).
2 See Foot's example (30) of the blue tit which lacks the blue patch on its head: we are assuming here this does not affect its desirability as a mate.
3 This point is the gist of Bernard Williams "representation problem" in his 2005a where he points out that beings with a culture and language represent things in various possible ways, and "where there is culture, it affects everything" (102).
4 Indeed it has been argued that "the harmony thesis" is false if applied universally (Stohr 2003). Even Aristotle argued that the courageous man should not regard with pleasure the prospect of dying on the battle field when virtue demands this. But the harmony thesis concerns temptation rather than pleasure: even if we should not take pleasure in virtuous action when for example giving sad news to a friend, and even if the grieving person has difficulty in doing what is required (because she lacks energy and her mind is overclouded by sorrow), we may still wish to claim that a person of perfect virtue will not be tempted to do what is wrong.
5 Dewey, 1944, p. 50, cited in Welchman, 2005, p. 147.
6 This is a notion of Nietzsche's, explained further in relation to the dynamic features of virtue in my 2005.
7 The example is adapted from Gross and McIlveen, 2000.
8 But see Swanton, 2003, Chapter 12 for the basis of such a view, and Dancy, 2004.
9 I claim there is such an imaginable case in Swanton, 2003.
10 It has been claimed (Das 2003) that such conceptions will be circular, invoking prior conceptions of right action, but if as is likely they will involve wide reflective equilibrium models with rich conceptions of the point and function of a given virtue relative to conceptions of a good human life in the relevant area, any "circle" will not be vicious.
11 For a good discussion, see Russell, 2009.
12 For a discussion of the problems the nonvirtuous self-improver poses for several virtue ethical accounts of rightness see Johnson, 2003, and for a reply see Russell, 2009.
13 I wish to thank Christian Miller for valuable editorial assistance.

Feminist Ethics

1 See Peggy MacIntosh, 2000, for a list of 46 privileges that whites have.
2 See Superson, 2009a, for a fuller discussion.

3 On this point, Hampton disagrees with radical feminist Andrea Dworkin (1987), who also invokes Kantian intrinsic value, but who believes that *all* heterosexual sex actually does in fact degrade women because it involves penetration of a woman by a man—mere biology makes it the case that the woman is objectified by the man, her humanity destroyed (Hampton 1999, 140–1).
4 I would like to thank Christian Miller for very useful substantive and editorial comments on this entry, which resulted in a much clearer presentation of these ideas.

Moral Particularism

1 The most prominent particularists are Jonathan Dancy and Mark Lance and Margaret Little; they often cite the work of Iris Murdoch and John McDowell as inspiration. Most moral philosophers aren't particularists, but most of them would grant that it is a position worth taking seriously.
2 These two roles that moral theories have been asked to play make different demands on moral claims. It is therefore possible that no moral claim, principle or otherwise, succeeds in playing both roles. Some philosophers deny that an adequate moral theory must be action-guiding.
3 Dancy (1993, 74; 2004, 85–7) notes that particularists agree. The general idea that moral facts are made to hold by other facts is discussed in Strandberg (2008) and Väyrynen (2009a).
4 The term "standard" is due to McKeever and Ridge (2006, 7).
5 Compare such standard examples of analytic truths as "Bachelors are eligible unmarried adult males" or "Nothing is both red all over and green all over."
6 Among particularists, Dancy holds the idiosyncratic view that basic moral knowledge is *contingent* a priori (2004, 146–8; for discussion, see McKeever and Ridge 2006, 159–69).
7 A good introduction to the topic of supervenience is McLaughlin and Bennett (2008).
8 Discussions of supervenience in the context of particularism include Dancy (1993, 73–8; 2004, 86–9), Jackson et al. (2000), Little (2000), McKeever and Ridge (2006, 7–8), and Strandberg (2008). See also Väyrynen (2009a, 298–9).
9 Dancy (2004, Ch. 2–4) explains well both the distinction between the contributory and the overall and problems with various attempts to analyze the former in terms of the latter.
10 See Ross (1930, Ch. 2). He grants that "prima facie duty" is a misleading label insofar as it suggests an epistemic notion (such as "what at first appears to be a duty"). He means moral considerations which do not simply vanish if they are outweighed by other, stronger considerations, but remain in force (and may ground residual duties of compensation, regret, and the like). This is how "pro tanto," as explained in the text, is to be understood.
11 Kagan (1988) and Dancy (2000). See also Berker (2007).
12 Dancy (1993, 2004) and Little (2000).
13 McKeever and Ridge (2006, Ch. 9) and Väyrynen (2008).
14 As McDowell (1979) emphasizes, and such generalists as O'Neill (1996), Crisp (2000), McKeever and Ridge (2006), and Väyrynen (2008) agree.
15 O'Neill (1996, 75).
16 Dancy (2004, 7).
17 Compare, for instance, the positions defended in Dancy (1993) and Dancy (2004).

18 McKeever and Ridge (2006) and Väyrynen (2006).
19 Jackson et al. (2000), as well as Peacocke (2004).
20 Moore (1903/1993). Very roughly, the Open Question Argument aims to show that no substantive moral claims are true merely in virtue of their meaning.
21 Holism can allow that some considerations may be invariable reasons, so long as they are so not *qua* reasons but because of idiosyncratic features, such as their particular content (Dancy 2000, 136-37).
22 A large selection of such examples can be found in Dancy (1993, 2000) and Little (2000).
23 Crisp (2000) and McNaughton and Rawling (2000).
24 Dancy (2004, 121–2) vs. McNaughton and Rawling (2000). See also Little (2000).
25 On these distinctions, see Dancy (2001; 2004, Ch. 3). Reasons, defeaters, and enablers can further be distinguished from "intensifiers" and "diminishers" (or "attenuators"), which can make a reason stronger or weaker in strength than it would otherwise have been.
26 Stratton-Lake (2000), Hooker (2000, 2008), and Raz (2000, 2006).
27 McNaughton and Rawling (2000) and Väyrynen (2006).
28 Schroeder 2011.
29 Dancy (1993), Little (2000), and Cullity (2002). Holism alone does not yield this view, for reasons might be context-dependent without being determined solely by features of context.
30 Dancy (1993, 26, 103; 2004, 111–17) and Lance and Little (2006a).
31 Väyrynen (2004), McKeever and Ridge (2006, Ch. 3), and Horty (2007).
32 Jackson et al. (2000), Väyrynen (2004, 2006), McKeever and Ridge (2005; 2006, Ch. 2).
33 Little (2000, 277), Stratton-Lake (2000, 129), and Dancy (2004, 82).
34 McKeever and Ridge (2006, 32–41) and Leibowitz (2009).
35 Väyrynen (2006, 2009b).
36 Horty (2007) and Schroeder (2009, 2011).
37 Ross (1930, Ch. 2), Gert (1998), McKeever and Ridge (2006, Ch. 7), and Hooker (2008).
38 Note that not all exceptionless generalizations count as genuine principles. Some are merely accidentally true and therefore lack the requisite modal implications. One example from outside morality would be "All nuggets of gold are smaller than 1,000 cubic meters."
39 This argument is due to McKeever and Ridge (2006, Chs. 6–7). For critical discussion, see Schroeder (2009) and Väyrynen (2009b).
40 There is a stronger claim in this vicinity, namely that the list of potential defeaters and enablers must be not only finite but also short enough that principles can exhaustively specify them all without becoming too complex to be possible objects of (human) thought. If principles failed to be cognitively manageable in this sense, generalism about standards might be epistemically irrelevant even if true. This alone would not be a problem for generalism about standards.
41 Pietroski (1993), Lance and Little (2006b, 2007), Robinson (2006), Väyrynen (2006, 2009b).
42 Lance and Little (2006a, 2006b).
43 Väyrynen (2006, 2009b) and Robinson (2006) develop two different accounts of this kind.
44 Little (2000), McKeever and Ridge (2006), Väyrynen (2009a, 2009b), and Leibowitz (2011).
45 The truth of holism would also complicate the use of hypothetical cases like the trolley problems in normative ethics, since one might not be able to generalize widely from them. Compare Kagan (1988) and Dancy (1993).

46 Similarly, the content of the correct moral standards need not depend on contingent facts about human psychology in the way that what counts as a valuable guide so depends.
47 Sunstein (2005), McKeever and Ridge (2006, 8–9), and Väyrynen (2008).
48 McNaughton (1988, 62, 190–3), Dancy (1993, 64, 67), and perhaps McDowell (1979).
49 Hooker (2000, 2008).
50 McKeever and Ridge (2006, Ch. 9) and Väyrynen (2008). See also Dworkin (1995).
51 Thanks to Christian Miller for excellent editorial comments on this chapter.

Biology, Evolution, and Ethics

1 Although I'm calling this the *normative* sense of "morality," not all questions about morality in this sense are normative or first-order ones. The first question above is a normative one, but the second is not: it is a *metaethical* or second-order question about morality in the *normative* sense, namely whether there are objective truths about what is good and bad, right and wrong.
2 This should not be understood as requiring explicit moral judgment in every particular case. There can be spontaneous acts of altruism, for example, that don't involve explicit moral judgment but still fall under the category of morality because they are implicitly informed by and interpreted through moral judgment: upon reflection one would judge the act to be morally appropriate, others might judge it to be morally praiseworthy, and so on.
3 One might wonder whether the capacity to *make* moral judgments and the capacity to be *motivated* by moral judgments are essentially associated, as I've suggested. On the view that the capacity to make moral judgments is an adaptation, they would be: it is only because such judgments at least often had practical effects on fitness that there was any selection pressure in favor of a capacity to make such judgments (or of a tendency to make certain classes of judgments rather than others). By contrast, on a by-product view, a capacity to make moral judgments might in principle emerge independently of a capacity to be motivated by them, and there might be a distinct account for the latter. It is also possible to hold that while a generic capacity for normative guidance is an adaptation, the capacity for *moral* judgment and motivation is a by-product. Thanks to Christian Miller for helpful comments here.
4 Though again, the existence of cultural universals would strictly be consistent with a nonnativist view, since one might also expect humans with the same cognitive resources facing similar challenges to arrive at similar solutions (Prinz 2008, 372).
5 Justifying (or normative) reasons are considerations that count in favor of something, such as a belief or action, as contrasted with explanatory (or motivating) reasons, which are considerations an agent (rightly or wrongly) *takes* to be justifying or normative reasons, thus explaining her belief or action. The same considerations can, of course, play both roles: the fact that smoking causes cancer may be a justifying or normative reason for believing that one should quit (and for quitting) and also be someone's explanatory or motivating reason for believing that she should quit (and for quitting). But they can also come apart: someone may *take* the fact that a certain act will cause a rival pain as a reason to do it, though that fact does not actually count in favor of so acting. For more on this see Parfit (1997).
6 The above point requires some qualification: one could take a purely scientific approach to causally explaining our moral beliefs without denying the existence of knowable moral truths if one held that the content of any moral truths we have grasped

is so closely tied to the evolutionary and other causal influences cited in scientific explanations that the two forms of explanation coincide: the scientific explanations may themselves constitute explanations in terms of grasping moral truths, given that the latter are simply functions of the same causal factors. If, however, moral truths are understood as having content that is *independent* of those causal factors, as they typically are, then the point in the text holds, since the explanation of beliefs resulting from grasping such truths would not simply coincide with the scientific explanations in terms of evolutionary and other causal factors (again, compare our grasping of complex mathematical or scientific truths). This issue will come up again later.

7 Parallel points apply to proposed scientific explanations for *theological* beliefs. If scientists purport to tell us, across the board, why people have theological beliefs or where such beliefs come from, by appeal to evolutionary causal influences on belief, say, then they are again relying on assumptions *external* to science, such as the assumption that there are no positive theological truths that some people may have come to know. This may raise no practical problems in cases where one's audience shares the atheistic assumption and expects only debunking explanations, and similarly with scientific explanations of moral beliefs directed to an audience of metaethical nihilists who think that morality is nothing but "a collective illusion foisted upon us by our genes" (Ruse 1986, 253). But even here one should be clear about what is coming from science and what is not.

8 For an articulation of moral realism and a survey of some current work on various forms of it, see FitzPatrick (2009) and Miller (2009).

9 For more on whether empirical moral psychology provides grounds for general skepticism about the efficacy of autonomous moral reflection, see FitzPatrick (2008).

10 In principle, a moral realist could hold that moral facts *are* reducible to facts about biological fitness in ancestral environments, with the good and the right understood ultimately in terms of maximal representation of copies of one's genes in succeeding generations, in which case faculties of moral judgment pervasively shaped by natural selection *could* be expected to track moral truths. The normative ethical view implied by such a view of moral facts, however, is a nonstarter and is not one that would be taken seriously by the moral realists Street is targeting.

11 Street's proposal is to adopt a radically subjectivist, antirealist account of value, whereby "evaluative truth is a function of how all the evaluative judgements that selective pressures (along with all kinds of other causes) have imparted to us stand up to scrutiny in terms of each other; it is a function of what would emerge from those evaluative judgements in reflective equilibrium" (Street 2006). If evaluative truths are just functions of a person's evaluative attitudes, then the alleged epistemic problems of using these attitudes to track *independent* evaluative truths are avoided.

12 The material in this paragraph and the next is drawn largely from FitzPatrick (2008).

13 Note that Street's deflationary take on autonomous moral reasoning goes even beyond Haidt's: he at least made an exception for philosophers (Haidt 2001, 828–9), while for Street, the claim about "saturation" with evolutionary influence is supposed to apply to "our" moral judgments quite generally, leading to the conclusion that realism leads to moral skepticism even for philosophers in connection with their most reflective and well-argued moral judgments. (For a more recent clarification and development of Haidt's social intuitionist view, see Haidt and Bjorklund 2008.)

14 For more about this and related arguments by Joyce 2006, see Copp 2008, FitzPatrick 2008, Enoch 2010, and Wielenberg 2010.

15 Thanks to Christian Miller for very helpful comments on this chapter.

Index